350

TESTED STRATEGIES TO PREVENT CRIME:

A Resource for Municipal Agencies and Community Groups

350

TESTED STRATEGIES TO PREVENT CRIME:

A Resource for Municipal Agencies and Community Groups

TAKE A BITE OUT OF
CRIME®

National Crime Prevention Council
1700 K Street, NW, Second Floor
Washington, DC 20006-3817

Publication Funded by
Bureau of Justice Assistance
Office of Justice Programs ▪ U.S. Department of Justice

This publication was made possible through Cooperative
Funding Agreement No. 94-DD-CX-K004 from the Bureau of
Justice Assistance, Office of Justice Programs, U.S.
Department of Justice. Opinions are those of NCPC or cited
sources and do not necessarily reflect U.S. Department of
Justice policy or positions. The Bureau of Justice Assistance
is a component of the Office of Justice Programs, which also
includes the Bureau of Justice Statistics, the National
Institute of Justice, the Office of Juvenile Justice and
Delinquency Prevention, and the Office for Victims of Crime.

TAKE A BITE OUT OF
CRIME

The National Crime Prevention Council is a private, nonprofit
tax-exempt [501(c)(3)] organization whose principal mission
is to enable people to prevent crime and build safer, more
caring communities. NCPC publishes books, kits of camera-
ready program materials, posters, and informational and
policy reports on a variety of crime prevention and
community-building subjects. NCPC offers training, technical
assistance, and national focus for crime prevention: it acts as
secretariat for the Crime Prevention Coalition, more than 130
national, federal, and state organizations committed to
preventing crime. It also operates demonstration programs
and takes a major leadership role in youth crime prevention.
NCPC manages the McGruff "Take A Bite Out Of Crime"
public service advertising campaign, which is substantially
funded by the Bureau of Justice Assistance, Office of Justice
Programs, U.S. Department of Justice. Proceeds from the
sale of materials, which are funded by public and private
sources, are used to produce more materials and to help
support the full range of NCPC's work, including the National
Citizens' Crime Prevention Campaign.

Cover photo © John Lund/TSI

Printed in the United States of America
December 1995

National Crime Prevention Council
1700 K Street, NW, Second Floor
Washington, DC 20006-3817
202-466-6272

ISBN 0-934513-05-8

The National Crime Prevention
Council is grateful to the
President's Crime Prevention
Council for helping to distribute
this document to a larger
audience. Points of view or
opinions expressed herein
do not necessarily reflect the
views, opinions, or official
position of the President's
Crime Prevention Council or
any of its members or
member organizations.

CONTENTS

FOREWORD xi

ACKNOWLEDGMENTS xiii

PUBLIC EDUCATION 1

Involve Media Representatives in
Coalition Work 2

Advocacy for Nonviolent Entertainment 3

Targeted Legal Services and Education 4

Local Public Service Advertising 5

Crime Prevention Programs on Local
Cable Television 5

Expand Access to Public Officials 6

Crime Prevention Information Centers 7

Outreach Through Community Media 8

Community Special Events and
Information Fairs 9

Speaker's Bureaus 10

Bibliography 11

COMMUNITY MOBILIZATION 13

Beautification Projects 14

Neighborhood-Based Service Centers 15

Organize Business Anticrime Groups 16

Promote Home and Business
Security Systems 17

Ensure Affordable Child Care 18

Violence Prevention and Problem Solving
Education for Children 19

Use College Students as Volunteers in Youth
Programs 20

Community Coalitions To Prevent Drug Abuse
and Drug-Related Crime 21

Crime Prevention Services for the Elderly 22

Special Community Events To
Promote Prevention 23

Provide Positive Alternatives to
Gang Activity 24

Reduce the Number of Handguns in
the Community 25

Community Support Programs for Mentally
Ill Offenders 26

Support Needs of Recent Immigrants 27

Community Job Banks 28

Use Codes and Ordinances To Prevent Crime ... 29

Use Media as an Ally 30

Faith Institution-Supported Mentoring 31

Nurture Community Groups and
Neighborhood Associations 32

Citizen Patrols 33

Local Government-Community Crime
Prevention Coalitions 35

Encourage Community Support for
Law Enforcement 36

Community Coalitions To Combat Crime,
Violence, and Drug Abuse 37

Broad-Based Community Programs To Support
Youth Development 38

Use Senior Citizens as Volunteers 39

Use Advances in Technology To Promote Safety
and Aid Community Crime Prevention 40

Performances To Reinforce Prevention Themes
With Youth 40

Crime Tip Rewards 41

Victim Assistance Services 42

Reinforce Community Standards Against
Violence 43

Neighborhood Watch 45

Create Access to Safe Urban Open Space 46

Directories of Services 47

Celebrate Neighborhood Accomplishments 47

Bibliography 49

YOUTH 51

Outdoor Challenge Education 52

School-to-Work Programs 53

Youth Leadership as a Community Resource 55

Dropout Prevention Focused on High-Risk
Elementary Students 56

Use Performing Arts To Build Healthy Bodies and
Minds 58

Recreation Centers 59

Crime Prevention Programs Targeted at
Female Youth 60

Implement Curfews for Youth 62

Support Youth Through Intergenerational
Programs 63

Community-Based Programs for Runaway and
Homeless Youth 64

College Students as Volunteer Resources and
Role Models 66

Counseling for Divorcing Parents 67

Peer-to-Peer Instruction 68

Crime Prevention Techniques for
Young Children 69

Values-Based Curricula 71

Safe Haven Facilities 72

Youth Advisory Boards 73

Surveys of Community and Youth Concerns 74

Local Coordination of Youth Policy
and Programs 75

Alternative Schools 76

Intensive Intervention With Adjudicated Youth and
Their Families 78

Community-Based Day and Residential Treatment
for Youth Offenders 79

Intensive Community-Based Supervision
and Reintegration 80

Teen Courts 81

Gang Prevention Programs for Female Youth 82

Surrogate Families 84

Gang Prevention Curricula 85

Individual and Family Therapy Programs 86

Court-Appointed Special Advocates 88

Adults as Career Mentors 89

Prenatal Care and Drug Abuse Prevention for
Pregnant Women 90

Family-School Partnerships 91

Community-Based Health Services
for Children 92

Victim and Witness Support 93

Graffiti Enforcement 94

Truancy Reduction Through Daytime Curfews ... 95

In-Home Counseling for Young Parents 97

Restitution to Victims 98

Teen Pregnancy Prevention 99

Parental Involvement Programs 100

Adults as Mentors 101

Rites of Passage Training 102

Community-Based Support for Domestic
Violence Victims 103

Date Violence Prevention for Teens 105

Community-Based Parent Education
and Support 106

Intensive Intervention To Prevent Foster
Care Placement 107

Youth-Designed and Youth-Led
Community Service 108

Schools as Community Resource Centers 109

Law-Related Crime Prevention Education
With Community Action 110

Crisis Hotlines 111

Bibliography 112

LAW ENFORCEMENT-COMMUNITY LINKS 115

Community Building Through Mobilization 116

Cooperate With Grassroots Organizations To
Address Problems 117

Analyze Crime Data To Focus Resources on
Local Problems 118

Police Sponsorship of Positive Activities
for Youth 120

Citizen Patrol 121

Partnership With Residents of Public Housing 121

Positive Youth Interaction With the
Criminal Justice System 123

Support Vulnerable Members of
the Community 124

Training in Prevention for Other
Local Agencies 125

Community Input on Improving
Court Systems 126

Educational Programs About
the Court System 127

Law Enforcement Involvement in Schools and
Surrounding Areas 128

Community Storefront Police Stations 129

Community Ombudsman 130

Intervene With Youth at Risk of
Gang Involvement 130

Crime Prevention Training for All
Department Staff 132

Partnership With City Agencies To
Prevent Violence 133

Law Enforcement-Led Multiagency Support for
Neighborhood Services 134

Law Enforcement-Sponsored
Community Events 135

Safe Havens 136

Community Meetings 137

Cooperate With Businesses 137

Partnerships in Rural Communities 138

Code Enforcement 139

Educate Residents About Law
Enforcement Operations 140

Multiagency Youth Service Support Teams 141

Focus on Quality-of-Life Improvements 142

Outreach to Diverse Communities To
Reduce Victimization 143

Translators and Multilingual Crime Prevention
Education Materials 144

Law Enforcement Programs for Youth From
Ethnic Minorities 145

Involve Residents in Community
Policing Planning 146

Police Cooperation With Residents To Identify
Community Needs 147

Mobile Service Vehicles 148

Bicycle Patrols 149

Police Cooperation With Residents To Reduce
Drug Trafficking 150

Bibliography 151

SAFE AND ATTRACTIVE PUBLIC PLACES 153

CITY-WIDE

High-Risk Business Security
Guidelines/Ordinances 155

CPTED Ordinances/Guidelines 155

Code Enforcement Teams 156

Utility/Employee Watch 157

Address Women's Concerns 157

Citizen Crime Prevention Councils 158

Safer Design of Public Areas
in Neighborhoods 159

Live-in Police Officers 160

Require Businesses To Remove Graffiti 160

Restricted Access to Selected Streets
or Neighborhoods 161

Apply Crime Prevention Through Environmental
Design to Parking Structures 162

Reduce Insurance Premiums for
Security Improvements 163

DOWNTOWNS/BUSINESS DISTRICTS

Business Crime Prevention Education 164

Community Safety and
Security Assessments 164

Fax Information Network 165

Workplace Safety Inspection 166

Promote Insurance Loss Control
Recommendations 166

Reduce the Amount of Readily Available Cash 167

Promote Hotel/Motel Security Standards 168

RETAIL BUSINESS

Employee Safety Training 168

Cardboard Police Officers 169

Ethnic and Culturally Sensitive Business
Crime Prevention 170

Control Cruising 170

Enhanced Lighting in Retail Districts 171

Display Business Address Numbers 172

ENTERTAINMENT DISTRICTS

Zoning Laws 173

Curtail Operating Hours 173

Traffic Control 174

Secure or Demolish Abandoned Buildings 175

Trash Patrol 175

Photograph/Videotape Illegal Behavior 176

Small Claims Suits 177

Put Workers in Public Places in Uniforms 177

Seize Customer's Vehicles 178

MALLS

Employ Security Staff 179

Provide Valet Parking 179

Bicycle Patrol 180

Mall Watch 181

Police Substations 181

Automated Teller Machine Safety 182

PARKS

Park Watch 183

Extended Park Operating Hours 183

Take Back the Parks 184
Restrict or Prohibit Alcohol Use 185

HOSPITALS

Restrict Access 185
Emergency Room Violence
Prevention Protocol 186
Hospital Watch 187

PUBLIC TRANSPORTATION

Exact Change Policy 188
CPTED for Subways 188
Prohibit Panhandling in Subways 189
Install Cameras on Buses 190
Remove Identification From Rental Vehicles 190
Taxi Security Screens 191
Security Escort Service 192
Highway Watch 192
Support Telecommuting, Teleshopping, or
Mail Ordering 193

SCHOOLS

Controlled Access to School Buildings 194
Closed Circuit Television Surveillance 195
Code of Conduct 196
Dress Code 197
Drug-Free Zones 198
Student Crime Watch 199
Gun-Free Zones 200
Crime Reporting Hotline 201
Student, Faculty, Staff, and Visitor ID Cards 202
Reduced Nighttime Lighting of
School Buildings 203
Volunteer School Security Patrols 204
Phones in Classrooms 205
Crisis Planning 206
School Resource Officers 207
Staff Training 208

PUBLIC HOUSING

Eviction 209
Enforcement of Trespass Law 210
Closed Circuit TV Cameras: Electronic
Surveillance of Public Spaces 210
Resident Initiatives and
Empowerment Program 211

Undercover Street-Level Drug Purchases 212
Access Control 213
Pay Telephone Incoming Call Elimination 214
Voluntary Resident Patrols 214
Tenant Screening 215
Crime Prevention and Awareness Training
for Residents 216
Cleanup Projects 217
Fencing and Other Barriers 218
Move Security Headquarters 219
Enhanced Lighting 220
Police-in-Residence Program 221
Bibliography 222

ECONOMIC DEVELOPMENT 223

"Incubate" Young Businesses 224
Early Warning Arson Prevention 225
Community Business and Housing
Development Planning 227
Community Beautification 228
Promote Business Involvement in
the Community 229
Ensure Supply of Affordable Housing 230
Enlist Resources of U.S. Department of
Housing and Urban Development and
Other Federal Agencies 231
Micro-Credits to Small-Scale Business 232
Targeted Lending 234
Business Watch 235
Bibliography 236

VIOLENCE 237

Comprehensive Curricula 238
Train Professionals To Recognize Child Victims .. 239
Public Dialogue and Community Mediation 240
Information Networks on Gang Activity 241
Multiagency Gang Interdiction Teams 242
Combine Corrections With Treatment 243
Target Serious Habitual Offenders 244
Restitution by Juvenile Offenders 245
Boot Camps 246
Teach Juveniles the Consequences
of Violence 247
Address Violence as a Public
Health Problem 248

In-School Probation 249

Diversion from Incarceration 250

Prevent Bullying 251

Assist Child Victims 252

Regulations and Ordinances on Gun Licensing ... 253

Promote Nonviolent Images of Youth 254

Involve Youth in Violence Prevention 255

Educate University Students About
Crime Prevention 256

Train School-Age Youth To
Mediate Conflicts 257

Support for Victims 259

Counsel Children Who Witness Violence 260

Family Therapy To Address Conflict
and Delinquency 261

Gun Court 262

Court Programs To Assist Victims of
Domestic Violence 263

Treatment for Male Batterers 264

Teach Teens To Prevent Dating Violence 265

Community Crisis Response Teams 266

Teach Entrepreneur and Job Skills to Youth 267

Corporate Support for Antiviolence Projects 268

Use State Laws and Ordinances To
Combat Gangs 269

Teach Children About Gun Safety 270

After-School Programs for Latchkey Children 271

Hold Parents Accountable for Their
Children's Behavior 272

Train Emergency Room Staff To
Prevent Violence 273

Incentives for Positive Behavior 274

Performance as Therapy and Education 275

Teach Male University Students To Prevent
Acquaintance Rape 276

Use School Organization and Policy To
Address Violence 277

Gang Prevention Through Community
Intervention With High-Risk Youth 278

Gun Interdictions 279

Bibliography 280

DRUGS 283

School-Based Curricula 284

Truancy Prevention 285

Parental Involvement 286

Before- and After-School Programs 287

Drug-Free School Zones 288

Incentives and Rewards for Healthy Choices 289

Easy Access to Prevention and
Treatment Services 289

Youth-to-Youth Antidrug Strategy 290

Alternatives to Drugs 291

Media Campaigns 292

Community Action 293

"Hot Spot" Strategy 294

Restrictions on Pay Phones 295

Community Partnerships 295

Churches as Resources 296

Involve Local Businesses 297

Enforce Local Codes and Ordinances 298

Hold Property Owners Accountable 299

Reinvest Assets Seized in Drug Raids 300

Enforce Bans on Alcohol Sales to Minors 301

Drug Courts 302

Empower Residents To Reclaim
Public Housing 303

Screen Tenants 304

Discourage "Happy Hours" 305

Ban Drugs From Public Events 306

Athletics for Drug Prevention 307

Drug Screening of Employees 308

Culturally Sensitive Drug Prevention
Programs 309

University Drug Policies 310

Mentors as Role Models 311

Arts-Related Prevention 312

Drug Activity Hotlines 313

Safe Design of Public Areas 313

Drug-Free Social Events for Youth 314

Job Training and Employment Opportunities 315

Train Those Who Serve Alcohol 316

Increase Police Presence 317

Educate Hotel and Motel Personnel 318

Make Drug Users Accountable 319

Prevent Gangs 320

Educate the Elderly About
Prescription Abuse 321

Prevention and Treatment Directed at Women ... 322

Leadership Training for High-Risk Youth 323

Bibliography 324

BIAS CRIMES 327

Court Monitoring 328

Diversity and Tolerance Education in Schools 329

Multilingual Reporting and Education Services ... 330

Culturally Based Youth Leadership and
Empowerment Programs 331

Ongoing Police-Cultural Organization
Service Partnerships 332

Rapid Response to Reported Incidents 333

Media Campaigns About Community Standards
for Tolerance 324

Counseling for Offenders Involved in
Hate Groups 325

Community-Based Dispute
Mediation Services 336

Support for Victims 337

Bibliography 338

PROPERTY CRIME 339

Graffiti Removal Policy/Tips 340

Discourage Graffiti Marketing 341

Graffiti-Resistant Materials 341

Offender Help With Paint-Outs 342

Adopt-A-Highway/Road 342

Restrict Sales of Graffiti Tools 343

Vandalism Prevention Curriculum 344

Community Cleanups 344

Home Security Inspections 345

Residential Building Codes 346

Insurance Premium Reductions 346

Operation Identification 347

Neighborhood Watch 348

Home Security Alarms 348

Street Access Restrictions 349

Increase Visibility and Surveillance 350

Cellular Telephone or Radio Patrols 350

Voice Mail Information 351

Outside Residential Lighting 352

Commercial Lighting 352

Business Watch 353

Display Business Address Numbers 354

Direct Deposit 354

Pay-Before-You-Pump Gas Policy 355

Score/Cut Vehicle Inspection Stickers 355

Protect Credit Cards 356

Use Security Sensor Tags 357

Fire Safety Education for Juveniles 357

Disseminate Automobile Theft
Prevention Devices 358

Anti-Theft Decals for Automobiles 359

Intervention To Prevent Recidivism Among
Juvenile Arsonists 360

Bibliography 361

RESOURCE LIST 363

INDEX 367

Foreword

"What works?"

"Has somebody tried . . . ?"

"What can we do about . . . ?"

"Why can't we . . . ?"

These are questions communities around the country ask as they roll up their sleeves to take on the challenge of reducing violence, drugs, and other crimes.

A cross the country in the past few years, there has been a groundswell of community partnerships to prevent crime and drug abuse. Collaborative, comprehensive efforts that address causes as well as symptoms, solutions as well as problems, are generating new energy and new working relationships at the local level, aimed at prevention rather than reaction. At their best, these partnerships involve all elements of the community and aim to build workable, lasting structures and institutions to establish and sustain community safety and security.

A major challenge for the Bureau of Justice Assistance is to help identify and spread the word about promising techniques and program ideas that can help prevent crime, in order to help communities develop and support the safe, strong neighborhoods and families which comprise safe communities.

In *350 Tested Strategies To Prevent Crime: A Resource for Municipal Agencies and Community Groups*, the National Crime Prevention Council has taken a major step toward helping us meet that challenge. By taking a novel approach—considering strategies rather than programs—this book helps communities focus on adapting and tailoring program ideas and crime prevention techniques to local needs and circumstances and to comprehensive plans. The strategies are vivid, real-life approaches rather than textbook theory. Program examples illustrate each strategy's practicality and promise.

Experience to date with such local partnership initiatives as BJA's PACT (Pulling America's Communities Together), and the Comprehensive Communities Program tells us that communities want to know what approaches give evidence of effectiveness, but they need to position these strategies in their own contexts. *350 Tested Strategies* lets them do just that.

Not every strategy will fit the needs of every community. But every community will benefit from thinking about whether and how these strategies can be useful. Strategic thinking helps bring to the table a wider range of partners to solve problems, leverage resources, and generate action. Any community will be enriched by developing a problem-solving attitude and approach as well as strategic perspective. *350 Tested Strategies* not only informs about crime prevention, but it engages all community residents in the task. That has for more than 15 years been the overarching goal of the National Citizens' Crime Prevention Campaign, which the Bureau of Justice Assistance is proud to support.

Nancy Gist, Director
Bureau of Justice Assistance
Office of Justice Programs
U.S. Department of Justice

December 1995

Acknowledgments

Ultimately, the value of crime prevention is that it "improves the quality of life for every community and its residents." These were the concluding words of the principles drafted in 1990 by the Crime Prevention Coalition, more than 130 groups— including federal agencies, national constituency organizations, and state crime prevention programs and associations— dedicated to promoting crime prevention.

This document is based on the premise that the key to effective crime prevention is cooperation and coordination among the criminal justice, social, economic, family, and other systems that make up a community. Prevention as a cornerstone of policy can reduce the burden on the criminal justice system—a burden felt at federal, state, and local levels as well borne by individuals and communities.

The Crime Prevention Coalition wrote in 1990:

Our aim is to build a foundation for crime prevention efforts within every community in the United States, to preserve and reclaim our neighborhoods, and to eliminate conditions that give rise to crime. To do so, we summon every citizen, civic and social group, government agency, and business to take appropriate steps to prevent crime.

That call to action offers the extraordinary promise of crime prevention to every community. Its manifestations are many; its opportunities are rich; and its rewards are extraordinary. It is our hope that this comprehensive collection of 350 tried and tested strategies reveals the richness in the innovations of local governments and communities throughout the nation. We present these strategies grounded in local realities as examples of approaches that can be applied to local issues and priorities. In recognition of the role of local governments in galvanizing community institutions and integrating programs, it contains many examples of how local resources were brought together to build safer, more caring communities.

Reducing crime is clearly one of the nation's most urgent social problems. Communities and local governments are the front line in the struggle to find practical and effective ways to build community, protect public safety, support families, encourage healthy youth, and improve residents' quality of life. We hope that committed community and local government leaders see the menu of strategies in this document as a tool to help them meet this most formidable challenge.

The ten chapters in this book highlight how communities and local governments have addressed crime problems and the conditions that lead to crime. Each chapter includes ten to fifty strategies in key topical areas: public education; community mobilization; youth; law enforcement-community linkages; safe and attractive public places; economic development; violence; drugs; bias crimes; and property crime. The chapters highlight the key components, partnerships, and potential obstacles for each strategy and profile established programs that employ the strategies. A reference bibliography concludes each chapter and offers opportunities for further research. The resource guide in the last section provides information on dozens of national, state, and local groups that provide resources and program examples. The index will help direct readers to key topic areas, programs, and strategies of particular interest. No one publication could capture the remarkably diverse and creative strategies and programs that have been developed by energetic and creative groups and individuals across the country. Omission here reflects our space limitations rather than the quality of these strategies and programs. Similarly, an exhaustive bibliography on any of these subjects would be in itself a major document. The bibliographies provided here reflect only a few of the many excellent writings on these topics. NCPC welcomes information on strategies, programs, and resources that enrich and expand upon this first edition. Correspondence should be sent to the attention of the Municipal Initiatives Unit.

This document was inspired by our work with local practitioners, state leaders, policymakers, and researchers who seek examples of the benefits of prevention. Many thanks go to the countless program and research organization resources that contributed information, ideas, and insight. The National Crime Prevention Council gratefully acknowledges the support of the Bureau of Justice Assistance (BJA), Office of Justice Programs, U.S. Department of Justice, and particularly Robert H. Brown, Jr., Chief of the Crime Prevention Branch. He encouraged us to pursue this mammoth undertaking and provided sustained support and encouragement as it was painstakingly compiled. Nancy Gist, BJA's Director, not only encouraged our work but graciously provided thoughtful framing in her Foreword.

The development and production of the document was spearheaded by the vision of Terry Modglin, NCPC's Director of Municipal Initiatives, who first noted the need for it during his work on the pioneering crime prevention planning effort by Texas' seven largest cities in the BJA-supported program, Texas City Action Plans to Prevent Crime. Research and selection of strategies, selection of consulting writers and compilation of the documents, and responsibility for several sections was managed by Theresa Kelly, originally a consultant writer to NCPC and now the Technical Assistance Coordinator for the Municipal Initiatives Unit. The entire document benefitted from framing and editing grounded in the considerable experience and thoughtful perspective of Jean F. O'Neil, NCPC's Director of Research and Policy Analysis and Managing Editor. Judy Kirby, Assistant Editor, provided extensive help in publishing the text and preparing it for production. Updates were researched by Chris Scileppi and other members of NCPC's staff. Jack Calhoun, Executive Director of NCPC, provided vision, valuable critique, patient perspective, and inspiration grounded in experience with community-based and local government programs across the county. Other NCPC staff who provided research contacts, suggested strategies, contributed to the text, and encouraged the process include Robert Coates, Michelle Cotton, Caren Garfield, Mac Gray, David Singh, and Alex Speier. Interns Suzie Easton and Sarah Hebrenk were key contributors to the research effort and initiation of contacts with resource agencies. Kim Anderson plowed pleasantly through the thankless task of preparing the document for final production. Her patience was a quiet but important resource.

Several able and experienced practitioners and writers contributed to this text, including Sarah Hay (Drugs, Law Enforcement), Pat Harris of the Virginia Crime Prevention Association (Public Places, Property Crime), Ray Konan (Economic Development, Community Mobilization), Chester Quarles of the University of Mississippi (Schools, Public Housing) and Bill Woodwell (Public Education). Their contributions made this publication possible, as the task was too vast to accomplish with staff resources alone. Sincere thanks go to them for their commitment, insight, and resourcefulness. This document is enriched because of their perspective, experience, and suggestions.

Public Education

"We're doing a whole lot but nobody seems to know it."

"We just can't seem to get it across to kids that there are alternatives to violence."

"All the media wants to do is focus on the problems and not on the solutions."

"It's hard to get people to comprehend the paramount role they play in preventing crime."

Public education is about more than sending out press releases or newsletters. It's broadening public support for and involvement in community crime prevention. It's about enlisting the media as a partner in determining program priorities and conveying positive messages to the public. And it's about laying the groundwork for the long-term behavior and attitude changes—on the part of citizens, the media, local government and others—that will help make crime prevention a way of life in your community.

Public education can encompass a wide range of activities. This collection of strategies demonstrates how crime prevention practitioners and others can *educate, motivate, organize, and mobilize* residents of their communities to prevent crime. These strategies include organizing a speaker's bureau, getting media representatives involved in local coalition efforts, and launching a community-wide campaign on behalf of nonviolent entertainment. This material is presented to help you consider the best way to make public education a priority for your community crime prevention program.

This section is not a complete overview of possible public education strategies. Rather, it is a sampling of the kinds of things that can work to get people and the media involved in preventing crime and violence; it also includes contact organizations so you can find more information.

Just as press releases and newsletters won't get the job done on their own, choosing just one or two of the activities outlined in this packet won't be effective. Public education campaigns work because lots of different things are happening, because different people are out there making the case, and because citizens are being exposed to messages in different venues and different situations. One public education priority is to do as many different things in as many different ways as you can. And because you can't do everything, another priority is to enlist others to help you achieve your goals:

■ Get together with community groups working on related issues—from poverty to economic development to youth services—to determine how they can help and what resources they can devote to public education activities on crime prevention.

- Reach out to local advertising, marketing, and public relations firms and other experts who might provide *pro bono* support and expertise.

- Convene a public education steering committee—with representatives from government, law enforcement, business, the media, and community and citizen's groups—to brainstorm about activities and divide responsibilities for getting the job done.

Community crime prevention initiatives have a wide array of local assets to draw on for designing and implementing public education strategies and activities like the ones presented here. Think about the assets available to you, and work with them to craft a long-term, sustainable public education campaign that makes crime prevention a community-wide concern.

Involve Media Representatives in Coalition Work

Strategy

Involve representatives of local media—newspapers, broadcast television, cable television, and radio—in crime prevention coalitions as a way of focusing media attention on prevention topics and tapping into the local media's expertise and resources.

Crime Problem Addressed

Media organizations are among the most visible and influential institutions in American communities. Media owners and managers often play active roles in the chamber of commerce and other prominent community, business, and professional groups; local television personalities are widely recognized, in many cases attaining celebrity status. Also, decisions made by editors, editorial writers, public affairs staff, program producers, and others can have a broad impact on community priorities and opinion. Involving media representatives in local coalitions can help assure that the media—and, in turn, the general public—is well informed on prevention topics.

Key Components

Media partnerships involve more than arranging for a public service announcement or a news story. Among the avenues to more active and rewarding relationships with the media:

- involving owners and senior management of prominent local media organizations in prevention task forces and other initiatives;

- asking reporters, editors, and program producers who regularly cover issues of crime and violence to join in discussions of the problem and possible solutions;

- ensuring that media representatives are on guest lists for community events, prevention workshops, parades, and other activities; and

- working with media representatives to help shape policies about violence in programming and to use the media to encourage positive responses to crime problems.

Key Partnerships

The key approach is to consider the media both a partner and a resource. Just as crime prevention practitioners can provide their media partners with information and guidance on how to respond to these issues, the media can help by framing messages, developing story ideas, and producing public service announcements, newsletters, and other critical communications.

Potential Obstacles

Media personnel are typically busy and may be reluctant to commit to or to take part in new projects or time-consuming activities. Additionally, concerns about the media's independence may keep editors and reporters from taking part in coalition efforts in an official capacity.

Signs of Success

When officials in San Antonio, Texas, were organizing a city crime prevention commission, they knew media involvement would be critical—but they did not know how critical. By inviting prominent local media figures to play a leadership role in the panel's deliberations and programs, the city created a partnership that has generated positive media coverage, as well as provided free broadcast equipment and facilities for public service announcements and other programming.

Applying the Strategy

The Utah Council for Crime Prevention sought to keep local media involved in policy discussions and program design by inviting media representatives to serve on the council's board on a rotating basis. Media personnel are also asked to participate in special prevention task forces organized by the council. Collaboration between the council and its media partners has resulted in locally produced television documentaries and public service announcements, as well as other activities raising public awareness of crime prevention throughout the state.

Contact Information

Crime Prevention Officer
San Antonio Police Department
711 West Mayfield
San Antonio, Texas 78211
210-207-7575

Executive Director
Utah Council for Crime Prevention
66 East Cleveland Avenue
Salt Lake City, Utah 84115
801-486-8691

Advocacy for Nonviolent Entertainment

Strategy

Encourage the public and the media to choose nonviolent forms of entertainment as a way of building public awareness of alternatives to violence.

Crime Problem Addressed

Violence is seeping into every facet of American society, from television and movies to music and advertising. According to the Center for Media and Public Affairs (based in Washington, DC), the number of violent scenes recorded during a sample of eighteen hours of broadcast and cable television programming jumped by more than two-thirds between 1992 and 1994. Such programming contributes to people's acceptance of violence as a normal, even preferred, way of dealing with conflict and anger. When the *Minneapolis Star Tribune* recently asked children to share their opinions on violence in the media, one child wrote, "I love violence. Violence is cool!"

Key Components

Urging people not to watch violent television programs, listen to violent music, rent violent videos, or go to violent movies *for just one day* can raise public awareness about excessive media violence and its possible impact on real-life violence and crime. It also sends a message to the media that violence is not so popular after all.

Key Partnerships

To have its intended effect, a community-wide "Turn Off the Violence" campaign requires extensive publicity. In addition to the media itself, community partners that can help spread the word include businesses, schools, libraries, park and recreation departments, religious organizations, and colleges and universities. Partners can sponsor alternative activities to violent entertainment and offer public education about media violence.

Potential Obstacles

Will the media cooperate in something so critical of its own activities? Generally, the answer is "Yes"—if project organizers are able to convince local media that this is a broad-brush campaign against *all* media violence, rather than an attack on a particular medium or specific programming. It is also difficult to quantify the impact of one day each year and to monitor the number of people who participate. Finding ways to demonstrate results—increased awareness, participation in alternative forms of entertainment—is key to gathering support.

Signs of Success

In June 1993, in response to increasing public concern about the depiction of violence in television programming, the major television networks announced a new "Advance Parental Advisory" to warn viewers about violent content in upcoming programs. The music recording industry has adopted similar voluntary advisories. Moreover, public pressure has sparked ongoing discussions in the movie, television, and music industries about the propriety of violent media content.

Applying the Strategy

A series of highly publicized violent crimes in Minnesota in the first half of 1991 led to the creation of the country's first "Turn Off the Violence" (TOV) campaign. For one day, people were asked to "turn off" violence by avoiding violent television programs, movies, and music. Related initiatives in community and schools were designed to teach nonviolent ways to solve problems. Minnesota's campaign was a success from the start. More than forty-five sponsors participated in the first year. Today, the campaign has been adopted by communities across the country.

Contact Information

Project Coordinator
Turn Off the Violence
Citizens Council
822 3rd Street, #100
Minneapolis, Minnesota 55415
612-340-5432

Targeted Legal Services and Education

Strategy

Encourage positive attitudes toward the law by building greater public understanding of the justice system and providing community-based legal assistance.

Crime Problem Addressed

Individuals often run into problems with the justice system simply because they do not understand it. Moreover, many lower-income people who need basic civil representation and advice cannot afford it. As a result, it is often difficult for people to feel that the law is on their side.

Key Components

A privately and publicly supported community-based public law office can act as a resource for neighborhood residents. Lawyers and staff encourage citizens to use their free services and come in with questions. These services are subsided by private sources and state and local government funds. In other activities, targeted materials and community outreach can provide community audiences—including teachers, students, and civic organizations—with helpful information about how the justice system works.

Key Partnerships

Building mutual trust between community residents and the attorneys who are there to help them is critical. The relationship between court representatives and the community is also important. A successful outreach and public education effort will rely on long-term partnerships with schools and local leaders. Finally, public information officers from the court system will need to work closely with the local media to publicize the resources that are available.

Potential Obstacles

A lack of public awareness about the availability of new products and services can doom court-system outreach efforts. Preconceived, negative attitudes about lawyers and the criminal justice system may also block use of such services. On the other hand, without proper planning, community-based service organizations may become overburdened and unable to serve a high volume of clients.

Signs of Success

A handbook distributed to judges and court administrators across the country in March 1995 focused on court-community relationships. *Citizens and Their Courts: Building a Public Constituency* is part of a long-term project partly funded by the State Justice Institute and sponsored by the Conference of Chief Justices and the Conference of State Court Administrators. The purpose of the project is to promote wider discussion of court-community partnerships. The handbook focuses on several states that have been successful in building public confidence and citizen involvement in their justice systems. A national video conference will continue the effort.

Applying the Strategy

The Neighborhood Defender Service (NDS) in Harlem, New York, has been representing people and educating local citizens about legal issues since December 1990. NDS has served more than 4,000 clients to date, building bridges between the justice system and the community and promoting local awareness about the legal system. The program's proven track record in reaching out to so many people who might otherwise become lost in the system has attracted continuing support from the Vera Institute of Justice and both the City and State of New York.

Contact Information

Public Information Officer
Conference of State Court Administrators
Office of the Administrator for the Courts
1206 South Quince Street
Olympia, Washington 98501
360-705-5319

Deputy Director
Neighborhood Defender Service of Harlem
55 West 125th Street
New York, New York 10027
212-876-5500

Local Public Service Advertising

Strategy

Educate the public about drug abuse and crime prevention through a local public service advertisement (PSA) campaign.

Crime Problem Addressed

Public service advertising is an effective way to increase awareness of urgent crime-related issues facing a community—including drug abuse, gang violence, and hate crimes—and to build consensus around possible solutions.

Key Components

Local PSA campaigns can take two forms. Some are produced locally, while others add a local "tag"—with sponsor identification and contact number—to national advertising. This second method greatly reduces the amount of work, time, and money required of the local PSA sponsor. PSAs of all types should be produced with an "action message," encouraging the audience to *do something* to address a problem facing them and their communities.

Key Partnerships

Locally produced PSA campaigns require close coordination between key community officials and an advertising agency willing to donate time and resources. To tailor national campaigns to local concerns, community officials need to work with the national sponsor. In both cases, partnerships with the media managers who make decisions about using PSAs are critical. Public service advertising depends on the media's willingness to donate valuable advertising time and space.

Potential Obstacles

At any given time, local media organizations may be confronted with 100 or more PSA campaigns competing for attention, support and, most importantly, advertising slots. What makes the difference between a PSA that gets used and one that doesn't is the media's judgment of whether or not the issue addressed is of *local relevance*—whether it's something that affects people in the community and that residents are concerned about.

Signs of Success

An independent 1993 survey of the impact of PSAs produced for the National Citizens' Crime Prevention Campaign—featuring McGruff the Crime Dog and his "Take A Bite Out Of Crime" message—found that the advertising had indeed affected people's awareness and behavior. Conducted on behalf of the U.S. Department of Justice, the survey of 1,500 American adults found that 80 percent recalled having seen or heard the McGruff advertisements and nearly one-third said they had learned from them. About one-fifth of those surveyed said that they had taken specific actions as a result of the PSAs, and almost half felt more personally responsible for preventing crime.

Applying the Strategy

"Do Drugs. Do Time." That's the warning at the heart of an innovative law enforcement campaign in metropolitan Phoenix, Arizona, that has relied heavily on locally produced PSAs. The campaign's aim is to reduce drug use and spur demand for counseling and treatment by alerting casual drug users to the possibility that they will be arrested. The program has attracted widespread community and media support, as well as funding and technical assistance from the Federal Bureau of Investigation, the Drug Enforcement Agency, the U.S. Attorney's Office, and state and local government.

Contact Information

Special Projects Director
Maricopa County Demand Reduction Program
301 West Jefferson, 8th Floor
Phoenix, Arizona 85003
602-506-7799

For a copy of the Department of Justice evaluation of the McGruff PSA campaign's effectiveness, call the Bureau of Justice Assistance at 1-800-688-4252 and ask for publication NCJ-144533.

Crime Prevention Programs on Local Cable Television

Strategy

Use public-access cable television programming to spotlight local police efforts and crime prevention activities and to educate residents about what they can do to Take A Bite Out Of Crime.

Crime Problem Addressed

Many individuals and organizations don't understand that prevention can be a successful strategy in reducing violence and other crimes. They are also unaware of complementary activities and programs in their communities.

Cable television programming produced by local police departments and government agencies can help bridge these gaps in public understanding while building awareness of local initiatives.

Key Components

Regular cable programming can be an effective forum for demonstrating the local police department's openness, its interest in dialogue with the community, and its commitment to creating a safer environment. Weekly, monthly, or quarterly programs can introduce members of the local police force, provide background and perspective on crime problems confronting the community, and offer advice on individual and neighborhood prevention efforts. Programs can also profile successful community crime prevention programs as models for other citizen-led initiatives.

Key Partnerships

The police department or other law enforcement agencies must forge a close working relationship with the local cable company, which assists in production and schedules programs. Program producers must also be in close contact with community crime prevention groups to ensure a steady flow of ideas and contacts for community features.

Potential Obstacles

A crime prevention cable show, of course, will have no impact if no one watches it; thus, working with the cable company to promote the show should be a priority. Also, the program won't attract a large audience on a continuing basis unless its production quality, topics, and format are engaging.

Signs of Success

Three out of every four Americans have access to cable. Moreover, half of cable subscribers watch their community public-access channels on a regular basis. In local success stories, the Oxnard Police Department in California has teamed with its local cable company to produce a weekly, one-hour prevention-oriented program that is the most popular offering on the local government channel. Since the show began, Oxnard reports a 50 percent decrease in burglaries despite population growth of more than 20,000 people.

Applying the Strategy

The Department of the Attorney General in Hawaii has taken on an unusual media role—producing a television talk show for teens. Called "Bridging the Gap," the program provides a platform for teens to voice their concerns about an array of prevention-related topics. Recent discussions addressed the problems of runaways, teen suicide, anger management, teen pregnancy, and date rape. The program airs quarterly on a public television station, a commercial channel, two cable channels, and a radio station.

Contact Information

Chief of Police
City of Oxnard
251 South C Street
Oxnard, California 93030
805-385-7430

Chief of Multimedia Resource Services
Hawaii Department of the Attorney General
810 Richards Street, Suite 701
Honolulu, Hawaii 96813
808-586-1416

Expand Access to Public Officials

Strategy

Broaden opportunities for citizens to express their concerns about crime, safety, and other issues in discussions with public officials.

Crime Problem Addressed

Even at the city or community level, Americans too often feel that their elected and appointed leaders are distant, inaccessible, and unaware of "real people's" concerns. As a result, citizens often lose the sense that they have a stake in the workings of their communities and that they can and should have a role in improving safety. Similarly, police and other public officials are often unaware of certain situations residents are facing. If people can be heard, problems that might otherwise be overlooked can be efficiently addressed.

Key Components

Citizens can address questions, comments, and concerns to local public officials in any number of ways, from town meetings and office visits to personal letters and call-in radio and television programs. To ensure broad participation, public events must be publicized well in advance. Another critical component of program design is implementing systems to ensure that citizen input will receive the attention and feedback it deserves.

Key Partnerships

The key partnership for achieving this goal is between public officials and citizens. Since one elected official cannot handle every concern, it is critical that citizen queries and concerns be relayed quickly to the appropriate government and public safety representatives. Elected officials must work closely with local agencies and police departments to ensure a timely and efficient response to priority problems and concerns.

Potential Obstacles

There are obvious constraints on how much time elected officials can devote to meeting with the public. Additionally, public events such as town meetings and call-in programs require considerable work and advance planning. Finally, unrealistic expectations can cloud citizens' opinions of local government as a force for good. Reconnecting the people to the process requires a better understanding of issues, policies, and government capabilities on both sides.

Signs of Success

People like to feel that they are a part of the process and that political leaders and policymakers are genuinely interested in their opinions and concerns. A nationally televised presidential debate in 1992 during which ordinary citizens asked questions of George Bush, Bill Clinton, and Ross Perot attracted the largest television audience in U.S. history, beating the *M*A*S*H* finale and the "Who Shot J.R.?" episode of *Dallas*. On the state level, Arizona recently coordinated a statewide interactive electronic town meeting to present the findings of a special commission on juvenile justice. The result? Capacity turnouts at "downlink" sites across the state and high rates of participation and follow-up from residents offering advice and opinions on a wide range of issues.

Applying the Strategy

In Corpus Christi, Texas, a year-long series of citizen town hall meetings played a critical role in the development of the city's action plan to prevent crime. "Our goal was to get input from every segment of the community—all income levels and all neighborhoods—and to offer a sounding board for people to express their opinions and concerns," recalls Larry Olivarez of the Corpus Christi Police Department. The meetings were held weekly in neighborhoods throughout the city and featured the mayor, police officials, and community leaders.

Contact Information

Program Manager
Administrative Office of the Courts
Arizona Supreme Court
1501 West Washington
Phoenix, Arizona 85007
602-542-9300

Community Service Officer
Corpus Christi Police Department
321 John Sartain
P.O. Box 9016
Corpus Christi, Texas 78469
512-886-2775

Crime Prevention Information Centers

Strategy

Set up an easily accessible resource center (either a community-based operation, a mobile unit, or an on-line service) where residents can obtain information about crime prevention and related issues.

Crime Problem Addressed

A Crime Prevention Information Center allows people to research crime statistics, find out about other communities' successes against crime, and tap into a wide range of resources providing information and guidance to support neighborhood prevention efforts.

Key Components

The most common type of prevention information center is the "store-front" police office, a neighborhood-based resource people know they can turn to for help. Among the other types of centers are a mobile police unit that visits high-crime areas regularly and an on-line database that allows residents to access prevention information from their computers.

Key Partnerships

Strong community-police relationships are critical to the success of neighborhood-based information centers. Store-front police or prevention offices often are staffed by community volunteers and also can be used for community meetings (e.g., Neighborhood Watch). On-line and mobile centers require outreach to the community and the media to alert people to their existence as a prevention resource. On-line networks can provide access to national prevention information databases such as PAVNET, the Partners Against Violence Network.

Potential Obstacles

Funding and effective allocation of police personnel are real concerns, especially for neighborhood-based information centers. Once one or two neighborhoods have centers, others will inevitably want one, too. One concern about on-line services is that there may be few users from disadvantaged communities—often a principal target of prevention initiatives—due to a lack of access to computers.

Signs of Success

Numerous police departments and community crime prevention efforts have established neighborhood-based centers to disseminate information and build prevention awareness. Using grants from the U.S. Justice Department's Bureau of Justice Assistance, New York City has put mobile-service vans to work as "Neighborhood Resource Centers" for three crime-plagued, low-income neighborhoods. The vans are staffed by a community policing officer, neighborhood volunteers, and a victims services agency coordinator; they provide everything from employment counseling to drug treatment referrals. "We use it as a mini station house," comments Lieutenant Tom Hoskins of the 72nd precinct in Brooklyn. A 1992 evaluation found that the mobile service centers had significantly increased cooperation between area residents and police.

Applying the Strategy

As part of the Texas Cities Action Plan to Prevent Crime (T-CAP), police in Dallas are putting together a computer-based prevention information center. Once on-line, the resource center will provide citizens with up-to-date information on all facets of crime prevention. T-CAP volunteers will conduct research to gather the information from resources around the country and will make it available both on-line and in printed form. As another example, The Community Information Exchange is a recently launched effort to provide neighborhood-based organizations and their partners with the information they need to revitalize their communities. The Exchange maintains five computer databases and seven computer bulletin boards containing information about successful community-building initiatives.

Contact Information

72nd Precinct
New York Police Department
830 Fourth Avenue
Brooklyn, New York 11232
718-965-6327

Dallas Police Department
Northeast Operations Division
9915 East NW Highway
Dallas, Texas 75238
214-670-4762

The Community Information Exchange
1029 Vermont Avenue, NW
Suite 710
Washington, DC 20005-3517
202-628-2981

Outreach Through Community Media

Strategy

Use community media resources, such as neighborhood and ethnic newspapers, to publicize information about events and issues of special concern.

Crime Problem Addressed

Mainstream media are limited in the amount of coverage that they will devote to crime prevention. When they do report on the topic, they usually provide a broad portrayal of what is happening and what can be done. Smaller community media, on the other hand, regularly report on issues specifically affecting the communities they serve. Whether they are published for residents of a specific neighborhood or for citizens of a particular race or ethnicity, community newspapers tailor their reporting to neighborhood or community concerns. As a result, they have a faithful following and often can mobilize citizens effectively against special threats or problems.

Key Components

Community media, including newspapers and radio and television stations, can report on crime and prevention topics in any number of ways. They can spotlight crime prevention activities and events in community calendars, broadcast community crime statistics, report on trends in community crime, and highlight successful prevention activities in the community. A successful outreach effort will help community media do all of these things and more.

Key Partnerships

Police and community organizations must work closely with the media organization's management and staff to make prevention a continuing priority. The community newspaper or radio station might be asked to become an active partner in community prevention efforts by sponsoring local events and allowing personnel to serve on special prevention task forces and committees.

Potential Obstacles

Running a newspaper or a broadcast station can be costly, and often communities with the most severe crime problems do not have the resources to support such endeavors. Also, community media are notoriously understaffed and may require a significant amount of encouragement and assistance to coordinate articles, calendar items, and events.

Signs of Success

A recent survey of readers of eighty-eight leading African-American community newspapers around the country illustrated the unique appeal of publications targeting specific population groups. More than 82 percent of those surveyed felt that the African-American newspapers dealt with subjects of special interest to them, while fewer than 60 percent felt the same way about the wider-circulation daily newspapers in their areas. Moreover, nearly 70 percent of those surveyed said they found "an understanding of their life" in the African-American newspapers; only 40 percent said the same thing about citywide newspapers.

Applying the Strategy

Crime Prevention Bulletin is a community newspaper in Washington, DC, devoted to "empowering communities to take back our streets." Published six times a year, the newspaper features photos and information about area fugitives, plus helpful and engaging articles on a variety of prevention topics. Since the *Bulletin* was first published in July 1994, it has led to the apprehension of thirty-six fugitives. The publication relies on financial support from area businesses, foundations, and individuals; it is distributed free in high-crime areas throughout Washington, DC, and neighboring jurisdictions.

Contact Information

Editor/Publisher
Crime Prevention Bulletin
107 South West Street, #274
Alexandria, Virginia 22314
703-683-8829

Community Special Events and Information Fairs

Strategy

Organize festive and informative special events to raise crime prevention awareness and bring people together as a community.

Crime Problem Addressed

Neighborhood events can help build the sense of community that is lacking in many American cities, suburbs, and rural areas today. Walking/running races, crime prevention information fairs, picnics, outdoor concerts, food festivals, and other events all can bring people together and create new respect and appreciation for a community among its citizens. Such events can also send important messages to people about supporting prevention and taking action against crime.

Key Components

Community special events can range from an information fair at a neighborhood police station or fire hall to a citywide crime prevention festival with music, food, information booths, and more. Yet no matter the event, an essential factor in its success will be the sponsors' efforts to make it both festive and informative. People need a special reason to attend, something in addition to the availability of good crime prevention information.

Key Partnerships

Large-scale community events are most effective and worthwhile when they involve as many people and organizations as possible. Heavy promotion is key—if possible, recruit a local radio station to broadcast live from the site. Recruiting large numbers of volunteers and support from neighborhood businesses and community groups is also essential.

Potential Obstacles

Events require a considerable commitment of time and resources on the part of their sponsors—financial and in-kind support from throughout the community is key. Also, weather can block outdoor events—make sure to have a rain date or back-up plan.

Signs of Success

In October 1995, the National Crime Prevention Council planned a nationwide crime prevention celebration called "America Against Crime" as a follow-up to the previous year's "America's #1 Challenge: U.S. Against Violence." Both the 1994 and 1995 events were structured around a five-kilometer running/walking race held in cities across the country. The 1994 event raised funds for local and national youth initiatives including Boys and Girls Clubs,

Police Athletic League programs, and activities of the National Citizens' Crime Prevention Campaign. Events for 1995, held in six cities from coast to coast, featured a "crime prevention expo" along with puppet shows, magicians, high school bands, and disc jockeys.

Applying the Strategy

In Cleveland, Ohio, city officials recently worked with the local ABC-TV affiliate to sponsor a citywide gun exchange at a local supermarket. Offering $75 in food vouchers in exchange for turned-in guns, the program collected nearly 2,500 guns and raised community awareness of important safety and prevention issues. A critical factor in the success of the effort, according to Tony Charles, the director of the Mayor's Office of Violence Reduction and Crime Prevention was the station's "relentless" promotion—through public service announcements, news stories, and other means both on and off the air. "They did a tremendous job," says Charles.

Contact Information

National Crime Prevention Council
1700 K Street, NW, Second Floor
Washington, DC 20006-3817
202-466-6272

Director
Mayor's Office of Violence Reduction and Crime
    Prevention
City of Cleveland
601 Lakeside Avenue
Cleveland, Ohio 44114
216-664-2220

Speaker's Bureaus

Strategy

Recruit and train speakers—representing law enforcement, community groups, and other organizations with prevention expertise—to address community gatherings and build support for crime prevention.

Crime Problem Addressed

Community associations, businesses, and schools are often looking for speakers to discuss issues of concern and answer questions at member, employee, or student gatherings. A key concern for many groups is how to prevent crime. Local trade group meetings, for example, can be a great forum for addressing specific concerns about crime—such as the impact of burglaries on local retailers—while detailing prevention measures. Other potential speaker's bureau "clients" might include large employers (for employee presentations); Neighborhood Watch groups; condominium or apartment building residents; the Rotary Club, Lions Club, and other fraternal organizations; and parent and citizen groups.

Key Components

The first step is to determine the local crime-related issues of most concern and develop an "inventory" of people able to address those issues in an expert manner. Next, it is important to train speakers—or, at the very least, to review a run-through presentation—to ensure that they have good communications skills and are giving the right messages. Finally, the success of a speaker's bureau depends on the community's awareness that it exists; publicity about the service is very important.

Key Partnerships

A speaker's bureau relies on strong partnerships between the speakers and the referring organization; between the referring organization and community groups that might use the service; and between the referring organization and untapped sources of potential speakers.

Potential Obstacles

Speakers need good communications skills to engage their audience and to ensure that their presentations have an impact. Also, community groups need to be aware of the availability of speakers, or else the service will be underused.

Signs of Success

The Arizona Crime Prevention Association regularly refers speakers for presentations throughout the state. Among the speakers who are "on call" through the association are experts on such topics as crime prevention through environmental design, violence in the workplace, multi-housing safety, and the prevention of ministorage theft—an increasing problem in many areas. After a series of recent presentations to ministorage facility owners, in fact, calls for service to police from the businesses dropped 50 percent. The program has documented similar reductions in service calls as a result of presentations to apartment building landlords and other groups.

Applying the Strategy

The Cultural Diversity Project in Fargo, North Dakota, is an effort to address the challenges and opportunities presented by the community's increasing ethnicity; the local minority population has doubled as a result of church-administered refugee resettlement programs. The project uses "Training Teams" of community residents who conduct diversity workshops for city employees, social service agencies, schools, and other groups. A speaker's bureau provides experts on topics including diversity, housing, and employment opportunities.

Contact Information

President
Arizona Crime Prevention Association
P.O. Box 408
Tucson, Arizona 85702
520-622-0683

Coordinator
Cultural Diversity Project
810 4th Avenue South, #417
Moorehead, Minnesota 56560
218-236-7277

Bibliography

Periodicals

Baker, Denise. TV Production Helps Youngstown Find Solutions. *Nation's Cities Weekly,* 13 February 1995, p. 11.

Killing Our Children. *A Chicago Tribune Reprint,* 25 January 1994.

Millions Celebrate National Night Out. *Catalyst,* National Crime Prevention Council, November 1994, p. 3.

Newspaper Bags Deliver Domestic Violence Information. *Catalyst,* National Crime Prevention Council, December 1994, p. 4.

Peirce, Neal R. A Generation That's Killing Itself. *National Journal,* 21 January 1995, p. 190.

Police and Cable Television Work Together in Virginia. *Catalyst,* National Crime Prevention Council, January 1995, p. 4.

Stepp, Laura Sessions. Youth Say TV Shapes Values: Poll Shows Majority Want Moral Guidance on Issues. *Washington Post,* 27 February 1995, p. B1.

Public Documents

American Bar Association. *Just Solutions: A Program Guide to Innovative Justice System Improvements.* 1994.

U.S. Attorney's Office. Cook County Crime Stoppers "Most Wanted" Television Program. *Resource Fair Program Summaries: Building Justice in Our Communities.* October 1994, pp. 12–13.

U.S. Attorney's Office. Greater Tyler Drug-Free Business Initiative. *Resource Fair Program Summaries: Building Justice in Our Communities.* October 1994, pp. 39–40.

U.S. Attorney's Office. Lewiston-Auburn Anti-Drug Coalition. *Resource Fair Program Summaries: Building Justice in Our Communities.* October 1994, pp. 21–22.

U.S. Attorney's Office. Media Simulcast, Fighting Back. *Resource Fair Program Summaries: Building Justice in Our Communities.* October 1994, pp. 30–31.

U.S. Attorney's Office. Operation RESIST. *Resource Fair Program Summaries: Building Justice in Our Communities.* October 1994, pp. 15–16.

U.S. Attorney's Office. Red Ribbon Celebration Day. *Resource Fair Program Summaries: Building Justice in Our Communities.* October 1994, p. 35.

U.S. Attorney's Office. Youth Court Watch. *Resource Fair Program Summaries: Building Justice in Our Communities.* October 1994, pp. 27–28.

Community Mobilization

Community-based action to prevent crime, violence, and drug abuse can help unify neighborhoods by bringing residents together in partnership with one another and with local government to reduce crime and the fear of crime. It builds neighborhood leadership and increases the ability of residents to resolve issues that affect public safety and the quality of life.

C rime prevention at the community level entails much more than ensuring the safety of homes and the occupants inside. Community crime prevention engages residents, addresses problems, mobilizes neighborhood resources, galvanizes local agencies to act, and revives civic energy and community spirit. Crime prevention at the grassroots level is most effective when it mobilizes the skills and resources of committed residents, community-based organizations, churches, parents, businesses, the elderly, and young people. Coalitions that link residents with local government can provide the spark needed to create changes in policies and institutions.

In different ways, each of the strategies in this chapter demonstrates what committed local and community leaders can accomplish when they enlist the resources and talents at hand.

Proven techniques to catalyze resident action to prevent crime include the following:

■ **Neighborhood-based services to help link families with needed assistance**—Since the Neighborhood Network Center opened in Lansing, Michigan, in 1990, crime in an area formerly known as a center of street drug trafficking and prostitution decreased by 75 percent. The Center, initiated through the city's community policing program, has improved resident access to housing, employment, health services, and educational support.

■ **Community coalitions to prevent drug abuse and drug-related crime**— Coalitions of concerned residents can be a potent force against drug-related crime, fear of crime, and community disintegration. Neighbors in Des Moines, Iowa, worked with local code enforcement agencies and police to close, renovate, or demolish drug houses at the owner's expense. In the northwest Bronx, a community coalition moved twenty-four families into a refurbished home and established "Safe Corridors" in the neighborhood for senior citizens.

■ **Special community events to promote crime prevention**—An anti-drug march through Philadelphia enlisted 3,000 community supporters from all walks of life. Their fear diminished by a common vision, participants filled six blocks as they marched through a neighborhood ravaged by drug dealing and chanted "No" to drugs.

■ **A reduced number of handguns in the community**—Handgun exchange programs have proven effective in both getting unwanted handguns off the streets and increasing public awareness of the dangers of guns and violence in America. In 1994, Cleveland's program netted 2,300 guns, with support from local media outlets and a supermarket chain. The city's churches helped with publicity and reinforced nonviolence in messages to their congregations.

■ **Neighborhood Watch**—Perhaps the most popular and proven community crime prevention strategy, Neighborhood Watch organizations work with police to organize groups of residents into a chain of individuals trained to notice and report criminal behavior. Their publicity and communication networks deter crime. A 1981 evaluation of a Seattle burglary prevention program proved that the combination of Neighborhood Watch, property identification, and home security surveys resulted in notable reductions in crimes.

The key to each of these successful strategies is that residents took action to establish or reinforce the community's standards against crime. They harnessed energy resources from all sectors of the community, built on their strengths, and illustrated that concerted action by committed individuals makes a real and lasting difference.

Beautification Projects

Strategy

Neighborhood and business district improvements—such as trash cleanups, landscape enhancements, and gardens—serve as a focus for community organizing and help communicate community standards of care, cohesion, and civility.

Crime Problem Addressed

The physical condition of neighborhoods and business districts conveys ownership, care, and purposeful maintenance and signals whether offenders should consider the area vulnerable to victimization by crime, violence, and drug trafficking. Most community-based crime prevention programs operated in cooperation with local government include periodic cleanup days or other efforts to beautify the area.

Key Components

Community organizations—usually in cooperation with local law enforcement, public works, parks and recreation staff—clean up public areas and abandoned lots. In some cases, the cleanup and the return of the public place to intended and unincumbered use is the desired result. In others, the cleanup results in the establishment of new green space, demarcation of neighborhood areas, a median strip improved with plantings, repaired sidewalks, or formation of a community garden. Staff and equipment from local government agencies are often borrowed to clear debris and trash, plant trees and shrubs, post signs, and maintain landscaping in public areas.

Key Partnerships

Community-based law enforcement officers and public works staff can help residents identify opportunities to implement beautification and improvement projects. Their equipment (bulldozers, front end loaders, rotor tillers, dumpsters, collection bins) make larger-scale projects possible. Local landscaping firms or other area businesses can be enlisted to help defray the cost of cleanup supplies and planting materials.

Potential Obstacles

Apathy in the community and cynicism about the benefit of "neatness" may dampen some residents' enthusiasm for cleanup efforts, community gardens, or landscape improvement projects. Publicity and coordination with other police-advised crime prevention projects help enhance the success of beautification efforts. Finding government funds to support continual effective maintenance can prove difficult in communities where budgets have been cut. Diligent volunteer patrols help support maintenance, and publicity helps protect areas from future deterioration.

Signs of Success

Through state and federal agency support, Long Beach, California, developed an Urban Forestry Program, planting 3,000 trees in the first three years. The landscaping improvements provide educational and employment opportunities for communities targeted for intervention through the Neighborhood Improvement Strategy. Two area neighborhood associations have since applied successfully for additional tree-planting grants. The Neighborhood Cleanup Program provides paint and tools to organized volunteer groups, which schedule cleanup projects designed to reduce blight throughout the community. Youth on probation provide additional labor as part of their required community service. Landscape improvements are linked with leadership development, community police centers, graffiti-removal teams, and recreational services for youth. In addition, a twenty-four-hour hotline allows residents to request graffiti-removal service.

Applying the Strategy

The St. Petersburg, Florida, Neighborhood Partnership Program includes infrastructure enhancement and beautification. In 1994, three neighborhoods were landscaped with trees, shrubs, and grass. Neighborhood grants offered through the program support the implementation of neighborhood improvement plans, which can include clean-ups, landscaping, and signs at the entrance to neighborhoods, as well as enhancement of parks and other public spaces. The program also coordinates housing rehabilitation and construction in targeted areas of the city. The impressive results of these projects are used to market neighborhoods and to promote neighborhood festivals.

Contact Information

Manager
Neighborhood Services Bureau
City of Long Beach
333 West Ocean Boulevard
Long Beach, California 90802
310-570-6066

Neighborhood-Based Service Centers

Strategy

Neighborhood-based service centers help link families with needed assistance and reinforce city government and community support for residents who utilize the center.

Crime Problem Addressed

This strategy aims to reduce all types of crimes. Unemployment, dilapidated housing, unmet needs for medical services, joblessness, drug abuse, and domestic violence are just a few of the conditions that contribute to the risk of criminal activity by adults and youth in a community. This strategy aims to minimize the impact of social conditions that foster crime by creating linkages to agencies that can address and remedy these conditions.

Key Components

The key component of this strategy is a neighborhood location for "one-stop" access to social services. The program is based on

■ cooperation between the neighborhood center staff and other government agency service providers (such as social workers, public health programs, educational programs, and community-based police);

■ support from other community resources (such as neighborhood churches, recreational programs, and service clubs); and

■ a knowledgeable and caring staff.

Multilingual and culturally competent staff are vital in diverse communities. In cities with more than one center, the services at each center are tailored to meet each community's needs.

Key Partnerships

The most important partnership for this strategy is between the neighborhood and the staff at the center. Such centers are most effective when they operate in partnership with the community, as well as with social service agencies, health providers, area schools, probation and parole offices, and the police department. Partnerships with community groups—such as local churches, charitable organizations, service clubs, and private rehabilitation services—are also key to program success, since these groups help legitimize the center with the community and ensure that its services meet the community's needs.

Potential Obstacles

One obstacle to this program can be agency bureaucracy that blocks the decentralization this strategy requires. The sharing of space and allocation of funds for shared support facilities at the neighborhood network center can also pose accounting and staffing challenges. Memorandums of understanding between agencies help clarify roles and responsibilities and ensure efficient delivery of services to the community.

Signs of Success

Research by the National Center for Community Policing resulted in development of a Neighborhood Network Center model that co-locates many social service programs with the community police office in neighborhood locations.

This strategy has been used successfully in several locations, including Lansing, Michigan. It adapts the decentralized model of community policing to the provision of other social services. The Lansing Neighborhood Network Center is co-located with the community policing officers, who coordinate a team of social service and health professionals. The program recruits area nursing students and others to provide health screening, employment services and job referrals, language interpreters, emergency housing and food assistance, recreational opportunities for youth, and education counseling for adults. Center staff and neighbors cleaned the area of trash, planted flowers, organized a garden-tool borrowing program, and closed several drug houses.

Since the Center opened in 1990, crime in the neighborhood has decreased 75 percent. Once an area of the city known for street drug sales, prostitution, and dilapidated rental housing, the neighborhood is now much safer. More residents have jobs and own homes, and community events occur regularly.

Applying the Strategy

In 1991, Miami police initiated Operation NEON (Neighborhood Enhancement Operation Network) to saturate designated areas with police officers and code enforcement agents. Neighborhood groups worked with police to identify problem areas and devise responses. The success of the project prompted the city to design NEON for thirteen areas of the city. The police department and the city base multiagency service teams in these areas, ensuring a cooperative approach to working with the community to identify problems and implement appropriate solutions. An integrated data system provides residents with neighborhood-based access to permit requirements, crime data, and information on social services available from the city or community-based organizations. Residents can also bring concerns to police officers and pay parking or permit fees at the neighborhood locations.

Contact Information

National Center for Community Policing
Michigan State University
School of Criminal Justice
560 Baker Hall
East Lansing, Michigan 48824
517-355-2192 or 800-892-9051

Lansing Police Department
120 West Michigan Avenue
Lansing, Michigan 48933
517-483-4663

Organize Business Anticrime Groups

Strategy

Business Watch groups deter, detect, and report crime in business and commercial districts.

Crime Problem Addressed

This strategy helps reduce many kinds of crimes against and around businesses: shoplifting, theft, burglaries, purse snatching, drug dealing, and vandalism. Just as citizen preparedness and surveillance in Neighborhood Watch programs reduce crime in residential areas, this strategy reduces crime against businesses and crime in commercial areas.

Key Components

A business anticrime council or Business Watch can establish links among businesses, as well as between businesses and the police. Business Watch participants take systematic steps with the police to reduce the opportunity for crimes to occur in and around business and commercial locations. Business personnel are trained to be eyes and ears for crime prevention and detection. Crime prevention officers and business leaders assist owners, operators, and employees in the following activities:

■ **Crime reporting**—Business people observe and report to police on crimes and suspicious activities that could lead to crime.

■ **Operation Identification**—All equipment, machines, etc., are marked with traceable identification numbers for deterrence and tracing.

■ **Robbery prevention**—"Easy prey" opportunities are eliminated.

■ **Burglary prevention**—Security measures are added to impede and detect criminals and to communicate with the police.

■ **Self-protection**—Merchants and employees learn to recognize dangerous situations, as well as ways to prevent, avoid, or flee them.

A business leader acts as a block security chief for the participating businesses. A police officer acts as liaison with the Business Watch group or business council. The local civic association or other community groups may also participate—extra eyes and ears, especially for periods when the businesses are closed. Business can be linked to each other and to the police through radio or facsimile machine message trees. Radio-equipped delivery and service vehicles should be enlisted in Business Watch activities. Window decals or signs can identify participating businesses, serving as a further deterrent to crime.

Key Partnerships

Key partnerships for this strategy include those between the business owners and the local business crime group. Together, they form a key partnership with the local police department, particularly with its crime prevention or watch liaison officers. Other partners can be the local citizens' association, church, chamber of commerce, or other groups interested in a safe and prosperous business sector.

Potential Obstacles

It is not always easy to convince busy business owners that they can significantly reduce the incidence of crime in and around their facilities and shops through their own efforts. On the other hand, early success in reducing crime may sow complacency. It is sometimes difficult to keep businesses active once the costs and threat of crime are reduced. Some police departments require a fixed percentage of businesses in the area to participate actively to qualify for "Business Watch" certification and support (such as signs, regular meetings, police briefings).

Signs of Success

The Detroit Police Department works closely with blocks of businesses to organize and guide Business Watch programs. The Crime Prevention Section is a significant part of the Detroit police force. It has developed extensive methodologies and materials for Business Watch, with emphasis on denying opportunity for criminal activity. It eliminates the "easy prey" temptation by training business personnel to identify potential crime indicators and report them to the police. The police officers provide blueprints for business groups organizing meetings and designating security chiefs. They also provide checklists on shoplifting prevention, bad check controls, internal theft precautions, premises security, and more. Crime rates have dropped in Business Watch areas.

Applying the Strategy

Many local police departments have documented significant reductions in reported crime where Neighborhood or Business Watch programs are instituted. The hundreds of members of the Business Crime Council of South Texas have provided crime prevention information to members representing various industries, participated in local crime prevention planning projects, supported youth programs throughout the area, and advocated for state and local crime-related legislation.

The Marathon County (Wisconsin) Sheriff's Department has developed a Fleetwatch Program: Employees of firms with two-way communication systems in their vehicles become extra eyes and ears for the police. They report on criminal and suspicious activity, helping to deter crime and identify criminals for apprehension.

Contact Information

Detroit Police Department
Crime Prevention Section
2110 Park Avenue, Suite 332
Detroit, Michigan 48201
313-596-2520

Marathon County Sheriff's Department
Wausau, Wisconsin 54403
715-847-0229

Promote Home and Business Security Systems

Strategy

Promotion of home and business security systems helps prevent property crime, educates residents, and encourages creation of neighborhood organizations.

Crime Problem Addressed

High rates of burglary, theft, and vandalism contribute to declining property values and tend to isolate residents who live in fear of victimization. This strategy reduces crimes against homes and businesses by disseminating information and products that protect those structures from unlawful entry.

Key Components

A key component of this strategy is public recognition that easy targets contribute to higher crime rates and that security devices in homes and businesses impede access and help reduce crime. Measures to improve security include common-sense precautions by police and community groups; security surveys of residences and businesses by police officers; assistance to victims of crime and elderly residents who cannot pay for additional security measures; donations of security services and products from area companies and community groups; and public information—to inform homeowners, businesses, and community groups—about crime prevention and the availability of crime prevention devices.

Key Partnerships

The central partnership is between the police and the community groups that want to implement this strategy. Other key groups are business associations, homeowners and homeowner associations, and crime-victim support groups. The media—radio, television, newspapers—make effective partners in informing the public and generating support for the project in the community.

Potential Obstacles

Home and business owners may lack information on devices and strategies that can increase security. Another potential obstacle for low-income residents and crime victims is the cost of security devices; sometimes this problem can be overcome with local government funds or donations from corporations or community groups.

Signs of Success

Police departments across the country send officers to Neighborhood Watch groups and homeowner association meetings to explain how simple steps—such as a dead-bolt lock and peep holes in front and rear doors—can deter would-be criminals from gaining entry.

In 1984, St. Louis, Missouri, launched Operation Safe Street with the slogan "Neighbors Standing Together Against Crime." The city urged all residents to install basic home security systems and keep porch lights on from dusk to dawn. New traffic flow patterns created a stronger sense of community and helped residents identify suspicious persons. In its second four-year phase, the city initiated a Home Security and Burglary Victims Program, supported by a nonprofit coalition of security professionals. Trained crews installed dead-bolt locks, peep holes, window bars, and other security devices in residential homes. This service cost $150 per home, but was free for the elderly and for crime victims. From 1980 to 1990, residential burglaries declined by nearly 50 percent, and automobile thefts also decreased.

Applying the Strategy

Seniors involved in the Retired Senior Volunteer Project (RSVP) of the Corporation for National and Community Service provided free in-home security assessments for their Phoenix, Arizona, neighbors during the nationwide Summer of Safety in 1994. Pairs of trained senior volunteers visited the homes of nearly a thousand area residents, offering advice on security improvements, examples of other burglary prevention techniques, and information on local crime watch and senior assistance programs available through the city and community-based organizations. Many residents reported that the visits from peers reduced their fear and equipped them to make decisions on increasing home safety.

Contact Information

Operation Safe Street
City Hall, Room 424
1200 Market Street
St. Louis, Missouri 63103
314-622-3444

Ensure Affordable Child Care

Strategy

Mobilization of community resources to provide quality, affordable child care helps support parents and ensures safe care for children of working families.

Crime Problem Addressed

This strategy protects children and supports families by ensuring the availability of reliable and affordable child care. The most immediate crime concerns are preventing the neglect and abuse of children and protecting the economic self-sufficiency of the family.

Key Components

The key components of this strategy include:

■ a government agency or a religious, nonprofit, school, university, health, or business group organized to provide and promote quality, affordable child care;

■ publicity to make residents aware of available services;

■ licensing standards to ensure safe and quality care in disperse locations; and

■ means to ensure participation by low- and moderate-income residents.

Key Partnerships

The most critical partnership for this strategy must exist between the child care providers and the parents of the children. That partnership needs competency, trust, and communication for the healthy growth of the child. Partnerships that are needed to support that central partnership involve the various groups in the community that provide child care, counseling, and funding assistance. For example, governmental, social, health, and educational services, local churches and other faith groups, service clubs, and nonprofit groups should all participate in this strategy. With encouragement and assistance, many businesses help with the child care needed by their employees, either at the job site, or through employee cooperatives, subsidies, and flexible time arrangements.

Potential Obstacles

One challenge is to get the complex system of community groups, including government programs, working together to assure the availability of quality, licensed, safe child care at a reasonable cost. Another task is to find the needed funding from employers or through government support. Local government funds to subsidize such services tend to be scarce, making partnerships with businesses and community-based providers even more important.

Signs of Success

Psychologists, criminologists, and social workers often trace the problems of youth crime and violence to dysfunctional families and to childhood abuse or neglect of the offenders. There are many groups—both governmental and nongovernmental—in every community with experience, people, and resources for helping to nurture children in healthy ways. When these groups are coordinated to ensure that children receive the care that they need, parents are free to find and do their jobs or get the education or training that they need, while their children are getting their health, social, and learning needs met, as well. More and more neighborhoods, communities, and cities have concluded that the availability and delivery of quality child care promotes healthy children, productive parents, successful families, and stronger, safer communities.

Applying the Strategy

In the City of Austin, Texas, the Opportunities for Youth Program (OFY) is establishing Child Care Management Services, supported by state and federal funds, to link low-income families with child care services. OFY is working to enhance child care services by collaborating with numerous locally funded child care initiatives. This program works with both families and child care providers, facilitating the efforts of both to ensure child care services for all children who need them.

In the spring of 1994, OFY established a second program called Youth, Family, and Neighborhood Vitality. It is designed to create a community of healthy children and families and strong neighborhoods for community revitalization. Austin's action plan provides several levels of support for children and families:

- child health care and early education opportunities at neighborhood health and education centers;

- parent training and counseling, as well as training and support for child care providers;

- improvement in schools and student learning through hands-on, problem-solving, and thematic learning; and

- Youth Opportunity Centers for middle and high school students, for tutoring, career education, recreation, cultural enrichment, and access to primary and mental health care.

The City of Austin is showing that it is possible to mobilize an array of community resources for quality child care. Many participants are now convinced that these resources are solid building blocks for healthier children and families, stronger neighborhoods, and safer communities.

Contact Information

Opportunities for Youth Program
Children and Youth Services Planning Unit
City of Austin Health and Human Services and Travis
  County Health Department
100 North IH-35, Suite 3500
Austin, Texas 78701
512-473-4100

Violence Prevention and Problem Solving Education for Children

Strategy

Community-based programs teach youth violence control and problem solving, thus preventing juvenile delinquency by providing critical decision-making and life skills.

Crime Problem Addressed

One-half million school-age children reported in a recent study that they spend at least part of their day concerned about violence. This strategy teaches children to reject violent responses to conflict by reinforcing positive and nonviolent means for resolving disputes. This strategy can help prevent drug abuse, gang violence, sexual harassment, and other problems of violence and crime. It empowers youth with the critical thinking and decision-making skills necessary to avoid the temptation of negative influences in their community.

Key Components

The key components of this strategy include the following:

- recognition by community institutions that violence is a learned behavior and that youth need specific skills to combat its influence in their lives;

- commitment from a community organization (church, youth group, recreation program) to promote violence prevention and positive decision-making and communication skills among the children involved in activities it sponsors;

- activities to encourage youth and their families to use violence prevention and communication skills in their home and community environment; and

■ support for these activities, from local government-sponsored youth programs, area businesses, and the media.

Key Partnerships

The central partnership in this strategy exists between the children and those who are helping them learn the violence prevention and communication skills. The community-based volunteer serves as a role model for the youth. Volunteers must also work in partnership with program staff and parents to ensure that the lessons of the program are reinforced at home and throughout the community. Area mental health professionals, counselors, religious leaders, and other community resources are valuable partners in providing training and counseling to adult volunteers and youth participants. Local community foundations and civic or service organizations can be valuable funding partners.

Potential Obstacles

The primary challenge is getting local community groups to include youth social skill development as a focus of their work. Overburdened with providing other needed services to the community, community groups and city agencies may not want to take on such a program. Programs run through religious institutions and service-oriented organizations can operate the programs with volunteers if adequate training is available.

Signs of Success

In 1987, a Detroit group of parents of slain children united to go beyond mourning to work toward positive alternatives to violence throughout the community. They founded the nonprofit organization, Save Our Sons And Daughters (SOSAD). SOSAD offers crisis intervention, counseling, training in violence prevention, multicultural conflict resolution, gang redirection, and bereavement support. This grassroots, community-based effort to teach peace and peacemaking skills has become a model for other communities. SOSAD expanded its positive impact by developing curricula for training other agencies, organizations,

school personnel, and community members in its problem-solving and crime-preventing techniques. With this active intervention and that of others, the number of children shot or killed in Detroit has declined each year since 1987.

Applying the Strategy

The August 1994 Crime Prevention Action Plan developed by the Greater San Antonio Crime Prevention Commission reports that community-based conflict resolution programs are effective in teaching young people non-aggressive methods for coping with conflict and resolving disputes. Accordingly, it has developed a city-funded conflict resolution program to serve neighborhoods, through the city Health Department. The program focuses on alternatives to violence, gang prevention, and aggression control, and it emphasizes positive behaviors.

In 1987, a small theater company formed in Minnesota with a focus on children and violence, seeking to provide alternatives through positive interaction and problem-solving. This grassroots program turns kids away from violence and toward positive interaction with family, peers, and the community. By 1989, the Climb Theatre group had brought its strategy of dramatic presentations (puppet shows, role plays) to over 60,000 children throughout the state. Parents report that children exposed to the interactive presentations used the techniques displayed to "cool down" and to help others to cool down, to talk about their problems, and to avoid fighting. The program offers services to thousands of children each year.

Contact Information

Save Our Sons And Daughters (SOSAD)
2441 West Grand Boulevard
Detroit, Michigan 48208
313-361-5200

CLIMB Theatre
500 North Robert Street, Suite 220
St. Paul, Minnesota 55101
612-227-9660 or 800-767-9660

Use College Students as Volunteers in Youth Programs

Strategy

College students help communities support youth through internships or volunteer work in tutoring, mentoring, social work, nursing, and law.

Crime Problem Addressed

This strategy provides additional resources to address local crime and violence problems, address neighborhood service needs, and support positive activities for youth.

Key Components

The first component is an agreement between the college or university and the municipal service agency or program that the students will assist. A second component is training and guidance for the college students. The third component is determining the services to be provided to the participating families or individuals, for example, family counseling or legal assistance, tutoring, or help in health clinics. The final component—often the most difficult—is evaluating the program's impact on crime prevention.

Key Partnerships

Key partnerships include those between the students and the families or individuals with whom they work and between the university and the local government programs in the service area. Businesses, faith institutions, civic groups, law enforcement agencies, and neighborhood organizations help identify communities in need and opportunities to use college student volunteers.

Potential Obstacles

One obstacle in such programs is the sustainability of relationships through the period of time needed to achieve the desired results. If the students are simply meeting a course requirement for a single term, the time may not be sufficient. The relative inexperience of the students could be another obstacle. Accordingly, it is very important that their involvement in the program be carefully defined and evaluated.

Signs of Success

In Austin, Texas, students from the University of Texas School of Social Work joined the Paths to Prevention (PTP) program of field internships. With federal funds shrinking and many municipal budgets diminishing as well, these internships permit services to more people than governmental programs can provide.

The PTP Program educates young children (from kindergarten through second grade) and their parents about gang prevention. It teaches children nonviolent conflict resolution, personal safety, drug use resistance, self-esteem, and cultural appreciation. Student social workers educate parents on communication skills, increasing empathy among family members, and building confidence and self-esteem in themselves and their children.

Applying the Strategy

In Lansing, Michigan, nursing students are working through a community-based service and police center to help meet the health care screening and immunization needs of a low-income neighborhood. The combination of services offered through the center has helped reduce crime in the area, built cohesion and stability among the resident population, and provided access to vital medical services at a low cost.

Contact Information

Paths to Prevention Program
Health and Human Services
P.O. Box 1088
Austin, Texas 78767
512-326-9210

Community Coalitions To Prevent Drug Abuse and Drug-Related Crime

Strategy

Community coalitions to eliminate drug sales and drug abuse help mobilize local resources against such offenses and reinforce resistance against all types of crime.

Crime Problem Addressed

Drug abuse is a known factor in many types of crime, including shoplifting, burglary, robbery, squatting in abandoned buildings, assault, child and spouse abuse, suicide, and murder. Early detection and corrective action can help prevent the spread of drug-related crime. Left unchecked, drug abusers can take over public places (such as parks and street corners), block walkways to school, and leave whole communities in fear. This strategy seeks to stop drug trafficking and drug abuse on the streets by mobilizing segments of the community in cooperation with law enforcement.

Key Components

Key components of this community-based and organized strategy to control drug abuse and sales can include the following:

- drug-free school zones;

- drug abuse prevention curricula in schools;

- parent education and counseling groups;

- after-school programs and activities for youth;

- drug-free home and apartment lease clauses;

- identification of and action against drug "hot spots;"

- allocation of community resources for rehabilitating drug abusers;

- youth employment and training programs;

- neighborhood beautification and revitalization; and

- community rallies against drugs.

Only a combination of strategies addressing the array of conditions that leaves a community vulnerable to drug sales and abuse will be effective against this multifaceted problem. Community group and local government cooperation in devising the strategy helps ensure that the activities will respond effectively to the needs and priorities of area residents.

Key Partnerships

Key partners in a community coalition are the mayor or city manager's office, law enforcement, juvenile justice authorities, public housing officials and resident groups, service clubs, civic associations, community organization representatives, religious communities, local media, and substance abuse treatment providers.

Potential Obstacles

All community groups say they are against drug abuse, but it may still be difficult to enlist their active participation in anti-drug campaigns. Reluctance comes from fear of retaliation, distrust of neighbors and the police, or the belief that the drug problems have grown too big to handle. To overcome these obstacles, a smaller group can start with a modest goal, such as deterring drug dealing on one corner or in one park. More people will join the effort as positive results are recognized.

Signs of Success

From 1990 to 1992, the U.S. Department of Justice, Office of Justice Programs, Bureau of Justice Assistance sponsored community-led drug prevention coalitions in ten cities. Through the Community Responses to Drug Abuse (CRDA) program, a national demonstration project, each community formed a multisector task force, defined its target area, engaged law enforcement as a partner, and developed a work plan. The reports on the project show that the strategy works:

■ Parks and street corners were purged of drug dealers and users, and returned to the people as safe areas.

■ Existing laws and regulations, such as statutes addressing nuisance and noise abatement, were used in creative ways to stop drug dealing.

■ Police closed drug houses by working with churches, neighborhood residents, the public health department, local utility companies, and the media.

■ Agencies and institutions changed their policies—for example, one public school agreed to keep its doors open longer to provide a safe place for the children of working parents.

■ Youth were offered new opportunities for positive fun and growth through mentoring, tutoring, and recreational activities.

■ Parents formed a community network to support one another in working to keep their children and communities drug free.

Applying the Strategy

In Hartford, Connecticut, schools strengthened drug-free zones and adopted drug abuse prevention curricula. In Des Moines, Iowa, drug houses were closed, renovated, or demolished at the owner's expense. The Public Housing Authority adopted the policy of terminating the leases of residents suspected of alcohol and drug trafficking. In Northwest Bronx, New York, a community coalition moved twenty-four families (most from the city's shelter system) into a refurbished home and established "Safe Corridors" for senior citizens. In Oakland, California, a community coalition closed dozens of drug houses, organized a neighborhood cleanup program, and purchased vacant industrial land for affordable housing units.

Contact Information

Hartford Area Rallies Together
660 Park Street
Hartford, Connecticut 06106
203-525-3449

Executive Director
Oakland Community Organization
7200 Bancroft Avenue, #2 Eastmont Mall (upper level)
Oakland, California 94605
510-639-1444

Crime Prevention Services for the Elderly

Strategy

Crime prevention and victim services help address the special vulnerability to crime and violence of some elderly people.

Crime Problem Addressed

Elderly people can be particularly vulnerable to the crimes of burglars, purse snatchers, petty thieves, and con artists. They fear crime, especially violent crime, and that fear causes many to remain in their homes. This strategy addresses their fear of crime and provides crime prevention services to minimize both fear and crime.

Key Components

The components of this strategy include the following:

■ a communication network to keep the elderly alert to potential crime;

■ information and training on how to report crime;

■ services to support elderly victims in dealing with the physical, emotional, and financial impacts of crime; and

■ access to products, training, and other services to help prevent victimization.

Key Partners

Key partners include the police, social services agencies, community groups, and religious groups. Volunteers can be used for escort or transportation services.

Potential Obstacles

One obstacle is the challenge of helping the elderly to protect themselves against crime without unduly raising their fear of crime. Fear of crime is a critical concern encumbering many elderly people. Crime prevention practitioners who work with senior citizens agree that knowledge is the best antidote to fear. Frequent interaction with other community members helps increase the sense of security and support for all neighborhood residents.

Signs of Success

Working with the police and social service programs, grass-roots community groups such as Neighborhood Watch can greatly reduce the fear of crime among the elderly and help keep them safe. Some religious and other community groups help the elderly by providing escorts and shopping or transportation services. Such services add greatly to the individual's safety and sense of well-being.

The Atlanta, Georgia, police department has a special Neighborhood Watch program that is tailored to older residents. It establishes a "buddy system" in which neighbors check up on one another, accompany one another to the bank, store, or doctor's appointment, and watch over homes when neighbors are away. All crime reports listing elderly persons as victims are forwarded to the crime prevention unit. Its officers contact the victim, call a neighbor or relative if the person is still fearful, make follow-up visits, and link the victim to any needed social services. The program serves hundreds of Atlanta's senior citizens each year.

Applying the Strategy

In Boston, Massachusetts, the Police Department's Senior Response Unit patrols 118 senior housing complexes, as well as meal sites, senior citizen centers, and other areas frequented by the elderly. The police have increased the residents' perception of the safety of their communities.

The St. Louis County (Missouri) Older Resident Program's (CORP) Crime Prevention Program gives senior citizens the social and mental stimulation that helps keep them alert and alive. Activities include an Opportunities Fair, a cable television show produced by retirees, crime prevention presentations at churches, social meetings and clubs, telephone reassurance, and help with insurance forms and legal documents. CORP protects elderly residents and boosts the spirit of older, home-bound individuals.

Contact Information

Director
St. Louis County
Older Resident Program's Crime Prevention Program
121 Marac Clayton Road
St. Louis, Missouri 63105
314-889-3516

American Association of Retired Persons
Criminal Justice Services-VOL
601 E Street, NW
Washington, DC 20049
202-434-2277

Special Community Events To Promote Prevention

Strategy

Special community events focus attention on crime prevention and help galvanize support for preventing crime, violence, and drug abuse and for improving the quality of life in the community.

Crime Problem Addressed

Some neighborhoods and municipalities use this strategy to focus attention on preventing the significant crime-related problems of the community, including drug trafficking or violence.

Key Components

The key components of this strategy include the following:

■ identification by residents of the central issue of concern, the purpose for the event;

■ a community group, coalition, or collection of residents to organize the rally, march, crime prevention fair, neighborhood party, vigil, or concert;

■ cooperation from local agencies and the police in providing information, services and facilities to support the event; and

■ publicity to help assure maximum community participation and reinforce community standards against crime.

Key Partnerships

Individual residents, crime prevention organizations, parent groups, civic clubs, religious congregations, and business owners can all be enlisted as partners in planning such events and implementing actions to address the problems which brought the community together. Police departments can provide educational materials and visible support for community members by their participation in the event; they can also help publicize the event throughout the community.

Potential Obstacles

Community events are most successful when the organizing groups include a broad representation of community members working together to address the community's problems and support the community's assets. Successful planning requires sufficient planning time and a media strategy.

Signs of Success

In Newport News, Virginia, Citizens Reclaiming Our Neighborhoods from Crime sponsored an antiviolence rally at a shopping mall. The mall, the police department,

the Girl Scouts, the fire department, the Mayor's Youth Commission, and many others supported this event. Saying "enough is enough" to crime, citizens organized a large, public rally in support of the police with the theme of "Back the Blue." The event also promoted formation of Neighborhood Watch programs. The whole community took back the streets of their neighborhood, showing community support for working with the police in making Newport News a safer place to live, to work, and to enjoy. The event inspired many, involved thousands of residents, and was well covered by the media.

Applying the Strategy

In Philadelphia, a "Weed and Seed" group banded together in a high-energy anti-drug march. Participants included 3,000 people from four schools, the Mayor, U.S. Department of Justice officials, educators, civic and political leaders, and the police. Marchers passing through a neighborhood ravaged by drug dealing filled six blocks as they chanted "No" to drugs.

Contact Information

Sergeant St. John
Newport News Police Department
2600 Washington Avenue
Newport News, Virginia 23607
804-247-8441

Provide Positive Alternatives to Gang Activity

Strategy

By providing positive alternatives to violent gang activities and tracking interaction with gang members, community groups can combat gang violence successfully.

Crime Problem Addressed

Surveys by the Office of Juvenile Justice and Delinquency Prevention (OJJDP) of the U.S. Department of Justice reveal increased youth gang activity in a rising number of cities. In recent years, youth gang activities have become more violent and more lethal. This strategy aims to reduce criminal youth gang activity and related juvenile delinquency by demonstrating the availability of more positive activities within the community.

Key Components

The key components of this strategy include community groups' recognition that gang activities involve violence and dangers to the individual members and to their communities; group resolve to identify, monitor, and reduce gang membership and activities; and a community-based effort to discourage young people from joining gangs.

Strategies to deter youth gang membership include education, counseling, and alternative activities, such as recreation and job training.

Key Partnerships

The key partnerships must exist among community groups providing services and must include community members who can identify the services most needed by youth involved in gang activity. The service providers, cooperating through a community organization, should include local schools, youth programs, recreation centers, religious groups, citizen patrols, and the police. Young people who are former gang members and staff of community organizations can form a variety of partnerships targeted to referring gang members to the program for support and services.

Potential Obstacles

One challenge is to reduce the fear of gang activity that can make some individuals and groups reluctant to get involved. Another is to gain the trust of the gang members, by listening to them and designing services that respond to their needs.

Signs of Success

According to OJJDP, the violence of gang activity is increasing. Gangs now operate across the country, even in smaller cities and formerly gang-free areas. Nationally, there has been a shift in strategies in the past forty years away from the social intervention approaches popular in the 1950s and 1960s to the suppression activities that started in the 1970s and continued into the 1990s,

However, respondents to surveys in several major cities with serious youth gang violence reported their belief that providing positive alternatives for gang members is the most effective strategy, with community organization being next most effective. Suppression strategies are considered to be less effective, except in conjunction with other approaches. Accordingly, OJJDP is focusing its gang prevention activities on comprehensive programs that include community-sponsored activities for youth, community organization to prevent and respond to gang activity, and police and court intervention both to interrupt destructive gang activity and to redirect the young person toward more positive community involvement.

Applying the Strategy

The Teens on Target program is helping youth become advocates for violence prevention. In collaboration with a school district, hospital, and rehabilitation center, Teens on Target trains urban youth who are at risk of participating in violent or gang activities to become health advocates for violence prevention. The program was started in Oakland and Los Angeles, California, two cities with high rates of youth violence. Teens on Target operates under the auspices of Youth ALIVE, a statewide public health agency that links public health information with community strategies to prevent violence by and against youth.

Established in 1989, the Teens on Target program provides peer education on violence and violence prevention at schools and conferences, educates professionals, informs the media on the causes of and solutions to violence, provides good role models, and urges policymakers to take action. Teenagers in the program make presentations to city, county, and state officials on a variety of topics including gun violence, family violence, street and gang violence, and violence related to drugs and alcohol. Thus, they serve as catalysts for more comprehensive community involvement with youth at risk and gang members and for mobilizing community resources to provide youth with opportunities that will reduce gang membership, violence, and victimization.

Contact Information

Teens on Target Coordinator
3012 Summit Avenue, Suite 3670
Summit Medical Center
Oakland, California 94609
510-444-6191

Reduce the Number of Handguns in the Community

Strategy

Buy-back programs and other strategies to reduce the number of handguns help reduce violence and other crime.

Crime Problem Addressed

Across the United States, an average of four people die from gunshot wounds each hour. Guns are the leading cause of death among males of all races ages fifteen to twenty-four. Firearms kill more teenagers than cancer, heart disease, AIDS, and all other biological diseases combined. A 1991 study of gun ownership and homicide published in the *New England Journal of Medicine* revealed that keeping a gun in a home nearly triples the chance that someone will be killed on the premises. Handguns accounted for six times the number of homicides committed by all other firearms combined. In homes with a gun, there is a five times greater chance that a family member will commit suicide. Treating a youth with a gunshot wound costs more than a year of college.

This strategy aims to reduce all crimes that involve guns, including assault, armed robbery, gang violence, and homicide. In addition, the strategy seeks to reduce accidents with handguns, many of which wound or kill children, and to reduce suicides, which occur much more often in homes where a gun is readily available.

Key Components

Among the key components of a gun buy-back strategy is the offer of incentives for people to turn in handguns, such as a cash payment, grocery store certificate, or concert tickets. Other important factors are a guarantee of anonymity for owners of illegal guns; numerous deposit sites to maximize gun-owner participation; publicity to advertise the gun turn-in program; and an educational component to reinforce the impact of gun violence and the importance of storing safely guns kept in the home.

Key Partnerships

The key partnerships are those between the sponsoring groups (often community organizations or local business leaders) and the police who receive and dispose of the guns. Another key partnership is between the sponsors and the media who help publicize the program and incentives. Schools, churches, youth groups, and civic, social, and service clubs should also publicize the program and encourage members to consider turning in their guns.

Potential Obstacles

One challenge is to ensure that guns can be turned in with no questions asked. Family members might be reluctant to turn in an illegal or unregistered gun if it would cause legal trouble. Another challenge is to find the donors to support the incentives used in a gun exchange program. Police may be reluctant to participate over concern about necessary resources to store the weapons and perform ballistics checks on the guns. The community should be educated to look at turn-in programs as one of many integrated strategies to reduce gun-related violence in a community.

Signs of Success

At the launch of the Cleveland, Ohio, gun exchange program in 1994, a city council member noted, "Handgun exchange programs have proven an effective way of getting unwanted handguns off our streets, as well as increasing the public's level of awareness to the dangers of guns and violence in America."

The Cleveland program netted 2,300 guns in 1994. The handgun exchange program provided a voucher for $75 worth of groceries for each operable handgun. Five churches served as neighborhood turn-in sites. Besides the Mayor's Office, other sponsors included a television station, a radio station, and supermarkets. Public media co-sponsorship helped assure that the word got out effectively. Cleveland's churches also reinforced the dangers of handguns used in violent acts and the benefits of the gun exchange program.

Applying the Strategy

In its six-day gun buy-back program, Norfolk, Virginia, collected 824 handguns, 235 shotguns and rifles, 1 machine gun, and 34 illegal sawed-off shotguns. Over the same period of time in 1992, Hennepin County, Minnesota, collected 6,000 firearms—1,000 per day! In a thirty-day period, St. Louis, Missouri, collected 7,500 guns.

Contact Information

Director
Violence Reduction and Crime Prevention
City Hall
Cleveland, Ohio 44114
216-664-4646

Center to Prevent Handgun Violence
1225 Eye Street, NW
Suite 1100
Washington, DC 20005
202-289-7319

Community Support Programs for Mentally Ill Offenders

Strategy

Community support programs for mentally ill offenders help create a positive environment for their return to the neighborhood, helping to reduce recidivism.

Crime Problem Addressed

This strategy addresses the criminal activity of mentally ill offenders, primarily crimes of theft, simple assault, and drug use. Community-based support and treatment systems for mentally ill offenders in the community are a cost-effective crime prevention tool, leaving more space in jails and hospital facilities for those who require secure detention.

Key Components

The key component of this strategy is a community-based group willing to work with mentally ill offenders to ease their re-entry into the community and keep them safe and crime free. Other components include referral systems to link offenders to community-based services; these referral systems should be based in hospitals, courts, and probation and parole programs. The supports provided may include medical and therapeutic services; money management counseling; housing and other support services; daily reporting by and monitoring of the clients; and a community education campaign to build acceptance of both the program and its clients.

Key Partnerships

The key partnership in this strategy exists between the community support program and the mentally ill offender. The offender must accept some supervision, take prescribed medication, and report daily for monitoring. Cooperation must also exist between the community support program and the sources of clients—such as the state hospital, probation and parole agencies, attorneys, hospitals, and the courts. Partnership and outreach to the host neighborhood for the facility is important to ensure the support of community residents and businesses. Collaboration with funding sources—governmental or private (for example, charitable organizations, hospitals, or foundations)—is also key to launching this strategy and implementing it on a long-term basis.

Potential Obstacles

Finding a welcoming host community for this kind of program can be one of the biggest challenges. Residents of a proposed location may fear that their safety, property values, and business success will be compromised. Proponents of this strategy must inform the community of the purpose and benefits of the program, explaining how it would be managed. Another challenge is locating local government resources to support the program. Some communities supplement local funds with volunteer counseling resources and in-kind donations of equipment, facilities, or expertise.

Signs of Success

The mentally ill offender requires more intensive monitoring than most probation departments can provide. A community support program can fill this need. The needs of the low-risk mentally ill offender can be met in the community at a lower cost than incarceration or forced hospitalization. For example, community support programs cost about $3,000 per person per year, while imprisonment can cost more than $30,000 per year. Hospitalization typically costs even more than imprisonment.

Applying the Strategy

In 1978, the city of Milwaukee, Wisconsin, noticed large numbers of mentally ill offenders in its courts and jails.

The Community Support Program (CSP) was established to reduce those high numbers, while effectively meeting the special needs of the mentally ill offender. The program is delivered through the Wisconsin Correctional Service, a private, not-for-profit organization that offers a community-based program for the mentally ill offenders. Many of these clients are diagnosed with conditions that require medication to control behavior. The criminal justice system uses formal legal authority to place these individuals into the program. CSP also accepts referrals of persons who are at-risk of committing an act that leads to arrest. Clients enter the program because it offers them needed social services and life supports, such as help with finances, housing, and jobs.

Milwaukee believes so strongly in the program's success that it has launched three additional community support programs—two private, and one governmental. The program has consistently achieved its goal of reducing the numbers of mentally ill in the courts and jails and has been praised by judges and social workers.

Contact Information

Wisconsin Correction Service
436 West Wisconsin Avenue
Milwaukee, Wisconsin 53203
414-271-2512

Support Needs of Recent Immigrants

Strategy

Formal programs and policies to support the assimilation and needs of recent immigrant groups help ensure the stability of those groups and reinforce positive opportunities for their development within the community.

Crime Problem Addressed

Crimes of domestic violence, assault, and property damage are reported to law enforcement less often in communities with recent immigrant residents. Language barriers, mistrust of authoritative institutions, and fear combine to result in low reporting rates. Local systems that help deter, detect, punish, and redirect criminal behavior may not be understood or seen as beneficial by residents new to the United States. This strategy aims to reduce the frequency of many kinds of crime in recent immigrant communities, through educating new residents and reforming policies and systems.

Key Components

Key components of this strategy include the following:

- recognition of recent immigrants' needs for information, services, and other support to help in their transition to life in American society;

- cooperation with community groups in surveying the needs of immigrant residents;

- policies and programs that ensure access to services needed by the immigrants;

- cultural awareness and language training for relevant local government employees;

- community-based transition assistance services to help educate new residents about communication and language skills, banking and managing family budgets, employment, conflict resolution, and crime reporting;

- victim and witness services in the language(s) of the immigrant community; and

- neighborhood-based services to help ensure access by residents in need.

Key Partnerships

Local government and community-based agencies combine services provided in the neighborhood and through law enforcement, social agencies, schools, churches, and civic groups. Some local governments, businesses, and other agencies advocate for support services delivered solely through culturally based community organizations.

Potential Obstacles

Locating or developing personnel with the appropriate multicultural skills may prove challenging. Mistrust and fear among recent immigrants and law enforcement personnel may require patience and long-term strategies to build cooperative relationships.

Signs of Success

This strategy will become increasingly important in the coming decades. Projected changes in demographic trends suggest that local government will need to pay greater attention to the needs of first- and second-generation immigrants from many diverse cultures.

Portland, Oregon, reports that following the establishment of programs to support recent immigrant Asian residents, those residents built cooperative relationships with the police, increased the rate with which they reported crimes, and noted that they feel safer in the community. La Familia Counseling Center in Sacramento, California, initiated successful outreach services after realizing that some newly arrived Hispanic immigrants felt too intimidated to ask for help from police or social service agencies.

Applying the Strategy

Honolulu, Hawaii, implemented cultural awareness training for police recruits to ensure their sensitivity in dealing with the substantial minority Asian-born population of the city. Residents report that the training resulted in officers who were better equipped to respond to their needs. In Milwaukee, Wisconsin, the Council for Spanish Speaking found that many people benefit from counseling on how to observe and report a crime and from victim assistance and help to prepare lawsuits to recover their losses. The Seattle Police Department similarly responded to the crime-related deaths of fifteen Asian residents; after their outreach to the immigrant communities, the number of murders dropped.

Contact Information

Community Policing Assistant
Portland Police Bureau Central Precinct
1111 SW 2nd Avenue
Portland, Oregon 97204
503-823-4636

Community Relations Division
Honolulu Police Department
801 S. Beretania Street
Honolulu, Hawaii 96813
808-529-3111

Community Job Banks

Strategy

Community job banks that also provide transportation assistance, educational support, counseling, and links to other social services help residents find secure employment, reducing their risk of involvement in criminal activity.

Crime Problem Addressed

Law enforcement officials and social researchers agree that reducing unemployment in an economically stressed community helps increase the stability of residents within the community, lessening the likelihood that residents will commit crimes.

Key Components

The most important component for this strategy is an interested community group with experience in helping local residents find jobs through a system of assisted job placement—a "job bank." The group operating the program is often a community development corporation, a business coalition, a council of civic associations, or a community-wide coalition of groups. A second component is a cadre of businesses willing both to inform the community job bank of openings for employees and to train newly hired employees. Such a program requires funding beyond that generated by placement fees charged to employers. Transportation, some training or counseling, and links to other social services are also important components for success.

Key Partnerships

Key partnerships include those formed between the job bank and

■ local government, for publicity and for links to government social services and other community organizations.

- businesses in or near the community that will share their needs for employees and help the job bank find or train local residents to fill those positions.

- government programs providing transportation, social workers for family counseling, and employment services.

- other community groups that can provide clothing, food, or tools as needed.

- community members who have personnel, occupational, child care, or counseling skills they can share.

- funding sources, such as foundations, philanthropists, corporations, nonprofit organizations, government programs, or individual contributors to fundraising campaigns.

These partnerships give community job banks an excellent chance to succeed in placing the unemployed in new positions.

Potential Obstacles

A common challenge in such programs is that some of the clients are difficult to place. Such clients may include those with little education or literacy, those with physical or mental disabilities, and the long-term unemployed. They may lack homes and family member support, and some may have been recently released from jail or a mental institution. However, the community job bank, with its links to other services and training programs, can help most of those who seek its services.

Signs of Success

Unemployment is a well-researched and documented risk factor for criminal activity. Secure employment helps end both the frustration of the unemployed and the potential likelihood of their involvement in criminal activity. Surveys reveal that in neighborhoods where the unemployment rates are twice the area average, crime rates, too, are often double the average of the communities with higher employment.

Applying the Strategy

The Weed and Seed Community Job Bank in Fort Worth, Texas, funded by the U.S. Department of Justice, has achieved much success. Residents who participated in community planning meetings realized that the priority problems in their neighborhood were crime, lack of economic development, and unemployment. They took the initiative to create the Weed and Seed Job Bank.

In two years, the Job Bank secured employment for nearly 900 community residents. The program placed 50 residents in jobs at the Dallas-Fort Worth Airport. The Department of Transportation also participates, donating three vans to transport residents to jobs and training sites. Community police officers often refer people to the job bank. Clients who fail a drug test are referred to a drug rehabilitation center, and those without a high school diploma are referred to classes. Other community agencies provide clothing and job-seeking skills training.

Contact Information

Weed and Seed Job Bank
1310 South Collard Street
Fort Worth, Texas 76105
817-534-3293

Use Codes and Ordinances To Prevent Crime

Strategy

Building codes and other ordinances provide local authorities with an effective tool for crime prevention and law enforcement.

Crime Problem Addressed

Enforcing sanitary, electrical, and other codes, ordinances, and laws can greatly help communities to counter crime, especially crimes related to neglected or vacant properties and public spaces. Such properties often attract substance abuse, drug trafficking, vandalism, prostitution, boisterous gatherings, and health violations. This strategy bolsters the resources of law enforcement agencies seeking to reduce crime at those locations.

Key Components

Concerns about crime at certain properties, on specific streets, or in public places are usually coupled with questions of compliance with occupancy codes, health standards, fire dangers, or illegal utility connections. In this strategy, local law enforcement collaborates with resident groups, the courts, public works departments, utility companies, and fire, health, inspection and code enforcement agencies to work with landowners to address violations of ordinances, codes, and laws governing use of property. Enforcement of codes culminates in legal sanctions and fines for non-cooperative property owners.

The strategy allows law enforcement to charge property owners, tenants, or residents who use public spaces with violations of the law that are easier to prove (exceeding occupancy standards, unhealthful living conditions, fire hazards, loitering, illegal utility hookups, etc.) than criminal charges for activities requiring witnesses or other evidence.

Key Partnerships

The partnership between residents and law enforcement prompts the identification of community concerns that can be addressed through code enforcement and other laws. Law enforcement agencies initiate partnerships with the other agencies, using them to develop multiagency inspection and enforcement teams to deal with problem properties and suspected criminal activities. Crime-reporting hotlines can help by receiving complaints from residents for follow-up by police or other agencies.

Potential Obstacles

Local government bureaucracy may slow the response of agencies to community concerns about crime-related issues and the need for code enforcement. Formalized interagency partnerships reduce the likelihood of delays. Reforming existing codes to build in graduated sanctions helps ensure compliance by property owners, even those outside the jurisdiction. Publicity of properties in violation also improves compliance by recalcitrant owners.

Signs of Success

Most states have a wide range of codes and laws on health, fire, and safety, including noise and nuisance abatement. Citizen groups across the country are starting to use these codes with increasing success. Most states also have Small Claims Courts, which are low-cost and "user friendly" for residents and groups with complaints.

Residents of Portland, Oregon, passed a Specified Crime Property Ordinance, resulting in the closure of over 400 drug houses. Nuisance abatement laws authorize private citizens, local agencies, or city attorneys to file civil suits against property owners who knowingly allow certain nuisances or misconduct to take place on their property. The laws subject property owners to both criminal and civil liability. These laws have eliminated graffiti, noise pollution, and gang activity, and their enforcement can lead to evictions, property condemnations, and prosecutions.

Applying the Strategy

Des Moines, Iowa, residents helped win enactment of a Specified Crime Property Ordinance. Police inform a property owner about criminal activity taking place at a particular property (drug dealing, gang violence, vandalism, under-age drinking parties). If proven illegal activity on the property does not cease within a specified time or if the owner does not cooperate with police to address the problem, the owner is fined and the property can be seized by the city; additional fines can be imposed for as long as the violations continue. As a result of this program, resident cooperation with police has improved, and remediation of problem properties now occurs with fewer bureaucratic delays.

Contact Information

Director
Citizens for Community Improvement of Des Moines
2301 Forest Avenue
Des Moines, Iowa 50311
515-255-0800

Use Media as an Ally

Strategy

Local media coverage of and support for community crime prevention help raise public awareness and encourage participation in community-based projects.

Crime Problem Addressed

This strategy advocates the use of local television, radio, newspapers, and other media to focus attention on community-based crime prevention projects and organizations. By highlighting such efforts, the media reinforces the community's standard in opposition to all types of crime and helps build crime prevention awareness among the public.

Key Components

Key tasks of this strategy include recognizing the power of the media as the public's source of information on a variety of topics; identifying media contacts; and establishing cooperation between community programs and media resources. The media should be asked to publicize community events and promote public education on crime prevention through articles, public service announcements, radio shows, news programs, and cable television shows.

Key Partnerships

Local crime prevention organizations must recognize their contacts in the public media as important partners in spreading the crime prevention message. Members of community-based crime prevention programs can begin to build partnerships with media sources by talking with reporters assigned to cover crime or community-related issues and by asking media sources for help in designing a public education campaign. Community leaders, key elected officials, church leaders, school board and Parent-Teacher Association members, philanthropists, and local celebrities often maintain contact with media sources who could be brought together to sponsor or support crime prevention activities in the community.

Potential Obstacles

Community groups may find it difficult to see local media as partners in crime prevention. Media of all types have frequently been characterized as part of the problem communities have with violence. Many communities now see the media as part of the strategy for educating the public and building public support for organizations and programs. Still, the media gravitate toward stories easy to understand and describe. To gather media support and coverage, community groups should attempt to design events or celebrations that clearly communicate their programs' successes and that highlight celebrity involvement, elected officials' participation, youth leadership, and dramatic visual or audio components.

Signs of Success

Crime and fear of crime consistently rank among the top fears of the American public in national and local surveys. Thus, a new crime prevention activity in which large numbers of people participate and achieve success locally is newsworthy.

In Memphis, Tennessee, the mayor, citizens, businesses, and community groups recently raised $1 million in donations for the police department through "Operation Drive Out Crime," which engaged local television and radio stations and the local newspaper as cosponsors.

The campaign relied on local television and radio news stories and public appeals, as well as newspaper public service announcements for publicity. When first approached, a local network television affiliate station had just begun a three-month anticrime campaign, so station managers viewed Operation Drive Out Crime as a welcome tie-in. That station produced promotional spots and aired them each night, often during prime time. The same station also included many news stories, often focusing on the department's need for resources.

A radio station also joined in the effort as a sponsor, running daily advertisements, highlighting the project during shows, and running weekly interviews with sponsors and police officers. The newspaper carried stories and contributed advertising. In addition, it included contribution envelopes in two different Sunday editions of the paper. Effective local publicity led to national publicity, and donations have poured in from across the state and around the country.

Applying the Strategy

Cleveland's mayor enlisted the sponsorship of a local television station and radio station for his announcement of the city's gun exchange and violence reduction and crime prevention initiatives. The television station not only helped to announce these very successful initiatives, it also operated the telephone banks for donations.

Contact Information

Operation Drive Out Crime
Coletta & Company
41 Union Avenue
Memphis, Tennessee 38103
901-528-0800

Faith Institution-Supported Mentoring

Strategy

Faith congregations that sponsor mentoring programs signal community support for families and youth and reinforce positive social bonds within the neighborhood.

Crime Problem Addressed

This strategy aims to reduce the likelihood of delinquent or criminal behavior within families and by youth through community reinforcement of values and consistent presence of caring community members. Social researchers often trace the problems of youth crime and violence to dysfunctional families, the stresses of economic deprivation, and to community standards for unhealthy, unproductive ways of dealing with conflict. This strategy addresses those problems through community role models.

Key Components

Faith community outreach to families, youth, and other residents in their communities simulates a supportive extended family. Volunteers from within the congregation can reinforce community values by engaging in the following kinds of activities:

- supporting parents in building better communication skills;

- helping locate jobs or training;

- mentoring youth;

- pairing youth with "surrogate" grandparents;

- facilitating connections with emergency food and housing assistance; and

- providing tutoring support to youth and adults.

Key Partnerships

Faith group or church members are linked to many other resources in the community through their professions, memberships in civic groups, connections to ethnic organizations, and other volunteer commitments. Pastors and lay faith leaders can encourage formal institutional programs, facilitate connections to existing community services, and promote participation through reinforcement of the core values of the faith-based community.

Potential Obstacles

Recruiting and training mentoring volunteers consumes a great deal of time. Once trained, the mentors face the challenge of building the trust needed for the families and individuals to share concerns. However, community-based volunteer mentoring programs are not costly and do not represent significant fundraising challenges.

Signs of Success

The Florence V. Burden Foundation—which has a special interest in crime, justice, and strengthening family and community—funded a demonstration initiative in three cities (Hartford, CT.; New York, NY; and Washington, DC) to explore ways that churches and divinity schools can support fragile families. The program matches parents in need with an adult mentor. Hundreds of volunteer

mentors were recruited from the congregations, trained at divinity schools, and placed with families in need.

This low-cost program re-creates extended family relationships, breaking the pattern of isolation experienced by many parents who are separated from their own parents and families. The nature and direction of each mentorship is determined by the parents and the mentor. The common elements are listening and problem-solving. By helping parents develop skills to provide a healthy, nurturing environment for their children, these faith communities have helped ensure positive development for thousands of youth.

Applying the Strategy

Baltimore's Bethel African Methodist Episcopal Church established an Outreach Center in 1975 as a means of rebuilding a dwindling church community and revitalizing its connection to an increasingly troubled neighborhood. The center began as a church-run center offering tutoring, job counseling, crisis assistance, a preschool, parenting classes, and space for meetings of neighborhood associations and block watch groups. The success of the Bethel Outreach Center resulted in the formation of a larger center separate from the church, even though the church remains the spiritual home of the center's volunteers and many of the families it serves. The congregation had grown by 50 percent by 1994 and the center continues to help thousands of youth and families.

Contact Information

Florence F. Burden Foundation Project
Yale Divinity School
409 Prospect Street
New Haven, Connecticut 06510
203-432-5345

Nurture Community Groups and Neighborhood Associations

Strategy

Local government support of community groups and neighborhood associations helps build neighborhood leadership and stability in those communities.

Crime Problem Addressed

The crime issues effectively addressed through this strategy include a variety of offenses and conditions related to crimes that affect neighborhoods: vandalism (including graffiti), dilapidated housing units, theft, burglary, gang activity, and drug dealing. Neighborhood and crime prevention organizations working to create healthier communities can help law enforcement agencies alleviate a broad range of problems concerning residents.

Key Components

Local government must commit to specific strategies to support and enhance neighborhood organizations interested in promoting healthy and safe communities. Speaker's bureaus serve as a training and coordinating resource for fledgling community groups. Local government agencies such as police departments and neighborhood service agencies often provide a variety of services. These service can include:

- grants to implement small neighborhood improvement and public safety projects;

- training in recruiting and using volunteers;

- leadership development;

- educational materials and information on successful organization and program strategies; and

- advice on fundraising.

Key Partnerships

Key partnerships include those that local government facilitates among civic associations, crime watch groups, local religious organizations, service and civic clubs, and community-based organizations that deliver services to youth, families, and neighborhoods.

Potential Obstacles

Obstacles to the formation of a block or neighborhood grassroots volunteer group include residents' apathy, doubts about their ability to help improve the neighborhood, and fear of crime in the area. Some residents not only feel powerless to make a difference but also lack the self-confidence to try. Furthermore, in lower-income areas, more families are headed by a single parent, some of whom may work more than one job to make ends meet—leaving little time or energy for volunteering.

Local government agencies can make available the resources, contacts, and support neighborhood groups often need:

- information on how to arrange and conduct meetings;

- neighborhood survey techniques and samples;

- guidance on how to access the news media; and

- how to form partnerships with other groups.

Volunteer or city staff facilitators can support such programs and lend objective advice.

Signs of Success

The National Association of Neighborhoods supports community groups by providing training, educational materials, and informative publications on building effective and safe communities at the neighborhood level.

The nonprofit Citizens Committee for New York City (CCNYC)—established in 1975 to help cushion the impacts of a severe fiscal crisis and reduced government-provided services—has fostered the development of hundreds of new block and neighborhood associations and nurtured many others. Training and information offered through the CCNYC's Leadership Institute promotes neighborhood self-help throughout the city.

CCNYC also provides community mobilization training for neighborhood groups. Free guides describe anti-drug and anti-poverty projects, community beautification, and neighborhood leadership development. CCNYC's Neighborhood Anticrime Center supports a citywide coalition of over 200 volunteer neighborhood groups, which have closed down drug houses, formed resident patrols, rid streets of drug sales, and trained residents in crime prevention reporting. Staff have trained 500 community patrol officers in the New York City Police Department and awarded hundreds of grants to community organization to support crime, violence, and drug-use prevention projects.

Applying the Strategy

In 1993, Hampton, Virginia, began the Healthy Neighborhoods Initiative, which builds on the strength of neighborhoods through the Technical Resource Center and Leadership Training Institute. This approach fosters cooperation among neighborhoods and enhances community groups' capacity to improve their quality of life.

St. Paul, Minnesota, supports a Safe City Initiative, which envisions a city where residents and agencies cooperate fully in identifying assets neighborhoods should use to address public safety issues. A primary focus of the effort includes reinforcing social support, opportunity, and development within the city's neighborhoods. Neighborhood safety audits help neighborhood groups and interdepartmental teams develop action strategies and a database of local public safety concerns. One district group and the area Neighborhood Development Company used the audit information to prepare a grant proposal to finance housing improvements.

Contact Information

Neighborhood Leadership Institute
Citizens Committee for New York City
305 7th Avenue, 15th Floor
New York, New York 10001
212-989-0909

Citizen Patrols

Strategy

Organized citizen patrols supported by local law enforcement improve public trust of police, protect the community from crime, and increase social cohesion among neighborhood residents.

Crime Problem Addressed

This strategy addresses all types of crime in a community, but has particular impact on street-corner drug dealing, prostitution, vandalism, and gang activity. Resident presence and visible control of an area can serve as a significant deterrent to these crimes.

Key Components

This strategy puts neighborhood residents, working in cooperation with local law enforcement, in visible foot or car patrols in the community to deter, detect, and report crimes. Key components include the following:

- a community group to organize the patrol volunteers and coordinate contact with the police;

- patrol volunteer recruitment;

- training in police procedure and crime reporting;

- communication networks to connect patrol members and the police, through radios or other technology;

- publicity material which makes clear the community's intention to protect itself; and

- a uniform to make patrol members visible to police and other members of the community.

While focusing on patrols through specific areas, many programs make a point to contact youth, conversing with them at "hot spots" of criminal activity and inviting them to participate in safe and positive activities.

Key Partnerships

Working together, the patrol organizers and local law enforcement officers publicize the program (to both law-abiding residents and criminals) and design needed training for patrol members. Friendships among neighbors helps strengthen communication networks and support for victims and patrol activities. Local businesses often support patrols by providing funds for patrol "uniforms" and communication equipment.

Potential Obstacles

Fear of crime and of retribution from criminals, apathy, and mistrust of police can prevent residents from participating in patrols. Opportunities to staff communication links or develop publicity materials allow fearful residents to support the program without putting themselves in danger. Police training of volunteers, community support, and large numbers of volunteer patrol members also help alleviate fear and increase the likelihood of success.

Signs of Success

Crime rates in Fort Worth, Texas, plunged by over 20 percent in 1993, the first year of heavy community participation in the Citizens on Patrol Program—a partnership between the police and local community groups. By early 1994, 1,500 residents had received 12 hours of crime prevention training, using it to deter and report crime in their neighborhoods. The nationally recognized program represents a cornerstone of the city's respected community policing program.

In Omaha, Nebraska, a father whose son was beaten by a gang founded MAD DADS—Men Against Destruction: Defending Against Drugs and Social Disorder. Starting with a few men, MAD DADS walked into the night to see what was going on and to try to get some of the wayward youth back on a better track. Now, its membership has grown to over 1,000 men and women who each volunteer up to hundreds of hours each year. Their mission is to save their community, one individual at a time.

Volunteers report criminal activity and communicate with gang-involved youth they meet on the streets. Publicity from local television stations elevated some patrol members to celebrity status, reinforcing their appeal with the youth. MAD DADS' mission and multicultural membership has enhanced racial harmony in Omaha. Patrols now use citizen band radios, cellular phones, and police scanners. By the end of 1994, this strategy had spread to dozens of cities, including a statewide program in Florida.

Applying the Strategy

The Brighton Neighborhood Improvement Program in Brooklyn, New York, started after residents grew tired of crime and substance abuse. A retired union organizer mobilized a group of retired residents in the community into a crime watch and patrol program, working cooperatively with law enforcement, the Coast Guard, and a local Marine Corps post. The group operates a jeep patrol, foot patrol, and drug busters program, all of which give police information about drug trafficking in the area. This successful program also offers to train other communities on starting patrols.

Contact Information

Citizens on Patrol
Fort Worth Police Department
350 West Belknap Street
Fort Worth, Texas 76102
817-877-8385

President
MAD DADS National Headquarters
3030 Sprague Street
Omaha, Nebraska 68111
402-451-3366

Local Government-Community Crime Prevention Coalitions

Strategy

Comprehensive local crime prevention plans are most effective when developed through a coalition of community groups, local government agencies, and other sectors.

Crime Problem Addressed

This strategy aims to reduce all types of crime. A comprehensive local crime prevention plan helps address goals and objectives that focus on particular crime problems, such as youth violence, drugs, property crime, and neighborhood deterioration. This strategy mobilizes affected groups to participate in reducing crime.

Key Components

The key components of this strategy to develop a comprehensive plan include the following:

■ support of key political leaders and law enforcement officials;

■ a commitment to a process open to all sectors of the community;

■ a vision shared to by all participants;

■ specific goals and objectives;

■ committees or task forces to study and develop recommendations on priority community issues—such as violence, drugs, guns, child safety, schools, gangs; and

■ review, evaluation, and amendment of the plan as conditions in the community change.

Key Partnerships

Key partnerships required for the success of this strategy include those among community residents, political leaders, municipal agencies, and the police department. City agencies responsible for implementing key components of the plan must develop written agreements governing relationships among their staff and reinforcing accountability for specific tasks. Other key partnership members include those whose input strengthens the plan: school officials; religious leaders; business owners; civic, social, and service clubs; neighborhood watch groups; chambers of commerce; and parent organizations.

Potential Obstacles

Community members may be reluctant to participate, doubting their input will be valued. Some residents of violence-plagued neighborhoods may have retreated from community involvement out of fear for their safety; these individuals are difficult to mobilize. Agencies that do not consider public safety issues as part of their mission may resist involvement, not wanting to place any other burdens on a strained budget. Political and business leaders sometimes view the planning process as labeling the area as "dangerous" and may not want to make such a statement which could result in additional demands for service from residents.

Signs of Success

In 1992, the mayors of the seven largest cities in Texas formed Mayors United on Safety, Crime, and Law Enforcement (MUSCLE). Later that year, with the support of the Bureau of Justice Assistance, the seven cities initiated local government-grassroots crime prevention planning projects involving all sectors of their communities. In San Antonio, a local ordinance established the Greater San Antonio Crime Prevention Commission, the nation's first legislatively created local crime prevention body. Its 29 members represent civic, religious, neighborhood, military, business, and government groups. After a year of work by five task forces (Youth and Education, Violent Crime, Business, Neighborhood, and Public Information), the Commission succeeded in developing a Crime Prevention Action Plan with specific goals and objectives.

Of the plan's fifty-six objectives, fifty-five were implemented within two years. These accomplishments included the following:

■ obtaining a $10 million increase in funding for youth recreation programs;

■ establishing a late-night curfew for teenagers;

■ initiating a locally developed gang prevention effort highlighted by a public education campaign;

■ establishing youth leadership development programs at area schools;

■ implementing school-based conflict resolution programs;

■ expanding community policing;

■ establishing a business crime commission;

■ garnering corporate support for mentoring programs; and

■ coordinating a week-long focus on prayer for violence prevention by area religious leaders.

Since the plan was implemented, youth victimization by crime during curfew hours has declined significantly, and overall crime has dropped each year.

Applying the Strategy

In 1993, the mayor of St. Petersburg, Florida, created the Neighborhood Partnership Department to increase government responsiveness to resident concerns and neighborhood issues, particularly public safety. The Department now works with sixty-five active neighborhood organizations, the Council of Neighborhood Associations, and the Federation of Inner-City Community Organizations. The Department links city agencies with residents to implement neighborhood plans, improve neighborhoods, address code violations, and implement community outreach programs.

A six-month-long intensive focus by police, fire, code, housing, public works and other agencies, Operation Commitment, in St. Petersburg, Florida, catalyzes implementation of neighborhood improvement plans developed cooperatively by residents. In addition, the Neighborhood Grant Partnership Program allocates funds for small grants to neighborhood associations for special events, landscaping, new road signs, or educational brochures. According to the city, the program has invested over $1.2 million in capital improvements; $300,000 is made available for neighborhoods to use for projects, $250,000 has been invested by nonprofit organizations, and about $500,000 worth of housing rehabilitation and construction has occurred. As part of Operation Commitment police resolved thirty-one of thirty-four public safety problem areas identified by residents; tons of trash were collected; miles of sidewalks were added; and over 100 streetlights were installed.

Contact Information

Greater San Antonio Crime Prevention Commission
San Antonio Police Department
Crime Prevention Division
214 West Nueva
San Antonio, Texas 78207
210-207-7575

Encourage Community Support for Law Enforcement

Strategy

Community support for police reinforces public safety and builds the foundation for continued cooperation to prevent crime.

Crime Problem Addressed

This strategy seeks to prevent crime by developing active, grassroots community support for the police. The goal is to reduce crime of all kinds, but especially street crimes that can be deterred by an active and visible presence of concerned community members and police. These street crimes include vandalism, mugging, purse snatching, car theft, open-air drug dealing, and gang violence.

Key Components

The key component of this strategy is for the community members to realize that broad-based, grassroots community support for the police bolsters public safety. The police department must also be committed to actively seeking the support of community members and organizations. The media must be enlisted to promote community education and mobilization and to show the community's support for law enforcement.

Key Partnerships

The key partnership for this strategy exists between the community and the police, visibly working together to prevent crime. Publicity—generated through radio and television stations, community and general circulation newspapers, and computer bulletin boards—encourages participation in community-sponsored events that focus on supporting the police. Community partners should include civic and watch associations, faith groups, schools, civic and service clubs, crime councils, chambers of commerce and other business organizations, and youth groups.

Potential Obstacles

A potential obstacle is that some groups may harbor suspicion toward the police because of past incidents or misunderstandings, or because they feel vulnerable to the police.

Signs of Success

In Memphis, Tennessee, a grassroots community coalition raised $1 million for sixty new marked police cars, $100,000 in the first three months alone. This community support for the police allows officers to drive their police cars home and for personal use around the city. This fringe benefit for the police raises police morale and positive recognition from the community. Even when off duty, officers leave their radios on and respond to crime reports in their vicinity. The community group sponsors include a bank, a grocery store, as well as television, radio, and print media. The mayor's office and many other community groups and businesses are also actively involved.

Applying the Strategy

The "Back the Blue" campaign in Newport News, Virginia, is another example of citizens rallying to support their police in a visible way. The organization Citizens

Reclaiming Our Neighborhoods from Crime sponsored an antiviolence rally at a shopping mall, with a wide range of supporters. Saying "enough is enough" to crime, citizens held a large, public rally, with information booths on how to organize crime watch programs. The goal was to get the whole community involved in taking back the streets of their neighborhoods.

Contact Information

Operation Drive Out Crime
Coletta & Company
41 Union Avenue
Memphis, Tennessee 38103
901-528-0800

Community Coalitions To Combat Crime, Violence, and Drug Abuse

Strategy

Mobilizing community coalitions for neighborhood revitalization through resident partnership with government will reduce crime and drug trafficking and improve the quality of life.

Crime Problem Addressed

This strategy effectively addresses drug trafficking, vandalism, abandoned housing, or any other public safety-related issues the local community identifies as priority concerns. The ultimate goal is to improve the overall quality of life of the community and to develop a feeling of cohesion and well-being among community residents.

Key Components

The first component of this strategy is a grassroots approach to local citizen empowerment. Another component is citizen identification of priority issues for action (for example, reducing the prevalence of alcohol and other drug use or drug trafficking). A third component is a partnership among residents and community organizations and local government—all working hand-in-hand to identify and solve problems. A fourth component is the development of strategies that residents and government officials can use to achieve specific goals, including identifying and gathering the needed community support and resources. Activities can include rallies and marches, youth recreation programs, parent-teen workshops, citizen crime patrols, media involvement, and intensive application of city services in targeted neighborhoods.

Key Partnerships

Key partnerships needed for this strategy include those formed among local residents working together to improve the local community. Coalition partners should include residents, parent groups, block watches, businesses, schools, and religious, civic, and service organizations. The third level of partnership is between the local citizens and groups and the local government agencies, particularly law enforcement.

Potential Obstacles

A common obstacle to mobilizing a community is the residents' fear, mistrust, and reluctance to get involved. One solution to this fear is to enlist those who have already engaged in joint action, even if for a completely different purpose. Another is to have residents invite the involvement of people whom they know. A second obstacle is that coming to quick consensus on one or a few problems or goals for immediate attention may prove difficult. Establishing clear priorities helps focus the effort and increases the potential for success.

Signs of Success

Community Responses to Drug Abuse (CRDA)—a demonstration project supported by the Bureau of Justice Assistance, Office of Justice Programs, U.S. Department of Justice and assisted by the National Crime Prevention Council (NCPC), demonstrates the success of this strategy. Ten economically distressed and crime-plagued urban communities across the country used grassroots resident partnerships with police to achieve results. They returned parks to local children and residents; built a high school; changed policies of local agencies; used codes, ordinances, and laws to shut down drug houses and curb street drug dealing and related violence; and made tutoring and recreational services available to local youth. The NCPC publication *Creating a Climate of Hope* catalogues the communities' successes.

Applying the Strategy

In the Pinellas County (Florida) Community Partnership Program, the communities of North Greenwood, Safety Harbor, and Tarpon Springs developed three distinct resident-driven community crime prevention partnerships, working hand-in-hand with the local government. Crime statistics in those communities show a reduction in drug-related arrests. In one community, overall crime has dropped 20 percent since the program began in 1992.

Contact Information

National Crime Prevention Council
1700 K Street, NW, 2nd Floor
Washington, DC 20006
202-466-6272

Broad-Based Community Programs To Support Youth Development

Strategy

Community organizations and local government agencies support the positive development of disadvantaged youth by providing a range of services.

Crime Problem Addressed

Juvenile delinquency and violent crime by juveniles can be prevented and reduced through outreach to youth with a variety of supportive services.

Key Components

The key component of this strategy is bringing the community to a new level of vitality and action by making it aware that it has resources—talent, connections, and access to government programs—that enable it to respond to the challenges it faces. The community must develop strong, confident self-advocacy. Finally, essential programs must be established: Services provided must include education and counseling for children, adolescents, young adults, families, and the unemployed.

Key Partnerships

The central partnerships in this strategy must exist between the organizers, those involved in education and recreation, faith groups that operate community programs, local university faculty and students, and other community groups and members. Other key partnerships are between organizers and youth advocates, and between the programs and the police and courts.

Potential Obstacles

One challenge is to find inspirational community-based leadership willing to work with local government to convince the residents of a disadvantaged community that they have considerable powers and skills to help turn their communities around.

Signs of Success

In one community in Puerto Rico, crime rates have dropped significantly (between 10 and 20 percent) and juvenile delinquency rates have dropped nearly in half (by 47 percent). At first, the police reacted with measured enthusiasm to community interventions for community rehabilitation of offenders; however, they began to cooperate with the community's advocates and outreach programs. As the police saw delinquency and crime rates dropping, their confidence and cooperation in community-based interventions and solutions increased.

Applying the Strategy

This strategy has been used successfully in Ponce, Puerto Rico, since 1969. A U.S.-trained sociologist founded Centros Sor Isolina Ferre in Ponce Playa—the poor port section of Puerto Rico's second largest city. Its delinquency rates were twice that of the rest of the city. The strategy helped a declining community tap its own human resources, take care of its own troubled youth, and revitalize itself.

In this program, young people are chosen and prepared to act as community advocates for other young people, who are involved with the police and courts. At first, the police saw these advocates as diverting arrested individuals away from the criminal justice system, but in time the police came see them as effective in rehabilitation. With their knowledge of the streets and the problems of troubled youth, the advocates become the big brothers and big sisters of the juveniles in trouble. Now, the police often call the Ponce Playa advocates before taking problem youth to jail. Once in satisfying employment, there is no room for violence to take root. Juvenile delinquency rates are reported to have dropped nearly in half.

The centers currently operate forty different community-based programs that provide education and counseling, offering services to children, runaways, dropouts, and the unemployed. Staff work with adolescents, single mothers, young adults, and families.

There are a number of community organizations, like Northwest Bronx Community Clergy Coalition (NWBCCC), that are assisting the residents of large apartment buildings to organize to begin to take care of themselves. Residents actively support one another's needs, with crime watch, day care, job search counseling, and maintenance of their buildings. These efforts lead to jobs, a sense of ownership and pride, sharper eyes and ears to aid the police, and crime reduction.

Contact Information

Centros Sor Isolina Ferre
P.O. Box 213
Ponce, Puerto Rico 00734-3213

Executive Director
NWBCCC
103 East 196th Street
Bronx, New York 10468
718-584-0515

Use Senior Citizens as Volunteers

Strategy

Senior citizens working with law enforcement provide valuable services, permitting officers more time to address crime in the community.

Crime Problem Addressed

The elderly can be vulnerable to crime and are often the special targets of some confidence schemes. A large portion of older persons live alone. They fear crime, and that fear restricts the mobility and quality of life of many senior citizens. Others, however, are joining with younger volunteers and working with their police departments to reduce all crime, including crimes against the elderly. This strategy gets the able elderly involved as volunteers in law enforcement to reduce crime and to apprehend criminals.

Key Components

Recruiting senior citizens as volunteers and clearly outlining the volunteers' roles and responsibilities is a vital element of a successful senior volunteer project. Such volunteer projects can address many needs of the senior population and the entire community: answering non-emergency calls, checking up on senior shut-ins, staffing citizen patrols, organizing crime watch groups, and helping maintain non-confidential records.

Key Partnerships

Key partnerships are formed between the volunteers and the police with whom they work. A key umbrella partnership that brings many of them together is TRIAD, an alliance of the American Association of Retired Persons (AARP), the National Sheriff's Association, and the International Association of Chiefs of Police. AARP provides training, organizational help, teaching guides, and other assistance for volunteer groups. This program operates at the community level through local police chiefs, sheriffs, and councils of senior citizens who work to combat crime against the elderly and to support law enforcement across the board. However, volunteering at a local police station can be done by seniors not part of these formal programs.

Potential Obstacles

One challenge for the police is to arrange for volunteer opportunities that can be accomplished a few hours at a time or within schedules that may vary from day to day. However, considering that elderly and other volunteers can add the equivalent of numerous new police officers to a department, this challenge is more than offset by the vol-unteers' contributions. Many senior citizens bring extra experience, good judgment, and a high degree of dependability to their work.

Signs of Success

The participation of senior and other volunteers in law enforcement is proving its effectiveness in many locations across the United States. Sheriff Ray Isgett, of Berkeley County, South Carolina, says that the work contribution of his volunteers is invaluable. Senior volunteers run the Berkeley Victims' Assistance Program. "If all my volunteers were to quit today," he estimates, "some services that the sheriff's office performs would be cut by 60 percent."

Deputy Chief David Baker of the Police Department of Alexandria, Virginia, says that volunteers are probably the equivalent of six to eight additional full-time police officers for the department. "We use them in communications, . . . in patrol, . . . in records, we use them in every facet of the agency." A senior citizen in one Florida county has helped recruit 3,000 volunteers for Citizen Observer Patrols (COP). The sheriff reports impressive results: "Not even one crime has been committed in some areas since (the COP volunteers) took over," he says. In another part of the state, Senior Sleuths screened junk mail solicitations to seniors for deception and fraud. This project resulted in fifteen indictments against the junk mail firms.

Applying the Strategy

In Smith County, Texas, when the sheriff told a civic group of mostly retired people that he needed volunteers to assist with law enforcement, thirty people wanted to help. He uses volunteers to accompany deputies on trips around the country to pick up prisoners. Other volunteers help in the secured areas inside the jail.

In Tacoma, Washington, a retired police captain now serves as AARP district director. He has led six AARP chapters in helping to run or oversee thirteen different law enforcement activities, including crime watch groups.

Contact Information

TRIAD
American Association of Retired Persons
Criminal Justice Services-VOL
601 E Street, NW
Washington, DC 20049
202-434-2277

Use Advances in Technology To Promote Safety and Aid Community Crime Prevention

Strategy

Advances in technology can be creatively applied to increase public safety and promote crime prevention.

Crime Problem Addressed

This strategy aims to reduce street crimes against residents by equipping crime prevention staff and volunteers with appropriate technology. It deters crime by improving the communication capabilities of community crime prevention programs and allowing residents to assist the police in apprehending criminal suspects.

Key Components

Successful implementation of this strategy requires organized community-based crime prevention groups that can use the technology (cellular phones, walkie talkies, fax machines, electronic mail) to communicate about crime threats in the area and to organize crime prevention or patrol activities. Such technology is most effective when the group works in partnership with law enforcement to identify public safety concerns and report criminal or suspicious behavior.

Key Partnerships

Partnerships between law enforcement and community groups can effectively recruit business support and other donations to supply the technology and equipment necessary. Community crime prevention group members can call on their employers or area businesses for support.

Potential Obstacles

One challenge is convincing the businesses with the technology or equipment needed that they should provide it without marketplace compensation. Another challenge is publicizing the new business-police-community coopera-

tion, so that the community learns about it and understands its benefits.

Signs of Success

In Oregon, the communications firm Cellular One, the Portland Police, and a citizens patrol tested cellular telephone communications and found them superior to the older police two-way radio system. In 1992, working with the Portland police, Cellular One established a Cellular Watch Citizens Patrol program that now supports fifty citizen patrols in cities and rural communities throughout Oregon and southwest Washington state. The Cellular Watch Program provides patrols with loaned phones, free air time, reflective vests, signs, hats, equipment training, and organizational support. This new program of business-police-community cooperation improved communications between and among community members, fostered community cohesion, and improved crime prevention at the grassroots level. A newsletter, the Cellular Watch Observer, reports on local patrol activities.

Applying the Strategy

In Oxnard, California, a monthly call-in television show links area Crime Watch members with police who share crime data and answer questions about crime trends throughout the city. In one Virginia city, business owners participating in a crime watch program receive information about crime problems in the area via a fax link to the police department. The service helps them identify potential threats to their businesses, suggests precautions, and provides information about suspects.

Contact Information

Public Safety Programs
Cellular One
1600 S.W. 4th Avenue
Portland, Oregon 97201
503-306-7336

Performances To Reinforce Prevention Themes with Youth

Strategy

Teenage performance troupes effectively convey prevention themes to their peers and younger audiences, demonstrating the performer's commitment to their community while building important self-esteem and leadership skills.

Crime Problem Addressed

The crime problems addressed effectively through this strategy include alcohol, tobacco or other drug abuse, vandalism, sexual assault, and other forms of violence. Education provided through theater and other performing arts strengthens resistance to peer group pressure and societal messages, that often seem to accept or promote violence and drugs.

Key Components

Community, university, or corporate sponsorship of youth theatre troupes is the essential first step. Adults trained in performance or production serve as volunteer coordinators or staff directors of the troupe, working with the youth performers to develop the vehicle for conveying prevention messages. Local repertory groups or university drama departments can provide facilities for rehearsal, production advice, and help with publicity. Written lyrics for songs, scripts, and follow-up exercises reinforce prevention messages with audiences after the performers leave.

Key Partnerships

Key partnerships often include a local church, school, library, or business or civic organization for practice and performance space. They can also include local professional actors, stage hands, sound and light systems advisors, and others who volunteer their time to train youth. Teacher or parent volunteers are valuable partners in publicity campaigns and as advocates for bringing the program into schools. Capital sponsorship—both governmental and private—is often critical. Publicity through the media helps, but posters in store windows and word of mouth can also prove effective.

Potential Obstacles

Experienced adult advisers with time to volunteer may not be readily available in every community. Steady funding support and outreach to nearby university and professional theater groups should yield results.

Signs of Success

Performance helps young audiences see options for understanding and coping with violence in their community. Young people learn best what they see and practice. Performances, videos, and songs with prevention messages are effective means of reaching a youthful audience. The adults who coordinate performance and media programs note that participants improve their sense of self-worth and develop communications and leadership skills, which strengthen them against peer pressure and the impact of violence in the community.

The successful Teen Connection Theater in San Diego involves twelve to fifteen teenagers per troupe. Eight years after its initial presentation of violence, gang, and substance abuse prevention vignettes before thousands of younger students in schools and at community locations, the program now includes youth leadership and peer mediation training. Participants are trained to be "facilitators of self-expression through the arts." The theater program enjoys the support of school systems and community groups throughout the region. *Teen Connection Teen Theater, A Practical Guide* outlines key components involved in supporting a youth prevention theater.

A prepackaged curricula for kindergarten through the sixth grade, the *Strategy on Elementary School Theater for Violence Prevention* is available through the Climb Theatre Company in St. Paul, Minnesota.

Applying the Strategy

Teenagers in Dallas, Texas, worked with the police department's audio-visual experts to produce a show for teens on prevention topics. Teenagers in Indianapolis produced effective public service announcements, including one titled "You Can't Live Your Dream if You're Behind Bars." A presentation on acquaintance rape developed by students at the University of Colorado raised awareness among freshman attending the orientation session and signalled the university's support for preventing this underreported crime.

Contact Information

Institute Director
Teen Connection Teen Theater
San Diego Youth and Community Services
3255 Wing Street, Suite 550
San Diego, California 92110
619-221-8622

Crime Tip Rewards

Strategy

Monetary rewards for crime tips encourage crime reporting.

Crime Problem Addressed

This strategy aims to encourage—through financial incentives and anonymity—reporting of criminal incidents by reluctant or fearful residents who have witnessed or have important information about a crime. Such reports provide information which helps local law enforcement apprehend criminal suspects, reduce crime, stop traffic in drugs and arms, and recover stolen property.

Key Components

A community group or city agency must administer a crime-reporting hotline and dispense rewards for valuable tips; local law enforcement personnel must be assigned to follow up on any tips received and help determine those who qualify for the cash (or other) rewards. Funds must be made available to pay rewards, and a telephone must be dedicated to receiving information from residents. Finally, written materials should describe the rewards, criteria for valuable information, and assurances that callers remain anonymous.

Key Partnerships

The central partnership in this strategy is the one between the program operators, police, and the public. The police must establish clear criteria for information that warrants rewards and, through written material and word of mouth, must ensure residents that the identity of callers will never be revealed. Law enforcement must cooperate in publicizing the program and developing cooperative relationships with the community to encourage residents to report criminal activity.

Potential Obstacles

Some residents will question payments to people simply for doing their civic duty. However, such concerns are often offset by the success that the program achieves in resolving cases.

Signs of Success

Begun in Albuquerque, New Mexico, in 1976, community-based Crime Stoppers programs have spread across the United States and around the world. The umbrella organization, Crime Stoppers International, focuses on the principle that someone other than the criminal has information that could solve every crime. The fear of reporting is overcome with anonymity, and apathy is overcome with rewards. Numerous communities have implemented this strategy, reporting successes in arrests of criminals and recovery of stolen and contraband property. During a recent five-year period, more than 200 crimes in San Jose,

California, were reported as solved with help from callers to the tip hotline. The existence of such a program makes many residents more observant and better detectors of criminal activity. When the community, police, and media all work together, this strategy reduces crime.

Applying the Strategy

Concerned about crime in the city and the surrounding area, the Savannah, Georgia, Chamber of Commerce established the "Savannah Silent Witness" program in 1983. The purpose was to spur residents to report crimes. The program supports police investigations, but it was set up outside the police department to overcome any reluctance to deal directly with the police. Rewards for tips vary with the severity of the crime, how critical the provided evidence is to the prosecution of the criminal, and the potential risk to the informant in coming forward with the information. Over its first ten years of operation, Savannah Silent Witness handled an average of 200 calls per month. Ten percent of the calls in that period contributed to the arrest of a suspect, to the recovery of stolen property, or to the seizure of illegal drugs or contraband.

In Savannah, San Jose, and most other communities using this strategy, recovered property and cash more than pay for the money paid to informants. Donations from the public fully support the Savannah program.

Contact Information

Crime Stoppers International
P.O. Box 30413
Albuquerque, New Mexico 87109-0413
800-245-0009

Savannah Silent Witness
P.O. Box 1027
Savannah, Georgia 31402
912-234-2020

Victim Assistance Services

Strategy

Community-based victim assistance services help relieve stress and other consequences of crime, reduce vulnerability to repeated victimization, and unite community support for crime prevention.

Crime Problem Addressed

This strategy is designed to reduce recurrence of all types of crime. Victim assistance can help prevent the same individual from being a victim again, help friends and family

members from falling victim to the same type of crime, mitigate the financial and emotional impact of crime, and help rally the community to action against crime.

Key Components

The key components of this strategy include the following:

■ a community group or law enforcement agency unit trained to support and assist victims;

■ victim assistance services, such as counseling, reporting, filing compensation or insurance claims, advocating with landlords and creditors, and advising on legal issues;

■ a forum for channeling emotional energy into community crime prevention activities, if the victim wishes to do so; and

■ a public information plan to raise community awareness of services and how to access them.

Key Partnerships

Victim assistance comes from a variety of sources, such as the police, faith communities, teachers, psychologists, and doctors. Sponsors of this program should establish a partnership with the media to help spread the word about community support for victims and to remind the com-

Potential Obstacles

One challenge is to reassure the victims and their friends and colleagues that it is normal for a crime victim to experience many different emotions, thoughts, and feelings. For example, numbness, fear, anger, a desire for revenge, and wanting to hide from others are all common responses. Another challenge is to relieve tension and channel the energy of those who wish to address the causes of crime and help prevent it. Workers who spend considerable time with victims need to be careful not to overinvest themselves to avoid "burn out." Training helps prepare volunteers for situations and emotions they will encounter.

Signs of Success

This strategy is working in the Ida B. Wells Public Housing Development of the Chicago Housing Authority. The Chicago Housing Authority was selected for a training and technical assistance project of the National Organization for Victim Assistance (NOVA). NOVA trained existing vic-

tim assistance staff and volunteers in public housing to meet the needs of survivors of homicide victims, victims of child violence, and victims of sexual assault. NOVA trained dozens of professionals and lay people to provide victim assistance. After this contract was completed and judged successful, the Chicago Housing Authority continued to contract with NOVA for additional training and technical assistance.

At the Ida B. Wells Development in October, 1994, two 11-year-olds pushed a 5-year-old child from a fourteenth-story window, while his brother, age 8, struggled to stop them. Many people saw this act of terrible violence or its immediate aftermath. There was widespread grieving in the immediate area. The victim assistance program provided both individual and group crisis intervention services, helping them to handle the intense grief and sense of despair that they felt. Many residents reported that they were helped by this assistance.

Applying the Strategy

In Oakland, California, an organization called Caught in the Crossfire sends young counselors into Highland Hospital to try to persuade teenage gunshot victims to avoid further violence. Each month, that one hospital treats ten teens wounded by violence. The program is run by Youth Alive, a nonprofit group committed to stopping youth violence. Trauma doctors say they help keep some gunshot victims, even a few involved in violence, from engaging in conduct that will increase their likelihood of returning to the hospital with new wounds.

Contact Information

Director of Victim Services
National Organization for Victim Assistance (NOVA)
1757 Park Road, NW
Washington, DC 20010
202-232-6682

Reinforce Community Standards Against Violence

Strategy

Organized violence prevention and awareness campaigns reinforce community standards of nonviolence and help mobilize residents to act to prevent violence in the community.

Crime Problem Addressed

Violent juvenile crime has increased in recent years. Juvenile arrests for murder increased by 51 percent between

1988 and 1992. In 1992, 129,600 juveniles were arrested for murder, forcible rape, robbery, or aggravated assault. Many psychologists believe—and some studies have supported the theory—that seeing violence or daily depictions of violence desensitizes both adolescents and adults to violence, leaving them more likely to judge such behavior as "normal." This strategy attempts to address the community environment by promoting nonviolence as the community standard for juveniles and adults.

Key Components

The first component of this strategy is establishing the goal to reduce exposure to violence, acceptance of violence, and use of violence in the daily activities of youth and adults. One facet of the strategy to achieve that goal is to reduce the violence youth see in their entertainment and activities. Also, young people must be taught conflict resolution and cooperation skills. Other components include the following:

- a coalition that includes representatives from local government programs, the school systems, faith communities, youth groups, the media, and business, civic, social, and service clubs;

- educational materials to increase awareness and guide action; and

- public activities to mobilize interest and participation in violence-free activities.

Key Partnerships

Key partnerships should involve community groups concerned about violence in cooperation with local faith institutions, schools, and libraries. The coalition should convey nonviolence messages to the community and develop positive activities for youth. In addition to raising awareness and providing education, the partners should provide facilities and support for activities. Businesses and merchant associations can be enlisted to help fund educational campaigns and community activities. Media partners can review their patterns of news coverage and attempt to balance violence and crime-related stories with positive stories about the community, particularly during hours when young people are among likely viewers.

Potential Obstacles

Maintaining volunteer participation in a long-term community antiviolence campaign can prove difficult. The impact of antiviolence campaigns will not surface immediately, so organizers should prepare to continue to schedule events, publicize the campaign, lobby local agencies for positive nonviolent activities for youth, and advocate to the media for nonviolent entertainment and news.

Signs of Success

Implementation of this strategy in Minnesota emerged in one community from a conversation between two crime prevention officers in 1991. They wanted to do something to try to reduce the kind of violence in several highly publicized violent crimes in the state. Thinking about all the violence in public entertainment, they wished that they could just take the knob in hand and "turn it off." From there, a partnership of forty-five organizations initiated a statewide campaign to "Turn Off the Violence." One preschool teacher reported that since celebrating their Turn Off the Violence Day, children who witness fighting are heard saying "turn off the violence."

Volunteer educators compiled a *Teacher's Education Idea Guide,* a curriculum for use in grades from kindergarten through high school, with lesson plans on conflict resolution and anger control. Reproducible brochures, a quarterly newsletter, and a *Community Action Guide* document the necessity of a campaign in every community to Turn Off the Violence. A "Turn Off the Violence Day" is celebrated in Minnesota every October—Crime Prevention Month. The success and the spirit of the campaign has been replicated in communities across the United States.

Applying the Strategy

In 1992 in San Antonio, Texas, a grassroots crime prevention planning team collaborated with local government officials to outline the need for increased public education and awareness about gang violence. Seeking to reinforce the community's values against violence, local media executives and residents developed their own gang prevention public service advertisements featuring local community and government leaders and youth. In addition, area ministers promoted the coalition's crime prevention action plan through a week-long commitment to sermons with antiviolence themes. Community involvement in implementing the plan and promoting nonviolent activity for youth continues.

Contact Information

Project Coordinator
Turn Off the Violence
P.O. Box 27558
Minneapolis, Minnesota 55427
612-593-8041

Neighborhood Watch

Strategy

Organized groups of neighborhood residents who watch out for criminal and suspicious behavior and report it to local law enforcement help prevent crime and promote cooperation among residents and with police.

Crime Problem Addressed

Ever day, neighborhoods across the United States confront any number of property and violent crimes and threats of crime. This strategy attempts to provide local law enforcement with additional eyes and ears to watch out for all types of criminal activity and promote neighborhood security.

Key Components

Perhaps the most popular and proven community crime prevention strategy, Neighborhood Watch calls for groups of residents in a designated area to become an organized chain of interconnected individuals trained to notice and report criminal or suspicious behavior near their homes. Local law enforcement provides training in crime reporting, alerts the group to potential crime threats, provides statistics and data on crime trends, advises leadership on how to recruit members, and helps design publicity campaigns and communication networks within the neighborhood and with watch groups throughout the jurisdiction. Other typical components include home security surveys, identification programs to mark valuable personal property, and signs alerting law-abiding residents and possible offenders of the boundaries of the watch community. Newsletters, telephone trees, and regular meetings facilitate communication among members.

Key Partnerships

Local law enforcement officials and residents form the crucial partnership in this strategy. Training from the police and help with recruitment and communication ensure the watch program's success and provides the basis for a sustained and broad-based community effort to promote public safety. Local media aid watch groups by publicizing recruitment drives and successes in crime prevention through citizen involvement.

Potential Obstacles

Apathy, civic disengagement, and fear are among the most common obstacles to forming a Neighborhood Watch. Education, usually via law enforcement, can overcome such obstacles. Since possible displacement of crime to other neighborhoods remains a concern for law enforcement, they seek to involve as many neighborhoods as possible to offset the potential displacement of crime. Also, volunteer momentum can wane if the program is narrowly focused and does not allow for a variety of roles that use residents' talents and respect the varying degrees of comfort with involvement in public safety programs.

Signs of Success

For over a decade, the National Association of Town Watch has promoted the Neighborhood Watch concept, encouraged community groups throughout the United States to pool resources in crime prevention efforts, shared crime prevention information with thousands of local organizations, and coordinated National Night Out, an annual August event where communities demonstrate their desire for peaceful neighborhoods through parties, cookouts, and crime prevention fairs. The Neighborhood Watch Advisory Board in one southwestern city facilitated participation by 230 neighborhood organizations in the 1994 National Night Out.

A 1981 evaluation of a Seattle community burglary prevention program provided proof that the combination of Neighborhood Watch, property identification, and home security surveys resulted in noticeable and statistically significant reductions in crimes targeted. The California Legislative Research Office recently called Neighborhood Watch "a proven program that reduces crime." The watch concept has been adapted throughout the United States and other countries to include Apartment Watch in areas with more densely concentrated resident housing.

Applying the Strategy

Neighborhood Watch groups in Sangamon County, Illinois, helped reduce burglary by nearly 50 percent, while crime rates rose throughout the rest of the state. Diligent activity by a watch program in Tucson, Arizona, resulted in 17 arrests and a 30 percent reduction in home burglaries in just three weeks, with three-fourths of the arrests of suspects made possible by tips from watch members in the area. Phoenix's Neighborhood Block Watch Fund was created by a citizen-initiated referendum to dedicate part of a local sales tax increase to expanding the already-successful block watch programs.

Contact Information

National Association of Town Watch
P.O. Box 303
7 Wynnewood Road, Suite 215
Wynnewood, Pennsylvania 19096
610-649-7055

Create Access to Safe Urban Open Space

Strategy

Accessible open space in urban areas contributes to the health and vitality of the community, contributing to its resiliency against crime and violence.

Crime Problem Addressed

Communities throughout the country have invested in parks to ensure the quality of life for residents, particularly young people and families. Open park grounds, playgrounds, and ballfields are vital recreational resources in metropolitan areas. According to the Trust for Public Land, roughly 80 percent of Americans live in metropolitan communities.

Key Components

Investment in parks and open spaces comes from both public and private sources. In some communities, investment has come from coalitions of corporate, community, and public agencies. In other instances, public acquisition or rehabilitation of lands for parks comes through bond sales, zoning restrictions to prohibit commercial development, estate bequests, and nature preserves.

Key Partnerships

Prospective public investment in parkland has to compete for resources with vital public works projects, such as public buildings, police and fire emergency agencies, hospitals, and schools. Partnerships with corporate leaders and community organizations can help build support for spending on parkland acquisition and maintenance, resulting in contributions of supplemental resources to the project. Neighborhood associations can help coordinate community advocacy for parks.

Potential Obstacles

Investment in parkland and open space can be expensive. City budgets are constrained by limited resources and challenged by many competing demands; officials may assign low priority to acquiring open space. Advocates for park investment should emphasize the multiple recreational opportunities, beautification benefits, and economic improvements that result from the revitalization of neighborhoods that follows rehabilitation of park areas.

Signs of Success

The Green Cities Initiative (sponsored by the San Francisco-based Trust for Public Land) helps local governments identify opportunities to develop parkland and coordinate financing for land purchase. Studies cited by the Trust reveal that crime drops when adequate parks and recreational activities are available in inner-city neighborhoods. According to the Trust, investment in parks creates job opportunities and increases property values in areas surrounding the open space, even as the park offers respite from stresses of urban life. Moreover, parks present a ready-made location for community events and recreation programs valued by community residents. In describing the need for the Initiative, the Trust states that "public open spaces are places where the seeds of sustainable communities take root—where people become neighbors and where cities become more livable."

In 1992, residents of Los Angeles County approved a Safe Neighborhood Parks Act, raising $540 million to acquire land and rehabilitate neighborhood parks. The Trust for Public Land helped the county leverage additional support from several local foundations and corporations. The Urban Los Angeles program also focuses on the developing community gardens and open space within the core inner city.

Applying the Strategy

The Clean-Land initiative in Cleveland helps to identify areas needing beautification through tree planting. The project was developed in response to the loss of hundreds of trees in downtown and inner-city neighborhoods. The city coordinates with Neighbor Woods, a volunteer tree-planting organization, to identify communities for tree planting and recruit resources. Advertising agencies donated publicity, and judges sentenced offenders to trash cleanup in tree-planting sites. In 1990, the project earned a National Arbor Day Foundation award for the investments it leveraged in planting over 1,000 trees.

Contact Information

Director of Public Affairs
Trust for Public Land
116 New Montgomery Street, 4th Floor
San Francisco, California 94105
415-495-4014

Directories of Services

Strategy

Directories of services that are provided by local agencies help residents, other service providers, and police officers identify opportunities to refer individuals and families to needed services.

Crime Problem Addressed

Residents of all kinds of neighborhoods will eventually require the services provided by a local government or community social, health, or employment service agency. Increased awareness of available services helps ensure that those in need will understand how to access those services.

Key Components

Service directories typically catalog services available from public and private sources in areas such as family support, counseling, employment training, health services, substance abuse treatment, and education. Distribution of the directory to residents and to service agencies helps reinforce coordinated referral to programs offering the support families and children need. Directories are commonly developed as a product of coalitions and interagency partnerships to assist neighborhoods.

Key Partnerships

Agencies should coordinate resources to develop, print, and distribute service resource directories. Neighborhood associations can identify community needs so that agencies and providers that address these needs can be included.

Potential Obstacles

Maintaining the directories and including updates can be a time-consuming process that a single agency may be reluctant to undertake. Neighborhood agencies can be asked to update the content as a trade-off for the local government department's commitment of resources to print and distribute it.

Signs of Success

Seattle's Youth Involvement Network represents the partnership of the community, city agencies, and youth. In addition to raising the community's awareness of issues facing Seattle youth, the Network developed the Youth Yellow Pages which lists youth-serving agencies. With the support of the public library and a local cable television company, the directory provides information on jobs, sports opportunities, legal assistance, and antiviolence programs.

Applying the Strategy

In Wichita, Kansas, the Neighborhood Initiative has pursued leadership training for residents, enhanced services for neighborhoods, and brought cooperation between public and private agencies in the two-county metropolitan area. The 1995 directory of services sponsored by the Initiative and printed with the cooperation of the local United Way includes hundreds of references to organizations that provide emergency family support, substance abuse treatment, mental health services, information on schools, health education resources, and job training centers. The directory is one vehicle for reinforcing the collaboration of local agencies on the Initiative.

Contact Information

Director of Intergovernmental Relations
City of Wichita
Office of the City Manager
455 North Main Street, 13th Floor
Wichita, Kansas 67202
316-268-4351

Celebrate Neighborhood Accomplishments

Strategy

Celebrating a community's accomplishments in planning and implementing anticrime projects and revitalization or redevelopment activities builds community pride and supports the sustainability of communities of all types.

Crime Problem Addressed

Residents of neighborhoods beset by crime and violence experience a great deal of fear. They may also feel that their community's problems are overwhelming, too large to be addressed by anything they could contribute. This strategy recognizes the need to promote the accomplishments, victories, and milestones of communities in order to demonstrate that local agencies support positive activity in those communities and that individual contributions are valued.

Key Components

Recognition can come in the form of awards ceremonies, small-scale events, or simple block parties to celebrate the conclusion of neighborhood revitalization projects. Media coverage of the events enhances opportunities to build support for the activity recognized. Neighborhood services agencies or local governments often coordinate events and also maintain networks of neighborhood associations and community planning groups.

Key Partnerships

Neighborhood service agencies should work with community groups to identify opportunities to note accomplishments of individuals and local projects. Media and other corporate resources can help underwrite the costs of events and awards.

Potential Obstacles

Recognizing community projects does not need to involve complicated or costly events. Recognition should be an predictable aspect of the collaboration between local agencies to promote the healthy development of neighborhoods.

Signs of Success

In 1994, St. Petersburg, Florida, initiated a Neighborhood Festival, a series of free parties to celebrate the outcome of community planning and improvement projects undertaken by groups throughout the city. The free events were so successful that the city decided to make it an annual event. Heavy local media coverage of the activities also highlighted the commitment to the community of local realtors and the Chamber of Commerce.

Applying the Strategy

Phoenix's awards program, "Celebrating Neighborhoods that Work," spurs competition among neighborhoods and profiles their accomplishments. The program recognizes successful outreach to residents, partnerships with diverse elements of the community, and efforts to reinforce the city's goals to solve problems at the neighborhood level. Groups that are organized to work through partnerships to improve the quality of life are eligible to apply for recognition through the program.

Contact Information

Neighborhoods that Work Program
Neighborhood Services Department
City of Phoenix
200 West Washington Street, 4th Floor
Phoenix, Arizona 85003
602-534-4444

Bibliography

Books

African-American Church Project. *Restoring Broken Places and Rebuilding Communities: A Casebook on African-American Church Involvement in Community Economic Development.* Washington, DC: National Congress for Community Economic Development, 1993.

Committee for Economic Development. *Rebuilding Inner-City Communities: A New Approach to the Nation's Urban Crisis.* Washington, DC: Committee for Economic Development, 1995.

Kretzmann, John P., and John L. McKnight. *Building Communities from the Inside Out: A Path Toward Finding and Mobilizing a Community's Assets.* Evanston, IL: Center for Urban Affairs and Policy Research, 1993.

Lofquist, William A. *The Technology of Prevention Workbook.* Tucson, AZ: Development Publications, 1989.

Guskind, Robert and Neal Peirce. *Against the Tide: The New Community Corporation 1968-1993.* Newark, NJ: Prudential Foundation, 1993.

Periodicals

Bennett, Amanda. Economist Demonstrates that Neighbors, Not Wardens, Hold Keys to Cutting Crime. *Wall Street Journal,* 7 December 1994, pp. B1-B2.

Bens, Charles K. Effective Citizen Involvement: How to Make it Happen: The Challenge of American Renewal. *National Civic Review,* Winter–Spring 1994, pp. 32–39.

Cellular Watch Patrols Fight Crime. *Catalyst,* National Crime Prevention Council, November 1994, p. 6.

The Life and Death of Neighborhood Watches. *Catalyst,* National Crime Prevention Council, July 1994, p. 1.

Neighborhood Offices Boost Police Resources. *Catalyst,* National Crime Prevention Council, April 1993, p. 6.

New Crime Prevention Alliance Launched To Help Americans Protect Themselves from Crime. *Community Crime Prevention Digest,* Washington Crime News Services, October 1994, p. 1.

The Newsletter of the Citizens Committee for New York City. *Citizens Report,* Spring 1994.

NLC's Database is a Rich Source of What's Working in Cities. *Nation's Cities Weekly,* 30 January 1995, pp. 7–8.

Officials Say Preventing Violence Far More Important than Jailing Results. *Community Crime Prevention Digest,* Washington Crime News Services, October 1994, p. 9.

Triad Partnership Increases Law Enforcement Support. *Catalyst,* National Crime Prevention Council, February 1994, p. 2.

Public Documents

American Bar Association. *Just Solutions: A Program Guide to Innovative Justice System Improvements.* 1994.

Community Development Corporations. *Building Communities that Work.* Washington, DC, 1994.

The National Assembly. *Building Resiliency: What Works!* Washington, DC, 1994.

National Association of Neighborhoods. *How Neighbors Are Helping Neighbors: A Profile of NAN Members.* Washington, DC, 1992.

National Center for Community Policing. *Community Policing Series.* "The Neighborhood Network Center: Part One." No. 23.

Teamworks. *A Place in the Marketplace: Making Capitalism Work in Poor Communities.* Washington, DC, March 1992.

U.S. Attorney's Office. Street Heat Anti-Drug Band. *Resource Fair Program Summaries: Building Justice in Our Communities.* Washington, DC, October 1994, pp. 18–20.

U.S. Attorney's Office. Violent Crime Initiative. *Resource Fair Program Summaries: Building Justice in Our Communities.* Washington, DC, October 1994, pp. 14–15.

U.S. Department of Justice. Bureau of Justice Statistics. *Highlights from 20 Years of Surveying Crime Victims: The National Crime Victimization Survey, 1973–1992.* Washington, DC, October 1993.

U.S. Department of Justice. Office of Juvenile Justice and Delinquency Prevention. *Innovative Community Partnerships: Working Together for Change.* Washington, DC, May 1994.

Westside Crime Prevention Program. *Westside Crime Prevention News.* February 1995.

Youth

Protecting youth and families from crime should be a cornerstone of our society. Yet youth in the United States are victimized by crime at rates significantly higher than adults. Furthermore, crimes—including violent offenses—are often committed by teenagers.

E ach day, thousands of young people live in fear of crime. Many attend school worried about guns, violence, and other crime. Too many children find it difficult to resist peer pressure toward drugs and violence. Every year in America, nearly three million cases of child abuse are reported and over 750,000 students drop out of school; in one recent year, over 130,000 youth were arrested.

Local and community action—by parents, youth, educators, health professionals, religious leaders, community organizations, recreation program directors, and others—can provide children and youth the skills and support they need to prevent victimization and to make healthy and safe choices. Committed local leaders and individuals can do much to help youth take advantage of opportunities to use their talents to help themselves, their peers, and their community. Youth-led projects that address social issues and public safety demonstrate the power that lies in the vision youth have of safer and caring communities.

Local governments and communities that have realigned policies and institutions to address the needs of children, youth, and families have seen how innovative approaches can reap unforeseen rewards. Communities that have implemented policies that promote individual responsibility among youth note that crime by youth decreases when those policies are implemented along with opportunities to pursue positive alternatives.

Local planning groups have collaborated around a common vision to prevent delinquency, help rear children in safe homes, and bring community assets to bear on social conditions that foster crime.

The fifty strategies in this chapter emphasize the important role many local actors play in securing a safe and stable community environment for children and youth. The successful means of protecting youth and preventing delinquency profiled in this chapter include the following:

■ **Neighborhood-based recreation centers**—Safe recreation facilities are vital sources of positive activity and learning for youth, and they are an important resource for connecting them to needed prevention services. A national study of nineteen city recreation programs revealed that police in those communities credited the programs with making significant contributions to reduced incidence of violence and other crimes. A late-night recreation and supplemental education program in Cincinnati helped reduce crime in one neighborhood by 24 percent after just three months. The reduction of crime was achieved at a cost of $.56 per youth participant.

■ **Late-night or daytime curfews for youth**—Many communities pursue local curfew ordinances as a strategy to combat youth violence. Juvenile crime in New Orleans decreased by 38 percent sixty days after implementation of the late-night curfew in 1994. New Orleans' ordinance holds both parents and juveniles accountable. Other city programs established at the same time offer youth support through job training and recreation.

■ **Values-based curricula**—Children benefit from school programs that instill values and positive character traits. Public schools in Dayton, Ohio, have established a comprehensive character education program. Teachers present one topic per week, which is followed by student discussion about basic societal values such as honesty, fairness, courage, loyalty, and tolerance. Since the program was initiated, school suspensions have dropped dramatically, academic performance has improved, and students say their schools feel safer.

■ **Alternative school sites**—Small-scale school environments that provide intensive tutoring and other services help youth with behavior problems and those at risk of academic failure. The Mat-Su Alternative School in Alaska has become a model for how alternative learning environments can help dropouts and delinquent youth. Students at this school have dropped out of school elsewhere, abused alcohol or drugs, or been placed on probation by juvenile court. Although 20 percent of the school's students are referred directly from the court system, only 3 percent become repeat offenders after attending the alternative school. Impressed by the results, state officials named it school of the year in 1994 and replicated the program across the state.

■ **Adults as career mentors**—Adults with business experience can help prevent delinquency by sponsoring youth in apprenticeships or mentoring programs. Over 1,400 USAA Casualty Insurance Company employees in several states mentor students; they work one-on-one with youth to foster academic skills and values such as dedication and responsibility. During one year in San Antonio, Texas, the number of USAA-mentored students with behavior problems dropped by 30 percent.

■ **Youth leadership and service**—Too often youth are viewed as a source of violence in the community, but not as a resource to help resolve crime and social problems. Youth as Resources (YAR), an initiative started in 1987, is a leading youth leadership and development model. YAR operates in more than forty communities in the United States, providing funding and technical assistance to youth-led community initiatives. In Chicago, seventh and eighth graders visit the elderly, running errands and doing chores for them. In Evansville, Indiana, young people renovated a resting area for children at the local zoo. In other communities, youth have built playgrounds and performed plays for younger children, plays which feature prevention themes. An evaluation of the effect of the program on its participants demonstrated that the program positively influenced attitudes toward delinquency, helped develop important leadership skills, and increased positive bonds to the community.

Outdoor Challenge Education

Strategy

Juvenile offenders who participate in rigorous outdoor challenge and therapeutic programs are less apt to commit additional crimes than their counterparts incarcerated in traditional juvenile detention facilities.

Crime Problem Addressed

Public fear of juvenile offenders has grown, along with the perception that the juvenile justice system has not always dealt successfully with the youth committed to its care. Significant numbers of juveniles who have been incarcerated in secure detention centers for even minor offenses commit further crimes within months after their release. Some portion of juveniles commits these crimes because they lack the self-esteem, self-reliance, spirit of cooperation, respect for others, and pride in themselves that society associates with law-abiding citizens. This strategy helps to reduce recidivism by using rigorous physical challenges and counseling to build these resiliency factors in youth participants.

Key Components

This strategy is an alternative to secure detention for all but the most seriously violent juvenile offender. The participants are removed from the negative environment that has fostered criminal behavior and placed in a positive, caring setting that offers physical and mental challenges, opportunities to build trust in adults and peers, and training in skills to make positive life choices. The best results are obtained if participation is optional and if those who take part make a serious commitment to the program. It is conducted in stages that allow the offenders to develop skills and encourages those skills to be challenged and refined through various activities. Follow-up care for the youth (e.g., group meetings, home visits, etc.) makes the transition back into the home environment as smooth as possible and enhances the likelihood that youth will maintain a lifestyle free of delinquent behavior.

Key Partnerships

Partnerships built on trust and respect among parents, youth, and adult program leaders are essential for the program to succeed. Cooperation between the placing agencies and the program administration is also key in ensuring placement of participants willing to commit to the rigorous program.

Potential Obstacles

One potential obstacle is the difficulty in building trust between the participants and their leaders. This can be overcome by patience and hard work. The negative effects of the neighborhood and peer associations can resurface once the program is over unless parental support and follow-up care are emphasized. Some of the more physically challenging programs are controversial among probation departments and other juvenile justice officials, who are concerned that the programs are too rigorous. However, judges tend to believe that the programs are more effective than traditional incarceration of similar offenders.

Signs of Success

VisionQuest is a confrontational outdoor challenge and rehabilitation program for juvenile offenders; headquartered in Tucson, Arizona, it has program sites throughout the country. VisionQuest takes juvenile offenders referred by juvenile courts, probation departments, or social services on a series of outdoor expeditions, or "quests." Participants are required to commit to the program for a minimum of one year and to complete three quests. The first quest is an orientation to ensure that each youth is fully prepared for later, more advanced quests. Quests can range from hiking trips to bicycle trips to mule packs and simulated wagon trains. Throughout the program, the participants also receive four hours of school lessons each day. At the completion of the program, the youth take part in HomeQuest, a continual transitional program to help the juveniles readjust to their home environments.

In 1987, the Rand Corporation, funded by the U.S. Department of Justice, evaluated San Diego County's VisionQuest program. That study revealed that "placement in VisionQuest is associated with a recidivism rate about half that of Youth Corrections Center graduates." The evaluation went on to note that "placement in VisionQuest reduced the one-year recidivism rate from 71 percent to 39 percent." The California Office of the Auditor General reported a 16 percent lower recidivism rate among San Diego VisionQuest participants than among their peers incarcerated for similar offenses in the Youth Corrections Center. Also a 1987 evaluation of ten Pennsylvania residential centers for juvenile offenders showed that the two centers that used VisionQuest had a 14 percent lower recidivism rate than the other eight.

Applying the Strategy

A less confrontational program approved by the Santa Fe Mountain Center was initiated in 1979 to encourage responsibility among juveniles through "adaptation to outdoor adventure and group living and to realize the value and power of group action." The center emphasizes communication skills, healthy risk-taking, and enhancement of self-esteem through mastery of new challenges. The successful program was given a Recognition of Program Merit by the National Association of Juvenile and Family Court Judges.

Contact Information

VisionQuest National, Ltd.
P.O. Box 12906
Tucson, Arizona 85732-2906
520-881-3950

School-to-Work Programs

Strategy

School-to-work programs help youth find jobs and sustain a successful transition to the work force.

Crime Problem Addressed

According to Massachusetts Institute of Technology economist Paul Osterman, "Roughly one-third of all high school graduates, and somewhat more high school dropouts, fail to find stable employment by the time they are thirty." The situation he describes is partly due to deficiencies in the academic skills and career preparation youth in most U.S. school systems receive. Lack of stable employment over time leads to economic instability and increased risk of involvement in crime for those youth and young adults from economically disadvantaged communities.

Key Components

The Center for Youth Development and Policy Research describes youth development as "an approach to youth programming and policy that stresses preparation and development—rather than prevention, deterrence and deficit reduction—as its ultimate goal, and the provisions of supports and opportunities as essential strategies." The Center and the National Youth Employment Coalition contend that school-to-work and other programs founded on youth development principles are successful when they integrate training, employment, education, and a network of social supports and services. The Coalition advocates expanding locally successful program models to a national level.

Successful local programs have included the following components:

■ a multiyear investment in the youth that begins early on and is directed to individual and age-appropriate needs;

■ opportunities for interaction with peers and adult role models;

■ education and skills training;

■ guidance on career choices as developmental and interest issues change over time; and

■ support from the community and service providers to help youth become productive citizens.

Beyond education and technical training, the programs also provide nurturing, guidance, and monitoring from teachers or workplace supervisors to respond to each youth's evolving needs and interests.

Key Partnerships

A successful program must engage schools in reassessing their curriculum for relevance to job training and career preparation. It should also organize the recruitment of public and private employers to support the project through internships, technical training, and loaned or donated equipment. The program must also be connected to resources that can help build community support. In addition, the program must include partnerships with all local government and community-based elements of the sectors that make up the social environment of youth. The services provided should include instruction; opportunities to learn and contribute in "real world" situations; and support from caring professional role models, loaned executives, and other adults as the youth sets goals and makes progress toward career and other objectives.

Potential Obstacles

Some programs have found it difficult to obtain the financial and volunteer support needed to maintain the long-term commitments vital to school-to-work transition programs. Continually reassessing the needs of participating youth and their progress requires staff activity and resources to gauge the program's effectiveness and adjust it to the needs of participating youth. In some economically disadvantaged areas, recruitment of employer participants is difficult and work opportunities are scarce. Some programs have responded successfully to that challenge by building partnerships with public sector and nonprofit employers, finding job and training opportunities for youth in those arenas.

Signs of Success

In 1993, Public/Private Ventures (in Philadelphia) completed a case study of five programs and related youth development literature for the U.S. Department of Labor. The study—*Strengthening Programs For Youth*—judged that the success of the local programs should be replicated on a national level, urging the Labor Department to redirect its youth programming and take a "leadership role in establishing and supporting programs aiming to promote the overall maturation of disadvantaged youth."

The federal School-to-Work Opportunities Act enacted in the summer of 1994 recognizes that the resources of effective locally driven and Labor-supported programs should be redirected and designed along youth development lines. It also recommends that such programs include adult role models and other support mechanisms that are tailored to age-appropriate needs, which are very different from those of adults in job training and career education programs.

Applying the Strategy

Moving Up is a program in New York City that offers youth comprehensive employment training, job retention and career advancement guidance, and placement services in a variety of technical and service fields. The relatively small inner-city program boasts impressive results. After one year of participation, 92 percent of participating youth had been placed in jobs, 74 percent had retained the jobs for that one year and 80 percent had avoided criminal activity.

The Quantum Opportunities Program (QOP)—a multiyear, comprehensive program piloted in five sites (San Antonio, Texas; Philadelphia, Pennsylvania; Oklahoma City, Oklahoma; Milwaukee, Wisconsin; and Saginaw, Michigan)—combines education, training, financial incentives, and other support to youth beginning in the ninth grade and continuing through high school graduation. The program served urban youth who were from welfare-supported households and were at risk of juvenile delinquency and becoming dropouts.

An evaluation conducted by Brandeis University determined that QOP participants were significantly more likely than non-participants to graduate from high school, pursue postsecondary education, or receive an academic achievement award. Additionally, QOP participants were significantly less likely to drop out of school or have children during the time period studied. The evaluation credited the success of the program to intensive support from adult workers, combined with training, financial incentives, and community service.

Contact Information

Andrew Hahn
Center for Human Resources
Brandeis University
60 Turner Street
Waltham, Massachusetts 02154
617-736-3800

National Youth Employment Coalition
1001 Connecticut Avenue, NW, Suite 719
Washington, DC 20036
202-659-1064

Youth Leadership as a Community Resource

Strategy

Foster the development of leadership in youth by providing them skills to help them make positive contributions to the community.

Crime Problem Addressed

All youth, including those who may be unaware of what they can offer, have energy, ideas, vision, and skills that can greatly benefit their communities. The success of countless community service projects that have substantial youth participation and leadership points to the strengths youth can bring to communities that are struggling with crime, violence, drug abuse, and quality-of-life issues. Literature on the risks and resources of communities demonstrates that efforts to bolster the skills of youth leaders help them resist the negative influences that are associated with delinquent behavior. In particular, such programs support youths' sense of control over some aspects of their lives, engenders altruism and caring for others, and enhances their belief in themselves and in positive prospects for their future.

Key Components

Many youth leadership development programs focus on opportunities for youth and adults to work together on issues of vital importance to the community. The young people help define and solve problems. The programs often involve youth participation in such areas as:

■ local government boards or advisory groups that set youth-related policy;

■ community service or charitable activities; and

■ public safety activities, such as community crime watch and school violence prevention programs.

In each case, youth are encouraged to develop their potential while contributing solutions to vital social concerns. Some programs focus on opportunities to build and harness the skills of youth leaders as teachers or counselors to their peers, offering positive peer role models in gang prevention, counseling, or drug abuse prevention projects. In these programs, youth are trained in self-discipline and self-esteem, positive life choices, refusal skills, conflict management, and strategies for sharing these skills with their peers.

Key Partnerships

Relationships between adults and youth that are based on mutual respect are key to successful youth leadership development programs. If the objective is youth participation in projects to serve the community, youth involvement must be substantial and include all aspects of decision-making; otherwise the program will have no legitimacy with youth who participate. If the objective is leadership skills for the youth to use in refining life skills, the program must include committed and caring adults who help set guidelines and serve as role models who have made positive life decisions. In many cases, implementing specific projects also requires resources for training, materials, or facilities.

Potential Obstacles

Programs may need to confront mistrust or preconceived notions that both adults and youth have about the other's role in or ability to contribute to the project's success. These barriers can be overcome through careful design of decision-making structures, team-building training, and opportunities for interaction that make everyone's skills evident. Participants in youth-led projects may not initially understand their own potential, which may need to be brought out through training, mentoring, and experience.

Signs of Success

Youth as Resources (YAR), an initiative started by the National Crime Prevention Council (NCPC) in 1987, is a leading youth leadership and development model. YAR operates in more than forty communities throughout the United States, providing funding and technical assistance to youth-led community initiatives. YAR programs are evidence that youth leadership can produce tangible results in the community.

In Chicago, over 100 seventh and eighth graders from Beethoven Elementary School visited senior citizens in their homes, providing companionship, running errands, and doing chores; these young people strengthened multi-generational ties in their community. In Evansville, Indiana, youth renovated a half-acre site at Mesker Zoo into a landscaped knoll to be used by young children as a rest and lunch area while visiting the zoo. Youth developed the idea, wrote the grant proposal, presented it to the school board of trustees, and initiated a publicity campaign. Longitudinal evaluations by the Lilly Endowment (a YAR financial supporter) concluded that YAR positively influenced antidelinquency attitudes and beliefs and helped to develop important leadership traits, including self-esteem, altruism, positive bonds with the community, social and communication skills, and civic responsibility.

The U.S. Department of Housing and Urban Development (HUD) supports youth leadership programs in public housing communities across the country, and it has placed youth leadership development at the forefront of its youth-serving program agenda. Creating an atmosphere supportive of youth leadership is at the heart of HUD's cooperative effort with other federal agencies to make public housing communities safe and drug-free.

Applying the Strategy

Youth residents of Macon, Georgia, public housing communities have been trained as state-certified teen community representatives, working under the supervision of a health professional to educate other youth about drugs, sexually transmitted disease, and pregnancy prevention. The Macon program is considered one of the most effective of the many youth projects run by the local housing authority.

In 1992, San Antonio, Texas, officials developed a network of leadership institutes for middle-school girls after they realized that programs aimed at violence and gang prevention had been disproportionately directed toward young males. The institutes in each school also teach skills in communicating effectively, resisting negative influences, and making positive life choices. The institutes are part of a comprehensive citywide effort to combat juvenile crime and victimization through a balance of prevention, intervention, and enforcement strategies.

Contact Information

Executive Director
Macon Housing Authority
2015 Felton Avenue
Macon, Georgia 31201
912-752-5070

Executive Director
National Center for Youth as Resources
1700 K Street, NW, 8th Floor
Washington, DC 20006
202-466-6272, ext. 151

Dropout Prevention Focused on High-Risk Elementary Students

Strategy

School dropout rates can be lowered through early intervention programs that are student-centered and teacher-led and that focus on the needs of children identified as being at risk.

Crime Problem Addressed

National estimates show that over one million students drop out of school each year, as many as one in four before scheduled graduation. School dropout rates, poverty, and crime are interrelated. Youth who do not graduate from high school are less likely than high school or college graduates to be able to find and sustain stable employment. States and local areas with the highest dropout rate also have high rates of crime, poverty, and enrollment in public assistance programs than other areas with higher school retention and graduation rates. The National Dropout Prevention Center estimates that billions of dollars in lost productivity, public assistance benefits, job training, and crime-related costs can be attributed to high rates of school dropout among youth.

Key Components

In a review of forty-seven local school dropout prevention programs in twenty-two states between 1986 and 1990, the National Foundation for the Improvement of Education (NFIE) found that key components to the success of these programs included the following:

■ early intervention with elementary-age children identified as at risk of dropping out;

■ strong school district support for applying resources toward this problem, including policies to empower teachers to make the curriculum engaging and interactive;

■ emphasis on building the self-esteem of the students through programs tailored to their needs, academic and otherwise;

■ high, yet reasonable, expectations for student performance; and

■ extensive collaboration with and involvement of parents and the business community.

The Comer School, a project affiliated with Yale University, attributed the success of its students and its low dropout rates to small classes, intensive parental involvement, clear expectations for student performance, a caring atmosphere, and a system of support for students needing assistance.

Key Partnerships

The partnership most vital to success is the one among the at-risk student, the parent(s), and the classroom teacher. The teacher is the front-line defense for a school system with a dropout problem—the first to notice academic performance, behavioral, and family-related issues that suggest a student is at risk for dropping out of school at a later age. Properly trained teachers are a vital resource for schools and parents seeking to identify at-risk children and provide them with support and guidance to increase their academic performance and reduce the chance they will drop out of school. Teachers and administrators can enhance the success of a dropout prevention program by collaborating with parents to involve them in school activities, helping them understand how to facilitate their child's academic progress, and collaborating with them to build community support for the program. Businesses can help by providing materials or equipment for schools or publicity for the program.

Potential Obstacles

The most common obstacle faced by school districts is measuring the extent of the dropout problem as a first step in designing a solution. A 1991 review of dropout program studies done by *The Washington Post* showed that dropout rates in most large U.S. cities "are full of statistical flaws and based on dubious data from overburdened school attendance supervisors." This issue can be addressed through a concerted effort of school administration to track dropout students in a consistent manner, aware of the impact of counting as dropouts those students who should not be, including those who were jailed, expelled, or transferred. The U.S. Department of Education provides guidelines to school districts on defining dropouts and collecting accurate statistics.

Signs of Success

Of the sites that took part in the NFIE-funded program, one-third leveraged outside support to continue the effort; 41 percent reported a significant improvement in elementary student test scores; 54 percent reported improved grades; 74 percent noted increased attendance among par-

ticipating students; and 80 percent said that student behavior had improved. In Las Vegas, Nevada, 76 percent of students involved performed at least one grade level better in two classes after the first year of the program. In Chattanooga, Tennessee, there was a tenfold increase in parent attendance at Parent-Teacher Association meetings.

Applying the Strategy

The Savannah, Georgia, school system has developed a continuum of programs to help its students. The effort begins in elementary school with the Services to Assist Youth (STAY) Team program. STAY screens students, assists them with academic and family problems, and provides some students with an alternative curriculum. The STAY Team includes a school counselor, suspension specialist, and additional staff who help connect students to needed services. In later years, students with academic difficulties are supported by the Comprehensive Competencies Program (CCP) and Transition Resource Teachers (TRT). The CCP lab program is designed to help students advance to their proper grade level with the help of individualized instruction. Teachers in the TRT program assist incoming ninth graders with course scheduling, and they provide long-term support and monitoring of academic, behavioral, and related family issues.

The Alpha Program at Blanton Elementary School in St. Petersburg, Florida, is a dropout prevention program that focuses on elementary school students; it was named a 1994 "Shining Star" program by the Southeast Regional Center for Drug-Free Schools and Communities. In existence since 1987, Alpha is a collaborative effort of the school, parents, and community-based agencies that has been judged very successful in several evaluations. End-of-year achievement tests show a minimum of six months growth in academic achievement among 95 percent of participating students. In addition, student behaviors improved, all parents who attended parenting classes reported learning at least four new skills, and no students have been reported for alcohol or drug abuse or treatment. Collaboration, training, and materials have been funded largely through corporate contributions.

Contact Information

Director
Alpha
Blanton Elementary School
6400 54th Avenue North
St. Petersburg, Florida 33709
813-547-7508

Carnegie Foundation for the Advancement of Teaching
1755 Massachusetts Avenue, NW
Suite 308
Washington, DC 20036
202-387-7200

Use Performing Arts To Build Healthy Bodies and Minds

Strategy

Performing arts programs build self-esteem, confidence, perseverance, and initiative among participating youth. All these qualities are important protective influences against involvement in delinquent behavior and substance abuse.

Crime Problem Addressed

Research analyzed by Dr. J. David Hawkins of Development Research Programs (DRP) indicates that many youth exposed to multiple factors that increase their risk of delinquency do not engage in that behavior. DRP research shows that those youth who resist delinquent behavior have specific "protective factors" that work against the risk factors, buffering their impact and enhancing the youth's ability to grow up healthy and safe. Hawkins groups these protective factors into three categories:

■ individual characteristics (i.e., positive social orientation);

■ bonding (positive relationships with family, other adults, and peers); and

■ healthy beliefs and clear standards for behavior from within the family, school, and peer groups.

Performing arts programs that build the self-esteem, poise, perseverance, teamwork skills, and initiative of young people help to support the youth's positive development and prevent delinquency.

Key Components

This strategy and the success of related programs depends heavily on the involvement of committed adults from the schools or community-based organizations. Beyond commitment, adults sponsoring or administering program activities must have specific performance or arts skills that they can pass along to the students. To be effective, these programs must not only be entertaining enough to attract youth, but they must also help youth develop perseverance, initiative, and teamwork skills through the effort to master a performance as an individual or within an ensemble. In addition, performances with specific messages about substance abuse, violence prevention, or cultural themes convey and reinforce healthy community standards and values, to both the participating youth and their audiences. Participants get a clear sense of their contribution to the community when they perform antidrug skits or violence prevention song-and-dance routines for younger students.

Key Partnerships

Local community-based and professional theater and dance groups often work in concert with schools and community organizations to support workshops and ongoing performance programs for youth. Where those collaborations are not possible, school personnel may develop the projects as part of drama, performance, or community service clubs. Most youth performance projects are supported by community groups and local businesses, which may donate performance space, transportation, and publicity for performances. In some cases, local corporations have donated materials and travel support to youth performance ensembles.

Potential Obstacles

Community-based programs sometimes find it difficult to maintain the involvement and support of adults with enough time, talent, and energy to sustain the project. Many local community-oriented performance groups for youth have received strong support from local university drama departments or professional theater ensembles that contribute time and talent as part of their commitment to the community. In addition, some projects find that space for rehearsals is hard to locate. The space issue can usually be overcome through partnerships between schools and community organization that allow the use of auditoriums for rehearsals or provide classes of younger children as audiences.

Signs of Success

Performing arts programs—encouraging development of talent, fostering cultural values, and conveying positive messages about staying in school and away from drugs—provide buffers against the risk factors that youth in disadvantaged communities face every day. One example of such a program is the youth "steel pan" Caribbean music group in Washington, DC. The program Self-Esteem Through Performing Arts: A Prevention Strategy for African-American Youth operates out of a local Boys & Girls Club and involves forty-five talented youth who perform at community festivals, benefit concerts, and other area events. All band members are recruited from an area of the city with a high concentration of violent crime, school dropouts, substance abuse, and public housing. The program supplements performances with information on drug prevention, tutoring, and the importance of parental involvement in activities. In 1994, all members of the group had at least a 3.0 average in school, and 85 percent were on the honor roll. Increasing numbers of parents were participating in group-sponsored activities.

The group has been designated a Shining Star program by the Southeast Regional Center for Drug-Free Schools and Communities.

Applying the Strategy

In 1991, the Austin (Texas) Independent School District adopted a performing arts character education program that uses dance as a medium to teach values and improve the self-esteem and confidence of elementary-school children considered to be at risk of dropping out of school. Ten- to fourteen-year-old students in the Believe in Me program learn and perform dance routines with the assistance of local professional instructors. Hundreds of students participate in the program each year, experiencing individual success within a group, developing self-confidence by mastering new skills, and channeling their energies and frustrations creatively. Believe in Me also uses curriculum guidelines to teach important lessons such as civic responsibility, citizenship, and public speaking. The program, patterned after one begun in New York through the National Dance Institute, was designated a model program by the Texas Attorney General and won a 1994 Criminal Justice Award.

Youth in Chicago's Cambodian community perform antigang and antidrug plays under the sponsorship of Travelers and Immigrants Aid (TIA), a community-based organization that assists Asian and African refugees. Written and performed by youth, the pieces convey vital prevention messages and foster self-esteem within a cultural framework familiar to young audiences new to the United States. The Refugee Substance Abuse Prevention Project of TIA also provides addiction prevention information and counseling for youth and adults.

Contact Information

Believe In Me!
4131 Spicewood Springs Road, Suite A3
Austin, Texas 78759
512-345-3357

Recreation Centers

Strategy

Neighborhood-based recreation centers are vital sources of positive activity and learning for youth, as well as an important resource for connecting them to needed prevention services.

Crime Problem Addressed

Youth from economically disadvantaged and crime-plagued communities often raise the concern that it is difficult for them to resist peer pressure to get involved in delinquent activity because of limited opportunities for attractive recreational or social activity. After-school recreational activities—offered through community centers, schools and local recreation departments—that are supplemented by educational opportunities such as tutoring and job placement services, help fill youths' free time with positive and safe activities. Late-evening recreation programs benefit older teens, helping to reduce youth-related crime.

Key Components

Recreation centers in neighborhoods rarely lack youth participants. The ball courts, swimming classes, art lessons, dance troupes, bands, martial arts instruction, and other activities often represent the sole outlet for formal sport and arts participation available to urban youth. The presence of recreation programs alone, however, does not tend to result in dramatic reductions in violent crime by or against youth.

When recreation is combined with supplementary educational activities—such as tutoring, education on drug abuse and health awareness, and job skills training—the recreation centers become a vital link in the community system supporting youth. Such centers often provide an oasis of safety and an alternative life choice to youth who reside in violence-plagued communities. Community support for such centers is strong, as they are often one of the few visible signs of comprehensive local services based in such neighborhoods. In addition, many centers have become home to a variety of health and prevention services for youth, as well as the center of youth-police partnership projects.

Key Partnerships

Residents and local organizations that operate recreation centers often work in partnership to develop programs to meet the needs of area youth and staff. Multiagency collaborations of the local government are nearly always involved in staffing the centers, providing services and referrals to youth and their families, and donating facilities and equipment. Schools can be helpful partners in identifying youth with academic and behavioral problems who may require support or services outside school. In turn, centers with tutoring programs can help schools track the needs and progress of students at risk of academic failure and dropping out. Local businesses can be partners in locating needed space and equipment, getting publicity for programs, and soliciting donations to support center activities or rehabilitate facilities. Youth in the community can help design programs and help peers and younger children with sports activities and homework.

Potential Obstacles

Local governments are finding it increasingly difficult to locate resources to support community-based recreation centers. It is incumbent upon local supporters to investigate innovative staff and budget plans for such centers, in order to make the best use of existing local government resources and to draw upon local reservoirs of corporate and nonprofit agency support. Many of the most successful programs started this way and have thrived through those partnerships.

Signs of Success

A national study of nineteen recreation programs by the National Parks and Recreation Association revealed that local law enforcement in these cities credited area youth recreation programs with significant contributions to reducing the incidence of crimes committed by and against juveniles.

Fort Myers, Florida, had a significant juvenile crime problem for several years. By 1990, juveniles had committed nearly 4,000 crimes, with 67 percent of crimes committed by repeat offenders, and a significant proportion by youth carrying firearms. Furthermore, the city of 50,000 was suffering from high rates of school suspensions and truancy. In response, the city applied for and received federal support for Success Through Academic and Recreational Support (STARS), a community recreation center-based program which enrolls thousands of area children in academic enrichment projects and organized recreation activities. The program's collaborators include the schools, police, housing agency, the Boys & Girls Club, and a local sorority. STARS' success stories include the following:

■ a nearly 50 percent increase in academic performance among participating students; and

■ a continuing decline in juvenile crime, including a two-thirds reduction in recidivism among eleven- and twelve-year-old offenders.

Applying the Strategy

In 1993, a late-night recreation and supplemental education program sponsored by the City of Cincinnati helped reduce juvenile crime in the Winton Hills community by 24 percent after just three months of operation. City officials attribute this reduction to the establishment of the center, which operates on a budget of roughly $60,000. The noted reduction in crime was achieved at a cost of $0.56 per youth participant.

San Antonio and Corpus Christi are two of the seven cities in Texas which recently developed comprehensive, citywide crime prevention plans through broad-based local government and community coalitions. Although each of the seven city plans included recommendations on youth recreation, these two cities put particular emphasis on the issue. In 1993, Corpus Christi developed a citywide youth sports network to coordinate youth activities. In the same year, San Antonio increased city funding for youth recreation by $10 million, as part of a comprehensive youth crime strategy which balances enforcement with prevention and intervention. Juvenile crime has since declined noticeably in both cities.

Contact Information

Director (Attn: Recreation)
Parks and Recreation
P.O. Drawer 2217
City of Fort Myers
Fort Myers, Florida 33902
813-338-2288

National Parks and Recreation Association
2775 South Quincy Street
Arlington, Virginia 22206
703-820-4940

Crime Prevention Programs Targeted at Female Youth

Strategy

Designing community-based delinquency prevention programs for the unique developmental needs of preteen and adolescent girls will reduce juvenile delinquency, school dropout, and early pregnancy.

Crime Problem Addressed

According to a recent study, 24 percent of high school girls reported having been abused, compared with 6 percent of high school boys. Girls with a history of abuse report doing

poorly in school, are at a higher risk for suicide, and have weak family support systems. In different communities, from four to seven times as many young men as women are involved with guns, but twice as many young women as men feel threatened by guns. Young women from communities with violent crime, alcohol or drug abuse, chronic unemployment, and other quality-of-life problems are at high risk for victimization. More of these women are becoming pregnant at an early age, dropping out of school because of poor chronic school performance or pregnancy, or abusing alcohol or illegal drugs. Low self-esteem, peer pressure to become sexually active, dating violence, and low expectations about school performance in families are major causes of developmental problems among young girls. Programs tailored to address developmental, socialization, and cultural issues will have the most success in preventing delinquent behaviors or poor life choices.

Key Components

Female adult mentors are very important components of programs serving female youth, who sometimes lack contact with positive female role models from whom they can learn specific life skills and receive specialized academic attention. Activities and services that are essential for healthy female development include the following:

- mentoring and tutoring;

- skills training in communication, conflict management, and decision-making;

- recreation and other activities to build self-esteem; and

- educational information on substance abuse prevention and self-protection from violence.

Community-based organizations (such as Girl Scouts, YWCA, and Girls, Inc.) often sponsor such efforts and unite their resources with area businesswomen, community service clubs, local government, nonprofit social service agencies, and school systems to identify at-risk girls who need healthy support systems. These groups also recruit volunteers, offer supplemental resources, and locate experts and materials when requested.

Key Partnerships

Sponsoring organizations usually work in partnership with:

- local schools to identify girls who would benefit from participation;

- area businesswomen to recruit volunteers as mentors, tutors, or other types of resource people; and

- a variety of community partners to publicize the project and recruit youth participants.

In some localities, community service groups assist these projects by helping with volunteer recruitment and fundraising drives.

Potential Obstacles

Some communities may not fully understand the particular developmental needs, pressures, and related issues that young girls confront as they mature into adolescence and young adulthood. Community groups that have information on the risk factors and delinquent behaviors most prevalent among girls will be better prepared to educate the community at-large on effective crime prevention strategies aimed at reaching female youth. Stereotypes and myths about male and female sexuality and conduct should also be addressed when implementing effective programs targeted at young females.

Signs of Success

Programs tailored specifically to girls have increased in number and popularity in recent years, largely out of increased awareness of the growing problems confronting female youth. Girls, Inc., established in 1945, is the nation's leading authority on girls. Operating a network of more than 300 centers in 135 cities nationwide, the organization develops and implements research-based programs that help girls build their capacity for economic independence and responsible adulthood. Their Preventing Adolescent Pregnancy program offers age-appropriate information for girls ages nine through eighteen, to help them avoid early sexual activity and pregnancy. Friendly Persuasion, a substance abuse prevention program for girls ages eleven to fourteen, helps girls develop the assertiveness skills they need to avoid substance abuse and develop strong leadership skills. The older girls use their knowledge and skills to teach younger children what they have learned. Teen Connections is an adolescent health program that puts girls in charge of improving health services in their communities.

Applying the Strategy

Just for Girls in Bradenton, Florida, has operated a life skills, educational support, pregnancy prevention, and drug abuse education and prevention program in cooperation with local government agencies and community groups since 1969. Tutoring, alternative education, refusal skills training, cultural awareness, and health education programs have had remarkable effects. Participating girls have had no pregnancies, improved their decision-making skills, and reduced their rate of school dropout. Standardized testing instruments demonstrated that participants who were in the program for at least four years had increased their self-esteem by 59 percent.

Contact Information

Executive Director
Just For Girls
920 14th Street West
Bradenton, Florida 34205
813-747-5757

Program Director
Girls, Inc.
30 East 33rd Street
New York, New York 10016-5394
212-689-3700

Implement Curfews for Youth

Strategy

Reinforce social controls on youth by using late evening curfews to help reduce youth crime and victimization.

Crime Problem Addressed

Delinquent and criminal behavior by youth is at its highest during evening and late-night hours. It is also during that time that many youths are victimized by crime, either as bystanders or in gang-related situations. Juvenile curfews are local policies that prohibit youth under the age of eighteen from being out on the street during late-night hours (most often from 11:00 p.m. to 6:00 a.m.), with few exceptions. Cities throughout the country have turned to juvenile late-night curfews as a strategy to protect the community at large, and law-abiding youth in particular, from juvenile offenders, many of whom are involved with gangs. The strategy has had notable impact on juvenile crime in cities in California, Arizona, and Texas, with many additional cities expressing interest in such policies since May 1994, when the U.S. Supreme Court upheld the Dallas juvenile late-night curfew as constitutional.

Key Components

A local ordinance or policy creating guidelines for the curfew hours, allowable exceptions, and sanctions is the most vital component of a juvenile curfew, since local police cannot enforce a curfew until it is agreed to by local officials and the public. The most effective juvenile curfew policies have been implemented in cities that view curfews as one tool within a multifaceted local strategy to deal with crime by and against youth through a blend of prevention, intervention, and enforcement approaches. The prevention component of the approach should include programs and activities to support the positive development of youth in the community and to ensure that youth and their families have access to services they need. Effective support programs include recreation programs, job banks, youth leadership programs, counseling, and support for parents and families with emergency needs for employment, housing, and substance abuse prevention services.

Some key issues local governments must consider include establishing provisions to allow "normal" activity, such as returning home from a job, athletic event, church-sponsored event, or other activity sanctioned by the community; discussing community norms about late-night activity by youth and about the potential effectiveness of a curfew; and reinforcing social controls on the youth through graduated sanctions that clearly hold both the youth and parents legally accountable. Most cities that have adopted curfews have found it helpful to review the May 1994 U.S. Supreme Court decision as a safeguard against constitutional challenges.

Enforcement of curfews generally involves law enforcement apprehension of violators, who are then transported to a recreation center or police substation to await processing by another officer or volunteer. The youth are only released into the custody of a parent. First offenses usually result in small fines levied against the offender. Repeat violations often result in increased fines and community service for the juvenile and fines levied against the parent. The cities with the most successful curfew policies also use the apprehension of the offender as an opportunity to discern the reasons for the violation (abuse in the home, gang involvement, substance abuse) and to refer the youth and the family to government or community-based service providers that can help address these issues.

Key Partnerships

Design and implementation of a successful juvenile curfew depends on several partnerships. Local policymakers and law enforcement must work together to determine whether a juvenile late-night curfew would be an effective and supported response to violent juvenile crime in that community. Second, lawmakers and police are more likely to get sustained support from youth, parents, and other adults in the community if they work with community representatives to design the curfew policy.

Potential Obstacles

Constitutional challenge and public opposition are the two biggest obstacles that communities interested in juvenile curfew policies must confront. The constitutional argument claims that curfews are an unfair challenge to the First Amendment's guaranteed right of assembly. Careful drafting of the document can ensure its constitutionality, and outreach to the community can foster public support and result in the creation of a broad-based prevention, intervention, and enforcement program that combats violent crime by and against youth. Public education about the protection a curfew can afford law-abiding youth will help build support among youth, who might otherwise view a curfew as an unfair restriction on their activity.

Signs of Success

In San Antonio, a nighttime curfew on youth under the age of seventeen has been credited with reducing nighttime juvenile arrests by 29 percent and youth victimization by violent crime during those hours by 85 percent in the first three years the curfew was implemented. The city, not relying on a curfew alone, has also set up additional youth recreation centers, thus providing positive opportunities for youth and gaining additional support from the community for the enforcement policy emphasized through the curfew. The success of the curfew policy has led the city to adopt tougher ordinances targeting truancy, graffiti, and youth possession of weapons; these ordinances have resulted in further reductions in juvenile crime and arrests.

Applying the Strategy

Phoenix, Arizona, implemented a juvenile curfew policy which has since been adopted in a modified form by numerous other jurisdictions. Supported by 93 percent of the residents in a recent poll, the curfew was established because of serious concerns about juvenile, particularly gang-related, violent crime during late-night hours. Combined with ordinances on juvenile liquor purchases and gun possession, the policy is credited with a 10-percent reduction in juvenile arrests for violent offenses during the first year of implementation. The curfew's effectiveness has since been enhanced by cooperation with the city's network of recreation centers, which now also serve as curfew drop-off, assessment, and service referral centers.

Juvenile crime in New Orleans decreased by 38 percent just sixty days after implementation of a late-night curfew in 1994. New Orleans' ordinance holds both parents and juveniles accountable. Other recently established city programs provide youth with opportunities for jobs through AmeriCorps and the Youth Action Corps. Oklahoma City and San Jose, California, have experienced similar success with curfews.

Contact Information

Patrol Administration
City of Phoenix Police Department
620 West Washington Street
Phoenix, Arizona 85003
602-534-2712

Youth Initiatives Manager
Office of Youth Initiatives
City of San Antonio
P.O. Box 839966
San Antonio, Texas 78283-3966
210-207-7196

Support Youth Through Intergenerational Programs

Strategy

Intergenerational programs that partner children with senior citizens expose youth to senior role models with diverse life experiences and help young people to develop a more positive self-concept and broader perspective on their futures.

Crime Problem Addressed

Most children today grow up without contact with an extended family including grandparents or older adults. Families are much smaller than previously, and many lack a strong adult support system. Children who grow up without positive adult role models have a limited sense of self and a narrow world view. They are more likely to get involved in delinquent behavior as they mature because they lack adult attention and understanding. This strategy attempts to address the general family and community issue of positive adult support, which all children need in order to grow into healthy and positive adults.

Key Components

This strategy creates opportunities for youth and older adults to interact in positive recreational opportunities, social events, or one-on-one mentoring and friendship situations. These activities are often organized by schools, local community centers, recreation centers, or churches. Sponsoring organizations often have extensive membership networks through which they can recruit older adult volunteers to match with interested youth. Some recreation centers organize intergenerational social and recreation activities to expose each age group to the other's experiences and break down barriers of misperceptions and understandings that may exist. Church-related and community-based programs may be designed explicitly to provide at-risk youth with surrogate grandparent role models who can provide the support and guidance formerly found in the traditional extended family. The church-based programs are particularly common in African-American communities, where traditions of extended family and community support for children are deeply rooted.

Key Partnerships

To ensure adult volunteer participation and outreach to youth and families in need, partnerships must exist between sponsoring organizations and the community. Sponsor organizations from the community often work with local recreation agencies to organize special events or provide space for senior citizens and children to interact through games, homework support, or other activities.

Potential Obstacles

Both children and older adults often have distorted notions about what people in the other age group are like, their activities and their interests. Programs using this strategy need to make a concerted effort to reach out to both groups to demonstrate the positive benefits that can come from increased contact with individuals from different generations with varied experiences.

Signs of Success

In Dade County, Florida, the Youth and Elderly Against Crime project is bridging the gap between at-risk youth and older adults. Operating in nine Dade County public schools in high-risk areas, the program brings together youth and older adults to identify and solve common problems in the community, create a safer environment, and stimulate positive interactions between the elderly and at-risk youth. Approximately 1,000 students participate in the program with support and assistance from law enforcement agencies, teachers, and administrators.

The Center for Intergenerational Learning at Temple University, in Philadelphia, Pennsylvania, serves as a national resource center and information clearinghouse for intergenerational programs. The center, established in 1980, develops and initiates numerous community- and school-based programs targeted at strengthening ties and breaking down barriers between youth and older adults. Their programs include the following:

■ Learning Retreats, an annual five-day residential retreat that brings together seventy-five persons, ages 14 to 100, to encourage open dialogue across the ages;

■ Linking Lifetimes, a multisite research and demonstration project that connects senior mentors to at-risk middle-school children and young offenders; and

■ Urban Initiatives, a program designed to help community organizations, churches, and schools in north Philadelphia develop intergenerational programs and engage students in service-learning projects that benefit the entire community.

Applying the Strategy

Grandfriends of Minneapolis, Minnesota, is operated by the Retired Senior Volunteer Program in that region and supported by the county, which started the program as a way of connecting young children with additional adult support and attention. Grandfriends volunteers spend time with children under six years old who go to day-care centers or live in group homes. They read with the children, play games, or help them with simple tasks. Established in 1983, Grandfriends believes that the relationships the children have built with the seniors enhance their self-esteem, social skills, and feelings of responsibility. Grandfriends volunteers say that they get as much benefit from the program as the children. Foster grandparent programs and church-sponsored senior mentor programs are increasingly popular throughout the country as volunteer projects, especially among American Association of Retired Persons and other national senior programs.

Contact Information

Grandfriends Coordinator
Retired Senior Volunteer Program of Greater
  Minneapolis
2021 East Hennepin Avenue, Suite 130
Minneapolis, Minnesota 55413-2723
612-331-4467

Program Developer
Center for Intergenerational Learning
Temple University
1601 North Broad Street, Room 206
Philadelphia, Pennsylvania 19122
215-204-6709

Community-Based Programs for Runaway and Homeless Youth

Strategy

Community-based programs provide residential, counseling, or service referral to runaway and homeless youth to help them regain the stability and support needed to maintain a lifestyle free of delinquent behavior, substance abuse, poor school performance, and violence.

Crime Problem Addressed

Each year an estimated 800,000 youth ten to seventeen years old run away from home or end up living on the streets. They do so for a variety of reasons, including:

■ family conflict and alienation;

■ physical, emotional, or sexual abuse;

■ behavioral problems or poor school performance;

■ substance abuse, their own or a parent's; and

■ related family-management problems.

Negative experiences in the home and school are reportedly the primary reason that 75 percent of the youth give for running away. Once away from even a modestly stable home life, youth on their own are at increased risk of victimization by crime and involvement in criminal behavior such as prostitution, robbery, gang violence, and substance abuse. Often, the crimes are committed as a means to gain money for survival. Drugs become an anesthetic to dull the impact of the perilous existence that frequently accompanies life on the street for a teenager. Community-based runaway youth services programs are vital support systems for youth who need help in securing a safe living environment or, in some cases, in uniting with their families.

Key Components

These programs are often administered by long-standing community-based organizations that offer a comprehensive range of services, including emergency shelter, clothing, food, social service and other referrals, counseling, health care, financial assistance, drug prevention awareness and education, AIDS prevention awareness and education, and help in reconciling the youth with their parent if appropriate or desired by the youth. Counselors who earn the trust of these youth can work effectively with them to identify their immediate and long-term needs for assistance; these counselors provide the cohesion for these programs, ensure that the services are meeting an individual youth's needs, and become a caring adult to whom the youth can turn for help.

Key Partnerships

Sponsoring agencies are most effective in their efforts when they work with local social service providers in linking youth with the assistance they need. In addition, most programs establish links with other service providers, government agencies, and community organizations for financial resources, facilities, and other program support. A variety of community service organizations provide volunteer assistance to these programs and recruit adult and peer helpers through membership networks.

Potential Obstacles

Effective delivery of such comprehensive services on an emergency and extended basis requires extensive staff and volunteer personnel, as well as the resources necessary to support them. Many community-based programs must sponsor ongoing fundraising drives and publicity campaigns to garner the support needed to keep their program operating effectively. Publicity is also vital to ensure that youth in need of the program's services are aware that it exists. Local public relations and advertising firms are often willing to donate professional services and advertising space as part of their commitment to the local community.

Signs of Success

The Sasha Bruce Youthwork organization in Washington, DC, an established local organization, operates several facilities for at-risk youth, including the city's only emergency shelter for runaway and homeless youth. In addition, the organization operates one home for teenage mothers and two long-term residential facilities for chronically homeless runaway youth where residents are required to go to school and contribute. Forty counselors and 100 volunteers help these youth secure apartments, jobs, and legal advice; they also provide individual and family counseling on life skills, drug abuse awareness, and AIDS prevention. Contact with the youth continues through counseling after they have left the facilities. The organization reports that 95 percent of the youth it helps attain more stable lives, with more than 75 percent returning home and 20 percent entering out-of-home placements, such as foster care.

Applying the Strategy

Aunt Martha's Youth Services (AMYS), a multiservice organization, provides a range of services to youth and families through a network of forty-eight programs located throughout communities south and west of Chicago, Illinois. In addition to crisis intervention and emergency assistance to families, diversion programs for youth at risk, and recreation programs, AMYS supports a network of private and group homes for runaway youth. A long-standing organization that is respected by the community, the program involves youth on its board, including them in project design.

The Family and Youth Service Bureau (FYSB) of the U.S. Department of Health and Human Services administers a number of programs targeted at rescuing runaway and homeless youth. The Basic Center Project funds 350 centers in communities across the country, centers designed to provide safe havens for thousands of runaway and homeless youth. Basic Centers offer support to agencies that provide crisis intervention services to runaway and homeless youth with a primary goal of reuniting them with their families or arranging for other suitable placements.

FYSB's Transitional Living Program for Homeless Youth helps homeless youth, ages sixteen through twenty-one, make a successful transition to self-sufficient living and avoid long-term dependency on social services or entanglement in the judicial system. This program addresses the reality that many youth flee their homes because of physical, sexual, and emotional abuse and that they often need long-term, supportive assistance that emergency shelters are not designed to provide. To date, eighty-six such projects are operating across the country.

Contact Information

Director of Public Relations
Aunt Martha's Youth Services
4343 Lincoln Highway, Suite 340
Matteson, Illinois 60443
708-747-2701

College Students as Volunteer Resources and Role Models

Strategy

College students—with their interests, perspectives, and experiences—are valuable volunteer resources and role models for programs serving younger people.

Crime Problem Addressed

In many communities, urban and suburban, children and youth are not well supervised by parents, who work long hours or for other reasons spend little time guiding their children. A variety of community-based recreation, after-school day-care, and other projects attempt to fill that gap and provide consistent support to children and youth. These programs offer supervised recreation and sports instruction, homework assistance, and education on drug and alcohol abuse, crime prevention, and self-protection. College and university students are valuable resources for these programs because they have flexible schedules and because they have interests and perspectives in common with youth, making it easy for at-risk youth to relate to them.

Key Components

College-age volunteer participation in programs may not correlate directly with a reduction in criminal or delinquent behavior by youth. However, the qualities possessed by college volunteers and role models provide a positive and rewarding atmosphere for youth participants. Many colleges and universities operate their own community-services projects, harnessing their students' energies and talents on behalf of at-risk youth, families, the elderly, the environment, and special populations, such as the physically challenged or refugees. In many instances, the students become involved through an internship, course requirement, or career-related interest, bringing specialized knowledge of the topic or service the program offers. On-campus community service clubs, fraternities and sororities, and athletic teams often coordinate special youth and community projects with their members and provide resources, such as sports fields, gyms, and concert halls.

Key Partnerships

Many universities have a student volunteer group, office, or coordinating council that keeps in contact with local youth agencies and community organizations, seeking opportunities to provide ongoing program support or staff for special events. Community organizations often pay particular attention to recruiting college-age volunteers, knowing how well youth respond to their guidance and opportunities to develop relationships with surrogate older siblings.

Potential Obstacles

Colleges and universities have, by definition, transient populations, so volunteer-supported programs that rely exclusively on them may suffer from turnover as the year progresses and class schedules and other commitments vary in intensity. Programs can overcome some of these drawbacks by building opportunities for the youth and students to develop relationships over time, making each more likely to remain active as program participants.

Signs of Success

The Campus Opportunity Outreach League (COOL) is a national organization dedicated to promoting university student involvement in community action. Through its newsletter, resource book, workshops, and technical assistance, it has provided guidance to countless universities on how to spur student involvement in community service projects, including those tailored to serving at-risk youth and promoting crime prevention. The COOL National Conference on Student Community Services brings together more than 2,000 college student leaders who are active in community service from across the country each year. In addition, COOL hosts an annual National Leadership Summit where 100 student leaders from coast-to-coast meet for five days to focus on a theme that will have an impact on COOL as an organization, as well as on its constituency.

Applying the Strategy

University of Washington students have volunteered at a local YMCA, tutoring, mentoring, and coaching youth who would otherwise have been at home unsupervised while their parents worked. University of Illinois students supervise, tutor, and share snacks with troubled youth from broken families in the area. They run a Big Brother-Big Sister program and treat the youth to dinners and discussions with students from different countries. Students from DePauw University in Indiana provide vital support to professional staff of the local Head Start Program, lending their assistance to young children developing basic language and social skills in preparation for starting school. Their volunteer contributions are counted among supports for the program as grant funding proposals are developed.

Contact Information

Director
Campus Opportunity Outreach League
1511 K Street, NW, Suite #307
Washington, DC 20005
202-637-7004

Counseling for Divorcing Parents

Strategy

Counseling divorcing couples minimizes the traumatic impact of the situation on children and improves relationships among family members.

Crime Problem Addressed

A family management issue such as prolonged and unresolved conflict among family members is a risk factor for juvenile delinquency and substance abuse, especially among children from divorced families, and particularly in families where domestic abuse occurs. Psychologists cited in a 1987 *Psychology Today* article stated that children of divorced parents suffer from loss of self-esteem and initiative, often resulting in poor school performance and difficult peer relationships. Furthermore, Louis Sullivan, former Secretary of Health and Human Services, said in a 1992 speech before the Council on Families in America that "fatherlessness is the greatest issue of our era. Approximately 70 percent of juveniles in long-term correctional facilities did not live with their fathers while growing up." According to research conducted by Judith Wallerstein, author of *Second Chances,* children who don't have regular contact with their fathers are five times more likely to be held back a grade in school; three times more likely not to graduate; five times more likely to be involved in juvenile delinquency; and three times more likely to be under the care of a psychologist. This strategy aims to accomplish two goals: minimize the often intense conflict between divorcing parents and maintain contact between both parents and the children.

Key Components

Programs that utilize this strategy often include a series of workshops or courses for parents to make them sensitive to the impact of divorce on children when family conflicts are not managed and when contact between parents and children is hostile or infrequent. Courses highlight strategies to help parents and children learn conflict management, to settle custody disputes fairly, and to help children cope with changes in the family structure and routine. An effective program must encourage ongoing contact and support by both parents, in particular the fathers, as well as counseling for children on dealing effectively with the absence of a parent.

Key Partnerships

Design and delivery of this type of program requires the participation and cooperation of representatives of the court, legal specialists in family law, and social services or child advocacy professionals. Successful implementation of the strategy is enhanced through connections to community-based organizations serving families and program curriculum evaluations that request feedback from adult participants. Parents who feel the program has benefited them can become powerful advocates for its continued use, even becoming informal recruiters for parent participants in communities where the program is voluntary.

Potential Obstacles

Voluntary programs may suffer if parents refuse to participate. Judges and family law specialists can help solve this problem by emphasizing use of the curriculum by family court litigants and by publicizing the program through their professional and personal networks. Programs that collect anecdotal or other comments on the value of the curriculum and include them in promotional materials will have a better chance of increasing the number of participants.

Signs of Success

Local and circuit courts that hear family cases are increasingly turning to parental counseling and education to ensure that divorcing parents remain mindful of the impact of divorce on children. Utah and Connecticut courts require all divorcing parents to attend parenting classes. Seventy-five percent of participating parents in Utah said the program should continue to be mandatory, and 90 percent rated it as worthwhile.

The Circuit Court of Cook County, Illinois, operates a lecture, videotape, and interactive discussion for divorcing parents on the impact of divorce on children. Focus on Children emphasizes skills and strategies that parents can use to avoid disputes with each other and to help the child cope with the divorce. Focus on Children is not a mandatory program, but many parents participate on the advice of their lawyer or a directive from the judge. Recognizing that some children experience the effects of divorce well past the time of court proceedings, Cook County officials are designing a system to track and follow up on participating families.

Applying the Strategy

Recognizing the need to intervene with at-risk families to prevent divorce trauma and domestic violence, Corpus Christi, Texas, has implemented court-ordered parental education classes for all divorcing parents seeking custody or visitation rights. The day-long Children Cope with Divorce curriculum, first implemented in 1993, helps parents to develop coping skills that will minimize the trauma suffered by the children in the family. The local family law association and family court judges worked together to design, publicize, and implement this successful program. All of the parents who took the course in 1994 (over 400) rated it very favorably. Local officials also established a Supervised Parent Visitation Center, essentially a neutral location where parents who cannot maintain amicable contact can drop off the child for pickup by the other parent. Volunteers trained in conflict management mediate between parents when necessary and chaperon controlled visitation situations. The two programs are part of a comprehensive citywide strategy to prevent crime, including violent crime within families.

The Non-Custodial Parents of Nebraska (NCPN) program—a coalition of parents, step-parents, grandparents, extended family members, and friends of children after divorce or separation—provides support, education, information, research, monthly meetings, and workshops supporting the fundamental right of children to responsible parenting. According to statistics, 90 percent of children live with their maternal parent after divorce or separation. NCPN, founded in 1988, encourages mediation and more participation and support by fathers to promote the welfare

and health of the child of a broken marriage. In 1993, the state of Nebraska spent nearly $24 million for its foster care program; increased "fathering encouragement" by the state has contributed to lessening this tax burden.

Contact Information

Director
Focus on Children
28 North Clark Street, Suite 600
Chicago, Illinois 60602
312-345-8850

Children's Rights Council NEIA, Inc.
P.O. Box 37387
Omaha, Nebraska 68137-5387
402-330-3353

Peer-to-Peer Instruction

Strategy

Providing young people with opportunities to help instruct younger children or their peers enhances the effectiveness of programs that aim to give children specific information and skills about substance abuse, violence, or victimization prevention. Furthermore, youth involved as peer teachers have their own self-esteem reinforced.

Crime Problem Addressed

Youth give many reasons for dropping out of structured learning environments: low self-esteem, personal problems, boredom, inability to communicate, and isolation, among others. These issues must be addressed if community youth-focused programs are to be effective. A program's impact is enhanced when the message is expressed by someone to whom the child or youth can readily relate, particularly a peer who they know faces the same pressures and challenges in school and the community.

Youthful presenters who convey messages as tutors or within entertaining formats such as skits, songs, dances, or puppet shows make learning potentially frightening facts fun and ensure that the knowledge is remembered. Programs that utilize this strategy also enhance the self-esteem of the youth presenters, helping them to understand their role in and value to the community. Furthermore, the act of presenting or performing the educational material in an entertaining way reinforces the concepts of a drug-free or violence-free lifestyle.

Key Components

The programs' success depends on the development of educational material appropriate for the age group of chil-

dren in the audience and adequate training for the youth who deliver the message. The youth presenters must both understand the material (e.g., facts about drugs or violence and their impact on children) and know how to interact with younger children or their peers; their interactions must strengthen and reinforce the positive messages. Youth who work with their peers or adults in community-based settings must also be familiar with the appropriate materials and learn conflict management and communication skills, thus enhancing their ability to work effectively and develop useful skills. This strategy has been used in schools, where older youth present antidrug or safety skits to elementary children; in community organizations, which have trained youth to work as outreach counselors with their troubled peers; and in community tutoring programs, where older youth help children in lower grades with homework while presenting themselves as positive and supportive role models.

Key Partnerships

Schools and community-based service or youth groups work together to recruit youth participants, including those considered to be at risk of dropping out or getting involved in violence or substance abuse. As the site for performance or tutoring programs, schools also help by working with youth to identify the strategies or issues where their help would be most useful and by providing the younger students who attend the programs or who need tutoring assistance. Community-based programs serving at-risk youth play a vital role, as they train youth as community workers or peer educators, connecting the talents of those youth to school or other local government-sponsored projects where their assistance is needed.

Potential Obstacles

Community or school-based programs using this strategy may encounter some opposition to the idea of using at-risk youth to teach their peers or younger students. This resistance can be overcome through concerted efforts when the youth are properly supervised and trained and when the long-term, positive effects of such participation on the at-risk youth leaders and participants are demonstrated. Other problems might include the at-risk youth diverting attention away from other important activities, such as their own school work. This issue can be resolved through a network of educators and trainers working together.

Signs of Success

The Intercultural Development Research Association developed the Coca-Cola Valued Youth Program, a cross-aged tutoring program that has affected the lives of more than 1,000 secondary students and 3,000 elementary school students in fifty-two secondary and elementary schools nationwide. The program focuses on turning the perceived liabilities of the at-risk youth into strengths and on reinforcing their self-worth and value. Involving at-risk students between the ages of twelve and seventeen, the program provides tutoring to younger children in the local school system. Its philosophy is based on learning, valuing, contributing, participating, excelling, involving, and supporting.

The students who participate as tutors and mentors have increased their own school performance, sharpened their communication skills, and improved their self-esteem. Only 1 percent of tutors (8 out of 747) dropped out of school from 1993 to 1994. Over 11 years, the findings have been consistent: The dropout rate remains below 2 percent, and participants' self-esteem, attitudes toward school, grades, achievement test scores, attendance, and discipline have all improved. The program is a nationally recognized model for dropout prevention, with waiting lists at every program site.

Applying the Strategy

The Neighborhood House of North Richmond, California, is the lead agency for a comprehensive community assistance program in that region. Neighborhood House was formed in 1956 and has been serving families and neighborhoods in Contra Costa County ever since. It has recently teamed with two other leading community institutions to formulate a program of additional services for the community. Included among them is a speaker's bureau of at-risk high school students who are trained to talk with younger students about drug abuse and gang prevention. The project is supported by The California Wellness Foundation.

The Real Alternatives Program agency in San Francisco's Mission District plans to train fifty youth as a "Peace Posse" of community violence prevention activists. The Macon (Georgia) Housing Authority and the State of Georgia have certified at-risk teens as community workers to present workshops to other youth on substance abuse and teenage pregnancy prevention. The authority considers the Students Taking a Right Stand program one of its most successful local crime prevention projects.

Contact Information

Coca-Cola Valued Youth Program
5835 Callaghan Road, Suite 350
San Antonio, Texas 78228
210-684-8180

Crime Prevention Techniques for Young Children

Strategy

Teaching young children basic crime prevention and self-protection techniques helps to keep them from being victimized by crime.

Crime Problem Addressed

Each year nearly three million children are reported abused in the United State, and millions more incidents go unreported. Four children die every day due to physical abuse by adults; more than 80 percent of abusers are a parent or someone close to a child. One in three girls and one in five boys are sexually abused by an adult at some time during childhood; one in thirteen children with a parent on drugs is physically abused, usually by the parent. Other statistics report that 84 percent of criminals were abused children.

Children are our most innocent victims, and without proper training and education they are our most vulnerable. This strategy aims to empower children with skills to make decisions and take actions that can protect them from victimization by physical or sexual abuse, abduction, bullying, or theft of personal belongings. It is particularly effective when delivered through age-appropriate educational materials or interactive teaching methods that help reinforce the messages of self-protection and preventive action.

Key Components

As noted, age-appropriate educational materials and techniques are vital to programs using this strategy. Simple and interactive techniques to convey key messages work best with younger children, while older children are able to learn through more complex techniques including group discussions and role playing. Teachers, day-care providers, and others who work with children must be trained by law enforcement officers or other specialists to ensure that they present appropriate information in ways most likely to reach the targeted age group without frightening the youth.

Some programs are implemented in schools or day-care centers by law enforcement officers and community organizations that serve youth. School systems often have counselors on hand following discussions of physical and sexual abuse, since this is a common time for children to disclose their victimization. Basic crime prevention and safety presentations by law enforcement officers and medical and fire emergency specialists create positive images of authority figures and teach small children about crime prevention and what to do in case of emergency.

Key Partnerships

Successful application of this strategy requires cooperation and partnership between the service provider (school-sponsored program, law enforcement, or community program), the teacher, and a parent or guardian. To ensure that the students are adequately prepared, it is important that the teacher is trained in making the presentation and responding appropriately and accurately to questions raised by young children. In addition, schools and police must work together to respond effectively when children report a crime.

Potential Obstacles

School officials may be concerned about how to handle reactions of children who have been presented with information on child abuse or abduction prevention. Police and school personnel can overcome this obstacle by working together and with parents to design a follow-up system for children's questions and crime reports; they must also ensure that the material presented is age-appropriate. The program must anticipate the potential legal issues and involvement by child protective and welfare agencies that may occur as a result of a report of child abuse or abduction.

Signs of Success

Thousands of schools and local law enforcement agencies have used child victimization and crime prevention information prepared by the National Crime Prevention Council and featuring McGruff the Crime Dog to educate young children. This material deals with inappropriate touching behavior; how to report a crime; and how to register bicycles with police so that they can be recovered if they are stolen. Law enforcement officers dressed as the McGruff character visit local schools, accompanied by an officer who presents the crime prevention information. In one Connecticut school, a five-year-old disclosed her sexual abuse to McGruff, providing more than sufficient evidence against the offender. This precluded the need for her testimony in court and saved thousands of dollars that would otherwise have been spent on a trial.

Housewise/Streetwise—started in 1982 by community volunteers in Greenville, South Carolina—is a child abuse victimization prevention program that works with the school system to provide educational programming for young children. The curriculum has helped over 65,000 Greenville third graders protect themselves and relinquish fear of disclosing sexual and physical abuse. Hundreds of children have reportedly disclosed abuse since the program began.

Applying the Strategy

Police, community, and local business leaders in Binghamton, New York, have set up a successful Stranger Danger and Child Molestation Prevention Program for physically and mentally challenged children and youth considered at special risk of victimization by such crimes. Hundreds of children and mentally challenged young adults have been empowered to feel more confident about their self-protection skills, and they now feel less vulnerable.

Trained volunteers in Houston, Texas, provide school children—from kindergarten through high school—with information on physical and sexual abuse, suicide prevention, and victimization prevention. The program—We Help Ourselves—is supported by the state, the local school district, and the regional United Way. Evaluations have deemed the program to be successful. Children report that they feel safer and more confident about what to do, and tests on very young students revealed they retained vital information from the hour-long presentation months after it was given.

Contact Information

WHO Project Director
2211 Norfolk Street, Suite 810
Houston, Texas 77098
713-523-8963

Office of the 13th Circuit Solicitor
Victim Witness Assistance Program
Courthouse Annex
Suite 113
Greenville, South Carolina 29601
803-467-8612

Values-Based Curricula

Strategy

Children benefit from curricula that help them develop values supportive of socially constructive behavior, including respect for others, fairness, honesty, and the responsibilities of individuals as members of a community.

Crime Problem Addressed

Educators and the public often express concern that children no longer learn values in school, that schools do not reinforce community values and that they do not teach children how to apply values in their relationships and daily life. The Search Institute study *Healthy Communities, Healthy Youth* focuses on what it terms "community strengths"—attributes that help reduce the likelihood of delinquent behavior. These strengths include motivated students with involved parents, structured religious activity, encouragement of prosocial behavior, responsible values reinforced in peer groups, and strong and supportive families. The study observes that "when we look at the strengths together, we find that few are reported as the norm. If these strengths do, indeed, contribute to community health by reducing at-risk behaviors, it becomes critical for communities to concentrate on building them."

Key Components

Most school curricula addressing this issue use a set of stories, discussions, classroom activities, and homework assignments to project basic societal values, including courage, conviction, justice, tolerance for social and cultural diversity, loyalty, optimism, and the rights and responsibilities of citizenship. The curricula materials are developed across the spectrum of age levels, using a variety of teaching methods and subjects for the different age groups. The messages are straightforward and become clear to the students through practice with their peers and reinforcement by adults in family and school situations.

The school-based curricula are sometimes reinforced through codes of conduct espoused in youth groups such as Boys & Girls Clubs, community service organizations, and religious institutions. The amount of training needed to deliver the material varies according to its complexity. Most school programs for children are fairly simple in nature and can be implemented without spending significant time on formal training sessions. School-based curricula are most effective when the values they promote are reflected in policies governing interactions among students, staff, and school personnel.

Key Partnerships

A school seeking to implement a values or character education curricula in the community should work with parents and other community members to review available curricula and determine which would best reinforce community values. Religious institutions, community youth groups, and the youth themselves should also be consulted. When values are conveyed through youth clubs or community service groups (e.g., Boy Scouts and Girl Scouts), the implication is that parents steer youths toward involvement in the groups, communities support the groups' activities, and youths agree to uphold the standards set by the group.

Potential Obstacles

Parents of public school children will have a variety of ideas about what the value and character curricula should contain and how the material should be conveyed. Communities can usually overcome this challenge by including parents and community members in the choice of curricula or related policies.

Signs of Success

The Heartwood Ethics Curriculum program for elementary school children was developed in 1985 by an attorney who had worked with juveniles and three elementary school teachers. This program was originally piloted in several Pittsburgh elementary schools; it is now used throughout that city, as well in twelve other states and two foreign countries. The program, for kindergarten to sixth-grade students, focuses on improving the students' understanding of seven core values vital to positive development and involvement in society: courage, loyalty, justice, respect, optimism, honesty, and love. Teachers use classic stories from different cultures to highlight one or more of the values and prompt discussion and application of those values among students. Evaluations document improved student knowledge and application of the core values and more open and tolerant classroom environments. Teachers believe the program provides a constructive strategy for fostering students' values and demonstrating their place in daily life.

Applying the Strategy

The Character Education Program of the Thomas Jefferson Research Center in Pasadena, California, is a widely used and well-evaluated curriculum on values and the constructive use of personal talents for the benefit of the community. Schools that have used the program report benefits including increased community support for the school, better student attendance, fewer discipline problems in classrooms, reduced incidents of crime and vandalism by or against students, and lower rates of student use of alcohol and illegal drugs.

In Dayton, Ohio, public schools have established a comprehensive character education program. Elementary-level teachers present one values-related topic per week followed by student discussions, performances, and publication of the issue within the school. Since the introduction of the program, suspensions have dropped dramatically, academic performance has improved, students say they feel safer, and teachers report that their school has more of a family atmosphere. In addition, the Allen School, where the program began, now ranks fifth in test scores out of the thirty-three Dayton elementary schools, up from twenty-eighth place before the program was implemented.

Contact Information

The Heartwood Institute
425 North Craige Street
Pittsburgh, Pennsylvania 15213
412-688-8570

Principal
Allen Classical/Traditional Academy
132 Alaska Street
Dayton, Ohio 45404
513-224-7369

Safe Haven Facilities

Strategy

Secured locations and zones free of drugs, violence, and guns encourage youth to use recreational and social facilities that provide an array of services to support their development. Such "safe haven" facilities and zones protect youth while discouraging potential offenders.

Crime Problem Addressed

The 1992 violent crime rate for youth ages twelve to fifteen was the highest ever reported in the United States. Large cities have the highest per capita crime rates, but violent crimes, including those committed by and against youth, occur in every type of community. Approximately 30 percent of crimes against youth ages twelve to nineteen take place in the street, and 14 percent occur near home. African-American youth from large urban areas are particularly at risk: African-American males between the ages of twelve and twenty-four are fourteen times more likely to be murdered than other Americans. Some of these crimes are committed near facilities where the youth engage in recreational, sports, or educational activities. Enhancing security at such facilities helps ensure that the programs are available to youth and that the positive activities hosted there are perceived as safe.

Key Components

Facilities and organizations that use this strategy generally offer an array of structured recreational, social, sports, and educational programs to youth in an environment that is protected by security personnel or police in combination with secure facility design such as restricted access. The facilities themselves are often community-based recreation centers run by the local government, charitable organizations, or Boys & Girls Clubs; the centers are staffed by employees and community volunteers. In addition to securing these kinds of facilities, localities are increasingly adopting ordinances that specify zones around recreation centers and schools as drug-free and violence-free. Special signs warn potential violators of increased penalties for criminal offenses committed within those zones.

Key Partnerships

This strategy is based on a partnership between the youth organization and the city agency with the authority to pass ordinances designating locations as safe haven zones. Community-based organizations or local agencies that operate such facilities or control enforcement of secure zones work in partnership with schools and local institutions to ensure that activities respond to the needs and interests of youth and that security measures are well publicized.

Potential Obstacles

Youths may have concerns about safety en route to the secured facility. The local recreation club located in a crime-plagued neighborhood in one southern city is underused because many children and parents fear the risks associated with travel to the facility. Some communities have addressed this concern by organizing escorts or "walking buddies," adults who volunteer to chaperon groups of children walking to activities at local recreation centers. Communities that pursue defined drug-free and weapon-free zones around schools must balance police assignments to enforcement duties with ongoing prevention projects of the department.

Signs of Success

Increasingly, schools with after-school and evening activities are following the lead of recreation centers and clubs by employing school or security personnel to keep the sites safe. In some cases, this means extending the hours or duties of existing school security personnel.

For Boys & Girls Clubs and facilities that offer similar services, safer facilities mean improved youth access to needed recreational activities. SMART Moves, a proven Boys & Girls Club-sponsored drug and alcohol prevention program, is an example of the vital programming these sites offer. A 1991 evaluation by a team of outside researchers found that "the influence of Boys & Girls Clubs is manifest in their [youth in public housing] involvement in healthy and constructive activities. Relative to their counterparts who do not have access to a Club, these youth are less involved in unhealthy, deviant, and dangerous activities." According to the study, communities that had a club used by area youth experienced 13 percent fewer juvenile crimes.

Applying the Strategy

The Challenger Boys & Girls Club in Los Angeles typifies the value area residents place on this kind of secure recreational facility. During the riots in 1992, community members actively guarded the building, protecting it while many nearby buildings were damaged or destroyed. This loyalty resulted from the facility's record as a secure and trusted site where neighborhood youth have the opportunity to engage in positive activities.

The Neighborhood Service Team partnership of a Garland, Texas, agency works with the local school district to oversee a "zero-tolerance" zone around an elementary school and nearby apartment building. Since the zone was established, major crime incidents in the area have declined.

Contact Information

Boys & Girls Clubs of America
1230 West Peachtree Street, N.W.
Atlanta, Georgia 30309-344794
404-815-5700

Youth Advisory Boards

Strategy

Youth advisory boards provide valuable input into local agency policy, helping to ensure policies are responsive to the needs and concerns of the youth population.

Crime Problem Addressed

Youth served by crime, violence, and substance abuse prevention programs and youth who have come into contact with law enforcement often complain that adults never ask them what they need, what would work with their peers, or how they perceive services or agencies. Youth policies created without regard to constituent opinion may be less effective and efficient in reaching their target audience.

Key Components

To address this problem, youth should provide input on policymaking and program design through membership on existing advisory boards or on a separate youth advisory council for local schools, law enforcement agencies, public housing authorities, community-based foundations, or health services agencies. Youth boards do not have formal policymaking power, but they provide necessary input on agency or school policy that affects them. Such youth advisors have participated in developing school and community-based drug and alcohol treatment programs, school violence prevention strategies, and gang prevention and intervention projects.

Key Partnerships

The most vital partnership for this type of program exists between the young people and the local policy body establishing the youth advisory panel. The panels are most often established in response to disturbances in local government-youth relations and are designed to permit youth participation in agency decisions and to improve youth-agency relations. Schools or other sponsoring agencies may need to provide youth with training in developing and implementing policy to ensure the success of this approach.

Potential Obstacles

Youth may be initially reluctant to participate, feeling that the board is more "lip service" than a real response to their legitimate concerns about the nature and quality of agency policy. A pattern of active attention and response to concerns will help address this issue and will likely result in competition among the youth for board participation. Council legitimacy and effectiveness are also enhanced if the youth participants represent the gender, ethnic, cultural, and economic composition of the community.

Signs of Success

The New Haven, Connecticut, police chief was concerned about police-community relations when he joined the force in 1991. The antagonistic relationship between police and youth and the high rate of youth crime and drug abuse in the city were of particular concern. In response, he increased efforts to implement community policing throughout the city and established the Board of Young Adult Police Commissioners (YAPC).

The goals of the YAPC include increasing the youth stake in community policing, providing citizenship mentoring for youth, and empowering young people to seek solutions to the issues that concern them. Although the

YAPC has no formal policymaking authority, it has become a vital link between local law enforcement and youth in the community. Since its establishment, YAPC has lobbied successfully to increase the capacity of residential drug treatment programs for youth, evaluated over 100 new police recruits, and influenced the local board of education to appoint a youth member. The board has become a national model for inclusion of youth and youth leadership in local law enforcement policymaking.

Applying the Strategy

State prevention officials and community-based programs in Kentucky have collaborated to establish the Kentucky Teen Leadership Conference. The event is an annual state-wide conference for youth leaders of school and community prevention projects and has fostered many ongoing local prevention projects. In each of the seventeen regions of the state, a twelve-member council of teens already active in drug prevention projects gathers to develop local alcohol, tobacco, and other drug abuse prevention plans for the coming school year. In addition, the program trains youth participants and adults in group dynamics, cultural sensitivity, team building, and leading group activities.

Since its beginning in 1987, the program has expanded to include a network of university students active in prevention projects on their campuses. The conference will soon publish a manual to help other communities that wish to design similar programs. Evaluation feedback from youth participants documents that the program has enhanced a variety of life skills, improved youth knowledge about the detrimental effects of alcohol and drugs, expanded participation in healthy activities, and successfully attracted youth for participation in prevention projects.

Contact Information

Prevention Consultant
The Adanta Regional Prevention Center
P.O. Box 3368
Somerset, Kentucky 42564
606-679-9425

Surveys of Community and Youth Concerns

Strategy

Surveys are an effective means of identifying community concerns about risk factors for juvenile delinquency and of engaging a broad spectrum of youth in communicating their concerns about community issues.

Crime Problem Addressed

Surveys of youth and adults help localities better understand community perceptions of risk factors for youth involvement in crime. Local governments with limited resources must be certain their programs will respond effectively to youth problems. Furthermore, by surveying youth about their use of community services and their perceptions of needed services, local agencies can better understand whether existing services need to be redesigned or augmented. Community support for local youth services is enhanced by using surveys and other means of program assessment.

Key Components

Surveys are often conducted by a variety of local groups, including law enforcement agencies, schools, youth service agencies, crime prevention commissions, and the youth themselves. Surveys typically aim to elicit comments on local risk factors, thus helping to define violence prevention and enforcement policy or to refine program goals and design. Surveys are also useful tools for engaging youth in discussion and projects focusing on crime and violence prevention.

Key Partnerships

The sponsoring agency will often work with area schools and youth advisory boards to identify groups of youth or neighborhoods that should be surveyed. Collaborating groups may also develop programmatic responses to concerns that the survey brings to light.

Potential Obstacles

Complex surveys may require more staff and time resources than local agencies or schools can provide, depending on the type of information solicited. Local groups may wish to hire area universities or private firms with survey expertise to design and implement surveys. Lack of public understanding can also be a barrier to the success of a survey. The sponsoring agency should explain to the community why the information is being collected and how it will be used. Implicit in the success of the survey is the local agency's commitment to share and act upon the survey results.

Signs of Success

The University of Nebraska surveyed 3,000 state residents, including youth, about risk factors for youth violence. Some of the youth had already had direct experience with violence. Thirty-five percent of young Nebraskan participants in the survey reported that they had been in a physical fight within the past thirty days, and more than 20 percent reported they had carried a weapon within the previous month.

The survey results were presented at public meetings where local and state policymakers, community groups, youth, and criminal justice officials came together to design a statewide, comprehensive youth violence prevention plan which was completed in early 1995. The plan includes youth input in the development of near-term and long-range strategies to address the priority risk categories for youth violence in Nebraska. The priority initiatives include employment opportunities for youth, mentoring projects, parenting education programs for young parents, youth violence prevention programs, conflict resolution and mediation training for youth service workers, and dropout prevention strategies.

Applying the Strategy

In 1992, the Youth Advisory Commission of San Leandro, California, surveyed 400 area youth to identify their most important concerns, preferred local activities, allocation of time, sources of information about issues that affect them,

and most appreciated aspects of their community. The results of the survey were very valuable, pointing out that one-third of students were interested in opportunities for community service; one-quarter of the teens wanted to participate in cultural diversity workshops; and nearly one-third would participate in peer counseling and support groups if they were established. Local officials now have a better understanding of what services the community wants and believes would be effective in preventing youth violence and juvenile delinquency.

Contact Information

Joe Jeanette
Office of the U.S. Attorney
7401 Zorinsky Federal Building
215 North 17th Street
Omaha, Nebraska 68101-1228
402-221-4774

Local Coordination of Youth Policy and Programs

Strategy

Local government coordination of youth-related agencies, policies, and programs helps ensure a continuum of effective and efficient services that promote youth development.

Crime Problem Addressed

Children and youth are victims of nearly two million violent and other crimes annually. An additional three million children are reported as victims of child abuse each year. More than 270,000 students in a 1993 survey stated that they had carried a gun to school within the past thirty days. A 1993 study of American teenagers by the University of Michigan Institute for Social Research revealed that one-third of eighth-graders and one-half of twelfth-graders had used an illicit drug. No one local agency or program can respond to these issues effectively. Coordination of local youth-related agencies and programs is essential to ensure that ever-diminishing local government resources are spent wisely to promote youth development and prevent youth-related crime and victimization.

Key Components

Localities should establish a standing coordinating council, board, or task force with the following tasks:

- Assess the needs and concerns related to children and youth.

- Set common goals and objectives for related programs.

- Review existing programs to eliminate overlap.

- Recommend how to fill gaps in needed programming.

Most local coordinating bodies develop around specific themes and targets for reducing youth crime and victimization, improving school attendance and performance, decreasing the incidence of teen pregnancy and drug use, enhancing recreational opportunities for youth, and improving the physical and emotional health of area children and youth. Strategies for achieving these broad goals are based on recognizing the reciprocal relationships among the family, school, home, and community environments in shaping the development of a child.

Agencies and groups involved typically include the mayor or city manager, the school system, community-based youth organizations, law enforcement agencies, parks and recreation services, social services agencies, health care agencies and providers, the courts and juvenile corrections, and public housing authorities.

Key Partnerships

The agencies involved in the coordinating council or board must agree on recommendations for youth-related policy and program goals at the direction of the mayor, city council, or county board. The staff or key contact for the policy board implements a public education campaign directed at building community support for the policy directions set by the council. Participating agencies collaborate to develop communication materials and proposals for foundation or corporate support for programs.

Potential Obstacles

Local agencies prefer to set their own goals for specific projects. Often those goals do not consider the implications beyond the narrow program focus. Agency personnel are therefore sometimes reluctant to participate in coordinating bodies, fearing infringement on their independence or program "turf." Mayors, city managers, and county leaders can set the tone for a successful coordinated policy effort by requiring agency participation and providing leadership; setting goals around topics that cross agency lines of responsibility (e.g., reducing youth violence); and reinforcing interagency coordination as the standard for agency behavior.

Local leaders must take care not to raise public expectations for significant additional local government spending. Instead, local government officials can educate the public on how improved direction and coordination of local youth-related policy can generate significant civic activity and help attract federal, foundation, and corporate funding.

Signs of Success

The mayor of Minneapolis established the city's Youth Coordinating Board (YCB) in 1986. The board "functions as an advocate, catalyst, and developer for collaborative planning and implementation of comprehensive services and systems benefiting children, youth, and families." YCB-directed initiatives include:

■ City Children 2007, a statement of vision and guiding principles for the board and partner organizations;

■ Minneapolis Way to Grow, a program which helps families and neighborhoods support the development of children up to six years old through community education and health services;

■ Neighborhood Learning Centers which promote school readiness, Head Start, child care, and home support; and

■ Minneapolis Youth Organization, which coordinates youth participation, recreation, and leadership projects throughout the city.

Now a model for similar local efforts throughout the country, the YCB has helped focus civic and local government energy toward youth and family programs.

Applying the Strategy

In 1992, the city manager of San Antonio created the Youth Initiatives Program (YIP) to coordinate ten city departments in developing and implementing youth programs. YIP has built on prevention, intervention, and enforcement strategies established through a concurrent citywide crime prevention planning process, creating an array of popular arts, recreation, mentoring, after-school, and employment programs for city youth. City officials believe that the 10 percent decrease in juvenile crime and more than 50 percent decrease in juvenile victimization by crime in 1993 resulted from the combination of YIP's youth opportunities programs with new enforcement measures (curfew, antitruancy, and graffiti prevention). Together, community participants have created a climate of opportunity and responsibility for the city's youth.

In 1986, Savannah, Georgia, established the Youth Futures Authority (YFA) to address youth problems, including teen pregnancy, substance abuse, and school failure. Supported by a grant from the Annie Casey Foundation, YFA now coordinates a variety of very successful after-school programs including, tutoring support, teen health clinics, and youth advocacy and peer counseling projects. The city has since made important progress toward reducing high rates of teen pregnancy.

San Francisco voters approved the establishment of a Children's Fund in 1993 to track money spent on youth services by all departments. The fund receives 2.5 percent of the local property tax to improve and expand children's services. A portion of the funding is set aside for community collaborations and public-private partnerships to deliver services. The fund is operated by a committee whose representatives include city departments and residents.

Contact Information

Minneapolis Youth Coordinating Board
202 City Hall, 350 South Fifth Street
Minneapolis, Minnesota 55415-1314
612-673-2060

Alternative Schools

Strategy

Alternative schools assist youth who have behavior problems and those at risk of failure, by helping them to focus on educational goals and remain in school.

Crime Problem Addressed

Each day over 2,000 youth drop out of school because of academic failure or behavior problems. Thousands of youth are suspended or expelled because of disruptive, violent, or criminal behavior. This strategy provides a structured environment with supervision, support, and focus to help students succeed academically and avoid behavior problems. The ultimate goals are usually reintegration of the student into the traditional school setting or achievement of a General Equivalency Diploma (GED). Alternative schools are useful strategies for dealing with youth having problems in school and those involved with the juvenile justice system.

Key Components

Alternative schools, or "learning academies," are small-scale school environments where a limited number of students receive intensive tutoring, consistent discipline with sanctions, and job training designed to improve their academic performance and build life skills. Some programs also include student participation in designing and implementing community service projects. The programs are run as separate sections of existing schools or as off-site programs serving students from several schools within a district or juvenile court jurisdiction.

Key Partnerships

School administrators work with teachers to identify students who would benefit from the alternative school setting. School officials also receive student referrals from juvenile justice agencies and the juvenile corrections system.

Potential Obstacles

Some local school systems have difficulty financing such programs, since they require a more intense concentration of teaching and other resources than traditional classroom environments. Believing that alternative schools benefit youth involved in the juvenile justice system, some local juvenile courts support alternative schools in their communities. Other programs receive support from local businesses and state juvenile justice programs.

Signs of Success

The Mat-Su Alternative School in Wasilla, Alaska, has become a model for what alternative learning environments can do for school dropouts and delinquent youth. Established in 1987 with 7 students, the school served 135 youth between the ages of sixteen and twenty-one during 1994; it provides a structured learning environment, discipline, and opportunities for community service.

The students at Mat-Su have dropped out of high school, abused alcohol or drugs, become parents, or been placed on probation by the juvenile court. In addition to intensive academic assistance, the school offers a teen parent program, a day-care center, nutritional advice, and counseling. The school also networks with thirty-four neighborhood organizations, linking with area food and clothing banks and devising community service projects. Each student is required to work in the school for a few hours each day, but participation in outside community service projects is considered a privilege available only to students with good behavior and academic records.

Although 20 percent of Mat-Su students are referred by the juvenile court, only 3 percent have again offended after attending the alternative school. Impressed by the results at Mat-Su, Alaska officials named it the state school of the year in 1994 and have replicated its educational and service programs in eight other Alaska schools. Many other states and localities have also modeled schools after Mat-Su.

Applying the Strategy

The Butz Learning Progressive Center (LPC) in Fort Stockton, Texas, was established in 1986 as an alternative learning environment for low-income, minority students at risk of dropping out. The school is designed to help students improve basic English and math skills and to support them in overcoming personal problems that affect their school performance. Students are referred to Butz LPC by their school, social service agencies, and law enforcement agencies. Since it opened, 217 of the 524 youth served have earned high school diplomas, 153 have earned GEDs, and 284 have passed the state exam required of exiting high school seniors. In 1988, the school was given the state Secretary of Education's Initiative for Assisting Disadvantaged Children Award. In 1991, LPC received top honors from the National Organization of Student Assistance Programs and Professionals.

Contact Information

Principal
Matanuska-Susitna Borough School District
1775 West Parks Highway
Wasilla, Alaska 99654
907-373-7775

Intensive Intervention With Adjudicated Youth and Their Families

Strategy

Intensive intervention promoting conflict resolution skills, communication skills, and drug and alcohol awareness is provided to youth and their families to discourage gang involvement and expand the community's capacity to combat youth gang violence.

Crime Problem Addressed

A 1990 study reported estimates of more than 120,000 members of youth gangs by police officials in thirty-five cities. This community-based strategy brings parents into the prevention and intervention process, ensuring that they have the communication and conflict management skills—as well as sufficient awareness of alcohol and substance abuse—to deter their children from involvement in youth gang-related violence and drugs.

Key Components

Programs that use this strategy usually work within a case management framework tailored to the specific problems of a particular youth and family. Programs offer parents a variety of skill-building workshops on conflict management, drug and alcohol abuse, effective communication, and effective discipline. Youth are also trained in these skills, with particular attention to depicting the results of gun violence and drug and alcohol abuse on individuals and the community. Some training sessions are presented to youth and parents, while other sessions target one group or the other. Sessions include discussions of the causes of and possible solutions to youth violence in the community, and they are usually supplemented by counseling.

Key Partnerships

Programs using this strategy are most often administered by community-based organizations in partnership with juvenile corrections agencies or the juvenile court system. Courts and law enforcement agencies cooperate by referring juveniles to the program for assistance. Counselors, police officers, and other health services experts staff the programs as employees or volunteers.

Potential Obstacles

The factors that encourage a young person to join a gang are complex and difficult to influence. Family violence or other problems at home may compel some young people to seek a surrogate family in a gang, while others may be influenced by peer pressure, a lack of self-esteem and refusal skills, or the lure of money from drug trafficking. Case management permits staff to tailor treatment and intervention, increasing the chances that a multifaceted

and intensive program will have a lasting impact on the youth. A program of at least several weeks duration contributes to this goal.

Signs of Success

The Gang Resource Intervention Team of the Multnomah County (Oregon) Community and Court Services Agency, a multiagency cooperative effort to reduce youth gang violence in the Portland area, takes a case-management approach to serving gang-involved youth between the ages of ten and nineteen who are referred by the county juvenile court. In addition to providing conflict management and drug and alcohol awareness education workshops to parents and youth, project staff also develop a personalized counseling and lesson plan for each youth. Other initiatives include a ten-week Weapons and Violence Reduction Program facilitated by adult inmates at a nearby prison and a hospital-sponsored curriculum on the impact of gun violence on victims and the community. District offices of the court are based in community facilities and mobilize efforts to involve youth, parents, and teachers in gang prevention.

Since 1989, 80 to 85 percent of youth participants have had perfect attendance records in program activities, and nearly 75 percent of youth participants over age sixteen who were on probation for previous assault or weapons charges have had no repeat referrals to the juvenile justice system in the first six months after completing the program. The success of the program has contributed to a 25 percent decrease in the number of African-American males in the juvenile correction system. GRIT staff believe that interagency cooperation has resulted in a program that truly responds to the needs of youth and the community. GRIT is currently working with a local university to assess changes in the attitudes of participating youth and parents.

Applying the Strategy

Modeled on a program developed through the Pennsylvania-based organization, Youth Advocate Programs, the Tarrant County (Texas) Advocate Program (TCAP) serves at-risk and adjudicated youth. Ninety percent of youth involved in TCAP of Fort Worth are gang-involved. TCAP assesses each youth individually, seeks out strengths of the youth and the family that can be fostered through intervention, and uses those strengths to design an effective program. The assessment is based on ten key areas of behavior, family circumstance, and previous history of delinquency. All TCAP youth participants come from the southeastern section of the city where gang activity predominates, youth unemployment is high, the resident population is transient, and family management and violence problems are prevalent.

The TCAP staff are recruited from the neighborhood being served, a policy that fosters bonding with youth and assures that the counselors have concrete knowledge of the challenges facing community residents. The program is funded by the Tarrant County Department of Juvenile Services. TCAP was credited with helping to reduce the number of area youth committed to state juvenile facilities by 44 percent after its first year of operation.

Contact Information

Supervisor
Gang Resource Intervention Team
Multnomah County Juvenile Justice Division
Community and Court Services
1401 N.E. 68th Street
Portland, Oregon 97213
503-248-3748

Community-Based Day and Residential Treatment for Youth Offenders

Strategy

Small community-based day and residential treatment programs for less violent juvenile offenders are at least as effective and less costly than large state-run residential facilities where violent and nonviolent offenders are mixed together.

Crime Problem Addressed

John DiIulio of Princeton University estimates that the direct societal cost of juvenile crime in the United States in 1992 was $17.2 billion. In 1992, 17.5 percent of all offenders arrested for violent crimes were juveniles. According to the National Council on Crime and Delinquency (NCCD), 95 percent of youthful offenders are arrested for nonviolent crimes. This strategy emphasizes a range of services that provide a variety of care options appropriate to the offense committed and the danger the offender poses to the community.

Key Components

State or county-supported community-based treatment programs serve juvenile parolees or probationers under seventeen years old and are based on the theory that personalized treatment near the offender's home is the most effective rehabilitation and prevention strategy. Youth in such facilities spend a few hours a day in classes working toward their GED and the balance of the day in counseling, vocational training, social and conflict management skills education, and supervised recreation. Some programs are organized exclusively for day treatment with only emergency residential facilities, while others are residential in nature. The length of participation by any youth varies from six to eighteen months. Research cited in NCCD's 1992 publication *Juvenile Justice: Improving the Quality of Care* states that critical components of successful juvenile corrections programs include the following:

■ continuous case management and assessment;

■ emphasis on preparing the youth for a successful return to the community;

■ opportunities for youth participation in decision-making;

■ clear and consistent consequences for behavior problems; and

■ family and youth counseling tailored to each participant's needs.

Key Partnerships

To deliver the needed services to less violent juvenile offenders, community-based programs work in close partnership with social services, counseling, and job training and placement agencies. Some state-supported programs work with a variety of public and private service providers to develop effective treatment for the youth.

Potential Obstacles

Community residents may be wary of having such facilities located near them. This concern can be addressed by:

■ inviting community members to serve on boards governing decisions about the facility;

■ describing the effectiveness of similar programs;

■ demonstrating the cost savings as compared to secure lockup facilities; and

■ assuring the community that violent offenders are ineligible for this program.

Despite the success of these programs, the public is calling for stiffer adult-style punishments for juvenile offenders of all types. This is a public policy issue requiring education and advocacy through media and agency strategies.

Signs of Success

Programs in Massachusetts, Missouri, and Utah serve as national models of successful and cost-effective local treatment programs for less violent juvenile offenders. Each state closed its large "training schools," which had previously mixed violent youth with vandals, truants, or status offenders. Each state has developed a network of small secure facilities to contain the most violent offenders and a range of community-based programs to offer a variety of educational, counseling, and other support services to less violent youth. According to an NCCD study, the recidivism rate for Massachusetts and Utah juveniles was as good or better than most other jurisdictions that placed offenders in large secure care facilities. A December 1994 article in *Governing* magazine noted that for every 100,000 juveniles in California, 450 are in large locked facilities, while only 55 out of every 100,000 in Massachusetts are incarcerated. Despite this differential, Massachusetts and Missouri have significantly lower recidivism rates than California.

Moreover, the cost of community-based care in these states is significantly less than the estimated $25,000–$30,000 per year required for incarcerating a juvenile. Additional NCCD-sponsored research estimates that Massachusetts saves $11 million each year by using community-based care. Massachusetts has been able to spend much of the money saved on job training and other programs to support the adjudicated youths' successful reentry into the community.

Applying the Strategy

The Southwest Key Day Treatment Program in Austin, Texas, serves parolees and probationers between the ages of ten and seventeen, providing a safe treatment environment within their community. Some youth spend ten or twelve hours a day in structured programming at the center; those with difficult family situations reside at the facility for six to nine months while receiving educational and other support. This counseling, vocational training, and recreation program has a recidivism rate 65 percent lower than standard parole programs in other parts of the state. The program is offered at twenty other sites in Texas and Arizona.

The Community Intensive Treatment for Youth (CITY) program in Birmingham, Alabama, offers nonresidential treatment to nonviolent juvenile offenders referred by the court. Each youth is required to develop a plan outlining the academic and personal goals that they will pursue with the support of staff. The program provides individual and group counseling for youth and in-home counseling for parents. CITY's tracking system of participants reveals that 70 percent of youth who graduate from one of the six sites statewide have no contact with the juvenile justice system for at least one year.

Contact Information

Program Coordinator
Community Intensive Treatment for Youth (CITY)
4308 42nd Street North
Birmingham, Alabama 35217
205-808-0001

Intensive Community-Based Supervision and Reintegration

Strategy

Intensive community-based supervision of juvenile offenders on probation is an effective tool for monitoring their behavior and ensuring successful reintegration into the community.

Crime Problem Addressed

A 1993 analysis of juvenile corrections programs cited in the National Council on Crime and Delinquency's (NCCD) *Images and Reality: Juvenile Crime, Youth Violence and Public Policy* concluded that 31 percent of juveniles housed in large secure training schools could be dealt with in less secure settings without threatening public safety. Some juvenile offenders are released into the community on probation. This strategy focuses on intensive supervision and monitoring of juvenile probationers as an alternative to incarceration for nonviolent offenders.

Key Components

Programs adopting this strategy are usually operated by county or other local juvenile probation agencies that provide intensive supervision and monitoring, as well as some training in problem-solving skills. Probationers are monitored in daily meetings with staff and, in some cases, with the electronic devices. Most programs also require the youth to keep up with schoolwork, hold jobs, and perform community service. Youth typically stay in the program for several months before being released from supervision. Intensive supervision programs check the behavior of the youths with a system of graduated sanctions, including temporary detention or suspension of privileges. Some programs also use community volunteers as mentors for the youth.

Key Partnerships

County or other local probation departments work closely with private and public sector employers to find jobs for the youth probationers. Once participants are hired, staff members coordinate with the employer to resolve any issues and ensure that the youth performs well. Programs often provide services for families also, to ensure their cooperation and commitment to the required regimen.

Potential Obstacles

Individuals may object to releasing juvenile offenders into the community, fearing that the intensive supervision will not be adequate to prevent additional crime. Public concerns can be allayed with education about the success of the program and youth participants, community participation on program boards, involvement of community mentors, and the support of judges and community leaders.

Signs of Success

The NCCD publication noted above cited studies done in the 1970s and 1980s on intensive supervision programs for juveniles in Utah and Michigan. Each study showed that recidivism among participating juveniles was lower than for juveniles remanded to traditional probation or incarceration. Since the mid-1980s, county juvenile courts in Pennsylvania, Arizona, and Indiana have instituted successful intensive supervision programs for juvenile offenders as an effective alternative to incarceration in large, often-overcrowded secure-care facilities.

Applying the Strategy

The Juvenile Intensive Probation Supervision (JIPS) program of Phoenix, Arizona, diverts nonviolent offenders from incarceration, placing them in a program of "accountability and consequences" with productive rehabilitative activities. Staff meet with participating youth at least four days each week and supervise them in community service or other jobs. Each youth must perform thirty-two hours of community service, complete a court-ordered treatment program and attend school. Program staff also meet with parents, employers, and schools officials regarding the progress of each participant. The program is now well-established in all fifteen Arizona counties. As of 1992, 70 percent of youth involved in JIPS completed the program successfully.

The Community Intensive Supervision Program of Allegheny County, Pennsylvania, supervises juvenile offenders found guilty of a variety of offenses, including robbery, gun possession, drug dealing, and property offenses. The Pittsburgh area program counsels, tutors, and electronically monitors youth as they complete 180 hours of community service and hold a job. The nine-month program also requires youth to undergo random drug testing. The community-based centers for the program are staffed by area residents, often young adults and former offenders who provide positive role models for participants. The county plans to expand the program in 1995, by opening additional centers in the community and providing job placement and a component on restitution to victims.

Contact Information

Juvenile Intensive Probation Supervision
Arizona Supreme Court
1501 West Washington Street, Suite 337
Phoenix, Arizona 85007
602-542-9443

Teen Courts

Strategy

Courts and sentencing procedures for youth that include judgment by their peers are an effective alternative to traditional juvenile justice system processing of nonviolent offenders.

Crime Problem Addressed

A 1994 report of the National Council of Juvenile and Family Court Judges contends that some local criminal courts have dismissed as many as 50 percent of juvenile cases forwarded to them. A December 1994 article in *Governing* magazine notes that adult courts in New York state have not taken action on 75 percent of cases involving juvenile offenders. This situation in New York and other states is due to the increasing frequency with which juvenile offenders are being referred to already-overburdened adult court and corrections systems. This strategy is one of several that local communities are adopting to process nonviolent juvenile offenders and assure a response that balances protection of the public with treatment and rehabilitation.

Key Components

Court programs using youth-involved sentencing procedures generally deal only with nonviolent misdemeanor offenders between twelve and eighteen years old. In some programs, youth who plead guilty of minor status offenses and rules infractions are tried and sentenced by groups of their peers. In the majority of the programs, a peer jury is involved in sentencing decisions about community service assignments once an adult judge (often a local attorney or prosecutor volunteer) has decided the case. Community service is a key component of sentencing for nearly all offenders found guilty.

Key Partnerships

The juvenile court supervises such programs, which are implemented in cooperation with local youth commissions, municipal agencies, and community organizations that oversee service project assignments, such as park cleanup and graffiti removal. The program staff consult parents when sentences are determined, with some jurisdictions even requesting parental permission to divert the youth from juvenile court processing.

Potential Obstacles

Teen Courts in some jurisdictions have faced opposition from policymakers who object to the expense of a separate court or believe the teen court system is too lenient on defendants. Teen Courts must keep records of decisions to ensure they can prove successes.

Signs of Success

Since the 1980s, teen courts and sentencing projects have become popular in many jurisdictions throughout the country, principally as a strategy for relieving local juvenile and adult court judges and prosecutors of heavy caseloads of minor offenses involving juveniles. One such program is the Hoffman Estates Peer Jury program in Illinois. The suburb west of Chicago established its program in 1983, focusing on rehabilitating nonviolent juvenile offenders through sentencing by their peers.

Devised by the city Youth Commission and local law enforcement agencies, the twenty-four-member teen jury recommends sentences for youth found guilty of minor offenses. Youth are usually required to make restitution to their victim and perform community service. The program has been so successful that it was featured in a 1994 National League of Cities publication *Exemplary Programs in Criminal Justice: Innovations at the Local Level.*

Applying the Strategy

The Moreno Valley (California) Youth Court was established in 1988 to give "specific youthful offenders an op-

portunity to take full responsibility for their actions and yet be diverted from the formal judicial system." Juveniles, ages twelve to eighteen, who have committed minor status offenses, other rules infractions, misdemeanors, and some felonies are prosecuted, defended, and adjudicated by high school students trained by the district attorney's office. The role of the judge is played by a volunteer prosecutor or defense attorney.

Eighty-five to 90 percent of youth court defendants complete the program successfully each year, and only 10 percent return to the juvenile justice system. Local officials praise the program, noting that the community service performed by the defendants saves the locality money in maintenance costs and time that otherwise would have been spent trying these cases in juvenile court.

The Houston (Texas) Teen Court operates in conjunction with the Teenage Community Alternative Program (TCAP). This program does not use the participation of youth from the community. The Houston court involves parents in substance abuse workshops with the offender and in decision-making about community service projects in lieu of fines, to deter first-time offenders from repeat involvement with the justice system. As of 1993, the Teen Court had processed over 1,000 juveniles, assigning all of them to community service projects through TCAP. This successful program received a 1994 Criminal Justice Model Program Award from the attorney general of Texas.

Contact Information

Deputy Zelon
Moreno Valley Police Department
14114 Business Center Drive
Moreno Valley, California 92553
909-697-8350

Gang Prevention Programs for Female Youth

Strategy

Gang prevention projects targeted to female youth are successful when they provide opportunities for positive activity and focus on risk factors, including the desire for friendship and belonging, a past history of family violence and gang involvement, and low self-esteem.

Crime Problem Addressed

Local law enforcement agencies report increased female participation in youth gangs and young females associating with gang-involved boys. According to a study on gang membership cited in the April 1994 Office of Juvenile Justice and Delinquency Prevention *Fact Sheet*, twenty-seven

cities report organized female gangs with an estimated 7,205 members. Los Angeles officials have estimated that 6 percent or more of gang members in that city are female. Many more young women in these cities are affiliated with male-dominated gangs through family connections or a personal relationship with a male gang member. This strategy recognizes that girls join gangs for different reasons than their male counterparts and that community-based programs to prevent female gang membership or affiliation must address these issues to achieve success.

Key Components

Programs adopting this strategy are most often operated by community-based and ethnically affiliated organizations that provide an array of services to the community. Some programs in cities with significant youth gang problems are administered in cooperation with the school system to maximize the number of participants. The aim of this program is to foster independence, self-confidence, and resourcefulness among gang-involved and at-risk teenage girls. Key components of these programs include recreation alternatives, cultural education, self-esteem building, violence prevention, health education, mentoring, and leadership development through service to the community. Counseling and case management ensure that program activities are tailored to individual needs. To confront the issues of the violent families and communities in which some of the girls live, most programs emphasize self-defense and personal responsibility within the context of community citizenship. Programs for high school students often offer career and job placement advice, providing positive alternatives to illegal activities.

Key Partnerships

Most programs using this strategy work with the police department to deliver self-protection and violence prevention education. They also work with local health professionals to educate female youth about drug and alcohol abuse, pregnancy prevention, and basic health and nutrition for young mothers and their children. Programs that identify school performance as an issue for participants place special emphasis on collaboration with school or community-based tutoring services. Others, which emphasize leadership skills and community involvement, collaborate with local businesswomen and other established women's organizations to recruit mentors and set up leadership projects and conferences.

Potential Obstacles

Girl gangs and female affiliation with male-oriented youth gangs receive less emphasis, fewer resources, and less attention from law enforcement and courts than most other local youth and delinquency problems. Community-based programs often work closely with local media to publicize their services and gain support for intervention with gang-affiliated young women.

Signs of Success

Participants at the 1993 Family and Youth Services Bureau's (FYSB) Forum on the Prevention of Adolescent Female Gang Involvement included representatives from eleven successful FYSB-funded projects across the country. Project representatives identified several factors that influence female gang involvement:

- self-esteem;

- domestic violence;

- high-risk sexual behaviors;

- pregnancy and parenting;

- drug and alcohol use;

- academic performance;

- cultural conflict; and

- adverse economic conditions.

Participants further agreed that their projects will continue to be successful only so long as they address the needs that young women, families, and communities have for the following:

- support groups;

- cultural awareness;

- youth leadership and empowerment;

- community awareness;

- collaboration among service providers;

- employment opportunities;

- spirituality; and

- consistent support for youth participants.

Applying the Strategy

The Seattle (Washington) Team for Youth operates a FYSB-funded project. The consortium of community organizations, local law enforcement agencies, parks and recreation departments, youth services agencies, and a school district began with support and empowerment groups for girls. Now called Beautiful Ambitious Ladies Able to Negotiate Commitment to Self-Esteem and Excellence (BALANCE), the program provides eleven- to eighteen-year-old girls alternatives to gang involvement through an array of services, including self-defense, setting boundaries in personal relationships, violence prevention, self-empowerment, career advice, and community involvement. BALANCE staff believe that the program teaches the young women how to make positive contributions to their families and communities and that participants are better prepared than their counterparts to make positive life choices about personal situations, careers, and raising children.

The Pueblo (Colorado) Family and Youth Services Bureau works with high-risk Hispanic youth in that community. Youth gangs in Pueblo are overwhelmingly Hispanic. In addition, nearly half of the crimes in the county are committed by girls, and girls were dropping out of school in alarming numbers. The agency runs the Movimento

Ascendencia (Upward Movement) program for gang-involved girls ages twelve to nineteen. The program focuses on cultural pride, public education through community and citywide media, leadership conferences for youth participants, career advice, and mentoring relationships with Hispanic adult women. Upward Movement attracted more than 100 youth and 100 adults to a recent leadership conference and recruited mentors from throughout the community.

Contact Information

Family and Youth Services Bureau
Development Services Group
Youth Gang and Drug Prevention Program
7315 Wisconsin Avenue, Suite 300E
Bethesda, Maryland 20814
301-951-0056

Surrogate Families

Strategy

Surrogate families that support youth in high-risk situations by facilitating bonding with positive adult role models and providing a structured environment for learning help many to move away from drug abuse or participation in gang activities.

Crime Problem Addressed

Dr. J. David Hawkins, a proponent of the social development theory of delinquency prevention, identified several risk factors for juvenile delinquency, including the following:

- low neighborhood attachment;

- transition and mobility;

- family conflict;

- alienation;

- academic failure and low school commitment; and

- a family history of high-risk behavior.

Programs that adopt the surrogate family strategy generate the protective factor of social bonding with caring adults, who convey clear standards of behavior to youth.

Key Components

Surrogate family programs are often located in residential facilities that offer youth informal mentoring and support from caring adults, emphasize academic achievement and setting of personal and career goals, and build skills in avoiding violence and drugs. The programs are typically staffed by community groups and assisted by adult volunteers from the neighborhood. The strategy underscores job preparation and academic performance as vital foundations for an independent and positive lifestyle, one free from involvement with gangs or drugs.

Residential programs are more intensive, offering a secure and structured full-time environment to youth from broken or dysfunctional families. Nonresidential programs involve intensive support from committed adult mentor volunteers who develop relationships with youth participants and provide key social services staff with insight into the needs and strengths of these youth.

Key Partnerships

Many surrogate family programs work closely with private industry councils to connect youth participants to jobs and job training. In addition, the programs coordinate with school and youth services agency officials to track progress and provide referrals to substance abuse treatment or other needed services.

Potential Obstacles

The primary obstacle to this strategy is locating adults and families who are interested in and suitable for playing the role of surrogate family. An effective program must involve long-term commitment from caring and supportive adults.

Signs of Success

In its 1994 report *Comprehensive Strategy for Serious, Violent, and Chronic Juvenile Offenders,* the Office of Juvenile Justice and Delinquency Prevention (OJJDP) concludes that negative family involvement factors—including parental rejection, inadequate supervision and discipline by parents, and family conflict—are predictors of delinquency and violence among youth. Providing surrogate families for youth in crisis is one of the strategies OJJDP recommends to address these situations and build protective factors important to healthy development.

The House of Umoja in Philadelphia, Pennsylvania, has provided a surrogate family for gang and drug-involved youth since 1969. The city-sponsored program was established by two parents concerned about the influence of youth gang members on their sons. Concerned that they might not be able to keep their children safe despite their best efforts, the parents decided to bring the gang-involved youth into their homes as members of a very unusual extended family. The parents had noticed that many of the gang members lacked connections to intact families, that they were often doing poorly in school, that few had prospects for legitimate work, and that many needed counseling to overcome substance abuse and other problems. Confident that many gang members would use support services that were readily available in a safe home environment, the couple set up a surrogate family or "intact family loan" for young men with few beneficial connections to their community.

The surrogate family sanctuary has grown into a full-service residential center for potential and current gang members and drug-involved youth, providing remedial education, vocational and educational counseling, life skills training, conflict management education, and opportunities for positive recreation.

Applying the Strategy

Family Augmenting Approach to Prevention is a successful neighborhood-focused effort based in Washington, DC, that pairs youth from high-risk environments with "supplemental parents." The volunteer parents spend weekends and after-school hours with youth in grades five through twelve. The city-supported program focuses on structured learning and recreation and reduction of risk factors for delinquency, including lack of bonding with caring adults, drug-involved parents, family conflict, social isolation, and low commitment to school. Participating youth have demonstrated improved school achievement and attendance, cultural pride, and bonding to the community.

Contact Information

House of Umoja
1410 North Frazier Street
Philadelphia, Pennsylvania 19131
215-473-5893

Gang Prevention Curricula

Strategy

Gang prevention curricula help elementary and middle school youth avoid gang activity by educating them about the impact of gangs on the community and by providing them with skills to resist peer pressure to become involved with gangs.

Crime Problem Addressed

Research compiled in 1991 on behalf of the U.S. Department of Justice documented an estimated 4,881 youth gangs, 249,324 gang members, and 46,359 gang-related crime incidents in 157 major cities. Experts cited in the 1994 National Institute of Justice report *Street Gangs: Current Knowledge and Strategies* note several reasons why youth join gangs, including identity, personal recognition, dysfunctional families, structure, protection, and a need to belong. This strategy addresses these issues by providing youth with a curriculum to help them build self-esteem, decision-making and conflict management skills, and positive connections to the community.

Key Components

Curriculum programs focus on the knowledge and skills needed by youth, including choices and consequences, anger and conflict management, acceptance of cultural diversity, the impact of violence and drugs on individuals and neighborhoods, future goals, and the responsibilities of citizenship. Delivered over several weeks, the programs employ discussions, role plays, supplemental activities such as community service, and participation of law en-

forcement officers and other leaders. Most curricula require students to take tests before and after participating in the program as a means of measuring changes in behavior, attitudes, and knowledge about the dangers of gang involvement and its impact on the community. Some programs supplement school-year classroom modules with summer instruction and activities, further ensuring that the students retain the key messages.

Key Partnerships

The key partnership in this strategy must exist between the school implementing the program and the local law enforcement agency that serves as a resource for both classroom activities and as positive adult role models.

Potential Obstacles

Teachers require training to undertake the curriculum, so participating schools must allocate time and funds for staff development activities. It may be difficult to reach youth already involved in a gang through a school curriculum project; such youth may require more intensive intervention than can be obtained in the school setting.

Signs of Success

The Federal Bureau of Alcohol, Tobacco and Firearms (ATF) helped design and implement one of the most effective gang prevention curricula for elementary and middle school youth. The Gang Resistance Education and Training (GREAT) program has separate curricula for elementary and middle school youth, and it supplements school-year activities with a summer component. GREAT is designed to "help children set goals for themselves, learn how to resist peer pressures, resolve conflicts without violence, and understand how gangs and youth violence impact the quality of their lives." Established through a cooperative relationship between the Phoenix (Arizona) Police Department and representatives from ATF, the program has trained nearly 1,000 officers from forty-four states in the curriculum.

An independent evaluation of students at ten GREAT sites, conducted by the Arizona State University Prevention Resource Center, revealed that the curriculum helped improve resistance skills, resulted in a drop in the number of children who wanted to be gang members, and contributed to a decline in the number of students with disciplinary problems. Students reported that GREAT had taught them that "police are not always against you, they can be good," and that they did not have to belong to a gang to be "cool." The students rated the conflict management portion of the curriculum as very valuable, noting that they planned to use their newly acquired communication skills to deal with problems more effectively.

Applying the Strategy

Each year, three full-time Phoenix police officers present the GREAT curriculum to over 6,000 students. Through English- and Spanish-language materials, the youth are taught how to appreciate and accept cultural differences within their communities, how to understand the impact of crime on individual victims and the community, and how to set short- and long-term personal goals. Phoenix police officers have also helped train their colleagues in Georgia and other states.

In 1988, recognizing the need to reach young students with the gang prevention message, the California Governor's Office created a gang- and drug-prevention curriculum entitled "Project Yes! Yes to Education and Skills." Developed for presentation to students in the second through seventh grades, Project Yes! links prevention information to traditional subjects through five central themes:

- responsible citizenship;

- cultural diversity;

- refusal skills;

- choices and consequences; and

- success and achievement.

The goal of the program is to equip students with the critical thinking skills and knowledge necessary for them to make informed decisions, set goals for success, and resist negative peer pressure. A 1993 evaluation survey of students revealed that 45 percent of seventh graders felt safer in the community and 33 percent said that they plan to avoid negative associations with peers. Teachers also reported improvements in students' behaviors and knowledge of the concepts presented. A longitudinal evaluation of the program is scheduled for release in 1995. Meanwhile, Project Yes! has been critically acclaimed in California and other states seeking a comprehensive primary gang-prevention curriculum for younger students.

Contact Information

GREAT Program
Bureau of Alcohol, Tobacco and Firearms
P.O. Box 50418
Washington, DC 20091-0418
1-800-726-7070

Individual and Family Therapy Programs

Strategy

Individual and family therapy to treat youth with emotional problems can prevent delinquent behavior and drug abuse linked with emotional conditions.

Crime Problem Addressed

Each year thousands of youth are arrested on criminal charges and for status offenses such as curfew violations. A portion of those youth suffer from emotional disturbances, exhibit behavioral problems, have difficulty managing anger, or come from families with few skills or resources. This strategy directs these youth toward mental health and therapeutic services that address behavioral and emotional problems in an effort to prevent delinquency and strengthen the family.

Key Components

Most programs that adopt this strategy offer youth both individual and group therapy to achieve the following:

- help reverse destructive behavior patterns;

- improve communication among family members and peers;

- teach coping and stress management skills; and

- treat violence and substance abuse problems.

Some programs treat youth on an out-patient basis or in the home, while others involve residential treatment for youth with serious behavioral, substance abuse, or family problems. Programs using this strategy represent a cost-efficient and effective community-based alternative to hospital treatment or incarceration for youth who do not require secure detention or aggressive treatments in such facilities. The most comprehensive programs also offer emergency counseling and intensive family intervention services, such as temporary out-of-home placement for children. Typically, therapy lasts for several months and focuses on changing family processes and individual behaviors and building skills that help both the parents and the youth maintain more positive behaviors.

Key Partnerships

Community organizations that operate therapy programs link youth to needed community-based mental health services through referrals and other assistance from schools and juvenile justice agencies. Some programs are organized around a consortium of community or local government agencies that provide a continuum of mental health services to youth and families. Case management of each patient provides an opportunity to tailor treatment to each youth's needs and establish cooperation among groups delivering therapeutic services and follow-up care.

Potential Obstacles

Communities that experience juvenile crime and violence may not initially be receptive to therapeutic treatments for offenders. Programs can overcome this by stressing the cost-effectiveness of community-based treatment of less violent offenders and reiterating the importance of communication and conflict management skills and family cohesion as factors in preventing juvenile delinquency.

Signs of Success

In its 1994 publication *Comprehensive Strategy for Serious, Violent, and Chronic Juvenile Offenders,* the Office of Juvenile Justice and Delinquency Prevention asserts that a variety of programs—including those that address the mental health of youth—are important opportunities for teaching positive values and reducing individual characteristics as risk factors in juvenile delinquency.

The Robert Wood Johnson Foundation funds community-based youth mental health projects in seven locations across the country, including the North Carolina Mental Health Service Program for Youth. That program has provided in-home or community-based services to youth with serious emotional disturbances and to their families in several rural counties of the state since 1989. The state-managed initiative offers diagnostic services and treatment for substance abuse and emotional and developmental disabilities; it also provides residential treatment when necessary. A Duke University evaluation team rated the program as successful in linking youth and families to needed services and helping them toward long-term solutions, improved family functioning, and positive behavior.

North Carolina also coordinates with the federal government in the Child and Adolescent Mental Health Demonstration Project at Fort Bragg. The U.S. Army established this pilot project in 1989 in partnership with the state Division of Mental Health, Developmental Disabilities, and Substance Abuse Services, primarily to serve dependents of active military personnel in the surrounding area. The program has met its goals, demonstrating that a federal-state partnership can coordinate a community-based consortium of services to provide cost-effective and successful treatment of youths. In 1992, the program served over 46,000 youth with a budget of $21 million, a fraction of what in-patient treatment could have cost, according to an evaluation conducted by researchers from Vanderbilt University.

Applying the Strategy

Specialized Treatment Services of Mercer, Pennsylvania, is a residential treatment facility which provides therapeutic services to youth, ages thirteen through eighteen, who cannot be placed in mental health facilities because of criminal behavior problems and who cannot be incarcerated in traditional settings because of their emotional and mental health status. Group and individual therapy lasts for at least eighteen months and focuses on modifying destructive behavior, managing anger and conflict, and resisting peer pressure. Family therapy begins while the youth is in residence and continues following release, where it is combined with mentoring and school-based follow-up services. The program reports that 82 percent of youth participants remain uninvolved with the juvenile justice system for the five-year period following treatment.

Contact Information

Department of Human Resources
325 North Salisbury Street
Raleigh, North Carolina 27603
919-733-0598

Court-Appointed Special Advocates

Strategy

The Court-Appointed Special Advocates (CASA) program helps protect abused and neglected children's rights within the court system and prevent further abuse and neglect by helping to design permanent and safe placement for the child.

Crime Problem Addressed

Each year nearly three million cases of child abuse are reported in the United States. Many of these cases are brought before juvenile and family court judges for review. The judge may employ a number of options to protect the child, including intensive family counseling or treatment, temporary out-of-home placement, or revocation of parental rights and eventual adoption. This strategy uses trained community volunteers to assist judges in making immediate and long-term decisions in the best interests of the child.

Key Components

CASA is typically operated by juvenile and family courts in cooperation with state or local social services agencies. Lawyers, judges, parents, therapists, social workers, and teachers work together to ensure a safe and permanent placement plan for each abused or neglected child whose case is brought before the court. The program coordinates the efforts of recruits and trains community volunteers to work with the victimized child. The volunteers give testimony at court hearings, meet with parents and service providers, and prepare reports on each case, including recommendations on treatment. CASA volunteers and supervisors work to preserve existing families wherever possible, and devise plans for permanent out-of-home placement when necessary.

Key Partnerships

A successful CASA program depends on cooperative relationships among the court officials and representatives of social, medical, school, and community services that assist abused and neglected children. These agencies must share information on cases, work with CASA to ensure that all appropriate services are provided on behalf of the child, and maintain a continuum of services that support permanent safe placement for victims of abuse and neglect. The court or agency that supervises the program volunteers must maintain relationships with community agencies serving children to ensure a supply of volunteer advocates and develop community-based placement alternatives for abused children.

Potential Obstacles

One of the biggest concerns with the program is appropriate selection and adequate training for volunteers to help them deal with children from such difficult circumstances. The program is most successful when volunteer advocates represent the variety of geographic, ethnic, and cultural characteristics of children and families that appear before the courts in abuse or neglect cases. To accomplish this goal, programs must concentrate on recruiting and training volunteers from affected communities. Coordinating the program with established community and volunteer groups can facilitate recruitment.

Signs of Success

The first CASA program was established in 1977 by a Seattle, Washington, judge concerned about the fate of abused and neglected children appearing before his court. Since then, CASA programs have been established in all fifty states and the District of Columbia. The Office of Juvenile Justice and Delinquency Prevention's *Comprehensive Strategy for Serious, Violent, and Chronic Juvenile Offenders* lists CASA among the programs it recommends to address family-related risk factors for juvenile delinquency.

The winter 1993 issue of the *Journal of Emotional and Behavioral Problems* reported that as of 1992, more than 28,000 volunteers were serving as child advocates, facilitating improvements in court-supervised programs to reunite and preserve families, prevent juvenile delinquency, and coordinate services for abused and neglected children and their families. The Seattle-based National Court-Appointed Special Advocate Association provides local courts and agencies with information on how to establish a CASA program. The association also provides training and workshops for local officials.

Applying the Strategy

The Court-Appointed Special Advocate Program of Baltimore—supported by grants from the state and foundations—was established in 1988 by a local judge and the University of Maryland School of Law and School of Social Work. The Baltimore CASA has provided comprehensive advocacy to over 500 abused and neglected children through the assistance of more than 350 specially trained volunteer advocates. Baltimore CASA staff and advisors have paid special attention to recruiting an appropriately diverse corps of advocate volunteers, half of whom are persons of color.

In addition to other duties, CASA volunteers work with the local Child in Need of Assistance Mediation Project to help families resolve conflicts prior to court proceedings. CASA also helps child victims through monthly Court School programs designed to familiarize them with court proceedings and prepare them to testify.

Contact Information

National Court-Appointed Special Advocate Association
2722 Eastlake Avenue East
Suite 220
Seattle, Washington 98102
206-328-8588

Adults as Career Mentors

Strategy

Adults with business skills and experience can help prevent juvenile delinquency by sponsoring youth in apprenticeship or business mentoring programs.

Crime Problem Addressed

Recent research and anecdotal reports consistently suggest that the presence of a caring adult is a vital element in successful youth-serving programs, including those programs that emphasize tutoring, mentoring, and preventing truancy or dropping out of school. Youth living in unsafe neighborhoods or confronting peer pressure to drop out of school or use drugs benefit significantly from the encouragement and support provided by adult volunteers in mentoring programs. In business apprenticeship programs, the adult conveys positive expectations for the youth's future and provides specific job-related skills, both vital buffers against negative environmental influences.

Key Components

Volunteer adult business or career mentors come from a variety of sources, including corporations, business associations, universities, professional organizations, and law enforcement agencies. Motivated by a desire to help youth needing inspiration to stay in school and plan for future jobs, the adult volunteers also expose participants to real-life job situations and skills needed to prepare for the world of work. Typically, business mentoring programs involve a variety of activities, including site visits, apprenticeships or internships in specific fields of interest, and educational seminars on job-related topics. A long-term relationship with the mentor is vital as the youth explores career possibilities, receives guidance on the responsibilities required of those who work, and acquires skills needed for particular professions.

Key Partnerships

Corporations, small business owners, professional associations, and law enforcement agencies that run business or entrepreneur mentor programs use their employee or membership networks to recruit adult volunteer mentors. Corporations sometimes operate Junior Achievement programs or encourage employees to work with area youth in apprenticeship programs as part of their community service commitment. Police departments that operate mentorship programs often work in partnership with public housing authorities and schools to identify youth who might benefit from a mentoring relationship with a law enforcement officer. Such programs educate participating youth about possible careers in police work, while also providing law-abiding adult role models.

Potential Obstacles

The success of business or career mentorship programs depends on sustained commitment on the part of the adult volunteer. Proper preparation and screening of mentor candidates is necessary to ensure a committed and effective corps of mentors. Businesses involving technology application may need to provide computer or other training as part of mentoring projects to ensure that youth receive the greatest possible benefit and realistic career exposure through the program.

Signs of Success

The Commonwealth Fund in New York City sponsors Career Beginnings, a network of twenty-two universities that operate mentorship programs for youth in twenty-one cities, including Bakersfield, California; Hartford, Connecticut; Memphis, Tennessee; Miami, Florida; and Rochester, New York. In a 1990 survey of 400 participating students and 400 adult mentors by Lou Harris and Associates, more than 50 percent of high school participants said that the relationship helped them improve their grades, stay out of trouble, and avoid drugs. Furthermore, 63 percent of the youth in the survey said that their mentors inspired them to go to college, and over half of these attended college within six months of high school graduation. Of those who chose to work instead, most were employed full time. Only 10 percent of participants were neither working nor in postsecondary education programs. Forty-nine percent of youth participants said that without their mentor they would not have chosen the same career or taken their current job.

Applying the Strategy

Over 1,400 USAA Casualty Insurance Company employees in six cities mentor students, working one-on-one with the youth to help foster academic skills and values such as dedication and responsibility. During one year in San Antonio, the number of USAA-mentored students who had behavior problems dropped by 30 percent. USAA also operates a Junior Achievement project, teaching practical business concepts and supplementing mentoring and tutoring offered to youth by their employees.

The YWCA New Entrepreneurs program in Omaha, Nebraska, helps fourteen- and fifteen-year-old students refine their career choices and develop entrepreneurial opportunities through a summer program of field trips, workshops, and internships in their fields of interest. The Pittsburgh Public Housing Authority works in cooperation with city police to operate the Junior Cadet program, a project pairing at-risk resident youth interested in law enforcement careers with police officers and agents from the Federal Bureau of Investigation. The Southern Bell Corporation sponsors a summer jobs program in Atlanta, Georgia, that places youth from public housing communities in apprenticeships at Head Start and day-care facilities located at housing agency sites.

Contact Information

Director
USAA—Educational Affairs
9800 Fredricksburg Road
San Antonio, Texas 78288
210-498-1055

Prenatal Care and Drug Abuse Prevention for Pregnant Women

Strategy

Prenatal care and drug abuse prevention programs for pregnant women and teenagers can help ensure healthy babies, preventing the developmental and behavioral problems caused by the alcohol and other drugs.

Crime Problem Addressed

The incidence of infant mortality and drug and alcohol-addicted babies is linked to the quality of prenatal care the mothers received. Low-income families sometimes do not have ready access to—or they do not seek—health care. Birth defects, developmental problems, and behavior problems occur in many children whose mothers have not received adequate prenatal care. Prenatal health-care programs for women in low-income communities can help prevent the occurrence of developmental problems that contribute to low academic achievement and the likelihood of problem behavior.

Key Components

Community-based clinics that run prenatal infant- and mother-care programs are often supported by funds and other resources from a combination of sources, including local and federal government agencies, private corporations, and nonprofit organizations. These facilities convey key messages—including the importance of early prenatal care and risk factors associated with low birthweight, alcohol, drugs, and smoking—to pregnant women and teens through aggressive outreach into targeted communities. Prevention programs typically use health professionals and paraprofessional resource workers to educate the mothers.

Key Partnerships

Most programs using this strategy are administered and supported through local and federal agency partnerships that coordinate needed health services in targeted communities, refer clients, and deliver follow-up services to infants and mothers. The coordination of service providers benefits each participating agency by helping to ensure efficient delivery of services to the women and children most in need. The key to client acceptance of the program is the involvement of women from the targeted community as outreach workers. Such staff can build relationships with the mothers while providing them with vital health information. Local corporations are also involved in many programs, donating funds for transportation, educational materials, and publicity.

Potential Obstacles

A key obstacle to successfully implementing prenatal health programs is getting health information to the women most in need and convincing them to follow this urgent medical advice. Some women who have already used drugs or alcohol while pregnant may be reluctant to receive help due to fear or shame. Others, who need and want the services, require transportation or child-care support in order to access them. Community residents trained as outreach workers can overcome some potential clients' fears and concerns, helping them understand the need for prenatal care and coordinating transportation to ensure that they receive that care.

Signs of Success

The Maternal and Child Health Bureau in the Public Health Service of the U.S. Department of Health and Human

Services sponsors a fifteen-city demonstration project on prenatal care for pregnant women and prevention of infant mortality and drug-addicted babies. Entitled Healthy Start, the program promotes community consortia and comprehensive service plans to bring prenatal care and information to pregnant women, with the goal of achieving a significant reduction in infant mortality. The program was established in 1991 and has already resulted in significant progress in many participating cities.

In New Orleans, Louisiana, local media have helped publicize Healthy Start by sponsoring Kids Health Fairs and medical screenings, transportation to services for pregnant women, information booths, and distribution of educational materials. In Washington, DC, the local Healthy Start program is credited with achieving a 10 percent reduction in infant mortality and low birthweights, as well as modest reductions in the number of infants who showed signs of exposure to drugs or alcohol during their mother's pregnancy.

Applying the Strategy

In 1991, concerned local officials in Virginia formed a state-wide network of 320 prevention programs to connect res-

idents in need with appropriate services. Project Link meets the medical and counseling needs of women in five of the state's major urban areas. The community-based, supportive, and nonpunitive approach is coordinated by a state interagency committee that provides technical assistance and training. At the local level, medical services are supplemented by child care, transportation, and help from paraprofessional "resource mothers" who come from the targeted communities. Researchers at the College of William and Mary report that in the two years that the project has been in operation, substance abuse among area women has decreased, parenting skills have improved, and the mothers' mental health is better.

Contact Information

Project Link Coordinator
Department of MHMRSAS
Office of Prevention and Children's Resources
P.O. Box 1797
Richmond, Virginia 23214
804-786-1530

Family-School Partnerships

Strategy

Family-school partnerships increase parental involvement in school activities and policy, creating a school environment that encourages and supports learning.

Crime Problem Addressed

Lack of positive contact with and support from parents and other adults is an important risk factor for juvenile delinquency. Parental involvement in schools—including cooperation with teachers, supervision of their children's homework, and parental participation in academic enrichment and recreation programs—helps support children's academic and social success.

Key Components

Programs using this strategy include any number of services to assist parents in becoming more involved, including the following:

■ parent-to-parent visits;

■ support groups;

■ activities to facilitate communication with the school; and

■ strategies to support and encourage the success of students.

Parent associations are a traditional source of such programs, providing advice on a range of issues including academic policy, security and violence prevention strategies, and dropout prevention projects. In some communities, members of parent associations set up after-school day-care, recreational, and tutoring programs for students.

Key Partnerships

School officials and parent associations must work in partnership for this strategy to be successful. Together, they need to identify what parents and students in the community need. They must design projects that can help remedy such problems as academic difficulty, crises in family management, and the need for after-school care.

Potential Obstacles

Parents' schedules, lack of understanding of the importance of their participation in school activities, fear of authority, and concern about school officials' involvement in child-rearing practices can all reduce the success of school-family partnerships. School policies that encourage parental participation on a range of issues help build the long-term relationships needed to create an environment that supports students' academic and social success. Schools should encourage formation of parent associations and should work with them on an ongoing basis.

Signs of Success

In *Strong Families, Strong Schools: Building Community Partnerships for Learning,* the U.S. Department of Education recommends that states pass legislation supporting family involvement in education. Specifically, they recommend parent-school partnerships, family-school coordinators, and teacher training in how to involve parents in supporting their children's educational and social development. The National Education Goals 2000 include "the promotion of parent involvement as a critical aspect of successful schools." As of 1994, only half of the states have mandated teacher training in parental involvement as a requirement for certification.

Applying the Strategy

The Atenville Elementary School in Harts, West Virginia, is improving parent-school communication through its Parents as Educational Partners Program. A church-based parent support center, home visits, and other communication tools are increasing parental involvement and enhancing student performance.

The Alpha collaboration in St. Petersburg, Florida, has made parental involvement a requirement in tutoring and dropout prevention programs. Nearly 100 percent of parents who attended the parent training programs learned new skills to help their children improve academically. The La Familia agency in Sacramento, California, plans to train parent association members and involve them in school violence prevention activities. The parents will also organize support for recreational activities for area youth.

Recognizing a need for safe after-school child care, parents and schools in Oakland, California, established Kids House, a network of private residences that provides safe care, snacks, and tutoring to area elementary students. Local foundations and area businesses support the program by paying parent caretakers and tutors. After only one year, 63 percent of students who took advantage of Kids House services had improved their grades.

Contact Information

U.S. Department of Education
600 Independence Avenue, SW
Washington, DC 20202
1-800-USA-LEARN
(for copies of *Strong Families, Strong Schools*)

Community-Based Health Services for Children

Strategy

Community-based health services for children and teens can help identify physical and emotional problems that could adversely affect the child's development and behavior.

Crime Problem Addressed

Researchers in the field of juvenile delinquency believe that there is a clear link between the physical and emotional health of children and their academic performance and behavior throughout school and beyond. Undiagnosed and untreated sight, hearing, or emotional problems will impair a child's ability to learn and perform in school, and may cause behavioral problems. When health problems are understood and treated, the child can be helped to perform and avoid the behavior problems and frustration associated with school failure.

Key Components

Children and families are treated in community-based centers or clinics and screened for needed immunizations, lead poisoning, hearing and vision problems, emotional and behavioral issues, nutritional needs, and dental problems. When disorders are found, the children are referred to treatment and provided supplemental educational assistance as appropriate. Teens are screened for mental health disorders; counseled on sexual matters; provided with substance and alcohol abuse treatment; helped to understand nutrition and wellness; and trained to recognize dysfunctional behavior in their peers. Some community health programs provide treatment to youth directly; others treat teens as part of a family unit and assess family management and health issues.

Key Partnerships

Community health-service programs work best when located in the communities most in need and coordinated with other trusted community-based organizations and programs. The programs should offer transportation and provide educational materials and counseling that recognize the ethnic and cultural diversity of the families and children served. Related community organizations sometimes help by providing interpreters for families with limited English skills. Local government and community organizations work in partnership with schools, churches, and ethnic and cultural groups to publicize the services and encourage participation. Programs targeted to teens often rely on peer clients as one means of recruiting other youth who need services.

Potential Obstacles

Some parents may not understand that certain behavioral, developmental, and medical problems are preventable or treatable. Fearing the cost of prevention services or wary that treatment may label the child, some parents may be reluctant to seek services. The presence of trusted community-based health-care providers, trained volunteers, and informal publicity from youth and families who have received services boosts awareness of affordable services.

Signs of Success

The U.S. government has supported the Women, Infants, and Children's Program (WIC) for more than twenty-five years. A comprehensive program that provides supplemental food, nutritional advice, and health screening to support the healthy development of children from low-income families, WIC has helped tens of thousands of women and children throughout the country. Continuation of federal assistance and screening is offered through federally supported Head Start preschool assistance programs in low-income communities. Children are often referred to community-based health services by Head Start project administrators. Additional local programs support child and teen health through local clinics based in schools or at community centers. Many programs receive federal support from the U.S. Department of Health and Human Services and local foundations and businesses.

Applying the Strategy

The Youth Futures Authority in Savannah, Georgia, serves hundreds of teens through the Savannah High School Health Center, the Teen Awareness Group, and the Teen Clinic in a low-income community. The services offered to youth at a variety of locations include the following:

■ physical and mental health assessments;

■ AIDS prevention education;

■ family planning and contraception advice for sexually active teens;

■ nutritional counseling;

■ treatment of minor illnesses and injuries; and

■ information on how to recognize dysfunctional behavior among their peers.

The high school health clinic is staffed by a nurse, nutritionist, and mental health counselor. Pediatricians, dentists, and nurses provide part-time support. Local officials see these services as important prevention tools in their efforts to reduce the rate of drug abuse, health problems, AIDS infection, and violent injuries among area youth. The number of teens seeking services continues to rise.

The Judge Baker Children's Center in Boston, Massachusetts, also includes mental health screening for children and youth. Originally offered through in-home visits and a specially staffed traveling van that served residents fearful of downtown mental health service providers and costs, the programs are now so well known and successful that the community van has been retired in favor of a community-based medical complex for children and families. The center's staff has diagnosed depression and mental illnesses and treated children who had exhibited poor school performance or behavioral problems. The nonprofit center has been serving families and children in Boston for more than fifteen years.

Contact Information

Judge Baker Children's Center
295 Longwood Avenue
Boston, Massachusetts 02115
617-232-8390

Victim and Witness Support

Strategy

Victim and witness support programs targeted to youth can help them deal with trauma, thereby minimizing the impact of violent incidents.

Crime Problem Addressed

Youth are victims of crime more often than members of any other age group. Those crimes may traumatize other youth who witness the incident or fear a similar fate. Many

youth violence research experts believe extensive exposure to violence on television and in other media desensitizes youth to the realities of violent crime and its effects. Victims, witnesses, and friends may seek retribution, not fully understanding the impact of their actions or the effect they will have on additional victims and the community. Victim and witness assistance programs help youth deal with their pain and frustration following violent incidents, thereby preventing additional violent crime.

Key Components

Counseling, discussion groups, and follow-up medical and school assistance is provided in these programs by social workers, specially trained police officers, and psychologists. The difficulties some young victims have in coping with violent incidents often extend well beyond the time spent recovering from physical injuries. These programs recognize that young people, like adult victims and witnesses, need to talk about their experiences and get assistance in coping with their feelings and understanding what happened. Such services may be offered as an emergency response to specific incidents in the community, in response to incidents that occur on school grounds, and as part of community-based crime prevention and victim assistance programs.

Key Partnerships

Local programs are usually the result of cooperative relationships among law enforcement agencies, emergency services, local hospitals, and mental health professionals. Law enforcement personnel in some cities summon trauma response teams of mental health professionals after violent incidents involving children and youth occur or refer youth victims to mental health professionals who coordinate such programs. In some cases, local programs work directly with schools to coordinate follow-up services and academic assistance to victims and witnesses who may have difficulties following exposure to serious violence.

Potential Obstacles

Local governments often have limited resources to support the traditional activities of law enforcement and social service agencies. Programs using this strategy may have to develop innovative and collaborative partnerships among agencies, hospitals, or local universities to fully support the range of services needed by victims and witnesses.

Signs of Success

The New Haven, Connecticut, police department offers counseling and treatment to young victims and witnesses through a partnership with area mental health professionals.

Since 1989, Youth Alive in Oakland, California, has sponsored Caught in the Crossfire, a victim-assistance program for youth who have been exposed to gun violence. The program sends trained youth counselors who have themselves been victims of violence to area hospitals to support their peers in avoiding further involvement with violent crime. The program has trained over fifty youth and served over 3,000 victims.

Applying the Strategy

The Youth Trauma Team in Washington, DC, responds to the scene of violent incidents where youth have been victims or witnesses. Psychologists, social workers, and trained police officers offer youth counseling to cope with their experiences. The city-supported service is supplemented by the Howard University Violence Prevention Project, a program offering youth victims and witnesses after-school activities, tutoring, cultural enrichment, and a summer camp. The Youth Trauma Team has provided an invaluable service in a city that experiences significantly high rates of youth-related violence.

Contact Information

Youth Alive
Summit Medical Center
3012 Summit Avenue, Suite 3670
Oakland, California 94609
510-444-6191

Graffiti Enforcement

Strategy

Strict enforcement of vandalism laws helps local police agencies identify gang members and prevent destruction or damage to property from graffiti.

Crime Problem Addressed

Many youth gangs use graffiti to mark territory, send messages, and intimidate rival gangs and community residents. Physical deterioration, including the presence of graffiti at many locations throughout a neighborhood, can increase residents' fears about their safety and reduce property values, in effect destabilizing the community. The damage and destruction such vandalism causes to public buildings costs large cities millions of dollars annually in maintenance and repair. Programs to remove graffiti and apply comprehensive prevention and enforcement strategies against vandals (often gang-involved youth) are an important component of a community's crime prevention and gang prevention strategies.

Key Components

Many localities have implemented antigraffiti ordinances, making youth and sometimes their parents legally accountable for damage and for possession of graffiti implements such as spray paints. Enforcement against graffiti vandals is most effective when implemented as part of a more comprehensive local strategy addressing the problems of youth gangs, including school-based curricula on gang prevention and counseling for gang-involved youth and their parents.

Key Partnerships

Antigraffiti programs are most often coordinated and implemented by police in cooperation with other local agencies, including schools that provide classroom time for gang prevention education programs and community-based groups or agencies that offer counseling to youth and their families. In addition, some urban police departments work with code-enforcement agencies to keep property free of graffiti and encourage businesses to donate materials for graffiti cleanup.

Potential Obstacles

Localities with many youth gangs that use graffiti for communication or intimidation may find it difficult to catch graffiti vandals or carry out graffiti cleanup of public and private properties. Some locations have attempted to prevent graffiti by coating walls of public buildings and transportation waiting areas with special paint products and surfaces that do not allow paint to stick.

Signs of Success

In Cathedral City, California, the police department operates one of the nation's most successful graffiti prevention programs. The Gang-Related Activity Anti-Suppression Program (GRASP) uses a combination of strategies to combat violent crime and destruction of property committed by youth gangs in the area. GRASP unit counselors and other police officers visit area schools to present gang-prevention educational programs to students and parents' groups and to provide specialized counseling to gang-involved youth and parents. GRASP also enforces strict antigraffiti ordinances aimed at identifying and prosecuting offenders and those caught with graffiti implements. The enforcement strategy involves serving search warrants on graffiti crew members, implementing sting operations to catch merchants who sell paint to underage youth, and cooperating with local schools in maintaining lists of graffiti vandals.

The combined enforcement and prevention approach of the GRASP program is credited with reducing the number of graffiti-related crimes in Cathedral City from 3,600 in 1992 to 400 in 1993. In addition, in 1993 all suspects in gang shootings that resulted in an injured or murdered victim were identified through the use of Gang Intelligence Files developed by the unit and were in custody of the GRASP unity within twelve hours.

Applying the Strategy

Cleveland, Ohio, has adopted a successful and low-cost strategy in response to graffiti vandalism of property. Through a coordinated effort entitled Walls of the City, local stations broadcast antigraffiti public service announcements on the radio and city agencies routinely notify property owners of ordinances that require them to keep their property graffiti-free. Outreach to local hardware stores has resulted in donations of paint and supplies for graffiti removal. The labor for graffiti removal and repainting projects is provided by gang-involved youth required to do community service for misdemeanor convictions. Graffiti has reappeared at only about 30 of the 200 chronic graffiti sites in the city.

From 1992 to 1994, Walls of the City sponsored community art education projects to cover graffiti-strewn walls with resident-designed murals depicting local interests. None of the murals has been damaged by new graffiti. In addition to the murals, the city has since redirected some of the graffiti artists toward more positive activities, such as attendance of the city's art museum school.

Contact Information

Youth Diversion Counselor
Cathedral City Police Department
68625 Perez Road
Cathedral City, California 92234
619-321-0111

Truancy Reduction Through Daytime Curfews

Strategy

Truancy rates are reduced by local policies and programs that reinforce social controls on the behavior of youth.

Crime Problem Addressed

All school-age children living in the United States are required to enroll in and attend school. A student who fails to attend school without permission from home or school is considered truant. Truancy is a "status offense," a violation of law that applies to youth, usually those under sixteen years of age. According to the National Dropout Prevention Center and other groups, reasons for chronic truancy vary widely and include lack of supervision at home, family problems, boredom, and substance abuse. In addition to violating school attendance laws, some of the more than two million truants each day commit crimes during daytime hours, when school is in session. Cities across the country have found that successful truancy prevention programs have resulted in fewer daytime burglaries and violent crimes committed by school-age youth.

Key Components

Stay-in-school policies support truancy laws that require youth to attend school. The main objective of such policies is to keep youth in school, preventing chronic truants from becoming dropouts. Additional objectives include reducing daytime property crimes and violent crimes committed by the truant youth. After returning truant youth to school or parents, police officers, school personnel, and community volunteers who staff truancy processing locations screen offenders and refer them to school-based or supportive services.

A system of graduated sanctions holding youth and parents legally accountable is a key component of antitruancy strategies. Such policies, which may range from fines to incarceration, are responsible for returning youth to school and decreasing their involvement in delinquent or criminal activities.

Key Partnerships

The partnerships most vital to the success of a truancy prevention program are those developed among the local law enforcement agency, the school, and other social services agencies that help youth and their families address the interrelated causes of truancy. The school's role includes communicating truancy policy to parents and students and providing law enforcement personnel access to well-maintained attendance records so that they can check on the status of possible violators of local truancy ordinances.

Law enforcement agencies not only apprehend truant youth, they also help schools identify chronic truants in need of scholastic or family support services and prevent daytime property and violent crime. Law enforcement officers and school personnel often work together in staffing drop-off or assessment centers for truant youth and help facilitate connections between the youth, their families, and social services agencies. In some communities, residents and parents are directly involved in truancy prevention programs, volunteering at drop-off centers or reporting neighborhood youth whom they suspect of truancy.

Potential Obstacles

Truancy prevention programs cannot be successful without community support. Therefore, it is essential that local law enforcement and school officials work with parent organizations, residents, and youth in the design and implementation of truancy prevention policy and programs. Successful intervention in the situation of any truant youth requires individualized needs assessment, and follow-up on treatment and service referrals. Where family management or supervision is a prominent issue, programs should pay particular attention to reinvolving parents in school activities and providing services to address that issue.

Signs of Success

School districts and police departments across the country have banded together to prevent truancy among middle and high school students, finding that as school attendance improves, the incidence of daytime burglary and violent crime decreases.

The Truant and Burglary Suppression (TABS) program in San Jose, California, helped that city reduce its dropout rate to 3.3 percent and resulted in a 50 percent decrease in daytime burglary rates. Following the success of a late-night juvenile curfew, San Antonio, Texas, passed a truancy prevention "daytime curfew" as an additional strategy for police officers to use in combatting juvenile crime. Implemented amidst strong community support and awareness, expanded youth initiatives, gang prevention, and education programs the San Antonio youth daytime curfew decreased juvenile crime during daylight hours, increased student attendance rates, and reduced repeat violations to only 10 percent. Baltimore, Maryland, and Charlotte, North Carolina, law enforcement and school officials have implemented similar truancy prevention programs with positive results.

Applying the Strategy

Responding to school system, police, and community concerns about high rates of truancy and juvenile crime, Oklahoma City, Oklahoma, started the Truancy Habits Reduced, Increasing Valuable Education (THRIVE) program in 1986. THRIVE operates a truancy prevention center staffed by police, social workers, school officials, representatives of the district attorney's office, and community volunteers who work together to counsel truant students and refer them to needed services. The program was so successful that after four years, the daily absenteeism rate had fallen from 10 to 4 percent and dropout rates had fallen by 50 percent. Since then, THRIVE has continued to benefit Oklahoma City students and the community, serving as a nationally recognized example of a successful truancy prevention program.

Contact Information

THRIVE
Department P
P.O. Box 18674
Oklahoma City, Oklahoma 73154
405-634-8081

In-Home Counseling for Young Parents

Strategy

In-home counseling services help young at-risk parents understand and foster their child's development, cope with the responsibilities of parenthood, and reduce the sense of fear and isolation that could otherwise lead to child abuse.

Crime Problem Addressed

This strategy addresses prevention of child abuse and later juvenile delinquency through intensive interaction with parents. First, it helps young at-risk parents cope with the frustration that can arise from not understanding their child's development and limited ability to communicate, reducing the likelihood that the parent might resort to abuse or neglect. Second, it helps parents prepare the child for school, addressing the belief that academic success is linked with reduced involvement in later delinquent behavior. Third, the skills it provides young parents foster the development of stronger and more positive bonds between parent and child.

Key Components

Programs that adopt this strategy often provide both home visits and support groups for parents. This intervention is most effective when it is begun early in the child's life and is continued through the child's enrollment in school. Trained program staff use home visits as an opportunity to educate parents about child development and to help parents manage frustration and anger. The program encourages reading to the child and other educational activities to help prepare the child for school. Home visits also include screenings to detect developmental delays so that they can be corrected early. Support groups provide the parents with an outlet for sharing frustrations and concerns. The strategy also provides a link to other services that may be needed. These types of programs are best promoted by former and present participants and are most successful if the participation is voluntary.

Key Partnerships

The most important partnership in this program is between the parents and the home visitor. Another key partnership is between the parents, so that they can provide each other mutual support.

Potential Obstacles

One problem is the potential lack of trust between the parents and the home visitor. Although most parents eventually trust the helper, in cases where trust is lacking, progress is difficult. Another obstacle is presented by parents who withdraw active support of their child's education once the child is in school. Also, parents who perceive the program as punitive rather than supportive will be reluctant participants; the program must be promoted as a resource for parents and as a means to enhance latent skills.

Signs of Success

The number of programs using this strategy has steadily increased over the years. Evaluations of various programs show a reduction in child abuse and neglect in families that take part, as well as an increase in school achievement for the children. Most of the programs are still relatively new and the children of the parents who have received help are still young, so long-term impacts and benefits are yet to be determined. Research studies cited by Ken Magid and Carole A. McKelvey in *High Risk: Children Without a Conscience* show that early positive social interactions such as the ones promoted between parent and child through this strategy decrease the likelihood of delinquent behavior.

Applying the Strategy

In St. Louis, Missouri, the Parents as Teachers program (PAT) focuses on families of all ages and socioeconomic status, providing in-home visits by specially trained parents to families from before the children are born until they reach kindergarten age. An evaluation done in 1991 by Research and Training Associates showed improved communication between parent and child as well as a dramatic decrease in reported child abuse. The report also showed an increase in resolving developmental delays among children in participating families. The program has now been expanded to over 1,300 sites in forty-three states, Washington, DC, and four foreign countries.

The Home Instruction Program for Preschool Youngsters (HIPPY) originated in Israel to help immigrant families. First brought to the United States in 1984, it has since been implemented at eighty sites, both rural and urban, in twenty-three states. Among those sites is Monticello, Arizona, where parents have witnessed positive overall changes in the family atmosphere.

The Center for Successful Child Development (CSCD) in the Robert Taylor Homes, a public housing community in Chicago, Illinois, has used this strategy since 1986. In addition to providing a community center offering day care and social gatherings for adults and children, the center trains former and present residents to serve as home visitors. The young children who have participated demonstrate improved social skills and readiness for school. Participating parents commented that they have been able to develop a stronger bond with their children and say that they have a better understanding of their child's development and needs.

In Elmira, New York, the Home Visitation Program uses nurses who work to develop individualized and respectful relationships with the parent(s). The program has been effective with parents identified as high-risk participants: young, unmarried, and poor. Among that group, the program is credited with a 75 percent decrease in reports of child abuse and neglect and a 56 percent reduction in the number of visits to the emergency room for illness or accidents.

Contact Information

Executive Director
Parents as Teachers National Center
10176 Coprorate Square Drive, Suite 230
St. Louis, Missouri 63132
314-432-4330

Restitution to Victims

Strategy

Requiring juveniles convicted of minor offenses to work to make restitution to their victims reinforces the accountability of the offender and helps prevent recidivism.

Crime Problem Addressed

According to the U.S. Department of Justice, over 90 percent of youth who are arrested are not charged with serious offenses. While not violent, the offenses do have financial and other impacts on the victims. This strategy gives the juvenile offenders an opportunity to repay the damages caused by their crimes, teaching them that their actions have consequences for which they must take responsibility and be accountable to the community. Such programs also tell the youth that they have skills that someone needs. Recidivism is reduced among offenders who make restitution to victims.

Key Components

This strategy requires the juvenile offender to work to earn the money to make restitution to his or her victims. It is generally used with first-time juvenile offenders convicted of minor crimes such as shoplifting, trespassing, illegal possession, and simple assault. Restitution can either be used to divert a juvenile from the justice system or as a condition of probation. In addition to the benefit of restitution to the victim, this strategy allows offenders to gain job skills. Failure to attend work or make restitution results in penalties levied against the juvenile.

Key Partnerships

Cooperation among the courts, area businesses, and local government agencies is necessary to ensure job and service opportunities for the juvenile offenders. Courts and law enforcement agencies must also work with victims to determine the restitution settlement. Parental support is beneficial, since it helps ensure commitment from the youth.

Potential Obstacles

A lack of support from the community and area businesses is a potential barrier to the success of this strategy. In addition, it is possible that offenders may view restitution programs as an easy diversion from the juvenile justice system and not as a serious commitment. This challenge can be overcome with strict sanctions against youth who fail to cooperate.

Signs of Success

A recent report by the Office of Juvenile Justice and Delinquency Prevention cited a 1991 study conducted by the National Center for Juvenile Justice indicating that recidivism is reduced "when juveniles agree or are ordered to pay restitution to their victims directly or through earnings derived from community service." The National Institute of Justice has also reported on studies which reach similar conclusions.

Applying the Strategy

Project Payback was initiated in Portland, Oregon, in 1986. Implemented through the county juvenile department and the area Boys & Girls Clubs, the program supplements minimum wage jobs with the city's water department and local businesses with privileges at the Boys & Girls Clubs, including eligibility to participate in a substance-abuse treatment program run by the club. At the club, participants can get involved in team sports, receive counseling, or enjoy other activities. The project reports that more than half of the participants earn enough money to repay their debts within one year, retaining 40 percent of their salary and contributing the rest to restitution. Many participants have also returned to school and sought additional job training.

In 1989, the rural community of Keene, New Hampshire, instituted the Earn-It restitution program through the Juvenile Conference Committee serving Keene and seventeen surrounding towns. The New Hampshire program is based on a model developed in 1973 by a Quincy, Massachusetts, district court judge. This voluntary alternative for youth prevents nonviolent first offenders from getting a juvenile record. The program manager assigns the youth a job with a nonprofit agency in the area, then requires that the youth contact the potential employer and interview successfully. Failure to complete the job in a timely fashion or committing another offense causes removal from the program and referral back to the court. More than 450 youth have been referred to the Earn-It program since February 1988, with over 75 percent of the youth successfully completing the program and 80 percent never again appearing in juvenile court.

Probation officers in Tuscaloosa, Alabama, refer some offenders to the County Juvenile Court Victim Restitution Program. The youth must make financial reparations to their victims and must also perform community service to repay the community. In 1993, the Alabama program reported that only 7 of the nearly 400 juvenile offenders it tracked reoffended after completing the restitution program.

Contact Information

Project Payback
Portland Boys & Girls Clubs
7602 North Emerald Street
Portland, Oregon 97217
503-289-8803

Teen Pregnancy Prevention

Strategy

Health and sex educations programs focusing on factors that influence the onset of sexual activity help discourage young people from early sexual involvement, reducing the likelihood of teenage pregnancy and the high risk of child abuse among children of teen parents.

Crime Problem Addressed

The Children's Defense Fund estimates that every day in the United States, 8,400 teenagers become sexually active, 1,340 teenagers have babies, and 1,115 teenagers have abortions. This strategy aims to prevent several types of crime. Teenagers, particularly those under sixteen, are generally not mature enough to rear children. The immaturity of young, unprepared parents can lead to neglect and abuse if they do not know how to respond to the child's behaviors and development or do not understand the long-term consequences of their actions. Neglect and abuse can cause the child to become socially "unattached" and more aggressive toward others. By helping prevent teenage pregnancy, this strategy is effective in helping prevent both child abuse and the violent crimes committed by adults who were abused as children.

Key Components

Traditional education techniques that instruct teens on the physical implications of sexual activity have not been exceptionally successful at reducing teenage pregnancy. In contrast, the key to this strategy is discussion with teens about their reasons for becoming sexually active and potential lifelong consequences of having sex. Through such discussions, teen participants examine attitudes toward sex, including its role in relationships, initiation of sexual activity as a "rite of passage," and the impact a baby would have on their lifestyle. Exploring reasons to put off or avoid sexual activity is also important to the success of this strategy, because it reinforces the teens' decision-making and critical thinking skills. Interaction between students and group leaders or teachers is beneficial in developing positive relationships between the two. This strategy is enhanced if it remains flexible enough to accommodate discussions about the students' concerns and allows some deviation from the prepared lessons. For example, many teens become sexually active in an attempt to fill an emotional void or because they think it is vital to attaining popularity; therefore, addressing self-esteem and societal influences is also valuable.

Key Partnerships

The key partnership exists between the teens and the adults who lead discussions and present the curriculum. That relationship must foster the trust required for youth to discuss these sensitive issues openly. Teachers or other adults must also foster cooperative relationships among the youth so they will feel comfortable discussing these issues among themselves. Programs should provide extensive training for all adult leaders.

Potential Obstacles

A potential obstacle for this strategy is a lack of trust between the group leaders and the students. The time and money necessary to train the group leaders can present another barrier. Also at issue is the difficulty of getting to the teens before they become sexually active. Once they have initiated sexual activity, it is more difficult to affect their behavior.

Signs of Success

External and internal evaluations conducted on programs that use this strategy show that the youth have reduced sexual involvement, more positive attitudes about remaining abstinent, and more positive attitudes about themselves in general.

In Atlanta, Georgia, Postponing Sexual Involvement, a ten-session program for eighth graders, began in 1983. This program uses eleventh- and twelfth-grade students to help younger teens understand that sex does not have to be a part of growing up. The peer educators, supervised by staff from Grady Memorial Hospital, involve the students in discussing and thinking about what leads teenagers to have sex (e.g., social and peer pressures). Through role-playing exercises, they practice how to deal with those issues and how to respond to difficult situations. Pre-tests and post-tests are used to indicate the students' level of sexual involvement. According to an evaluation appearing in the January-February 1990 issue of *Family Planning Perspectives*, "by the end of eighth grade, students who had not had the program were as much as five times more likely to have begun having sex than were those who had had the program." In addition, 95 percent of those who had not had sex before the program felt it made them more prepared to remain abstinent.

Applying the Strategy

In Chicago, Illinois, middle-school students have an opportunity to take part in either Peer Power for girls or ADAM (Awareness and Development for Adolescent Males), extracurricular programs that focus on creating strong relationships between teens and adults and among the teens. Teens learn reasons and ways to say, "no," to sex and, "yes," to a productive life. They also take field trips to businesses and places of interest and participate in recreational activities. After taking part in this program, twice as many participants were abstinent; among those who were sexually active, most used birth control. Before the program, a majority of participants believed that having a child at sixteen would not be a problem. After the program, a majority of participating students said they believed in waiting until at least age twenty-two.

Project First-Class Male in Fort Lauderdale, Florida, a program of the local Urban League, promotes sexual abstinence among males twelve to eighteen years old. Counselors and volunteers emphasize family planning, self-esteem, career goals, and parenting skills for young men who are already parents. The program serves approximately 150 youth each year and reports an 85 percent success rate in preventing new pregnancies in partners of participants.

Contact Information

Grady Memorial Hospital
Teen Services Program
Box 26158
80 Butler Street, S.E.
Atlanta, Georgia 30335-3801
404-616-3513

Parental Involvement Programs

Strategy

Programs and mechanisms that incorporate parental involvement in raising drug-free children help reduce drug use and strengthen community antidrug norms.

Crime Problem Addressed

When drug information and antidrug behaviors learned at school are not reinforced at home, young people are more likely to turn to substance abuse.

Key Components

The most important components of a parent-based strategy for drug prevention are factual education and support from other parents or community groups. Parent drug prevention efforts should include education about the signs and symptoms of drug use and information about drug paraphernalia. Parents should also be aware of resources in the community if they are concerned that their children might be involved with alcohol or other drugs. An effective parent program:

- strives to strengthen communication between parents and children;

- supports parents who refuse to allow alcohol or other drugs at parties;

- provides information about sources of alcohol and drugs; and

- supports parents who are trying to keep their children drug-free.

In some communities, parents sign a pledge that they will not permit young people to bring alcohol or other drugs into their homes. Some parent programs also teach effective parenting skills.

Key Partnerships

Parents should work in partnership with the youth themselves, school personnel, law enforcement, community-service providers, and other residents in the community who observe young people in after-school or evening activities. In some communities, youth organization leaders and athletic coaches have worked effectively with parents interested in combating youth drug use.

Potential Obstacles

Denial is a serious barrier in the effort to help parents whose children are involved with alcohol and other drugs. Additionally, some parents may judge others, creating hostility within the parent support group. These barriers can be addressed through the expertise of trained family counselors or drug abuse prevention specialists who are effective in communicating without expressing judgment.

Signs of Success

In *Adolescents at Risk*, J. D. Dryfoos reviews the success of adolescent drug prevention programs and concludes that the availability and involvement of a caring adult in a parenting role is the "hallmark of effective prevention programs."

Project Info in Whittier, California, puts this strategy to use by working closely with youth and family members of youth who show early warning signs of drug or alcohol abuse. Initially a research project, the program now provides direct services. A recent evaluation highlighted a 4 percent recidivism rate for youth participants.

Applying the Strategy

In Houston, the Self-Help for African People through Education (SHAPE) program formed a Parent Awareness Network (PAN) to unite the community in the fight against drugs and crime and to improve neighborhood conditions. With help from local schools, the parents met weekly at the schools and at a housing development and signed a pledge to work in partnership to keep their children drug-free.

The Scott Newman Center, headquartered in California, has been part of a strong movement to increase parental awareness of drug problems and how they affect families. The Center's program Neighborhoods in Action assists existing neighborhood groups by providing drug education and prevention materials, teaching basic parent-child communication skills and techniques, and helping resolve problems that arise with drug use.

The Parents' Communication Network of Minnesota connects more than 10,000 families in the state with newsletters and other printed materials addressing problems with alcohol and other drug use, parenting skills, guidelines and restrictions for parties, and other issues that are of concern to parents of elementary and teenage children. The network also keeps parents apprised of effective antidrug education curricula, legislative efforts to prevent problems with substance use, state and national resources in drug prevention, and health issues.

Contact Information

Program Coordinator
Parents' Communication Network of Minnesota
National Federation of Parents for Drug-Free Youth
P.O. Box 24392
Apple Valley, Minnesota 55124
612-432-2886

Neighborhoods in Action
Scott Newman Foundation
6255 Sunset Boulevard
Suite 1906
Los Angeles, California 90028
213-469-2029

Adults as Mentors

Strategy

Caring adults who serve as mentors to at-risk youth build resiliency and academic skills in those youth, helping prevent juvenile delinquency.

Crime Problem Addressed

Recent youth development research highlights the importance of the consistent presence of a caring adult in helping prevent juvenile delinquency and increasing school success and social development. Adult mentors are a stable source of encouragement and support, communicating values and providing models of dedication and dependability vital to youth.

Key Components

Volunteer adult mentors are often recruited by schools and community-based youth service agencies from a variety of sources, including churches and senior citizen organizations. Mentors are traditionally assigned to work one-on-one with a single student, and they are often involved in educational assistance such as tutoring in specific subjects, teaching practical life and job preparation skills, and informal counseling and discussion with youth through social interaction.

Referred in many cases by local services agencies, churches, schools or juvenile courts, mentors are carefully screened to ensure they are appropriate and stable role models and to match them with particular youth in need of assistance. Mentors bring a number of qualities to the relationship with the youth, including specific skills or interests in common with the youth, experience or aptitude to help the youth with specific school performance problems, and long-standing positive ties to the community and its institutions. In most cases, attempts are made to match youth with a mentor of the same gender, race, and cultural background.

Key Partnerships

Community service groups, youth-serving organizations, churches, synagogues, and schools that sponsor mentor programs use their own membership networks to recruit adult mentors from within the communities where the youth live. Religious or culturally based organizations often add particular values education components to their programming to reinforce their beliefs and standards for the development of youth. Local government agencies, in many cases the school system, sponsor programs or provide meeting space to youth and mentors as a means of enhancing the chances for that youth to achieve academic success through the tutoring the mentor provides. In some cities, mentors are selected from senior citizen groups or older members of religious congregations as a way of bridging understanding and support between age groups.

Potential Obstacles

Sustained commitment and participation of qualified adult volunteers is vital to the success of youth mentor programs. As most participating youth have experienced broken commitments, sustained adult commitment is essential. Busy community residents may find it difficult to make the commitment to dedicate the time and effort needed to support youth effectively. Some adults may be turned off by the extensive nature of volunteer screening processes in more elaborate and established programs. Also, it may be difficult for mentors to provide all of the support that some youth need, so referrals to supportive service agencies and community organizations are very important. Training mentors how to recognize needs of youth and work with school or service agency case managers can help address these issues.

Signs of Success

In a 1989 nationwide poll about mentoring programs conducted by Lou Harris and Associates, 73 percent of participants said their mentor had helped them raise their expectations and 59 percent said their grades had improved.

Big Brothers and Big Sisters of America (BB/BS) is the oldest established youth mentoring program in the United States. In operation for over ninety years, the national organization oversees over fifty BB/BS agencies in the fifty states and the District of Columbia. In 1992 alone, over 60,000 youth were matched with adult mentors. Evaluations and anecdotal comments from youth and adult participants rate the program as very successful in helping youth and providing positive service opportunities for adults.

One to One (OTO) is a national organization that sponsors mentoring programs in localities across the country. Founded in 1989 by a group of educators, business people, and philanthropists, OTO matched over 2,500 youth with mentors during 1993, brokered mentoring program partnerships with over 300 businesses and created a program of investment accounts to give over 150 youth a start as entrepreneurs. Most recently, OTO, BB/BS, the Points of Light Foundation, and Cities in Schools have entered into a mentoring program partnership sponsored by the Corporation for National and Community Service.

Applying the Strategy

Cherokee County Schools in South Carolina established a mentoring program in 1992 in response to concerns about high dropout rates and serious problems with alcohol and other drug abuse among students. Community groups, businesses, the school, and law enforcement have all recruited adults as mentors, providing assistance to twice the number of youth as in the first year of the program. When interviewed, the student participants revealed that the mentors helped them improve their confidence levels and their self-esteem.

The Fairfax County (Virginia) Juvenile and Domestic Relations District Court Services recently implemented a mentoring program to help court-involved youth prepare for positive and productive lives in their communities. The mentors in this program act as a liaison to court counselors, the youth's family, and the school system. They help the youth improve school performance, set goals for postsecondary education and job training, and locate employment. The Volunteer Sponsor Program has actively and successfully recruited African-American, Latino, and Asian adults as mentors—an important strategy, since more than one-third of court-involved youth come from those cultural backgrounds.

Contact Information

Vice President for Communications
One to One Partnerships, Inc.
2801 M Street, NW
Washington, DC 20007
202-338-3844

Rites of Passage Training

Strategy

Community-based faith institutions and other organizations help prevent juvenile delinquency and reinforce the community's sense of appropriate values by providing "rites of passage" and life skills training for at-risk youth.

Crime Problem Addressed

Research on juvenile delinquency identifies a number of risk and protective factors that contribute to the likelihood a juvenile will be delinquent or that help prevent that same youth from falling prey to negative influences or individuals. Specifically, youth development literature points to a belief in self and a sense of optimism and faith (including religious) in what the future holds for them as key factors in creating resilient youth. Life skills training in social development, personal goal setting, and values education can help bolster these resiliency factors in youth.

Key Components

So-called "rites of passage" training is one method used by some community-based and religious organizations to provide African-American males with a base of skills and role models for pro-social and positive behavior consistent with community standards. Based on African cultural traditions of important lessons and skills which must be learned at key stages in life, such programs—often implemented through local religious organizations—include mentoring by adults, tutoring, informal counseling, and specific training and values-based education in life skills development.

The training typically involves several components, including the following:

- **spirituality and values**—understanding the basis for ethical rules and appropriate social behavior;

- **values clarification**—responding to societal influences, which tend to reinforce violence and other negative social behavior; stressed as a natural component of religious instruction;

- **money management**—emphasizing the importance of planning for the future through legitimate employment; and

- **health and hygiene**—preventing pregnancy and AIDS, the role of personal hygiene in health, and the health effects of violence.

Key Partnerships

Key partnerships generally involve church or other community members who help identify youth in need of services and adults who can deliver skills training and support youth making difficult transitions through adolescence.

Signs of Success

There are few formal evaluation data on programs using this strategy. However, many communities and religious organizations believe in their value and have incorporated such training into regular programs for youth.

Project Image is a confederation of twenty Chicago churches providing rites of passage training to hundreds of youth through cooperative partnerships with area schools. Role models from the churches assist young African-American males between the ages of eight and eighteen, individuals who are considered at risk of engaging in delinquent behavior or dropping out of school. Over the years, the number of churches, schools, mentor volunteers and youth participants has steadily increased, as has the enthusiasm for the effectiveness of the services it offers. Anecdotal comments of participants praise the program's ability to use trusted community volunteers to provide at-risk youth with comprehensive life skills training and guidance on building a positive connection to the community and its values.

Applying the Strategy

The Jane Boyd Harambee House in Cedar Rapids, Iowa, operates a rites of passage training program similar to Project Image. Focused on building participants' self-esteem and sense of personal responsibility, the training has been very successful. Youth involved have improved their academic performance and reported positive changes in their family relationships.

Sisters in Spirit—in Omaha, Nebraska—is a mentoring program that reaches out to African-American females who are eleven to fifteen years old. Women from the community present rites of passage training, which they believe is very helpful in empowering young teens with skills to cope successfully with their transition into adulthood. The program also emphasizes community involvement and cultural awareness.

Contact Information

Project Image
765 East 69th Place
Chicago, IL 60637

Community-Based Support for Domestic Violence Victims

Strategy

Community-based counseling and support services help victims of domestic violence understand their rights under the law and provide refuge and services, helping to prevent additional instances of victimization.

Crime Problem Addressed

Recent statistics indicate that domestic violence is a growing national problem. According to research cited by the National League of Cities, nearly 500 women across the country are battered every two hours, and women who stay in violent relationships are at a 75 percent greater risk of being killed by the batterer than those who leave the relationship. Children of those families are also at significant risk. Factors associated with domestic violence often include adults with alcohol and other drug abuse problems, poor relationship and communication skills, and a past history of violent behavior. Factors that can contribute to battered partners (usually women) staying in physically abusive relationships include economic dependence and fear of their partners.

Key Components

Community-based domestic violence prevention and intervention programs typically offer victims and their children a variety of emergency services to meet their needs for housing, child care, food, medical assistance, and crisis intervention. These groups help prevent additional cases of domestic violence by providing counseling and information on self-protection and prevention and referrals for legal services as needed. Community-based groups also work with police and the court system to protect victims and ensure that offenders are prosecuted. Programs for victims are most effective when community service agencies, legal institutions, and public safety officials cooperate in addressing the needs of individual victims and advocating solutions that provide them protection.

Key Partnerships

Community-based victims' services or women's organizations often focus on providing services to domestic violence victims and coordinating with the legal system to ensure that batterers are prosecuted. Counselors and other health professionals and volunteers provide group and individual counseling, referral to medical services, and crisis hotlines. Community service organizations also work with victims who wish to file charges against their batterers, educating them on the criminal justice process, reporting procedures, and self-protection. Trained law enforcement and court personnel, sometimes from special domestic violence or family units, help victims file criminal complaints and obtain restraining orders.

Potential Obstacles

Victims of domestic abuse are often afraid of the batterer, unaware of services available to help them and their children, and embarrassed to admit that they are victims of abuse. The victims often have to be persuaded that alternative and more positive living circumstances exist and that they can pursue legal action against the offender. Programs administered through community service organizations have difficulty keeping up with the demand for emergency shelter and medical services. It is particularly difficult to retain volunteers for counseling and advocacy assistance and to obtain funding for services.

Signs of Success

Countless community-based organizations provide services to victims of domestic violence. The King County (Washington) Department of Judicial Administration has, for many years, provided a coordinated court system, law enforcement, and community services response to domestic violence in that region, advocating for victims and referring them to a full range of services. In Philadelphia, Pennsylvania, the police department and district attorney's office provide services to over 15,000 victims annually through the Women Against Abuse program.

In addition, local and state governments across the country have passed legislation and established programs to protect and support victims and potential victims. In 1994, the National League of Cities' Women in Municipal Government caucus affirmed the value of community-based victims' services programs and asserted that court, health, public safety personnel, and local elected officials should be trained to understand the dynamics of domestic violence and assist strategies.

Applying the Strategy

Mujeres Latinas en Acción (Latin Women in Action) Domestic Violence Program in Chicago provides information and referrals to police, emergency shelter for women and their children, court advocacy programs, education about the victims' rights within the court system, Spanish-language educational materials and support groups, community education and advocacy, child care, and crisis hotlines for Latina women on the city's west side. The organization is an important community-based resource for victims who might not otherwise be aware of available services because of language and transportation barriers.

The Quincy, Massachusetts, municipal court system designed a strict pretrial probation and drug treatment program for batterers and developed procedures for informing victims of the array of services available to help them cope with the physical and emotional trauma of abuse. In the three years since the program has been in effect, many more women have pursued abuse claims through the court and more abusers have completed treatment or substance abuse programs. In addition, Quincy experienced no homicides related to domestic violence in 1991 or 1992, while neighboring jurisdictions without these programs experienced more than a dozen in the same years.

Contact Information

Mujeres Latinas en Acción
Quincy District Court
Domestic Violence Program
1823 West 17th Street
Chicago, Illinois 60608
312-226-1544

Date Violence Prevention for Teens

Strategy

Dating education and date violence prevention programs help prevent domestic violence within teen and young-adult relationships.

Crime Problem Addressed

Women in the United States are more likely to be victimized through assault, battery, rape, or homicide by a current or former male partner than by all other offenders combined. Tens of thousands of women, including youth, receive treatment for injuries resulting from such abuse. Patterns leading to violence that are developed in teen and young adult relationships are very likely to repeat over time if young women fail to develop communication skills, conflict management skills, and self-esteem. In this strategy, communities attempt to prevent the establishment of negative patterns leading to violence.

Key Components

The primary goal of dating violence prevention and intervention projects is to discourage young women from accepting violent and emotionally abusive treatment in their interpersonal relationships. Typically delivered to teens through cooperation between school systems and community service groups, these programs include curricula on identifying abusive behavior, counseling and discussion sessions about situations that can lead to violence, and training in effective communication. Some programs also use peer education.

Key Partnerships

Community service organizations that support domestic violence victims are increasingly providing early education and support services to teens who are just beginning to date. These organizations deliver crisis counseling and support services, and they often help school districts develop curriculum modules on communication and conflict management skills and dealing with abusive behavior. Local health, public safety, and counseling professionals are often involved in programs targeted to teen dating violence prevention, providing counseling, crisis management, and medical services.

Potential Obstacles

As with their adult counterparts, teen victims of dating violence are often reluctant to seek assistance and embarrassed to admit that they have been abused. In addition, young women lacking communication skills and not understanding abusive behavior may not realize that they are in an abusive situation. This situation is prevalent among youth who come from families where violence and abuse are the norms of behavior within adult relationships.

Signs of Success

The Dating Violence Intervention Project in Cambridge, Massachusetts, began in 1988 through collaborative effort between a successful local treatment program for male batterers and an emergency shelter and support program for battered women. The program providers were concerned that the violent behavior they witnessed had become entrenched, beginning in teenage relationships and being reinforced over time. Since then, the program—now offered in high schools in the Boston area—has become a model for similar efforts in many parts of the country.

The pioneering Dating Violence Prevention Project has developed into a full-service and education program for area teens. The services it provides include the following:

- training through school assemblies and information sessions around the theme "Respect—it can't be beat!";

- mini-courses on communication and conflict management skills;

- hotlines and other counseling support services;

- peer leader programs for students trained to educate other youth; and

- training for school staff to identify signs of abuse among the student population.

Students and staff uniformly report that the program has been effective in helping students recognize an abusive relationship and to cope with abuse.

Applying the Strategy

The Fresh Start Program in the south suburbs of Chicago is operated by a youth-serving community-based agency and provides training sessions for teens, including discussion sessions and role plays.

Additional resources for teen dating violence prevention programs include the King County (Washington) Rape Relief organization, the Southern California Coalition Against Domestic Violence (in Santa Monica), and the Minnesota Coalition Against Domestic Violence (in St. Paul). Each organization provides dating violence prevention services and related information.

Contact Information

Dating Violence Prevention Project
P.O. Box 530
Harvard Square Station
Cambridge, Massachusetts 02238
617-868-8328

Community-Based Parent Education and Support

Strategy

Community-based parent education and support systems enhance parents' knowledge of ways that they can support the development of their children. Through a focus on family management and problem-solving skills and referrals to other needed services, families whose children are at risk can help those youth avoid later problems with delinquency.

Crime Problem Addressed

Lack of family management and communication skills, as well as literacy and chronic employment problems, make effective parenting difficult, particularly in impoverished communities. Communities that assist parents—by providing education and training in communication skills, counseling services, referrals to job training, and housing assistance—help those families transfer skills to their children, preventing delinquency and family violence.

Key Components

Community-based programs that adopt this strategy typically deliver a comprehensive array of services, including the following:

- parent-education classes in child development;

- skill building and educational enhancement programs for children;

- communication and family management training;

- counseling;

- literacy classes; and

- referral to job training, housing assistance, and other services.

Key Partnerships

The most effective community programs using this strategy work in partnership with a variety of social service agencies and schools to design programs and coordinate services for families. The program provider also works with other community groups to publicize the services and recruit families to the program, using community newspapers and newsletters to advertise support available to families. The programs are typically based in neighborhood centers in economically deprived communities with significant crime problems, problems often related to family violence and youth delinquency. The community organizations that deliver the services are often funded by a combination of local government, community foundation, and corporate resources.

Potential Obstacles

Recruiting families into the programs can be difficult, since those with serious management problems and service needs are sometimes reluctant to seek assistance. Information about available services can be communicated through community-based newspapers, newsletters, public events, or schools; these means can help to educate parents about how those services could be helpful to them. Another challenge is encouraging parents to take a larger role in designing effective programs. In addition, maintaining funding support for such programs is a constant concern.

Signs of Success

The Avance (Progress) program in San Antonio, Texas, was established in 1972, one of the first programs of its kind in the nation. Avance now serves thousands of individuals annually, at six sites located throughout the city. Supported by a variety of local government, federal, and corporate sources, Avance is nationally recognized as a model of a community-based program supporting child development, family literacy, and child abuse prevention. Avance's Even Start program focusing on family literacy and parenting education is a national demonstration model program.

Applying the Strategy

By 1991, Maryland's Friends of the Family—a network of community-based drop-in centers for families—had grown from four to thirteen centers, providing services to more than 3,000 families each year. A primary focus of the Maryland program is Family Start, an intensive effort that supports 120 low-income families in Baltimore in fostering their children's potential and achieving economic independence.

Connecticut's Department of Children and Youth Services supports fifteen Parent Education and Support Centers throughout the state. An independent evaluation of the centers demonstrated that participating parents gained increased confidence in their parenting skills and reported significant reductions in family conflicts.

Contact Information

Executive Director
Avance Educational Programs for Parents and Children
301 South Frio Road
San Antonio, Texas 78207
210-270-4630

Intensive Intervention To Prevent Foster Care Placement

Strategy

Families at risk of having a child removed from the home due to neglect, abuse, or delinquent behavior benefit from intensive intervention to prevent delinquency associated with the youth's disconnection from family structures.

Crime Problem Addressed

Research shows that lack of consistent family discipline and support are contributing factors to delinquent behavior. In addition, the readjustment of adjudicated youth to life in their communities is more successful when they can return to a supportive family environment than when they are placed in foster care or other out-of-home placement. Out-of-home placement should be a last resort, used only when the dysfunction in the family cannot be repaired successfully.

Key Components

Programs using this strategy most often involve the cooperative efforts of a number of mental health and other local government social agencies and the juvenile justice system. Youth are referred to the services of a community-based program by the court system because of abuse or delinquent behavior and a belief that the family is not equipped to support and care for the youth adequately. Family assistance includes counseling all family members, mentoring the parents, teaching communication skills, identifying community support systems, and (for some families) providing funds to meet emergency housing and food needs. These services are typically delivered by a combination of social workers, parent aides, and representatives from other local government agencies.

Key Partnerships

Social workers and other family support professionals must work closely with juvenile and family court personnel who refer families and juveniles to the foster-care system. Community-based organizations often provide centers for program activities, including respite-care facilities for use by parents and juveniles on an emergency basis.

Potential Obstacles

In the recent past, the typical response of the court system and social services agencies to family crises involving abused children and delinquent youth had been referral to out-of-home placement, often long-term foster care. Now, in cases where the family management problems can be resolved, intensive services help repair and preserve family structures. Court and social services systems programmed to refer youth to out-of-home placement must be educated about the beneficial effects of intensive services for preserving families and savings available to the local government when the cost of these services is compared to foster-care placement.

Signs of Success

Maryland's Intensive Family Services (IFS) system has been in operation for several years, employing a social worker and parent aide to deliver two to three months of intensive and emergency support to families throughout the state. Families at risk of having one or more children placed in foster care volunteer to participate, receiving parenting training, counseling, and emergency assistance with rent, food, and medical care as needed. In recent years, over 90 percent of children participating in the program have avoided foster-care placement, a figure that improved in the year after families received services through the state-supported program. Moreover, significant cost benefits have been achieved; a "normal" placement in foster care costs $11,500 per year per child, whereas IFS spends only $2,400 per family.

Applying the Strategy

The Walbridge Caring Communities Program in Walbridge, Missouri, assists African-American families in the area through a collaboration of local education, mental health, and related services agencies. Using an Afrocentric approach to family counseling, the program has helped participating families keep children in school, improve academic achievement, and prevent foster-care placement of hundreds of children. Prevention services include culturally oriented educational presentations, employment and parenting programs for parents, respite child care for stressed parents, and preemployment training for adults. Intervention services include drug abuse and other counseling services and intensive in-home therapy for families.

Family Preservation Services of Nevada serves families referred by the child protection and juvenile justice systems in that state. With funding from a combination of federal, state, and local government sources, the program seeks to empower families to provide adequate and safe care for children by supporting the families' strengths and helping them identify solutions to family conflict and management problems. The intensive in-home services are offered to families on the philosophy that children's emotional and physical needs are best met within their families whenever those situations can be made safe and supporting. The Idaho Youth Ranch provides similar services to residents of that state.

Contact Information

Fern Blake
Social Services Administration
Department of Human Resources
311 West Saratoga Street
Baltimore, Maryland 21201
410-361-4600

Youth-Designed and Youth-Led Community Service

Strategy

Youth-designed and youth-led community service programs teach specific skills and prevent delinquency by providing youth opportunities to bond with and improve their communities.

Crime Problem Addressed

One of the key components of a youth's development toward an independent and productive adulthood is bonding with society and society's institutions. That bonding is more likely to occur when youth recognize their stake in society and how their specific contribution can improve the conditions of others in the community. Youth with positive connections to their community, a stake in its future, and enhanced academic and job-readiness skills are better protected against community risk factors they may face growing up.

Key Components

Key to the success of youth community services programs is youth participation in designing, selecting, and implementing projects, including those that offer opportunities to learn specific skills. Successful youth services programs also support themes noted in youth development literature as most directly correlated to resilience to violence and delinquency, including the following:

■ a sense of control over some aspect of their lives;

■ a sense of altruism and caring for others and the community;

■ consistent presence of a caring adult;

■ belief in themselves; and

■ optimism and faith in what the future holds for them.

Key Partnerships

Key partnerships in youth services learning programs must be formed among the following:

■ adults, who mentor youth participants and provide project support when needed;

■ youth volunteers, who take on leadership roles in designing and delivering service projects; and

■ community-based organizations or local government agencies, which coordinate community service programs and recruit youth volunteers and adult mentors.

In many communities, schools play a vital role as the mobilizing and organizing force in youth community services programs, sometimes requiring community service as a condition of graduating from high school. In addition, local government and corporate leaders often play a role, identifying possible service projects or long-term community service opportunities for youth.

Potential Obstacles

Many adults, including local government and community leaders, do not recognize the capacity of youth to design and lead community service projects. These adult leaders must be educated to involve youth in decision-making on community service and other local programs that affect them.

Signs of Success

The importance of community service in developing positive social attitudes has recently been highlighted by the public safety component of the National Community Services Trust Act. One program model for that initiative is Youth as Resources (YAR), a project begun by the National Crime Prevention Council in 1987 and now in use in more than forty localities in the United States. Through YAR, youth choose the community problems on which they will work, design programs in conjunction with adults in non-profit and community organizations, and present their approaches to a central board composed of teens and adults. Then, with funding, the youth carry out and assess the impact of the projects.

YAR has been successful in a variety of contexts, including schools, community-based organizations, and youth detention facilities. In Fort Wayne, Indiana, students produced a video on the effects of drug abuse on users, their families, and their friends. Young men at an Indianapolis group home serving delinquent males renovated a run-down park and playground equipment in the neighborhood. YAR has recently expanded to offer service opportunities to youth in public-housing communities in major cities.

Longitudinal evaluations of YAR demonstrate that two to four years after participation, youth identified themselves as strong supporters of voluntarism, as well-connected to their community, and as more focused and thoughtful in their personal and educational goals. The YAR programs evaluated in juvenile-care settings documented the program's efficacy as a change agent for youth and institutions. YAR also positively influenced prosocial, antidelinquency attitudes and beliefs, including self-esteem, altruism, and bonding with the community.

Applying the Strategy

Seeking an outlet for its research, the National Center for Service Learning in Adolescence developed the Early Adolescent Helper Program. This youth employment and service program began in New York City in 1982 and is now located in more than twenty schools as a course or club activity. Students work with younger children as helpers in child-care centers, as partner helpers for the elderly in senior-care facilities, and in other related projects. Community service activities are supplemented by weekly educational seminars for youth participants ages twelve to seventeen. The center considers the "structured reflection" of the weekly seminars key to enabling students to learn from their service experiences. While assuming these responsibilities, students also improve their academic performance, increase their self-esteem, and develop positive relationships in the community.

Contact Information

National Center for Service Learning in Adolescence
Center for Advanced Study in Education
Graduate School and University Center of the City
   University of New York
25 West 43rd Street, Suite 612
New York, New York 10036-8099
212-642-2945

Schools as Community Resource Centers

Strategy

Schools that serve as a resource center to students and their families during non-school hours help build positive partnerships between the community and the school system. Such partnerships foster the bonding of student and parent to the school and help ensure a supportive learning environment.

Crime Problem Addressed

Research noted in the U.S. Department of Education's 1994 report *Strong Families, Strong Schools: Building Community Partnerships for Learning* shows that "greater family involvement in children's learning is a critical link to achieving a high-quality education and a safe, disciplined learning environment for every student."

Key Components

A variety of nonprofit private and local government entities have established schools in their communities as support centers for youth and their families. They focus on coordinating services available through community organizations, provide direct education support services to students, and host community meetings before, during, and after school hours. They seek to prevent student dropouts, build relationships among parents in the neighborhood and with school administrators, increase parents' involvement in the community, and provide a safe location for health education and employment services for parents. They connect students with mentors, counsel them on careers and about peer pressure, offer sports activities and classes in creative arts, and promote community service. The programs make best use of the school building and promote the school as a resource and a center of community activity.

Key Partnerships

Community organizations and schools work with residents to identify community needs and design the array of services available through the school. The school officials must coordinate with each participating organization to design services, locate resources to support the center, and track the services provided and referrals to outside agencies. Parents and other neighborhood leaders must be involved in decisions about the center's priorities and hours of operation.

Potential Obstacles

The coordination of community agencies and city-sponsored service providers in consideration of the community's need can be challenging. Effective coordination helps maximize existing resources and helps convey to the community the school's and other agencies' investment in responding to the community's needs.

Signs of Success

Cities in Schools (CIS)—one of the nation's largest nonprofit school-serving organizations—is dedicated to educational support, violence prevention, networking social services for families and youth, and helping students make a successful transition from school to work. Established in 1977, CIS now serves over 175,000 students and families annually in 264 communities in nearly thirty states. Several states have initiated CIS programs, providing training and other support to communities in the program. The program estimates that it facilitates efficient use of over 70,000 school and social agency staff hours every month.

Applying the Strategy

The city-sponsored Beacon School initiative in New York City serves the communities and student populations at 37 programs in all five boroughs of the city. The sites are managed by community-based organizations, which subcontract with other groups to provide services in response to needs articulated by parents and students. The organizing group coordinates design of services through a community advisory board, including school officials, residents, and service groups. There are a range of programs provided at the schools (primarily elementary schools) during extended hours including:

- family activities;

- narcotics anonymous meetings;

- homework help;

- a health clinic;

- conflict resolution workshops;

- job training; and

- workshops for young parents.

A typical Beacon School is open and available to the community for 200 percent more hours than a traditional school. There is at least one Beacon school in each community school district in the city. Access to needed services and additional guidance from supportive adults has built positive attitudes in youth from Beacon School communities. The success of the program has leveraged support from foundations and the private sector.

Contact Information

Cities in Schools
1326 Fifth Avenue, Suite 808
Seattle, Washington 98101
206-461-8521

Project Manager
New York City Department of Youth Services
44 Court Street
Brooklyn, New York 11201
718-403-5200

Law-Related Crime Prevention Education With Community Action

Strategy

Comprehensive classroom instruction in crime prevention can build awareness among youth and increase their understanding of the impact of crime on individuals and the community. Where it is supplemented by action in service to the community, it reinforces positive behavior and choices by youth.

Crime Problem Addressed

Many teens are still unaware that they are the age group most often victimized by crime. Many do not know they can help protect themselves and the communities in which they live. Teens, like most adults, often do not fully comprehend the impact that crime has on the community as well as on individual victims. Without that knowledge, teens, adults, and communities are at increased risk of victimization by crime.

Key Components

Comprehensive classroom instruction in crime prevention can build awareness among youth if it includes information on the following:

- the impact of crime on individuals and neighborhoods;

- the importance of reporting crime;

- developing skills to resolve conflict through nonviolent means; and

- facts about preventing specific types of crime.

Even more effective, in terms of impact in the community, is an action-oriented component that supplements classroom work. The classroom education helps build knowledge and change attitudes. The action component engages youth in translating the classroom knowledge into positive crime prevention behaviors.

Key Partnerships

School-based programs should coordinate with community crime prevention groups, health professionals, law enforcement, and other local resources to expose students to positive community leaders and opportunities for community service.

Potential Obstacles

Students' attitudes and behaviors are shaped by many influences that extend beyond the school environment. Key to the success of curriculum programs is providing students with skills to apply communication and decision-making skills to their lives in and out of school.

Signs of Success

In 1985, the National Crime Prevention Council and the National Institute for Citizen Education in the Law combined to empower teens to make themselves and their communities safer, founding the Teens, Crime, and the Community (TCC) program. TCC offers students in grades seven through twelve comprehensive classroom instruction, in an infusion format, on a variety of crime prevention topics. TCC also encourages students to develop crime prevention projects for their school or community. These projects have included violence prevention education campaigns, service to a victim assistance group, and formation of school-based crime watch groups. Since its inception, TCC has been implemented in more than forty states, reaching over 500,000 youth through school and community-based programs.

An independent 1992 evaluation of TCC in ten Iowa schools revealed that the program helped prevent delinquent behavior in students by affecting their "belief in ethical rules, their attitude toward associating with delinquency-prone peers, self-reporting behaviors," and their sense of altruism. Key to these changes were cooperative learning, participation in a chosen project, and connection with community resources through the action projects. In addition, students in nearly every TCC program evaluated from 1989 to 1992 demonstrated an increased knowledge of the risks and nature of victimization, ways to prevent crime and how to assist victims.

Applying the Strategy

The Law-Related Education Program for Adjudicated Youth in Meade County, South Dakota, focuses on providing programs for "low-ability" readers, developing curriculum materials targeted to high-risk youth, and integrating back into the community youth who have been adjudicated by and diverted from the juvenile justice system. The program coordinates court, probation, law enforcement, drug treatment, and school personnel on behalf of the students. The program won the state's award for best curriculum in 1992. It has since been replicated in several other school districts throughout the state.

Contact Information

Teens, Crime, and the Community
National Crime Prevention Council
1700 K Street, NW
2nd Floor
Washington, DC 20006
202-466-6272, ext. 155

Director
Statistical Analysis Center
South Dakota Attorney General's Task Force on Drugs
500 East Capitol Avenue
Pierre, South Dakota 57501
605-773-6313

Crisis Hotlines

Strategy

A network of anonymous and widely available crisis hotline counseling and support services helps youth or adult clients with the challenges of peer pressure, stress, substance abuse, violent behavior, and fears which result from victimization.

Crime Problem Addressed

Parents stressed by child rearing and youth feeling isolated from peers or family members both need the support of caring professionals and volunteers who can provide counseling and related services. Since the services focus on improving relationships and choosing healthy behaviors, the programs help address risk of delinquency among youth and increase the ability of parents to deal with their children in healthy, nonviolent ways.

Key Components

Community organizations that serve targeted populations such as teens or parents network with service providers and recruit volunteers to make information available to individuals in need. Programs offer a variety of services, including crisis hotlines, support groups, resource information, counseling services, and health care. Volunteers who work on the hotlines and facilitate discussion groups are trained by social service and health care agency staff.

Key Partnerships

This strategy requires coordination of service providers to receive referrals and offer assistance to individuals in need. Public education resources coordinated to publicize services ensure that individuals or families in need are aware of the support available to them.

Potential Obstacles

Locating the resources required to adequately screen and train volunteers can present a challenge for crisis support services. Many programs recruit former recipients of such services and train them to support others in need.

Signs of Success

Parents Anonymous is a statewide, grassroots network of volunteers who assist parents with parenting challenges. The free counseling and support services include discussion groups, crisis hotlines, and educational materials on parenting. The services focus on building communication skills, decreasing the isolation of parents, and building healthy family relationships. The program is affiliated with the Seattle Violence Prevention Project, a coalition of city- and community-sponsored organizations.

Applying the Strategy

The Niagara County Hotline and Drug Abuse Program was established in 1971 to provide crisis counseling ser-

vices through the county's mental health and substance abuse agency. The services provide vital support to low-income residents. In 1990, the program organized a anti-drug march to publicize the need for counseling and treatment services in the low-income and racially diverse communities of the county. The march united a group of service providers in the Niagara community.

Contact Information

Program Coordinator
Niagara County Department of Mental Health, Alcohol, and Drug Abuse
775 Third Street
Niagara Falls, New York 14302
716-278-1825

Parents Anonymous
1-800-932-HOPE (in Washington state)
206-233-0139 (in the Seattle area)

Bibliography

Books

Blyth, Dale A., and Eugene C. Roehlkepartain. *Healthy Communities, Healthy Youth: How Communities Contribute to Positive Youth Development.* Minneapolis, MN: Search Institute, 1993.

Cave, George, Hans Bos, Fred Doolittle, and Cyril Toussaint. *JOBSTART: Final Report on a Program for School Dropouts.* New York, NY: Manpower Demonstration Research Corporation, October 1993.

Embry, Dennis D. *Reducing Youth Violent Crime by 50% with Proven Research-Based Interventions through a Community-Wide, Partnership Approach.* Atlanta, GA: U.S. Centers for Disease Control and Prevention, 1994.

Jackson, Gail, ed. *Exemplary Programs in Criminal Justice: Innovations at the Local Level.* Washington, DC: National League of Cities, 1994.

Jones, Michael A., and Barry Krisberg. *Images and Reality: Juvenile Crime Youth Violence and Public Policy.* San Francisco, CA: National Council on Crime and Delinquency, June 1994.

Krisberg, Barry. *Juvenile Justice: Improving the Quality of Care.* San Francisco, CA: National Council on Crime and Delinquency, 1992.

Kyle, John E., ed. *Children, Families and Cities: Programs that Work at the Local Level.* Washington, DC: National League of Cities, 1987.

Lofquist, William A. *The Technology of Prevention Workbook.* Tucson, AZ: AYD Publications, 1989.

McCarthy, William H., David R. Jones, R. Leo Penne, and Lucy R. Watkins. *Reducing Urban Unemployment: What Works at the Local Level.* Washington, DC: National League of Cities, October 1985.

Mendel, Richard A. *Prevention or Pork? A Hard-Headed Look at Youth-Oriented Anti-Crime Programs.* Washington, DC: American Youth Policy Forum, 1995.

Sundlee, Craig A., and Willie Stapp. *Youth Action Teams: A Primer for Youth Participation.* San Rafael, CA: Social Action Research Center, 1979.

Periodicals

Allen, Pam. The Gould-Wysinger Awards: A Tradition of Excellence. *OJJDP Model Programs 1993.* U.S. Department of Justice, Office of Juvenile Justice and Delinquency Prevention, February 1994.

Answers to Kid Crime. *USA Today,* 22 February 1995, p. 10A.

Drugs, Delinquency, and Other Data. *Juvenile Justice,* Office of Juvenile Justice and Delinquency Prevention, Spring–Summer 1994.

Family and Youth Services Bureau. *Connections: FYSB Youth Gang Prevention Program Update,* Summer 1994.

Henderson, Andre. The Graffiti War. *Governing,* August 1994, pp. 40–44.

Lemov, Penelope. The Assault on Juvenile Justice. *Governing,* December 1994, pp. 26–31.

Meyer, David, and John E. Kyle. Survey Clarifies Ways To Steer At-Risk Youths Toward Future Success. *Nation's Cities Weekly,* 9 January 1995, p. 6.

Mitchel, Leslie. Healthy Families America: Preventing Abuse by Supporting Parents. *Violence Update,* October 1994.

Petersilia, Joan. Crime and Punishment in California: Full Cells, Empty Pockets, and Questionable Benefits. *California Policy Seminar Brief,* May 1993.

Prisons No Cure for Young Criminals. *Florida Sentinel,* 16 January 1995.

Stepp, Laura Sessions. The Crackdown on Juvenile Crime: Do Stricter Laws Deter Youths? *Washington Post,* 15 October 1994, p. A1.

Youth Employment. *Home Front,* U.S. Department of Housing and Urban Development, Washington, DC, Summer 1994.

Public Documents

American Bar Association. *Just Solutions: A Program Guide to Innovative Justice System Improvements.* 1994.

American Youth Policy Forum. *Prevention or Pork? A Hard-Headed Look at Youth-Oriented Anticrime Programs.* Washington, DC, 1995.

Annie E. Casey Foundation. *The Plain Talk Planning Year: Mobilizing Communities to Change.* Spring 1995.

Carnegie Council on Adolescent Development. *Consultation on Afterschool Programs.* Washington, DC, 1994.

Center for the Study of Policy Attitudes. *Fighting Poverty in America: A Study of American Public Attitudes.* Washington, DC, December 1994.

Citizens Committee for New York City Neighborhood Anticrime Center. *How To Start a Youth-Run Peer Counseling Project.* New York.

Commonwealth Fund. *Pilot Survey of Young African-American Males in Four Cities.* New York, March 1994.

Developmental Research and Programs. *Communities that Care.* Seattle, WA, 1993.

Governor's Council on Adolescent Pregnancy. *Prevention Strategies.* Baltimore, MD, March 1992.

Majority Staff of the Senate Judiciary Committee. *Catalogue of Hope: Crime Prevention Programs for At-Risk Children.* Washington, DC, April 1994.

National Association for the Advancement of Colored People. *Youth at Risk: A Community Re-entry Program.* Fort Lauderdale, FL.

National Center For Education Statistics. *Dropout Rates in the United States: 1993.* Washington, DC, 1993.

National Crime Prevention Council. *Changing Perspectives: Youth as Resources.* Washington, DC, 1990.

National Crime Prevention Council. *Charting Success: A Workbook for Developing Crime Prevention and Other Community Service Projects.* Washington, DC, 1992.

National Crime Prevention Council. *Given the Opportunity: How Three Communities Engaged Teens as Resources in Drug Abuse Prevention.* Washington, DC, 1992.

National Institute of Justice. *Boot Camps for Adult and Juvenile Offenders: Overview and Update.* Washington, DC, October 1994.

National League of Cities. *Education: Everybody's Business.* Washington, DC, 1992.

National League of Cities. *The State of America's Cities: The Eleventh Annual Opinion Survey of Municipal Elected Officials.* Washington, DC, January 1995.

National Parks and Recreation Association. *Beyond "Fun and Games": Emerging Roles of Public Recreation.* Arlington, VA, October 1994.

Office of the Attorney General. State of Texas. *Juvenile Justice Handbook for Cities: How the System Works and Resources for Texas Cities to Combat Juvenile Crime.* Austin, TX, September 1994.

Office of the Attorney General. State of Texas. *The Texas Attorney General's Model Program Report: 1994 Criminal Justice Award Winners.* Austin, TX, Summer 1994.

Task Force on Youth Development and Community Programs. *A Matter of Time: Risk and Opportunity in the Nonschool Hours.* New York, NY: Carnegie Corporation, December 1992.

U.S. Attorney's Office. Cedar Rapids Youth Leadership Program (CRYLP). *Resource Fair Program Summaries: Building Justice in Our Communities.* Washington, DC, October 1994, pp. 17–18.

U.S. Attorney's Office. Onondaga County Youth Courts. *Resource Fair Program Summaries: Building Justice in Our Communities.* Washington, DC, October 1994, pp. 31–32.

U.S. Department of Housing and Urban Development. Office of Policy Development and Research. Office of Public and Indian Housing. *Together We Can . . . Meet the Challenge: Law Enforcement Strategies and Practices to Eliminate Drugs in Public Housing.* Washington, DC, March 1994.

U.S. Department of Justice. Bureau of Justice Statistics. *Highlights from 20 Years of Surveying Crime Victims: The National Crime Victimization Survey, 1973–1992.* Washington, DC, October 1993.

U.S. Department of Justice. National Institute of Justice. *Reducing School Crime and Student Misbehavior: A Problem-Solving Strategy.* Washington, DC, June 1986.

U.S. Department of Justice. National Institute of Justice. *Street Gangs: Current Knowledge and Strategies.* Washington, DC, August 1993.

U.S. Department of Justice. Office of Juvenile Justice and Delinquency Prevention. *Comprehensive Strategy for Serious, Violent, and Chronic Juvenile Offenders.* Washington, DC, December 1993.

U.S. Department of Justice. Office of Juvenile Justice and Delinquency Prevention. *Fact Sheet #12: Gangs.* Washington, DC, April 1994.

U.S. Department of Justice. Office of Juvenile Justice and Delinquency Prevention. *Office of Juvenile Justice and Delinquency Prevention: 1993 Annual Report.* Washington, DC, 1993.

U.S. Department of Justice. Office of Juvenile Justice and Delinquency Prevention. *OJJDP Model Programs 1990: Preserving Families To Prevent Delinquency.* Washington, DC, April 1992.

U.S. Department of Justice. Office of Juvenile Justice and Delinquency Prevention. *What Works: Promising Interventions in Juvenile Justice.* Pittsburgh, PA, October 1994.

U.S. Department of Justice. Law-Related Education National Training and Dissemination Program. *Law-Related Education for Juvenile Justice Settings.* Washington, DC, 1993.

Western Regional Center. *Sharing Your Success: Summaries of Successful Programs and Strategies Supporting Drug-Free Schools and Communities.* Portland, OR, August 1991.

Youth Alive. *Teens on Target: Youth Advocates for Violence Prevention.* Oakland, CA.

Youth Employment. *Home Front,* U.S. Department of Housing and Urban Development, Washington, DC, Summer 1994.

Law Enforcement—Community Links

Traditionally, relationships between the community and law enforcement were based in a reactive philosophy: The police responded to crimes as quickly as possible, instead of attempting to forge proactive partnerships to prevent crime before it happened.

Protecting the public against crime is most effective when residents cooperate to identify and prevent the most pressing problems in their area. Bringing the police into contact with the neighborhoods that they serve can forge positive relations based on trust, helping reduce resident fear of crime while improving the ability of officers to work with communities to solve crimes when they happen.

Law enforcement must be responsive to the crime problems identified by the community, if a strong partnership is to exist. This partnership can be built through regular meetings, in which residents discuss crime problems and possible solutions with local officers. In order to ensure the success of this approach, officers must demonstrate that they are taking the recommendations of the citizens seriously and eager to work in partnership.

The Board of Young Adult Police Commissioners in New Haven, Connecticut, has improved relations between youth and police officers and has a youth advisory voice for the Chief of Police. Other areas have instituted public meetings on a regular basis to ensure that police respond to the greatest concerns of their communities. A program in Maryland created by the U.S. Attorney brings citizens into contact with professionals in the legal community to ensure that the limited resources of the criminal justice system are used in ways in which they can make the greatest impact.

Outreach programs to specific groups can restore a sense of community and reduce the antagonism between the police and disaffected populations. Law enforcement-supported work with youth and gang members through social activities—such as sports or after-school programs—provides positive alternative activity and can help prevent violence and gang involvement. A Dorchester, Massachusetts, program that organizes activities between youth and officers has resulted in a decline in juvenile violent crime.

Increased police patrolling of public housing areas reduced crime by 25 percent in one complex in North Carolina, while other programs have established police-sponsored activities to prevent youth in public housing from turning to gangs for social activity. Police substations—police mini-departments in areas with above-average crime rates—have also proven effective in reducing the incidence of crime and the social deterioration associated with it.

Police can also facilitate the development of community organizations that recognize, report, and act to reduce crime. Citizen patrol groups, for example, can prove effective in establishing channels of cooperation between law enforcement and local residents. Citizen patrol groups establish a strategy of community policing in which residents and businesses monitor their areas for suspicious activity and contact police when they observe irregular or potentially criminal conditions. This program strikes an ideal partnership between citizens and the police, giving the public a sense of control over its area while bringing in the police before residents resort to vigilantism. At the same time, police response time to crimes is improved by the active monitoring of neighborhoods. A community policing program in Fort Worth, Texas, reduced crime by almost 25 percent.

Police agencies can also encourage citizen grassroots organizations that mobilize to prevent crime. When local groups identify a problem, the police can assist by providing enforcement and information. Citizens who take it upon themselves to counsel troubled youths, for instance, can receive police assistance in identifying the parts of their city where help is most needed. Law enforcement can provide grassroots groups with statistical and informational assistance, while also publicizing local causes. MAD DADS (Men Against Destruction: Defending Against Drugs and Social Disorder)—a grassroots organization in Omaha, Nebraska—cooperated with police to reduce gang-related killings to zero in just one year of operation.

Another measure to increase resident cooperation with law enforcement, surveys reveal vital information about the public's perceptions of the court system. Feedback from members of the public who participate in the court process allows the justice system to improve court services; positive responses to complaints about the court system also increase citizens' faith in the legal system. Other actions undertaken to increase the ease with which the court system can be used—such as information telephone lines that make courts more user-friendly—help to demystify the legal process and allow those who have to enter a courtroom to do so with a positive impression. A municipal court in Portage County, Ohio, produced informational pamphlets to explain courtroom procedure, increasing the accessibility of the legal system.

Law enforcement can also cooperate with other governmental agencies in the community to overcome crime threats. Working with social service agencies in areas plagued by crime brings needed attention to neighborhoods that are often suffering from extensive neglect. The police can also cooperate with regulatory agencies to counter areas of suspected criminal activity; municipal ordinances of health and safety departments can often force deteriorating areas that are vulnerable to crime to clean up. In Oakland, California, the police worked with state regulatory agencies to shut down or destroy over 200 buildings that had been exploited for illegal businesses and criminal purposes.

The thirty-five strategies in this chapter explore the following approaches to crime prevention:

- successful community policing strategies and other ways law enforcement can build trust and partnerships with residents;

- community policing and problem-solving methods to identify and address community concerns about crime, violence, gangs, and substance abuse; and

- officer training to be sensitive to the needs of the area.

Reinforcing the public stake in taking care of the community can best be achieved through cooperation with police that balances crime and safety concerns while maximizing the efficiency of police resources. Partnerships in which citizens feel involved in the actions of law enforcement agencies create the best prospects for successful crime prevention and reduction.

Community Building Through Mobilization

Strategy

As part of a comprehensive community-building strategy, law enforcement can take active measures to help mobilize the community to decrease its vulnerability to crime.

Crime Problem Addressed

Communities that mobilize to work in partnership with law enforcement can decrease crime, decrease the fear of crime, contribute to a secure environment for residents, and develop a healthy working relationship between residents and the police. With this partnership as a basis, other community-building activities can contribute to the social and economic health of the community.

Key Components

Community mobilization often hinges on a crisis or upon an incident in a community that brings residents together in shared anxiety, fear, or rage. Turning these emotions into action takes leadership, coordination, focus, direction, and planning, as well as expertise on the part of community institutions such as law enforcement. Following the initial burst of interest, community mobilizers should gather a group of leaders representing a wide range of interests and population groups. This planning group must reach consensus on the nature of the problem and the most effective solutions.

Resources—both funds and volunteers—can strengthen the mobilization campaign. Shared communication is also key for a successful strategy to cause change in a community. Some communities have mobilized solely for the purpose of distributing accurate information about a specific problem. Others have formed long-term anticrime groups, such as Neighborhood Watch, Block Watch, or Crime Watch.

Key Partnerships

Although the community often takes the lead, law enforcement and other community agencies—such as regulatory, health department, code enforcement, and transportation agencies—can serve as effective partners. Youth frequently bring tremendous enthusiasm and energy to a community mobilization project and should not be overlooked as a valuable resource. Religious groups can contribute both volunteers and meeting space.

Potential Obstacles

Long-term community mobilization groups have to address several obstacles. Often volunteer leaders and workers suffer from burn-out, the end of enthusiasm and energy for a specific activity. To reduce burn-out, members should be involved in other types of activities such as citywide food and clothing drives; workshops on violence, rape prevention and self-defense; welcome committees for new neighbors; or volunteer work with shelters or food banks. A remedy for Block Captain burn-out is to ask someone else to co-chair and divide the responsibilities.

A second obstacle can be the size of the groups. One Neighborhood Watch organization in Newport News, Virginia, reports that 35 homes is a manageable number. If the group expands, they can no longer meet in residents' homes or backyards.

Signs of Success

In eleven months, the Oakland (California) Crack Task Force—a committee initially mobilized because of the scourge of crack houses in their neighborhoods—reached over 8,000 residents with information on crack, family addiction, and AIDS. Based on early successes, the group is now providing broad-based education services and a network for collaboration among community groups, government agencies, law enforcement, religious institutions, and the private sector.

Applying the Strategy

Residents of Oakland, California, knew the city was in crisis when drug use—especially of crack cocaine—rose more than 2,200 percent over a ten-year period. The drug culture had affected over 70 percent of students in grades seven through twelve. Thousands of women of child-bearing age were using drugs. The need for education and action was clear, and the residents responded by convening the area's top experts to meet the challenge. The group has chosen knowledge as its primary force against the problem and has successfully brought antidrug education and drug prevention programs to thousands of Oakland residents.

In Newport News, Virginia, the Newport News Coalition received funding from the County Council because of its success in rejuvenating area Neighborhood Watch groups. In mid-1994, the Coalition comprised 220 active Neighborhood Watch groups with 18,000 members.

Contact Information

Director
Oakland Community Partnership
440 Grand Avenue, Suite 210
Oakland, California 94610
510-251-6344

Newport News Crime Watch Coalition
P.O. Box 6361
Newport News, Virginia 23606

Newport News Police Department
Community and Public Affairs
2600 Washington Avenue
Newport News, Virginia 23607
804-247-8786

Cooperate With Grassroots Organizations To Address Problems

Strategy

Law enforcement works collaboratively with existing grassroots community action organizations to focus on specific local problems.

Crime Problem Addressed

When law enforcement supports the community-building efforts of an existing organization, the community benefits from a stronger network built on citizen concern and law enforcement expertise. Law enforcement can collaborate with grassroots groups by providing information and professional support, thus strengthening the bond between law enforcement and the community.

Key Components

In order for this law enforcement strategy to work effectively, law enforcement should support the goals and activities of the existing organization. Law enforcement can help community groups by educating them about crime prevention techniques and methods of reporting crime and drug activity. Existing community groups can rely on law enforcement for increased attention to local "hot spot" areas and as a source of useful crime data. Law enforcement can also support existing groups at special community events, neighborhood meetings, and community patrols. Publicity and community information-sharing about local crime problems and anticrime campaigns are also valuable to increase support.

Key Partnerships

Law enforcement can work in a supportive partnership with local chapters of large national organizations, such as Mothers Against Drunk Driving, as well as with small local groups of parents, neighbors, youth, business owners, or others who have organized to address and resolve one or more specific identified community problems. Local media and business can serve as partners by publicizing efforts and successes and by donating resources to a local campaign. Parent groups, such as the Parent Teacher Association (PTA), and local service clubs are valuable support partners.

Potential Obstacles

When grassroots community groups mobilize to focus on concerns such as increased drug activity, speeding traffic, or vandalism, they usually request the assistance of law enforcement or other municipal agencies. If asked to work with an existing group, law enforcement must be careful not to interrupt or slow community momentum by ignoring community leaders, assuming the lead, and leaving the community behind. Within reasonable safety guidelines, law enforcement should provide supportive expertise, while permitting the organization to be responsible for directing a local anticrime campaign.

Signs of Success

Collaboration between law enforcement and existing community organizations usually brings success both in re-

solving local problems and in strengthening bonds between the community and law enforcement. In Omaha, Nebraska, collaboration between a concerned group of fathers and the local police resulted in cutting gang-related killings from thirteen in one year to zero the next and in removing 2,500 firearms from a community in three years.

A group of concerned African-American men mobilized to help make schools and neighborhoods safer for their children. Men Against Destruction: Defending Against Drugs and Social Disorder (MAD DADS) assumed the roles of mentors, social chaperons, community protectors, and street counselors. They have worked with law enforcement to remove gang activity, decrease drug sales and use, assist runaways, and discourage illegal behavior among youth through visits to local jails and prisons. Since its inception in Omaha, MAD DADS has expanded to twenty-three other communities.

Applying the Strategy

Residents of a Waterloo, Iowa, neighborhood enlisted the support of police to close down bars that had been selling alcohol to minors. They transformed one abandoned bar into a recreation center for area youth.

The Sunset Park neighborhood in New York City attacked the problem of prostitutes by petitioning police and city officials for help and by writing to the prostitutes' customers (using addresses gained from license plate numbers) to threaten them with exposure and prosecution. The effort resulted in more than 700 arrests and longer jail terms for prostitution.

Contact Information

President
MAD DADS
3030 Sprague Street
Omaha, Nebraska 68111
402-451-3500

Analyze Crime Data To Focus Resources on Local Problems

Strategy

Law enforcement can gather and analyze crime data from the community to focus resources on specific local trends and problems.

Crime Problem Addressed

Communities have increased confidence and trust in their criminal justice system when law enforcement takes a

proactive approach to a series of specific problems, rather than responding to individual crime incidents as separate unrelated events. Police crime analysis experts can document and assess specific community crime problems through closer communication and information-sharing between law enforcement and community residents.

Key Components

Effective crime data analysis requires accurate and thorough data-gathering techniques:

- monitoring daily police reports and calls for service;

- surveying community residents and businesses;

- interviewing social services and other agencies;

- analyzing arrest reports; and

- documenting crime activity through videotapes and other surveillance.

Officers should receive special training in effective data gathering. Analysis of the data can pinpoint when and where identified types of crimes are occurring, permitting police to tailor responses—and prevention techniques—to the problem. Community cooperation and involvement are critical elements of gathering crime data and helping to implement such effective solutions as establishing a high-visibility community patrol, strengthening Neighborhood Watch programs, convening a drug-abatement task force, or conducting community meetings.

Key Partnerships

In order to gather accurate data for crime analysis and problem solving, neighborhood patrol officers must work closely with community residents, business owners and staff, and other people who observe activities within a neighborhood or community. Information from other municipal agencies—such as code enforcement, housing, and transportation—can augment crime data and help pinpoint causes and trends.

Potential Obstacles

Inaccurate reporting is a prime problem when law enforcement gathers data from individual area residents. In some communities, law enforcement has trained citizens how to observe for certain details when viewing suspicious or criminal activity. A second obstacle is the tendency to reach a conclusion before all data have been analyzed. It is better to wait until the full range of information has been collected before action is prescribed.

Signs of Success

Police intervention in a California urban business area plagued with crime resulted in decreased crime and increased business, according to post-intervention surveys. With effective data-gathering and analysis, police were able to address the problem successfully. One restaurant reported that sales had gone up by 50 percent after the police had removed the source of the problem. A review of statistics showed that property crimes had decreased and shoplifting arrests increased. The business owners formed an association and now meet regularly with law enforcement to discuss areas of mutual concern.

When businesses in the Harbor Plaza section of Santa Ana, California, complained to police that criminal activity was having a detrimental impact on their sales, law enforcement collected information and implemented a directed response, based on the area's crime data. Relying on data gathered from the community, police focused attention on the increased transient and homeless population that was illegally panhandling around stores and restaurants, driving off customers. The police implemented a five-phase response, ridding the area of the problem and restoring healthy sales and customer confidence to local businesses.

Applying the Strategy

The police department in Tucson, Arizona, developed a systems approach to policing, based on systematic analysis of data gathered from the departments of sanitation, transportation, housing, planning, and parks and recreation. This information was supplemented by surveys of school officials, religious leaders, and business people. The police department was able to pinpoint problems, such as a rash of burglaries occurring in some neighborhoods, and devise a strategy to intervene.

Contact Information

City of Santa Ana Police Department
24 Civic Center Plaza
P.O. Box 1981
Santa Ana, California 92702
714-647-5061

Police Sponsorship of Positive Activities for Youth

Strategy

Law enforcement officers and other members of the criminal justice system can develop mutual trust with community youth by spending time with them in activities that provide healthy alternatives to violence and crime on the street.

Crime Problem Addressed

Young people, particularly teens, are often hostile to law enforcement officers, seeing them as "the authorities" or as adults who get involved only when there is trouble. Law enforcement and other criminal justice system members can face a substantial challenge when trying to develop close bonds with young people. However, a strong police-youth link can help young people make healthy anticrime, antidrug choices.

Key Components

Young people are more likely to accept the friendship and counsel of members of the criminal justice system within a social or activity-oriented environment, such as in a youth center or on a sports field. Trust and integrity are critical to the success of a police-youth relationship, although sometimes trust is slow to develop. Law enforcement can nurture trust through honesty, shared experiences, and mutual respect. Once trust is established, young people are more likely to accept personal and family-related advice, tutoring and other educational assistance, job counseling, and health information and guidance.

Key Partnerships

Young people can benefit from a strong link with all members of the criminal justice system as well as with other elements of the community, such as media, business leaders, neighborhood leaders, health professionals, and others. These partnerships are more likely to flourish where young people feel at home, such as youth activity centers or other community gathering places. A shared activity or experience is often the linchpin of a successful youth-adult relationship.

Potential Obstacles

Just as trust is the backbone of a solid relationship, breach of trust can irreparably ruin a relationship between a young person and an adult. Members of the criminal justice system who choose to work closely with young people must be honest, loyal, and trustworthy as well as serve as role models for high integrity and moral standards. It is also critical to honor commitments; disappointment is a difficult challenge for young people.

Signs of Success

In many communities, law enforcement officers have been able to develop successful relationships with young people by working with them after school, in the evenings with youth clubs, or on weekends for special outings. By eliminating the "threatening" aspect of the police presence, law enforcement officers have succeeded in teaching young people about the dangers of gangs, violence, drugs, AIDS, and other problems. According to a spokesman for one after-school drop-in youth program, "a new level of communication between police and the youth has been one of the highlights of the program."

Crime rates among youth have declined in Dorchester, Massachusetts, where police officers are regular members of the Dorchester Youth Collaborative, a youth center that is participating in a police-community partnership. The officers have broken down barriers with the youth by joining them in basketball games, working with them on weight lifting, and accompanying them on field trips. Having gained their trust, the officers can teach youth to resolve problems and mediate with other youth, instead of resorting to violence.

Applying the Strategy

In Portland, Oregon, the police department established a Police Activities League (PAL) with other law enforcement agencies, businesses, and individuals. They conduct year-round sports events to reduce gang and drug activities among the community's youth.

Houston established its Police Athletic League in 1983. The popular program operates in partnership with area professional sports teams, local churches, the Boys & Girls Club, the Chicano Family Center, and the city's Parks and Recreation Department. The League provides sports programs, educational field trips, and community service projects, reaching close to 1,000 youth, ages ten to seventeen, each year.

Contact Information

Executive Director
Dorchester Youth Collaborative
1514-A Dorchester Avenue
Dorchester, Massachusetts 02122
617-288-1748

Citizen Patrol

Strategy

Law enforcement can train citizens to monitor and report unsafe or suspicious conditions in their own neighborhoods through citizen patrol groups.

Crime Problem Addressed

If citizens feel empowered to make a difference, they will be willing to cooperate with law enforcement to rid their area of crime. This police-community link ensures that specific neighborhood problems are addressed and resolved and that neighborhoods employ prevention techniques to deter crime from returning.

Key Components

Police train volunteer neighborhood patrol groups to drive or walk through neighborhoods; the patrol groups use portable radios to relay information to a group leader or directly to police about criminal activity, code violations, graffiti, and drug or gang activity. It is important for patrol groups to meet regularly to discuss schedules and other organizational details. In some communities, volunteers ride with patrol officers and attend patrol workshops to train for the program.

Key Partnerships

All residents who are responsible members of a neighborhood can team up with law enforcement in a volunteer citizen patrol group. Police patrol officers and training personnel should work closely with citizen volunteers, who can be elderly residents; members of a church, synagogue or other religious institution; members of ethnic organizations; a group of parents; or a teen service club. The media can be partners, bringing public attention to the problems and the patrol's success.

Potential Obstacles

Several challenges can affect the success of a citizen patrol group. If the group is not properly trained, some of its members can become too vigilant in their efforts to decrease specific problems. It is critical that patrol members follow specific procedures, focusing on observation and reporting. Patrol members who conduct themselves irresponsibly should be assigned to other activities, sent for retraining, or requested to leave the patrol.

Signs of Success

Crime reports from the Federal Bureau of Investigation for 1993 showed that Fort Worth, Texas, reported a 24 percent drop in crime, credited in part to the citizen patrol program. Police captain Randy Ely of Fort Worth noted the group, Citizens on Patrol (COP), has "helped improve police response time and ensure [the police] have the right resources dispatched to a crime scene. But as importantly, [our citizen patrol] has created a method for residents to make a significant contribution to crime prevention."

COP has made life safer in some Fort Worth, Texas, neighborhoods. More than 2,200 volunteers in ninety-six of the city's neighborhoods take part in the program that is being given credit for reversing crime trends. Members—who undergo twelve hours of training—wear identification badges, T-shirts, hats, and jackets with the COP logo.

Applying the Strategy

In Chicago, the Edgewater neighborhood faced a serious arson problem in an area of rundown and abandoned buildings. Residents agreed to organize and patrol areas where buildings might be subject to arson (backed up by communication through two-way and citizens band radios) and report suspicious activity to the police.

In Washington, DC, the Cabbies on Patrol program solicited help from taxi drivers in reporting crime. Police developed a reward program if an arrest resulted from a cab driver's observations about crime or planned crime (drivers report to 911 or the program's special number).

Contact Information

Fort Worth Police Department
350 West Belknap Street
Fort Worth, Texas 76101
817-877-8023

Partnership With Residents of Public Housing

Strategy

Law enforcement can demonstrate its commitment to safety in public housing by becoming acquainted with residents and implementing crime intervention and prevention programs that address needs identified by residents.

Crime Problem Addressed

Public housing complexes can present special security and safety challenges due to large, often transient populations; unsupervised young people; clusters of newly settled immigrant populations; few play areas or youth resources; and structural or maintenance problems.

Key Components

A link between law enforcement and public housing residents must be built upon a visible and highly responsive police presence in public housing. Many cities are assigning regular police foot patrols to be available to public housing residents for a wide range of services, including organizing residents in citizen crime prevention patrols and attending residents' association meetings. Some patrol officers live in the public housing units they cover, increasing their social and informal contact with residents. In housing units with large groups of refugees or immigrants, law enforcement can work with special service agencies to help youth and families in need of assistance with language problems; practical day-to-day activities such as grocery shopping; crime prevention and personal safety; and social adjustment in their new surroundings.

Key Partnerships

A multiagency partnership—including law enforcement, the housing authority, and resettlement and social services—can establish and sustain a program to address the wide variety of needs of public housing residents. Additionally, law enforcement and public housing residents can work together more effectively if they have the cooperation of local resident leaders, such as tenant association officials, as well as housing management. When working with ethnic groups, it is critical to have an influential member of the group serve as liaison to law enforcement and housing authorities.

Potential Obstacles

A serious obstacle to success in public housing programs is the residents' feeling that the crime problem is too pervasive and overwhelming, that residents are powerless to make a change. This concern can be addressed by starting with a small program: Choose a manageable activity, such as cleaning up trash in a nearby playground, that will have guaranteed success. The program can then build on that success once the residents realize that they can make a difference.

Multicultural tension can also create problems within a housing area. Law enforcement officers can begin by getting young people of all ethnic backgrounds together on a sports field or at a picnic. Children who are friends often encourage their parents to become acquainted. Sharing a common goal, such as beautifying a building or campaigning for better hall lighting, can also bring ethnically diverse families together.

Signs of Success

In a public housing complex in North Carolina, law enforcement worked in partnership with residents to decrease drug activity, arrest dealers, and bar nonresidents from the property. After the cooperative program had been in effect for several months, calls to police from the public housing residents fell by 25 percent. Attitudes about safety and the police have also improved.

In 1990, Greenville, North Carolina, police launched community partnership programs in six public housing communities by having specially assigned officers go door to door to collect information from residents. The department established a police office at one of the housing complexes to demonstrate its long-term commitment to the residents. After several years of collaborative effort between police and residents, drug activity has been replaced by basketball teams, Boy Scout and Girl Scout troops, and a baseball league.

Applying the Strategy

In Honolulu, the police department has worked collaboratively with the Interagency Council for Immigrant Services to address specific problems of ethnic groups in public housing. They hold classes, teaching basic skills such as banking and shopping, as well as dispute resolution techniques. In return, police recruits receive cultural sensitivity training from members of the ethnic groups.

In Louisville, Kentucky, police have established ministations in several public housing facilities. The stations provide an opportunity for increased positive contact between police and residents.

Contact Information

Program Coordinator
Greenville Housing Authority
1710 West Third Street
Greenville, North Carolina 27834
919-830-4073

Informational Resources Section
Honolulu Police Department
801 South Beretania Street
Honolulu, Hawaii 96813
808-529-3351

Positive Youth Interaction With the Criminal Justice System

Strategy

Young people can feel empowered to address crime problems in their communities through formal communication with police policymakers and the judicial system.

Crime Problem Addressed

Often young people feel alienated from the decision-making that affects their lives and their communities. By opening the doors for a formal collaboration between the criminal justice system and youth, communities can tap into a valuable resource for anticrime and antidrug prevention ideas.

Key Components

A collaborative partnership that encourages young people to learn about the judicial system should involve observation, education, and participation at all stages of the system. Students can spend time in a busy law office with an attorney or law clerk willing to explain the impact of different legal situations. Court personnel can walk students through courtroom procedures and permit them to observe a trial. In some cases, young people have been appointed or elected to a youth police board where they can formally conduct meetings, debate issues, research and gather information, and present policy advisories on matters concerning youth and police in the community. Students can then report back to their classrooms and disseminate information to their peers.

Key Partnerships

School personnel can work with the mayor, chief of police, district attorney, local judges, and corrections officials to set up a program that will expose high school students to the day-to-day operations in all phases of the criminal justice system. This partnership not only increases a young person's knowledge about the judicial system in the community, it also strengthens the bond between the judicial and school systems.

Potential Obstacles

At the practical level, time is a serious challenge to any adult-youth educational program. In order for a young person to learn about the criminal justice system, judicial officials and staff must set aside time from their daily professional obligations—a requirement that can be diffi-cult to meet. Additionally, adults working with youth must take the young people seriously. If they feel that they are being patronized or that the adult is not genuinely interested in their concerns, the youth will lose interest in the program. Adults must learn to view youth as a valuable resource in the community.

Signs of Success

In New Haven, Connecticut, the city's 22-member Board of Young Adult Police Commissioners has developed a position on city curfew for youth; organized a focus group on drugs and violence for the Chief of Police in all six public high schools; successfully lobbied the state legislature to preserve and expand adolescent alcohol and drug treatment programs; and successfully raised funds to support an AIDS hospice program for adolescents.

Its membership is drawn from a cross-section of the city's neighborhoods: One member is elected from each of the city's six high schools, and sixteen members are appointed by the Mayor. Although the group has no formal policymaking power, the department does listen to its recommendations. This formal link between law enforcement and young people in the community has improved relations in New Haven.

Applying the Strategy

The Los Angeles Municipal Court arranges for tenth- and eleventh-grade students at James Monroe High School to experience their city's judicial system. Students work with judges, attorneys, and other judicial employees, viewing the court system in action.

Contact Information

Community Youth Coordinator
New Haven Police Department
One Union Avenue
New Haven, Connecticut 06519
203-946-6276

Director
Public Affairs Office
Los Angeles County Courthouse
110 North Grand Avenue
Los Angeles, California 90012
213-974-6358

Support Vulnerable Members of the Community

Strategy

Law enforcement can work directly with the community members who are most vulnerable to crime to create innovative, prevention-oriented solutions to specific crime problems.

Crime Problem Addressed

Special populations—such as the elderly, the handicapped, retirees, or people on public assistance—are often particularly vulnerable to crime's effects. These residents feel they have a greater stake in their communities when they can contribute to the prevention or solution of neighborhood problems that affect them. A joint problem-solving effort contributes to improved relations between police and the citizens with special needs whom they serve.

Key Components

An effective, collaborative prevention or problem-solving effort depends strongly on clear and accurate communication between residents and the police. Residents must understand the limits of their power to take action to resolve a problem. Police must understand the fears and concerns of the residents. A successful partnership balances the ideas and suggestions of the residents with law enforcement's authority to make substantive changes. Frequently, a joint problem-solving collaboration results in innovative and unique strategies.

Key Partnerships

All members of a neighborhood or community can help law enforcement with local crime prevention or problem-solving. Usually, the segment of the community most affected by a crime will work closely with law enforcement; however, other community residents—such as business owners, students and members of the school system, the elderly, and physically challenged residents—have successfully collaborated with law enforcement to create safer communities. In some cities, local chapters of national organizations, such as the American Association of Retired Persons, have been involved with community-law enforcement collaborative crime prevention efforts.

Potential Obstacles

Special populations—such as the elderly, the handicapped, and retirees dependent on receiving checks through the mail—are often reluctant to seek special assistance for personal safety problems. They may feel that they have little power and control over their circumstances and that there are no solutions to their problems. Local law enforcement can address these fears by talking with organizations, addressing the problems of special populations, and encouraging them to work with police to reduce their victimization.

Signs of Success

Since 1985, the Warminster Township (Pennsylvania) Police Department has worked to train the Neighborhood Watch group. Volunteers in the group:

- held workshops in the neighborhoods;

- distributed crime prevention educational materials;

- visited shut-ins;

- developed a video on personal safety for the disabled; and

- helped deaf, blind, and senior residents of the community.

Applying the Strategy

The Binghamton (New York) Police Department set up Stranger Danger and Child Molestation programs for physically and mentally challenged children at area summer camps and schools. Local restaurants, the television station, and a theater owner support the program, which provides McGruff presentations with messages to reinforce self-esteem and reduce vulnerability. The department has uncovered several cases of abuse, resulting in arrests or protective orders.

In 1993, the seventh police district in Chicago became the first in the nation to house a bank's automatic teller machine (ATM). Vulnerable residents in the district, many of whom use the convenient ATM system for currency exchange, had been frequent victims of robbery after receiving their money. The police station ATM was the idea of District Commander Ronnie Watson, who approached officials at Chicago's Marquette Bank. Bank officials, residents, and law enforcement have promoted use of the new ATM, teaching other residents how to use it. Community leaders also see the new machine as an economic opportunity for residents in the seventh district. The Monroe Foundation, a nonprofit agency that supports community development initiatives, sees the idea as increasing access to banking in a traditionally underserved community.

Contact Information

Chief
Warminster Township Police Department
Bucks County
Henry and Gibson Avenues
Philadelphia, Pennsylvania 18974
215-443-5000

Training in Prevention for Other Local Agencies

Strategy

Law enforcement will experience greater cooperation and success with crime prevention programs if other municipal agencies can learn prevention principles and techniques and if law enforcement, in turn, can learn about the techniques and goals of other city agencies.

Crime Problem Addressed

Often employees of government agencies work at cross-purposes, primarily because of a lack of communication and understanding of their respective missions and programs. A greater mutual understanding of the roles and activities of different government agencies will eliminate duplication of effort and help to implement and coordinate important community programs.

Key Components

Crime prevention training for non-law enforcement government employees should provide clear instruction on the basic goals and objectives of specific crime prevention activities and programs. The training instructor should have good communication skills and should distribute printed materials. The instructor should define all terms that may be unfamiliar to non-law enforcement personnel and should allow ample time for questions. Similarly, law enforcement officers can benefit from training sessions conducted by city planners, engineers, and transportation officials, among others, whose programs may complement or overlap crime prevention programs.

Key Partnerships

Law enforcement personnel will derive great benefit from a clearer understanding of the programs and techniques of other government agencies, such as the departments of recreation and parks, transportation, social services, city planning, code enforcement, and health.

Potential Obstacles

Several obstacles can interfere with an effort to encourage representatives of municipal agencies to learn more about other agencies' duties and professional techniques. It can be challenging for professionals from diverse disciplines to understand specific terminology and definitions, making

basic professional principles seem foreign. Additionally, there can be turf wars, with battles over agency authority, resources, and areas of expertise. A multiagency summit might require a skilled facilitator to help resolve any difficulties that might arise.

Signs of Success

Law enforcement officers in Ann Arbor, Michigan, who are trained in the principles of Crime Prevention Through Environmental Design (CPTED) have the opportunity to work closely with city planning officials. Using a two-tiered training program, city planners and other non-law enforcement personnel learn about the fundamentals of CPTED in a seminar that presents the strategies of natural access control, natural surveillance, and territorial reinforcement. In return, the crime prevention officers learn the functions and operations of the city planning department and the site plan review process. They also attend review meetings and public hearings and learn to read blueprints. The site plan review process for new buildings is incorporating CPTED principles because trained law enforcement officers are involved in studying the probable impact of the development on crime in the area.

Applying the Strategy

Involving department heads throughout the city has been a hallmark of the community policing program in Hayward, California. The city attorney conducted training for the police department on how her department would work with them to resolve neighborhood problems.

Salt Lake City, Utah, requires all city departments to take responsibility for crime prevention. Total quality control councils throughout city government seek opportunities for non-law enforcement agencies to become involved in crime prevention.

Contact Information

Crime Prevention Unit
Ann Arbor Police Department
100 North Fifth Avenue
Ann Arbor, Michigan 48104
313-994-2979

Community Input on Improving Court Systems

Strategy

By gathering information from citizens, court constituency groups, and professional and non-professional court employees, the court system can learn how to improve court services.

Crime Problem Addressed

Community residents often perceive the court system as inflexible and intimidating. By permitting residents and others to offer opinions and suggestions on court services, the community develops a more positive attitude toward the courts, and the courts can benefit from valuable input from the community.

Key Components

Key to gathering information from the community about the court system is the type of instrument used to solicit opinions and data. Several types of survey instruments, or less formal information-gathering devices, can be used, such as telephone surveys, exit surveys of court users, suggestion boxes, and focus group interviews of court users and employees. The data must be classified accurately and interpreted by analysts with competency in surveying and in the procedures of the court system. Following the survey, it is important that resultant changes in the court system be made public.

Key Partnerships

All users of the court system—litigants, jurors, law enforcement officers, witnesses, attorneys, and judges—can benefit from suggestions and ideas from people who have come in contact with local courts. Community residents and court system personnel can work in partnership to devise a system that is more responsive to the community's needs.

Potential Obstacles

A survey to gather information will be most valuable if designed by a professional familiar with court services, as well as with public surveying. A local public surveying firm or university might be willing to assist with designing a court system survey. Once the information is gathered and analyzed, it is critical that court officials make the public aware of changes due directly to comments and suggestions gathered by the survey or interviews.

The court must convince the community that it is willing to make changes, or the public will see the survey as a public relations exercise.

Signs of Success

The nation's first community court, the Midtown Community Court, serves several neighborhoods in Manhattan. The court's Community Advisory Board coordinates outreach to residents and keeps the court aware of community issues. Focus group interviews and surveys that the Board has conducted periodically since the court was established in 1993 reveal that expanded court services—which resulted from community input—have increased residents' knowledge of the court and their satisfaction with how it serves the community. In 1994, the National Association for Court Management awarded the Midtown Community Court the Justice Achievement Award for improved services, constructive sentences, and responsiveness to community input.

Applying the Strategy

The Virginia Judicial Council established the Consumer Research and Service Development Project on recommendation of the Commission on the Future of Virginia's Judicial System. After gathering data from consumers of the state's court system, the Commission found that consumers thought that:

- the courts treated minors unequally;

- litigation was not handled expeditiously;

- the courts needed more effective ways to help citizens understand basic court procedures and services; and

- alternative dispute resolution methods should be used more frequently.

Contact Information

Senior Planning Analyst
Office of the Executive Secretary
Supreme Court of Virginia
100 North Ninth Street
Richmond, Virginia 23219
804-786-6455

Educational Programs About the Court System

Strategy

Courts can become more user-friendly if court personnel take the time to educate the public about terminology, procedures, and expectations.

Crime Problem Addressed

For many people, the prospect of appearing in court is frightening and intimidating. They don't know what to expect or how to behave once they have entered the courtroom. Often, their fear gets in the way of their ability to testify with accuracy and confidence.

Key Components

Educating the public about the court system can be a relatively simple task. Court personnel can produce pamphlets or videos on a variety of topics:

- how to be a good witness;

- citizens' rights;

- types of court cases;

- the appeals process;

- traffic laws;

- juvenile problems; and

- probate laws and procedures.

In court buildings, personnel can erect signs in several languages to direct the public to the appropriate offices, waiting rooms, or courtrooms. In some communities, court clerks have attended seminars to train them how to be more helpful to the public. One state has installed a telephone system that gives citizens who dial a toll-free number access to more than sixty prerecorded messages about the court system.

Key Partnerships

Court employees can meet with members of the community to solicit ideas for making the courts more user-friendly. Experts can help translate key documents and explanatory pamphlets or signs into languages used by ethnic groups in the community. Court personnel can speak to local groups, such as civic groups or community or tenant associations, to try to demystify the court process.

Potential Obstacles

Courts in this country are typically overworked. One serious obstacle to this program can be allocating time to a public educational project. Volunteers could be a valuable asset to portions of this program.

Signs of Success

Just Solutions, an American Bar Association report on successful programs, includes a profile on municipal courts in Michigan, which use a toll-free telephone system for distributing information. Court staff note that people who used Tele-Court before appearing in court are more informed and their requests or procedures are processed more quickly.

Applying the Strategy

The Portage County (Ohio) Municipal Court wanted to have a better image in the community and launched a public information campaign to help people feel less intimidated by the court system. Officials produced a series of 24 pamphlets, written in everyday language, to explain step-by-step the process of court appearances. They also produced public service videos explaining new drivers license and driving-under-the-influence laws. They installed magazine racks and vending machines in public areas for people waiting to go to court. According to the project director, "We believe it is possible to lessen the trauma usually experienced by those who appear in court."

Contact Information

Project Director
Portage County Municipal Court
214 South Water Street
Kent, Ohio 44240
216-678-9100

Law Enforcement Involvement in Schools and Surrounding Areas

Strategy

Law enforcement can work more closely with schools to identify concerns of the neighborhoods that surround schools, student hangouts, parks, and athletic fields.

Crime Problem Addressed

Many young people are wary of developing friendly relationships with law enforcement officers. By working closely with schools and students, law enforcement officers can address not only problems identified by young people, but also those concerns of neighborhoods near schools or areas where young people gather.

Key Components

Some law enforcement agencies assign officers to serve as a liaison with schools (school resource officers) and neighborhoods surrounding schools. Liaison officers maintain contact with school personnel and with student leaders to build trust. Officers often attend PTA meetings and back-to-school or open house events. In some communities, school resource officers have encouraged nearby businesses to participate in mentor or adopt-a-school programs, providing equipment, volunteers, tutors, and other resources. The students then identify that business as a friend to their school, improving school-neighborhood relations.

Key Partnerships

Law enforcement can be effective school-based partners not only with students and teachers, but also with school support staff. For example, school bus drivers are frequently aware of problems in neighborhoods or with young people. Officers can also work closely with parents, neighborhood association leaders, residents, tenant organizations, and businesses that are located near schools.

Potential Obstacles

In some communities, school officials have been reluctant to have uniformed law enforcement personnel present at schools. It may take time to develop a comfortable relationship with school officials and neighborhood residents. One approach is to begin by meeting with officials and neighborhood leaders in an informal setting, just to get acquainted and learn about each other. Developing a mutually beneficial partnership may take several meetings.

Signs of Success

After the tragic murders of five students in 1990, the University of Florida Police, the Alachua County Sheriff's Department, and the Gainesville Police Department formed a partnership to support the "Together for a Safe Campus" program on the Gainesville campus of the university. The campaign enhanced student awareness of security systems already in place:

- rape prevention and personal safety training;

- crime prevention demonstrations;

- "Think Smart" posters;

- an escort service; and

- emergency telephone networks.

Brochures offered students living in dormitories and in off-campus housing a do-it-yourself checklist for security measures. As a result of dramatic changes in student safety prevention behavior, violent crime on campus decreased 26 percent and the crime prevention unit of the university police department remains an important resource for ensuring student safety.

In San Jose, California, an 11 percent drop in reported crime was attributed in part to a community policing program that encouraged officers to spend more time at school with students. This program started because of a proliferation of drive-by shootings and gangs.

Applying the Strategy

In Santa Ana, California, one school located in an area heavily populated with gangs worked with a school resource patrolman to educate parents and students on anti-gang techniques. More than 150 parents attended meetings that provided information on parenting, recognizing gang activity, and how police respond to gangs. While parents were in the meeting, other patrol officers were talking with students in a separate room and answering questions about gangs. Working closely with another school, the school resource officer was able to add a crossing guard at a busy street, providing a safer environment for the students.

Crime near a college campus became an opportunity for a partnership among the City of Columbus, the State of Ohio, Ohio State University, the Franklin County Sheriff's Office, and the Columbus Police Department. The Community Crime Patrol puts two-person, radio-equipped teams of patrollers into the neighborhood during potential high-crime hours to act as observers and crime reporters. A number of these paid, part-time jobs are filled with college students interested in careers in law enforcement.

Contact Information

Media Educational Coordinator
University of Florida Police
Building 51, Museum Road
Gainesville, Florida 32611
904-392-1114

Community Storefront Police Stations

Strategy

Law enforcement can more effectively bring police services to residents by establishing a substation or storefront policing program in the community.

Crime Problem Addressed

Although high-visibility patrol officers walking the streets of an area improve the relationship between law enforcement and the community it serves, a working police office who deals with specific local problems within a community increases the residents' perception of police commitment to the community.

Key Components

Often, storefront police operations or substations are the result of resident requests for increased protection and services in a neighborhood. In return, the residents frequently provide volunteer assistance to help operate the storefront. Other social services and community information can be located at the storefront; thus the locations serve as a central resource for community aid, such as victims' assistance and youth programs. Law enforcement can also establish a mini-station or substation in a neighborhood shopping area, a previously abandoned building, a public housing building, or in a trailer parked in an accessible location. The guiding principle of a storefront or decentralized police station is to encourage residents and police officers to become neighbors, learning about and assisting each other.

Key Partnerships

Storefront service delivery sites can be the collaborative effort of law enforcement, social service agencies, health programs, antidrug programs, youth and family services, and other assistance needed by a neighborhood or community. Media can be valuable partners in publicizing services provided by storefront or mini-stations.

Potential Obstacles

Funding is usually the primary obstacle to decentralizing police services. If costs can be shared among the resources of many agencies, a storefront or substation can be made more economically feasible. Neighborhood volunteers can help with office work and other duties.

Signs of Success

A storefront in Dorchester, Massachusetts—staffed with one Vietnamese woman serving as community liaison and three full-time police officers assigned to assist her—provides a wide range of services to the neighboring Vietnamese community. The storefront staff give presentations on crime prevention to English as a Second Language (ESL) classes and distribute brochures on crime and gang prevention techniques. They also arrange for court translation and assist with community organization, reaching the community through posters and newspaper advertisements. The station has successfully brought crime response, crime prevention, and other assistance to a neighborhood with a large Vietnamese population. According to the Community Service Officer, "When residents see you are making an effort and spending time with the community, they trust you."

Applying the Strategy

A storefront police station in Houston, Texas, has not only reduced residents' fear of both personal and property crime, it has also helped to reduce disorder in the community, according to residents' reports.

In Abington Township, Pennsylvania, the police department has decentralized service by equipping a mobile mini-station to bring services to any troubled neighborhood. Staffed by police officers and citizen volunteers, the mobile station also carries representatives of other service providers, such as drug and alcohol abuse counselors, health professionals, and nutritionists. The vehicle is also a mobile station for Abington Hospital.

Contact Information

Safe Neighborhood Administrator
Boston Police Department
Area C-11
40 Gibson Street
Boston, Massachusetts 02116
617-343-4339

Community Ombudsman

Strategy

Law enforcement can establish a community ombudsman to increase public access to the police department and to advise callers to the police about the range of available services.

Crime Problem Addressed

Community residents in some cities have expressed confusion about police non-emergency services. They have encountered difficulty in reaching the appropriate officer or office to get information about a policing or community matter. Such difficulty leads to apathy and discourages a beneficial relationship between the community and the police department.

Key Components

Law enforcement agencies in many cities have developed community relations boards as a means of receiving community input about resolution of resident complaints about police services. Law enforcement ombudsmen in other agencies answer a telephone line or staff an information desk that offers information about non-emergency police organization and public safety services. The ombudsman must be highly informed about and familiar with organizational information and must be able to interact well with the public. The position could be staffed with a paid officer, a paid support staff person, or with a community volunteer who has been trained. The ombudsman could also mail out flyers or other printed information in response to calls about specific services.

Key Partnerships

Community organizations provide volunteers to help operate the ombudsman service. Law enforcement agencies also work with community-based organizations to publicize the service in hopes of diverting non-emergency inquiries and complaints from the 911 emergency telephone system. Citizen boards recruit members through political appointment, usually with consideration of neighborhood, ethnic, racial, and other interest group diversity.

Potential Obstacles

Ombudsmen must be diplomatic and skilled at presenting information courteously. They must also be problem solvers, able to connect the caller with the proper service. Law enforcement agencies with community relations boards have to provide members with input into department policy if they hope to overcome resident apathy about the legitimacy of such groups.

Signs of Success

Corpus Christi, Texas, included establishing a community ombudsman among the goals agreed to by a grassroots government coalition, which drafted a crime prevention plan for the city in 1993. Residents with non-emergency crime reports and complaints about service can meet with the Station Duty Officer (SDO) in precinct stations. The SDO and personnel who staff the telephone response unit have handled over 30,000 inquiries and minor incident reports, freeing other officers for patrol duty.

Applying the Strategy

Community residents active on law enforcement policy boards in Salt Lake City, Utah, are pleased with regulations on the behavior of law enforcement officers. The police chief believes handling citizen complaints is now more efficient because of the visibility and input of the citizen members of the board.

Contact Information

Corpus Christi Police Department
P.O. Box 9016
321 John Sartain Road
Corpus Christi, Texas 78469
512-886-2775

Intervene With Youth At Risk of Gang Involvement

Strategy

Law enforcement can provide alternatives to gang involvement to youth who are involved in or exposed to gang activity, by offering information, mentors, role models, and positive relationships.

Crime Problem Addressed

Young people who are vulnerable to gang involvement are often very difficult to reach through traditional youth programs. They have a strong need to belong to a "family"— a group that professes to care about them—and they develop tight bonds to their fellow gang members. A program that understands and addresses these needs can offer guidance to young people, as well as help combat community gang activity.

Key Components

The primary element of a successful youth antigang program is the development of trust for specific law enforcement officers and other adults who work with youth. The officers must be patient, honest, and credible. They should be trained to work with young people, and they must understand how and when to set limits in their negotiations with youth. A youth antigang program should include the following components:

- education and information;

- community-building activities that provide alternatives to the appeal of gang membership;

- leadership training;

- job and skills training;

- counseling; and

- follow-up services.

Ideally, an antigang program should also convey a sense of "family" to a young person.

Key Partnerships

Trained law enforcement officers can successfully collaborate on antigang programs with other service agencies, institutions, and individuals:

- parents;

- health and mental health agencies;

- schools;

- religious organizations;

- community leaders;

- businesses;

- ex-gang members; and

- ethnic leaders.

Potential Obstacles

It is critical that adults who work in partnership to provide assistance to young people attracted to gang membership fully understand that a prime reason kids join gangs is to have a sense of belonging and caring. A serious obstacle to the success of an antigang collaborative program could lie in a multidisciplinary approach in which all participating professions claim to have a different answer to the problem. Program leaders much reach consensus on the problem and on the solutions before the program is implemented in the community.

Signs of Success

In a youth antigang program (Youth Intervention Program) in Jacksonville, Florida, law enforcement officers first approached the problem of youth who were already in gangs. After successfully convincing some youth to drop out of their gangs, the program focused on preventing other youth from joining gangs. According to representatives of the Sheriff's office, which sponsors the program, the antigang activities have generated positive relationships between law enforcement and youth. Teens now approach police to get advice about their problems.

Applying the Strategy

In Phoenix, Arizona, Gang Resistance Education and Training (GREAT) focuses on gang prevention by sending law enforcement officers into school classrooms to teach young students about gang-related violence, the dangers of drug use, conflict resolution, and cultural prejudice. The eight one-hour sessions approach the problem formally; informally, the GREAT program sponsors a summer camp that reinforces positive attitudes against gangs. Law enforcement officers are permitted to contact parents of suspected gang members and refer them to existing social programs that address the gang phenomenon. The GREAT program is now offered nationwide through a partnership with the federal Bureau of Alcohol, Tobacco, and Firearms.

In San Bernardino, California, the school system and the police department jointly sponsor a Junior Police Academy for students in the fifth and sixth grades who might be vulnerable to the appeal of gang membership. The cadets, who must be accepted for the program, proudly wear uniforms one day a week and are involved in the school safety patrol program, civic events, parades, and community service activities.

A multicultural gang diversion program in Fort Worth, Texas, provides antigang workshops, parent services, counseling, and English as a Second Language classes to gang members and their families.

Contact Information

Phoenix Police Department
Community Relations Bureau
620 West Washington
Phoenix, Arizona 85003
602-262-7331

Crime Prevention Training for All Department Staff

Strategy

Police departments can extend crime prevention training to all members of the department who have personal contact with community residents, with the goal of disseminating crime prevention techniques to residents during routine and non-emergency operations.

Crime Problem Addressed

Traditionally, the specialized police department crime prevention unit is seen as a referral agency for beat officers who are asked about crime prevention techniques. Because of this pattern of specialization, beat officers have missed many opportunities to instruct parents, youth, business owners, and other community residents about crime prevention. Instead, questions have been referred to a crime prevention unit that is also busy with conducting organized programs such as Drug Abuse Resistance Education (DARE) and Neighborhood Watch. Consequently, community residents sometimes have to wait to receive the benefit of their police department's crime prevention knowledge.

Key Components

Training beat officers to know and understand the importance of crime prevention techniques can take the form of a series of workshops, created collaboratively with the training unit and the crime prevention unit. These workshops can include crime prevention videos, work sheets and other printed material, and discussion sessions with crime prevention specialists. Beat officers can also accompany crime prevention officers to community meetings or schools when crime prevention is the topic of instruction. It is helpful for the department to recognize the importance of crime prevention training through incentives or professional recognition and awards.

Key Partnerships

Law enforcement training is usually implemented internally, with the training unit taking the lead. The crime prevention unit can be a valuable partner in creating materials for the training sessions. Other crime prevention agencies, such as the state crime prevention organization, private security groups, and drug prevention groups can provide helpful assistance in workshops and on-the-beat training.

Potential Obstacles

Law enforcement departments report that the primary obstacle to training all officers in crime prevention techniques is resistance among veteran officers who are not as willing to embrace change as are younger officers. Attitude change can occur with patience, time, and successful crime prevention results.

Signs of Success

Recruits in Tempe, Arizona, are trained in crime prevention and problem-solving. The centralized crime prevention unit of the department provides an eighty-hour crime prevention course required of all Police Resource Officers, the city's designation for community policing officers assigned to patrol specific quadrants or neighborhoods. The unit also works with other city agencies and the private sector, providing security-based reviews of plans of new building construction.

Applying the Strategy

In New Haven, Connecticut, as part of a department-wide change to a more holistic form of police service delivery, all officers received eight hours of basic crime prevention, including residential and commercial security and alarm systems. The department also created an incentives program, modifying the criteria for the Chief's Award of Merit to include crime prevention training. Suggested crime prevention tips were read out at each roll call meeting, and all officers were given access to a computerized record of crime data and analysis to show how crime prevention affects crime trends. A post-training staff report showed that crime prevention training of all officers resulted in at least 25 percent of them regularly conveying crime prevention information to city residents.

Contact Information

New Haven Police Department
Neighborhood Services Unit
One Union Avenue
New Haven, Connecticut 06519
203-946-6299

Partnership With City Agencies To Prevent Violence

Strategy

Law enforcement can decrease the incidence of violence in a community by working in formal partnership with other agencies to implement multifaceted approaches to incidents or trends in community violence.

Crime Problem Addressed

While law enforcement has always been effective in reacting to a violent emergency situation, it can also team up with other agencies and individuals in the community to prevent violence, address the causes of violence, and ensure that victims receive appropriate care.

Key Components

An effective partnership between law enforcement and the community to address violence should have, according to several communities, at least the following five components:

■ a violent offender removal program to respond to existing violence and be available for crisis intervention;

■ a community-oriented policing component to bring together law enforcement and the community to identify and solve local problems related to crime or violence;

■ a partnership program between law enforcement and social service providers to ensure that victims of violence receive proper follow-up care;

■ a safe haven program that provides community members a secure environment for healthy nonviolent activities; and

■ a neighborhood revitalization component that builds community health through a strong economy, provides positive alternatives for youth, and educates residents about avoiding violence.

Key Partnerships

A community antiviolence strategy can rely on the expertise and experience of a wide variety of agencies (mental health, schools, recreation), private groups and professionals (violence victims' groups, counselors, medical professionals), and neighborhood groups (Neighborhood Watch, youth clubs, athletic groups, social organizations) to work closely with law enforcement and the court system to decrease and prevent violence. The court system can order a violent offender to get professional help. A multiagency task force can provide a formal structure to a comprehensive antiviolence effort in the community.

Potential Obstacles

Victims of violence often fear retaliation and, out of this fear, refuse to report a violent crime or refuse to press charges against the perpetrator, particularly if that person is a family member. Victims also fear that they will suffer a sense of social isolation and stigma if they bring charges. It is critical to have highly trained law enforcement personnel respond to calls about family violence or child abuse. In many cases, police departments have a social services professional respond to the call with the patrol officer to attend to the emotional needs of the victim.

Signs of Success

In Union City, New Jersey, a Police-Community Partnership has organized to address community problems and help prevent the incidence of violent and other crimes in parts of the city. The program is guided by a steering committee that is responsible for communication and coordination of the four-point program to:

■ intervene in incidents of violence and remove violent offenders;

■ encourage close bonds with the community through community policing;

■ provide secure areas for residents; and

■ strengthen the quality of life in the community through economic revitalization.

Applying the Strategy

The Memphis (Tennessee) Police Department's Family Trouble Center is a collaboration between police and mental health professionals for crisis intervention focusing on domestic violence. The authority of the police department is necessary to control and stop the violent episodes. Once the immediate threat is resolved, the mental health counselors assist the family in finding nonviolent ways to resolve conflict. The center uses volunteers, most of whom are graduate students in the counseling and social work professions, and offers services at no cost.

Contact Information

Union City Police Department
619 Bergenline Avenue
Union City, New Jersey 07087
201-863-4889

Law Enforcement-Led Multiagency Support for Neighborhood Services

Strategy

Law enforcement can coordinate and integrate multiagency neighborhood support teams to improve the quality and timeliness of service delivery.

Crime Problem Addressed

The problems of some neighborhoods are a complex interweaving of poverty, inadequate housing, joblessness, neglected children, and no relief from crime. By coordinating services with other local agencies, these situations can be addressed more effectively, decreasing duplication and cost.

Key Components

Community services' collaboration depends on information-sharing, support from agency and municipal leaders, a consensus on local problems and solutions, and a shared sense of leadership and responsibility. In addition, residents must feel empowered to be a part of the problem-solving process, learning the basics of planning, budgeting, and decision-making. Successful neighborhood service teams rely on a committed staff that can develop a rapport with community residents. Staff must know the resources and limitations of their own agencies and be flexible when working with other team members and the community. It is also important that the team be able to deliver tangible benefits quickly to reinforce trust among the residents.

Key Partnerships

The neighborhood team must reflect the complexity of local problems and include representatives from law enforcement, youth and family services, the school system, the recreation agency, the local housing authority, the court system, health agencies, and job placement and training agencies, among others. The team must also include representatives from all segments of the neighborhood or community, including businesses, groups with special needs (such as the elderly), and ethnic groups.

Potential Obstacles

Some neighborhood teams begin as a well-funded group, but when budgets in the participating agencies are tightened, the multiagency programs can lose funding. If public funding erodes, teams should look to local businesses, churches, and neighborhood volunteers to take over some of the team's obligations. A second problem is the fact that building partnerships can take a long time, and representatives from a variety of disciplines may have initial difficulty in finding common ground when identifying and designing solutions for problems.

Signs of Success

Statistics show that crime has dropped significantly in neighborhoods where the Norfolk (Virginia) Police Assisted Community Enforcement (PACE) program has collaborated with local agencies and residents to offer integrated service delivery.

PACE teamed up with local service agencies to tackle complex problems in six public housing areas and four residential neighborhoods particularly susceptible to drug activity and drug-related crime. The program is divided into three areas:

■ support services made up of representatives of city agencies, neighborhood groups, business, and religious leaders;

■ a Neighborhood Environmental Assessment Team; and

■ a Family Assessment Services Team.

PACE has made sweeps of neighborhoods to identify and arrest suspects, has increased patrols, and has met regularly with residents and agency representatives. Residents report that the program has facilitated access to city agencies and cut red tape. Program participants also report that fear of crime has decreased.

Applying the Strategy

The Neighborhood Resource Team in Dade County, Florida, has focused on public safety, housing, jobs, community tensions, and youth activities in Dade County neighborhoods. This group has revitalized tenant councils and recruited a full-time Community Street Coordinator for alternative youth activities.

Contact Information

Chairperson
PACE Support Group
302 City Hall Building
Norfolk, Virginia 23510
804-664-4626

Law Enforcement-Sponsored Community Events

Strategy

Law enforcement can work more effectively with local residents if it has first established a trusting relationship, beginning with non-threatening events such as community social activities.

Crime Problem Addressed

Law enforcement and other agencies that develop programs to resolve identified problems in local neighborhoods might encounter resistance from residents unless there is first a relationship built on mutual trust. Getting to know residents through social activities can be an important component of building that trust.

Key Components

Building trust between law enforcement and residents—particularly in troubled neighborhoods—can begin with social events such as neighborhood picnics, holiday parties, school events, and other non-professional activities that permit police and residents to become acquainted personally. The events can be sponsored by the police department or by a committee of residents and law enforcement and should be free of charge. Child care and youth activities should be arranged. The event can feature a concert, sports contests, or other activities that put residents and police together in an informal atmosphere. It is critical that law enforcement follows up in the community with other social events or meetings to provide information and build on the established trust.

Key Partnerships

Community social events can be arranged by law enforcement in conjunction with community leaders. Businesses, schools, the religious community, and other sectors can take part in planning social events and can donate awards, T-shirts, food, or entertainment. The media can play an important part in publicizing the event.

Potential Obstacles

Lack of follow-up can be a serious problem after a law enforcement-sponsored social event for the community or neighborhood. Community residents must feel that law enforcement officers care about their concerns and are willing to listen to their problems. Law enforcement could schedule a community meeting for the week after the picnic or party, inviting all community residents to a question-and-answer session about police services and community concerns.

Signs of Success

In Lansing, Michigan, the participants in the Neighborhood Network Center (a coalition of law enforcement and other service providers) have worked with neighborhood groups to organize Christmas parties, cookouts, neighborhood beautification programs, community fairs, and fundraising events to pay for future neighborhood projects. Every month, residents are invited to come to the Center for a potluck dinner, followed by Caring Area Residents meetings to coordinate social activities across several individual neighborhoods.

Social events have contributed to a healthier, more trusting relationship between police and residents. Volunteers, area churches, businesses, and students have become involved, some donating space in the community for parties, meetings, and youth recreational programs.

Applying the Strategy

In Rochester, Minnesota, law enforcement works closely with the Intercultural Mutual Assistance Association to provide crime prevention information to youth while conducting recreational and social events. The Association serves the city's Cambodian, Lao, and Vietnamese communities.

One element of a community policing program, neighborhood festivals showcase communities throughout St. Petersburg, Florida, allowing them to show off improvements to the media, the public, and neighborhood groups.

Contact Information

Neighborhood Network Center
Lansing Police Department
735 East Michigan Avenue
Lansing, Michigan 48912
517-483-7663

Safe Havens

Strategy

Law enforcement and other community partners can establish a safe haven where young people can enjoy a secure, healthy environment supportive of drug- and crime-free activities.

Crime Problem Addressed

Community programs to help youth make healthy choices—staying in school, staying out of gangs, setting and achieving goals—often fail if the young person has no alternative to an unhealthy environment. Safe havens support programs that reinforce a youth's choice to be a drug-free, positive contributing member of the neighborhood.

Key Components

Although the number and variety of activities offered at a safe haven are important, key to the success of a safe haven is a youth's compliance with rules and regulations. These rules should be formulated with the participation of the youth as well as with adult leaders, counselors, law enforcement, and others involved with the program. A safe haven board with wide community representation can set and maintain standards of acceptable conduct within the boundaries of the building or site. If possible, a safe haven should be accessible at all times with an adult available; if the location can be accessible only at certain hours, it is important to coordinate those hours with times when youth need alternative activities, such as after school, in the evenings, and on weekends. Volunteers can assist with sports activities or other events offered at the haven.

Key Partnerships

A safe haven governing board should include representatives from law enforcement; the municipal department of parks and recreation; youth organizations such as Boy Scouts, Girl Scouts, and Boys & Girls Clubs; social services; and community groups such as religious institutions, schools, and businesses.

Potential Obstacles

To be successful, a safe haven must codify and enforce a rigid set of regulations that ensure its purpose: to provide an antidrug (including alcohol), antiviolence, anticrime environment. It must be made clear that certain behaviors will not be tolerated, and the managing group must agree on and enforce consequences for breaking the rules. A second challenge is keeping the program fresh and appealing for all participants. When young people become bored, they are more likely to break the rules or stay away. Funding can also be a challenge; business donations, resources from other agencies and private groups, private sector donations, and volunteers can all be solutions.

Signs of Success

The Trenton, New Jersey, Safe Haven program has successfully offered a drug-free environment at three public middle schools after school and in the evenings. The program has attracted youth and adult participants, with one Safe Haven school averaging between 85 to 125 people per evening. The Safe Haven program is a collaboration between law enforcement, education, health, recreation, and community groups. It offers a wide variety of activities for youth and adults after school and in the evenings at several middle schools in targeted neighborhoods.

Applying the Strategy

The Union City, New Jersey, Safe Haven program is part of a Police-Community Partnership Program to decrease crime and strengthen the cooperation between residents and law enforcement. The program is held in a school gymnasium near the Union City Recreation Building and is open seven days a week from 3:00 p.m. to 9:00 p.m. Youth are welcome to participate in activities such as swimming, cheerleading, cooking, basketball, dances, field trips, and workshops on drug awareness, nutrition, AIDS, and first aid. The center also provides information about city services and police assistance.

Contact Information

Union City Police Department
615 Bergenline Avenue
Union City, New Jersey 07087
201-863-4889

Community Meetings

Strategy

By holding a series of meetings at several locations in the community or region, law enforcement and other criminal justice system leaders can develop a list of community concerns and expectations both about specific crime problems and about the delivery of services.

Crime Problem Addressed

In order to make informed decisions about the allocation of resources for an effective criminal justice system, leaders must hear directly from community residents about their fears and how they see the role of the criminal justice system in their communities. This information must then be incorporated into community plans to decrease crime and the fear of crime and to improve service problems perceived by the public and by other components of the criminal justice system.

Key Components

Community meetings, conducted by leaders of state, county, or municipal criminal justice agencies, must be well publicized several weeks prior to the meeting date. The meeting should be held at a time and place easily accessible and convenient to the majority of community residents. Each meeting's agenda should be limited to several key topics, and the resultant list of concerns should be published and distributed in the community. Information gathered from concerned residents should be the focus of future initiatives and programs.

Key Partnerships

Organizers should develop lists of invitees from key organizations in the area, such as court action groups, legal assistance groups, victims' groups, ethnic groups, special needs groups, crime prevention organizations, corrections officials, elected officials, law enforcement and other criminal justice system agencies, and community residents. It is important that high-profile officials conduct these meetings to underscore to the public that their concerns will have bearing on criminal justice policy.

Potential Obstacles

The public often misunderstands the language and terminology of the criminal justice system. It is important that these meetings avoid that jargon and that they respond to the concerns of the lay public rather than experts and specialists. It is also critical that follow-up meetings or other public contact convey to the community that its input is valuable and can serve as the basis for substantive and procedural change. One-time meetings can lead to skepticism among community residents.

Signs of Success

In Maryland, the newly appointed U.S. Attorney undertook a series of community meetings to involve residents in ongoing interaction about concerns and problems in the state's criminal justice system. The meetings resulted in increased involvement—not only by residents, but also by members of law enforcement organizations, who subsequently attended seminars on state grant resources. The U.S. Attorney's Office also adopted a change in organizational structure to concentrate increased resources on violent crime, forming a Violent Crime Coordination Group to improve information sharing and networking with state and local police and prosecutors.

Applying the Strategy

The Mayor's office in Cleveland, Ohio, organized six town hall forums, where residents were encouraged to air their views on the direction of the proposed community policing program. In addition, residents were asked to complete surveys ranking crime problems the city should address. The forums attracted an average of more than 300 people per meeting.

Contact Information

United States Attorney
District of Maryland
United States Courthouse, Room 604
101 West Lombard Street
Baltimore, Maryland 21201-2692
410-962-2458

Cooperate With Businesses

Strategy

Law enforcement can develop a mutually beneficial relationship with local businesses to address specific crimes that affect a community's economic—and therefore general—health.

Crime Problem Addressed

Crime in commercial areas sometimes drives away local businesses, taking jobs and neighborhood stability with them. When local businesses leave because of crime problems, drug and crime activity takes over abandoned buildings, keeping fearful residents inside their homes. A link between law enforcement and business owners can address problems specific to commercial areas or neighborhoods supporting small, locally owned commercial establishments, maintaining community vitality.

Key Components

It is important that law enforcement approach specific business crimes analytically, identifying trends that are prevalent in one area but may be minimal or absent in another. Each cluster of crime problems must be addressed with the help of the local business owners who are most affected by the problems. Solutions may include increasing patrols, changing transportation patterns, enforcing loitering laws, increasing private security, or modifying public lighting or alleyway access.

Key Partnerships

A business-law enforcement partnership can also effectively draw upon the resources and cooperation of the local chamber of commerce, business-related service clubs, unions, private security firms, media, city planners, and residents of neighborhoods where businesses operate.

Potential Obstacles

In some communities where businesses have been vulnerable to crime, business owners and managers have not immediately welcomed police suggestions for crime prevention measures. In one instance, the manager chose not to make changes because of the "inconvenience"; however, after he was a victim of crime he chose to modify the environment around his establishment to reduce the possibility of crime. A police-business partnership may take time to cultivate.

Signs of Success

In Edmonton, Alberta (Canada), police discovered that downtown crime was prevalent around hotels that attracted the city's tourists. Through a collaborative program with local hoteliers, the police helped decrease the incidence of crime by suggesting architectural and other changes that would decrease the opportunity for crime. The Edmonton police department attacked crime around these hotels by recommending lighting and other architectural changes to hotel and motel owners. In addition, they have worked with the Alberta Liquor Control Board to mandate the use of plastic and safety glass in drinking glasses and bottles, after a British study showed that in England four out of five injuries from assault are caused by beer bottles and glasses.

Applying the Strategy

A car dealership in the southwest established a graffiti paint-over campaign, which now includes the police department and dozens of other area businesses among its partners. The police department helps by advising the paint-over crew about dangers in specific neighborhoods and providing escorts when requested. Other city agencies provide paint to support the project.

In Santa Ana, California, business owners in the Harbor Plaza worked successfully with police to pinpoint specific crimes that were driving away business. The police documented and analyzed a series of incidents and were able to implement effective prevention measures.

Contact Information

Edmonton Police Service
Community Based Policing Project
9620 103-A Avenue
Edmonton, Alberta
Canada T5H0H7
403-421-3333

Partnerships in Rural Communities

Strategy

With few sworn personnel, law enforcement agencies in rural areas can particularly benefit from a partnership with local agencies and with neighboring jurisdictions to address identified crime and personal safety concerns.

Crime Problem Addressed

Small law enforcement agencies serving rural communities may find many urban area personnel-intensive strategies difficult to adapt to their departments due to lack of resources and criminal specialists and to geographical constraints such as sparsely settled farmland. A team approach to problem-solving can supplement a small department's resources, using the existing community structure and local network to identify problems and plan and implement solutions.

Key Components

The basic components of a rural law enforcement partnership strategy are identical to those used by large urban agencies:

- identifying a problem;

- forming a task force of local leaders and experts;

- planning a strategy;

- setting a budget;

- mobilizing the community;

- implementing the strategy; and

- evaluating the results.

The difference faced by a rural agency can be a greater reliance on other agencies and volunteers to resolve or prevent local problems. Law enforcement agencies might also have to rely more heavily on resources outside the community, such as those found in a neighboring urban area or in state or federal agencies. In rural areas, residents often have developed a closely knit social and business structure that can serve as a network for identifying and addressing problems.

Key Partnerships

In rural areas as in other locales, all community members can work together to ensure the safety of the community. Law enforcement can take the lead, providing information about drug use and crime to schools, youth, parents, local merchants, agricultural and business leaders, and town service providers. Churches and other religious institutions, often a dominant part of a rural community, are especially valuable as vehicles for communicating information to residents.

Potential Obstacles

In a rural community where law enforcement traditions may be deeply instilled, change may come slowly. Police or sheriff's department officials may resist working with the community as a partner, and turf issues may be strong among local organizations. It might be advisable to have the task force chaired by a citizen who is highly influential in the community and has demonstrated leadership and skill in managing a diverse group of residents.

Signs of Success

In a rural part of California, farmers worked together with four local sheriff's departments, the Farm Bureau, the state Department of Food and Agriculture, and district attorneys' offices to reduce crop theft through stricter market controls and identification of stolen produce. In 1989, the California avocado-growing industry lost approximately $10 million due to theft. The partners hired a field manager to serve as an industry-wide crime prevention coordinator and function as liaison between the growers and the sheriffs' departments. The group now publishes a quarterly newsletter, has established a reward program for the arrest of thieves, has mounted a publicity campaign, and has installed a toll-free Avocado Theft Hotline.

The problem has not been completely eradicated, but the thefts have dropped substantially. Additionally, farmers report heightened confidence in the sheriffs' departments, and local law enforcement is more informed about agricultural theft.

Applying the Strategy

In Richmond, Maine, a rural town of about 3,000 residents, the police department established an advisory board and consulted with other jurisdictions that had successful neighborhood-oriented policing programs. They gained information by networking, holding cluster meetings, and sharing data. The department distributes a newsletter and gives reports to the media to inform community residents about police strategies, programs, and successes.

Contact Information

California Avocado Commission
Field Manager
Avocado Theft Prevention Program
440 State Place, Suite A
Escondido, California 92025
619-743-4712

Code Enforcement

Strategy

Law enforcement can work closely with code enforcement agencies and residents to identify and address problems with crime in neighborhoods through enforcement of a variety of municipal and state codes.

Crime Problem Addressed

When it is difficult to bring direct criminal charges against a criminal, such as a clandestine drug manufacturer, police can curtail activities by enforcing municipal standards and codes. Observation and reporting by community residents are particularly valuable in this partnership.

Key Components

Enforcing codes involves a series of steps that require cooperation from several segments of the community. After the problem is identified by residents or by the police, police and housing records can identify the landlord who is sent a letter of abatement. The letter is usually followed by inspections conducted by police, health, public works, fire, housing, or utilities personnel. If the owner complies with the required changes, no further action in required. However, if the landlord does not comply, a court hearing can result in receivership, demolition, or rehabilitation of the building into an acceptable community structure.

Key Partnerships

Police and citizens can work with a wide range of municipal enforcement agencies, including the electric and gas companies, the telephone company, and city agencies for planning, building, health, transportation, sanitation, and fire prevention.

Potential Obstacles

Community residents who work with police to identify crime-related problems are frequently concerned about fear of retaliation. Police can help allay these fears through an anonymous tip program that does not require callers to identify themselves.

Signs of Success

In 1988, the Oakland (California) Police Department developed a program with city, county, and state regulatory agencies and the neighborhood-based Oakland Commu-

nity Organization to close down crack houses and other illegal businesses. Since the beginning of the program, more than 200 crime-and drug-inviting sites have been destroyed or turned into clean, legally occupied, safe buildings.

Applying the Strategy

In Hayward, California, the police department has formalized a Code Enforcement Team comprising representatives from a variety of agencies to abate buildings associated with criminal activity. Members meet to address problems and strategies that affect the team's ability to collaborate on neighborhood concerns.

Police and citizens have cooperated to close drug houses for health code and housing violations in Houston, Texas; Hartford, Connecticut; and Chicago, Illinois.

Contact Information

Beat Health Unit
455 Seventh Street, B-48
Oakland, California 94607
510-615-5808

City of Hayward Police Department
300 West Winton Avenue
Hayward, California 94544-1137
510-293-7058

Educate Residents About Law Enforcement Operations

Strategy

Law enforcement outreach programs educate residents about police activities and increase community support for law enforcement and prevention.

Crime Problem Addressed

Community residents are often uninformed about services provided by their law enforcement agency and about successes of apprehension and prevention programs in the community. This lack of information can lead to apathy or even hostility among residents and law enforcement.

Key Components

Law enforcement agencies can bring important information to the public through large community meetings, citizen academies, small seminars, public classes on police services, printed information, and even local television and radio talk shows. Law enforcement can also work closely with judicial partners—such as the court and corrections systems—to educate the community about problems and

solutions. Printed materials that explain new programs can be distributed at meetings or through other channels such as community fairs. Law enforcement agencies can publicize programs through newsletters, and the media can be a strong partner in disseminating police-related information to the community.

Key Partnerships

Efforts to disseminate law enforcement information can be the focus of a partnership between the department's public affairs officer and other specialists, the media, community groups (such as business or service clubs), youth program officials, and any other public forum. Police service information brochures can be distributed at centers where residents seek assistance for other concerns, such as health, drug problems, food assistance, or housing.

Potential Obstacles

It is important that public information be honest and comprehensive. Public cynicism can increase if meeting presenters are not forthcoming and available for questions. As is the case with all meetings, it is also important for presenters to be organized and skilled in public speaking.

Signs of Success

The Citizen Police Academy in Lakewood, Colorado, provides groups of fifteen residents with first-hand opportunities to participate in a nine-week training course on police operations. They listen to and comment on responses to 911 emergency calls, act out mock arrests, role play an officer being interviewed about a crime by the media, and receive instruction in the law and police procedures. The success of the adult program resulted in expansion of the academy to include a youth component. Parents of youth participants report positive changes in their children's attitudes toward the police. Community-wide attitudes now are more supportive of the police as a result of this program.

Applying the Strategy

The Portland (Oregon) Police Bureau has created a Community Policing Media and Outreach program to commu-

nicate more effectively with residents about the Bureau's activities. It also conducts a community policing workshop for citizens, providing the opportunity for officers and residents to meet and discuss police services.

In Tempe, Arizona, the police department has implemented a Communications Network to enhance the exchange of information related to drug demand, crime, and police services. Newsletters are given to residents and business owners with information about drug and crime prevention. The Network also meets regularly with schools, religious groups, and a Coordinating Committee made up of representatives of the city's public and private sector.

Contact Information

Training Agent
City of Lakewood Police Department
445 South Allison Parkway
Lakewood, Colorado 80226-3105
303-987-7353

Multiagency Youth Service Support Teams

Strategy

A multiagency approach to the problems young people face can improve chances of reducing youth victimization, delinquency, and drug involvement.

Crime Problem Addressed

Although law enforcement can curtail drug use and crime through apprehension, a multiagency approach can more successfully identify causes of drug and crime involvement, deal with needed treatment, employ community prevention resources, and address such related issues as parenting, school truancy, and joblessness.

Key Components

Teams of experts, drawn from public and private agencies, can address youth issues in a community and serve as advocates and information resources for young people and their families. The team can help identify neighborhood problems and bring the resources of a wide variety of disciplines to resolve them. It is important for the team to have a shared vision and to be able to work closely together, sharing official and anecdotal information. A well-informed team will be less likely to permit a troubled youth to "fall through the cracks" of the system and will be able

to offer a range of solutions to a single problem or to multiple problems. The team can also help identify trends in youth problems and help design and implement prevention techniques to stop or slow the trend.

Key Partnerships

School officials and trained youth counselors, social workers, juvenile court officials, neighborhood leaders, recreation leaders, health professionals, parents, religious leaders, and youth can all work together to identify and resolve youth problems in the community. Businesses can help with job programs, and community leaders and social organizations can provide volunteer opportunities to assist in community-building programs.

Potential Obstacles

As with many partnerships, turf battles can become a serious obstacle to reaching a consensus on community youth problems. Also, child-raising practices vary among economic populations and ethnic and racial groups, making standardized programs difficult to implement. Finally, parents are often in denial about problems their children are encountering, and they may be hostile to outside intervention.

Signs of Success

In Cincinnati, Ohio, Youth Support Teams are active in a number of community activities, from removing glass from playgrounds to removing parking meters from a residential area to increase neighborhood safety. The teams work closely with youth-related agencies in the community to coordinate needs assessments, identify neighborhood problems, and provide technical assistance to groups working with youth. The Department of Education is involved as a strong partner by providing healthy recreational activities for youth. Community-Oriented Policing officers help coordinate summer youth programs and serve as counselors and mentors to young community residents.

Applying the Strategy

Seattle's police department works with city agencies on two youth-serving programs. In the Joint Parks Department and Police Guild Program, police union volunteers work with older youth in late-evening recreation programs. In the Youth Intervention Program, human services, police, schools, and community agencies cooperate to design gang prevention programming and intervention with gang-involved youth.

Contact Information

Director of Neighborhood Services
Human Services Division
2 Centennial Plaza, Suite 700
805 Central Avenue
Cincinnati, Ohio 45202
513-352-1948

Focus on Quality-of-Life Improvements

Strategy

Law enforcement can help reduce crime in neighborhoods by addressing quality-of-life problems raised by residents, such as loitering, vandalism, graffiti, and unsupervised youth who create public nuisances.

Crime Problem Addressed

For many community residents, unhappiness with community conditions stems from the seemingly small problems that directly affect levels of fear, annoyance, and inconvenience. Although some problems raised by citizens may not fall under the purview of traditional policing, police attention to residents' concerns can add to community satisfaction with police services.

Key Components

Face-to-face neighborhood patrols are the cornerstone of responses to quality-of-life issues in a community. When police patrol on foot, they are more likely to talk with residents and be seen as community members, rather than as reactive police officers. Many police officers have found that residents, once fearful of coming out of their houses, are more encouraged to do so when they see police foot patrols and they know that their concerns, no matter how small, will get attention.

It is important for foot patrols to learn residents' names and, if possible, find solutions to some of the quality-of-life problems concerning the neighborhood. In some cases, the problems can be resolved easily. In others, solutions may come from a team approach, involving other agencies or members of the community. Problems can include

leaves that have not been cleared from sidewalks, causing safety concerns; street lighting that needs to be replaced; graffiti that is contributing to a run-down look in the neighborhood; loud teenage gatherings late at night; and broken glass in parks.

Key Partnerships

When residents turn to local police officers to help with neighborhood problems, police can work closely with other government agencies, volunteer groups, youth who are willing to work to make the community beautiful, and elderly residents who can be encouraged to report problems while they are happening. Local crime prevention groups can also help by teaching residents about basic personal safety techniques if fear of crime is a serious problem in the community.

Potential Obstacles

Although police officers are willing to handle many concerns raised by individuals in the community, it is important that police not overload their time with problems that can be more readily solved by others. Police should learn to refer residents to appropriate agencies and service providers to solve problems outside their areas of expertise. A resource reference directory could be distributed to neighborhood residents.

Signs of Success

Since its creation in 1975, the Citizens Committee for New York City has worked closely and effectively with law enforcement to improve the quality of life in New York neighborhoods. Police have worked with residents and other agencies to clean up parks and streets, erase graffiti from buildings, and help organize citizen block groups to monitor problems and design solutions. The Committee has had measurable success restoring feelings of safety and pride to city neighborhoods.

Applying the Strategy

Police officers in Long Beach, California, are important members of multiagency Neighborhood Improvement Teams. The neighborhood cleanup program supplies community groups with materials for tree plantings and graffiti paint-overs. The police department refers juvenile probationers to help the program as part of their community service. In addition, police and other agencies provide residents training in nuisance abatement, property owners'

responsibilities, documenting neighborhood problems, and pursuing claims in court.

Contact Information

Neighborhood Anticrime Center
Citizens Committee for New York City
305 Seventh Avenue
New York, New York 10001
212-989-0909

Manager
Neighborhood Services Bureau
City of Long Beach
333 West Ocean Boulevard
Long Beach, California 90802
310-570-6066

Outreach to Diverse Communities To Reduce Victimization

Strategy

Law enforcement can help reduce victimization among newly settled ethnic groups by teaching them practical crime prevention techniques.

Crime Problem Addressed

Newly settled ethnic families are vulnerable to a wide variety of crimes because they are often afraid to report crime to law enforcement. This fear can stem from an abusive practice of law enforcement in their native country and from a failure to understand that the police can help them protect themselves from crime.

Key Components

The cornerstone of any relationship between the police and an ethnic community is trust, a bond that is not always simple to develop. In order for police to teach ethnic groups how to protect themselves from crime, communication and ethnic tradition barriers must be overcome through cultural and sensitivity training, patient instruction, and special information-sharing. Teaching ethnic populations about police procedures and services can assist in developing a good working relationship between law enforcement and non-American cultures.

Key Partnerships

Police must often rely on the services of translators, interpreters, community liaisons, religious leaders, and other trusted members of an ethnic community to develop an effective crime prevention program for ethnic groups.

Schools can also assist by including crime prevention techniques in classroom instruction and special ESL classes.

Potential Obstacles

Many newly settled refugees and immigrants choose to stay within their own community, rarely attending public meetings or classes where they might learn about crime prevention or other important issues. Women raised in cultures where their role in the family in relation to men is different than in the United States may not feel comfortable leaving their homes to attend classes or meetings. Some law enforcement agencies have solved these problems by holding meetings in neighborhood sites, religious buildings, or even family homes and by offering child care.

Signs of Success

In Portland, Oregon, the police department has developed an Asian Law Enforcement Advisory Council to address problems encountered by ethnic populations in the city. The department sponsors cross-cultural training for police officers and offers 24-hour-a-day interpreter services. It also offers information on gang and crime prevention at community meetings and to ethnic families. Ethnic leaders work with the department to report crime and resolve problems in their neighborhoods.

Applying the Strategy

In Lowell, Massachusetts, police officers include a tour of the police station in their crime prevention program for newly settled refugees to help them learn about police services and to show them law enforcement in operation. In nearby Revere, Massachusetts, the police department has extended Operation Crime Watch to ethnic neighborhoods that have experienced crime.

Contact Information

Portland Police Bureau
1111 Southwest 2nd Avenue
Portland, Oregon 97204
503-823-4198

Translators and Multilingual Crime Prevention Education Materials

Strategy

Translators and interpreters can provide a valuable service to make the criminal justice system accessible to non-English-speaking residents.

Crime Problem Addressed

According to the 1990 census, one out of seven people living in the United States speaks a language other than English at home. Many people who have settled in the United States from other countries and cultures feel that non-English speakers are at a disadvantage because of unequal access to the U.S. criminal justice system and lack of understanding of police procedures and crime prevention resources. The Federal Court Interpreters Act of 1978 established the right of non-English speakers in federal courts to have certified interpreters.

Key Components

Increasing access to the criminal justice system for non-English speakers requires training interpreters and translators for both adult and juvenile courts. Interpreters and translators, many of whom may be volunteers, assist court personnel and non-English speakers both inside and outside the courtroom. It is imperative that the volunteers undergo cultural sensitivity training, as well as training to introduce them to the terminology of the court system. Some cities have had important documents—such as Miranda rights, civic rights, brochures documenting court and other legal procedures, and crime prevention educational materials—translated into languages of ethnic groups in the community.

Key Partnerships

All members of the criminal justice system who are involved with the court system and law enforcement can benefit from training and seminars on cultural diversity problems. Colleges and universities may be able to provide interpreters and translators as a service to the court. Groups that help resettle refugees, such as Mutual Assistance Associations, can also provide expert guidance on court translation. Some police departments have hired

community relations officers to assist non-English speakers when they are required to appear in court.

Potential Obstacles

Several obstacles interfere with effective interpretations and translations in court. Frequently, the court interpreter is skilled only in literal interpretation instead of understanding idioms and subtle nuances in the language. In addition, cultural and legal differences can contribute to misunderstandings that can affect the way information is presented to a judge or jury. Basic judicial concepts are sometimes not explained clearly to non-English speakers, adding to semantic confusion. A New Jersey Supreme Court Task Force study found that more than two-thirds of interpreters frequently used in state courts had no training in law and legal terminology, and nearly nine out of ten had no interpreting training at all.

Signs of Success

The Fairfax County (Virginia) Bar Association has developed the Civil Translators Pilot Program, conducting seminars and providing reference materials for 100 volunteer translators for the County's Juvenile and Domestic Relations Courts. The program is funded through the American Bar Association's Immigration Pro Bono Development Project.

Applying the Strategy

The ethnic crime prevention program in Lincoln, Nebraska, developed a series of videos in Vietnamese to be shown on the public access cable television channel. The videos explain a wide array of police services and include techniques for ensuring personal safety and reporting crimes. Crime reporting by members of that community has increased.

Contact Information

Director
4110 Chain Bridge Road, Room 303
Fairfax, Virginia 22030
703-246-2740

Law Enforcement Programs for Youth From Ethnic Minorities

Strategy

Law enforcement and other members of the criminal justice system can develop close bonds with young people who are members of ethnic minority groups by teaching them about the U.S. criminal justice system and helping them learn how to resist drug use and violence.

Crime Problem Addressed

Young people from other cultures who have resettled in the United States face problems as teenagers as well as problems of cultural adjustment. Frequently they feel alienated from their elders, who are less ready to adopt the customs of their new country, and they need special attention from community leaders who can gain their trust through cultural understanding and shared activities.

Key Components

Cultural leadership training is critical to the success of any multicultural program to help young people keep their lives drug- and crime-free. By working closely with refugee and immigrant youth to meet their social-adjustment needs, law enforcement can develop the trust required to build a relationship that will help steer them away from victimization and from involvement with drugs, crime, and gangs. Youth programs must integrate a respect for the person's native traditions, while assisting the young person to understand and adapt to American culture. A culturally sensitive program should have access to competent interpreters and translators.

Key Partnerships

Young people from ethnic minority groups can benefit from the assistance of all members of the criminal justice system, who can explain American laws, procedures, and legal expectations. Religious institutions and others who have sponsored the resettlement of newcomer families can work closely with law enforcement to ensure that ethnic youth and their parents have access to United States systems that address problems with social adjustment, physical and mental health, language, routine daily customs, and job training.

Potential Obstacles

The most serious obstacle to a trusting relationship between law enforcement and ethnic minority youth link is the problem of stereotyping. Each ethnic youth presents a unique set of challenges, because of both cultural background and the ability to adapt to new circumstances. Similarly, the perception of law enforcement will differ among ethnic groups, based on experiences in the native country. To avoid stereotyping, law enforcement must be knowledgeable about the cultures of ethnic groups in the community.

Signs of Success

In Willows, California, ethnic tensions among youth have decreased since a Community Service Officer began meeting regularly with Asian youth and parents of youth in gangs. The Officer has been successful in helping the youth focus on school and helping parents relate more effectively to their children.

Applying the Strategy

The Center for Urban Expression, part of the Dorchester (Massachusetts) Youth Collaborative, sponsors Common Ground, a violence and substance abuse prevention program for African-American, Asian, and Latino youth ages ten to thirteen. The Massachusetts Committee on Criminal Justice has helped establish this program, which focuses on the special needs of immigrant and refugee young people. The program is held at a youth center that also features a basketball tournament and weight training competition. A bilingual outreach worker is a member of the staff.

In Portland, Oregon, police meet with ethnic youth at pizza restaurants and other informal locations to hear their concerns. The youth can attend summer field trips, and during the school year, specially trained officers help them with their homework and encourage them to stay in school.

Contact Information

Program Director
Center for Urban Expression
Dorchester Youth Collaborative
1514-A Dorchester Avenue
Dorchester, Massachusetts 02122
617-288-1748

Involve Residents in Community Policing Planning

Strategy

By bringing residents into the community policing planning process, law enforcement can facilitate positive relations between the police and residents, relations that are essential to addressing resident concerns about crime and safety.

Crime Problem Addressed

Many U.S. communities and neighborhoods face serious problems with quality-of-life issues, lack of services, property crime, youth violence, drug trafficking, and other environmental factors. Typically, police responded to such problems in an incident-driven and reactive fashion; they control the particular incident, but have limited long-term impact on crime prevention. Such techniques do not allow residents to become partners in crime prevention and control and to address their concerns about crime and safety. As a result, many communities have poor or ineffective relationships with the local police and there is no mutual cooperation to address resident concerns. Community-oriented policing, which builds cooperative relationships with residents, reflects the importance of police-resident cooperation. Partnerships in the formative stages of community-oriented policing initiatives can enrich the effectiveness of this approach.

Key Components

The concept behind community policing is that the most effective way to deal with crime is to supplement traditional approaches with police-resident cooperation in identifying and responding to problems that contribute to the likelihood of criminal behavior in the community. Community-oriented policing encourages residents to share the responsibility of building safer and more healthy communities. Community Policing Officers (CPO) are encouraged to build positive relationships with residents, involving the residents in crime prevention and control through recognition and use of community resources. During the planning stages of a community policing initiative, all efforts should be made to engage residents by asking for input on analysis of neighborhood crime problems and by involving community groups in crime prevention. Ignoring residents in the planning stage may result in diminished receptivity of residents to the initiative and less effective relationships with community groups. Neighborhood forums, surveys, or informal dialogues can facilitate the involvement of residents in the planning process and help ensure a mutually acceptable and effective community policing program.

Key Partnerships

Effective community-oriented policing requires a relationship of trust and mutual cooperation between police and local residents. Residents must be aware that police officials view their input as valuable and necessary. Effective design of patrol beats and crime prevention programs depends on understanding neighborhood and community issues. Dialogue with residents and community groups brings these issues to light.

Potential Obstacles

One expert in the field remarked that "community policing is a mindset, not just another program." The success of a community policing initiative thus requires the entire department's understanding and commitment to its philosophy. Because community policing requires restructuring traditional law enforcement approaches and forming new relationships with residents, efforts must be made to impart clear information to the community about the program and what the police hope to achieve through these organizational changes. Some police departments even contract with community leaders, who help plan, support, and maintain community policing projects in specific neighborhoods.

Signs of Success

In 1990, the Bureau of Justice Assistance of the U.S. Department of Justice awarded eight localities funds to implement community policing initiatives. In the Innovative Neighborhood-Oriented Policing Program (INOP), residents and police worked together to plan and design the community policing program. INOP was successful at many levels. Many sites reported that community-oriented policing had diminished drug trafficking, alleviated residents' fear of crime, improved police-citizen relations, and bolstered community involvement in crime control and prevention projects.

Applying the Strategy

Input from community residents on the development of a community policing initiative was a primary goal of the city government in Cleveland, Ohio. The mayor's office organized six town hall forums, where residents were encouraged to air their views on the direction of the proposed community policing program. In addition, residents were asked to complete surveys on the most pressing violence and crime problems in their city and to propose solutions to those problems. The concerns identified were followed up by city officials within a few days of the forum, a signal that resident input was desired and would be valued.

The forums attracted an average of 300 residents. Many residents who attended also signed cards stating they would like more information on volunteering for the Department's community relations committee, Neighborhood Watch organizations, and neighborhood patrol groups. Dozens of new Neighborhood Watch groups were founded in neighborhoods throughout the city through this process.

Contact Information

Director
Office of Violence Reduction and Crime Prevention
City Hall
601 Lakeside Avenue
Cleveland, OH 44114
216-664-4646

Police Cooperation With Residents To Identify Community Needs

Strategy

Identification of residents' need for services by community policing officers (CPOs) helps gain cooperation among local agencies to bring those services to the community and its neighborhoods.

Crime Problem Addressed

Typically, police have responded to crime-related problems in a community in an incident-driven, rapid-response fashion. This approach quells the momentary threat, but does not address the causes of the problem or the concerns of the residents about conditions in the neighborhood that contribute to the likelihood of crime. In community policing, the most effective way to deal with crime is to supplement traditional law enforcement approaches with police-resident cooperation through identification of and response to resident concerns. Often, residents' concerns about crime go beyond incidents of criminal activity to a need for assistance from social services or other agencies. This strategy directs CPOs to learn about the community's needs for services from local agencies and service providers other than the police department. The strategy recognizes that the police department alone cannot resolve the community's concerns, but that a network of agencies must cooperate in assisting residents of troubled neighborhoods.

Key Components

In this strategy, law enforcement agencies and social service providers, job placement agencies, and youth service organizations coordinate their activities on behalf of neighborhoods that have demonstrated an array of crime-related problems and social needs. The implementation of this cooperation can take the form of co-located services in a neighborhood site, coordinated outreach and information to clients in specified areas, or cooperative provision of services for the maximum benefit of the residents needing assistance.

Key Partnerships

Effective community policing requires a relationship of trust and mutual cooperation between police and local residents. Understanding and awareness of the community's need for youth programs, employment assistance, safe recreation facilities, medical or social support services, sanitation, and substance abuse treatment is imperative for an effective community policing program. CPOs can work with neighborhood councils, crime watch groups, or tenant organizations to build the relationships that help bring such concerns to light.

In this strategy, the CPO facilitates connections between the residents and agencies from whom they need new or expanded services. The CPO develops an understanding of the community's needs and then helps resident organizations or neighborhood groups advocate for services in the area or improved access to centrally located services.

Potential Obstacles

Because community policing requires restructuring traditional law enforcement approaches to crime prevention and establishing new types of cooperative relationships with residents, law enforcement must make a strong effort to communicate clearly with the community about what they hope to accomplish with the residents through community policing. Police officers should be extensively trained to work with residents to identify common concerns in the community and to elicit resident suggestions about how these concerns could be addressed. Some police departments hire community residents to work directly with the CPOs in their neighborhood.

Signs of Success

Since early 1990, the Sparrow Estates neighborhood of Lansing, Michigan, has benefitted from the Neighborhood Network Center. The Center was established after the area's CPO began discussing the crime-related problems of the neighborhood with residents and seeking their ideas about possible solutions. This full-time neighborhood service center hosts a variety of government and nonprofit service providers. Services provided in this donated space include:

- parenting classes;

- substance abuse and job counseling;

- health care advice;

- dropout prevention assistance;

- interpreters for non-English speaking residents; and

- a base of operations for law enforcement and code enforcement agency activities to close drug houses in the area.

The center now also serves an adjoining neighborhood. After three years, the two neighborhoods have seen a 75 percent reduction in reported crime. The law enforcement-led problem-solving team has also closed several drug houses, connected residents with job opportunities, or-

ganized programs for area youth, coordinated visits to home-bound elderly, and supported community cleanup projects. Area residents credit the Center and the CPOs with restoring a "real neighborhood feeling" to an area once known as one of the city's primary locations for drug trafficking and street prostitution.

Applying the Strategy

As far back as 1987, the police department and residents in Savannah, Georgia—working with other agencies—had established a partnership designed to increase the quality of life in distressed neighborhoods. Supported by city, state, federal, and private funds, the Showcase Neighborhood Program sought to bring important services into targeted neighborhoods. The successful program earned the city a City Livability Award from the U.S. Conference of Mayors in 1990.

Contact Information

Neighborhood Network Center
Lansing Police Department
735 East Michigan Avenue
Lansing, MI 48912
517-325-6497

Mobile Service Vehicles

Strategy

Mobile service vehicles staffed by community policing officers (CPOs) and representatives of service agencies provide a variety of communities with access to needed assistance.

Crime Problem Addressed

Neighborhoods with serious crime, violence, drug abuse, and quality-of-life problems are usually also neighborhoods that are underserved by local government and private social service agencies. Neighborhood-based services would be ideal for such communities, but that is often not possible in municipalities with limited city funds. Frustration grows in communities that believe their needs are not being met. The social conditions that prompt the need for services also contribute to the likelihood of continuing problems with crime and violence.

This strategy addresses those underlying social conditions by using multipurpose mobile service vehicles to provide services to several neighborhoods on a rotating basis; the vehicles ensure that the service provider reaches the maximum number of residents in need at the minimum cost to any single agency or organization. Police involvement, in cooperation with other service providers, helps establish a basis for positive relationships with res-

idents and gives the CPOs a presence in each neighborhood and a base of operations for work in each community.

Key Components

In this strategy, police combine resources with local social service agencies to sponsor a mobile office or service vehicle that takes needed services to neighborhoods:

- medical care;

- substance abuse counseling;

- job referral service;

- emergency housing assistance; and

- support for domestic violence victims.

In addition to providing services to residents, the presence of the vehicle deters criminal activity in the neighborhoods it visits. The mobile van gives police and other agencies the ability to respond quickly, as service needs in neighborhoods changes. For police, the vans provide a vantage point for understanding the crime problems of the neighborhood, even for conducting surveillance.

Key Partnerships

Effective community policing requires a relationship of trust and mutual cooperation between police and local residents. The establishment of a mobile service van should result from problem-solving discussions where police and residents have identified neighborhood concerns and service needs. Often, resident associations serve as a key partner with police in solving problems.

Potential Obstacles

The cost of the vehicle and the personnel resources to staff it present the most significant obstacles to this strategy. Police and other contributing agencies can combine resources to fund the purchase of the van or mobile home, which is often marked as a police vehicle. The police department can offset the burden by seeking corporate or community resources to buy the vehicle or to publicize the services that neighborhoods can receive through participating agencies.

Signs of Success

New York City was one of eleven sites that participated in the Innovative Neighborhood-Oriented Policing Program (INOP) sponsored by the Bureau of Justice Assistance, U.S. Department of Justice, and one of several that used mobile service vans. The goal of the New York City program was to use a large van as a mobile resource center for three low-income and crime-plagued neighborhoods.

The vans were staffed by CPOs and neighborhood volunteers. They provided services as well as information about other service providers in the area. Services included employment counseling, information on emergency food and housing support, health screening, AIDS education, referrals to substance abuse treatment, and information on community events.

The 1992 evaluation of the INOP program cited in *The Challenge of Community Policing*, by Dennis Rosenbaum, showed that the mobile service van service centers had significantly increased cooperation between residents and police and had improved community relations with the department.

Applying the Strategy

In Abington, Pennsylvania, the Community Policing vehicle is a twenty-foot mobile mini-station that supports CPOs' work in the neighborhoods. It provides decentralized police services and allows other local agencies space for neighborhood-based services. On occasion, the vehicle has been used during daylight hours as a base for observing illegal activity, resulting in several arrests.

Contact Information

Abington Township Police Department
1166 Old York Road
Abington, Pennsylvania 19001
215-885-4450, ext. 620

Bicycle Patrols

Strategy

Community policing officers staff and coordinate bicycle patrols of neighborhoods and business districts to deter crime, identify problems, and respond to incidents.

Crime Problem Addressed

Bicycle patrols can facilitate cooperative relationships between residents and police, as they increase police visibility in an accessible way. Depending on the geography and climate of the community, the bicycle patrols can also be highly effective as an enforcement tool. They are quiet and quick; they can pursue suspects through some areas that police cars cannot reach.

Key Components

The concept underlying community policing is that the most effective way to deal with crime is to build police-resident cooperation in identifying crime-related issues and responding to crime. Bicycle patrols are valuable because they increase enforcement capabilities and flexibility. In addition, residents and business owners perceive officers who patrol on bicycles as more approachable.

Typically, police department bicycle patrols are a separate unit designated to patrol business districts or neighborhoods. Training in police work and community relations is often supplemented by strict physical conditioning. Many police departments raise private funds to purchase bicycles or use assets seized in drug cases to finance the unit. In some cities, sporting goods manufacturers and bicycle stores have donated equipment for use by the officers. Bicycle patrol officers have even sponsored youth-officer riding clubs as a strategy for improving relationships with area youth.

Key Partnerships

Partnerships with businesses and residents can be helpful in raising funds to support the program.

Potential Obstacles

One obstacle to the strategy is the seasonal nature of its usefulness in some communities. Long and cold winters are not hospitable conditions for patrol on bicycles. In some southwestern and southern cities, officers have found it uncomfortable to wear bullet-proof vests while on patrol during summer months. Bicycle patrols have been used in business and tourist districts during summer months when crowds are heaviest. Raising funds for the equipment and adapted uniforms for the officers can present an obstacle, but one which can be overcome through partnerships with businesses and residents. Fundraising events can also help build community support for the police.

Signs of Success

The bicycle patrol program in San Antonio, Texas, began in 1990 in response to downtown merchants and residents concerned about crime. The police department bicycle unit started out as a subset of an established foot patrol program. It is now supported by private donations from merchants eager for increased visibility of patrol officers in the downtown area most frequently visited by tourists. To date, bicycle patrol officers have made close to 7,000 arrests and enjoy the continuing support of a growing number of area businesses and residents.

Applying the Strategy

The Civil Bicycle Patrol in Orange County, Florida, was conceived and is run by civilians who work in close cooperation with police and the sheriff's department. The volunteers report suspicious activities and deter crime through their visibility in areas not always covered by police patrols.

Abington, Pennsylvania, police officers participate in a part-time bicycle patrol. Working in close cooperation with the department's Bureau of Narcotics Investigation, the officers are able to arrest suspects and reduce drug sales in targeted areas, increasing resident confidence in the department's commitment to rid the neighborhoods of drug trafficking. Side benefits of the program include increased apprehension of suspects in thefts at a nearby shopping mall. This resulted from bicycle patrol officer pursuit of suspects through parking lots at the request of mall security.

Contact Information

Bicycle Patrol Supervisor
San Antonio Police Department
240 East Houston Street
San Antonio, Texas 78205
210-207-7764

Police Cooperation With Residents To Reduce Drug Trafficking

Strategy

Police and residents work in partnerships to prevent drug trafficking and substance abuse.

Crime Problem Addressed

Communities across the country struggle to address drug trafficking, a crime problem that has taken on crisis proportions in many localities. In rural and urban settings, it has been demonstrated that an active drug trade precipitates and perpetuates the disintegration of neighborhoods. By supplementing traditional law enforcement methods with community policing approaches, community members become partners in drug-trafficking prevention, maximizing the effectiveness and efficiency of the police.

Key Components

Police and residents use patrols, neighborhood problem-solving meetings, "hot spot" reporting cards, anonymous tip lines, and crime data analysis to identify high drug-trafficking locations, track suspects, and deal with landlords and business owners who facilitate drug trafficking.

Key Partnerships

All community members are affected by the ills of drug trafficking, and all hold a stake in improving their neighborhoods. Police-resident partnerships help residents take an active stand against drug trafficking in their neighborhoods. In this capacity, residents are viewed as valuable resources who can provide police with valuable information, organize street patrols, support recreational activities for youth in the community, or facilitate enforcement tactics.

Potential Obstacles

Fear is one of the greatest issues facing residents who live in neighborhoods with significant drug trafficking. Residents may be reluctant to become vocal, visible opponents of drug traffickers. Resident fear cannot be abated overnight. Skilled community and police leadership working in cooperative partnerships can build trust and encourage resident participation to address drug dealing in safe and effective ways.

Signs of Success

Tempe, Arizona, is a densely populated suburb of Phoenix, about a three-hour drive from the border of Mexico. In 1990, Tempe was chosen to participate in the U.S. Department of Justice-sponsored Innovative Neighborhood-Oriented Policing (INOP) initiative. The focus of the city's community policing program was to reduce drug-related crime in neighborhoods through partnerships among law enforcement, community organizations, and local residents. A police "beat team" was set up with the following goals:

■ develop intelligence and information systems to support drug enforcement and demand reduction;

■ implement a communications network and information hotline with citizen groups, to educate them on drug prevention and involve them in drug and crime prevention efforts;

■ coordinate enforcement activities;

■ expand recreational and educational programs staffed by team members; and

■ enhance existing community outreach programs.

In addition, the city developed a citizen police academy, where residents received training in community policing and were encouraged to play an active role in implementing the program.

The 1992 evaluation of INOP rated Tempe's community policing program as extremely effective, particularly on the issues of reducing drug trafficking and drug-related crime, decreasing fear among residents, and enhancing community organization and involvement.

Applying the Strategy

The South Seattle (Washington) Crime Prevention Council is another example of a successful police-community partnership. Formed in 1988, the group targeted suspected drug locations with aggressive patrols, followed up on citizen hotline reports of crack house locations, and investigated citizen complaints of drug activity in public and private housing. Police followed up on more than 1,200 citizen reports in just one year, closing crack houses and enforcing violations by landlords. The Seattle Police Department has been a national leader in supporting community crime prevention strategies since the 1970s.

Contact Information

Director
Community Policing Bureau
Seattle Police Department
700 3rd Avenue, Room 540
Seattle, Washington 98104
206-684-5701

Bibliography

Books

Eck, John E. *Criminal Justice Abstracts.* Buffalo, NY: Willow Tree Press, 1993.

Goldstein, Herman. *Problem-Oriented Policing.* New York: McGraw-Hill, 1990.

International City/County Management Association. *Source Book: Community-Oriented Policing: An Alternative Strategy.* Washington, DC: National Institute of Justice, October 1994.

Jackson, Gail, ed. *Exemplary Programs in Criminal Justice: Innovations at the Local Level.* Washington, DC: National League of Cities, 1994.

Rosenbaum, Dennis P. *The Challenge of Community Policing: Testing the Promises.* Thousand Oaks, CA: Sage Publications, 1994.

Periodicals

Bike Patrol Rolls Over Crime. *Catalyst,* National Crime Prevention Council, May-June, 1994, p. 4.

Donahue, Michael E. A Comprehensive Program to Combat Violent Crime: The Savannah Experience. *The Police Chief,* September 1993, pp. 12–22.

Inkster, Norman D. The Essence of Community Policing. *The Police Chief,* March 1992.

Lutton, Linda. Victory at Mount Vernon: Neighbors Say Goodbye to Gangs and Graffiti and Take Back Their Park. *Neighborhoods,* Winter 1995.

Peddling Prevention. *Catalyst,* National Crime Prevention Council, November 1993, pp. 4-5.

Rush, George E. Community Policing: Overcoming the Obstacles. *The Police Chief,* October 1992.

Sparrow, Malcolm K. Implementing Community Policing. *Perspectives on Policing,* U.S. Department of Justice, National Institute of Justice, November, 1988.

Public Documents

California Department of Justice. *Community-Oriented Policing and Problem Solving.* November 1992.

California Department of Justice. *Community-Oriented Policing and Problem Solving: Definitions and Principles.* April 1993.

Community Policing Consortium: International Association of Chiefs of Police, National Sheriffs' Association, Police Executive Research Forum, Police Foundation. *Understanding Community Policing: A Framework for Action.* Version 7.6. 1994.

National Center for Community Policing. *Community Policing Series.* "The Neighborhood Network Center: Part One." No. 23.

North Carolina Department of Crime Control and Public Safety. *From Projects to Communities: Crime Prevention in Inner-City and Public Housing Communities.* November 1993.

U.S. Attorney's Office. *Resource Fair Program Summaries: Building Justice in Our Communities.* October 1994.

U.S. Attorney's Office. District of Maryland. *Community-Based Initiatives Program: Summary Report.* Baltimore: 11 July 1994.

U.S. Department of Justice. *Community Policing: A Survey of Police Departments in the United States.* National Center for Community Policing, Michigan State University, 1994.

U.S. Department of Justice. Bureau of Justice Assistance. *Understanding Community Policing: A Framework for Action.* Washington, DC, August 1994.

U.S. Department of Justice. National Institute of Justice. *Community Policing in Seattle: A Model Partnership Between Citizens and Police.* August 1992.

U.S. Department of Justice. National Institute of Justice. *Rural Crime and Rural Policing.* October 1994.

Safe and Attractive Public Places

Crime prevention means much more than protection of individuals within their homes. Safe and thriving communities need parks, downtown shopping areas, business districts, schools, and public housing communities where residents can feel protected from the threat of crime and violence.

The maintenance of public areas in which people can interact is critical in fostering the sense of community that is needed to empower and motivate residents to prevent crime and rebuild their cities. The 86 strategies in this chapter are divided into ten crime problem areas:

■ **City-Wide** (twelve strategies)—Perhaps more important than any single strategy to address a specific crime is an overarching commitment to increase citizens' perception of safety and a general sense that crime prevention actions are occurring. Key programs that can address all crimes include safety inspections, such as those which reduced crime in public housing by 62 percent in Danville, Virginia, and Crime Prevention Through Environmental Design (CPTED) programs, which use the planning and design of an area to make residents feel secure in their environment, both indoors and outdoors. City crime prevention councils encourage partnerships between businesses and residents that identify and address crime issues.

■ **Downtown/Business Districts** (seven strategies)—Businesses can take numerous actions to discourage crime. Business Watch programs create partnerships between the police and local businesses to increase awareness of crime trends and take preventive measures such as safety inspections to make workplaces crime-resistant. A Seattle Business Watch cut crime by almost 50 percent. Other safety recommendations can come from insurance companies or municipal inspectors who evaluate the security of a business district.

■ **Retail Businesses** (six strategies)—Individual retail businesses can use highly innovative strategies to reduce the risk of crime. City and state governments can improve safety by enacting high-risk business security guidelines and ordinances that identify areas that have particularly high crime rates or businesses that are especially vulnerable to illegal activity. A Gainesville, Florida, ordinance requiring a number of measures, such as two clerks at night, alarms, and drop safes, was credited with eliminating three-quarters of store robberies. Stores have taken independent action to discourage crime by limiting the amount of cash in registers and placing life-sized cardboard police officers in visible parts of the establishment to deter would-be criminals.

■ **Entertainment Districts** (nine strategies)—Red-light districts and concentrations of entertainment within a city often suffer from corresponding concentrations of criminal activities, particularly drug trafficking and prostitution. CPTED measures

153

can accomplish a great deal in ridding an area of these undesirable behaviors. Zoning laws can prevent the over-accumulation of entertainment industries that spur crime, such as bars, liquor stores, and adult book stores. Restrictions on turning and parking can also inconvenience criminal businesses and prevent their incidence. The securing or demolition of abandoned buildings can have a substantial impact on crime, as evidenced by a study in Austin, Texas, showing that there was no crime in two-thirds of abandoned but secure buildings, whereas 83 percent of abandoned and unsecured buildings were crime hotspots.

■ **Malls** (six strategies)—Shopping malls are often vulnerable targets of crime and theft. To deter crime, it is important to maintain a police or security presence at virtually all times. Accordingly, many malls across the country have instituted 24-hour security staffs to ensure business safety at all hours. Bike patrols at malls also increase the visibility of security staff, making criminal activity riskier. Some bike patrols have led to reports of up to 69 percent reductions in crime.

■ **Parks** (four strategies)—Parks and recreational public spaces can serve as sources of civic pride and as centers for social activities that prevent crime. If left to deteriorate, however, parks become centers of criminal activity and symbols of municipal decay. The public should be encouraged to maintain parks through Take Back the Parks programs that encourage residents to clean up local recreation areas and increase surveillance to prevent crime and to provide centers for activity. Other programs have capitalized on accessible parks; a midnight basketball program in Phoenix, Arizona, organizes basketball games during the times when crime occurs most frequently, from 10 p.m. to 2 a.m., and has achieved a 55 percent reduction in juvenile crime.

■ **Hospitals** (three strategies)—Hospitals are becoming increasingly susceptible to theft and violence, compounding the traumas of physical injury and illness with the victimization of crime. Preventive measures include restricting access to prevent wandering visitors from stealing possessions and assigning police or security guards to emergency rooms to prevent violence.

■ **Public Transportation** (nine strategies)—The appearance and actual security of public transportation facilities has a great deal to do with residents' perception of crime in their city. Subways can be high-risk areas for crime, engendering an atmosphere of fear among passengers. City ordinances to ban panhandling in subway stations have resulted in a number of benefits, including lower crime rates in the subways (a New York subway ban on panhandling reduced crimes by 15 percent), a greater will-

ingness to use public transportation, and more positive perceptions of the homeless population. Subway station design can use better lighting and visibility to tighten security and alleviate fears of crime. Buses can lower the risk of theft by enacting exact fare requirements and using an inaccessible coin deposit safe.

■ **Schools** (fifteen strategies)—All too frequently, schools are unable to perform as centers of learning because of the presence of violence and crime within them. Countering this trend requires increased surveillance to keep criminals and strangers outside of schools in conjunction with increased internal security to stop students from committing crimes. A number of programs exist to achieve the goals of CPTED: Lafayette County, Mississippi, restricts the number of doors through which visitors can enter the school, uses closed-circuit television cameras, and has volunteer security patrols in order to make sure that people who don't belong on school grounds don't go there; the required wearing of school identification cards allows strangers or intruders on school grounds to be spotted immediately; turning off the lights after school stops vandalism by preventing graffiti from being visible. Schools can bolster their internal security by having codes of conduct and dress codes that establish community rules and discourage gang behavior. Student crime watches and crime hotlines also create a climate intolerant to crime among the student population. Around the country, drug-free and gun-free zones have abated major crime threats on school grounds.

■ **Public Housing Communities** (fifteen strategies)—Public housing communities often experience significant violence and other crimes. Some offenders are residents; many others are visitors, illegal occupants of residential units, or trespassers. Without action to protect them, residents and visitors suffer injury, law-abiding residents live in fear, and public areas of the community go unused or deteriorate. As in any other neighborhood, when residents collaborate with one another, property management, and police, crime is reduced. Property managers and police in Mobile, Alabama, enforce provisions of resident leases which prohibit criminal activity; in one 18-month period they evicted 90 crime-involved residents. Enforcement of trespass laws helped make public communities in Tampa, Florida; Baltimore, Maryland; and other cities safer for law-abiding residents and their families. Closed-circuit television surveillance of lobbies and hallways in New York City's Bronxdale complex helped police identify drug-dealing suspects without endangering residents. Saginaw, Michigan's resident patrol in public housing trains residents to use portable radios to notify police of intruders and trespassers. More than 15,000 residents of New York City's public housing had volunteered for resident patrols as of 1994.

CITY-WIDE

High-Risk Business Security Guidelines/Ordinances

Strategy

Voluntary security guidelines or mandatory ordinances establish safety and security requirements for retail businesses at high risk of violent crime.

Crime Problem Addressed

High-risk business security guidelines or ordinances address robbery and other crimes that may accompany it: assault, rape, and murder.

Key Components

Businesses at high risk of being victimized by violent crime are identified. They may be located in high-crime neighborhoods, open 24 hours per day, have only one or two staff during late-night hours, and sell alcohol. Police and businesses work to develop security guidelines that address cash control, employee training, lighting, store layout and design, staffing, and store appearance. The retail industry may seek voluntary compliance, or local ordinances may be necessary.

Key Participants

The policing agency, local retail businesses, and business associations must work together to promote the safety of high-risk businesses.

Potential Obstacles

Retail businesses are resistant to security ordinances. Many do not support requirements to have two clerks on duty during late-night operations.

Signs of Success

The Southland Corporation developed security guidelines that emphasized reducing the opportunity for crime by making stores less attractive to robbers. From 1975 to 1986 their stores had a 37 percent reduction in robbery, and the average theft amount decreased from more than $130 to less than $40 (Crowe, Erickson & Scott, "Set Your Sights on Preventing Retail Violence," *Security Management,* Sept. 1987). In Gainesville, Florida, a late-night security ordinance is credited with a 74 percent robbery reduction from 1986 to 1989 (Virginia State Crime Commission, "Violent Crimes in Convenience Stores," 1993).

Applying the Strategy

Florida's 1990 Convenience Store Security Act focuses on retail stores operating between 10 p.m. and 5 a.m. that report a serious violent act. It requires that these stores set up alarms and video cameras, drop safes, security lighting, training, height markers, increased visibility, and cash management procedures.

Contact Information

Florida Bureau of Criminal Justice Programs
Office of the Attorney General, The Capitol
Tallahassee, Florida 32399-1050
904-487-3712

CPTED Ordinances/Guidelines

Strategy

An ordinance or guideline establishes local Crime Prevention Through Environmental Design (CPTED) standards.

Crime Problem Addressed

CPTED ordinances address a broad range of violent and property crimes, including robbery, assault, burglary, larceny, auto theft, vandalism, and drug dealing.

Key Components

CPTED is action to design the physical environment in ways that reduce or remove identifiable crime risks. The following steps are involved: (1) Organize a small group representing planning, zoning, building, and crime prevention to develop the CPTED initiative. (2) Provide CPTED training to the planning group and orientations to the police department, community groups, business leaders, and economic development officials. (3) Develop a list of CPTED initiatives to incorporate into zoning, redevelopment, or economic development. They should address lighting, security hardware, street and building access control, visibility, and landscaping.

Key Participants

CPTED ordinances require a partnership that includes government leaders and planning staff, police, community groups, architects, and developers.

Potential Obstacles

It may be difficult to interest and organize the variety of individuals and professions necessary to develop a CPTED ordinance. Many see CPTED as having high up-front costs. CPTED works best with new construction. CPTED for existing structures and neighborhoods will be more involved and costly.

Signs of Success

CPTED guidelines that began as a plan to reduce crime in the North Trail Neighborhood in Sarasota, Florida, became an accepted part of the local planning process. The

guidelines helped created active, attractive, and safe streets. The Ringling School of Art and Design, which was in an unsafe neighborhood, developed a strong sense of place and was treated with respect following remodeling using CPTED design guidelines. Litter was reduced and sculptures placed in open view were not defaced (*Catalyst*, National Crime Prevention Council, Oct. 1993).

Applying the Strategy

Sarasota, Florida, organized a CPTED Task Force under the authority of the city manager. It recommended amending the city's zoning law to establish a special zoning district where CPTED was a major component in business revitalization. Later, a resolution in support of CPTED for all city land development and redevelopment projects was adopted.

Contact Information

City of Sarasota
Planning and Development Department
P.O. Box 1058
Sarasota, Florida 34230
813-954-4195

Code Enforcement Teams

Strategy

Teams are organized to enforce federal, state, and local laws, codes, and ordinances to intrude on the crime-generating activities of occupants or owners of property where illegal activities occur.

Crime Problem Addressed

Code enforcement teams address many crimes, including drug sales, gambling, illegal liquor sales, and other serious crimes often associated with these activities, such as rape, robbery, and assault.

Key Components

Locations where illegal activities are taking place are identified. The public should be encouraged to report locations where the illegal activities are occurring. The enforcement and regulatory resources of the locality are coordinated to use the full force of federal, state, and local law to intrude on the activities of crime-generating sites. Health, building, and fire codes are used to have these locations brought into compliance or closed down.

Key Participants

The police; prosecuting attorney; courts; health, building, and fire code officials; fire marshall; alcohol regulators;

and property managers and residents must cooperate to identify and control crime-generating properties.

Potential Obstacles

The variety of participating organizations presents problems of organization, and often the code enforcement process can be very bureaucratic. For code enforcement to be effective, other local government departments must respond quickly to issues. It will also be difficult to locate property owners and hold them accountable for their property.

Signs of Success

The Oakland, California, Police Beat Health program worked with housing, health, and fire officials to reduce criminal activity at 424 properties from 1988 to 1991. The police also offered a program to landlords to teach them how to control or remove illegal activity from their property ("Beat Health Staff Report," Oakland Police Department, 1991).

Applying the Strategy

The Dallas, Texas, Police Department has SAFE teams that address blighted buildings, crack houses, and similar properties with teams of law enforcement and code enforcement personnel.

A neighborhood planning team composed of key city agencies and neighborhood groups was organized by the New Haven, Connecticut, police to monitor activities in high-crime neighborhoods and to focus crime prevention strategies.

Contact Information

Dallas Police Department
4230 West Illinois
Dallas, Texas 75211
214-670-6809

Utility/Employee Watch

Strategy

Businesses and government agencies that have two-way radio communications are organized to report dangerous or suspicious situations.

Crime Problem Addressed

These programs address crimes that occur in public view; they can be a valuable resource in reporting safety hazards and emergencies such as accidents and fires.

Key Components

Businesses or organizations that have two-way radio communication capabilities with staff traveling through the community by vehicle are asked to report suspicious activities. Reporting requirements are established between the policing agency and the participating organizations. A training manual is prepared and used to teach employees how to recognize and report dangerous and suspicious situations. Police staff are oriented on the purpose and operation of the program.

Key Participants

Businesses or organizations that have two-way radio communication are key players in this strategy. Public utilities and local governments have provided significant support for this strategy in many localities. Reporting must be coordinated through the central dispatching office of the policing agency.

Potential Obstacles

Maintaining the interest of workers may be difficult. An incentives program can be developed to recognize them for their support. There may also be some indifference from police patrol personnel who might view some of the reports as unimportant or a waste of time.

Signs of Success

In Salem, Oregon, the workers of the Valley Garbage and Recycling Association made more than 400 reports that have helped to foil car thieves, help catch burglars, and save lives in accidents (*Foundations for Action,* National Crime Prevention Council, 1990).

Applying the Strategy

The Fleetwatch Program operated by the Springfield, Illinois, Police Department involves more than 100 companies. It includes public utilities, moving companies, tow trucks, cable companies, repair trucks, and sanitation trucks. They have helped apprehend criminals, find weapons, and locate lost children.

Contact Information

Springfield Police Department
617 Jefferson Street
Springfield, Illinois 62701
217-788-8392

Address Women's Concerns

Strategy

Develop crime prevention programs from a woman's perspective.

Crime Problem Addressed

Reducing fear of sexual assault and other physical attacks is the primary goal of this approach. The fear of being victimized by men leads many women to change their lifestyles, which can have a detrimental impact on the quality of their lives.

Key Components

Surveys are conducted to determine which situations and people generate the most fear among women when out in public. Particular attention is paid to the unconscious behaviors women engage in to avoid unsafe situations. The opinions of men are compared with those of women. Based on the research, crime prevention proposals that address the fears expressed by both groups are developed. A public education campaign is designed to make men aware of behaviors that make women uneasy in public. This perspective approach can be used for other groups, such as the elderly, children, or the disabled.

Key Participants

Community, victims', and women's groups need to work with the police and researchers to develop a greater understanding of women's perceptions of safety.

Potential Obstacles

Some men may see this approach as a feminization of crime prevention. British research found many men were unwilling to make behavioral changes recommended by study groups.

Signs of Success

The British Home Office researched male behaviors that frightened women and made them uncomfortable in public.

A handbook of tips for men to help them make women feel safer was developed. Tips included the following: don't sit too close to a woman riding alone on public transportation; if walking in the same direction as a woman on her own, don't walk behind her but cross the road and walk on the other side ("Helping Women Feel Safer," *Crime Prevention News,* British Home Office, Fall 1989).

Applying the Strategy

The Safer Cities initiative in Toronto took a similar approach. Grassroots women's organizations conducted research to identify the public places where women feel unsafe. Crime prevention strategies were developed to address the fear of crime by focusing on urban safety and design. The program has been duplicated in Montreal, Winnipeg, and Ottawa.

Contact Information

Faculty of Environmental Studies, York University
355 Lumberg Bldg.
4700 Keele Street
North York, Ontario M3J1P3
416-736-5252

Citizen Crime Prevention Councils

Strategy

A council of community representatives to provide support and advice on public safety issues.

Crime Problem Addressed

Crime prevention councils are organized to address all types of crime.

Key Components

A partnership is formed among the police, government, citizen groups, professional organizations, and business to identify crime problems and develop programs to address them. Members should represent a wide variety of community interests. The council should be a formal organization with elected leaders and bylaws. It should serve in an advisory role and have the ability to influence crime prevention policy. Government may provide funds to support council activities.

Key Participants

Neighborhood Watch supporters, civic groups, community and business leaders, the police, and government organize to form a volunteer advisory council.

Potential Obstacles

Finding individuals with strong leadership skills who are willing to devote volunteer time can be a challenge. Local government and the police may be unwilling to give the council a meaningful voice in developing crime-related policies and programs.

Signs of Success

The Citizens Committee for New York City evaluated neighborhood block associations. It found that strong and durable block associations increase the ability to prevent and combat crime. It found that a strong sense of community at the block level produced greater commitment to anticrime activities, that residents of organized blocks were more aware and less fearful of crime, that active associations were most likely to report crimes to the police, and that the most successful associations had a well-developed system of communication (*Research Update,* California Department of Justice, 1989).

Applying the Strategy

The Citizens Committee for New York City also organized a Neighborhood Leadership Institute, which has trained more than 500 persons on how to lead block associations and tenant groups. In addition to coordinating the city Block Watch program, the Crime Watch Coalition in Newport News, Virginia, has coordinated drug and child abuse prevention workshops, self-defense classes, and support groups for crime victims. The city provides $12,000 annually to support the coalition.

Contact Information

Citizens Committee of New York City
3 West 29th Street
New York, New York 10001
212-684-6767

Safer Design of Public Areas in Neighborhoods

Strategy

Neighborhoods can reduce drug-related activity through environmental changes that make their communities less vulnerable and hospitable to drug dealers.

Drug Problem Addressed

Some communities are perfect hideaways for drug dealers and users. The lighting is poor, the streets permit speeding traffic and traffic patterns that enable quick-getaways, signs are in disrepair, and there are no sidewalks for residents.

Key Components

Crime and drug activity can be reduced if a neighborhood or community is physically designed to provide protection for its residents. Physical changes or improvements can include erecting and maintaining better outdoor lighting, installing and enforcing traffic control signs and lights, closing or limiting access to streets to avoid through traffic, building fences, cleaning up bushes and shrubbery in parks and other public places, installing or repairing sidewalks, and removing abandoned vehicles.

Key Partnerships

Community residents can team with municipal planners, architects, city agencies, law enforcement, traffic engineers, and utility companies to create a safer environmental design in their neighborhoods.

Possible Obstacles

Often, municipal governments are unwilling to work with neighborhoods to improve the physical layout and design of their area to reduce the presence of drug dealers and other criminals. The process frequently takes time because of the requirements of surveying, analysis, bidding for contracts, and delegating funds, all of which require patience from neighborhood residents. In addition to technical issues, there are also issues of eliminating residents' fears, establishing trust between law enforcement and residents, and working to design a model that not only increases safety but promotes neighborhood beautification.

Signs of Success

In the fall of 1992, residents in the Five Oaks community of Dayton, Ohio, joined forces with local police and city planners to institute a Neighborhood Stabilization program. Based on the premise of creating defensible space, 35 iron gates and 26 alley barricades were installed around the Five Oaks community. The gates and barricades were effective in closing off open space previously occupied and used as a main thoroughfare by drug dealers and prostitutes. According to a report from Dayton's Office of Management and Budget, the initiative resulted in a 50 percent decrease in violent crime and a 24 percent decrease in nonviolent crime.

Applying the Strategy

In the east-side peninsula of Bridgeport, Connecticut, an area referred to locally as "Beirut" where 10 percent of the state's homicides occurred in one year, local police authorities and city planning officials implemented a street modification program called the Phoenix Project. Street barriers were installed in heavy drug traffic areas to create "loop" streets coupled with traffic control devices (signs, signals, markings, and gates), making street entrances one-way, turn-offs onto side streets difficult, and traffic flow easier to manage and monitor. The project involved a ten-component community intervention plan including community mobilization, increased tactical enforcement, and a multilaw enforcement sting operation targeted at removing dangerous gang and drug leaders from the streets. The overall initiative resulted in an approximate 75 percent decline in crime and the lowest crime rate in the area since 1972.

Contact Information

Bridgeport Police Department
300 Congress Street
Bridgeport, Connecticut 06604
203-576-7611

Dayton Police Department
Professional Standards Division
335 W. Third Street
Dayton, Ohio 45402
513-449-1311

Live-In Police Officers

Strategy

Incentives encourage police officers to live in high-crime neighborhoods.

Crime Problem Addressed

Having police officers living in high-crime communities addresses all types of crime, but more important, it addressees the public's fear of crime and sense of security.

Key Components

There are a variety of options to encourage police officers to move into high-crime neighborhoods. Public housing authorities have the option of providing apartments in public housing communities at little or no cost. Privately managed apartment communities can also provide apartments at little or no cost. Another option is to provide low-interest mortgage loans to encourage police officers to buy homes in high-crime neighborhoods. Local governments use grant money or foundation donations to provide these low-interest loans.

Key Participants

Local governments working with public housing authorities, apartment management companies, and lending institutions can develop a variety of living options for police officers in high-crime neighborhoods.

Potential Obstacles

Traditionally, police officers have tended to move away from the communities they police. High-crime neighborhoods are also likely to be unattractive to police officers with families. Because this living arrangement is a benefit of employment for participating officers, it will be taxed as income.

Signs of Success

A public housing resident in Elgin, Illinois, stated that "a dramatic, drastic and significantly important change for the better in the living conditions there as a result of having police officers living there." The U.S. Department of Housing and Urban Development has approved accommodations for 135 officers to live free in public housing communities over the past five years (*Crime Prevention News,* May 1994).

Applying the Strategy

The Cops on the Block program in Savannah, Georgia, offers police officers 4 percent loans to buy homes in high-crime neighborhoods. Similar reduced loan programs are used in Columbia, South Carolina, and Wichita, Kansas. Police officers live in public housing at no cost in Milwaukee, Wisconsin, and Alexandria, Virginia.

Contact Information

Savannah Police Department
323 East Oglethorpe Avenue
Savannah, Georgia 31412
912-651-6667

Require Businesses To Remove Graffiti

Strategy

Identify business locations prone to graffiti and require them to remove it promptly.

Crime Problem Addressed

Graffiti is a significant vandalism problem for businesses and communities throughout the country. Beyond the defacing of property from graffiti, the strategy aims to prevent drug sales, robberies, and other crimes which may result in an area where long-standing graffiti signals disorder and decline in a neighborhood.

Key Components

City policy which establishes standards requiring business owners to paint over or remove graffiti is the first step. The ordinance sets out graduated sanctions against property owners who do not take action to address graffiti vandalism. The sanctions include letters from the public works or police department, followed by fines and other penalties for those who do not remove graffiti within set timelines. Property owners are informed of the policy through communication from the city. The city also publicly announces the policy to ensure that all property owners and vandals understand the sanctions and the city's commitment to zero tolerance for graffiti. Most cities who initiate such policies also inform property owners of volunteer or city-sponsored assistance available to help them with graffiti removal.

Key Partnerships

Neighborhood associations, business watch groups, and local business federations can help police and public works departments identify properties with significant graffiti problems and coordinate resources to repair the defaced property.

Potential Obstacles

It may be difficult to get property owners who live out of the area or who do not demonstrate a commitment to the neighborhood to comply with the removal ordinance. The system of graduated sanctions provides the city agency with options to encourage compliance. Fees paid by the owners who do not voluntarily comply can be used to support equipment and supplies to remove graffiti from problem properties. Some localities publish the names of property owners fined as a strategy to promote their compliance. In other cases, business owners complain that they should not be held accountable for damage that others do to their property. The availability of volunteer (or required community service) resources helps address business owners' concerns about the cost of compliance.

Signs of Success

The Community Crime Prevention/SAFE Program in Minneapolis assists property by providing information packets on how to remove graffiti. The police department helps out by providing graffiti removal materials and equipment to residents and businesses.

Applying the Strategy

Cleveland (OH) requires businesses to remove graffiti within specified time frames. Businesses who do not respond to the initial notification can be fined or have liens placed on their property. Police and the courts help property owners by supplying materials, community volunteers, and juveniles sentenced to help with removal of graffiti as their punishment for "tagging" or other minor property offenses.

Contact Information

Department of Neighborhood Services
Room 310-1/2 City Hall
350 South 5th Street
Minneapolis, Minnesota 55415-1388
612-673-3095

Restricted Access to Selected Streets or Neighborhoods

Strategy

Control access to streets and neighborhoods, making travel inconvenient for non-residents.

Crime Problem Addressed

Access restrictions aim to prevent burglary and larceny in residential and business areas, but for some locations may also help prevent easy access by those who wish to buy drugs or commit other crimes and escape quickly. The restrictions can also help address traffic flow and redirect out of town traffic away from residential districts.

Key Components

The restrictions or street closures are based on analysis of area crime problems and review of traffic patterns to determine how redirection of streets or blockades on certain streets could help address the problem. The restrictions are made possible by installing permanent or semi-permanent barriers, and establishing one-way directions for specific streets. The analysis by the police is supplemented by input from traffic engineers and street planners about the style of barrier which would best suit the purposes of the policy. Evaluation of the plan by fire officials helps ensure that response time is not adversely impacted by street changes. The changes are discussed with residents and businesses to determine how to address security concerns without unduly inconveniencing their routines or ability to survive.

Key Partnerships

Interagency coordination in the design and application of the policy builds support for the policy and helps increase the likelihood that street restrictions will help reduce crime without creating problems for fire and other emergency response teams. Cooperation of residents and businesses is essential to understand the impact of the restrictions and build support for expenditures associated with the barriers, street signs, and additional police patrols.

Potential Obstacles

Those who live outside the restricted access area may resent the inconvenience or restriction from entering certain areas as an infringement on their ability to travel as they please. The policy decision to restrict streets or block access must be viewed in balance with safety benefits, public opinion, and the impact of closures on residents and businesses.

Signs of Success

Crime in Bridgeport, Connecticut is the lowest it has been in nearly twenty-five years following imposition of street closures and access restrictions in a neighborhood adjacent to the interstate highway. Previously, unrestricted access to the low-income neighborhood had facilitated outsider travel to the area to buy illegal drugs. Redesign of traffic patterns, bisected intersections, and reduced ingress and egress into the area resulted in a significant reduction in all types of crime within three months. Established after significant public hearings and extended discussions with fire officials and street planners, the policy continues to enjoy significant support among neighbors and businesses.

Applying the Strategy

A Dayton (OH) policy restricting traffic patterns in three neighborhoods resulted in a 50 percent decrease in violent crime and a two-thirds decline in traffic through the residential communities.

Redirection of traffic and new speed controls, parking restrictions, and street closures in public housing communities in Knoxville (TN) helped those neighborhoods achieve a 35 percent reduction in overall crime and a significant reduction in the number of drive by shootings.

Contact Information

Mayor's Office
45 Lyon Terrace
Bridgeport, Connecticut 06604
203-576-7201

Apply Crime Prevention Through Environmental Design to Parking Structures

Strategy

Use of Crime Prevention Through Environmental Design (CPTED) concepts reduces opportunity for all types of crimes and addresses security concerns of residents using such facilities in business districts and shopping malls.

Crime Problem Addressed

This strategy addresses all types of property crimes (theft from vehicles, vandalism against vehicles) and crimes against individuals (assault, robbery, rape) which occur in enclosed parking facilities. It helps to reduce the opportunity for such crimes by paying attention to design issues which can increase surveillance and promote the use of the structures.

Key Components

The effectiveness of the strategy is enhanced if the security issues are addressed at the design stage. If that is not possible, security issues can be reviewed and alterations made based on an analysis of crime data and usage of the facility. Security reviews include lighting within the structure, controlled access to the facility, installation of signs reminding drivers to lock car doors, removal of cars left in the facility beyond a specific number of days, and coverage of walls with white or light paint to reduce the number of dark shadows in the facility.

Key Partnerships

City policy which requires security issues to be addressed at the design level is the optimal situation. If that is not in

place or possible, the police should build a relationship with the property owner and suggest security upgrades which would address crimes in that specific location. Frequent users of the facility should be surveyed about their fears, past victimization, and ideas on how to increase the security of the facility.

Potential Obstacles

Property owners may be reluctant to spend money on security upgrades. Police can help owners understand the benefits of that expenditure by pointing out that security problems may lead to people avoiding the facility or that a user victimized in the facility could bring legal action against an owner for failure to implement security procedures. A reduction in incidents could help the owner reduce insurance costs as well.

Signs of Success

Toronto (Canada) amended its by-laws to increase security in existing parking structures. The policy now includes all mixed use and commercial garages (new and existing structures). City officials promoted use of the garages and provided drivers with reminders about how to secure their cars and take precautions while in the facility. Within a year, 97 percent of the city's 750 garages had complied, reducing crime in parking facilities throughout Toronto.

Based on the Toronto example, laws in Vancouver (Canada) specify minimum design, lighting, signage, and maintenance in parking facilities. The laws apply to new facilities. The city is investigating the possibility of partnerships with the local power utility to provide enhanced energy efficient lighting for parking structures.

Applying the Strategy

According to a security expert, malls in California and Knoxville (TN) reduced crime in mall parking facilities by as much as 25 percent after they instituted CPTED security enhancements.

Contact Information

CTPED Liaison
Vancouver Police Department
312 Main Street
Vancouver, British Columbia
CANADA V6A 2T2
604-665-5065

Reduce Insurance Premiums for Security Improvements

Strategy

Use state or city policy to require insurance premium reductions for businesses or homeowners who install recommended security measures.

Crime Problem Addressed

The policy is intended to encourage residents and business owners to take action which helps reduce the incidence of burglary, home invasion, and vandalism.

Key Components

Local or state insurance regulators work with police to identify basic security enhancements which can reduce the vulnerability of homes and businesses to property crime. They establish a policy which mandates homeowner insurance premium reductions for people who install basic devices such as window locks, deadbolt door locks, alarms, or other access control and early warning techniques. The techniques and devices which qualify property owners for reductions vary from state to state. In other cases, insurance companies offer residents reductions as part of their strategy to limit the loss of profit through claims filed.

Key Partnerships

Police and neighborhood watch groups can help build awareness among property owners of the reductions available. Police can also help residents understand the value of specific techniques and products, advising them on how to prioritize expenditures on products available. Insurance agents can provide homeowners with a list of devices and techniques which qualify for reductions. Community groups can advocate to insurance companies for reductions where they are not required through state or local policy.

Potential Obstacles

Some homeowners may have difficulty finding funds to implement some security measures, particularly alarms and more expensive devices. City or state policy can provide support to low-income residents through loans or support to those who have been previously victimized. Insurance companies can provide discounted coupons for specific items by working with product manufacturers or retailers.

Signs of Success

Texas mandates insurance premium reductions for home security improvements. The policy has helped reduce burglaries among those who have taken advantage of the policy. The rate reduction requirements on companies operating in the state has become part of how they market services to homeowners.

The New York-based Insurance Information Institute helps homeowners and companies evaluate techniques which help secure homes and businesses from crime.

Applying the Strategy

A community-based organization in Baltimore (MD) organized residents and advocated successfully for insurance premium reductions for homeowners who install security devices. They recruited other companies to donate motion detectors, locks, lights, and fencing supplies for low-income residents. The pilot program will seek similar benefits for apartment dwellers by working through landlords to build awareness of available premium reductions and security concerns. The program also focuses on fire safety awareness and fireproofing of homes.

Contact Information

Insurance Information Institute
110 William Street
New York, New York 10038
212-669-9200

DOWNTOWNS/BUSINESS DISTRICTS

Business Crime Prevention Education

Strategy

A curriculum on small retail business crime prevention strategies is used by marketing education teachers to teach marketing education students in high schools.

Crime Problem Addressed

The crime prevention curriculum course addresses all types of crime faced by businesses: robbery, burglary, assault, shoplifting, credit card and check fraud, employee theft, refund fraud, and substance abuse in the workplace.

Key Components

A committee representing education, business, and crime prevention is organized to develop a crime prevention curriculum for retail businesses for high school marketing education students. The curriculum should address robbery, burglary, shoplifting, fraud, employee theft, and drugs in the workplace. It should include an instructor's guide and student workbooks. Marketing education teachers should have a brief orientation at which they receive an instructor's guide, which includes a detailed set of overheads to accompany the training manual. Marketing education teachers should use the instructional material to teach retail business crime prevention to students. The students should also receive a student's manual.

Key Participants

Local schools, law enforcement, and business can work together to provide training to marketing education teachers and students interested in a business career.

Potential Obstacles

Local schools have many demands placed upon them. Introduction of another new curriculum may meet with some resistance or indifference.

Signs of Success

Sixty full-time marketing education teachers in Fairfax County, Virginia, are using the curriculum to teach 3,800 marketing education students. A survey of marketing education teachers statewide was very positive about the curriculum.

Applying the Strategy

A small retail business crime prevention curriculum has been used in school systems throughout Virginia. The training program has been presented to nearly 9,000 high school students. In 1995, NationsBank was considering supporting the project in its nine-state banking area, and Visa U.S.A. was studying the possibility of nationwide distribution.

Contact Information

Project Director
Virginia Tech Hampton Roads Center
418 Pembroke Four
Virginia Beach, Virginia 23462
804-552-1880

Community Safety and Security Assessments

Strategy

Safety and security assessments of neighborhoods, schools, and business districts are conducted.

Crime Problem Addressed

Safety and security assessments address all types of crime.

Key Components

The physical boundaries of the area to be assessed are clearly defined. Data about crimes, arrests, and radio calls from the police, as well as demographic data and land use plans from the community planning department, are obtained. An assessment team, which can include representatives from police, health, building inspections, fire, traffic, community groups, education, social services, and housing management, is organized. The team is familiarized with the location and background data and conduct an on-site inspection. The inspection should assess the physical condition of the area and how it may deter or encourage crime. Residents and other users are interviewed. Government policies and practices related to how the area is served are reviewed. A report of findings is made, with recommendations to correct deficiencies.

Key Participants

Residents, community organizations, the police, and local government officials can work together to conduct community assessments.

Potential Obstacles

Strong support from the local government must be achieved because of the broad range of government services and data involved. The assessment process can be very labor intensive and should be reserved for high-risk neighborhoods.

Signs of Success

In Danville, Virginia, overall crime in public housing was reduced by 62 percent from 1990 to 1992 after changes based on a safety and security assessment were implemented. Police domestic calls decreased 38 percent and fight calls dropped 19 percent ("Safety Assessment for the Danville Housing and Development Authority," Virginia Crime Prevention Association, 1992).

Applying the Strategy

The National School Safety Center has developed a school safety assessment process that examines school management, student behavior, and the school building and surrounding property. The Virginia Crime Prevention Association uses a community safety and security assessment process to assess the safety and security of public housing communities.

Contact Information

Virginia Crime Prevention Association
P.O. Box 6942
Richmond, Virginia 23220
804-266-7506

Fax Information Network

Strategy

A fax network alerts businesses to crime problems or patterns in the commercial community.

Crime Problem Addressed

The fax information network will provide timely information about a variety of crimes against businesses, including robbery, burglary, shoplifting, bad checks, and credit card fraud.

Key Components

The police department on its own or in conjunction with a business organization establishes a fax network. Information on current crime problems or trends is faxed to participating businesses. A schedule can be established for sending a regular fax broadcast; the network can also be used to send time-sensitive material, such as information about an armed robbery ring working the business area or the photo of a child missing in the neighborhood.

Key Participants

The police department, businesses, and business organizations must be linked together by fax machines.

Potential Obstacles

Participation is restricted to businesses that have fax machines. The system must deliver timely and accurate information or the businesses may lose confidence in it.

Signs of Success

US West has established a fax broadcast service for the Rocky Mountain Business Watch. It has distributed 3,000 crime alert bulletins to 13 police department and 250 businesses in the Business Watch network. Subscribers pay $100 for the service. Information about the US West service can be obtained by calling Business Watch (800) 947-4770 ("US West Establishes New FAX Service," *Crime Control Digest,* March 22, 1993).

Applying the Strategy

The Police Department in Dallas, Texas, is implementing a Fax Alert program that will link businesses and crime watches to the police department. It will provide information on crime trends and suspect descriptions and warn of crime patterns from area to area. The program is provided at no cost by Fax-Net 1, a non-profit group in Phoenix, Arizona.

Contact Information

Dallas Police Department
Community Policing Support Unit
2020 North Lamar, Suite 300
Dallas, Texas 75202-1799
214-670-4427

Workplace Safety Inspections

Strategy

Government agencies responsible for workplace safety conduct inspections of high-risk businesses to reduce crime-related safety hazards to employees and customers.

Crime Problem Addressed

The most recent National Crime Victimization Survey found that one in seven of all violent crimes occurs in the workplace. This strategy addresses murder, rape, robbery, and assault in the workplace, primarily in retail settings.

Key Components

The agencies responsible for workplace safety must accept crime as a workplace safety issue. They must cooperate with the police and businesses to identify the workplaces at most risk for violent crime and develop strategies to reduce the risks. The strategies can include design changes to stores, violence prevention training for employees, use of cameras and alarms, and improvements in lighting. Enforcement can be done separately or through a partnership agreement between the police and workplace safety agencies.

Key Participants

Government agencies responsible for workplace safety and businesses are the key participants. Crime prevention staff from the police should serve as advisors.

Potential Obstacles

Businesses are likely to resist this intrusion into the workplace as another set of government regulations. Government agencies responsible for workplace safety may not agree that crime is a workplace safety issue. Police departments may also see this as an infringement on their authority.

Signs of Success

The Indiana Department of Labor fined a drug store where three employees were murdered $1,000 for violating the Occupational Safety and Health Act of 1974. It found that the employer did not furnish a place of employment that was free from recognized violent crime hazards and had not introduced procedures to reduce the crime hazards and had not properly trained employees.

Applying the Strategy

The State of Washington developed standards for Late Night Retail Workers Crime Protection. It established authority for the Department of Labor and Industry to ensure that retail establishments that operate from 11 p.m. to 6 a.m. provide crime prevention training to their employees and establish crime prevention procedures to reduce the risks of crime and violence.

Contact Information

Division of Industrial Safety and Health
Technical Services HC-432
P.O. Box 207
Olympia, Washington 98507-0207
206-586-1851

Promote Insurance Loss Control Recommendations

Strategy

Businesses and organizations implement crime prevention recommendations made by insurance carriers.

Crime Problem Addressed

Insurance carriers rate businesses and other insured organizations based on their crime risk. The ratings address all types of crime, including robbery, assault, burglary, and larceny. The focus for a particular set of ratings will depend on the type of property being rated.

Key Components

Insurance industry crime risk ratings for businesses and other organizations are used to encourage them to implement recommended crime prevention strategies. The ratings are produced by individual insurance companies and by insurance rating organizations. The insurance industry conducts loss control evaluations of all the organizations it insures. These evaluations address loss related to automobile liability, general liability, product liability, worker's compensation, fire, and crime. Locations are classified by type of operation and business activity. The insurance industry relies on current practice by the police community and corporate security to develop recommendations to identify and reduce crime risks.

Key Participants

Police agencies, business groups, and civic groups can work with the insurance industry to identify risks and implement crime prevention recommendations.

Potential Obstacles

A main principal in the insurance field is that if you have a risk, you should insure against it. The ratings are offered only as advice to businesses and organizations. The businesses and organizations that follow the advice are expected to have a lower exposure to crime, and their losses from crime are expected to be less, possibly resulting in lower insurance costs.

Signs of Success

The Best Underwriting Guide for Commercial Standards is an industry standard for writing all types of insurance and is a primary reference for insurance risk managers across the country.

Applying the Strategy

The A.M. Best Company has developed a comprehensive guide to assist in writing insurance for a variety of settings. Individual insurance carriers may also develop their own rating guide.

Contact Information

A.M. Best Company, Inc.
Oldwick, New Jersey 08858
908-439-2200

Reduce the Amount of Readily Available Cash

Strategy

Cash control reduces the amount of cash readily available in cash registers.

Crime Problem Addressed

Reducing the amount of cash that is readily available deters robbery and assault.

Key Components

Research has shown that the amount of cash on hand is a primary factor in whether or not a robber will attack a particular store. Small businesses can discourage robbers by keeping as little cash as possible in the register. Options are to transfer the cash to the bank frequently or to purchase a safe to store the cash until it can be deposited. A policy should be set limiting how much cash can be in a cash register at one time, especially when it is dark. Signs can be posted that only $50 is in the cash register at any given time, to discourage robbers.

Key Participants

The business owner must establish a cash handling policy and make sure that employees adhere to it.

Potential Obstacles

Transferring the cash can be a nuisance and can add to the time it takes to transact sales.

Signs of Success

A study of convenience store robbery in the 1970s found that the amount of cash on hand was one of the primary factors driving robbery. It was determined that the majority of robbers would not rob a store if the take would be $50 or less. In response to this research, Seven-Eleven convenience stores implemented a $50 cash restriction policy. The policy had a dramatic effect on robbery. From 1975 to 1985, robberies decreased by 65 percent (The Store Safety Issue, National Association of Convenience Stores, 1990).

Applying the Strategy

The policy for cash handling established by Seven-Eleven set a standard for the industry that is now used by most major convenience store chains and gasoline retailers.

Contact Information

Loss Prevention
Southland Corporation
2711 North Haskell Avenue
Dallas, Texas 75204
214-828-7451

Promote Hotel/Motel Security Standards

Strategy

Hotels and motels implement minimum security standards.

Crime Problem Addressed

Security standards not only protect travelers from burglary and larceny but can also reduce robbery and assault. Hotel and motel employees are also protected.

Key Components

Most states have laws requiring hotels and motels to protect the safety of their patrons. Safety can be achieved by establishing security standards for the operation of the hotel or motel. Standards typically address door and window locks, peepholes, safes for valuables, lighting, and access to lodgers. Standards have also been established by hotel/motel associations and by travel groups that rate hotels and motels. Determine which hotels and motels in the locality have established security standards. If local hotels and motels are not meeting company safety standards, they should be notified in writing. If corrections are not made, the appropriate rating organization can be contacted. Many organizations restrict their lodging needs to hotels and motels that meet recognized security standards.

Key Participants

Police departments, crime prevention groups, travel organizations, and businesses should work with hotels and motels to encourage the broadest support of the security standards.

Potential Obstacles

Many security and safety problems will be found in small hotels or motels that have no obligation to meet industry security standards. Franchise hotels or motels of large chains usually have no obligation to meet company standards on issues such as security.

Signs of Success

Super 8 Motel mandates that a motel replace a door lock if a key is missing and redo the whole motel lock system if a master key disappears. The Central Florida Hotel and Motel Association developed 19 recommended security and safety standards for its members in response to perceptions about hotel safety in southern Florida (*Lodging Hospitality,* March 1993).

Applying the Strategy

The American Automobile Association (AAA) enhanced its security standards in March 1993. The standards are a component of the system used by AAA to rate hotels and motels throughout the United Sates and other countries.

Contact Information

American Automobile Association
1000 AAA Drive
Heathrow, Florida 32746
407-444-7000

RETAIL BUSINESS

Employee Safety Training

Strategy

Retail employees are trained to avoid dangerous or life-threatening situations.

Crime Problem Addressed

The training provides information needed to deter or avoid rape, robbery, and assault.

Key Components

The types of physical attacks that are most likely to occur in the retail environment must be determined. Considerable research has been conducted by the convenience store industry which is useful to all retail businesses. Store security procedures should be established and incorporated into a training program. The training should be part of introductory training for new employees and offered periodically for current employees. Employees should be taught how to maintain a store environment that will not attract robbers and if a robbery does occur, how to handle it without escalating it to a serious physical assault.

Key Participants

The business owner must work with staff and security consultants or the local police department to develop an effective training program.

Potential Obstacles

There are continuing costs involved with any training program. Small businesses may find it difficult to provide effective training for employees. Employees who frequently violate security policies defeat training objectives.

Signs of Success

Georgia Power Company's Security Awareness Program began in 1982 as bulletin board tips for employees. It expanded to serve the entire community. Information is provided on burglary prevention, child protection, travel safety, office safety, drug prevention, and antirobbery techniques for customer service representatives. A manual, *Security Awareness for Employees,* was published. In 1989 more than 100 classes in crime prevention were provided for employees and community groups (*Foundations for Action*, National Crime Prevention Council, 1990).

Applying the Strategy

The National Association of Convenience Stores has developed employee training programs to reduce violent crime in convenience stores. Model training programs, support materials, and videos are available.

Contact Information

National Association of Convenience Stores
1605 King Street
Alexandria, Virginia 22314-2992
703-684-3600

Cardboard Police Officers

Strategy

Full-size cardboard photos of policemen are displayed in stores to discourage shoplifting or disorderly behavior.

Crime Problem Addressed

Use of full-size photos of police officers can discourage shoplifting and in bar settings can discourage drinking and driving.

Key Components

Full-size photos of police officers are mounted on cardboard stands. The photos are distributed to retail businesses, bars, and other establishments, which are encouraged to display them to discourage crime.

Key Participants

The police department and businesses can work together to create and display the cardboard photos.

Potential Obstacles

There will be some costs associated with producing enough of the cardboard photos to have an impact.

Signs of Success

A full-size cardboard photo of a police officer can have an effect similar to an actual police officer. A study conducted by the University of Chicago found that persons wearing a uniform in public, whether employed by government or the private sector, reduced fear of crime. Women were are more impressed than males by the presence of a uniform ("Reducing Fear of Crime Through Occupational Presence," *Criminal Justice and Behavior*, March 1983).

Applying the Strategy

The Buffalo Grove, Illinois, Police Department issues full-size police photos to display in stores. The use of such photos began with the Houston Police Department in 1991 and now is used by many others.

Contact Information

Houston Police Department
61 Reisner
Houston, Texas 77002
713-247-5550

Ethnic and Culturally Sensitive Business Crime Prevention

Strategy

Business crime prevention services can take into account the special needs of different ethnic groups and cultures.

Crime Problem Addressed

Many small businesses are owned by persons from ethnic or cultural groups whose needs are not addressed by the usual business crime prevention services offered by the police. Many of these businesses may suffer from higher rates of crime because owners do not understand crime prevention and are reluctant to report crime.

Key Components

Police departments should identify the members of ethnic and cultural groups running small businesses in their locality. It must be determined if language or cultural perceptions are inhibiting the business owners from asking for or even wanting crime prevention or other services offered by the police department. Police staff should be briefed on the cultural background of business owners and residents they serve. Crime prevention information may need to be printed in other languages or offered in a different format.

Key Participants

The police department will need to work with ethnic business organizations, refugee resettlement groups, religious groups, and other organizations that provide services to ethnic or cultural groups.

Potential Obstacles

Overcoming the typical stereotypes that many police officers will have of various ethnic groups will be a significant challenge, and these groups may have to change how they view the police. The police department will also have to make arrangements to provide translation services.

Signs of Success

In Portland, Oregon, the police meet regularly with Hmong community leaders and clan heads to discuss problems in their community. As a result of a better understanding between the police and refugees, refugees are more comfortable in reporting crime, and community members are experiencing both a decrease in crime and a sense of increased protection (*Building and Crossing Bridges*, National Crime Prevention Council, 1995).

Applying the Strategy

The Westminster, California, Police Department provides a Neighborhood and Business Watch program that relies on outreach meetings, crime prevention presentations, a resource center, and translation services for its Vietnamese and Hispanic citizens.

Contact Information

Westminster Police Department
8200 Westminster Boulevard
Westminster, California 92683
714-898-3315

Control Cruising

Strategy

Programs control cruising in automobiles by youth.

Crime Problem Addressed

Controlling cruising can help curb disorderly behavior, public drinking, fights, and traffic congestion and help reduce the fear of crime cruising tends to generate among adults and the elderly.

Key Components

Unsupervised locations where youth congregate to "see and be seen" are identified. Youth are surveyed to determine why they cruise. Traffic patterns are studied to see if they are contributing to the problem. A community task force develops strategies to control cruising. Strategies might include better lighting and trash collection, stricter enforcement of traffic laws, and street closures or restrictions. Strategies to channel the cruising energy of youth might include designating a cruising area that is less disruptive to business and traffic flow or supervised activities that appeal to cruisers, such as cars shows.

Key Participants

The police, traffic safety staff, businesses, and youth must work together to develop strategies to control cruising, while providing youth other opportunities to express themselves.

Potential Obstacles

If not planned properly, cruising control techniques may just move the youth from one area to another to cruise.

Signs of Success

Boise, Idaho, feared that a plan to revitalize the downtown area was placed in jeopardy because of the large number of youth who were cruising downtown. After a study of cruising was completed, a task force was put together and cruising control measures were introduced. Lighting was improved, a police mini-station was established, and the YMCA and YWCA started sponsoring alternative activities for youth during the cruising hours. The cruise route remained the same, but because of changes, the cruising caused less traffic congestion and fewer public order problems.

Applying the Strategy

The police in Boise used a community-oriented policing approach to control cruising. They recognized that using enforcement strategies to close down the cruising in one location would not solve the problem. A comprehensive approach was needed to address problems that cruising behavior identified.

Contact Information

Boise Police Department
Administrative Support Division
7200 Barrister Drive
Boise, Idaho 83704
208-377-6770

Enhanced Lighting in Retail Districts

Strategy

Enhance lighting along streets and in parking areas of commercial and retail districts.

Crime Problem Addressed

Minimal lighting helps criminals who would vandalize property, steal vehicles, or commit violent crimes against patrons of businesses avoid detection and escape without detection. The strategy attempts to increase the ability of business owners, patrons, and passersby to notice criminal activity, reducing the attractiveness of the area for potential criminals.

Key Components

Lighting design and installation consultants from private firms or utility companies help business owners understand the value of lighting in attracting customers, protecting customers and employees using the facility or parking areas, and reducing opportunities for vandalism to occur without detection. Business Watch groups request basic security surveys from local police experts who recommend enhanced lighting as part of a comprehensive security strategy for the property. Lighting helps business owners maintain surveillance of their own and other business during operating hours and helps police see suspects fleeing the scene of a crime or suspicious activity.

Key Partnerships

The utility company can help business owners identify the best lighting design and products to meet their security needs. Police can help business owners organize a business watch group to understand how lighting and other security improvements would help protect their customers, employees, and the investment in the facility.

Potential Obstacles

Investments in lighting can be costly. Consultations from utility and police experts can help offset the costs of the products. The business owners must be educated about how to understand the benefit of enhanced lighting and security to bringing in customers and reducing losses through insurance claims on property damage and injuries to customers or employees.

Signs of Success

A study by the U.S. Department of Justice revealed mixed results about the reductions in crime from installation of lighting in commercial districts, but did highlight that significant reductions in fear of crime among residents and customers resulted when uniformed lighting was installed in commercial areas. Reduced fear of the area can be correlated with a willingness of residents to frequent businesses in the area.

Applying the Strategy

The Illuminating Engineers Society publishes security standards for interior and exterior lighting for industrial complexes, sports facilities, and retail establishments. Their Lighting Handbook outlines the security benefits of enhanced lighting.

A comprehensive economic development project along several business district corridors in Charlotte, North Carolina has focused on security enhancement among other key issues. City officials and businesses are inves-tigating partnerships with the local utility company police to provide security surveys and advice to business owners about how lighting could help reduce crime and provide an atmosphere attractive to potential customers.

Contact Information

Illuminating Engineering Society of North America
345 East 47th Street
New York, New York 10017
212-705-7926

Display Business Address Numbers

Strategy

Local policy which requires that business display promi-nently their address helps customers find the location and help police and other emergency personnel find the location when they receive a report of a criminal incident. The displays can help individuals unfamiliar with the area avoid confusion and vulnerability to crime by those who notice them as outsiders.

Crime Problem Addressed

Display of addresses helps new customers and visitors to the area avoid looking vulnerable to crimes such as auto theft and robbery. In addition, it helps police and fire emer-gency personnel respond quickly to incident reports in commercial districts.

Key Components

The police department encourages businesses to display their numbered address prominently on the surface of the building or signage visible from the street. Business or neighborhood crime watch groups and insurance compa-nies can provide advice on placement of the numbers and help with installation of signage and purchase of materials for small businesses.

Key Partnerships

Business watch groups can help each other understand the value of prominent address and business name markings and provide loans or volunteer assistance to install the products.

Potential Obstacles

Long-established business owners may believe they al-ready have enough visibility with their frequent customers and not worry about the need for prominent signs and numbers. Police and fire officials can help them understand the impact of unclear address markings on those agencies' ability to respond efficiently to emergencies.

Signs of Success

An increasing number of localities have established ordi-nances requiring businesses to display address numbers prominently in view of passersby. Ann Arbor, Michigan requires all homes and businesses to display numbers in plain view. The police department offers business owners security reviews which help them identify additional tech-niques which can enhance security for employees and cus-tomers.

Applying the Strategy

Several companies now offer illuminated number signage and curbside number displays as a security device for businesses. The products range in cost, though most rep-resent a minimal expense for the benefit they provide.

Contact Information

Crime Prevention Unit
Ann Arbor Police Department
Ann Arbor, Michigan 48104
313-994-2979

ENTERTAINMENT DISTRICTS

Zoning Laws

Strategy

Zoning laws are used to restrict or prohibit activities likely to generate crime.

Crime Problem Addressed

Zoning laws can be used to control and restrict prostitution, gambling, illegal liquor sales, drug sales, and other illegal or quasi-illegal activities.

Key Components

An analysis of crime, arrest, and service calls is conducted to determine community hotspots. Hotspots are plotted against the addresses of bars, liquor stores, video arcades, strip clubs, and adult book stores to see if these areas have high rates of crime or generate high levels of police calls. Zoning laws are developed to restrict locations of offending activities in residential neighborhoods or near schools or churches. Some communities have restrictions on the number of such businesses in a given block; other communities restrict them to one well-defined area to allow for concentrated police surveillance and enforcement.

Key Participants

Citizen groups must work with local and/or state government to develop or amend zoning laws to protect the public from crime and other illegal activities.

Potential Obstacles

Crime has normally not been an issue addressed by zoning. Zoning officials may have to be encouraged to use zoning laws to prevent and control crime. There is likely to be resistance from developers, builders, and business to expanding the scope of zoning laws.

Signs of Success

In *Young* v. *American Mini Theaters,* the U.S. Supreme Court found that zoning can be in the community interest if it is done to control secondary effects attributed to adult businesses, such as increased crime rates and neighborhood deterioration. As a result of this case, many localities, including Boston, Seattle, and Dallas, have passed zoning laws to restrict adult-oriented activities considered to be generators of crime and neighborhood disorder (Irving Sloan, *Regulating Land Use: The Law of Zoning,* 1988).

Applying the Strategy

Virginia amended the state's zoning law in 1993 to include protecting the public from crime as one of the purposes of zoning. A federal appeals court upheld zoning to regulate adult bookstores in Prince Georges County, Maryland. The zoning prohibited adult bookstores from being located within 1,000 feet of a school or 500 feet of a church.

Contact Information

Zoning and Administration
Prince Georges County
14741 Governor Oden Bowie Drive
Upper Marlboro, Maryland 20772
301-952-3195

Curtail Operating Hours

Strategy

Operating hours of businesses that are likely to generate crime and disorder are curtailed.

Crime Problem Addressed

Curtailing the late-night operating hours of small retail or service businesses addresses the robbery, assault, and disorderly behavior they tend to attract.

Key Components

Certain types of businesses are likely to generate crime and disorder problems because of the items they sell or entertainment they provide. Data are gathered about crimes, arrests, and radio calls to determine if these incidents take place late at night. Local guidelines or ordinances are developed to curtail the operating hours of these businesses. As an alternative to restricting their hours of operation, it may be possible for these businesses to enhance security during late-night operations by adding more staff, using surveillance cameras, and improving lighting.

Key Participants

Lawmakers can work with the police, regulatory agencies, businesses and employees to identify and assist businesses that have high levels of crime during late-night hours.

Potential Obstacles

Some stores are required by their franchise agreement to be open 24 hours per day. Many businesses rely on their late-night hours and the convenience they provide to their customers to stay profitable.

Signs of Success

Extended operating hours exposes a business to more crime opportunities. The Florida Independent Gasoline Retailers Association and Service Station Dealers of Flor-

ida opposed mandatory 24-hour operation of convenience stores and service stations because of concerns about worker safety. A University of Florida study found that closing a convenience store during the late-night hours was one (of two) of the most effective measures to reduce convenience store robbery ("Study of Safety and Security Requirements for At-Risk Businesses," Florida Office of the Attorney General, 1991).

Applying the Strategy

Many states have laws restricting the sale of alcohol during the early morning hours. Responding to concerns about late-night robbery of convenience stores, Akron, Ohio, developed an ordinance requiring convenience stores to curtail late-night operations.

Contact Information

Akron Police Department
217 High Street
Akron, Ohio 44308
216-375-2244

Traffic Control

Strategy

Traffic control measures are used to inconvenience customers of illegal activity.

Crime Problem Addressed

Street prostitution and illegal drugs sales can be discouraged by making them inconvenient for the purchasers.

Key Components

Illegal activities are conducted along public streets at certain times and in certain areas. The local or state agency responsible for the roads should be able to develop traffic control strategies that will make it inconvenient for customers in automobiles to access these services. Strategies will typically include turn restrictions and parking prohibitions. These restrictions will most often be necessary from late at night to early in the morning.

Key Participants

Police departments, businesses, and crime prevention groups must enlist the help of road and highway officials to restrict traffic in target locations.

Potential Obstacles

Road and highway officials are concerned with the efficient movement of traffic, so arguments to restrict traffic must be very convincing. Residents and businesses in the tar-

geted areas may also resist traffic restrictions because they will be inconvenienced.

Signs of Success

A traffic control and intensive enforcement plan in London resulted in a significant reduction in traffic circulating in a red-light district in a residential neighborhood. The plan reduced the level of noise and congestion and made the streets safer. Twelve months after the implementation of the traffic changes, serious crimes decreased by 50 percent ("Developing More Effective Strategies for Curbing Prostitution," *Security Journal*, Vol. 1, No.3, 1990).

Applying the Strategy

The Washington, DC, Police Department worked with roads officials to establish turn restrictions in areas of the city where street prostitution was a public safety problem accompanied by serious traffic congestion. The nighttime turn restrictions discourage customers from driving by the prostitutes by limiting their ability to circle the blocks frequented by the prostitutes.

Contact Information

Community Relations Unit
Metropolitan Police Department
300 Indiana Avenue, NW
Washington, DC 20001
202-727-4283

Secure or Demolish Abandoned Buildings

Strategy

Abandoned buildings that are being used to conduct illegal activities are secured or demolished.

Crime Problem Addressed

Securing or demolishing abandoned buildings denies hiding places for illegal drug sales; prostitution; storage for guns, drugs, or stolen property; and places where homeless people congregate.

Key Components

Abandoned buildings in high-crime neighborhoods may be used for illegal or inappropriate purposes. Owners of these properties should be identified and asked to make the properties habitable or have them demolished. Local or state condemnation laws can be used to have these properties condemned. In some states, the National Guard has demolished abandoned buildings.

Key Participants

Local housing officials and the police must work with neighborhoods and property managers to identify buildings that are no longer fit for human habitation and must secure them or use local condemnation authority to remove them.

Potential Obstacles

The condemnation process can be very long and drawn out. Even if a property is condemned, there may not be sufficient resources to demolish it.

Signs of Success

A study of abandoned buildings in Austin, Texas, found no illegal activity in 66 percent of 59 abandoned but secure residential buildings. Illegal activity was found in 83 percent of 24 unsecured abandoned buildings. Drug activity was found in 19 percent and sex and prostitution activities in 20 percent. In Newport News, Virginia, the burglary rate in a crime-ridden apartment complex dropped 35 percent after 100 apartments that were vacant or beyond repair were boarded up ("Abandoned Buildings: Magnets for Crime," *Journal of Criminal Justice,* Vol. 21, 1993).

Applying the Strategy

The Norfolk, Virginia, Police Department uses a code enforcement team to identify abandoned building that harbor crime. Patrol officers are encouraged to report all such buildings on their beat. Some buildings that were beyond economic repair have been demolished. The city is also negotiating with the Virginia National Guard to provide demolition services.

Contact Information

Norfolk Police Department
206 Monticello Avenue
Norfolk, Virginia 23501
804-441-2261

Trash Patrol

Strategy

Police officers conduct organized searches of public trash receptacles in high-crime neighborhoods looking for drugs and illegal firearms.

Crime Problem Addressed

The searches aim to affect drug sales and violent crime in high-crime neighborhoods by denying criminals hiding places for drugs, weapons, and cash.

Key Components

Police officers conduct an organized sweep and search of trash cans, supercans, dumpsters, and other public trash receptacles in neighborhoods with a high incidence of drug dealing. Because large trash receptacles may be involved, searching officers should be prepared to dive into and closely search large piles of trash and garbage.

Key Participants

The police agency cooperates with property owners, including public housing authorities and apartment managers, to conduct the trash searches.

Potential Obstacles

The police agency must ensure that it has the authority to search the trash under consideration. Because much of the searching may take place in public housing or low-income neighborhoods, support from the public housing authority or property manager is important. Searching trash and garbage will not be a pleasant task.

Signs of Success

Police officials in Richmond, Virginia, searching one night in one neighborhood found two assault rifles, two pistol-grip shotguns, four pistols, and an assortment of drugs and cash. All had been stashed in trash cans in areas where drug dealers are known to work. As a result of the searches, death threats have been made against police officers going into that neighborhood.

Applying the Strategy

The Richmond, Virginia, Police Department and the Virginia Department of State Police joined forces in 1995 to conduct searches of trash receptacles in high-crime communities. They are locating two to three weapons per search as well as drugs and cash.

Contact Information

Richmond Police Department
501 North Ninth Street
Richmond, Virginia 23129
804-780-6801

Photograph/Videotape Illegal Behavior

Strategy

Photographing or videotaping illegal or quasi-illegal behavior in public brings attention and embarrassment to the participants.

Crime Problem Addressed

Photographing or videotaping persons soliciting prostitution or engaging in drug sales helps discourage those activities from taking place in public view.

Key Components

Many people who engage in illegal activity on public streets do not want to be identified. Using a still or video camera to record these activities may discourage the illegal behavior. Citizens or the police can photograph persons involved in street prostitution or drugs sales. If made up of citizens, the team should be composed of two or more persons, preferably working from a vehicle. Signs advertising that the illegal activity is being photographed may also help to discourage the activity. If the police are supporting the filming activity, the photos or film can be turned over to them.

Key Participants

Citizens or members of Neighborhood Watch can organize teams to photograph illegal activities in public. The police can be also be a partner or assume complete responsibility for the filming.

Potential Obstacles

This crime prevention strategy must be strictly controlled. Transactions in public view are the only activity that should be filmed. Singling out and identifying particular individuals can expose the filmers to civil litigation. Filmers should avoid any confrontation with the people they are filming. The activity can be dangerous, especially if drugs are involved.

Signs of Success

A Neighborhood Watch member in Portland, Oregon, photographed drugs deals, wrote down license plate numbers, and reported suspicious activity to the police. The result was no more drug houses on the block and an area virtually free of crime (*Foundations for Action*, National Crime Prevention Council, 1990).

Applying the Strategy

Residents of Methuen, Massachusetts, began videotaping flagrant activity between prostitutes and their customers. The Neighborhood Watch sends out two-person teams to videotape activity. The tapes are turned over to police. Signs are posted warning of the videotaping. The police in Fredericksburg, Virginia, videotape drug transactions and broadcast them on cable television.

Contact Information

Fredericksburg Police Department
615 Princess Anne Street
Fredericksburg, Virginia 22401
703-372-1055

Small Claim Suits

Strategy

A small claim civil suit is filed against the landlord of property that is being used illegally.

Crime Problem Addressed

Filing a small claim civil suit against a landlord can address any activity that a neighbor or community considers a nuisance, including illegal activities such as drug sales or use, gambling, and prostitution.

Key Components

Evidence should be gathered of the suspected illegal activity. Evidence may include suspicious visitors, loud noise and music, threats to neighbors, heavy auto or foot traffic, gun shots, etc. Before bringing suit, it is necessary to demand that the landlord correct the identified problems. If the landlord refuses to correct the problems, a claim may be filed. The landlord should be notified of the suit.

Key Participants

Residents can work on their own or with the support of the police and housing, zoning, and other officials to sue landlords whose properties harbor crime.

Potential Obstacles

Because this is a legal proceeding, it will require that residents be willing to attend hearings and see the process through. It is often difficult to determine the actual owner of a property.

Signs of Success

A community group in South Berkeley, California, sued the owner of a drug-plagued building known as the "Pink Palace" and won a $36,000 judgement against the landlord. The neighbors of a crack house in San Francisco won $2,000 each after they sued the landlord to force him to clean up the property ("How to Eliminate Crack Houses in Your Neighborhood," Legal Aid Society of Alameda County, 1991).

Applying the Strategy

The California Drug Abatement Act was amended to allow private citizens and the city attorney to bring suit in civil court against property owners who allowed drugs to be used or placed on their property. This approach has been used by residents in Oakland and Berkeley, California.

Contact Information

Beat Health Unit
455 Seventh Street, B-48
Oakland Police Department
Oakland, California 94601
510-287-6368

Put Workers in Public Places in Uniforms

Strategy

Government and private employees who work in public wear uniforms to increase the perception of safety.

Crime Problem Addressed

Putting individuals in uniform creates an official presence or feeling of guardianship that tends to reduce the public's fear of crime. This can result in a greater use of the area by the law-abiding public, thus attracting even more law-abiding users.

Key Components

Employers of government or business workers who are in public performing their job on a regular basis are encouraged to have these employees wear uniforms and to place as many uniformed employees in public as practical. Employees can be encouraged to wear their uniforms to and from work.

Key Participants

Police departments and crime prevention groups can work with local governments and businesses to convince them of the value of placing their workers in uniforms to help reduce the fear of crime.

Potential Obstacles

Some employees may not like to wear uniforms, and some may prefer not to wear them to and from work.

Signs of Success

A study conducted by the University of Chicago found that persons wearing a uniform in public, whether employed by government or the private sector, reduced fear of crime. Women were more impressed than men by the presence of a uniform. Persons working in locations where they had a vested interest also generated greater feelings of safety ("Reducing Fear of Crime Through Occupational Presence," *Criminal Justice and Behavior,* March 1983).

Applying the Strategy

The National Park Service found that a uniformed employee acted as a deterrent to illegal activity and created a feeling of safety for users of a hiking trail in Mount Rainier National Park.

Contact Information

National Park Service
College of Forest Resources, University of Washington
Seattle, Washington 98195
206-545-7404

Seize Customers' Vehicles

Strategy

The personal vehicles of customers trying to pick up street prostitutes are seized.

Crime Problem Addressed

The vehicle seizure strategy attacks street prostitution and the violent crimes of robbery and assault that may accompany it.

Key Components

The policing agency identifies locations where street prostitution is occurring and arrests individuals attempting to buy the services of prostitutes. This is typically accomplished in a "sting" type operation where police officers act in the guise of prostitutes. Once the customers solicit, they are arrested and their vehicles confiscated.

Key Participants

The local policing agency is the primary participant, but it may be assisted by citizen crime prevention groups working to remove crime from their neighborhood.

Potential Obstacles

There is concern about the constitutionality of seizing vehicles at the time of arrest. Some contend that individ-uals are being penalized before they are convicted. Court challenges to this practice are pending in several states.

Signs of Success

In St. Paul, Minnesota, arrests for prostitution dropped from 245 in 1990 to 75 in 1993 after police began seizing customers' vehicles ("The War Against the Sex Trade," *Governing,* April 1994). Seizing vehicles resulted in a 90 percent decease in prostitution and vehicle traffic in neighborhoods in Hartford, Connecticut (*Crime Prevention News,* March 1993).

Applying the Strategy

The Portland, Oregon, Police Department began seizing vehicles in 1989. In the first two and one half years after the seizure policy was implemented, 605 customers found themselves without their vehicles. About one in five of the vehicles was forfeited to the police. Similar programs have been established in Milwaukee, Wisconsin; Long Beach, California; and Washington, DC.

Contact Information

Portland Police Bureau
1111 S.W. 2nd
Portland, Oregon 97204
503-796-3126

MALLS

Employ Security Staff

Strategy

Employing a mall security staff deters crime and provides crime prevention services to merchants and customers.

Crime Problem Addressed

A mall security staff can address all types of crime problems that may confront a mall and will also help reduce shoppers' fears about crime.

Key Components

The mall management must make arrangements to organize and employ security staff. The mall can either create and staff an in-house security force or contract with a private security company. The mall must make sure that security staff meet applicable state standards for private security personnel. Consideration can also be given to hiring off-duty police officers to augment the mall security staff.

Key Participants

The mall manager should work with a security consultant to determine the mall's security staffing needs or consult with a private security company. Mall businesses should also be asked to provide input into the security staffing plan.

Potential Obstacles

A mall security staff will be expensive, especially if off-duty police are employed. Employing a security force or using off-duty police officers will also expose the mall to liability because of the possibility of inappropriate action by the security staff.

Signs of Success

A survey of 49 shopping malls by Brookstone found that 100 percent of the malls had 24-hour security, 90 percent conducted security training for retail tenants, 76 percent assisted merchants in conducting surveillance, 65 percent maintained an information alert network, 27 percent apprehended shoplifters or other wrongdoers, and 14 percent had arrest authority ("Securing America's New Town Centers," *Security Management,* June 1992).

Applying the Strategy

Union Station Mall in Washington, DC, contracts with Burns International for its guard force, which is maintained 24 hours a day. The Rouse Company has 88 facilities throughout North American and uses only in-house security officers. Their security officers undergo a 32-hour training program, and ongoing training is mandatory.

Contact Information

International Conference of Shopping Centers
665 5th Avenue, 11th Floor
New York, New York 10022
212-421-8181

Provide Valet Parking

Strategy

Valet parking for mall patrons reduces their fears about going to and from their cars.

Crime Problem Addressed

Valet parking at malls can protect shoppers from robbery and assault and can also have a significant impact on their fear of crime.

Key Components

The shopping mall should survey its customers to determine if fear of crime in the parking lot is affecting their shopping habits. The mall staff should determine exactly where and at what times people are most fearful. A valet parking area must be set aside within the mall, which may require changes to traffic patterns. The mall can make arrangements with a parking service company to provide valet parking for customers. The mall should advertise the availability of the service and the locations of the valet parking service.

Key Participants

The mall must assess the parking and shopping needs of its customers and make arrangements with a parking service company.

Potential Obstacles

If the service is not well advertised it will not be used. The valet service should be offered free or at as little cost as possible.

Signs of Success

Regency Mall in Richmond, Virginia, established a valet service in response to customer concerns about parking lot safety. An average of about 120 of 200 spots reserved for valet parking were used. The customers using the service had very positive comments about it (*Security Management,* Feb. 1993).

Applying the Strategy

Lenox Square in Atlanta experimented with using off-duty Marines to escort shoppers to their cars. Regency Mall invested $10,000 for signs, blockades to direct traffic, and advertising. A service contract was established with a parking contractor. The mall charges a $3 fee to customers for the valet parking.

Contact Information

Security Director
Regency Mall
Parham and Quioccasin Roads
Richmond, Virginia 23230
804-740-7467

Bicycle Patrol

Strategy

A bicycle security patrol program patrols parking lots and other exterior areas of shopping malls.

Crime Problem Addressed

The security bicycle patrol addresses personal crimes against shoppers and employees such as robbery and assault, auto theft, theft from autos and vandalism to autos, and disorderly and suspicious behavior. Bike patrols can also assist in apprehending lawbreakers who are fleeing from the mall.

Key Components

The most physically fit members of the security staff can be asked to volunteer for the bike patrol, or new staff can be hired. They should be trained on patrolling, riding on stairs, jumping curbs, negotiating through crowds, traffic safely, and how to use the bike as a defensive weapon. Bikes and biking attire must be purchased. Several types of uniforms will be needed for hot weather, cold weather, and rain. Patrol times and beats must be established. The bike patrol should be used in coordination with vehicular patrol of parking lots, not in place of it.

Key Participants

The mall manager must find willing and qualified security staff to participate in the bike patrol.

Potential Obstacles

Some malls may not have security staff who are fit enough for patrolling on bikes. Bike patrolling will result in more workplace injuries, which will most likely mean higher insurance costs.

Signs of Success

The Rouse Company conducted a before-and-after study of crime in the parking lots of two shopping centers. The study found a 69 percent crime decease at Fashion Island and a 40 percent decrease at North Star Mall after the bike patrol was introduced ("A Bicycle Build for Security," *Security Management,* June 1993).

Applying the Strategy

The success of the bike patrol at the two test malls has led to the establishment of a bike patrol at all Rouse facilities. Bicycles are also being used by many police departments to patrol residential and business neighborhoods.

Contact Information

Corporate Security
The Rouse Company
10275 Little Patuxent Parkway
Columbia, Maryland 21044
410-992-6325

Mall Watch

Strategy

A watch program in malls encourages businesses to watch out for each other and report suspicious situations.

Crime Problem Addressed

A watch program in a mall will primarily focus on the crimes most mall businesses face: shoplifting, bad checks, and credit card fraud. The watch can also help control disorderly behavior in the mall.

Key Components

The mall manager working with local police organizes mall business into groups just as one would organize a neighborhood into blocks for Neighborhood Watch. The businesses should review their security procedures and prosecution policies. Those polices should be communicated to mall security and the police. A communication system should be established among each of the mall groups to pass on information about suspicious persons or situations. The mall security or local police can be brought in to give lectures on business crime prevention.

Key Participants

The mall manager, the mall security department, and the local police can work with mall businesses to set up the watch.

Potential Obstacles

The mall management cannot compel businesses to participate in the mall watch. The problems typical of a Neighborhood Watch will be found in a mall watch.

Signs of Success

The Woodfield Mall in Schaumburg, Illinois, employed a full-time business awareness officer to set up a mall watch and to provide crime prevention services to businesses. The awareness officer conducts security assessments of each of the mall stores. The Woodfield Mall also participates in a mall fax network involving 20 shopping centers in the Chicago area (*Security Management,* Nov. 1991).

Applying the Strategy

The Detroit Police Department organizes watch programs in business districts. The department trains owners and staff to recognize criminal behavior and report to police and mall security. The department also provides checklists on shoplifting prevention and store security. These services have contributed to lower crime rates in areas where businesses organized watch groups.

Contact Information

Security Manager
5 Woodfield Shopping Center
Schaumburg, Illinois 60173
708-330-1555

Police Substations

Strategy

Locating police substations or offices in shopping malls creates a police presence and provides crime prevention services.

Crime Problem Addressed

The location of a police office can address the typical crime faced by shopping malls: shoplifting, bad checks, and credit card fraud. It may also affect disruptive behavior in the mall and may have a limited impact on activity in mall parking lots. The police office may also increase the perception of safety for mall shoppers.

Key Components

The mall manager must make a space available for the police office. The police department must decide how it wants to assign personnel to the office. For example, will it be staffed during mall operating hours only? Some departments use a combination of sworn personnel and civilians to staff mall offices.

Key Participants

The mall manger and police department must work together to implement a mall police office.

Potential Obstacles

Mall space is very expensive. Maintaining a mall police office will require a substantial commitment by the police department. If regular hours are not established for the police office, the public may not find it useful or a deterrent.

Signs of Success

A police mini-precinct and safety awareness office in Potomac Mills Mall outside of Washington, DC, received more than 2,100 visitors in a ten-month period from 1992 to 1993. Police and volunteer staff distributed nearly 12,000 pieces of safety awareness material (Prince William County, Virginia, Police Department, internal memo, Sept. 1993).

Applying the Strategy

The Sunrise, Florida, Police Department maintains an office at the Sawgrass Mill Mall that is staffed by an officer while the mall is open. Four on-site holding cells have been set up for detaining arrested persons. Emergency medical technicians have also been placed on mall property.

Contact Information

Sunrise Police Department
10440 West Oakland Park Boulevard
Sunrise, Florida 33351
305-746-3600

Automated Teller Machine Safety

Strategy

Minimum security standards are established for automated teller machines (ATMs).

Crime Problem Addressed

Security standards for automated teller machines are intended to reduce robbery and the assault that may accompany it.

Key Components

Banks must study and assess their ATM crimes to determine the primary problem areas. Procedures for reporting ATM crime should be established by the banks and the police. Security personnel must work with bank marketing personnel to review site selection procedures and other ATM marketing decisions. Issues to consider in developing guidelines are site selection, surveillance cameras, lighting, visibility, panic communications, roving patrols, operating hours, and customer awareness.

Key Participants

Banks acting on their own initiative or as the result of local or state legislation can develop and implement minimum security requirements for ATM safety. Reporting and response policies should be established with the police.

Potential Obstacles

Quite often, decisions about location and operation of ATMs are marketing based, not security based. Bank security personnel must make a strong case for security.

Signs of Success

A study of ATM crime by New York City found that lighting inside 95 percent of the ATM locations was good, but 26 percent had broken or faulty vestibule entry locks, allowing access to anyone. Only 22 percent of the sites had security cameras, but 75 percent had a telephone or intercom providing access to bank personnel. Believing that ATM security standards are necessary to protect the public, New York City and the states of California, Nevada, Georgia, Washington, and Oregon have passed ATM security legislation.

Applying the Strategy

Ann Arbor, Michigan, developed guidelines to enhance the safety of consumers without discouraging the placement of ATMs in locations convenient to consumers' homes and workplaces. The guidelines address ATM location, lighting, landscaping, electronic monitoring, crime in the immediate neighborhood, and consumer education.

Contact Information

Ann Arbor Police Department
100 North Fifth Avenue
Ann Arbor, Michigan 48104
313-994-2979

PARKS

Park Watch

Strategy

A program that enlists users and neighbors to watch over park property.

Crime Problem Addressed

A Park Watch program can address all types of crime.

Key Components

The park staff must enlist the participation of park users and neighboring residents. The users and neighbors are encouraged to report suspicions or illegal activity. A special telephone number can be provided to report criminal activity or maintenance problems that need attention. A nearby Neighborhood Watch group can be encouraged to adopt the park and volunteer to check periodically for litter and damage. Signs can be posted that the park is protected by a Park Watch.

Key Participants

Park staff can work with nearby resident and users to watch out for parks.

Potential Obstacles

As with all watch programs, generating and maintaining interest will be a challenge. In some areas, the parks have been taken over by drug dealers and gangs, which may be very intimidating to people who would like to participate in a Park Watch.

Signs of Success

A campground watch established in a state park near San Clemente, California, produced a 15 percent drop in burglary and an $8,000 decrease in property loss ("Safety in the Parks," *Security Management,* 1982).

Applying the Strategy

The U.S. Park Service has established a Park Watch program along the Blue Ridge Parkway. It enlists the support of park neighbors and campers to make the park safer. Information on safety and security is provided by park rangers. A toll-free number is available to call to report suspicious activity.

Contact Information

Superintendent
Blue Ridge Parkway
200 BB&T Building
Asheville, North Carolina 28801
704-298-0398

Extended Park Operating Hours

Strategy

Extended park operating hours encourage youth to engage in recreational activity rather than becoming involved in criminal acts.

Crime Problem Addressed

Extending the operating hours of a park encourages youth to engage in positive recreational activity rather than getting involved in criminal acts.

Key Components

Park staff must determine the types of activity they want to provide during the extended hours. The surrounding neighborhood should be canvassed to make sure that the late-night activity is not going to adversely affect the area.

Staff must be on site and structured programs should be provided. Consideration can be given to providing education as well as recreation programs. Minimum age limits of youth allowed to participate should be established and well communicated.

Key Participants

Park staff must work with the community to set up schedules and programs for extended recreation hours.

Potential Obstacles

Extending hours will require extra staff. Some localities now have curfew laws that may create some problems for extended recreation hours. Residents living near parks may be disturbed by people playing sports at 2 a.m.

Signs of Success

In the summertime, when Phoenix, Arizona, basketball courts and other recreational facilities are kept open until 2 a.m., police calls reporting juvenile crime drop by as much as 55 percent ("Healing America's Cities," The Trust for Public Land, 1994).

Applying the Strategy

The City Manager of Glenarden, Maryland, found himself reading too many obituaries about young people, so in 1986 he founded a midnight basketball league (MBL) to give young people a safe, structured, and supervised alternative from 10 p.m. to 2 a.m., when they are most vulnerable to the drug culture and the crime it spawns. Games were followed by workshops on drug abuse, employment and sexual responsibility. In 1995, 38 localities were identified as having MBL leagues.

Contact Information

MBL of Monmouth County
201 Alpine Trail
Neptune, New Jersey 07753
908-988-9491

Take Back the Parks

Strategy

Citizens with government support engage in activities to take parks back for legitimate recreational use.

Crime Problem Addressed

In many cities, parks have been taken over by youth gangs and drug users, denying them to the law-abiding public for their intended recreational use.

Key Components

Citizens must organize to take back their parks. They must organize to help clean and repair the parks and to report suspicious and illegal activity to the police. Residents must also use parks in large enough numbers on an ongoing basis to ensure that the drug use and other illegal activity is discouraged. This can be accomplished by providing interesting play equipment and organizing recreation activities that interest law-abiding children and adults. Residents must insist that local government maintain parks and that vandalism or other damage be immediately repaired.

Key Participants

Community residents working with park administrators and the police can take parks back for community use.

Potential Obstacles

Many people are fearful of challenging the disorderly or lawbreaking people who drove them from the park in the first place. Repair and continued upkeep of the parks may be costly.

Signs of Success

The Alisco-Pico Recreation Center in Los Angeles serves 850 children each week, offering 19 sports, cultural, and academic programs. In 1980, a resident found that the area park had no programs and was dominated by gangs and graffiti. The resident organized the business community and secured funding to rebuild the park and set up programs ("Taking Back the Parks," *Parks and Recreation,* April 1991).

Applying the Strategy

In the summer of 1989, Philadelphia community groups held block parties and barbecues in drug-infested parks and street corners to disrupt drug-dealing activities. The "Noble Neighbors" group in Chicago organized a candlelight vigil and took back a small park that had become a center for drug activity.

Contact Information

American Parks and Recreation Association
1800 Silas Dene Highway No. 1
Rocky Hill, Connecticut 06067
203-721-1055

Restrict or Prohibit Alcohol Use

Strategy

Alcohol use in public parks or other public recreation areas is restricted or prohibited.

Crime Problem Addressed

Restricting or prohibiting alcohol use discourages disorderly behavior, violence, and drunk driving.

Key Components

Residents can collect information about incidents of disorderly behavior, violence, and drunk driving in recreation areas where alcohol consumption is allowed. They should then determine whether restriction on public use of alcohol is a local or state authority. (In many states public consumption of alcohol is prohibited, but in some states it is not.) Other cities can be contacted to find out how their laws have fared against legal challenges. This information can be presented to government leaders and with the request that restrictions be placed on the use of alcohol.

Key Participants

Citizens' groups, businesses, and the police can work together to define areas where alcohol consumption may be contributing to community disorder.

Potential Obstacles

Many business owners in resort towns may oppose this move because of the impact it may have on their business. A ban on drinking will place additional enforcement duties on the police department.

Signs of Success

After a prohibition on alcohol on its public beaches was established, the City of Galveston, Texas, saw arrests for disorderly conduct decrease from 125 to 36 and arrests for drunk driving decrease from 67 to 19 in the first six months of 1994 versus 1993. In 1993 there were also three murders on the beach. The Fourth of July weekend normally brought with it fighting and scattered shooting. But after the ban there were no recorded incidents of violence, even though the crowds were the biggest seen in seven years ("Dry Beaches," Dallas, Texas, *Morning News,* July 24, 1994).

Applying the Strategy

The Mayor of Ft. Lauderdale, Florida, visited Galveston to talk about how his city banned alcohol on all of its beaches in 1987 and how the city went from a spring break party town to a draw for international visitors. Residents along the beach in neighboring Galveston County are upset that thousands of partyers from the city have moved to their beaches.

Contact Information

City Manager
P.O. Box 779
Galveston, Texas 77553
409-766-2150

HOSPITALS

Restrict Access

Strategy

Access to laundry rooms, storage closets, heating and cooling rooms, certain stairwells, and other sensitive areas in hospitals is restricted.

Crime Problem Addressed

Restricting access in hospitals will address theft of property from the hospital and patients as well as assaults on staff and patients.

Key Components

Hospital security staff must work with hospital administrators to manage access into and within the hospital. Doors opening to stairwells and the outside should be identified. Rooms containing attractive targets, either in value or ease of theft, should be located away from stairwells and elevators. If attractive targets must be located by stairwells, elevators, and exterior opening doors, proper locks should be installed on the doors of the high-risk areas and procedures put in place to ensure that they are properly secured. Signs that identify attractive targets should be removed. Identification badges should be worn by staff, and visitor badges should be issued to all visitors.

Key Participants

Hospital security staff and hospital administrators can work together to increase security for high-risk areas of the hospital. Enlisting the cooperation of visitors by posting the visitation rules can also be helpful.

Potential Obstacles

Changes to the layout of the hospital may be cost prohibitive. Emergency exits needed for escape during fires cannot be closed or obstructed. Many staff resist wearing identification badges.

Signs of Success

A 1989 study of hospital theft found that areas of the hospital with controlled access had lower rates of theft.

Another study found higher theft rates for rooms located near an escape route.

Applying the Strategy

At Children's Hospital in Washington, DC, access to hotspots such as the hospital pharmacy is strictly limited. No signs are used to identify other sensitive locations such as executive offices and the credit union. An electronic card system is used to control access throughout the hospital.

Contact Information

Director of Security
Children's National Medical Center
111 Michigan Avenue, NW
Washington, DC 20010
202-884-2065

Emergency Room Violence Prevention Protocol

Strategy

Emergency room staff are trained to respond to violent patients and situations.

Crime Problem Addressed

Developing protocol and training emergency room staff to adequately respond to violence in the emergency room will help reduce the likelihood of physical attacks against staff, visitors, patients, and police officers.

Key Components

As they treat an ever-increasing number of violent crime victims, emergency rooms and their staff are becoming more exposed to violence. Emergency violence prevention protocols should be developed and staff trained to handle violent patients and situations to ensure that the emergency room itself does not become a victim. Nonviolent crisis intervention training should be provided to teach staff how to diffuse violence in the emergency room. The protocol should also address public access to emergency services and the hospital, procedures to check for and handle weapons, control of family members and visitors, and ground rules for working with security staff and the police in the emergency room.

Key Participants

Emergency room staff must work with security, the police, and other emergency workers to develop protocols for handling violence and its victims.

Potential Obstacles

Medical staff are interested in helping the sick and injured. They may be resistant to policies that place other concerns ahead of treating patients.

Signs of Success

A 1993 study by the American College of Emergency Physicians found that many hospitals were adopting enhanced measures to address emergency room violence. Fifty-two percent reported the use of panic buttons, 34 percent use closed-circuit television, and 27 percent place security personnel in emergency rooms during high-risk hours. Other measures were training, visitor control, and metal detectors ("The Emergency Room View on Violence," *Security Management*, April 1994).

Applying the Strategy

Henry Ford Hospital in Detroit, Michigan, made many changes to its procedures because of lax security in the emergency room, where even the security staff had concerns about its own safety. A committee of emergency room staff, hospital administrators, and security was created to develop new procedures. Changes included restricted access, closer screening of patients, and new visitation rules.

Contact Information

Director of Security
Henry Ford Hospital
2799 West Graham Boulevard
Detroit, Michigan 48202
313-876-2600

Hospital Watch

Strategy

Hospital staff are organized and trained to watch for and report dangerous situations.

Crime Problem Addressed

A Hospital Watch can address all types of crime problems.

Key Components

The hospital should be organized into watch groups by building or floors, with one hospital staff person assigned to each watch group to coordinate activities. A regular newsletter can be issued to provide staff with information about security-related problems and suggestions. Watch leaders should be given enhanced crime prevention training. All hospital staff should be given a basic orientation class on crime prevention, followed with periodic training on related topics. To make watching easier, all staff should wear identification badges. If practical, temporary ID badges should be issued to all visitors. A telephone number should be established to report problems, and signs should be posted that the facility has a Hospital Watch program.

Key Participants

Hospital security staff and administrators can organize all levels of hospital employees to establish a Hospital Watch. Participation should also be sought from vendors and other persons who visit the hospital for business purposes.

Potential Obstacles

A Hospital Watch will face the typical apathy problems faced by most watch programs. Because hospitals have so many doors with all types of staff and visitors coming and going all the time, watching for unusual activity will be difficult.

Signs of Success

A 50 percent reduction in crime was recorded after the introduction of a Hospital Watch program at Poole General Hospital in Dorset, England. The watch involves 35 coordinators from all staff disciplines: doctors, nurses, porters, and cleaners (*Crime Prevention News,* Home Office—Great Britain, Summer 1990).

Applying the Strategy

Security staff of Bellevue Hospital conducted a detailed study of crime on hospital property. It found theft the most frequently reported crime, with most occurring on the ground floor in one building. To increase surveillance, a Hospital Watch program was established, security patrols were increased, and surveillance cameras were placed in strategic locations.

Contact Information

Director of Hospital Police
Bellevue Hospital Center
462 First Avenue
New York, New York 10016
212-562-4141

PUBLIC TRANSPORTATION

Exact Change Policy

Strategy

Users of public buses are required to have exact change to pay fares.

Crime Problem Addressed

Exact change has had a dramatic effect on reducing the robbery of bus drivers. The reduction in robbery has also resulted in fewer assaults and murders of bus drivers.

Key Components

The local transportation company establishes a policy that all bus riders must have exact change. No arrangements are provided for the bus driver to make change, and the exact change is normally deposited into a secure fare box which the driver cannot open. Notices placed on the exterior and interior of the bus notify riders that exact fare is required.

Key Participants

The transportation company establishes the policy requiring exact fare and then relies on the willingness of the public to tolerate this minor inconvenience.

Potential Obstacles

Exact fare has become a standard practice with most bus companies throughout the country.

Signs of Success

From 1963 to 1968 the nation's bus systems experienced a fivefold increase in bus driver robberies and a tenfold increase in driver deaths. The shooting of one driver and the murder of another in one month in 1968 led to the enactment of an exact fair policy by the bus system in Washington, DC. This change sharply reduced attacks on drivers. Systems across the country have adopted exact fare, and today robbery and attacks on bus drivers are rare ("Reduction of Robberies and Assaults on Bus Drivers," Stanford Research Institute and the University of Columbia, 1970).

Applying the Strategy

This strategy is now a standard practice in most localities throughout the United States.

Contact Information

American Public Transit Association
1201 New York Avenue, NW, Suite 400
Washington, DC 20005
202-898-4000

CPTED for Subways

Strategy

Crime Prevention Through Environmental Design (CPTED) is used to build a subway environment that deters the opportunity for crime.

Crime Problem Addressed

The use of CPTED in subway construction will help deter and control all types of crime and help create an environment that is clean, well-lighted, and safe.

Key Components

CPTED is action to design the physical environment in ways that reduce or remove identifiable crime risks. Because of the cost of subway construction, it is vital to incorporate CPTED into the original design. A security design group should include architects, security and police, and the subway authority. Other cities where CPTED was a design component of the subway can provide input. CPTED design principles should address visibility, access control, lighting, security hardware, landscaping, resistance to vandalism, and maintenance.

Key Participants

Incorporating CPTED subway construction requires participation from security and police, architects, builders, and the subway authority.

Potential Obstacles

It may be difficult to interest and organize the variety of individuals and professions necessary to incorporate

CPTED into subway design. Many see CPTED as having high up-front costs. CPTED works best with new construction. CPTED for existing facilities is more complicated and costly.

Signs of Success

The Washington, DC, subway opened in the early 1970s. Because of the fear of crime, CPTED became one of the more important design components of the system. It was designed to discourage crime by providing excellent visibility, good lighting, and vandal-resistant materials. The subway has had fewer than five murders and averages about 100 robberies per year, many of which take place around bus stops and not in the subway (Washington Metro Crime Prevention Unit, 1993).

Applying the Strategy

CPTED changes implemented by the New York Transit Authority have substantially increased the overall perception of security by passengers. Unfortunately, because the changes modified existing construction, they were very expensive. As the Washington subway continues to grow, CPTED remains a primary design requirement to keep passengers safe.

Contact Information

Crime Prevention Unit
Metro Transit Police Department
600 Fifth Street
Washington, DC 20001
202-962-2135

Prohibit Panhandling in Subways

Strategy

Begging or panhandling in subways is prohibited.

Crime Problem Addressed

Panhandling or begging creates an impression among the public that an area is unsafe. A survey by Columbia University showed that nearly 70 percent of the public believes panhandling should not be allowed. Many people feel intimidated or coerced by beggars or panhandlers.

Key Components

Local governments must carefully craft laws to prohibit or restrict individuals from begging for money on subway property. The laws should address the specific activities to be prohibited and where they are prohibited. The police department and transit authority should collect detailed information on the detrimental effects of panhandling on the public's right to use the subway system safely.

Key Participants

Local government officials must work with the police, government attorneys, and groups that provide support services to the homeless and similar persons.

Potential Obstacles

Many groups that provide support services to the homeless and poor may find this type of legislation discriminatory. The panhandling law must be very specific; if it is too broad it may be successfully challenged in court.

Signs of Success

The New York Transit Authority banned beggars from subways, lost the right to do so in district court, and then won back the right on appeal. Polls showed that sympathy for the plight of beggars and the homeless actually increased among ridership after the ban was affirmed by the courts. Felonies deceased in the subway by 15 percent following the ban ("The Broken-Window Theory of Urban Decay," *This World*, March 15, 1992).

Applying the Strategy

Philadelphia discourages panhandling by asking the public not to give money to panhandlers. In addition to banning beggars, the New York system has also focused on pickpockets with the passage of a jostling law. It allows the police to arrest individuals who bump into or jostle people to commit pickpocketing. This and other steps are part of a comprehensive plan the New York Transit Police have implemented over the past few years to make the subways safer.

Contact Information

New York City Transit Police Department
370 Jay Street
Brooklyn, New York 11201
718-330-8658

Install Cameras on Buses

Strategy

Video cameras on buses record and discourage illegal and disruptive behavior.

Crime Problem Addressed

Installing video cameras on buses can diminish vandalism, theft, assault, and disorderly behavior.

Key Components

Transportation routes that experience high levels of crime and disorder should be identified and video cameras installed on those buses. Camera boxes can be placed on all of the problem buses, but cameras will actually be installed in only a few of the boxes. The boxes themselves should act as deterrents. The fact that cameras are installed and that they will be used to bring charges against offenders should be publicized. Charges will be brought for illegal activity recorded by the camera and the results publicized.

Key Participants

The transportation company can make arrangements to obtain and use video cameras on its vehicles.

Potential Obstacles

There are minimal up-front costs for the installation of video cameras. If the program is not given significant publicity, especially when someone is caught because of the cameras, it may have limited effect.

Signs of Success

A bus company in North Shield, England, installed two active and three dummy video cameras on 24 buses. The use of videos on the buses was well publicized. Vandalism declined for the whole fleet, reducing seat repair costs by two-thirds. Other benefits were fewer assaults on drivers, less fare evasion, and fewer complaints about bad driving ("Video Cameras and Bus Vandalism," *Situational Crime Prevention Successful Studies,* 1993).

Applying the Strategy

The Greenville County, South Carolina, school district rotated 15 video cameras among 70 video camera boxes on its 332 school buses. The cameras and camera boxes were installed to record and deter disruptive behavior by students on school buses. The project was so successful that the school district ordered 15 more cameras and 70 more camera boxes.

Contact Information

Greenville County School District
P.O. Box 2848
Greenville, South Carolina 29602
803-241-3100

Remove Identification From Rental Vehicles

Strategy

License plates and company logos that identify vehicles as rental vehicles are eliminated.

Crime Problem Addressed

Removing markings that identify rental vehicles should make it more difficult for criminals who would attack tourists or business travelers unfamiliar with their surroundings.

Key Components

Car rental companies must decide if they want to remove rental identifications from their vehicles. This may be necessary only in high-crime areas or areas with a large tourist population. The rental companies must devise a system to keep track of their vehicles without advertising that they are rental cars. The companies must also make arrangements with states that issue vehicle rental license plates to discontinue that practice.

Key Participants

Rental companies can remove their company identifying logos and must work with state motor vehicle departments that issue identifiable license plates for rental vehicles. Travel groups such as the American Automobile Association can also be key players.

Potential Obstacles

In states where identifiable license plates are issued for rental cars, changes in state law or regulation may be required to stop the issuing of rental license plates.

Signs of Success

Alamo Rent-A-Car got permission from the state of Florida to relicense 20,000 of its rental cars in southern Florida. Alamo also removed its company logos.

Applying the Strategy

The Automobile Association of Florida urged car rental agencies in the state to remove license plates and logos that identify rental vehicles. Hertz removed all company logos or other rental identifiers from its cars. Hertz also worked with the state of Florida to discontinue issuing unique license plates for rental cars.

Contact Information

American Automobile Association
1000 AAA Drive
Heathrow, Florida 32746
1-800-926-4222

Taxi Security Screens

Strategy

Security screens are installed in taxicabs between the driver and passenger compartments.

Crime Problem Addressed

Security screens protect taxicab drivers from robbery and assault.

Key Components

The taxicab company or driver, if independent, must consider the various security screens that are available and decide on a model that provides security to the driver while having the least impact on communications between driver and passenger. Some localities have mandated security screens, but in many areas company policy decides whether screens are required.

Key Participants

Taxicab companies and drivers are the primary participants. Local government may also become involved if it chooses to use its regulatory authority to improve driver safety.

Potential Obstacles

Many drivers claim that security screens limit visibility, interfere with communication, and reduce tips. Many in the industry claim that screens currently available have deficiencies. In many cities, "gypsy" taxis operate without a license and usually prefer to operate without screens. In New York City, 35 of the taxicab drivers murdered in 1993 were "gypsies."

Signs of Success

The New York City Taxi and Limousine Commission recently began requiring that all cabs have bullet-resistant partitions and emergency lights installed. Nearly 1,200 cabs are affected by this law. The Metropolitan Board of Trade, which represents 1,764 cabs, says that all of its taxis have security screens and that in the past 20 years only one driver has been murdered, and that was outside the taxi (*New York Times,* Jan. 16, 1994).

Applying the Strategy

The City of Los Angeles recently enacted a mandatory law for taxi screens. The International Taxicab and Livery Association supports the use of screens but believes that screens presently available have many deficiencies. In response to the need for a better screen, the association is developing a new screen that will provide safety with as little negative impact as possible on passengers. A prototype of the new screen should be available within the next year.

Contact Information

International Taxi Cab and Livery Association
3849 Farragut Avenue
Kensington, Maryland 20895
301-946-5701

Security Escort Service

Strategy

Special transportation or escort services are offered to individuals in high-risk locations.

Crime Problem Addressed

Transportation escort services primarily address the fear of crime by offering travelers secure transportation from one point to another.

Key Components

Populations who are restricting their travel because of fear of using public transportation must be identified, as must the times that escort services are most needed. Arrangements should be made to provide low-cost transportation services to these special populations. The availability of the service should be advertised. If the services allow women or other populations to have greater employment freedom, corporate or government sponsorship may be provided.

Key Participants

Local governments or special-interest groups can work with transportation companies or car dealerships to obtain vehicles.

Potential Obstacles

This type of service will have to be subsidized because of the small population it will serve. The major costs will be personnel to drive the vehicles and the vehicles themselves.

Signs of Success

In 1988, women in Bristol, England, who did not feel safe using other forms of transportation at night were provided a low-cost door-to-door lift service. A similar service was started in Bradford, England, in 1989. Service was offered for women from 6 p.m. to 10 p.m. Monday through Saturday for a very low fee. The service averaged about 350 passengers per week. Employers liked the service because it gave greater working freedom to their female employees ("Safer Cities for Women," *Town Planning Review,* Vol. 63, 1992).

Applying the Strategy

The Local Intercampus Mobile Operation (LIMO) program at Marquette University uses five 15-passenger vans driven by students to offer free escort-service for students. LIMO operates from 6 p.m. to 3 a.m. There are set routes, but students can request special pick-up services. In two years LIMO logged more than 350,000 transports.

Contact Information

Department of Public Safety
Marquette University
749 North 16th Street
Milwaukee, Wisconsin 53233
414-288-5625

Highway Watch

Strategy

A watch program is organized so that highway truck drivers can observe and report suspicious or illegal activity along highways and at truck stops and rest stops.

Crime Problem Addressed

A watch program along highways and at rest stops and truck stops can address all types of crime.

Key Components

The police can work with trucking companies to encourage truckers to use CB radios or cellular telephones to report suspicious or dangerous situations on the highways. Truck stops can also be incorporated into a business/neighborhood-style watch. Managers and users of truck stops can look for missing or abducted children and fleeing felons wanted by the police. Crime prevention training programs can be set up for drivers, travelers, and truck stop employees. In essence, the truck stop could be treated like a small community.

Key Participants

The police can work with truck companies and drivers, truck stop operators, highway personnel, travelers, and tourism authorities to use truck drivers as extra eyes and ears.

Potential Obstacles

The obstacles to a watch program like this would be those typical of any Neighborhood Watch: apathy and a drop in interest after concern about a given tragic event subsides.

Signs of Success

The Pennsylvania State Police began the Pike Watch program with truckers and truck stops in 1990. The program began with the Pennsylvania Turnpike and later expanded to Interstates 79, 80, 81, 83, and 84. From 1990 to 1992, ten motor carrier companies joined the program. State Police departments in other states are considering copying the program.

Applying the Strategy

The American Truckers Association has adopted the Pennsylvania Pike Watch program and is beginning a new national program called Road Watch. The program was recently begun in New York, with a planned expansion to nine other states.

Contact Information

American Truckers Association
2200 Mill Road
Alexandria, Virginia 22314
703-838-1912

Support Telecommuting, Teleshopping, or Mail Ordering

Strategy

Individuals fearful about crime can use technology that allows them to work or shop by computer, telephone, television, and mail.

Crime Problem Addressed

Telecommuting, teleshopping, and mail order allow individuals fearful about crime to avoid areas or times when they feel unsafe working or shopping. This can reduce their exposure to robbery, assault, larceny, and vandalism.

Key Components

Telecommuting requires that businesses change working hours and conditions to allow individuals to work by telephone modem and computer from the home. The worker will need to have the computer equipment and software at home to communicate with the office. Teleshopping is available in communities with cable television service. Mail order catalogs make it possible to shop by mail. These crime prevention options could be discussed at a Neighborhood Watch meeting.

Key Participants

Individuals wishing to telecommute must make arrangements with their employers. Individuals can subscribe to a cable television service in their locality to gain access to home shopping channels on television.

Potential Obstacles

Telecommuting requires significant changes in the work environment for employee and employer. Communications equipment and software are necessary. Cable service is not available in all communities, and some people cannot afford the cost of cable television service.

Signs of Success

Telecommuting as a crime prevention strategy has not been evaluated. However, telecommuting should expose persons to less workplace violence while providing a presence in the home and neighborhood that can help reduce burglary. The National Retail Federation's research found that fear of crime, frustration with poor store service, and increased comfort with new technologies could prompt 40 percent of all shoppers to try home shopping in the next two years ("Retail Forecasting at New York Convention," St. Paul Pioneer Press, Jan. 31, 1994).

Applying the Strategy

Many organizations are experimenting with telecommuting. Stampede Technologies has developed a software package called Remote Office that allows the user to access any server, printer, mainframe, or desktop computer from the home.

Contact Information

SSSmith and Associates
8572 Old Stage Road
Waynesville, Ohio 45068
513-897-0654

SCHOOLS

Controlled Access to School Buildings

Strategy

By limiting and controlling access to school buildings, school officials enhance safety and security for staff and students.

Crime Problem Addressed

Sixty-nine percent of students who responded to a recent survey and who have been victims of violence in or around their school believe people who do not belong can easily enter their school. Only half of the students who had been victims of violence believe that interior areas of their school are safe. This strategy reduces student and teacher victimization by nonstudents who do not belong on the school campus. It recognizes the problem of school-age or other criminals entering schools for the purpose of committing a crime. It recognizes that youth who have been expelled may return to the school to commit criminal acts or that adults may enter the campus to victimize students or staff.

Key Components

Drug pushers, gang members, and students who have been suspended or expelled may attempt to enter schools to commit crimes. Preventing unauthorized entry will have a favorable impact on and support any school security program.

In this strategy, school officials secure all exterior doors so that they can be opened only from the inside. Access is limited to one entrance in each building, usually one in the front of the building and visible from a main street. Staff and students exiting from any other door are instructed to not let anyone they do not recognize enter through that door and to direct such persons to go around to the front of the building. The single access point is monitored by school staff or security personnel. Legitimate visitors sign in and are issued passes that they must wear while inside the school. Visitors who do not wish to identify themselves or their purpose for entering are not allowed into the school.

Key Partnerships

School boards, superintendents, principals, and parent organizations should band together to ensure that schools are secure. While creating limited access or "choke points" may be inconvenient for casual entrance by parents and other visitors, the limitations significantly deter the potential for crime within the building and therefore should be communicated to parents and staff as a crime prevention and security measure. Support for the measure can be enhanced if staff and parent concerns are addressed in the design of the school's security plan.

Potential Obstacles

Many students, staff, and parents do not want the inconvenience of walking or driving to specific entrances supervised by school staff. Especially during inclement weather, reasonable complaints about access will be made. Discussion with and education of each affected group will help alleviate many concerns and will build support for this security measure.

Signs of Success

Access limitation is a strategy used throughout the country. The Chicago Public School District removed most outside door handles on all but the front door of all its school buildings. Doors are locked 24 hours a day, even when the school is in session. Panic bars allow exit from the building in case of emergency. An alarm sounds if the doors are opened without permission from school staff.

Applying the Strategy

After a stranger abducted a third grader from a local elementary school in Oxford, Mississippi, this strategy was among the first security measures implemented by the school district. Mothers of students now monitor entrances and hallways to ensure that access is gained only by legitimate visitors. The school is now much safer.

Contact Information

Assistant Superintendent of Education
Lafayette County
P.O. Box 110
Oxford, Mississippi 38655
601-234-3271

Closed Circuit Television Surveillance

Strategy

Installation of closed circuit video cameras in schools with a high incidence of crime can help deter crime within the school, on buses, and in parking areas.

Crime Problem Addressed

Half of student victims of school violence surveyed in 1994 believe the interior areas of their school are not safe. A significant percentage of crimes committed against youths occur in or near school. The whole gamut of offenses committed on school grounds is addressed through this initiative. Natural fields of surveillance reduce crime at any location. School policies that place teachers and other staff in hallways help reduce crime. Closed circuit television cameras are additional "supervisors" whose electronic recording capability is useful in getting an accurate account of events that occur in their field of view.

Key Components

This strategy involves placement of video cameras at several points along hallways, in common areas such as lunch rooms and student locker areas, and on the exterior of buildings in areas near the main entrance and parking lots. The closed circuit cameras allow school staff in the main administrative or security office to view, simultaneously, activity in each of these locations. School officials can then dispatch security personnel or other staff to subdue fighting students, calm disturbances, or assist an injured student or staff member. As the cameras scan the areas within their view, they also record activity that security officials may need to review at a later date if an incident occurs. Some schools mount cameras on school buses to deter violence among students and to discourage anyone who would attempt to harm a student from boarding the bus.

Coupled with a policy limiting access through one door only, closed circuit television (CCTV) can also be used at that doorway to view all parties who enter, including visitors signing in with staff monitoring the entrance. If a visitor came to school to commit a crime, the visible CCTV camera would serve as a deterrent because it reminds the individual that his or her image is being recorded. Similarly, students who would deal illegal drugs in a hallway or stairwell or assault another student or a staff member are deterred by the presence of the CCTV camera. The cameras essentially serve as extra security staff and supplement security personnel who cannot otherwise monitor all areas simultaneously.

Key Partnerships

The school district, which must train all personnel who will use the equipment, should have the school board set policies governing the use of the CCTV system and the information it records. Parents, students, and staff should be involved in decisions about placement of the cameras to ensure that placement responds to the crime concerns of everyone.

Potential Obstacles

Cameras and monitors are relatively inexpensive, but wide angle and zoom lenses, weatherproof housing for outdoor cameras, and mounts for cameras can be very expensive. In addition, the assistance of a security consultant may be necessary to ensure maximum effectiveness in the placement of the correct number of cameras. These costs can be absorbed by school districts, but usually at the expense of other items in the school budget.

Many students and some parents initially object to placement of cameras as an intrusion on their privacy. The best way to overcome these objections is to communicate the security concerns that prompted the decision to install the cameras and to provide information of their effectiveness in deterring crime problems in the school.

Signs of Success

The National School Boards Association documents the successful implementation of CCTV technology in many school districts in its 1993 report, *Violence in the Schools: How America's Schoolboards Are Safeguarding Your Children.* Security expert Lawrence J. Fennelly also advocates use of CCTV in schools in his 1992 work, *Security Applications in Industry and Institutions.*

Applying the Strategy

Lafayette County, Mississippi, schools now use CCTV on school buses. Permanent mounts are affixed in each bus, and the more expensive cameras are moved at the discretion of school officials. Misbehavior by children has declined dramatically since installation. Use of CCTV by Foley Public Schools in Minnesota has curtailed thefts of student property from hallway lockers.

In 1992, the Topeka, Kansas, public schools developed a comprehensive district-wide security program. In 1993, the district added installation of CCTV to the program. Although students initially resisted the intrusion of the cameras and complained about being watched all the time, they are now among the policy's biggest advocates. The cameras now mounted and active in each of the district's six middle schools and three high schools are credited with contributing to a decline in crime within school buildings. Other key elements of the successful security program include photo ID badges for students and teachers, a system of crisis management plans for each school, and hand-held metal detectors.

Contact Information

General Director of Secondary Education
Topeka Public Schools
624 Southwest 24th Street
Topeka, Kansas 66611
913-233-0313

Code of Conduct

Strategy

A code of conduct outlining acceptable and unacceptable student behavior establishes clear rules and helps to create in the school an atmosphere that deters crime and violence.

Crime Problem Addressed

Nearly 40 percent of local officials surveyed in 1994 by the National League of Cities stated that school violence in their community had increased noticeably in the previous five years. Order within the school and discipline of violent and disruptive students are both effectively addressed through this strategy.

Key Components

A student code of conduct clearly spells out definitions of acceptable and unacceptable behavior and outlines a system of graduated sanctions (detention, suspension, expulsion) for violations. The code is usually designed by a combination of school officials, parents, faculty, and student representatives. Teachers are responsible for describing the policy to students, who receive it in writing and must signal their agreement to abide by it by signing a copy. Some policies also incorporate a system of rewards for students who exhibit good behavior. Many schools also have peer review boards that recommend penalties for students with discipline problems. Adherence to policy and application of sanctions without exception helps to increase compliance with the policy and adherence to the rules of the school.

Key Partnerships

School officials, parents, and students should all be involved in designing the code and in developing materials for communicating it to students and parents. This involvement will help build support for the policy and ensure that all parents and students understand the potential consequences of acceptable or unacceptable behavior.

Potential Obstacles

The system must be logical, fair, and subject to appeal within the school system. According to the Southeastern Regional Vision for Education, effective codes "are written with student input, and clearly define the roles, the rights, and the responsibilities of all persons involved in the school." Some parents initially perceive a student code of conduct as being unfair and overly strict. They should be advised that codes of conduct are meant to reinforce positive behavior as well as set out consequences for inappropriate or dangerous behavior. With that understanding, parents often become more supportive as they realize that the policies help keep their children safe in school.

Signs of Success

The National School Boards Association (NSBA) highlights successful codes in seven cities in four states in a 1993 report on school violence control and prevention policies. Seventy-six percent of the districts surveyed by NSBA in 1993 reported use of a student conduct or disciplinary code as part of a violence control measure. The National School Safety Center also credits student codes of conduct as a successful strategy in its 1990 *School Safety Check Book*.

Applying the Strategy

The Montgomery, Alabama, Public Schools established a "code of good student behavior" for all students in the system after hearing of growing concerns over bullying and more serious student behavior issues. The school district developed a booklet for students and parents that outlines classroom behavior guidelines and consequences, school rules about cheating and other infractions, and sanctions against illegal activities (assault, vandalism, presence of drugs and weapons). The policy outlines a range of age-appropriate consequences for violations. After the first year of implementation, incidents of violence and behavior problems declined noticeably. The code is part of a comprehensive security program that includes security guards in schools, drug abuse prevention education, and conflict mediation training for teachers.

Contact Information

Security Chief
Montgomery Public Schools
P.O. Box 1991
Montgomery, Alabama 36104
334-269-3937

Dress Code

Strategy

A school board policy restricting wearing of gang-related, sexually explicit clothing or clothes bearing violent messages or sayings advocating illegal activities helps reinforce discipline and minimize the potential for violent confrontation in the school.

Crime Problem Addressed

Seventy-eight percent of school districts responding to a recent national survey said their schools had reported serious student-on-student violence. Some of the violence occurring in schools is related to the presence of gangs and conflicts that arise among rival gangs. The gangs are recognizable through the wearing of specific colors or other identifying garments. The dress code is one element of school district policy to combat gang activity and the violence that often accompanies it.

Key Components

The strategy focuses on gang activity within a school. To require a dress code, the school must demonstrate a connection between establishment of a dress code and its impact on gang activity. The policies typically prohibit wearing of specific colors associated with area gangs, certain sports franchise merchandise, or certain kinds of jewelry. Many school dress codes also prohibit wearing of sexually explicit T-shirts or other garments that display messages advocating use of drugs, violence, or otherwise illegal behavior. Some schools go beyond prohibiting certain clothing and require uniforms similar to those of private or parochial schools.

Key Partnerships

School administrators, parents, teachers, and students must each have a voice in designing a dress code policy. Some schools have even negotiated dress code policies with gang members as part of an effort to keep the school neutral territory in gang disputes.

Potential Obstacles

There are some constitutional impediments. Schools must associate dress code policy with reasonable concerns about safety and must relate restrictions on clothing to security concerns. Some parents and students object to such policies, characterizing them as restrictions of personal freedom of choice. Open and honest communication with parents and students about the objectives of the policy can help to build support for its implementation. Policies based only on gang colors can backfire if gang membership or color affiliations of gangs change.

Signs of Success

Forty-one percent of all schools and 52 percent of urban schools surveyed in 1993 reported use of student dress codes as part of a crime and violence prevention strategy. Dr. Chester Quarles, professor and director of criminal justice programs at the University of Mississippi, notes the large number of successful school dress code policies in *Staying Safe at School,* one of a series of monographs designed to educate teachers about effective school safety strategies.

Applying the Strategy

Tacoma, Washington, adopted a "no gang colors at school" policy as part of a strategy to address an increase in gang-related drive-by shootings. Tipton Community School Corporation in Indiana has a policy restricting the wearing of clothes that "disrupt the school, interfere with health or safety, or promote vulgarity." Each of these districts feels confident that the dress code policies have helped reduce the incidence of violence and conflict among students and improved student and staff perception of safety within the school.

San Juan Capistrano, California, schools adopted a dress code policy in 1993. The centrally developed policy gives individual schools the flexibility to develop more restrictive prohibitions if school officials and parents feel it is necessary. Flyers and information packets describe to parents the policy, which is in effect in all schools. The policy prohibiting baseball caps and baggy pants, clothing considered unsafe, garments that display obscene symbols or slogans that denigrate specific groups of people, or anything that promotes illegal activity has helped to alleviate some violence problems associated with the dozen gangs active in the area. The number of suspensions has also declined significantly in many schools.

Contact Information

Assistant Superintendent of Secondary Schools
Capistrano U.S.D.
32972 Calle Perfecto
San Juan Capistrano, California 92675
714-489-7224

Drug-Free Zones

Strategy

Establishing areas in and near schools as drug-free zones helps to prevent drug dealing and use and enhances the safety of the school environment for students and staff.

Crime Problem Addressed

Drug trafficking to children is reduced inside schools, in school bus and parking areas, and in other locations within a specified distance of the school that are designated as drug-free zones. This strategy uses increased penalties and prison sentences for those caught dealing drugs within 1,000 feet of a school.

Key Components

While drug dealing is already illegal, the local ordinances that establish drug-free zones add significant time (often two to three times the sentence for a similar offense outside the zone) to prison sentences for those caught dealing drugs within the specified distance around a school. The community and potential offenders are informed of the policy and the boundaries of the zone via signs within the designated area and through publicity from the police department, school officials, and community organizations. Informal publicity occurs as those arrested in the zone spread word about the strict sentences they received. This informal publicity encourages drug dealers to move to other parts of the community, away from areas where children congregate. Although displacement of the activity is not the ideal result, the strategy at least helps ensure that children are protected from drug dealing and the violence that sometimes accompanies it.

The strategy also supplements drug abuse prevention activities within the school, adding emphasis and visibility to such programs and reminding students who would use or sell drugs of the penalties involved should they be caught. Drug-free schools have students sign covenants stating they will not use drugs at school. Some schools notify students that lockers are school property and remind them that lockers can be searched by school officials who suspect they contain illegal drugs or weapons. Schools with very serious drug problems sometimes even use drug-sniffing police dogs to conduct random searches of student lockers.

Key Partnerships

Lawmakers must work with school authorities and criminal justice personnel to designate the area a drug-free zone and to publicize the program within the community and to parents and students. Local police must cooperate with the community to arrest and seek convictions for offenders caught dealing illegal drugs in the zone. Local

prosecutors and judges must commit to applying the tougher sentences in such cases.

Schools can create support for the program by designing comprehensive drug abuse prevention programs that build an antidrug and anti-alcohol bias among the students. Student support can also be built through student-designed publicity for the drug-free zone and through communication to students about the convictions achieved by local law enforcement and prosecutors.

Potential Obstacles

Prison officials may resist establishment of drug-free zones if their facilities are already crowded and would have difficulty absorbing additional detainees for such long sentences. Some judges may resist applying the policy to juvenile offenders. Policies involving locker searches or other student-related enforcement may face opposition from students or parents on constitutional grounds. Open and clear communication with all parties affected by the policy should help alleviate their concerns. The policy should apply to locker searches and other, stricter, enforcement measures only in situations where there is serious disruption or danger in the school caused by drug dealing and drug abuse.

Signs of Success

Legislation mandating establishment of drug-free school zones was enacted by Congress in 1986. In 1988, the legislation was expanded to include other areas where children congregate, such as playgrounds, recreation and youth centers, and business areas that attract children.

In *The Winnable War: A Community Guide to Eradicating Street Drug Markets*, Roger Conner and Patrick Burns advocate establishment of drug-free school zones as one of the strategies communities should consider to fight drug trafficking. While pointing out that effective policies must be widely publicized and posted, the authors note "[while] some critics argue that drug-free school zone legislation is more symbolic than effective, proponents of the law point out that this 'symbolism' results in real jail time. In addition, there is some evidence to suggest that drug dealers are moving their operations away from drug-free school zones. In New Jersey, for example, some dealers have said in wiretapped conversations that they refrain from locating their operations near schools in order to avoid harsher sentences."

Applying the Strategy

In 1989, a new state drug-free school zone law prompted the Seattle Police Department to establish the program in city schools, at school bus stops (3,300 sites), and in parks. The policy added nearly two years to the average sentence handed down to an offender convicted of dealing illegal drugs. Signs were posted around and in the city's 175 schools and throughout 40 city parks. Students, parents, teachers, and others helped publicize and build support for the program by distributing flyers.

The program has been very successful. Since 1990, local prosecutors have convicted 250 offenders. Arrests within the zone dropped noticeably after 1992, when word of the program had spread throughout the city. Frequent drug dealing in areas around Seattle's schools has nearly been eliminated. Parents who used to patrol the parking lots and bus stops have withdrawn those patrols, believing the immediate threat to their children has abated.

Contact Information

Crime Prevention Unit
Seattle Police Department
610 3rd Avenue
Seattle, Washington 98104
206-684-7555

Student Crime Watch

Strategy

Student crime prevention or crime watch groups help to ensure the safety of students and staff and play an important role in establishing a school environment that does not tolerate crime.

Crime Problem Addressed

A substantial percentage of victimization of juveniles by crime occurs in or around schools. These crimes include theft of property from lockers, bullying, assault, and destruction of personal property. This strategy addresses all types of crime and disorder in a school. By involving students in safety and security issues at the school, it teaches students to be responsible for their own behavior and for the welfare of the school community.

Key Components

In this strategy, students work together in a commitment to create a crime-free school environment. Students in a crime prevention or crime watch club educate their peers about crime and crime prevention, commit to reporting suspicious or criminal activity on campus, and serve as supplemental security assistants by patrolling playgrounds, cafeterias, and school buses.

Students in the group organize informational assemblies, recruit their peers into crime prevention projects within the school and community, publicize crime-reporting hotlines, distribute information to students on crime-related topics, act as liaisons with the community's Neighborhood Watch program regarding observation of school property during off hours, and serve as role models for their peers by demonstrating a commitment to remain crime-free and active on behalf of the school community.

Key Partnerships

School board members, principals, school staff, and students must be encouraged to work together to ensure a safe school environment. This strategy is one element of such a program. The school crime watch represents a recognition that school officials alone cannot protect the school, staff, and students.

Potential Obstacles

Some school administrators do not believe that students can or should perform security functions or assist with crime prevention activities within a school setting. In instances where the school environment is violent, parents may be reluctant to see their children involved in activities they may perceive as making them vulnerable to crime or retaliation from student offenders. To be effective, student crime watch programs must be communicated as part of an overall school strategy of "zero tolerance" for crime. In that way, student involvement in crime prevention becomes the norm of student behavior, not the exception to indifference, fear, or delinquency.

Signs of Success

Youth Crime Watch of America, Inc. (YCWA), a non-profit organization, empowers and motivates students to "create crime-free and drug-free schools and communities" through establishment of Youth Crime Watch programs. YCWA provides materials, workshops, and on-site training for schools and communities seeking to initiate YCWA programs. It also facilitates the exchange of crime prevention information and ideas among student groups across the country via the organization's newsletter and other materials. The Miami-based group has helped to establish very successful Youth Crime Watch programs in middle and high schools throughout the state of Florida and around the country.

Applying the Strategy

School safety patrols and crime watch-style groups have been used successfully for decades. In 1975, students at Parkdale Senior High School in Prince Georges County,

Maryland, banded together to patrol their parking lot to deter larceny from student vehicles. After a short while, incidents of larceny from student vehicles dropped from an average of 30 per month to zero. The success of the program prompted continuation of patrols and formation of a Student Security Advisory Council that continues to this day. The Tiger Patrol in the W.R. Thomas Middle School in Miami monitors the hallway to prevent bullying and victimization of students. It also actively discourages vandalism. Seymour Vestermark, Jr., and Peter Blauvelt, authors of *Controlling Crime in the School,* believe in the concept of student crime watch and patrols and assert that students often do a better job than adults of settling student disputes and preventing confrontations and crime within schools.

Contact Information

Youth Crime Watch of America
Dadeland Towers North, Suite 320
9300 South Dadeland Boulevard, Suite 100
Miami, Florida 33156
305-670-2409

Gun-Free Zones

Strategy

Establishing policies prohibiting the possession of guns in schools and within a set distance of school buildings helps to secure schools from gun-related violence and crime.

Crime Problem Addressed

The strategy recognizes the inherent danger of concealed firearms in the possession of gang members, drug traffickers, and fearful students. A survey by the National Centers for Disease Control and Prevention indicates that about 135,000 guns are brought into schools every day. According to the Office of Juvenile Justice and Delinquency Prevention, nearly 20 percent of all offenders arrested in 1991 while carrying guns were juveniles.

Key Components

Localities designate school buildings, school bus stops, and the perimeter area around school buildings as weapon-free zones, where possession or use of a firearm, knife, or other weapon carries additional penalties for the offender. Youths caught with a gun in the zone are usually suspended (in some cases expelled) by school officials and may face criminal charges. Like the drug-free school zone concept, this strategy aims to deter offenders from carrying and using a gun or knife in the zone by imposing increased penalties. The policies may displace such activities to other areas of the community. Even so, school and law enforcement officials believe that the policies are very effective in securing areas frequented by school-aged youth and staff while school is in session.

The designated areas are marked by special signage and publicized throughout the community. In addition to enhanced sanctions, most school districts where such policies are in place also have implemented antiviolence and gun education programs to reinforce among students the belief that carrying guns and knives to school is not safe and should not be tolerated by them and their peers.

Key Partnerships

Lawmakers must work with school authorities and criminal justice personnel to designate gun-free zones and to publicize the program within the community and to parents and students. Local police must cooperate with the community to arrest and seek convictions for offenders caught handling guns in the zone. Local prosecutors and judges must commit to applying the tougher sentences in such cases.

Schools can create support for the program by designing comprehensive gun violence prevention programs. Student support can also be built through student-designed publicity for the gun-free zone and through communication to students about the convictions achieved by local law enforcement and prosecutors.

Potential Obstacles

Some communities resist the policies out of concern that the accompanying publicity will label the community as one with a gun violence problem. Local policymakers in some communities worry that expulsion of students caught with guns just releases dangerous students into the community and removes them from educational opportunities. Many communities in this situation have developed alternative (off-site and separate) education programs for such students, combining traditional curricula with violence prevention education. Implementing such policies and alternative education programs can be costly for school districts. Some have not aggressively pursued these policies out of a concern about costs or because they have determined that guns are not currently a significant problem in their district. As of 1994, the federal government was considering withholding some federal funds from districts that did not adopt expulsion as the sanction for students caught with guns. Costs can be minimized through partnerships with businesses to share expenses and with law enforcement to develop prevention education programs for students.

Signs of Success

In 1990, Congress passed and the president signed the Gun-Free School Zones Act. The law directs school districts to develop policies to keep students and staff safe from guns and other dangerous weapons. Following the successful drug-free zone concept, many local districts have adopted weapon-free zones within and around the school, in many cases developing "zero tolerance" policies that direct severe sanctions (including expulsion) of students caught with guns or other dangerous weapons. Communities in states as diverse as Oklahoma, Washington, California, Missouri, and Pennsylvania have had success with this approach. The National School Safety Center and the authors of *Violence In Our Schools, Hospitals, and Public Places* endorse weapon-free school zones as an effective violence and crime prevention measure. A 1994 federal court of appeals decision called into question the ability of states and localities to enforce the law when it declared Louisiana's law unconstitutional. Localities should consult their state attorney general for advice on implementing a policy inspired by the federal legislation.

Applying the Strategy

The San Diego, California, school district, under the direction of the School Police Services director, devised a zero tolerance policy for weapons on campus policy. The policy prohibits weapons on campus, on buses, and at school-sponsored activities. Posters and bumper stickers publicize the program to students and staff. Parents and youths receive written descriptions of the policy and sanctions against students who violate it. In order to attend certain preferred schools, students must sign a contract that they will not bring a gun or weapon to school or fight with other students. Since the policy was enacted in 1991, the number of gun-related incidents in schools has declined annually. Many students and parents have expressed support for the policy, believing it has helped make school buildings safer.

Contact Information

Director, Police Services
San Diego Unified School District
4100 Normal Street
San Diego, California 92103-2682
619-293-8053

Crime Reporting Hotline

Strategy

Anonymous hotlines or similar services allow students to report incidents of crime, weapons, or drug violations in schools, thus reducing fear of retribution and preventing additional incidents.

Crime Problem Addressed

Forty percent of 700 cities responding to a 1994 survey by the National League of Cities reported that school violence had increased significantly over the past five years. One of every four communities surveyed reported incidents resulting in serious injuries or death in the previous year. Hotlines can be used to address any crime, disorder, or disruptive behavior. They are particularly effective in encouraging students to report incidents that threaten the security of other students and school faculty. The reputation of the reporting system as truly anonymous greatly enhances the likelihood that it will be used frequently.

Key Components

School administrators develop the reporting system in cooperation with the local law enforcement agency, school board, state education department, or area crime watch group. The program is sometimes a supplement to a school crime watch or community crime reporting program. In many schools, the program is operated from an office within the school and is staffed by security, law enforcement, or school personnel. Callers anonymously report the presence of weapons or drugs, crimes they have witnessed, or pending fights among students. Donations and some school funds are used to support rewards for reports. Rewards typically are between $25 and $100, depending on the resources available to the program and the information given in the report.

Key Partnerships

For the program to work well, the school must distribute information on the program to students and staff and ensure that the program is viewed as part of a broad-based effort to promote a crime- and drug-free school. Students, local businesses, and community groups can be recruited to design, fund, and help distribute educational materials about crime and violence and drug abuse prevention and to build awareness and acceptance of the anonymous reporting system. Neighborhood crime watch and reporting groups can build support for the programs by building relationships with school principals and helping them to understand the role of anonymous reporting systems in creating a safe school environment.

Potential Obstacles

The expense of establishing the reporting system can present a challenge for some school systems. Reporting systems need at least one phone line, or more if the school is large or the system is heavily used. Training for school or law enforcement personnel who staff the system and refer calls about serious incidents to the police is an additional required expense. Some school reporting systems are connected to the area 911 service, creating a potential impact on that system. Partnerships among school officials, law enforcement agencies, and administrators of the 911 system can help address such impacts.

Signs of Success

The National School Safety Center (NSSC), in its publication, "School Crisis Prevention and Response," recommends that school districts pursue an array of crime and violence prevention strategies, including incentives or encouragements for students to report suspicious and criminal activity. The NSSC states that such programs are an important part of a comprehensive school-based violence prevention strategy. The 1993 Southeastern Regional Vision for Education report, "Reducing School Violence: Hot Topics and Usable Research," recommends a school crime reporting system as a means of protecting students and staff and "enlisting support for preventing violence."

Applying the Strategy

Elementary, middle, and high schools in Seattle and Tacoma, Washington, use posters describing the program to promote participation of their successful school-based crime, drug, and weapon reporting system; this practice has helped to reduce gun- and drug-related incidents involving students.

Contact Information

Office of the Superintendent of Public Instruction
Old Capitol Building
P.O. Box 47200
Olympia, Washington 98504-7200
360-753-5595

Student, Faculty, Staff, and Visitor ID Cards

Strategy

Identification cards for students, faculty, staff, and visitors increase the visibility of individuals who do not belong in the school building and make the facility safer for all who use it.

Crime Problem Addressed

This strategy focuses on increasing the visibility of trespassers, intruders, and suspended or expelled students through identification cards for students, staff, faculty, and visitors. In the MetLife Insurance Company-sponsored 1994 survey, *Violence in America's Schools: The Family Perspective*, nearly two-thirds of students polled said they believed it would be easy for people who don't belong in their school to enter the building. An identification card system, particularly when combined with access control procedures, deters individuals with no legitimate business in the school from attempting to enter the building and reduces opportunities for on-campus crimes, violence, and drug dealing by unauthorized outsiders.

Key Components

Schools using identification cards issue them to students and staff at the beginning of the school year. Students, faculty, and staff are required to display valid identification cards to enter the building. Usually color coded to differentiate between student classes, and between faculty and staff, the cards are worn throughout the day by everyone in the school building. The visitor ID card is usually larger than any other, making it noticeable and distinctive from those worn by students and staff.

Visitors are issued temporary identification cards after showing a driver's license and signing in as they enter the building. Signs at the main entrances notify visitors that identification is required to enter the school building. The school district purchases, leases, or contracts with a vendor company to provide the identification cards. Each school using the identification system has a distinct card to reduce the likelihood that students or staff could enter without authorization.

Key partnerships

The superintendent and school board must authorize the use of an identification card system and agree to expend funds necessary to implement it. Parent organizations and students should be consulted and informed about the role identification cards are expected to play in the comprehensive security planning for school facilities. Extensive communication with staff, parents, and students is necessary to ensure successful implementation of the policy.

Potential Obstacles

Identification cards can be expensive, particularly for a large school district with many students, faculty, and categories of staff. Administration of the system must be carefully maintained to ensure adequate accounting of students, staff, and faculty transferred into, within, or out of the school system. In addition, some school districts have difficulty staffing school entrances to check ID cards and to sign in visitors. Many districts use staff or faculty to check IDs; others obtain assistance from local law enforcement agencies or volunteer parents. In some school districts, the identification card doubles as the school lunch account card. Combining the two systems on one card reduces costs.

Signs of Success

The Southeast Regional Vision for Education's 1993 report, *Reducing School Violence: Hot Topics and Usable Research,* recommends students and staff ID cards as one of many successful strategies for "keeping unauthorized persons off campus" and ensuring the safety and security of students and staff.

According to a 1993 study by the National School Boards Association, 32 percent of all school districts surveyed reported successful use of student and staff photo ID card systems. The rate of use was 41 percent in urban school systems. The report highlights seven districts in six states that use the systems with success.

Applying the Strategy

In Oklahoma City, Oklahoma, each school's emblem is displayed on a photo ID card worn by students, faculty, and staff. As part of a security enhancement plan implemented in 1992, visitors and temporary maintenance workers must check in and be escorted to their destination within the school. Costs assessed for lost cards help minimize replacement costs. Other security measures include metal detectors, full-time presence of police officers in school buildings, and closed campuses during lunch hours. Since the comprehensive policy was implemented, the number of unauthorized visitors and the number of guns found on campuses have declined.

Contact Information

Director of Information
Public Services Department
Oklahoma City Public Schools
900 North Klein Avenue
Oklahoma City, Oklahoma 73106
405-297-6615

Reduced Nighttime Lighting of School Buildings

Strategy

School authorities turn off interior and exterior lights at school buildings at night to reduce opportunities for vandalism and other crimes to occur during those hours. Businesses and neighborhood residents call the police to report lights on during those hours.

Crime Problem Addressed

This strategy addresses acts of nighttime burglary and after-hours vandalism, including graffiti, by turning off interior and exterior lights that can illuminate building surfaces and entrances and make visible school equipment desired by burglars.

Key Components

The "lights out," or total darkness strategy, is based on the belief that darkness reduces the attractiveness of the school as a target for criminals, including graffiti taggers and burglars. In addition to turning off the interior and exterior lights at the school, the school publicizes the program with area residents and businesses, asking them to report to police any lights they see at night. Police who patrol the area know to investigate activity at the school

if they notice lights. Security experts and psychologists have theorized that vandals who cannot view the destruction they have caused are less inclined to commit the act.

Key Partnerships

School boards and school superintendents must approve a "lights out" policy. School officials must train faculty and staff to turn off all interior and exterior lights at the conclusion of scheduled activities on campus. Neighbors must be educated on how to report lights at the building during late-night hours. Similarly, police officers must be briefed on the policy so that they will understand that lights visible during late-night hours signals that criminal activity may be occurring and should be investigated.

Potential Obstacles

The main obstacle is the perception among most people that enhanced lighting increases security. While that is true for public areas in use and buildings where entrances are used during nighttime hours, school buildings not in use during late-night hours do not need to be illuminated. The evidence indicates that it is appropriate to look at reduced lighting as a security enhancement in such situations as schools during off hours.

Signs of Success

The San Diego Unified School District has used a lights-out policy since 1974 with a great deal of success. A National School Safety Center publication quoted the district's school police chief: "In addition to reducing crime, having total darkness after hours has saved the District over $2 million in utility bills. It was a radical move because we had been brainwashed . . . for years that the more lights, the less crime. To the contrary, I think lights help a burglar to see where the equipment is. We've told the community, 'if you see a light come on, call the police'. . . . A dark and silent school is effective against property crime."

Applying the Strategy

In his 1981 book, *Effective Strategies for School Security*, the director of security for the Prince Georges County, Maryland, school system advocates the lights-out policy and details how the policy has been implemented successfully in his county since the late 1970s.

Contact Information

Director, Police Department
San Diego Unified School District
4100 Normal Street
San Diego, California 92103-2682
619-293-8053

Volunteer School Security Patrols

Strategy

Parent volunteers provide additional supervision and basic security assistance in schools, helping to prevent crime and keep the building safe for students, faculty, and staff.

Crime Problem Addressed

The focus of the strategy is to assist in creating a school environment in which disciplinary problems, disruptive behavior, violence, and criminal activity are seriously curtailed by enhancing the supervision of students through use of volunteer security patrols.

Key Components

Volunteer security assistants at schools can include parents of students, retired residents of the area, or others from the community who have time to devote during school hours. Usually, parent volunteers supervise youths in the hallways, cafeterias, and on school playgrounds and ball courts. Certain schools also use the volunteers as security help at social, extracurricular, and sporting events. Some schools pay parents or other adults a small stipend, but most of these patrols are volunteers. Most volunteer patrols wear distinctive clothing to make them visible to students who may need help and to signal to outsiders that the students are closely supervised.

Key Partnerships

School administrators should work with parent and teacher organizations, school security personnel, and students to plan the roles and responsibilities of volunteers as supplemental security staff and how the volunteers will respond to criminal or delinquent incidents on campus.

Potential Obstacles

The primary obstacle to the strategy is likely to be resistance from school administrators and staff to the idea of using volunteers as security help. School staff may be reluctant to take on the responsibility of supervising and training the volunteers. Additionally, school districts are concerned about liability issues associated with injuries to volunteers caught in violent confrontations or trying to stop fights. Many schools resolve this issue by putting parents or other volunteers on the school payroll at a level of compensation that ensures coverage by workers' compensation and other insurance maintained by the school system.

Signs of Success

Only 13 percent of schools surveyed currently utilize the services of volunteer security patrols. The National School Board Association advocates and profiles successful volunteer patrol programs in a number of school districts throughout the country in its 1993 publication, *Violence in the Schools: How America's School Boards Are Safeguarding Your Children*.

Parent security patrols and related programs are also advocated in *Staying Safe at School*, a guide for teachers written by Dr. Chester Quarles, professor and director of the criminal justice program at the University of Mississippi. In one such program, in Oxford, Mississippi, mothers of students patrol the hallways to ensure that only authorized visitors may enter the school building.

Applying the Strategy

In the suburban Chicago community of Matteson, Illinois, the Woodgate Fathers organization has become a vital resource for the local elementary and secondary schools, supplementing school security staff and modeling for students and other adults a commitment to the school and the community through organization of special events for youths. The group publicizes and promotes its activities within the community, using brochures and community meetings to recruit other adult members and to gain the cooperation and involvement of students. The group has also created a youth advisory committee to explore ways to enhance communication between parents and youths in the area.

Dads on Patrol has operated in Houston, Texas, schools for many years. In Cornwall, New York, parents are paid to patrol hallways and supplement security staff.

Contact Information

Elementary School District 159
6131 Allemong Drive
Matteson, Illinois 60443
708-720-1300

Phones in Classrooms

Strategy

Schools that equip each classroom with a telephone for use by teachers in a medical, disciplinary, or crime-related emergency provide both teachers and students with a means to get help.

Crime Problem Addressed

The strategy helps to improve a teacher's ability to get rapid response to crime, drug, medical, and discipline-related emergencies in classrooms, on playgrounds, or in cafeterias. The situations of concern include student intimidation or threats to peers or teachers, severe discipline problems, or incidents witnessed from the classroom.

Key Components

The school system provides each classroom and major activity area in the school with an emergency phone through which teachers can request assistance from school officials or police. The phone, portable radio, or intercom system also allows teachers to report suspicious or dangerous activity occurring in the hallway, in the parking lot, or in nearby classrooms. The rapid reporting increases the likelihood that a perpetrator will be caught and that security staff or police will be able to avert escalation of violent confrontations.

Key Partnerships

In most settings, phone systems are funded fully by the school district. In some cases, community organizations, parent-teacher groups, and teachers' unions have supported initial costs of installing such systems. School districts will need to establish a relationship with local law enforcement agencies to obtain training for teachers in the appropriate use of the emergency phones.

Potential Obstacles

School administrators may be reluctant to admit that the security issues in their school are serious enough to warrant installation of phones in classrooms, or they may be concerned about costs. In schools with very serious security issues, phones may become a vital component of a strategy that demonstrates to students and faculty that the district wishes to ensure rapid response in the case of emergencies.

Signs of Success

Twenty-two percent of school districts surveyed in 1993 by the National School Boards Association reported safety benefits from using phones in classrooms. Security consultant Peter Blauvelt and his coauthor advocated on behalf of phones in classrooms in their 1978 book, *Controlling Crime in the School.* The 1989 National Education Association-sponsored book, *School Violence: A Survival Guide for School Staff,* also advocates phones in classrooms as part of a comprehensive school security program.

Applying the Strategy

School staff and students in Oneida County, New York, report that they feel much more secure since phones were installed in each middle school and high school classroom. Response in cases of medical and disciplinary crises is now almost immediate. The Liberty Central School District in New York created an in-house 911 phone system to respond to similar situations. All schools in Monroe County, Kentucky, now have telephones in each classroom.

Contact Information

National School Boards Association
1680 Duke Street
Alexandria, Virginia 22314
703-838-6722

Crisis Planning

Strategy

Comprehensive crisis management policies prepare school administrators and staff to respond appropriately to violence, criminal acts on campus, and natural emergencies. The policies cover response after the fact but also include prevention and intervention actions that should be taken by staff.

Crime Problem Addressed

The strategy addresses not only a school's preparedness to deal with natural disasters but also the disruption and chaos that can follow gang-related or other violent incidents, serious accidents, or suicides involving students. The crisis response plan can help avert escalation of violent incidents by ensuring that administrators address school security issues and the need for law enforcement or medical assistance in a rapid and efficient manner.

Key Components

Development of crisis policies covers three phases: organization of a crisis management team; establishment of plans of action for the team during specific kinds of emergencies; and training for crisis teams, faculty, and students in how to respond in case of emergencies, including violent incidents, on campus. The policies cover such issues as the protocol for reporting incidents, designating safe places on campus, handling groups of students and providing for their safety, and notifying parents and others in the community as the situation warrants. Most schools have well-understood policies for responses to such natural disasters as tornadoes or floods. However, many schools do not have policies that specify the roles and responsibilities of staff and faculty in case of student abduction, gang violence, shooting incidents at the school, or large-scale fights among students. Such policies help ensure that faculty, staff, and students know how to report an incident and can locate safe places on campus or outside the building, and that school administrators and staff can mobilize the appropriate law enforcement and medical assistance. The policies may also include provisions for counseling students and staff following violent incidents or deaths of students or staff. For the policy to be effective, all staff and students must be educated and trained in it. In addition, parents and others in the community must be aware of the policy and how they can contact the school in case of emergencies.

Key Partnerships

The school board, principals, teachers, parents, school staff, and student representatives should all play a role in designing the crisis management policy, determining training needs of staff who will use it, and setting guidelines for prevention, intervention, and post-crisis action.

Potential Obstacles

Because some school boards do not believe that violence or crime-related crises will affect their districts, they may not emphasize crisis management planning for such incidents or they may be less than willing to develop such policies. Parent groups and teachers can convince reluctant administrators to pursue crisis management planning by reminding them that, while occurrences requiring use of the policy may be rare, rapid and effective response is as vital as in any natural disaster or emergency.

Signs of Success

School security expert Bob Nations highlights the importance of preparation for crisis response by local school districts. In *Comprehensive Crisis Management Planning*, he asserts that schools should set up specific and well-publicized policies regarding response to serious disruptions and crisis situations at school buildings (including those related to violent incidents). He further states that schools should develop a "crisis action team" including the principal, counselors, health professionals, teachers, and representatives from local law enforcement and mental health agencies with specific responsibilities for prevention, intervention, post-incident follow-up, or emergency response to the crisis.

Basing their advice on research and information from successful local experiences, Eugene D. Wheeler and Dr. Anthony Baron outline detailed action steps for schools considering crisis management planning in their 1994 book, *Violence in Our Schools, Hospitals and Public Places: A Prevention and Management Guide.*

Applying the Strategy

The Dallas, Texas, Independent School District developed an extensive crisis management planning mechanism in 1987. Initially a suicide prevention and intervention program, the program expanded to include response to gang-related violence among students and assaults on teachers. By 1992, the district had developed a crisis management emergency handbook for principals and a resource manual for post-crisis services available to schools throughout the district. The district-wide plan incorporates school-based violence prevention plans developed by school administrators, parents, and teachers. Basic security procedures are addressed in the plan, along with directions for establishing crisis management communications systems and using parent liaisons to update the community. Since then, the district has surveyed schools to determine how well the plans fared during crisis drills. The majority of the schools that responded reported the plans helped them to organize a more effective response for use in real emergencies.

Contact Information

Crisis Specialist
Psychological/Social Services
Dallas Public Schools
12532 Nuestra Drive
Dallas, Texas 75230
214-982-1400

School Resource Officers

Strategy

Security or police presence at schools helps to reduce opportunities for unwitnessed crimes. The presence of school resource police or security officers reduces fear of crime and violence among students, faculty, and staff.

Crime Problem Addressed

School resource officers address the gamut of crime and drug activity that occur in schools. Properly trained and integrated into the school administration, these officers can be viewed as an asset and resource to the school and not simply a disciplinary force to "catch" student criminals and delinquents.

Key Components

Security officers, police officers (often youth or gang specialists), and school counselors trained in security are assigned to patrol school buildings during school hours, to develop positive relationships with students and staff, to recognize and respond to security threats on campus, and to deter crime through their visible presence in the school and at school-sponsored activities. The officers may also sponsor or lead specific educational (drug prevention, conflict management) or recreational activities on campus as a means of building positive relationships with students. Some schools have established mentoring programs, pairing school resource officers with students who have discipline problems.

Key Partnerships

Administrators, teachers, and staff usually encourage the presence of law enforcement officers or security personnel in a school, believing that their presence helps protect all who use the building from crime and violence. Parents aware of the program usually support it fully and can be powerful advocates for funding to cover the costs of assigning law enforcement personnel to the school.

Potential Obstacles

Administrators in some school districts do not want security personnel or police officers in their school, fearing that the school atmosphere will appear less open and more concerned about crime. Many districts have difficulty finding funds to support assignment of law enforcement personnel and may be concerned that security funds divert funding from educational programs. Supplemental funds from the school district or law enforcement agency can remedy this situation. In addition, some principals may be reluctant to turn over some element of disciplinary control, even to trained police officers. Partnerships among school officials and police in planning the roles and responsibilities of officers can help address such concerns.

Signs of Success

The National Association of School Resource Officers advocates placement of law enforcement officials in schools on a full-time basis to supplement security and prevention education provided by school staff. The association notes that this approach has been successful in thousands of communities across the country, helping to reduce violence, improving law enforcement-school relations, and enhancing positive images of law enforcement among students and staff. The association offers advice as well as pertinent publications and other materials to schools looking to establish such programs.

Applying the Strategy

The Arlington, Texas, comprehensive crime and violence prevention plan, developed in 1993, called for 10 additional school resource officers for the city's schools. The officers have been hired and assigned, further enhancing security at the schools and fostering positive partnerships among officers, students, and school staff. The Montgomery, Alabama, Public School District now assigns security officers to every high school and junior high school in the area. In the Phoenix, Arizona, School District, two police officers are assigned to each of several high schools. During the summer months, the officers are reassigned to gang prevention programs.

Contact Information

National Association of School Resource Officers
4222 Old Dominion Road
Orlando, FL 32812
407-898-5491

Staff Training

Strategy

Crime and violence prevention training builds the abilities of school personnel to prevent and respond to incidents in the school.

Crime Problem Addressed

On-campus crime is now a fact of life in many schools. Fifty-five percent of students surveyed in 1994 said they had been the victim of a fight or threat during the previous school year. The National School Boards Association call this "the epidemic of violence in the school." Schools are also more likely to be burglarized than nearby businesses. Many school districts across the country spend more money to repair the effects of vandalism then they do on the cost of new textbooks. This strategy aims to provide teachers, administrators, and staff the training and skills to prevent and address on-campus crime.

Key Components

Researchers Patricia Larke of the Texas A&M University and Norvella Carter of Illinois State University summarized strategies proven effective when implemented by trained teachers in "School Violence: Preparing In-Service Teachers." They note that teachers should be trained in the following skills:

- improving the school climate through after-school activities;

- non-conflict mediation;

- recognizing the impact of social influences such as poverty and racism on student behavior;

- promoting empathy among students for the concerns of others;

- helping students control impulses to react violently when challenged;

- teaching students problem-solving skills;

- communicating with parents to get them to reinforce lessons from the classroom;

- building self-esteem in students through praise and recognition; and

- using and teaching students to use resources in the community to address their needs.

Successful training programs for school staff also include training in implementation and enforcement of school disciplinary and security procedures. Uniform application of these rules establishes the standard of behavior in the school and helps protect students, teachers, and staff.

Key Partnerships

Teachers, administrators, and other school staff should plan training as a group so that sessions address the concerns of all school personnel and the skills they need to protect themselves and students.

Potential Obstacles

Schools whose budgets are strained by diminished resources may find it difficult to identify funds to support training. School administrators can argue for training resources if they can compare the investment in training with what the school system spends on responses to crime and violence.

Signs of Success

The University of Virginia's Youth Violence Project began in the spring of 1993. Representatives from youth agencies, law enforcement, schools, parents, elected officials, and business leaders developed a pilot program to help teachers deal with violence in the schools. The Virginia Youth Violence Project uses problem-solving training in psychology, sociology, criminal justice, and public policy to help teachers understand factors that contribute to youth violence. The university receives assistance on the project from the FBI's Behavioral Sciences Service Unit and National Academy. By 1995, several hundred teachers and administrators had been trained, and many had created strategy teams to implement projects in their schools. The state's model was recognized by the Governor's Commission on Violent Crime and is under consideration for replication by other states.

Applying the Strategy

The schools of education in Mississippi have all recognized the sudden spiral of youth violence and disorderly behavior at school. The Continuing Education Division of the University of Mississippi has sponsored school violence prevention workshops for school staff since 1992. The Educational Leadership Academy of Mississippi State sponsors a three-day school crime prevention seminar. The Education Service Center of the University of Southern Mississippi has sponsored a four-day school crime prevention and control seminar since 1990.

Contact Information

Project Director
University of Virginia
Youth Violence Project
418 Pembroke Four
Virginia Beach, Virginia 23462
804-552-1890

PUBLIC HOUSING

Eviction

Strategy

Cooperation among housing authority administrators, residents, and police results in identification and eviction of drug pushers from within the community.

Crime Problem Addressed

The focus of this program is to reduce the sale of drugs by arresting drug traffickers, evicting them, and rearresting them as trespassers should they return. Reducing drug sales also reduces robbery, prostitution, burglary, and auto theft. Fear of crime among residents declines as drug dealing and related crime go down.

Key Components

The strategy recognizes that some drug-pushing criminals make their living within public housing complexes. Many of these criminals are trespassers, intruders, or illegal (not authorized on the lease, whether they reside there or not). *Tackling Drug Problems in Public Housing*, a report on the Chicago Housing Authority, demonstrated that 80 percent of crimes in the city during 1990 occurred on housing authority property. Public housing residents often live in fear of gang activity and drug dealing.

In this strategy, the property management and police enforce lease provisions that hold tenants responsible for the behavior of residents and guests in that unit. In cases involving multiple family members in one home, implementation of the strategy may focus on one person living in the unit, such as an adult child of the leaseholder. A parent who allows the child back on the premises loses the lease.

Use of eviction policies reinforces the value that all residents have the right to live peacefully. Those who choose not to live by acceptable standards must leave, since residence in public housing is a privilege and not a right. It also reinforces accountability with families.

In April 1989, the U.S. Department of Housing and Urban Development (HUD) published a policy that leases on HUD-controlled properties must include a provision allowing eviction of "any member of the household, or person under the tenant's control" who engages in drug-related behavior. If illegal drugs are found in the apartment, the leaseholder is in violation of this policy and may be evicted.

Key Partnerships

Key partners include public housing management, residents, resident initiative groups, and law enforcement. Property managers provide residents with opportunities to report or otherwise help identify problem tenants who deal drugs or commit other crimes. Membership in resi-dent patrols and apartment watch groups supports other residents by diminishing the vulnerability and visibility of individuals who assist the effort.

Potential Obstacles

Local courts have interpreted public housing as the "housing of last resort" for some low-income residents. Courts with this view resist evictions as an enforcement tool. Looking at the rights of the individual resident, magistrates often hesitate to evict residents who are clearly violating the law.

Signs of Success

Carl Harass, in "How to Evict Drug Dealers from Public Housing," outlines management techniques and partnerships that have proven successful in protecting law-abiding residents. The article highlights successful eviction initiatives pursued by HUD-supported authorities.

Applying the Strategy

In 1988, the New York City Housing Authority requested the assistance of U.S. marshals. Armed with court orders, the marshals arrested drug pushers, seized their leases, and caused their eviction. This was the first time civil procedures of the federal drug laws had been used to seize federally subsidized public housing leases. This weapon can be used in other jurisdictions where local efforts have failed.

To ensure cooperation in Atlanta, Georgia, the housing authority has a permanently assigned detective serving as a staff liaison between the authority and the police department. The officer spends a lot of time working in lease enforcement. His presence also allows housing authority administrators access to arrest data. The arrest of a public housing tenant in Atlanta requires eviction. The arrest is considered proof the lease was violated.

In Mobile, Alabama, Sergeant Jack Dove of the Public Housing Interdiction Through Community Policing Program estimates that he spends approximately 60 percent of his time on screening and eviction matters. His efforts have resulted in the eviction of more than 90 crime-involved residents over an 18-month period.

Contact Information

Director of Office of Resident Services
Atlanta Housing Authority
709 Peachtree Street, N.E.
Atlanta, Georgia 30365
404-885-1339

Enforcement of Trespass Law

Strategy

Identification of nonresident trespassers and criminals who live on housing authority property helps police and property management determine which individuals should be removed from the premises.

Crime Problem Addressed

Crime problems on public housing property include unlawful drug sales, prostitution, sale and distribution of stolen merchandise, gang participation, and vandalism. Property managers and security attempt to separate those who have a right to be there from trespassers and intruders.

An estimated 70 to 90 percent of those arrested in public housing communities are intruders or trespassers, not residents. The policy is most effective in communities where access to the property is controlled by security and design of traffic patterns and fencing. Trespassing rules are difficult to enforce in an open or open-access community.

Key Components

Nonresidents are approached to ascertain if they have been invited to a particular residence. Intruders and trespassers are asked to leave by housing authority police officers, contractual security officers, or public police officers. Those who do not leave voluntarily and those who continue to trespass are arrested. Housing authorities with vehicular or pedestrian access control and security officers turn away uninvited nonresidents at the point of access.

One way to assist in the enforcement of trespassing laws is to create a "resident pass" and identification program for the authorized tenants who are formally recognized and accepted on the lease agreement.

Restricted access to the community, a neighborhood crime watch, or similar people-empowerment programs enhance the success of the strategy. In some communities this program is restricted to specific hours. Many communities, for instance, will support programs which help protect children and youth who live there.

Key Partnerships

Partners include public housing management and security, residents, resident groups, and law enforcement.

Potential Obstacles

In many instances 24-hour contractual or proprietary security officers will be needed to control vehicular and individual access points. Housing authorities will be required to make the necessary financial commitment to fund this security emphasis.

Signs of Success

Tackling Drug Problems in Public Housing: A Guide for Police reviews how legitimate visitors can register at entrance gates with security officers for visitor passes. Trespass prevention programs have been successfully conducted in Denison, Texas; Greensboro, Georgia; Clearwater, Florida; and Tampa, Florida.

Applying the Strategy

Recent HUD-sponsored security reviews of public housing communities administered by the Oakland, California, Housing Authority; the Tacoma, Washington, Housing Authority, the Tampa, Florida; Baltimore, Maryland; and Atlanta, Georgia, authorities recommended trespass enforcement strategies. Each community was able to identify and deter trespassers who had or were likely to commit crime on the property.

Contact Information

Commander, Public Housing Section
Chicago Police Department
1121 South State Street
Chicago, Illinois 60605
312-747-3526

Closed Circuit TV Cameras: Electronic Surveillance of Public Space

Strategy

Police and security officers, with the approval of housing authority administrators, purchase and install closed circuit television (CCTV) units for areas commonly used by drug traffickers and other criminals.

Crime Problem Addressed

The focus of this program is to reduce the sale of drugs by increasing surveillance, both visual and electronic. The videotape record of the sale can be used as evidence to obtain conviction in court. When the word gets around that both drug traffickers and customers are being apprehended, the drug sale problem in the community will diminish.

Key Components

Many drug pushers make their living on public housing properties. Because of the expense of intensive police patrols and undercover operations, many cities feel unable to offer full-service police operations to public housing. In fact, some cities justify this refusal economically because few housing authorities contribute directly to the tax base of the jurisdiction. Police authorities are, however, willing to prosecute ideal cases that are presented.

An exterior or interior CCTV operation with protective casing, heater, and dehumidifier offers an ideal way to assist police in curtailing drug activity. These cameras can be "fixed" or immovable, looking constantly at a single location, or they can be equipped with an electronic base that can be manually manipulated by a security officer at a separate location. In some cases the equipment is set up to move constantly, increasing the view of the officers monitoring the equipment.

The outside equipment is installed at appropriate locations where a low-light camera can scan the participants involved in any criminal activity. In large public housing administrations, this equipment can be moved, as appropriate, to minimize the expense of purchasing multiple units.

Key Partnerships

Public housing management, HUD grant makers, residents, resident initiative groups, and police authorities enable the purchase and proper installation of this equipment.

Potential Obstacles

While CCTVs are inexpensive, the outside covers, electronic bases, and the installation procedures are not. Also, an employee must monitor these devices at appropriate hours, so there is a constant security personnel expense. There is also a constant maintenance requirement, as electronic equipment breaks down and has to be repaired. The equipment is normally monitored at the times crimes are most likely to be committed. The officers monitoring the equipment usually turn the recording devices on when it appears that a crime is being committed, is about to be committed, or just has been committed.

Signs of Success

"Crime, Drugs and Subsidized Housing," by D.B. Bryson and R.L. Youmans, lists CCTV as one of several successful tactics for improving security.

Applying the Strategy

The monograph *Architectural Design for Crime Prevention* describes the successful use of CCTV at the Bronxdale Houses Apartment Complex of the New York City Housing Authority. Used primarily in lobbies and hallways, this equipment was also used outside to help identify drug-dealing suspects on the property.

Contact Information

U.S. Department of Housing and Urban Development
New York Regional Office
26 Federal Plaza
New York, New York 10278-0068
212-264-6500

Resident Initiatives and Empowerment Programs

Strategy

Housing authority administrators give logistical aid to resident initiative groups seeking ways to develop a safer and more secure community.

Crime Problem Addressed

The whole gamut of street crimes is addressed through this initiative.

Key Components

Basically, it is a residential security approach that encourages residents to understand that if they want a safe community they must help obtain it. Safety isn't the police officer's or firefighter's responsibility. Those who want security for their children and all the residents in their development, must help "clean up" (take out the trash), involving those whose activities are a threat to all citizens. They must help develop initiatives to cause the arrest of trespassers and the eviction of deviating tenants. Those who want safety must keep the fire code by cleaning up and disposing of flammable debris.

Key Partnerships

Public housing managers, residents, resident initiative groups, HUD, police officers, and crime prevention specialists at all levels are the key partners.

Potential Obstacles

The most formidable obstacle is the attitude of tenants. Fear, concern, ignorance, and the hesitancy to get involved are aspects of the problem. Many residents think that "whatever the effort, it won't make any difference. Nothing we do can help."

Signs of Success

The Chicago Housing Authority developed the nationally acclaimed Clean Sweep operation. While this approach was comprehensive and involved changes in public housing authority policy and the use of public police officers and detectives, it was still created at the insistence of a group of residents living in public housing.

Applying the Strategy

In Tacoma, Washington, there were 85 drive-by shootings during the first six months of 1991. While only a portion of these were in public housing, the fear for all children resulted in the creation of Residents in Force for Freedom (RIFF) at the Tacoma Housing Authority. These public housing residents simply insisted that there were ways to deal with the moral decay and public violence.

Contact Information

Special Projects Coordinator
Leasing Department
Tacoma Housing Authority
902 South L Street
Tacoma, Washington 98405
206-207-4456

Undercover Street-Level Drug Purchases

Strategy

Housing authority administrators, with the endorsements of residents, resident initiative groups, and police and/or security authorities, seek the infusion of funds to assist in undercover purchases of illegal narcotics.

Crime Problem Addressed

The focus of this program is to assist police authorities in making undercover narcotic purchases. These purchases can result in buy/bust operations in which the perpetrator is immediately arrested at the time of the sale. In some investigations, long-term surveillance and additional undercover buys may be completed in order to get retail drug sales personnel, suppliers, and those who smuggle or manufacture street drugs.

Key Components

Police drug enforcement units make undercover buys and arrest drug pushers. Grants come from HUD and state or local authorities dealing with deterrence, arrests, evictions, and abuser treatment programs. Money transferred to the police department, earmarked for use against drug dealers selling in local developments, will normally be used well, used appropriately, and appreciated.

Key Partnerships

Public Housing management, residents, resident initiative groups, HUD funding programs, and law enforcement officials will all be involved in this program.

Potential Obstacles

One potential obstacle for this strategy is the public housing management group that has had difficulty dealing with local law enforcement agencies. Cooperation from residents can be difficult to obtain in areas where they feel intimidated about assisting police or property managers.

Signs of Success

The Tacoma, Washington, Police Department received HUD monies from its housing authority to establish SET (Special Emphasis [Police] Teams). The Tacoma Police Department increased police patrol operations, used the HUD financing for undercover buys, and arrested several major drug dealers and gang members trafficking in drugs. Residents agree that the housing authority development is a safer neighborhood today.

Applying the Strategy

The Oakland Housing Authority cooperated with the Oakland street drug unit. Many arrests, convictions, and evictions resulted.

Contact Information

Director of Housing Management
Oakland Housing Authority
1619 Harrison Street
Oakland, California 94612
510-874-2520

Access Control

Strategy

Housing authority administrators, in cooperation with residents and city or county officials, agree to limit casual access into public housing. A permanent guard post and altered secondary access points assist with this strategy.

Crime Problem Addressed

The strategy addresses all types of crime, as it deters criminals who would come onto the property of a public housing community to engage in illegal activity, including violent gang activity, drug dealing, theft, and other crimes.

Key Components

All security devices and techniques are designed with the following aims:

- Deter criminals from attacking.

- Detect them if they do attack, so that a police (or other) response may be initiated.

- Delay them so that they can be apprehended before achieving their objective.

- Deny them access to particular targets (*Understanding Crime Prevention*, 1986).

These measures are accomplished by physical security and procedural security activities. The physical security includes gates, fences, roadblocks, and guard posts. Procedural security is accomplished by the work habits of the guard at the gate. Procedural security will require that legitimate guests to the properties be allowed access, but trespassers, intruders, or troublemakers be denied access.

Properly staffed, guard posts (also called kiosks) will screen all pedestrians and vehicles as they enter the housing complex. Resident pedestrians, both children and adult, will be issued housing authority identification cards. Authorized vehicles will be issued housing authority-approved parking permits.

Those attempting to enter the area without housing authority identifiers will be stopped. If a driver says "I'm here to visit Mrs. Jones in Building 310, Apartment 2-B," then the guard will telephone Mrs. Jones for permission. Persons identified as gang members, troublemakers, or drug traffickers are denied access.

Physical access control and checkpoints are used to screen undesirable visitors. Walls, fences, and gates, as well as the guard post, can prevent most trespassers from intruding.

Key Partnerships

Resident councils often ask police or property management to implement a version of this strategy. City engineers and policymakers become involved in approving altered traffic flow, blocking and fencing certain streets, and placing guard houses adjacent to public thoroughfares.

Potential Obstacles

Some housing authorities do not control or maintain the streets within the facility. Blocking a street, fencing a street, and otherwise altering a neighborhood traffic flow must be approved by city or metro officials. This request may also be challenged by non-residents who live near the properties and would be inconvenienced by the proposed changes. Also, police, fire, and other emergency services will need access.

Signs of Success

Access control through a kiosk or other checkpoint or barrier was part of the foundation of the redesign of the Clason Point development in the South Bronx section of New York City. Completed in 1972, the variety of redesign techniques were based on creating what researcher and expert Oscar Newman termed "defensible space." In addition to lighting changes and delineation of formerly public space as private space for specific units, the project controlled access to the development through installation of fencing to enclose the area behind each block. Following these changes, crime decreased by more than 50 percent. According to an article on the project by HUD Secretary Cisneros, "Defensible Space: Deterring Crime and Building Community," the percentage of tenants who felt they had the right to challenge the presence of strangers on the property nearly doubled.

Applying the Strategy

In Tacoma, Washington, the amount of space required of a garbage truck to turn around and make a U-turn was considered a major determinant in deciding which streets could be modified for one-directional traffic and which could be blocked from thoroughfare access.

In Oakland, California, a consultant recommended an electronic gate system that could be opened by an access card. Emergency personnel could use this gate. One alternative to traditional permanent fencing in areas where police want to discourage auto traffic is flexible "knockdown" vehicle barriers made of plastic and rubber (*The Winnable War*, 1991).

Contact Information

Director of Housing Management
Oakland Housing Authority
1619 Harrison Street
Oakland, California 94612
510-874-2520

Pay Telephone Incoming Call Elimination

Strategy

Housing authority administrators, residents, and resident initiative groups petition local phone companies to alter public pay phones so they cannot receive incoming calls. In some cities, only seven-digit numbers can be called. A drug pusher with a beeper cannot be contacted because beepers require at least nine and sometimes 11 numbers.

Crime Problem Addressed

This focus reduces the sale of drugs from public areas and restricts the casual calling of wholesalers for resupply in the streets.

Key Components

This tactic recognizes that drug dealers need to communicate with their customers and their wholesalers. Home and office phones are often avoided because of the fear of discovery by parents or employers. Also, a phone tap on a public phone is more difficult to obtain. A violator using it could more easily claim that a particular call was made to someone else or deny making that call.

Key Partnerships

Cooperation is required from public housing management, residents, resident initiative groups, law enforcement authorities, and phone company policymakers.

Potential Obstacles

There may be some resistance to the curtailing of services, both from within the community and from the phone company. However, this practice is imperative if local crime prevention efforts are to be effective.

Signs of Success

The Winnable War: A Community Guide to Eradicating Street Drug Markets by Roger Conner and Patrick Burns of the American Alliance for Rights and Responsibility advocates removal or alteration of public telephones from areas frequented by dealers and buyers. The strategy is noted as one of the techniques successfully applied by communities throughout the country.

Applying the Strategy

In San Diego, so many drug dealers were clustered around the public telephones on certain corners that residents were unable to use them. The San Diego Police Department pursued an initiative to have the phones dedicated only to outgoing calls, preventing drug dealers from receiving orders by phone. This tactic was also used successfully in Tacoma, Washington.

Contact Information

American Alliance for Rights and Responsibilities
1725 K Street, NW Suite 1112
Washington, DC 20006
202-785-7844

Voluntary Resident Patrols

Strategy

Public housing administrators work with concerned residents, both adult and juvenile, to provide training and logistics for a voluntary neighborhood patrol.

Crime Problem Addressed

The volunteer patrol concept tends to inhibit almost all larcenies, burglaries, and premise robberies. Also, pressures are directed toward loiterers, trespassers, drug pushers, and troublemaking nonresidents. The voluntary patrols also tend to reduce the fear of all crime for housing residents and their neighbors.

Key Components

In working to eliminate drug and prostitution markets from the street, patrols often use informational tactics against potential users and clients. They distribute brochures about their group and seek interviews with the media. This increased visibility virtually guarantees a more significant presence in their neighborhood. In working with police officers, some tenant patrols use video cameras. They pan the streets periodically, taking down the license tag numbers of persons in the drug/sex zones. After police assist in getting the addresses of the owners of the vehicles, a post card is forwarded to the owners.

In most communities, the patrols are fully staffed by volunteers. Usually the housing authority furnishes jackets, flashlights, and perhaps handcuffs. In other situations, unarmed officers are actually employed by the housing authority.

Key Partnerships

Public housing management, residents, resident initiative groups, and law enforcement authorities are key partners. In some cases, housing authority proprietary or contractual security organizations may also participate in this effort.

Potential Obstacles

On occasion the police resist voluntary efforts. Some police administrators see these volunteers as vigilantes and not responsible citizens. Citing the fear of a volunteer being injured or killed, the police also question the motives of the volunteer groups. Quite often the police attitude is, "I'm the cop on this beat. I don't need or want any help." Yet this attitude also lowers citizen participation and increases the prevalence of crime. Research clearly indicates that violence by drug dealers against citizen patrols is rare. Volunteer groups should insist that all members work together in unit patrols and not go off on their own. Volunteer applicants who have aggressive or combative attitudes should be screened from these groups.

Signs of Success

Resident patrol members in New York City's public housing communities work to reduce vandalism, loitering, and more serious crime. They report loiterers and suspicious parties in hallways, lobbies, and elevators. The patrols have also included youth who serve as escorts to seniors traveling through the community. As of 1994, more than 15,000 resident volunteers participate. The housing authority reports that buildings with active patrols experience fewer crimes, including vandalism, and have increased social cohesion among residents.

Applying the Strategy

Saginaw, Michigan's resident patrol in public housing uses trained residents to assist police in identifying intruders and trespassers through portable radios and monitoring of the surveillance equipment stationed throughout the development.

Contact Information

Saginaw Police Department
612 Federal Street
Saginaw, Michigan 48607
517-759-1229

Chief
Tenant Patrol Division
Department of Community Affairs
New York City Housing Authority
250 Broadway, Room 1905
New York, New York 10007
212-306-2866

Tenant Screening

Strategy

Housing authority administrators employ staff or contractors to investigate and screen all tenant applicants who are seriously being considered and who meet all other local and national HUD-mandated standards.

Crime Problem Addressed

The focus of this approach is to reduce the acceptance rate of families who cause trouble or who have gang members, convicted criminals, or active drug traffickers or drug addicts residing with them.

Key Components

The strategy recognizes the social harm caused by certain types of criminals, whether adult or juvenile. These dysfunctional families (about 6 to 7 percent) often cause disproportionate problems within public housing and threaten the stability of the entire community. Prostitutes, drug pushers, and families with gang members residing in their homes are extreme risk housing clients and must be screened during the application process. Also, consideration should be discontinued for heads of households whose boyfriends or girlfriends are currently involved in criminal or troublemaking activities.

Key Partnerships

Public Housing management, law enforcement, private security agencies, and tenant screening agencies may be run by commercial apartment specialty realtors. It should be emphasized, however, that the traditional tenant screens run by realtors do not include adult and juvenile criminal record checks. This is why a public/private contract should be obtained through a local police or sheriff's unit.

Potential Obstacles

Some private security and resident screening firms are not authorized to have access to local, state, and national criminal justice record systems. This is why a public police agency partnership is so important. Since this screening approach will require a considerable commitment on the police agencies' part, some type of grant program might be used to reimburse the police agency for its time.

Some police agencies would be happy to help "clean up" public housing. Others apparently prefer to keep criminal zones isolated to particular environmental areas (like public housing) and away from downtown or residential areas. These police agencies fear that disrupted isolation will redistribute crime to other areas and other precincts.

Signs of Success

In Mobile, Alabama, the Public Housing Crime Interdiction Through Community Policing Program eliminated more than 200 unsuitable tenant applicants. Sergeant Jack Dove, of the Mobile team, estimated that he spends about 60 percent of his time on screening and eviction matters.

The U.S. Department of Housing and Urban Development publication, *Together We Can . . . Meet the Challenge* describes the success other communities have experi-

enced deterring undesirable applicants through a screening process.

Property managers in the San Francisco Bay area have discovered that working in concert with each other and employing a reporting service have improved their residential screening procedure. By utilizing the services of a private rental screening reporting system, housing agencies have been able to improve the screening of prospective residents and thus protect their developments from drug trafficking and crime.

Applying the Strategy

The Housing Authority of Alameda, California, uses a private company, the National Tenant Network (NTN), to run background credit checks and screen applicants. NTN provides standard credit reports, which housing managers have long been able to order on prospective renters, but also offers access to a computerized network of information on past resident performance that included evictions and lease violations.

New Haven, Connecticut's housing agency screens applicants by checking police records and credit history of prospective tenants. Current residents help through their participation on tenant screening committees.

Knoxville, Tennessee's police department uses police officers to take applications for public housing. The housing agency believes the presence of the uniformed officer deters many potential criminals from applying.

Contact Information

Executive Director
City of Alameda Housing Authority
701 Atlantic Avenue
Alameda, California 94501
510-522-8422

Mobile Police Department
2460 Government Boulevard
Mobile, Alabama 36606
334-434-1701

Crime Prevention and Awareness Training for Residents

Strategy

Resident groups and individual residents learn how to report crimes to authorities and how to assist police and property management prevent crime in public housing communities.

Crime Problem Addressed

This strategy addresses the skills of residents to help each other and law enforcement authorities identify and address

crime and crime-related issues in the public housing community. Training programs provide residents with information and skills they need to keep their communities safe.

Key Components

Crime prevention, crime deterrence, and post-crime response are covered in workshops offered at a citizens' police academy or by members of the crime prevention unit of the local police agency. Attendees are taught how to call in crime reports and how to work with police and housing authority security who respond to crime-related situations in their neighborhoods. This program addresses resident concerns about all types of crime and increases the level of understanding between the police and residents.

Key Partnerships

Resident or tenant associations, housing authority management, police academy trainers, and the crime prevention unit of the local law enforcement agency cooperate to put on crime prevention programs for residents.

Potential Obstacles

In housing authorities where language barriers between management, police, and residents represent an obstacle, interpreters can help. In Tacoma, Washington, the housing authority brought in Cambodian and Laotian interpreters to assist the SAFE STREETS organization in its Drug and Gang Elimination Program training.

Sometimes authorities must assist in creating a safer environment before residents will even consider participating in the most basic and rudimentary of programs. Many residents fear that their homes will be attacked in their absence, especially if they were to attend SAFE STREETS, Neighborhood Watch, or gang elimination programs. Police and resident patrols can help by watching those locations while sessions are held.

Signs of Success

Jackson, Mississippi, brings in interested participants from the greater metropolitan area. Students are first trained at the academy, meeting many local officers who discuss some of the crime problems and potential solutions to these problems in the communities represented in the class. Officers also pass out business cards, and participants now know that instead of calling a police department, they can call a particular officer who is prepared to render every assistance possible. Citizens are taught that emergencies take precedence over a "barking dog" complaint or that of a "loud" party. In addition to riding in a patrol car for a few hours on patrol, the students come in contact with the magistrate courts, county courts, circuit courts, and prosecutors at the county and district levels. On occasion, bail bondsmen are brought into the training session, so residents can understand how that system deals with persons accused of crime and who may return to their communities. Each professional who participants in sessions for residents explains his or her role and attempts to dispel any misunderstandings about the adult and juvenile justice system.

Applying the Strategy

The SAFE STREETS program in Tacoma, Washington, used several professional crime prevention officers, many with former criminal justice agency experience. The participation programs were sound. Not only were residents taught how to use the police and justice system, they were taught how to interact and how to manage a resident initiative drug and gang program.

Contact Information

Community Affairs Division
Jackson Police Department
327 Pascagoula Street
P.O. Box 17
Jackson, Mississippi 39205-0017
601-960-1389

Cleanup Projects

Strategy

When resident groups, city agencies, and law enforcement combine forces to clean up trash and debris in public housing communities, they improve the image of the area, reduce opportunities for criminals to hide unnoticed, and help eliminate places where drugs and weapons can be illegally stored with ease.

Crime Problem Addressed

The focus of this program is to reduce the number of interior hiding places for drugs, decrease barriers (e.g., discarded furniture or trash) that may present obstacles in a police chase, and reduce the opportunity to use outdoor locations (dense underbrush, abandoned cars, discarded household items) to store drugs or disguise criminal activity. The strategy also addresses general neighborhood disorder, which contributes to the perception of danger and vulnerability of an area to criminal activity and victimization.

Key Components

Often initiated by residents, cleanup programs typically also engage housing authority maintenance crews, local police (in case weapons, guns, or other evidence is discovered), city sanitation or public works crews with equipment and transportation to haul away trash and debris, and parks and recreation departments that can suggest ideas to beautify the area and maintain it over time. Some communities have called upon local outposts of the National Guard or state public works agencies with large construction equipment to help remove trees, trash, furniture, appliances, and abandoned vehicles and restore the cleared area for its original purpose. Many programs follow up the community-based activity of a cleanup with a campaign to encourage residents not to litter or abandon vehicles, and broker agreements with city agencies to enhance refuse collection and maintenance at the properties.

Key Partnerships

Housing authority management, residents, resident groups, sanitation and parks departments, law enforcement, and civic organizations all participate in cleanup programs. National Guard units, local construction firms, private trash haulers, and area businesses each represent potential resources to support collection, removal, and transport of material cleaned off the grounds. Businesses can also provide publicity for the program and donate materials for a neighborhood celebration after the cleanup is completed.

Potential Obstacles

Clearing debris does require local government resources. Residents argue that sanitation and maintenance services should be part of daily routine in their communities. The managing authority is likely to argue that residents should take on some responsibility for maintenance of the area. Both are correct, so both groups should cooperate in the cleanup program and commit to expend or locate outside resources to keep the area clear. No single local agency is likely to have the resources to undertake a major cleanup effort, so collaboration to implement the project and locate residents and outside resources to help is essential to the success of the strategy.

Signs of Success

The Tacoma, Washington, Housing Authority had a crime problem with a large ditch filled with underbrush known as the gulch, which meanders through the city, not only in the housing authority communities, but throughout residential and business districts. The gulch cuts through housing authority property and offers concealment to burglars, robbers, gang members, and drug pushers. Police have received many reports of offenders fleeing residences and cars running into the gulch and away from apprehension. The housing authority cleared it out, created a pathway along its banks, and built footbridges at key crossing points. One of the city's least attractive features suddenly became a visual and recreational asset for residents. To accomplish the project, the police and the housing authority called in the National Guard's heavy construction-style equipment to remove abandoned cars and large debris. The Guard also provided people to help residents with other cleanup activities. Police, pleased because criminals fleeing into the gulch could be pursued more easily and in view, believe the area is now safer.

Applying the Strategy

As part of recent cleanup drives in Tampa, Florida, residents joined with the Solid Waste and Parks Departments to remove 88 tons of trash from the streets in and around the city's public housing communities.

Contact Information

Special Projects Coordinator
Tacoma Housing Authority
902 South L Street
Tacoma, WA 98405
206-207-4456

Fencing and Other Barriers

Strategy

Housing authority administrators, in cooperation with residents and HUD grant sources, install fences or other barriers to help redirect traffic flow and discourage entrance by nonresidents.

Crime Problem Addressed

Drug traffickers and gang members are usually trespassing. In fact, David Echols, the executive director of the Housing Authority for the City of New Haven, Connecticut, estimates that "85 percent of those arrested on housing agency properties do not live here."

Key Components

The central focus of this strategy involves design and installation of fencing high enough to create a difficult barrier to pedestrians. Most fences installed are at least six feet tall. The fence must enclose the development, help control access, and be constructed in a way that permits privacy while not obstructing the view from common areas and the streets around the complex.

Key Partnerships

Public housing management, residents, resident initiative groups, and law enforcement should be partners in the decision to install fencing and design fencing that is functional but not isolating to the residents.

Potential Obstacles

Some residents will resist the fencing approach because it will inconvenience them. "I will have to walk another block to shop. I like the bus stop on this street, I don't want to go over there." But until access control is a fact of everyday life, none of the residents will ever be safe. When security versus convenience becomes the priority, the majority of residents will support a fencing approach where it seems appropriate. Staffed security kiosks, trespassing law enforcement, and access control policies enhance the effectiveness of fencing as a deterrent to crime. Cost is another potential obstacle. Public housing authorities may find it difficult to locate the funds to install fencing, though support is available to many localities through federal programs. The cost of the fencing must be weighed against resources needed for other security enhancements or other capital improvements.

Signs of Success

In *The Winnable War: A Community Guide to Eradicating Street Drug Markets*, the authors assert that fences help prevent drug-related crime. They state, "fences can be extremely effective in cutting off dealer escape routes and channeling foot traffic to one or two monitored avenues."

Applying the Strategy

The Little Rock, Arkansas, Police Department worked with the housing authority to fence specific areas and reroute traffic around public housing. The strategy greatly reduced street level narcotics trafficking throughout the developments.

Two public housing developments in Oakland, California, installed a $1.1 million tubular steel fence around the perimeter of the complex of buildings. Residents reported they felt unsafe on many occasions until the fencing cut down on traffic, deterred drug traffickers, and discouraged prostitutes who had frequented the area. The fencing does not make this community seem particularly distinct in its security procedures, since almost all privately owned apartment complexes in the area maintained fencing for similar reasons. Previously, as the only development, business, or warehouse in the area that did not have adequate environmental protection, Oakland's developments had become vulnerable to criminals.

Contact Information

Little Rock Police Department
Organized Crime and Intelligence Division
700 West Markham Street
Little Rock, Arkansas 72201
501-371-4700

Move Security Headquarters

Strategy

Housing authority-operated security/police organizations move their headquarters into the most dangerous housing areas of their jurisdiction. If this is not possible for space reasons, mini-stations are a viable alternative.

Crime Problem Addressed

The focus of this approach is to reduce the sale of drugs and crime associated with drug trafficking through choosing a high-profile location for security headquarters. Traffickers feel very uncomfortable selling within sight of a police station. Purchasers are less likely to come into the area at all.

Key Components

The strategy recognizes that drug-pushing criminals make their living within public housing communities. The "move the headquarters" approach redistributes police and housing authority security resources to the most drug-intensive, and often the most violent areas of the complex. Moving the police/security headquarters to a visible location intensifies the police presence generally and increases the number of random patrol operations in the area as officers travel to and from other areas. The location is labeled and staffed at all times to ensure surveillance of the premises and to deter residents or outsiders from criminal activity. The location can also serve as the site for a reporting hotline for residents to alert security of incidents on the grounds. This strategy is most effective when combined with fencing and access-control tactics.

Key Partnerships

Public housing administrators, residents, and housing police/security administrators and officers are partners in this endeavor. Residents should be consulted about the choice of locations, as they know about traffic and activity patterns and where criminal activity tends to occur.

Potential Obstacles

The expense of moving an established security location or security administrative office would be the most salient potential obstacle. In addition, the possible danger to security officers from the location chosen can represent a barrier to their participation. Some communities have experienced retaliation against these locations even when residents and staff are in the vicinity. The management must institute procedures to deal with potential dangers and response to specific incidents of vandalism or other crime.

Signs of Success

The Knoxville, Tennessee, Police Department used to send officers to public housing communities in response to calls from residents or management. The department now places a two-person mobile unit in each of its public housing communities on weekend evenings, when criminal activity is at its peak. The presence of the officers, who receive extra training in drug enforcement and how to work with residents, has helped reduce crime. Since the program began, the housing authority has donated several

apartments for mini-stations where officers can take reports and use the telephone and restroom. Resident support for the program is consistently very high.

Applying the Strategy

The HUD manual *Winning the Fight Against Drugs* highlights the successful pioneering efforts of the Manchester, New Hampshire, Housing Authority. The Oxford, Mississippi, Housing Authority established a police mini-station in the C.B. Webb Apartment Complex; crime has declined as a result.

Contact Information

Deputy Director
Knoxville Community Development Corporation
P.O. Box 3550
Knoxville, Tennessee 37927
615-521-8606

Enhanced Lighting

Strategy

Enhanced outdoor lighting that illuminates walkways and perimeter areas increases safety and security of residents and reduces crime.

Crime Problem Addressed

The focus of this program is to illuminate dark areas, eliminate the possibility that crimes can casually be committed in secret, and increase the visibility level for all citizens. This approach illuminates drug pushers, prostitutes, gangs, and predatory criminals, who don't want to be identified. Take away the cover of darkness, and they will be afraid to use an illuminated area.

Key Components

Illuminating an area, in and by itself, can positively affect a consensual crimes marketplace. Adding aggressive police patrol operations, tenant patrols, and mobile videotaping of violators and purchasers will cause drug marketers, prostitutes, and street criminals to move elsewhere. Lighting strategies focus on perimeter areas, entry points to buildings, walkways, and parking areas. Installation is usually done by the housing authority, but may be designed in cooperation with the local utility company or public works department.

Key Partnerships

Police, housing authorities, and power companies all play a part in this program. Power utility companies have lighting experts who can work with police and the housing management to increase security through lighting techniques. Architects in city agencies and the private sector can also provide advice on placement and lighting styles.

Potential Obstacles

It is expensive for governments to "light up the night." And criminals often shoot out exterior lights with firearms or high-power slingshots. There are several security lamp systems that are hard to damage. While security light covers are much more expensive, they are worth the expense in the decrease in crime and in the increase of commercial operations.

Signs of Success

Lighting was a key element in the crime prevention strategy developed by the Greenwich, Connecticut, Drug-Free Public Housing Task Force, a community-wide coalition of tenant leaders, police, other agencies, and housing authority managers. The recommendations in the 1988 plan also included programs for children. Development of tenant associations contributed to reductions in crime and increased interaction among residents.

Applying the Strategy

In the Housing Authority of Tacoma, Washington, the lights were inadequate on the streets. Residents were issued free lightbulbs and given a power bill break when they agreed to participate in the light program. To participate, they agreed to leave their exterior front and rear entrances illuminated every night.

Contact Information

Chief of Police
Greenwich Police Department
P.O. Box 1404
Greenwich, Connecticut 06830
203-622-8000

American Institute of Architects
1735 New York Avenue, NW
Washington, DC 20006-5292
202-626-7300

Police-in-Residence Program

Strategy

Housing authority administrators that offer free or reduced-cost housing to police officers in exchange for after-hours order maintenance, patrol, or participation in security programs will experience less crime.

Crime Problem Addressed

The focus of this program is to reduce the sale of drugs by arresting traffickers and evicting the ones who live in public housing. Public order problems are also addressed by the continuing presence of the officers.

Key Components

The officer(s) are moved into the more volatile housing areas. The best "police" apartments are adjacent to, and in sight of, the primary drug sale areas. The presence of these officers will dramatically lessen the sale of drugs at this location. This effort should be just one component of an intensive community policing plan.

Key Partnerships

Public housing management, residents, resident initiative groups, and law enforcement officials should agree that this idea has merit and it is "the right thing to do." This neighborhood invitation is very important. The idea will not work as well if the "good" people in the community are hostile to it.

Potential Obstacles

The program should recruit young, single officers and provide incentives for them to live in the community. Officers with families are far less likely to participate. Still, many officers will not want to participate for fear of violence or retaliation from unlawful residents or trespassers. The police agency must ensure that the community receives police protection during hours when the resident officer is away on duty elsewhere. Otherwise, crime patterns will simply adapt to the officer's shift assignments.

Many police administrators are so sure that the Resident Officer Program won't succeed that they will not even attempt to ask for volunteers. Communities in California, Washington State, Mississippi, and many other states have successful officer residence programs.

Signs of Success

Phoenix's Police Officer Placement Solution program recruits officers to live in rent-free public housing units. The program was developed in response to the request of a neighborhood association looking for a way to enhance the security of the area. The police department, the Neighborhood Services Agency, and residents cooperate in the recruitment process. Officers who volunteer also patrol the area nearest to where they live. The city believes the program is an important step toward building a partnership between key agencies and the neighborhoods they serve.

Applying the Strategy

The Manchester, New Hampshire, Housing Authority asserts that it was the first to institute an officer in residence program. The long-standing program now has several volunteer officer participants annually.

Contact Information

Phoenix Police Department
Central City Precinct
1902 South 16 Street
Phoenix, Arizona 85034
602-495-5005

Bibliography

Books

Clarke, Ronald V., ed. *Situational Crime Prevention: Successful Case Studies.* 1992.

Quarles, Chester L. *Staying Safe at School.* Thousand Oaks, CA: Corwin Press, Inc., 1993.

Wheller, Eugene D., and S. Anthony Baron, Ph.D. *Violence in Our Schools, Hospitals, and Public Places: A Prevention and Management Guide.* Ventura, CA: Pathfinder Publishing of California, 1994.

Periodicals

Brown, DeNeen L. Anti-Violence Program Doesn't Get Far at Cardozo: Students Wary of Effort to Rid Neighborhoods of Guns. *The Washington Post,* January 26, 1995, p. DC 1.

Jefferson, Bob. The On-Off Dilemma of Public Lighting. *American City & County,* August 1994, pp. 60–70.

Kovaleski, Serge F. For Potomac Gardens, Safety Means Life Behind an Iron Curtain. *The Washington Post,* May 8, 1994, p. B1.

Level Two-Crime Prevention Through Environmental Design. *FBI Law Enforcement Bulletin,* June 1994, p. 10.

The Mesa Crime-Free Multi-Housing Program. *FBI Law Enforcement Bulletin,* June 1994, pp. 8–9.

Mueck, Cpl. Robert P. Student Involvement in Campus Security: A Model Approach. *Campus Law Enforcement Journal,* March–April 1994, pp. 28–30.

National School Safety Center, Malibu, CA. *School Safety,* Fall 1994.

Padgett, Ingrid. Neighborhood Stabilization Works For Dayton Community. *Nations Cities Weekly,* September 5, 1994.

Sanchez, Rene. Expulsions Becoming Popular Weapon in U.S. Schools. *The Washington Post,* January 20, 1995, p. A1.

Valentine, Paul W. Baltimore Patrols Cited in Decrease in Downtown Crime. *The Washington Post,* March 28, 1994, p. B5.

Public Documents

Ann Arbor Police Department. *Crime Prevention Through Environmental Design.*

California State Department of Educational School Climate and Student Support Services Unit. *Safe Schools: A Planning Guide For Action.* Sacramento, CA, 1989.

Citizens Housing & Planning Council. *How To Get Drug Enterprises Out of Housing.* New York, NY, 1994.

Harvard University Graduate School of Education. *Coping With Violence in the Schools: A Report of the 1993 Summer Conference of the Center for School Counseling Practitioners.* Cambridge, MA, 1993.

Metropolitan Life Insurance Company. *The Metropolitan Life Survey of The American Teacher 1994.* New York, NY, 1994.

National Crime Prevention Council. *Preventing Crime in Urban Communities: Handbook and Program Profiles.* Washington, DC, 1986.

National School Boards Association. *Violence in the Schools: How America's School Boards Are Safeguarding Our Children.* Alexandria, VA, 1993.

National School Safety Center. *Weapons In Schools: NSSC Resource Paper.* Malibu, CA, August 1993.

N.C. Department of Crime Control and Public Safety. *From Projects to Communities: Crime Prevention In Inner City and Public Housing Communities.* Raleigh, NC, November 1993.

Southeastern Regional Vision for Education. *Reducing School Violence: Hot Topics: Usable Research.* Greensboro, NC, March 1993.

U.S. Department of Justice, National Institute of Justice. *Drugs and Crime in Public Housing: A Three-City Analysis.* Washington, DC, March 1994.

U.S. Department of Justice, National Institute of Justice. *Preventing Interpersonal Violence Among Youth: An Introduction to School Community, and Mass Media Strategies.* Washington, DC, November 1994.

U.S. Department of Justice, National Institute of Justice; and U.S. Department of Education, Office of Elementary and Secondary Education. *The Smart Program: School Management and Resource Teams.* Washington, DC.

U.S. Department of Justice, National Institute of Justice. *Update on NIJ-Sponsored Research: Six New Reports.* Washington, DC, April 1994.

University of Alabama-Birmingham, Office of Vice President for Administration. *The Spatial and Temporal Patterns of Fear of Crime: An Examination of Their Characteristics.* Birmingham, AL, October 30, 1993.

Economic Development

Economic underdevelopment is both a cause and a symptom of crime. Crime is an important factor in businesses' decisions to take flight from the places where it occurs, thereby worsening the economic problems that underlie an area's deterioration.

A s jobs depart with businesses, crime becomes an increasingly popular means to achieve economic survival. Without the prospect of economic opportunity in a community, deterrence from law enforcement will often fail, as no visible alternative to crime exists. When drug dealers and criminals are the wealthiest members of a community, crime will develop a frighteningly strong appeal among youth.

The physical deterioration that accompanies the financial decline of an area also acts as a source of crime. As businesses begin to leave a region, local governments lose the tax revenues necessary to maintain civic projects. As budgets fall, crime prevention programs and law enforcement funding are reduced, in turn leaving the area vulnerable to greater criminal activity. Vacant buildings left behind by departing businesses and landlords serve as havens for drug dealing and other crimes.

Economic development opportunities create the promise of jobs, thereby increasing the stability of the community and reducing its vulnerability to crime. Successful commercial areas, affordable housing near sustainable employment, and better physical conditions prevent the development of social tensions that act as sparks for criminal activity. The revitalization of communities through tax incentives, infrastructure improvements, and aggressive civic marketing campaigns for new jobs can be a potent force for reducing crime.

Partnerships among small businesses, government, and residents are critical to achieving a community environment ready for sustained growth. The organization of local community development groups focuses attention on what is needed to improve civic conditions, encouraging citizens and businesses to recognize their important role in rebuilding the neighborhood. Development planning groups create the infrastructure needed to obtain government, business, and private grants that act as a launching point for commercial improvement.

Citizens can help encourage good business and low crime rates by sprucing up neighborhoods and business areas—simple projects such as planting flowers and cleaning up trash signal a neighborhood's concern and refusal to let commercial areas be overrun by crime, while creating a more inviting business atmosphere with better prospects for success.

Businesses must be included in crime prevention strategies and economic development to stabilize the dislocation associated with shifts in patterns of economic activity. Business Watch groups deter and detect crimes, and security surveys help identify how stores and other business locations can be made more secure.

Increasing the availability of credit to support the establishment of new businesses enhances an area's financial vitality, generating commercial activity and increasing employment prospects. The empowerment of local groups and individual entrepreneurs stabilizes the community and increases the prospects for cooperative relationships between businesses and residents, reducing opportunities for crime. The South Shore Bank in Chicago emerged more than two decades ago as a group dedicated to local development through the provision of loans based not on collateral, which its targeted borrowers often lacked, but on trustworthiness. The cooperation of a business in local community development has proven mutually beneficial, spurring the creation of several new local enterprises and the recovery of once-threatened neighborhoods while creating a profitable locally based banking corporation.

Development planning groups are important in considering the type of business that can best improve the area's economic strength while minimizing crime. Some types of infrastructure improvements actually reduce the natural surveillance that deters crime. Some types of facilities and businesses tend to be accompanied by increases in certain crimes. Research shows that neighborhoods in transition, whether developing or deteriorating, are more susceptible to crime than stable neighborhoods. It is critical that planning not neglect the pitfalls that can accompany economic development, since overlooking crime as a development issue could prevent the success of budding enterprises.

This chapter highlights ten strategies for creating a business environment that is safe from crime. These strategies have successfully stimulated business activity by creating the capital necessary to start new ventures. Loan assistance programs in which a bank cooperates with a community to encourage growth have consistently proven successful. Local subsidies can provide the means to develop the physical infrastructure for the creation of small businesses, while national institutions such as the Department of Housing and Urban Development have made investment in abandoned areas attractive through tax credits and outright grants.

Strategies for economic development must also go beyond financial provisions. This chapter explores how businesses can help build communities and how communities can spur businesses. Methods for ensuring high-quality, affordable housing that avoids gentrification are examined. Examples of successful efforts to build businesses that provide for the needs of their local communities are also reviewed. The underlying goal of these growth strategies is to ensure that new economic development strengthens social ties through the cooperation of businesses and the areas in which they operate.

"Incubate" Young Businesses

Strategy

Helping businesses to start up and to grow in "incubators"—nurturing environments of successful business people, training in entrepreneurial and related skills, and helpful support services—improves economic conditions in neighborhoods and leaves them less vulnerable to crime.

Crime Problem Addressed

This strategy addresses the crime rate, which tends to rise as jobs, stable businesses, incomes, and economic opportunities decline. Residents of communities with these conditions can experience a reduced sense of control over their future and diminished feelings of self-worth, sometimes leading to theft, vandalism, drug dependency, and family violence. Helping such individuals to reclaim or establish control through steady incomes and jobs can be a positive and productive remedy for communities with high crime rates.

Key Components

The main goal of the business "incubator" program is to produce successful graduates—new businesses with good plans that are financially sound, independent, and geared to thrive. The specific objectives of an incubator could include economic diversification, jobs and self-help opportunities in an inner-city neighborhood, or transfer of technology from university research to business application.

Business incubators, often run by community development groups or by private entrepreneurs, help new businesses grow by providing the following:

- space for a number of businesses under one roof;

- flexible space allocations and lease terms;

- an on-site incubator manager and business advisor;

- organized interaction with business and technical advisors;

- financial counsel and assistance; and

- business interaction with other firms in the same incubator.

Incubators commonly screen participating businesses to ensure a mix of businesses and identify business potential of small-business owners seeking assistance. Although space, services, and management assistance have often been shared by businesses, incubators began in the 1960s out of the need to put abandoned factory buildings to use. The incubation experiment funded by the National Science Foundation sought to foster entrepreneurship, and the initiatives of successful entrepreneurs and investor groups involved sought to transfer their know-how to new companies in a supportive environment.

Key Partnerships

The core partnership is between the tenant entrepreneur or business and the incubator management. The incubator encourages partnerships with other businesses and sources of support. Incubators are created and run by local governments, economic development agencies, community development corporations, colleges and universities, private management firms, and various combinations of these organizations. A growing number of incubators are cosponsored by large commercial firms, such as Corning and Digital Equipment Corporation.

Potential Obstacles

The quality of the incubator depends on the quality of the managers and the networks they provide. Some work better than others, and all work better for certain business types than they do for others.

Signs of Success

Since 1985, the National Business Incubation Association (NBIA), based in Athens, Ohio, has been providing training and a clearinghouse for information on incubator management and development. New incubators are forming at an average rate of one per week, some for specialized technical businesses. NBIA reports that more than 80 percent of the firms that have ever been incubated are still in operation—far above the figures for all businesses started, most of which fail in the first few years. In the past twelve years, the number of business incubators has increased 30-fold to more than 500. Thirty percent of

incubated businesses "graduate" annually and become independent.

Applying the Strategy

Chicago's Fulton-Carroll Center for Industry (FCCI) began in 1980 as the cornerstone for revitalization of a desolated industrial neighborhood. In its first eleven years, FCCI created 127 jobs per year, with a net gain of more than 1,000 jobs. Only 14 percent of its incubated firms have failed. Eighty percent of the jobs created are held by disadvantaged groups, and 41 percent of businesses created are owned by disadvantaged groups. FCCI has helped many families out of poverty and off welfare. It has helped start many micro-enterprises, but its goal is to fast-start companies that grow quickly to millions of dollars in annual revenues. Its seventy incubator tenants generated about $40 million in annual gross sales as of 1994. The surrounding neighborhood's commercial property vacancy rate has dropped sharply and real estate values increased by more than 500 percent since FCCI was established. The FCCI incubator has done a lot for individuals, families, and community revitalization.

Other successful incubators include the Milwaukee Enterprise Center in Wisconsin, the Franklin Business Center in Minneapolis, Minnesota, and the Homewood Brushton Incubator in Pittsburgh, Pennsylvania

Contact Information

Fulton-Carroll Center for Industry
2023 West Carroll
Chicago, Illinois 60612
312-421-3941

National Business Incubation Association
20 East Circle Drive
Suite 190
Athens, Ohio 45701
614-593-4331

Early Warning Arson Prevention

Strategy

An Arson Early Warning and Prevention Program identifies and treats properties in danger of arson and fire before they are burned.

Crime Problem Addressed

Arson rates fluctuate from one geographic area to another but remain a serious crime and economic issue in many older, distressed urban areas. Arson seems to come to

certain communities in waves. In North Flatbush, New York, sixty-nine suspicious fires occurred in one year alone. In 1994, suspicious fires burned scores of homes and thousands of acres of woodland in the west. Arson can result in deaths, injuries, loss of homes and businesses. Gutted buildings create eyesores that blight neighborhoods and communities. Property loss, even from just one fire, can reach millions of dollars. Worse, arson and arson "copycats" can cause community disintegration.

Key Components

The following are key components of the anti-arson strategy for businesses:

- organization of a community, municipal agency, or business group to coordinate education of the public, collection of data related to incidents of arson, and communication about arson threats against businesses;

- establishment of community links among the police and fire departments, code enforcement officials, and insurance companies;

- installation of an arson early warning system to alert business and property owners;

- design of an arson prevention education program with easily understandable information for homeowners and businesses;

- preparation of a manual or information document that can be disseminated in the community; and

- coordination of action against fire code violators, fire hazards, and abandoned or neglected properties.

Key Partnerships

Key Partnerships include those between the concerned community or business group and its members, the police and fire departments, and municipal code enforcement officials. Additional important partnerships are with the fire insurance companies that insure properties in the community. Ideally, cooperative working relationships will also exist between the project managers and the owners or managers of properties in the community.

Potential Obstacles

Obstacles may include the difficulty of finding and engaging the absent owners of properties with high levels of code violations and arson risk and achieving thorough surveillance and security in very large, densely populated areas. Litigation may be necessary in tough code enforcement and condemnation cases. Careful and determined self-help measures for property owners might often reduce these obstacles to manageable proportions. Low arrest and conviction rates are often the most difficult obstacle to community action against arson.

Signs of Success

Working under a Ford Foundation grant and in cooperation with the Institute for Social Analysis (ISA), the Flatbush Development Corporation (FDC) cleared new ground with this innovative strategy. In the four years of the project (1982 to 1986), suspicious fires in North Flatbush declined from sixty-nine in 1982 to sixteen in 1986—a drop of 77 percent. Over the same period, the number of serious "all-hands" and "greater alarm" fires dropped nearly as much—from twenty-three to six per year—a 74 percent decline.

FDC kept good records to predict and act on properties at high risk of arson. Four key variables identified as predictors of arson-endangered properties were (1) serious building code violations, (2) fires of unknown origin in the past, (3) vacancy rates, and (4) the number of units in the buildings. FCC was aggressive in its role as community catalyst by distributing fire safety information to landlords and tenants, organizing tenants for fire safety, scheduling fire marshall inspections where and when needed, ensuring fire insurance company intervention (or policy cancellation) for neglected properties to reduce the risk of intentional fire setting by owners, and obtaining safety code enforcement and property condemnations as necessary. Some properties were sealed and secured, others inspected and repaired, and still others rehabilitated and beautified. By 1986, arson had declined dramatically to the lowest levels in eleven years.

Applying the Strategy

FDC was the first to implement this strategy. FDC worked closely with the Peoples Firehouse in Brooklyn, New York, with Kensington Action Now in Philadelphia, Pennsylvania, and with the New York Neighborhood Anti-Arson Center in New York City in the development of its successful arson prevention programs.

Contact Information

Director of Community Relations
Flatbush Development Corporation
1418 Cortelyou Road
Brooklyn, New York 11226
718-469-8990

Community Business and Housing Development Planning

Strategy

Bringing community members together in action planning for a balanced, healthy community with good housing, jobs, shopping, health care, recreation, etc., helps to protect the community, making it less likely to experience crime.

Crime Problem Addressed

This strategy for a balanced, healthy community aims to reduce crime at its base or origins by reducing hardship, frustration, and pessimism, which can lead to criminal behavior. The goal is to raise community cohesiveness and pride, to help individuals grow in dignity and self-respect from a foundation of decent housing, good jobs, and a well-kept neighborhood.

Key Components

The key components of this strategy are as follows:

■ organization of community members (individual residents, civic groups, churches, businesses, banks, key government agency representatives, etc.) into a community action group or community development corporation;

■ identification of basic needs of the community (for example, teen recreation facilities, jobs for the unemployed, better affordable housing, stores for necessities, health care);

■ formation of a goal or set of goals for creating the kind of balanced, healthy community that the residents want;

■ development of objectives to achieve the results in cooperation with government agencies and other community groups; and

■ implementation of plans for community action around established objectives.

Key Partnerships

The key partnerships include those between members of the community (individuals, organizations, or groups) who want to achieve the community development goals and ally groups who can help make it happen: political leaders, government agencies (local, county, state, or national), foundations, corporations, lending institutions, the media, and influential individuals and groups from both inside and outside the community.

Potential Obstacles

The first challenge is to assemble a core group of individuals or organizations committed to the sustained hard work necessary to build a better community. Some vested interests or those supporting different approaches may oppose a community's desire to be independent and self-sufficient. A serious obstacle can be getting the capital or credit for housing, job training, or other services needed. Perseverance and key partnerships with influential individuals, groups, and government and private sector institutions can solve many problems along the way.

Signs of Success

The federal Enterprise Zone (EZ) and Enterprise Community programs, established in the Omnibus Budget Reconciliation Act of 1993, awarded the first grants late in 1994. The programs were born out of a recognition that economically distressed communities needed flexible tools (block grants, tax breaks, new partnerships with community groups) to achieve economic goals and improve cohesion and stability within neighborhoods.

Awardees were selected in part because of their ability to demonstrate strong partnerships with and involvement of community groups in formulating long-term plans for economic growth and sustained community development. The Kentucky Highlands Investment Corporation, an EZ awardee, worked with community groups and the private sector to attract $33 million in commitments from banks in the region to create capital for business and other investments.

Applying the Strategy

New Community, in the Central Ward of Newark, New Jersey, is one place where this strategy has worked on a large scale. The local community organizers started in 1967 with a complex of 120 apartments—a first step in meeting the need for decent, well-maintained, low-cost housing. They found allies in the suburbs, in a few corporations and foundations, and in state government.

Next steps included planning a new urban community with housing, health, commercial, and educational facilities to serve needs expressed by residents. Day care facilities were established along with a restaurant, spa, and wellness center. Through an agreement with a supermarket corporation, New Community obtained a supermarket for the area that helped attract other businesses—all parts of a balanced, healthy community. Since New Community began, hundreds of jobs have been created for Central Ward residents.

Contact Information

New Community Corporation
233 West Market Street
Newark, New Jersey 07103
201-482-0682

Community Beautification

Strategy

Beautification of a community makes it more attractive to the law-abiding residents, which makes the area less attractive to those who might otherwise gather for criminal activity.

Crime Problem Addressed

Abandoned buildings, vacant lots, and unused parks signal neighborhoods in disarray and attract criminal activity. In such areas, residents tend to avoid problem neighborhoods, especially at night, out of fear of victimization. The visible deterioration and crime problems in these areas can spread to neighboring properties if left unchecked. When one store closes and gets boarded up, nearby businesses often lose customers. Beautification and restoration efforts can help address such safety and economic concerns.

Key Components

Key components of the beautification strategy include the following:

■ organizing property owners and lessees, police, zoning office representatives, leaders of the larger community, and other interested parties to discuss the locations in need of beautification;

■ defining the problem or target property or area needing beautification and recruiting those willing to work on it;

■ setting the beautification goal (simple trash cleanup or enhancement of the public area with landscaping, lighting, etc);

■ gathering available resources (volunteers or city staff, money for materials, equipment, landscape shrubbery, etc.) from the municipality, property owners, and tenants, or in-kind support from local businesses and community organizations; and

■ keeping the group together for other beautification activities.

Key Partnerships

Key partnerships are formed:

■ among the local residents themselves;

■ between them and the property owners and lessees;

■ with the police and other municipal personnel; and

■ with local businesses, chambers of commerce, and merchants associations that have business and community interests in enhancing the area through beautification. Area youths and religious groups might also be recruited to join in these partnerships.

Potential Obstacles

Nonparticipation by owners of problem properties can be an obstacle; another is the lack of sufficient resources for the actual beautification project. Police and other municipal agencies can often overcome nonparticipation by enforcing codes and zoning ordinances, or through condemnation or seizure for back taxes.

Signs of Success

Community beautification raises community and individual pride, and often brings a community closer together for common activities, with noticeable crime reduction effects.

The New York City-based Trust for Public Land (TPL) supports dozens of groups throughout the nation in their efforts to rehabilitate dilapidated properties and parks into green spaces accessible for the community's recreational needs. TPL helped one New York City neighborhood convert derelict land into community gardens. In Los Angeles, TPL helped clean up and secure lands for an urban river parkway.

Applying the Strategy

Pond Street in New Haven, Connecticut, suffered from the presence of illegal drug sales, trash, loiterers, and noise complaints from residents. The Block Watch resolved to take back some of its territory by planting flowers along curbsides and in a blighted lot on the corner. With 100 percent participation of their group, they turned the neighborhood into a beautiful garden. Other cleanups and beautification seemed to flow naturally. The beautification idea has now spread to nearby streets. Besides the visual benefits of beautification, crime has receded.

In California, the Alameda County Transit Authority joined with Oakland residents to remove graffiti on buses. Unemployed youths were offered the jobs of cleaning the buses. It appears that the graffiti cleanup has led to much less new graffiti being added. Small-business owners, corporate executives, civic officials and the police joined together in supporting these Bay Area United Youth who have been empowered to lead others in the community with positive, visible results, including other cleanups.

Contact Information

Pond Street Watch
c/o New Haven Police Department
One Union Avenue
New Haven, Connecticut 06519
203-946-6269

Crime Prevention Unit
New Haven Police Department
One Union Avenue
New Haven, Connecticut 06519
203-946-6269

Promote Business Involvement in the Community

Strategy

Promoting ethics in business and in the workplace for honesty, safety, and service to the community both decreases employee theft and helps to create a community climate conducive to economic development and less likely to attract crime.

Crime Problem Addressed

This strategy aims to reduce "white collar" crime, such as false advertising, marketing scams, product switching, sale of unsafe products, environmental damage, and many other types of less visible crime. It does so by promoting good business ethics and service to the community. This saves money for businesses and customers, saves jobs, and helps free police to concentrate on other crime-control activities.

Key Components

The goal of this strategy is a business community that acts ethically, does not tolerate crime, and serves the community. The key components of this strategy are as follows:

- adoption of ethical standards by businesses, covering all employees and operations;

- commitment to apply ethical standards including conduct with customers, company support for community service, and corporate involvement in the community;

- promotion of standards of ethical business practice for viewing by employees, the public, and other businesses;

- acknowledgment and awards for businesses in the community that have adopted and operate by sound ethical standards; and

- information for other businesses to learn of the ethical commitments of the best and to follow their good example.

Key Partnerships

Key Partnerships should be formed with the local chamber of commerce, other business associations, individual businesses, government offices, and with consumer, civic, and service organizations in the community. Since more than 90 percent of the nation's business schools provide training in business ethics, they, too, are good candidates for partnership in carrying out this crime prevention strategy.

Potential Obstacles

Companies with a good ethics culture are often very receptive, while those that seek profits by cutting corners on quality, safety, or honesty may be less receptive to community programs to enhance ethics. Citizen reporting of false advertising and consumer fraud can help to ensure good business practices and a low-crime commercial sector.

Signs of Success

The bestselling book by author Stephen R. Covey, *The 7 Habits of Highly Effective People,* describes how ethics and good character are the core bases for personal effectiveness and business success.

"Doing Right for Your Bottom Line" (*Business Ethics,* October 1992, pp. 99–104) concludes that, in some cases, companies that increase their community involvement are more likely to show an improved financial position.

Rotary International is a worldwide service club network of more than one million members, most of whom are business owners and managers. Rotary has a four-point test that it promotes in its own and its communities' businesses: (1) Is it the truth? (2) Is it fair to all concerned? (3) Will it build goodwill and better friendships? (4) Will it be beneficial to all concerned? The club's motto is "Service Above Self; They Profit Most Who Serve Best." Many members firmly state that is their experience.

Applying the Strategy

Since its founding in the 1930s, Motorola has been clear in its affirmation that high standards and good business go naturally together. Its statement is, "We will always act with constant respect for people, and with uncompromising integrity." The company gives its staff, worldwide, a booklet, *For Which We Stand: A Statement of Purpose, Principles and Ethics.* One main component is a commitment to honesty, integrity, and ethics; another is the goal to be a good corporate citizen by contributing to the economic and social well-being of every community in which the company operates. Motorola actively encourages its employees to participate in the community. One of its steps to good customer relations is to allow community use of its communications systems in support of Neighborhood Watch programs to report crime. Motorola is also an important corporate partner of the National Crime Prevention Council, providing support to publications and projects.

Contact Information

Motorola, Inc.
1303 East Algonquin Road
Schaumburg, Illinois 60196
708-576-5000

Ensure Supply of Affordable Housing

Strategy

Neighborhood cohesion and economic stability are enhanced in areas where the continuing supply of dispersed, affordable housing is assured.

Crime Problem Addressed

Densely concentrated clusters of high-rise, publicly assisted apartment complexes, away from centers of economic activity, experience high rates of crime. These rates apparently drop when residents feel a sense of pride in their dwelling places and join in community action with their neighbors. This strategy helps to reduce conditions that sometimes increase the likelihood of crime by providing affordable housing for the less affluent in dispersed areas, in low concentrations, and integrated into their work communities.

Key Components

This strategy works best in areas that are growing or redeveloping, and that have room for new developments. Key components include the following:

- development of a city-wide or county-wide plan to require lower cost housing units in all sizeable new housing developments;

- changes in the municipal code and zoning ordinance to provide a firm legal basis for the program and thus avoid challenges;

- requirements to make developers set aside a portion of new units, say 15 percent, for moderately priced dwelling units (MPDUs) to be sold or rented at below-market rates to those of low or moderate income;

- acquisition by the municipality of a portion of these MPDUs for its subsidized, low-cost housing program;

- allowances for the developer to provide MPDUs at other sites, if condo or other fees would raise total costs of MPDUs too high; and

- incentives for developers to participate in the program by allowing some limited exceptions to density limits.

Key Partnerships

The key partnerships are those that are established among the different municipal offices involved: housing, plan reviewing, zoning, etc. The cooperation of the builders and developers is essential and is obtained by legal requirement and by giving greater-than-normal density allowances (saving the land costs for the extra units allowed).

Potential Obstacles

This strategy requires that new, sizeable development take place and that local zoning authority impose its MPDU mandates. Builders' and developers' objections are possible, but may be avoided by offering greater density authorization that would give the developer an economic advantage to offset the cost of units subsidized. Potential opposition from local citizen groups may be muted by the legal mandates and by hopes for an improved community atmosphere and the possibility of a reduction in crime.

Signs of Success

Montgomery County, Maryland, has successfully implemented this strategy over a twenty-year period with few problems and many major successes. Moderate- and low-priced housing is now available throughout the county, and racial and economic integration is a simple fact of life. In the belief that doing so would assist economic development in the city's neighborhoods and downtown, Bloomington, Indiana, recently added affordable housing requirements to a new community development plan for the area.

Applying the Strategy

Montgomery County, Maryland, has been at the forefront in implementing this development strategy. This county of nearly 800,000 residents is north of Washington, DC. In the 1970s and 1980s it changed from a bedroom community for the nation's capital to a regional employment center. In the same period, the shortage of affordable housing became acute.

In the early l970s, the county developed an innovative, county-wide inclusionary zoning/density allowance program known as the Moderately Priced Dwelling Unit program. Now, 12.5 percent to 15 percent of every subdivision or building of fifty units or more in zones with lot sizes less than one acre are made available as MPDUs. The zoning law allows for a density allowance of up to 22 percent over normal density for developers who provide the MPDUs. This is the virtual equivalent of free land to the developer for the MPDUs, making the developer a cooperative partner in their production, cost-free to the county. Accordingly, more is left in the county housing budget for assistance to very low income households. Pro-

gram requirements are put in the County Code and Zoning Ordinance. The county's housing authority has the right to purchase up to one-third of the MPDUs, and it can provide below-market-rate mortgage financing for qualified purchasers.

More than 8,000 affordable units have been created in Montgomery County. MPDUs now comprise nearly 3 percent of all county housing. In 1990, the average MPDU purchaser had an annual income of around $27,000, compared with the county average income of about $68,000. Two-thirds of the units sold are going to first-time home buyers. Economic and racial integration are direct products of this program. The high crime rates of many high-rise, publicly assisted projects have been avoided.

Partly inspired by Montgomery County's success, neighboring Fairfax County in Virginia enacted a similar MPDU program in 1994.

Contact Information

Coordinator
Montgomery County Department of Housing &
Community Development
51 Monroe Street
Suite 908
Rockville, Maryland 20850
301-217-3705

Enlist Resources of U.S. Department of Housing and Urban Development and Other Federal Agencies

Strategy

Use U.S. Department of Housing and Urban Development (HUD) resources and incentives for revitalizing and developing distressed neighborhoods—both urban and rural.

Crime Problem Addressed

Inadequate jobs, lack of decent housing, and economic deprivation or lack of economic opportunity are risk factors and community conditions that can lead to crime. When these conditions afflict large numbers of people in crowded inner-city areas, there is a danger of incidents and misunderstandings igniting significant crime problems, as in the disturbances in Los Angeles after the Rodney King police assailants' trial. This strategy can reduce crime generally by revitalizing individuals and communities through social integration and economic opportunity.

Key Components

The key components of this strategy are as follows:

■ review of federal program resource availability;

■ identification of federal programs that offer opportunities and benefits to the local community or municipality;

■ mobilization of the effort needed to apply and meet the conditions for successful applications, or simply utilization of the programs that are available;

■ tapping of available federal resources and incentives for maximum local benefits; and

■ coordination of the local distribution of these resources and incentives for fairness and impact.

The following kinds of HUD programs have been made available to localities in recent years:

■ Community Development Block Grants: Annual grants to cities and counties to develop viable urban communities with decent housing and expanding economic opportunities, principally for low- and moderate-income persons, or to prevent or eliminate slums and blight. Detailed citizen participation plans must be developed and followed.

■ Empowerment Zones and Enterprise Communities: The goal is to help some of the most impoverished communities across the country "jump start" their revitalization. Ingredients are special tax incentives, including employer wage credits for creating jobs, Social Services Block Grants for business investment and better housing, a 50 percent exclusion of capital gains for certain business investments, and gain deferral for reinvestment in a Small Business Investment Company (SBIC).

■ Community Development Corporations: Twenty such designations are offered. The corporations would be qualified to receive up to $2 million, with the donors receiving up to a 50 percent tax credit over ten years.

A related effort is the Small Business Administration's commitment to targeting some of its lending and community development tools to small and minority-owned businesses in distressed communities and underserved markets.

As of early 1995, new proposals include the following:

■ The President's Community Development Banking and Financial Institutions Bill, to provide credit for the needy.

■ The proposed Neighborhood Leveraged Investments for Tomorrow (LIFT) program as a catalyst for community coalitions working for community revitalization and balanced growth.

■ The proposed Community Reinvestment Act, whose regulations focus on actual lending and investment in low-income communities.

■ The Economic Development Initiative, which would authorize $50 million for fiscal year 1995 to add grants to help subsidize the costs of Section 108 Loan Guarantee programs for economic revitalization.

Key Partnerships

Participating federal agencies, political leaders, and citizen groups are key partners.

Potential Obstacles

Not all federal programs that are authorized and announced get the full funding envisioned. Programs have selection criteria that limit eligibility. Some, like Empowerment Zones, are limited to specific numbers of communities, so many deserving communities may be passed over. However, the application process itself can help bring communities together with focused plans for vital community development.

Signs of Success

Many local experiences and broader studies have shown that disinvestment—declining property values and the flight of investment—is associated with higher crime rates. Investment in the community, when combined with broad-based community involvement in improving housing and jobs, generally cuts crime rates. Based on these principles, HUD has a number of programs that provide and promote investment in communities while requiring or encouraging broad-based community involvement. The goal is citizen-based community revitalization that restores communities, resulting in less crime.

Applying the Strategy

Locations where the different referenced federal resources and incentives have been used successfully may be available through the contact office below.

Contact Information

Field Offices of HUD around the country.

Assistant Secretary for Community Planning and
     Development
U.S. Department of Housing and Urban Development
451 7th Street, SW,
Washington, DC 20410-7000

Micro-Credits to Small-Scale Business

Strategy

Business micro-credits—small-scale, revolving loans to those deemed poor credit risks by the normal banking system—help to create self-employment and jobs for neighbors.

Crime Problem Addressed

This strategy reduces unemployment and some of the financial desperation often associated with the potential for crime and delinquency in neighborhoods.

Key Components

The business micro-credits strategy gives individuals and very small businesses the opportunity to obtain small loans (perhaps $500 to $6,000), even if they have no track record and no collateral, putting them outside the regular banking system. The special micro-credits lending authority can be a community development corporation, a non-profit organization, a government program, a special program of a standard bank, or a small business incubator. The following are key components of this strategy:

- a group of individuals in need of capital to start or expand business opportunities;

- borrower responsibility (individually or shared with peer group) for repayment of loans;

- start-up capital with which to launch the initial round of loans;

- systems for borrower counseling, or coaching for success and savings;

- repayment collection; and

- recirculation of repaid monies to new individual borrowers or peer groups of borrowers.

The concept is a very small-scale version of the technique used by the state's local grants to finance major public works projects.

Key Partnerships

The key partnerships include those between

- the organization providing the micro-credits and familiar local organizations that can help find numbers of worthy and willing borrowers;

- the handful of individuals who form a solidarity peer group of small-loan borrowers, each guaranteeing repayment by the few others in their group; and

- the lender organization, borrowers, and local banks that hold and, perhaps, lend the funds.

Potential Obstacles

It can be difficult to find enough micro-credit borrowers to bring these programs to true economies of scale, whereby overhead costs can be fully covered by the credit activities themselves. Pay-back collections can be challenging, but with good program planning they can match or exceed those for normal bank lending.

Signs of Success

The strategy was developed by an economics professor in Bangladesh who was frustrated by local banks' refusal to lend money to the poor who needed it when they lacked the required collateral. He started by lending money from his own pocket so that the poor could get a better start in their small-business activities. The loans were repaid, and in 1983, the gratified professor established the Grameen Bank for lending to the poor. The bank now has operations in half of all the villages of Bangladesh. The poor are empowered to escape dependency and poverty. Repayment rates are excellent—99 percent.

Accion International and Foundation for International Community Assistance (FINCA), two U.S. non-profit organizations, used this micro-credits model in Central and South America, bringing credit and capitalism to the poor. They enable cottage industries to start up, expand, and create jobs for others as they grow.

Now these two organizations, and others, are adapting these models to American cities and towns. Acknowledging the success of such programs, the $30 billion Crime Bill of 1994 authorizes $270 million for community economic partnerships to establish lines of credit to stimulate business and employment opportunities for low-income, unemployed, or under-employed citizens.

Applying the Strategy

In 1991, Accion International started a successful micro-loan program in Brooklyn, New York, focusing on Hispanics. The typical business served is a small store-front operation or one run from the home by a woman, often a single parent. Many have no employees outside the family. Most serve the neighborhood or local market. Accion International is now seeking to create effective programs on a national scale.

FINCA started a similar Neighborhood Business Banking Program in greater Washington, DC, and another micro-loan program in rural Minnesota, in 1993.

The Association for Enterprise Opportunity (AEO) has been established to assist organizations involved in micro-credits and self-employment.

Contact Information

Technical Support Manager
FINCA International, Inc.
1101 14th Street, NW, 11th Floor
Washington, DC 20005
202-682-1510

Vice President for U.S. Operations
Accion International
733 15th Street, NW, Suite 700
Washington, DC 20005
202-393-5113

Targeted Lending

Strategy

Lending targeted to areas where needed credit is scarce or simply unavailable strengthens the economic vitality of those areas and builds stability in the neighborhood.

Crime Problem Addressed

Areas with blighted commercial strips, low rates of home-ownership, inadequate and overcrowded housing, and a declining jobs base often have high crime rates. Targeted lending to these areas can create affordable housing, homeownership, jobs, and stability, all of which help alleviate social conditions that contribute to the likelihood of crime.

Key Components

Components of the targeted lending strategy by local government can include the following:

■ requiring banks that locate in the area to serve a variety of neighborhoods;

■ opening, creating, or redirecting and energizing a local bank;

■ creating a for-profit real estate development company to acquire and rehabilitate housing and commercial properties;

■ creating a nonprofit community development company to secure government, business, and private party grants;

■ targeting lending and development in the problem area by using incentives wherever possible;

■ mobilizing support from inside and outside the targeted community; and

■ achieving visibility and publicity for each success to change the area's image to one of positive growth momentum.

Key Partnerships

The key partners in this targeted lending strategy are local neighborhood residents and the banks themselves.

■ Local residents and outside supporters become depositors with the target-lending bank (or community credit union/program).

■ The Federal Deposit Insurance Corporation is an ally of the bank, the depositors, and the community by insuring the deposits.

■ The bank acts as a financing partner in a real estate or community development company by earmarking and targeting its lending in the community in need.

■ A non-profit community development company is often allied with its funding supporters (government, businesses, individual and group donors), and perhaps with the bank and real estate development company, through their common efforts.

Potential Obstacles

Economically deteriorating communities often experience an exodus of long-established businesses and families. Those who remain may be thinking more about their own departures than about investing themselves and their money in the community. In the face of such pessimism, it may be difficult to get most residents committed to long-term efforts to start targeted lending and community development projects. Getting the needed capital for lending can be very difficult and demand a lot of determination and perseverance by local economic development agencies and state regulators. Good community organization and public relations are key to achieving the credibility needed to persuade people to invest their time, efforts, and money in a struggling community. Even when target-lending operations are working well, it may still be difficult to match returns to investors in more prosperous communities.

Signs of Success

Targeted lending makes funds available for renters to become homeowners, entrepreneurs to become housing rehabilitators, jobless persons to become business operators, and small businesses to become bigger businesses. Congress recognized the positive effects on crime reduction efforts by authorizing $270 million in the $30 billion Crime Bill of 1994 for lines of credit to community development corporations for business and employment opportunities for low-income, unemployed, or underemployed citizens.

The strategy works best in conjunction with community development companies and business incubation programs that nurture new, small businesses and help them to grow by ensuring that they will be able to borrow money to finance expansion.

Applying the Strategy

In the early 1970s, South Shore Bank in Chicago, Illinois, dedicated itself to reversing local community decay by targeting its lending to local community development. The bank has spent two decades seeking out borrowers where more traditional banks fear to tread—inner-city areas deemed too high a risk for lending. Specializing in loans to acquire and renovate small apartment buildings and in loans to new, local businesses, South Shore Bank has stimulated neighborhood revitalization while remaining profitable. The bank keeps a positive loan repayment rate, not by requiring collateral, which its targeted borrowers seldom have, but by knowing its neighborhood and its business and individual borrowers. Now, other banks compete for lending in the improving South Shore neighborhoods.

Inspired by its success in Chicago, South Shore Bank led the effort to export the target-lending strategy to Arkadelphia, a one-hour drive from Little Rock, Arkansas.

After purchasing Arkadelphia's Elk Horn Bank, the bank began to revitalize the rural area by mobilizing capital for poor but determined small-business entrepreneurs. South Shore has helped start similar targeted lending programs in the Upper Peninsula of Michigan and in Kansas City, Kansas.

Baltimore's plan for implementing federal assistance offered through a 1994 Urban Empowerment Zone grant award includes commitments by several local banks to provide $50 million in loans to businesses and residents within the targeted zone.

Contact Information

South Shore Bank
71st and Jeffery Boulevard
Chicago, Illinois 60649-2096
312-288-1000

Business Watch

Strategy

Business Watch programs deter and detect crimes and diminish opportunities for crime.

Crime Problem Addressed

This strategy reduces many types of crimes, including shoplifting, theft, burglary, purse snatching, and vandalism against and around business. Just as citizen preparedness and surveillance in Neighborhood Watch programs have led to a reduction of crime in residential areas, this strategy can reduce crime against businesses as well as other crimes.

Key Components

Business Watch primarily establishes links among small businesses, and between them and the police. Basically, Business Watch is businesses (sometimes with community groups) taking systematic steps to reduce opportunities for crimes in and around business locations. It includes training business personnel to be eyes and ears for the police. In Business Watch areas, crime prevention police officers and business leaders assist business owners, operators, and employees in:

■ reporting crime: effectively observing and reporting to police on crimes and suspicious activities that could lead to crime;

■ operation identification: marking all equipment, machines, etc., with traceable identification numbers for deterrence and tracing;

■ robbery prevention: eliminating "easy prey" crime opportunities;

■ burglary prevention: adding security measures to impede criminals, detect criminal activity, and communicate with the police; and

■ self-protection: learning to recognize dangerous situations, and learning how to prevent, avoid, or flee them.

Business Watch programs often have a business leader act as the block security chief for the participating businesses. One or more police officers are usually assigned to be the liaison with the Business Watch group. The local civic association or other community groups may also participate, lending extra eyes and ears, especially for periods when the businesses are closed. Sometimes the businesses are linked to each other and to the police through radio or fax machine message trees. Radio-equipped delivery and service vehicles may also become part of Business Watch.

Key Partnerships

Key partnerships are those among the businesses and business people themselves and their organization and leaders. They, in turn, form a key partnership with the local police department, and especially with its crime prevention or watch liaison officers. Other partners can be the local citizens' association, church, Chamber of Commerce, or other groups interested in a safe and prosperous business base in the community.

Potential Obstacles

Sometimes it takes time to convince busy business owners that they can to a large degree control the incidence of crime in and around their operation. It can be difficult to keep businesses active in Business Watch when the costs and threat of crime have been reduced. Some police departments require a fixed percentage of businesses in the area to participate actively to qualify for Business Watch recognition and support (such as signs, regular meetings, etc.).

Signs of Success

Many local police departments have documented significant reductions in reported crime where Neighborhood or Business Watch programs are instituted. For example, burglary rates in Seattle, Washington, were cut in half in Watch neighborhoods. When St. Louis, Missouri, introduced its city-wide crime prevention and Watch programs, substantial reductions were realized in both violent crimes against persons and property crimes.

Applying the Strategy

The Detroit Police Department has worked very actively with blocks of businesses to organize and guide Business Watch programs. The Crime Prevention Section is a very

significant part of Detroit's police force. It has developed extensive methodologies and materials for Business Watch, with emphasis on eliminating opportunities for criminal activity. It eliminates the "easy prey" temptation by training business personnel in the skills of perceiving potential crime indicators, protecting themselves, and reporting to the police. Police officers provide blueprints for business groups organizing meetings and designating security chiefs. They provide checklists for shoplifting prevention, bad check controls, internal theft precautions, security of premises, and more. The Detroit police have documented lower crime rates in Business Watch areas.

The Marathon County Sheriff's Department in Wisconsin has developed a Fleetwatch program: employees of firms with two-way communications systems in their vehicles become extra eyes and ears of the police. They report on criminal and suspicious activity, but do not physically intervene. The Department has supported Farm Watch in rural areas. There, many ginseng growers were experiencing thefts of crops and plants. After Farm Watch with its citizen patrols was instituted, there were no documented ginseng thefts over a two-year period.

Contact Information

Detroit Police Department
Crime Prevention Unit
2110 Park Avenue, Suite 332
Detroit, Michigan 48201
313-596-2520

Marathon County Sheriff's Office
Wausau, Wisconsin 54403
715-847-0229

Bibliography

Books

African-American Church Project. *Restoring Broken Places And Rebuilding Communities: A Casebook On African-American Church Involvement In Community Economic Development.* Washington, DC: National Congress for Community Economic Developments, 1993.

Committee for Economic Development. *Rebuilding Inner-City Communities: A New Approach to the Nation's Urban Crisis.* Washington, DC, 1995.

Schweke, William, Carl Rist, and Brian Dabson. *Bidding for Business: Are Cities and States Selling Themselves Short?* Washington, DC: Corporation for Enterprise Development, 1994.

Periodicals

Budd, Claire Patton. Kirkwood's Commitment Brings Opportunity to Annexed Neighborhood. *Nation's Business Weekly,* January 9, 1995, p. 8.

Valentine, Paul W. Baltimore Patrols Cited in Decrease in Downtown Crime. *The Washington Post,* March 28, 1994, p. B-5.

Public Documents

U.S. Department of Justice, Bureau of Justice Assistance. *Business Alliance: Planning for Business and Community Partnerships.* Washington, DC, August 1994.

Washington State Crime Prevention Association. *Business Watch Manual: Preventing Crimes Against Businesses.* SAFECO Corporation, August 1993.

Violence

Violence is one of the most pressing social problems and important public health issues in American society.

T he fear that so often accompanies violence threatens the nation's civic life because it makes citizens retreat from community activity in search of security. Violence among youth has increased significantly over the past decade, leading many localities to view youth as the problem's source. The costs of violence burden local and community institutions: violence drains the budgets and staff of schools, hospitals, businesses, courts, and social service agencies. Prevention and enforcement can effectively address violence in communities.

Effective violence prevention addresses an array of causes through partnerships of local government and community residents. Innovative approaches to violence at the local level recognize the need to sanction violent offenders and support victims. Community and local government action can prevent additional victimization because such action signals community standards and a commitment to residents' safety and security.

The strategies highlighted in this chapter represent a sample of varied local responses to violence. In each case, the communities involved achieved results when they drew on grassroots energy and resources, as well as local government partnerships with other community sectors. Important partners include parents, youth, schools, churches, and other community organizations.

This collection profiles the following successful, cost-effective local partnerships.

■ **Restitution to victims.** Repayment of damages to victims enhances offenders' accountability. Among youth offenders who participate in the Earn-It restitution program sponsored by Keene, New Hampshire's municipal court, 80 to 85 percent do not become repeat offenders. The sentencing alternative requires that nonviolent offenders set aside two-thirds of their earnings from court-arranged jobs as restitution to the individual or institution they victimized.

■ **Conflict mediation training for youth.** Young people need communication skills and an ability to deal with anger in nonviolent ways. New York's Resolving Conflict Creatively Program is cosponsored by the city's public schools and Educators for Social Responsibility. Seventy percent of teachers involved in the nationally recognized program has resulted in less name-calling, less classroom violence, and more cooperation and understanding among students. The program has helped teachers understand the value of letting students take responsibility for solving their problems with peers.

237

■ **Support for victims of domestic violence**. Assistance to victims prevents additional violence because it demonstrates the community's support. *Family Violence State-of-the-Art Court Programs*, a 1992 publication of the National Council of Juvenile and Family Court Judges (Reno, Nevada), examines eighteen of the best court programs that support victims of domestic violence. The publication identifies elements common to successful programs, including services to victims and batterers, coordination with prosecutors, and efforts to change laws affecting victims and their children. Services for victims include education regarding their legal rights, help filing charges and obtaining protection orders and custody, and help obtaining medical, counseling, legal, and financial support through agencies outside the court system.

■ **Prevention of dating violence**. Acquaintance rape and other violence can result from an inability to build healthy adult relationships. Those who run the Boston-based Mentors in Violence Prevention (MVP) Project believe that student athletes enjoy a high status that increases their influence over peers. For this reason, it is especially important to educate student athletes about rape, battering, and sexual harassment. Using what it calls the *MVP Playbook*, the program guides students through role plays and discussions about on-campus parties, alcohol and its effect on dating relationships, harassment of gay and lesbian students, and violence in relationships. The program challenges male students to develop strategies for dealing with abusive behavior by a fellow student. In addition to working on campus with fraternities and student government, program personnel train student ath-

letes to make their own presentations to middle and high school classes.

■ **Strong state laws to combat gang violence**. Careful drafting of state laws on street gang activity requires knowledge of gangs' nature, extent, and relationship to crime. California's attorney general, legislature, and governor cooperated in designing a wide array of laws to combat gang violence in communities throughout the state. The partnership resulted in enactment of the California Street Terrorism Enforcement and Prevention Act, which focuses on criminal street gangs. The act provides for felony prosecution of active gang members, felony penalties against adults who coerce youth into joining a gang, and possible life terms in prison for murder convictions involving drive-by shootings. It also outlines penalties for graffiti vandalism and sale of illegal weapons. Other provisions call for publication of a gang prevention resource guide for community organizations and in-service teacher training in preventing gang violence and drug abuse.

Cathedral City, California, applied the law to combat the city's gang problem. After the Gang Related Activity and Suppression Program (GRASP) used the law to identify gang members and enforce against their violence and graffiti vandalism, community incidents of graffiti dropped by more than two-thirds.

These strategies disprove the notion that violence is either inevitable or so inveterate that individual and community action can't make a difference. They show that community action and government commitment hold the promise of a nonviolent society.

Comprehensive Curricula

Strategy

Comprehensive curricula on violence prevention can reduce victimization, encourage victim assistance, and convey vital information about the dangers of violent conduct and firearms.

Crime Problem Addressed

Violence against and by elementary school students is a widespread reality. Violence prevention curricula can improve young children's understanding of appropriate social behavior and reduce their impulsive and aggressive behaviors.

Key Components

Teaching materials and methods must be age-appropriate, impart problem-solving and communications skills, and

teach ways to resolve conflict and handle anger and stress. Effective materials and methods include written lessons and exercises, videos, role plays, and discussion groups. Bringing violence prevention into the classroom reinforces the value of nonviolence for all students and establishes the teacher as a resource for children who have questions about resolving conflicts.

Key Partnerships

Many school systems have successfully relied on counselors, nurses, or other specialists to supplement teachers' efforts to teach nonviolence. The participation of these other professionals gives students a sense of a supportive network of adults available to help them resolve problems in a nonviolent way.

Potential Obstacles

Materials geared to the wrong age group will not produce the desired effect on students. School systems must carefully review available curricula to determine which would work best with their student population. When curriculum programs provide materials for different age groups, the same students can participate over a number of years, improving their chances of long-term skill development and information retention.

Signs of Success

The Committee for Children, a Seattle-based nonprofit organization founded in 1979, has developed Second Step, a set of comprehensive curricula for preschool through eighth grade. Through role plays, discussions, and videos, children gain empathy, self-control, problem-solving and communications skills, understanding of appropriate behavior, and the ability to manage anger. The program is designed to benefit all children, not just high-risk students. First piloted in 1987, the program serves over a million children annually, primarily in school settings. Program materials for preschool through fifth grade are available in Spanish as well as English. The committee also offers training videos and technical support to those who implement the program.

An evaluation of the preschool/kindergarten curriculum showed that participants' violence prevention knowledge and skills surpassed those of nonparticipants. The study also noted that preschool and kindergarten children increased their social skills knowledge after completing the program. Evaluations of the curriculum for grades 1 through 3, 4 through 5, and 6 through 8 yielded similar results.

Applying the Strategy

Richmond Youth Against Violence bases its strategies on an eighteen-session curriculum for sixth graders, an eight-session format for ninth graders, and a peer mediation program in middle schools. Violence prevention facilitators in each school counsel students. Parent and neighborhood involvement strengthens the program. Reportedly, participation in the Virginia program has decreased students' fear and hostility, increased their problem-solving skills, and reduced fighting on school grounds.

Contact Information

Committee for Children
172 20th Avenue
Seattle, Washington 98122
206-322-5050 or 800-634-4449

Train Professionals To Recognize Child Victims

Strategy

Hospital personnel, lawyers, justice system officials, and psychiatrists should receive training that enables them to recognize child victims of violence and abuse, understand their special needs, and act as their advocates.

Crime Problem Addressed

According to a 1994 article in *Parade* magazine, each year approximately two million children are physically or sexually abused, while untold others are neglected or emotionally harassed. Other research indicates that firearms are the fifth-leading cause of accidental death for children under fifteen; one in six pediatricians has treated a child for a gun-related injury. This strategy aims to train health care, legal, and other professionals to recognize child abuse, treat children who are victims of violence, and act as their advocates.

Key Components

Professionals likely to encounter child victims need training and cross-training in appropriate legal and medical procedures for dealing with child abuse, recognizing child

victims and treating them effectively, and becoming involved in community projects that serve children in need.

Key Partnerships

Agencies and institutions with staff who regularly interact with or treat child victims must recognize the benefits of coordinating the efforts of well-trained professionals. Law and medical schools can provide trainers. Professional associations can also cooperate in creating training programs and fostering cooperation among their members who staff key agencies.

Potential Obstacles

Professionals such as lawyers and physicians may be reluctant to admit shortcomings in their ability to recognize and assist child victims. Formal training agreements among institutions help generate and sustain cooperation among individuals in the system.

Signs of Success

The Chicago-based Civitas Initiative grew out of a local lawyer's concern about the treatment of abused children within the court and foster-care bureaucracies. The program cross-trains law and psychiatry students to improve each group's understanding of legal procedures, ability to evaluate medical reports, and use resources available to assist victims.

In the program, law students train with emergency room doctors, ride with police officers responding to calls, and join social workers in home visits to affected families. In turn, psychiatry students attend law school classes and monitor court proceedings. The U.S. Department of Justice (DOJ) and the American Bar Association have endorsed the program. Area prosecutors and local government agencies that serve children's needs have pledged to continue cooperative training agreements.

Applying the Strategy

Baylor College of Medicine, in Texas, has expanded its cross-training program to include thirty psychiatry residents and medical students who will serve the community through area hospitals and clinics that treat children.

The American Academy of Pediatrics and the Center to Prevent Handgun Violence sponsor educational and training materials for pediatric health care professionals through the Stop Firearm Injury program. The program provides doctors and others with brochures, posters, reading lists, and other information to help them recognize child victims of gun violence and refer victims and their families to other service providers as needed. Thousands of physicians have received and used the materials.

Contact Information

American Academy of Pediatrics
141 Northwest Point Boulevard
P.O. Box 927
Elk Grove Village, Illinois 60009-0927
708-228-5005

Public Dialogue and Community Mediation

Strategy

Community-based public dialogues help identify neighborhood issues and resolve disputes among groups.

Crime Problem Addressed

The strategy addresses a wide array of neighborhood issues, including intergroup relations, nuisance abatement, landlord-tenant complaints, threats, vandalism, and other disputes that could escalate into violence.

Key Components

Systems through which to refer cases from community groups, the courts, police, and other city agencies help community-based mediators identify neighborhood issues requiring resolution. Volunteer mediators and discussion leaders help disputants recognize issues of concern, accept responsibility without threats, and identify strategies to resolve the conflict. Formal hearings serve as the setting for discussion of complaints, lending structure and credibility to the grassroots process. Some local groups use a more informal system of discussion leaders, working through community organizers and other informally established community leaders.

Key Partnerships

Schools, police, probation agencies, and area courts advance the program by referring cases for resolution. Such referrals relieve schools and the law enforcement system from the burden of dealing with disputes that neighborhood leaders could resolve. Youth serve as vital partners in mediating school-related disputes. Community newspapers and grassroots word-of-mouth networks help publicize the community dialogue and mediation services.

Potential Obstacles

Community-wide education that informs residents of this method of conflict resolution can be difficult to finance. Community newspapers and other local communications networks help increase the program's visibility and spread word of success. Courts and other institutions help reinforce the program's value by referring cases.

Signs of Success

The Community Board Program in San Francisco uses community activism to resolve conflict among groups. Schools, courts, public housing councils, juvenile corrections facilities, and other local government agencies refer cases for mediation by staff or volunteers. Hearings run by trained volunteer youth or adult mediators serve as the forum for airing and resolving disputes. The cadre of three hundred mediators work out of more than eighty donated sites, mostly in neighborhood settings. Requests for mediation and other services reached 1,200 in 1991 and have grown steadily since. Services expanded to include peer mediation in juvenile correction facilities. Staff members of social service agencies and the community board also mediate between child protection workers and families.

Applying the Strategy

The Study Circles Resource Center of the Connecticut-based Topsfield Foundation advocates formation of community-level study circles or discussion groups as a means of discussing issues and resolving problems among neighbors. The center publishes *The Study Circle Handbook: A Manual for Study Circle Discussion Leaders, Organizers, and Participants*, a guide to forming local study circles. A discussion guide shows communities how local groups are using discussion circles to resolve neighborhood disputes. The Common Enterprise group of San Antonio, Texas, emphasizes building the community, resolving conflict, and achieving consensus "across broadly diverse and contentious communities."

Contact Information

Executive Director, Community Board Program
1540 Market Street, Suite 490
San Francisco, California 94102
415-552-1250

Topsfield Foundation
P.O. Box 203
Pomfret, Connecticut 06258
203-928-2616

Information Networks on Gang Activity

Strategy

Information and communication networks among law enforcement agencies and the general public help identify gang leaders and track their activities in and across jurisdictions.

Crime Problem Addressed

This strategy aims to provide law enforcement agencies with the up-to-date information they need to identify, track, and apprehend violent juveniles who belong to gangs. The problems addressed through this strategy include assaults and homicides associated with gang-related drug trafficking and conflicts among rival gangs.

Key Components

Networks of agencies, usually headed by law enforcement, share information on contacts with known or suspected gang members, looking for changes in their behavior, associates, or involvement in criminal activity. Shared information includes photos, arrest records, intelligence on ongoing investigations, and resource lists of services to which a gang-involved youth could be referred. The means of sharing the information varies by community but may include newsletters, on-line networks, fax links, and reports on changes in the behavior of youth following their participation in prevention and intervention programs. In many communities the network's mission includes a prevention component and outreach to parents of gang-involved youth.

Key Partnerships

Agencies outside of law enforcement are key partners in this strategy. Local government and community-based social service agencies, recreation programs, counseling resources, and family outreach projects represent a continuum of supports that can be brought to bear on behalf of juveniles.

Potential Obstacles

Concern about legal restrictions on sharing confidential records of juveniles may result in minimal agency participation. Careful law enforcement agents may initially choose not to open records of investigations and enforcement activity to other agencies' staff. Legal consultation and careful interagency planning can yield a policy that provides useful information without violating a juvenile's right to privacy.

Signs of Success

Yonkers, New York, established Operation I.D. to identify gang-involved and at-risk youth and change their behavior. In the program a network of city agencies assist participating youth with job referrals, counseling, and outreach to parents. Law enforcement officers work directly with the youth, advising them and, when necessary, arranging home visits by Community Affairs Division staff to determine the extent of family problems. Parental responsibility ranks high among the program's priorities. The year before the program began, gang activity increased by 66 percent; the year after, it increased only 3 percent.

Applying the Strategy

Fresno, California's Law Enforcement Gang Information Network provides information that helps local police capture gang-involved criminal suspects. The school district, local Boys & Girls Club, county probation department, district attorney, and Fresno police and county sheriffs departments have participated.

Columbus, Ohio's police department observes gang members and has them self-report so that police can target leaders whose activities should be monitored. The department distributes a newsletter on gang activities during morning roll call, providing patrol officers with current information on activities of the area's known gang leaders. The information proves valuable to investigations of gang-related incidents.

Contact Information

Planning and Management Unit
Yonkers Police Department
104 South Broadway
Yonkers, New York 10701
914-377-7350

Multiagency Gang Interdiction Teams

Strategy

Multiagency representation on gang interdiction teams reinforces the support systems for rehabilitation of gang members, helping to turn them from gang activity.

Crime Problem Addressed

This strategy represents an integrated local government effort to enforce against crimes related to youth gangs, particularly the violent offenses that devastate communities. The team's multidisciplinary nature increases its ability to deliver services to gang-involved youth and its capacity for community outreach.

Key Components

Teams led by law enforcement and representing multiple agencies include school personnel, residents, youth diversion counselors, staff of the district attorney's office, probation department personnel, and, in some cities, university research staff who provide support for crime analysis. The teams share information but also develop coordinated gang-enforcement strategies, including dissemination of prevention information and apprehension of gang leaders and others involved in gang activities.

Key Partnerships

The enforcement team should represent youth services, law enforcement, the juvenile justice system, and other agencies that address juvenile crime. Schools can help prevent gang-related crime by providing opportunities for gang-enforcement team members to interact with students.

Potential Obstacles

Agency "turf" issues and institutional biases against certain prevention or enforcement strategies may initially impede cooperation. Cooperative funding arrangements and formal policies detailing team members' roles and re-

sponsibilities help eliminate interagency conflicts and increase the potential for successful collaboration.

Signs of Success

In Cathedral City, California, reported incidents of graffiti dropped from 3,600 in 1992 to 400 in 1993. The police department heads GRASP, which focuses on graffiti abatement. The GRASP team receives support from the school system and includes a bilingual diversion counselor and a community representative. Team members have presented prevention programs to area students, initiated a media campaign against gangs, and involved parents in weekly meetings to discuss local youth-related policies on drug enforcement and probation. GRASP's success has made it a model of interagency cooperation throughout the region.

Applying the Strategy

The Tri-Agency Resource Gang Enforcement Team of Westminster, California, combines the efforts of law enforcement staff and researchers from California State University to counter the city's youth gang problem. Westminster hired a deputy district attorney, an investigator, and a probation officer to operate the team, which has based its work on the university's findings. Cooperation within the team has resulted in creation of a database on key gang leaders and recidivist gang members and has led to more convictions of gang-involved offenders, including seventy-six gang members in sixty-two separate cases. A combination of probation checks, restraining orders, and investigative work has reduced gang activity within this community.

Contact Information

Chief of Police
8200 Westminster Boulevard
Westminster, California 92683
714-898-3311

Combine Corrections With Treatment

Strategy

Correctional facilities for violent juvenile offenders reduce recidivism when incarceration is combined with treatment, opportunities for achievement, and aftercare focused on reintegration into the community.

Crime Problem Addressed

The National Council on Crime and Delinquency cites Federal Bureau of Investigation (FBI) estimates that in 1992 more than 3,200 juveniles were arrested for murder and nearly 130,000 were arrested for other violent crimes. While most youth arrests are for property crimes and status offenses (curfew violations, truancy), the number of youth committing serious violent offenses challenges states and localities to reduce recidivism among these dangerous offenders.

Key Components

The most effective programs provide individualized rehabilitation, treatment, and case management services to a small population in a secure facility; use a system of rewards and sanctions to modify behavior; promote bonding with pro-social adults and empathy with victims; and offer aftercare services to support offenders' reintegration into the community.

Rehabilitation services include treatment assessments and individualized therapy over six to nine months. Treatment is often vigorous, using group sessions and role plays to promote nonviolent expressions of emotion, instill empathy for victims, and encourage personal responsibility. In addition, many programs require detainees to work at the facility or demonstrate progress in therapy or academics in order to obtain privileges. Aftercare helps a small number of released offenders find employment, deal with family conflicts, and avoid criminal behavior.

Key Partnerships

Some programs' primary partner, the adult justice system, refers clients processed as adults back to the juvenile system for treatment and incarceration. In such cases, the juvenile program's residential facility must maintain a close partnership with the adult system to ensure referrals along established criteria. Programs that incorporate community reintegration emphasize partnerships with local employment programs; community-based, residential treatment facilities; and family support services—to increase the likelihood that the treatment's effects will last beyond the detention term.

Potential Obstacles

The combined costs of intensive treatment and small staff-to-participant ratios in aftercare services can seem prohibitive unless compared to the expense of the juvenile's recommitment to residential detention. An absence of community-based aftercare programs that provide follow-up services diminishes the chances that a released youth will maintain the progress achieved during treatment. Comparing participants' recidivism rates with those of juveniles who have not received treatment or other services is complicated unless control groups are delineated at the intervention's outset. Treatment groups' small size makes careful selection of a control or comparison group a key component in evaluating the program's impact.

Signs of Success

The DOJ-sponsored Violent Juvenile Offender (VJO) Program established small-scale residential treatment, behavior modification, achievement, community reintegration, and neighborhood supervision services for violent juvenile offenders in Boston, Detroit, Memphis, and Newark. The program aimed to strengthen participants' bonds with the treatment providers in the institutions, encouraged achievement by rewarding appropriate behavior, and provided participants with individualized psychotherapy. A 1990 evaluation by Rutgers University researchers revealed that "VJO programs can reduce recidivism and serious crime among violent juvenile offenders." In Boston and Detroit, where aftercare and community reintegration components were comprehensive and well implemented, participating youth had significantly fewer rearrests, and for offenses that were significantly less serious, than youth who did not participate.

Applying the Strategy

Located in the Everglades and operated by Associated Marine Institutes, a seven-state network of juvenile programs based in Tampa, the Florida Environmental Institute is a secure treatment facility for serious and violent juvenile offenders. Youth referred by the adult justice system average eighteen prior offenses and eleven prior felonies. During a residential stay that averages nine months, youth receive counseling, work at the facility, and gradually reintegrate into their home communities. The program's last phase involves release under a strict curfew and close follow-up by staff who help with job hunting and offer support in dealing with family conflicts. A follow-up study revealed that only one-third of participants were convicted of new crimes within three years of their release from the program. Only 36 percent of tracked youth returned to juvenile court, compared with 47 to 73 percent of youth in programs lacking treatment and reintegration components.

Contact Information

Violent Juvenile Offender Program
School of Criminal Justice
Rutgers University
15 Washington Street, 12th Floor
Newark, New Jersey 07102
201-648-1305

Target Serious Habitual Offenders

Strategy

Comprehensive action and targeted enforcement helps law enforcement agencies identify and apprehend serious, habitual juvenile offenders. Such programs are most effective when combined with community-based services aimed at reducing additional offenses by the same individual.

Crime Problem Addressed

An estimated 6 to 8 percent of juveniles are responsible for 80 percent of juvenile crime. State and local laws that restrict sharing of records on adjudicated cases involving juveniles have limited agencies' access to vital information on repeat juvenile offenders. Decisions of the juvenile justice system based on incomplete information on past offenses have resulted in sentences for habitual offenders that may not adequately protect the public. This strategy focuses on identifying and apprehending repeat offenders and ensuring that sentencing suits the crime committed.

Key Components

Established by the DOJ's Office of Juvenile Justice and Delinquency Prevention (OJJDP), the Serious Habitual Offender Comprehensive Action Program (SHOCAP) encourages information sharing among local law enforcement, probation, correctional, and social service agencies, as well as prosecutors, schools, and community-based organizations that serve youth.

The program's focal point is a database that lists serious, habitual juvenile offenders and integrates information gathered by all agencies and maintained by a local or state agency. Only staff of participating agencies can access the database's information. Profiles on each youth enhance case management and encourage interagency referrals for family support, therapy, and other aftercare services that reduce recidivism. In addition, participating agencies agree to procedures that address pretrial procedures, plea bargains, and sentences. Schools help the system by reporting crimes to the police, particularly those relating to serious, habitual offenders. The police monitor youth identified through the program, who sign a contract agree-

ing to a rehabilitation plan. Youth are removed from the SHO list after they show a year of good behavior as determined by the program's standards.

Key Partnerships

The relationships among participating agencies determine a SHOCAP's success. The agencies must establish procedures for sharing information and keeping the database updated. The program's success is enhanced when state agencies coordinate SHOCAPs in neighboring jurisdictions. Such coordination addresses concerns about offenders attempting to avoid sanctions by committing crimes in other communities. The partnership among agencies must also include outreach to community-based organizations that serve youth and families and can respond to the needs of youth who have been incarcerated.

Potential Obstacles

State policy prohibiting or limiting access to juveniles' records impedes SHOCAP implementation. Partnerships among local agencies and among localities can overcome this problem through education of state policymakers and community members concerned about confidentiality and "labeling" youth. Local officials should emphasize that the database's function is to facilitate assisting the youth and ensuring sanctions in line with community standards against violent crime.

Signs of Success

The Illinois Criminal Justice Authority administers the state's SHOCAP, OJJDP's pilot program. The Illinois program's database has enhanced the juvenile justice system's credibility by ensuring appropriate and consistent treatment of chronic juvenile offenders. The SHOs in the Illinois program are supervised by probation officers while they perform community service or work to pay restitution. A health center provides therapy, crisis intervention, and substance-abuse treatment referrals. The state's Department of Children and Family Services receives information on offenders victimized by child abuse or neglect.

The program's success has led the Illinois General Assembly to develop a policy allowing each county to develop SHOCAPs within guidelines that respect state confidentiality laws.

Applying the Strategy

Oxnard, California's SHOCAP helped identify the community's "top 40" juvenile offenders. Record sharing that increased the number of apprehensions and provided prosecutors with vital information helped reduce juvenile crime by 38 percent within four years. SHOCAP was implemented in conjunction with citizen patrols, a crime prevention program on local cable TV, community policing, and crime prevention surveys of residents' homes. In 1994 the city's crime rate was the lowest in twenty years.

Contact Information

Director, Drug Information and Analysis Center
Illinois Criminal Justice Information Authority
120 South Riverside Plaza, Suite 1016
Chicago, Illinois 60606
312-793-8550

Restitution by Juvenile Offenders

Strategy

Restitution to victims reinforces youth offenders' accountability to victims and the community while building self-esteem and job skills likely to help prevent repeat offenses.

Crime Problem Addressed

Nationwide, 16 percent of all arrests in 1992 involved juveniles younger than eighteen. According to the FBI, nearly 85 percent of arrests of juveniles involved property crimes and other nonviolent offenses. When the value of property stolen or damaged can be assessed, restitution programs enhance offenders' sense of personal responsibility, build empathy for victims, and reinforce consequences for criminal behavior.

Key Components

Restitution programs typically originate as a sentencing alternative imposed by the juvenile justice system on nonviolent offenders. Court-ordered community-service programs require juvenile offenders to work at jobs in public agencies or community organizations and contribute one-half to two-thirds of their stipend as payment for damages they caused. The sponsoring agency provides the stipends, although some programs require youth to work without pay at nonprofit agencies or city departments.

Many restitution programs have expanded to include education in job skills, life skills, values, and prevention. Some programs also include academic enrichment and tutoring for offenders or referrals to community-based service providers. Restitution programs are usually operated by juvenile courts, probation agencies, or community-based agencies working under contract for the court.

Key Partnerships

The program's effective operation requires that public agencies, community organizations, or private firms make jobs available to youth offenders. The juvenile justice agency and the court must develop an outreach program to build community support for this sentencing alternative and locate job opportunities for the youth participants. Community-based agencies can help support the program by integrating the work component with life-skills classes and job training and by helping participants understand how work builds self-esteem.

Potential Obstacles

Community members may advocate for incarceration of nonviolent, as well as violent, juvenile offenders. The agencies administering the program must concentrate on providing the youth with an array of services that bolster community acceptance as they help prevent additional offenses. Through its restitution provisions and its required training in job and survival skills, the program should concentrate on making youth more responsible and accountable.

Signs of Success

Eighty to 85 percent of youth offenders who participate in the Earn-It restitution program sponsored by the municipal court in Keene, New Hampshire, do not become repeat offenders. The sentencing alternative requires that nonviolent offenders set aside two-thirds of their earnings from court-arranged jobs to pay restitution to the individual or institution they victimized.

Applying the Strategy

Youth in the Juvenile Work Restitution Program in Graham, North Carolina, are assigned to work sites where they are supervised by the community agency that administers the program. Participants also attend a self-esteem and job-training course. The program reinforces personal responsibility and accountability by requiring that the youth write letters of apology to their victims.

Following a somewhat different model for restitution, California's juvenile justice system requires youth detainees to attend an "Impact of Crime on Victims" course as part of the crime prevention and law-related education curriculum. Since 1990 the California Youth Authority has invited victims advocates to speak to the youth, who have raised funds for specific victims and for community-based victims services programs. The program has given the youth social, problem-solving, and teamwork skills.

Contact Information

Earn-It Program Manager
Earn-It Keene Program
City Hall
3 Washington Street
Keene, New Hampshire 03431
603-357-9811

Director, Almanac Friends of Youth
124 West Elm Street
Graham, North Carolina 27253
910-228-7563

Boot Camps

Strategy

Physical conditioning, leadership, and counseling in a military-style setting diverts juvenile offenders from more expensive long-term residential detention while building life skills and discipline that the youth need to avoid criminal behavior when they return to the community.

Crime Problem Addressed

States and localities faced with overcrowding in juvenile detention facilities and concerned about public demands for tough sanctions on juvenile offenders have turned to juvenile "boot camps" as one method of preventing recidivism. Juveniles spend less time in boot camps, with their military-style discipline and conditioning programs, than in prison.

Key Components

Military-style physical conditioning and leadership training form the basis for the programs, which imitate, in a residential setting, a boot-camp orientation lasting 90 to 120 days. At any given time, the programs serve many youths, including those who would otherwise have been incarcerated. Whether their participation is mandatory or voluntary, the youths typically serve less time than those who are incarcerated.

Typically, current and former military personnel or law enforcement personnel from neighboring jurisdictions provide the training in physical conditioning and leadership. Program sites have included former military installations and facilities built by juvenile courts and correctional agencies.

Additional services include counseling, educational enhancement, and aftercare that includes help finding a job and intensive community supervision for a period following release.

Key Partnerships

Juvenile justice system partnerships with correctional agencies, military resources, and community-based programs help increase the likelihood that discipline imparted during the program will last through reintegration into the community. The program administrator must seek program support from local and state legislators by informing them that participation reduces recidivism and helps avoid the need for expanded juvenile detention facilities.

Potential Obstacles

Some members of the juvenile justice system oppose boot camps because they consider them too punitive and fear that their military-style discipline is abusive and may reinforce the type of confrontational and violent behavior that the detainees have already exhibited. Others in the community object to a program if its staff fails to reflect the youth population's diversity or its setting is far from the detainees' home communities. The program should establish clear goals for participants and definite selection criteria so that program interventions can be evaluated and revised as needed. Evaluations have shown that aftercare is critical.

Signs of Success

As of 1993, fifty-nine state and ten local boot camps had been established for adults in twenty-nine states. The nine boot camps for juvenile offenders typically offer significant counseling and rehabilitation services in addition to community reintegration programs.

In a 1993 Government Accounting Office study of boot camps, eleven of the twenty-six states surveyed reported that their programs helped reduce overcrowding in juvenile facilities. A recent National Institute of Justice (NIJ) report cites a New York Department of Correctional Services study that concluded, "without the boot camp program, the department would need 1,846 more beds." The same NIJ report cites Louisiana's estimate that its boot-camp program saved 154 beds.

Applying the Strategy

The About Face Program is a juvenile boot camp for non-violent males, aged fourteen through seventeen, sentenced by the Memphis, Tennessee, juvenile court. A Memphis State University evaluation found some promising changes among the 245 participants: an average improvement in academic achievement scores of one grade level; improved math and vocabulary performance; and changes in important psychological measures such as risk of addiction, commitment to goals, and attitudes about law and order. Although nearly half of the participants were rearrested during a twenty-month follow-up, that rate is considerably less than the rate among incarcerated youth who did not participate in the program. Also, program participants showed a dramatically reduced incidence of rearrest on cocaine-related charges; in general, those who were rearrested had committed much less serious offenses than rearrested nonparticipants.

Contact Information

Director of Operations, About Face
Youth Service USA
314 South Goodlet
Memphis, Tennessee 38124
901-452-5600

Teach Juveniles the Consequences of Violence

Strategy

Hospital-based or community programs that demonstrate the stark, lifelong consequences of violence for victims and offenders encourage offenders and other youth to avoid violent behavior.

Crime Problem Addressed

According to OJJDP-sponsored research, annually almost 7 percent of U.S. youth are victims of violent crime, and there are fourteen youth victims for every violent youthful offender arrested. Research by the National Association of Children's Hospitals and Related Institutions shows that the average cost of treating a child wounded by gunfire is more than $14,000, enough to pay for a year of college. Some experts estimate that the country spends as much as $14 billion annually to rehabilitate gunshot victims, many of whom require long-term stays in specialized treatment facilities.

Key Components

In the typical program, hospital-based and other health professionals give presentations to at-risk youth or youth offenders. The presentations detail the physical and other consequences of head and spinal cord injuries, examine risky violence-related behaviors of youth, and highlight the impact on injured victims and perpetrators through testimonials on the trauma caused by injury. Some programs include field trips to hospital trauma centers and films depicting consequences of violent and other risky behavior. Youth are referred to these programs by schools, court-sponsored programs, and community reintegration programs for juvenile offenders.

Key Partnerships

Programs dealing with violent behavior's physical consequences are based on partnerships among health professionals, the juvenile justice system, community-based programs serving at-risk or violent youth, and schools. While the health care facility presents an appropriate forum for the program, participation by community agencies that serve victims and by community-based counseling programs enhances the program's success.

Potential Obstacles

Busy hospital and trauma center staff may find it difficult to set aside time to administer and deliver the program. Additional resources from the health care facility, law enforcement, or community-based victim assistance services support program implementation. The stark details of violence's physical consequences can themselves be traumatic; the program must be carefully designed so that it sensitizes youth without unduly frightening them.

Signs of Success

The Southeastern Michigan Spinal Cord Injury Center operates an effective program in which paraplegic and quadriplegic victims of gun violence give youth presentations that demonstrate violent behavior's consequences. The testimonials reach the students in a way that lectures cannot. The program has developed effective partnerships among police, schools, and victims groups.

In 1989 the D.C. Hospital Center launched the Washington Community Violence Prevention Program. In two weeks of classes, middle school students receive instruction from a team of trauma nurses, victims from the community, and a lawyer. The program also includes field trips, education in administering first aid, training in conflict management, and realistic discussion of the extensive physical and emotional rehabilitation that victims of violence often require. Teens consider the program effective because it personalizes violence and reminds them that they must take responsibility in order to remain safe.

Applying the Strategy

The Think First program offered through the Head and Spinal Cord Injury Prevention Program of the Rehabilitation Institute of Chicago teaches students about injuries' consequences and leading causes, including violence and other risky behavior. In addition to viewing videos and holding discussions with health care professionals, the youth participants talk to victims of traumatic injury caused by violence. The institute tailors the program and

presentations to the audience, ensuring that the students share similar ethnic backgrounds with the speakers and victims.

Contact Information

Washington Community Violence Prevention Program
Washington Hospital Center, Room 4B-46
110 Irving Street, NW
Washington, DC 20010
202-877-6267

Coordinator, Head and Spinal Cord Injury Prevention
   Program
Rehabilitation Institute of Chicago
345 East Superior Street
Chicago, Illinois 60611
312-908-6000

Address Violence as a Public Health Problem

Strategy

Curricula and programs that focus on violence as a preventable public health problem encourage involvement of a wide array of community resources to address violence and its causes.

Crime Problem Addressed

From 1988 to 1994 the homicide rate among males fifteen to nineteen years old rose 154 percent, according to the Centers for Disease Control and Prevention. The American Psychological Association reports that homicide is now the leading cause of death for African-American youth. As reported in *Health Affairs* magazine, in 1987 physical injury from violent crime cost about $10 billion in health-related expenses and $23 billion in lost productivity; it also caused a reduction in the quality of life equivalent to $145 billion. The public health approach to violence focuses on prevention, particularly on education and action aimed at reducing violence-related risk factors.

Key Components

A successful public health campaign against violence requires violence prevention curricula, community coalitions, a public awareness campaign that involves the mass media, and clinical education and training.

Community- or school-based programs must foster conflict mediation, students' ability to manage anger, and other violence prevention skills in youth, teachers, and agencies that serve youth.

Coalitions should focus on identifying and addressing neighborhood-level risk factors for violence. Schools, par-

ents, community groups, the clergy, and business leaders all have resources to contribute. Coalitions spur local agencies and others to form a network of services. Referrals can connect youth and families to organizations and resources that work to prevent violence.

Community-wide campaigns, publicized through the mass media and through community-level resources, raise awareness about violence's impact on the community, help recruit resources to community-based coalitions, and reinforce community standards against violence by promoting healthy, nonviolent behavior.

Physicians, nurses, and other health care providers should be trained in violence prevention techniques, including ways to counsel youth and teach them to manage anger.

Key Partnerships

The group coordinating the campaign must seek broad representation of the community and key youth-serving organizations to ensure that the coalition reflects the array of resources that support violence prevention. Hospitals, clinics, and state health agencies must be mobilized to communicate violence prevention as a priority in their institutions. Business leaders can assist with resources needed to launch the public awareness campaign.

Potential Obstacles

Community residents' perceptions that violence is an intractable problem can be difficult to overcome. Effective community coalitions and coordination of services can overcome fear and inertia. A commitment, on the part of local political leaders, to ensuring coordination of service providers helps to address concerns about referring youth and families to those able to provide the assistance they need.

Signs of Success

In 1982 the Boston City Department of Health and Hospitals initiated a program to prevent youth violence. The program centered on a ten-session curriculum developed by physician Deborah Prothrow-Stith. Initially used in high school classrooms, the lessons—which present violence statistics and address ways to avert violence—have since become the building blocks of a more comprehensive effort to reach the whole community with information on preventing violence.

The nationally known program, which incorporates education and training for youth-serving agencies, has trained over five thousand individuals and two hundred agencies as of 1993. In addition, the Boston Violence Prevention Project contributed to the formation of the Community Coalition to Prevent Black Homicide, spurred development of the "Friends for Life, Friends Don't Let Friends Fight" media campaign and "Increase the Peace" weeks, distributed "teen survival" booklets at health and community centers, networked service providers, and trained nurses in methods of counseling youth hospitalized with intentionally inflicted injuries. Other city-sponsored efforts to increase community policing and partnerships

between youth and police have enhanced the program and contributed to declining youth homicide rates for each year from 1990 to 1994.

Applying the Strategy

The Injury Prevention and Control Unit of New Jersey's department of health focuses on violence prevention in the state's three urban areas with the highest rates of death from gunfire. The unit has trained health care professionals to recognize youth at risk for violent behavior, developed policies for physician referral of cases involving violence, and involved youth in advocacy of prevention policies. The agency is also involved in a statewide task force on school violence.

The Adolescent Violence Prevention Project of Hartford, Connecticut's city hospital includes a violence prevention curriculum. Supported by a local foundation, this successful program has resulted in a community-level coalition, has increased coordination among agencies that serve area youth and families, and has launched the "Chill B 4 It Gets 2 Hot" media campaign.

Contact Information

Boston Violence Prevention Project
Department of Health and Hospitals
1010 Massachusetts Avenue, 2nd Floor
Boston, Massachusetts 02118
617-534-5196

In-School Probation

Strategy

In-school probation keeps the nonviolent offender connected to the educational setting, helps ensure discipline, and enhances compliance with behavioral standards through intensive supervision provided by the probation officer.

Crime Problem Addressed

Daily, school districts throughout the country confront concerns about keeping juvenile probationers connected to the educational system whenever possible while maintaining discipline in the school. Police and probation departments view in-school probation as a strategy for monitoring the activities of youth on probation in a confined setting that provides a place for meetings with school officials, families, and youth-serving agencies.

Key Components

Probation agencies and school departments coordinate the placement of probation officers in school buildings. They

cooperate to address behavior standards for the students, assist with academic difficulties, and address absenteeism and discipline problems. The programs, which often teach school staff about the probation agency and teach probation personnel about the schools, show how services can be combined to avoid duplication and improve assistance to youth on probation and their families.

Key Partnerships

The participating agencies develop referral procedures, implement programs for involving parents, and establish links with substance abuse treatment, counseling, and other services needed by youth and their families.

Potential Obstacles

School officials and community leaders who oppose school-based probation usually do so because they believe that students on probation should be expelled or placed on long-term suspension to prevent them from disrupting the school environment. Communities without alternative school settings for such students should be encouraged to understand how in-school probation reinforces the discipline required in the school environment while keeping the youth in class and out of trouble in the community. The assignment of probation officers to the school should alleviate the concerns of some school officials who worry about the prospect of supervising students with a history of violent or other criminal offenses.

Signs of Success

Since 1990 the Juvenile Probation Department of Lehigh County, Pennsylvania, has assigned officers to four of the school district's middle schools. In 1993 the program expanded to include placement of probation officers in each of the two secondary schools. The officers serve as a liaison between the school and families, ensure that students on probation remain in school, intervene with referrals to treatment services when they encounter students with substance abuse problems, and participate with school staff in Student Assistance Program Teams. A project evaluation revealed a decrease in disciplinary problems in participating schools, including suspensions and detentions, and a decrease in absenteeism. The program has since been duplicated in twenty-nine other Pennsylvania locations. The Pennsylvania Commission on Crime and Delinquency offers the program to other counties.

Applying the Strategy

The Straight Talk About Risks Project in Conroe, Texas, combines in-school supervision of junior high school youth on probation with educational support. The program helps reduce disruptive behavior and build self-discipline among young probationers.

Contact Information

Chief Juvenile Probation Officer
Lehigh County Courthouse
455 Hamilton Street
P.O. Box 1548
Allentown, Pennsylvania 18105
610-820-3143

Pennsylvania Commission on Crime and Delinquency
P.O. Box 1167
Harrisburg, Pennsylvania 17108-1167
717-787-2040

Diversion From Incarceration

Strategy

Diversion of juvenile offenders into intensive monitoring and support programs in community settings provides localities with a less costly and more effective strategy for reducing recidivism among juveniles who have committed less serious offenses.

Crime Problem Addressed

Statistics cited in a *U.S. News & World Report* article indicate that juvenile crime increased by 250 percent from 1984 to 1994. The National School Boards Association reported in 1993 that one in four schools is vandalized each month, resulting in $200 million in maintenance and repair costs borne by local taxpayers. A National League of Cities survey of seven hundred cities revealed that school violence significantly increased from 1990 to 1994. This strategy aims to provide the juvenile justice system with an effective sentencing alternative for cases involving juvenile offenders convicted of property crimes or less serious violent crimes without sacrificing public safety.

Key Components

Typically developed in response to overcrowding in juvenile detention facilities and based on the belief that stability reduces the likelihood of rearrest, juvenile diversion programs include an array of community-based services to support the youthful offender, prevent reoffending through supervision, and promote academic and employment success. Programs are operated by juvenile courts or by community-based agencies under contract to the court.

An extensive evaluation of each youth provides casework staff with information needed to develop individualized treatment, supervision, and referral plans for each offender. Regular in-home meetings with families, school consultations, and any needed referrals to counseling and substance abuse treatment services help caseworkers track the progress of the youth assigned to them. The program staff serve as role models and mentors, keeping in almost daily contact with the youth and acting as their advocates within the juvenile justice and social service systems. Program staff may include court personnel, specially trained community organizations or university students, or social workers.

Key Partnerships

A successful program requires small caseloads for staff so that they have time to develop partnerships with the youth, family members, counselors, and others assisting the youth. Formal agreements among participating agencies help establish staff roles and responsibilities and ensure proper monitoring of the youth's progress in the program.

Potential Obstacles

Community members may resist diversion programs, believing that they represent inadequate punishment for juvenile offenders and may put the public at risk of additional victimization. Clear standards for participation must be developed to exclude the most violent offenders. Programs should track participants and collect information that demonstrates cost savings compared to incarceration and reduced recidivism among participants compared to that among other juveniles detained for similar offenses.

Signs of Success

The Michigan State Diversion Project for juveniles is based on the premise that juvenile offenders respond better to intervention implemented outside the juvenile justice system. Believing that the youth's family and community provide the best context for successful treatment, the program's implementers set up intensive monitoring, home visits, and school follow-up. The average age of youth participants was fourteen; on average, they appeared in court one and a half times for status offenses, property crimes, or less serious crimes against persons. The program paired different youth with different contacts—juvenile court staff, family members, or university students who stressed relationship building.

An evaluation of the program supports the view that connection with the juvenile justice system might increase the likelihood of rearrest. Sixty-seven percent of the youth paired with court personnel reoffended within two years, compared with only 46 percent of those in the group that focused on family relationships and 33 percent of those paired with a university student who emphasized relationship building.

Applying the Strategy

The Juvenile Upgrading Motivating Program in Cleveland, Tennessee, serves delinquent youth through the county juvenile court. A partnership between the court and the school system, the program provides judges with a sentencing alternative for juveniles who have committed minor offenses. The program focuses on improving student motivation, academic performance, and school attendance and on preventing rearrest. Students arrive at school at 7 a.m. for breakfast, group therapy, and educational progress reviews. Some students are permitted to opt into the program as part of a dropout prevention strategy agreed to by parents and school administrators. The program has become popular with school administrators and court officials who are pleased that discipline problems have declined, academic performance has improved, and attendance has improved for most student participants.

Contact Information

Department of Psychology
135 Snyder Hall
Michigan State University
East Lansing, Michigan 48824-1117
517-353-5015

Prevent Bullying

Strategy

School-based assistance programs for victims of bullies help prevent additional confrontations and establish a school climate in which fear and intimidation are not tolerated.

Crime Problem Addressed

As noted in the National Association of Secondary School Principals' *Report to Parents*, one in ten students surveyed in a study of 15 percent of the nation's students reported having been harassed or attacked by bullies. A study by Norwegian researcher Dan Olweus estimates that 2.1 million bullies and 2.7 million of their victims attend American schools. This strategy aims to prevent bullying, whether verbal or physical.

Bullying's consequences continue throughout a student's school years and beyond. Research shows that boy bullies will display life-long aggression problems if no one intervenes. One study found that boy bullies have a one-in-four chance of having a criminal record by the time they are thirty years old, whereas only one in twenty children who do not bully is likely to become a criminal. Research reveals that mothers who were aggressive as girls are more likely to punish their children harshly.

Key Components

School-based programs to prevent bullying typically focus on counseling bullies and their victims, teaching victims assertiveness, and establishing clear school policies that reinforce consequences for aggressive behavior. School officials train teachers and other staff to recognize bullies and their victims and refer both to counseling. School policies about fighting, taunting, and other bullying behaviors are made clear to both students and parents.

Key Partnerships

Schools and parents must cooperate in setting and communicating standards for student behavior that will be enforced when students bully others. Whenever possible, counseling programs should involve parents so that lessons about aggressive behavior can be reinforced at home.

Potential Obstacles

Parents who taunt or physically abuse their children may present an obstacle to school staff attempting to convey to students the importance of nonaggressive behavior. School staff must attempt to involve parents and provide them, when appropriate, with referrals to outside counseling and support resources. Some school officials may be reluctant to believe a serious bullying problem exists in the absence of a large number of fights on school grounds. School staff should be trained to notice signs of verbal bullying and intimidation and trained to understand them as just as serious as physical fighting.

Signs of Success

Dr. Olweus, who has studied programs successful in preventing bullying, recommends seven strategies: (1) adult supervision at recess, (2) strict enforcement of clear rules for student behavior, (3) consistent, nonphysical punishment of students who misbehave, (4) assistance to bullying victims that helps them to assert themselves, (5) parental encouragement that students develop and maintain friendships, (6) clear and positive communication between parents and school officials, and (7) clear and swift reaction to persistent physical or verbal bullying. Within its first

two years, a program based on these principles reportedly cut bullying incidents in half at the forty-two participating schools.

Applying the Strategy

The anti-bullying program in the schools of Southern Westchester County, New York, counsels bullies individually and in groups. The program provides incentives for bullies to change their behavior, cooperate with peers, and empathize with victims. Reportedly, this successful program's most effective aspect focuses on increasing victims' assertiveness, through counseling, role playing, and group discussions.

Set Straight on Bullies, an examination of bullying problems by the National School Safety Center (NSSC), provides insights on strategies that schools should consider. The NSSC also publishes other useful resources for school districts.

Contact Information

National School Safety Center
4165 Thousand Oaks Boulevard, Suite 290
Westlake Village, California 91362
805-373-9977

Department of Personality Psychology
University of Bergen, Box 25
N-5014 Bergen, Norway

Assist Child Victims

Strategy

Coordination of victim assistance services focused on the developmental needs of child victims of crime or abuse helps prevent additional victimization.

Crime Problem Addressed

Statistics reviewed by the National Council on Crime and Delinquency indicate that "childhood death at the hands of parents or guardians is much more prevalent than children being killed by other children. Estimates indicate that perhaps as many as 5,000 children die each year as a result of mistreatment and abuse from parents and guardians, and over 165,000 children are seriously harmed." A 1995 National Crime Prevention Council (NCPC) publication, *Preventing Violence Against Women*, highlights research on child abuse's long-term effects on victims. The document notes that "being abused as a child increases a person's risk for arrest as a juvenile by 53 percent, as an adult by 38 percent, and for violent crime by 38 percent." These statistics point out the importance of intervening early to mitigate abuse's effects on young victims.

Key Components

Many local and county agencies play a part in addressing the causes of violence, including family violence against youth. Coordinating those services among family courts, health professionals, counselors, prosecutors, and police helps ensure that appropriate services reach all victims in the family. Services for children include age-appropriate counseling, emergency housing for victims of domestic violence, and health evaluations of children from families in which spousal abuse has occurred. Task forces help social service agencies, law enforcement, the court system, health professionals, and school officials understand how to coordinate services that address youth's needs at home and in school.

Key Partnerships

Agencies' ability to meet victimized children's needs requires continual policy coordination regarding information sharing, service referrals, and enforcement against adult offenders. Schools and community-based organizations serving families and children should be encouraged to refer parents and children needing assistance to the task force or participating agencies.

Potential Obstacles

Policies, organizational structure, and budget issues sometimes make it difficult to coordinate services. Umbrella organizations that coordinate services for children reduce duplication of services and help meet the needs of child victims by ensuring that adult victims and offenders are treated or prosecuted. In some jurisdictions, one agency's political power, legal authority, or expertise results in its assuming leadership in matters of program coordination and delivery to youth victims.

Signs of Success

In the mid-1980s the staff of Boston's Children's Hospital helped establish Advocacy for Women and Kids in Emergencies (AWAKE). The program trains hospital staff, police officers, social workers, court staff, and nursing students in advocacy for mothers and children from families experiencing domestic violence. Staff of participating agencies help mothers receiving treatment at the hospital obtain legal advice, assistance from the courts, additional medical care, counseling, and help from support groups. The program also conducts counseling sessions and support group discussions specifically for children. Recently the program has expanded to include an advocacy program for women and children in a nearby housing project. In its first week, the housing project program received ten referrals.

Applying the Strategy

In 1992 a planning coalition on crime prevention formed between the grassroots and city government of Corpus Christi, Texas, recommended improved coordination of services to children and families. The Commission on Families and Children developed programs in parent education, child protection, and family support to address concerns about child abuse and the trauma experienced by children and adults when parents divorce. The commission has helped courts, social agencies, police, and schools better coordinate services.

In response to increasing child abuse and violence in schools in 1991, the Mental Health Association of Montgomery County, Maryland, helped organize a panel of local and county agencies to investigate how to better coordinate services to youth and families in the Washington, DC, suburbs. A conference of mental health, school, police, child welfare, and health service agencies resulted in formation of a task force to investigate how to improve referrals and delivery of services. Task force members successfully petitioned to retain two judgeships in the juvenile court to deal with cases involving children.

Contact Information

AWAKE
Children's Hospital
300 Longwood Avenue
Boston, Massachusetts 01225
617-355-7979

Regulations and Ordinances on Gun Licensing

Strategy

Licensing regulations and ordinances for gun dealers help localities control gun dealers' qualifications and promote gun safety education of those choosing to purchase guns from dealers.

Crime Problem Addressed

Guns kept in the home are more likely to be used in a suicide or the accidental shooting of a family member than in apprehension of a burglar or other intruder. In 1988 alone, firearms resulted in 1,501 unintentional deaths and were used in 18,169 suicides. Too often young children suffer gun-related injuries because they experiment with guns stored carelessly in their home. This strategy aims to prevent gun-related injuries by focusing on licensing requirements for gun dealers and imposition of ordinances requiring information on gun safety education on firearms sold by licensed dealers.

Key Components

Coordination between state and local law enforcement to develop gun safety education requirements for licensed gun dealers includes tags or labels identifying health and safety risks of firearms that occur when they are not operated properly and stored securely. Stiffened federal regulation of licenses for gun dealers aims to weed out licensees who do not receive or sell weapons on a regular basis. Implementation of licensing restrictions and gun safety education helps control the conditions under which legal firearms enter the community. Nineteen states have implemented statutes restricting handgun possession to adults over age twenty-one.

Key Partnerships

State and local legislatures and law enforcement agencies should cooperate to develop licensing requirements and safety education programs. Partnerships with associations of licensed dealers help ensure compliance with ordinances and regulation; representatives of such associations should be included among those who help review proposed ordinances and legislation.

Potential Obstacles

Some gun dealers and owners may view such policies as infringing on their right to sell legal weapons. Partnerships with local law enforcement and regulatory agencies help to ensure that dealers understand the audiences' potential benefits. The greatest obstacle is perhaps the large number of guns traded and sold illegally, a problem that cannot be addressed through licensing restrictions and local ordinance.

Signs of Success

A 1992 report by the Violence Policy Center revealed that the United States had more licensed gun dealerships than gas stations—280,000. In response, the Bureau of Alcohol, Tobacco, and Firearms (ATF) implemented stiffer licensing requirements and raised the licensing fee from $30 to $200. Applicants must now be fingerprinted, certify that they have complied with local laws and ordinances, and pass through more extensive background checks aimed at weeding out unscrupulous dealers. The National Alliance of Stocking Gun Dealers welcomed the new policy, which resulted in a 19 percent drop in the number of licensed gun dealers within three years.

Applying the Strategy

Concerned about accidental and intentional gun deaths in the area, in 1994 officials in Fulton County, Georgia, designed local legislation requiring that an information tag on gun education and safety be placed on each firearm sold through a licensed dealer. Failure to display the tags carries a fine of $500 and imprisonment not to exceed sixty days. Local law enforcement agencies monitor the county's 260 licensed dealers. Since the law passed, county agencies have been deluged with calls from other jurisdictions that want to adopt similar laws. The program's total cost is less than $10,000, including printing and delivery of the tags and posters that explain the program.

In 1995 Pasadena, California, became the nation's first city to pass a local ordinance requiring registration of handgun ammunition purchases. Established at the insistence of Pasadena's police chief and the eight hundred members of the Coalition for a Non-Violent City. Though largely symbolic, the ordinance is one component of a comprehensive antiviolence strategy that incorporates policing enhancements, a crackdown on gangs, and numerous prevention programs. According to one city council member who supported the legislation, "Voting 'yes' affirmed that we will take any step, no matter how small, that is going in the right direction."

California does not permit purchase of a gun until the potential buyer has taken a gun safety course or passed a test on gun safety. Minnesota added conviction on spousal abuse charges to the list of violations that prohibit purchase of a firearm in that state.

Contact Information

Violence Policy Center
1300 N Street, NW
Washington, DC 20005
202-822-8200

Fulton County Department of Information and Public
   Affairs
141 Pryor Street, SW, Suite 3090
Atlanta, Georgia 30303
404-730-8305

Promote Nonviolent Images of Youth

Strategy

Television and radio programs and print media offer opportunities to promote prevention of youth violence and convey positive images of youth concerned about their community's safety.

Crime Problem Addressed

A 1995 American Medical Association (AMA) study gave the United States a D grade on efforts to reduce violence. As reported in *USA Today*, by the time they reach junior high school, children have seen eight thousand killings and a hundred thousand other violent acts on TV. According to the OJJDP report *Juvenile Offenders and Victims: A Focus on Violence*, "with some notable exceptions, percentage increases in juvenile and adult arrests have been roughly similar over the past 10 years." Many youth complain that a media focus on violent and irresponsible youth distorts the reality of America's youth. This strategy aims to use the media to portray positive images of youth and provide a forum in which youth can discuss strategies for preventing violence. Through this forum, youth can increase awareness among their peers and adults.

Key Components

Building on the idea of local cable TV and radio shows featuring community crime prevention and "Teen Summit," a teen talk show that airs weekly on Black Entertainment Television, many cities are initiating televised discussion forums for youth in their communities. Believing that information about violence helps identify solutions as well as problems, these programs air youth's views and show teens concerned about public safety and violence prevention.

Typically produced by the youth themselves, the programs address issues related to violence, such as family, relationships, media images of youth, entertainment, racism, drugs, and gangs. Often the shows give youth a chance to make policymakers and other adult guests aware of their concerns. The youth involved in the program's production also learn job skills.

Key Partnerships

The program's success relies on partnerships among youth leaders, organizations that serve youth, and the media. University media departments and media outlets can provide professionals to guide youth working on a production job, helping them to develop program content, obtain publicity, and recruit guests. City and community-based agencies help by providing information on programs to prevent violence, statistics on violence, and other information key to the development of program content.

Potential Obstacles

Business-oriented media outlets could be reluctant to help develop reality-based youth programming, believing it too controversial, confrontational, or unlikely to attract a large audience. Ultimately, media outlets control program content, so their perspective must be considered and balanced with youth participants' views. Increased publicity or boosted ratings achieved through the show's popularity could provide a powerful incentive for media outlets to air youth-oriented programming on violence prevention.

Signs of Success

In February 1994, members of New Haven, Connecticut's Anti-Crime Youth Council met with local media representatives to suggest ways the media could help prevent violence and "more responsibly report on school violence and youth activities." Sponsored by a New Haven congresswoman, the council is a youth leadership program and violence prevention coalition of students from New Haven and seventeen surrounding communities. The discussion resulted in a plan to produce a series of hard-hitting teen talk shows focused on preventing youth violence and modeled on the mission of the Corporation for Public Broadcasting's National Campaign to Reduce Youth Violence. After the program was promoted at high schools throughout the region, the first "Choices" program aired on six cable stations in November 1994. The episode featured the topic of youth violence and debate among youth participants. Six months later a second program focused on the connection between youth violence and the music industry. The council plans additional episodes of the popular program.

Applying the Strategy

Proyecto Pastoral, a church-based community organization in east Los Angeles, offers programs in which youth supervise younger peers and help prevent gang-related and other violence. In addition to providing youth with recreation and training in conflict management, the programs include employment projects in five area public housing communities. Supported by the California Wellness Foundation, the organization produces a quarterly newsletter and plans to produce a youth-oriented talk show, "Tell It Like It Is," in partnership with a local cable affiliate. The residents and local agencies who are working together believe that the show will provide an important forum through which to inform the broader community of the positive contributions and concerns of east Los Angeles youth.

Contact Information

New Haven Anti-Crime Youth Council
c/o Congresswoman Rosa DeLauro
265 Church Street
New Haven, Connecticut 06510
203-562-3718

Involve Youth in Violence Prevention

Strategy

Youth should be involved in planning and carrying out strategies to prevent violence in their communities. They contribute a valuable perspective on the problem as they build skills that will help them make positive contributions to their neighborhoods.

Crime Problem Addressed

As indicated by OJJDP statistics, the risk of being a victim of violence has increased 17 percent for youth aged twelve to seventeen and 24 percent for young adults aged eighteen to twenty-four. In 1991 nearly 1.5 youth were victims of violent crime. OJJDP reports that juveniles were responsible for approximately one in five violent crimes. The potential for victimization of youth and perceptions that most violence is caused by youth have led many communities to mobilize youth to help solve one of society's most pressing problems.

Key Components

Youth who participate in projects to prevent crime and violence play many roles: they join task forces of planning coalitions, volunteer in community-based prevention projects, mediate conflicts in schools and the community, perform in prevention-focused programs for younger children, counsel peers, and organize neighborhood antidrug and anticrime events. Many successful programs involve at-risk and other teens. The element that unifies the diverse activities is openness to full participation by youth whose leadership, commitment, experience, and skills support the community's goals.

Key Partnerships

Partnerships in preventing youth violence should include youth at all levels of activity. Their role should be considered as vital as that of adults.

Potential Obstacles

The attitude of some adult policymakers and leaders that youth are the source of communities' violence problems is a difficult bias to overcome. Forums in which youth can present their views help raise awareness of the skills and experience that the community's youth have to offer. Training youth to advocate prevention increases their ability to have a long-term effect on policy and programs.

Signs of Success

Youth as Resources programs in over twenty communities in several states empower youth to address social issues in their neighborhoods. Concerned young people identify issues, develop strategies, and manage budgets. Com-

munity boards disperse funds to youth to implement projects to fight crime and violence. Youth participants have developed antidrug videos for their peers, built playgrounds, painted over graffiti, counseled their friends, and supported programs for elderly neighbors and crime victims. Supported by the NCPC, evaluations of the program reveal that it builds leadership and altruism among participants as it enables them to help prevent crime in their cities.

Applying the Strategy

Teens on Target is a peer education program established by Youth Alive in partnership with Oakland, California's Unified School District and Pediatric Spinal Injury Service. Formed after two high school students were shot by peers, the program trains high-risk students to advocate violence prevention by educating and mentoring their peers and younger children on gun violence, drugs, and family conflict. The youth arrange trips to local hospital emergency rooms to give their peers a first-hand look at violence's impact on victims.

Decatur, Georgia's Ujima project involves the community's youth in "Peace in the Streets" rallies, unit campaigns, antiviolence projects, and other activities that serve the community's interests.

The Indochinese Mutual Assistance Association in San Diego plans to train more than a hundred youth to serve as mentors and tutors. The community-based collaborative of ethnic and social service organizations provides culturally based violence prevention and leadership training to Cambodian, Hmong, Lao, and Vietnamese youth in the city's southeastern neighborhoods.

Contact Information

Youth as Resources
National Crime Prevention Council
1700 K Street, NW
Washington, DC 20006
202-466-6272, ext. 151

Educate University Students About Crime Prevention

Strategy

Educating university students about crime prevention increases their ability to protect themselves and encourages them to assist victims.

Crime Problem Addressed

Crime on university campuses is an ongoing problem. Thousands of students, many of them away from home for the first time, live on campuses in close quarters. Often,

university students know little about protecting themselves or recognizing potential crime risks. State legislation and the federal Higher Education Amendments of 1992 have reinforced standards for campus police services, the safety of campus grounds and buildings, and services for victims. High-profile crimes at universities have resulted in requirements that school administrations report on-campus crime to the police.

Key Components

Many universities now provide crime prevention information and victim services to secure the campus for students and staff. Crime prevention activities include safety awareness orientations for incoming students; training for dormitory staff; seminars for students on preventing sexual assault; programs that educate male students about rape awareness and prevention; escort services and shuttle buses; emergency phones at key locations throughout the campus; educational, counseling, medical, and legal support services for victims; personal defense classes; and strict behavior codes for students that call for sanctions against those who commit crime.

Key Partnerships

University officials should bring students, faculty, and staff into a partnership to identify security and crime concerns on campus and develop solutions that include student participation as peer counselors, security assistants, trainers, and speakers.

Potential Obstacles

University officials may be reluctant to develop crime prevention programs out of a fear that such programs could label the school as one with a crime problem and drive away potential students. Student inaction about potential victimization or the need to support victims can be overcome through education and outreach through student leaders. Students who binge drink are especially vulnerable to crime because their senses and judgement are impaired. In a 1994-released AMA survey of nearly eighteen thousand college students, 47 percent of students who binge drink reported several problems, including unprotected or otherwise dangerous sexual activity. It is difficult to estimate how many sexual assaults occur when the offender, the victim, or both are incapable of thoughtful judgement.

Signs of Success

In 1990 the murders of five University of Florida, Gainesville, students in their off-campus apartment shocked and frightened the school's students and administrators. Basing its safety campaign on information gathered from the NCPC's *Together for a Safe Campus* kit, the campus police began a major public education effort to protect students, faculty, and staff from crime. The police boosted awareness of an escort service and emergency phone network and made crime prevention presentations to students. The program was a striking success. In the first few weeks alone, the number of students using the escort service quadrupled. Violent crime on campus dropped 26 percent during the 1990 fall semester. By fall 1991, the program was inundated with requests for presentations on crime prevention.

Applying the Strategy

George Mason University, in Virginia, recently hired a Sexual Assault Services Coordinator to supplement the campus's crisis and victim services. The coordinator provides educational programs, training, and advocacy; intercedes with faculty in behalf of victims; and works with the campus police on emergency communication systems, a speakers bureau on crime prevention, and orientation sessions for students and housing staff.

Contact Information

Together for a Safe Campus
Public Information Officer
University of Florida Police
Building 51, Museum Road
P.O. Box 112150
Gainesville, Florida 32611
904-392-1114

Coordinator, Sexual Assault Services
George Mason University
Fairfax, Virginia 22030-4444
703-993-4364

Train School-Age Youth To Mediate Conflicts

Strategy

Nationwide many schools and communities have implemented student training in conflict mediation. School-based programs in conflict mediation give youth participants the communications, decisionmaking, and anger management skills they need to remain resilient against violence in their community.

Crime Problem Addressed

In 1993 Southeastern Regional Vision for Education surveyed more than five hundred teens on violence in school: 83 percent had witnessed a fight, 16 percent had seen a student assault a teacher, 20 percent had seen a student threaten to use a knife, and 7 percent had witnessed a threat made by someone armed with a gun. Many of these situations resulted from poor communication among peers, taunts or threatening language, lack of clear and consistent standards of conduct, and fear. This strategy aims to train students so that they can mediate conflict among their peers and give other youth more effective communications and problem-solving skills.

Key Components

School-based mediation programs improve students' communication skills and train students in violence prevention so that they can mediate conflicts among their peers. When a dispute occurs on school grounds, the parties involved seek out a teacher or the program's adult coordinator. The coordinator, who is usually the youth participants' mentor, assigns peer mediators to intervene and attempt to resolve the dispute without violence, through the parties' mutual agreement and commitment to a contract with set standards for conduct. Conflict resolution through mediation often substitutes for detention or suspension of youth involved in fights, verbal threats, or intimidation of others on school grounds. Training for student mediators must be age-appropriate and develop skills in active listening, effective communication, and anger management.

Programs should also train teachers, administrators, and staff to ensure that they interact with one other and with students in recommended ways. School administrators recruit youth mediators. A key strategy of successful programs is to recruit students whose gender, race, economic status, academic performance, and age reflect the student body's diversity.

Key Partnerships

School administrators and staff should team up to train students. They should track the program's impact on fighting, suspension rates, disciplinary referrals, and student opinions on crime and safety. Students and parents should be consulted on the program's design and given information that encourages use of recommended techniques in the family and community. Religious leaders and other key figures in the community should reinforce the program in their daily work. Local businesses can help support information dissemination that advances the program's goals.

Potential Obstacles

Lack of adequate funds for staff to train students and faculty and coordinate mediator assignments is a major obstacle to a peer mediation program. Also, convincing students and staff that violence can be prevented can be difficult. A group of mediators representative of the school community can promote nonviolence to all sectors of the student population.

Signs of Success

The New Mexico Center for Dispute Resolution has developed a nationally recognized curriculum of dispute resolution and conflict management. Already successful at implementing community mediation programs, the center began the school-based program to help ensure that young students are introduced to nonviolence as their environment's social norm. The program has two primary components—a curriculum designed to give youth vital skills and dispute mediation by peers assisted by a teacher/trainer. Now operative in most of the state's elementary schools, the program will soon expand to include students in middle and high schools.

A comprehensive evaluation showed significant gains in conflict resolution and social skills among participants, dramatic reductions in on-campus fighting, and increased self-confidence among students. The center also offers an array of effective mediation services for parents and for youth in correctional facilities.

Applying the Strategy

New York's Resolving Conflict Creatively Program is cosponsored by the city's public schools and Educators for Social Responsibility. Seventy percent of teachers involved in the nationally recognized program say it has resulted in less name-calling, less classroom violence, and more cooperation and understanding among students. The program has helped teachers understand the value of letting students take responsibility for solving their problems with peers.

In Kansas City's high schools, volunteers from the *Lawyers Association's* Young Lawyers section train student response teams to mediate conflicts. The teams encourage students involved in disputes to avoid confrontation at school.

Contact Information

New Mexico Center for Dispute Resolution
620 Roma Avenue, NW, Suite B
Albuquerque, New Mexico 87102
505-247-0571

Support for Victims

Strategy

Community-based victim assistance programs operated in partnership with policing agencies effectively combine support for victims with education aimed at preventing additional victimization.

Crime Problem Addressed

In the NIJ-sponsored study *Understanding and Preventing Violence*, researcher Jeffrey Roth notes that 2.9 million Americans were victims of serious but nonfatal violence in 1990. Roth cites *National Victimization Survey* statistics indicating that 3.1 million assaults occurred that same year. Though daunting, these statistics don't include many cases of domestic violence. And, as Roth notes, "no statistics fully capture the devastating effects of violence on local communities—their economies, neighborhoods, and quality of life." This strategy aims to increase community support for victims of crime.

Key Components

Victims of crime need a variety of support systems to help them deal with the physical, emotional, financial, and legal consequences of their victimization. Services offered by community-based programs include help coping with the trauma of violent victimization, help filing victim compensation claims and insurance forms, help accessing long-term rehabilitation treatment, hospital visitation, self-protection education to help prevent revictimization, advocacy and liaison with the police regarding filing a complaint and making a statement, crisis intervention and support groups for victims, and guidance through court proceedings. Community-based groups often train police officers to deal with victims and be able to refer them to the array of supportive services available throughout the community.

Key Partnerships

Community volunteers active in crime prevention, hospital and other health professionals, police officers, emergency services personnel, and former victims can combine forces to help victims by establishing a network of services for victims.

Potential Obstacles

Distribution of resource directories throughout the community and at agencies that serve victims, as well as public education campaigns that advertise service providers, can remedy low awareness of local government and community-based resources that assist victims.

Signs of Success

Since 1981 Philadelphia's community-based program Northwest Victims Services (NVS) has worked on behalf of crime victims in four police districts, serving four hundred thousand of the city's residents. NVS strives to meet victims' emotional, social, and financial needs while serving as a community resource that increases safety and reduces fear among residents. A primary purpose of NVS is to increase cooperation among community groups and city agencies. On average, NVS annually assists 1,800 victims, 75 percent of whom are victims of violent crime. Paid staff and volunteers provide crisis counseling and referrals, support victims through court proceedings, help meet victims' medical and financial needs, help victims fill out compensation and insurance claims, and advise victims on ways to prevent crime.

Dozens of local residents have helped train police to work with victims, established block watches in their neighborhoods, and created a network of organizations that assist victims. Other programs involve hospital visits and, in cooperation with police, education offered through the Crimes Against the Elderly and Retired Unit.

Applying the Strategy

Fairfax County, Virginia's police department established the Victim Witness Assistance Program, which offers counseling, aid to witnesses, confidential 24-hour assistance, crisis intervention, and support groups. Free of charge, the Fairfax Peer Survivors Group offers families of homicide victims services that help them recover from emotional trauma. The group encourages such families to investigate policies and laws that support victims, educates them about crime prevention, helps them network with other victims and support services, and publishes a quarterly newsletter. Police and victims have also campaigned for state laws to assist victims.

Contact Information

Northwest Victims Services
6008 Wayne Avenue
Philadelphia, Pennsylvania 19144
215-438-4410

Fairfax County Victim Witness Assistance Program
Fairfax County Police Department
3911 Woodburn Road
Fairfax, Virginia 22030
703-691-2131

Counsel Children Who Witness Violence

Strategy

Counseling and treatment for young children who have witnessed violence helps prevent them from viewing violence as an appropriate response to stress, anger, or conflict.

Crime Problem Addressed

Like adult victims, children who witness family violence are especially likely to respond to conflict, anger, or stress with violence. In addition, they are vulnerable to traumatic stress disorder, which can impair their ability to perform in school, develop healthy relationships, and deal with conflict in nonviolent ways. This strategy aims to provide child victims with psychological counseling and other support so that they can cope with trauma.

Key Components

Typically offered through trained hospital staff or volunteer health professionals, services focus on counseling to help overcome the trauma experienced by children who have witnessed violence. Usually the children belong to families troubled by spousal abuse. Counselors teach anger management, stress reduction, and techniques for resolving conflict. Some programs operate hotlines and train teachers and personnel in the criminal justice system. Health professionals, teachers, police, and family court personnel refer the children to the programs.

Key Partnerships

School, police, hospital, and court personnel trained to understand the needs of children who witness violence can support the program by referring children in need. Volunteer psychologists and other health professionals help reduce the program's costs.

Potential Obstacles

Perceptions about the cost of treatment may keep parents, educators, or others from referring children from low-income families. Lack of awareness that such services are available at little or no cost to those in need prevents children from obtaining help unless health personnel and police publicize the program to youth and organizations that serve youth.

Signs of Success

Research indicates that young children who see violence accept it as appropriate unless someone intervenes with counseling and education. Alert to this reality, health personnel and police in New Haven, Connecticut, have teamed up to provide counseling to young children who witness violence. The police identify children who have witnessed violence reported to them and refer those children for therapy. The program, operative for more than a decade, has served thousands of area children.

The Child Witness to Violence Project at Boston City Hospital counsels child witnesses and their family members. Since 1992 the program has provided advocacy services and trained child care, health, and criminal justice personnel to recognize traumatic stress in children who have witnessed violence. Across town at another hospital, the Good Grief Program supports children who have experienced—in many cases, witnessed—the death of a family member or friend from violence. Like Boston City Hospital's project, the Good Grief Program consults parents, teachers, and school administrators regarding children's progress in the program.

Applying the Strategy

Following the recommendations of a Child Victim Witness Advisory Committee, California's attorney general implemented a Child Victim Witness Pilot Project that uses trained interviewers and multidisciplinary teams to counsel and process witnesses in child abuse and related cases. An evaluation of the two-county project revealed that it has helped streamline and otherwise improve local investigations.

Contact Information

Director, Child Witness to Violence Project
Boston City Hospital
Division of Developmental and Behavioral Pediatrics
818 Harrison Avenue
Boston, Massachusetts 02118
617-534-4244

Family Therapy To Address Conflict and Delinquency

Strategy

Counseling from a trained therapist helps families manage conflict and address antisocial or delinquent behavior in children. Treatment emphasizes positive family interactions and clear standards for behavior.

Crime Problem Addressed

Each year in the United States, thousands of children enter out-of-home care because of family conflict or delinquency and millions experience significant conflict resulting from a family divorce. In 1991 alone 2.7 million incidents of child abuse were reported. Each year an estimated half million children run away from home, a quarter of whom are reported as unwanted by their parents or guardians. Researchers consistently link delinquent and violent behavior of juveniles to the absence of a supportive family environment. This strategy aims to prevent family conflict and disintegration through counseling and education of all family members.

Key Components

According to research conducted for the OJJDP and catalogued in *Guide for Implementing the Comprehensive Strategy for Serious, Violent, and Chronic Juvenile Offenders*, effective therapies for family conflict and disintegration typically focus on children's antisocial behavior, poor family management, conflict within the family, and other problems that prevent family members from interacting in a positive way. Interventions promote bonding, healthy beliefs, and clear standards of behavior, through reinforcement of positive behaviors. Therapy programs typically follow up on participants a year after the intervention's conclusion, to determine whether behavioral changes were sustained.

Key Partnerships

Therapy programs that establish partnerships with schools and hospitals increase referrals of families needing services. Juvenile court and school officials can supply important information about family therapy's long-term effects on juvenile delinquency and family functioning.

Potential Obstacles

Families required to undergo therapy are less likely to benefit than those who participate by choice. In addition, families who enter therapy to prevent conflict and delinquency should be treated differently than those attempting to reverse parents' antisocial behavior or children's delinquency.

Signs of Success

According to the OJJDP guide mentioned above, "two meta-analyses have demonstrated the general effectiveness of marital and family therapy in reducing family conflict, family management problems, and children's antisocial behavior." In addition, "for families with children or adolescents with behavior problems or parents with mental health problems, family therapy significantly improved post-test family interaction, child behavior, and parents' level of functioning in comparison to other therapeutic interventions." Another study examined a Utah program that reinforced desired behaviors, trained parents and children in communications skills, and developed techniques for reforming behavior. In that program, "significantly fewer siblings of identified delinquents whose families received . . . therapy had juvenile court records" than did siblings of delinquents whose families received less intensive therapy or none at all. This effect lasted up to three and a half years after the therapy's conclusion. The recidivism rate among identified delinquents whose families had participated was significantly lower (26 percent) than that among youth whose families had not participated (47 to 73 percent).

Applying the Strategy

The Silver Spring Neighborhood Center in Milwaukee offers therapy and counseling to delinquent youth and their families. The program's goal is to identify and address the causes of negative behaviors and associations in youth assigned to the program after being arrested for delinquency or less serious violent offenses. For delinquent youth aged nine to thirteen, the program provides therapy and recreation, group discussions, and group family therapy. Within one year of the program's inception, many participants showed improved self-esteem and family relationships. Only one-third of the youth continued to show antisocial, destructive behavior.

Contact Information

Department of Psychology
University of Utah
Salt Lake City, Utah 84112

Silver Spring Neighborhood Center
5460 North 64th Street
Milwaukee, Wisconsin 53218
414-463-7950

Gun Court

Strategy

Local courts that deal exclusively with gun law violations reinforce community standards against violence and ensure swift punishment of violators.

Crime Problem Addressed

According to FBI statistics, handguns were used to murder 13,220 people in the United States in 1991 alone. That figure represents a 10 percent increase from 1990. According to the 1994 DOJ report *Guns and Crime*, "In 1992, people armed with guns committed nearly one million violent crimes." ATF statistics indicate that U.S. citizens privately own more than 210 million firearms, 71 million of which are handguns. Increasing concern about violent crime committed with guns has led many states and localities to pass legislation stiffening penalties for felony violations of handgun possession laws. This strategy addresses cases involving violations of those laws by segregating those cases from others, requiring quick resolution, and ensuring swift punishment of those convicted.

Key Components

Modeled after drug courts and other local courts devoted to particular issues, gun courts take only cases that involve violation of firearm possession laws or the use of guns to commit a crime. The courts commit to resolving the case within a specified time and ensure mandatory prison terms for those convicted. The segregation of gun-related cases builds expertise among the prosecution and judicial staff, enhances familiarity with repeat offenders' records, and helps eliminate or reduce case backlogs and uneven application of sentencing guidelines.

Key Partnerships

A partnership of court, police, and prosecutors aids in assigning cases to the specialized court. Publicity about the court builds public support for assigning court personnel to a single-issue court system and for sentencing applied through the court. Court partnerships with state legislatures improve the chances of changing laws to permit mandatory sentences for gun-related cases.

Potential Obstacles

Local and state judiciaries sometimes resist formation of issue-specific courts, believing that one such court begets another, posing the threat of increased court-system fragmentation and cost. Some defense lawyers claim that issue-specific courts give undue weight to the charges against the defendant, reducing the chances for a fair trial. Gun courts' success in expediting cases, applying stiff but appropriate sentences, and relieving other sectors of local courts from the burden of multiple gun cases constitutes strong evidence against such opposition.

Signs of Success

Within four months of implementing a gun court, Providence, Rhode Island, convicted twenty defendants on gun charges, sent them to jail, and reduced the backlog of gun-related cases by two-thirds. In a survey of gun cases prior to the court's establishment, the city found that only about 25 percent of defendants had gone to jail and only 10 percent had received a jail sentence of more than two years. In the new gun court, all cases are tried within sixty days and most convictions carry mandatory prison terms, including ten years to life for a third offense. The court is popular with the public, which appreciates the resultant swift and sure punishment for violators. The mayor garnered program support from both the National Rifle Association (NRA) and local advocates of gun control. The NRA has already spent $10,000 on billboards, placed around the city, that announce, "Gun Court Is Now in Session."

Applying the Strategy

Concerned about the rising number of juveniles caught with firearms, the family court in Birmingham, Alabama, created a juvenile gun court in 1995. Since state laws prohibit juveniles from carrying guns, the court has considered penalizing parents or requiring that they attend an education program on gun safety.

Contact Information

Assistant Administrator, Superior Court
250 Benefid Street
Providence, Rhode Island 02903
401-277-3288

Court Programs To Assist Victims of Domestic Violence

Strategy

Court-based domestic violence programs that help victims understand court proceedings, exercise their right to prosecute their abuser, and obtain referrals to services outside the court system enhance victims' ability to make informed decisions, reducing the likelihood of additional victimization.

Crime Problem Addressed

According to the 1995 NCPC publication *Preventing Violence Against Women*, women in the United States annually experience an estimated 1.8 to 4 million assaults by husbands or boyfriends. Studies by the AMA and others indicate that 20 to 30 percent of women who seek medical treatment in hospital emergency rooms do so because they have been physically abused by a partner. In most jurisdictions, police who respond to calls involving domestic violence must arrest a suspect unless there is a compelling reason not to. Such policies and heightened public awareness of domestic violence have increased the number of cases before local courts. This strategy aims to prevent additional victimizations by ensuring that court systems are sensitive to victims' needs.

Key Components

Court-based programs for victims of domestic violence are more recent than community-based organizations and specialized police units. The programs' goal is to enhance the court system's effectiveness in responding to physically abused spouses, particularly by increasing victims' awareness of the court's readiness to take action against the offender. Training for court personnel focuses on understanding victims' financial, emotional, and medical needs and informing victims of their legal rights, such as the right to obtain a protective order or pursue their abuser. The programs also seek to increase cooperation among courts, police, prosecutors, and community advocates for victims.

Key Partnerships

Court partnerships with victim advocacy groups and shelters facilitate training of court personnel in dealing with victims and ensure awareness among court personnel of community-based services for victims.

Potential Obstacles

The court may resist providing services to victims because of potential costs or the belief that court personnel are not trained to provide such services. Local and state law can help establish expectations for family courts and increase the likelihood that victims of domestic violence will receive consistent treatment. The court's advice to victims must be tempered by the knowledge that no one set of prosecutorial responses or victim services is appropriate in every case. Each victim's case and concerns are unique and call for whichever techniques are best suited to preventing additional victimization.

Signs of Success

Family Violence State-of-the-Art Court Programs, published in 1992 by the National Council of Juvenile and Family Court Judges (Reno, Nevada), examines eighteen of the best court programs that support victims of domestic violence. The publication identifies elements common to successful programs, including services to victims and batterers, coordination with prosecutors, and efforts to change laws affecting victims and their children. Services for victims include education regarding their legal rights, help filing charges and obtaining protection orders and custody, and help obtaining medical, counseling, legal, and financial support through agencies outside the court system.

Applying the Strategy

Seeking to go beyond enforcing the law against those who commit domestic violence, the city of Quincy, Massachusetts, in 1977 designed Emerge, a strict pretrial probation and drug treatment program for offenders, and developed procedures for informing victims about the services available to help them cope with the physical and emotional trauma of abuse. In the few short years since Emerge's inception, many more women have pursued abuse claims through the court and more abusers have completed treatment programs. In 1991 Quincy experienced no homicides related to domestic violence, whereas neighboring jurisdictions that lack programs like Quincy's each experienced more than a dozen.

Contact Information

Center for the Prevention of Sexual and Domestic
    Violence
1914 North 34th Street, Suite 105
Seattle, WA 98103
206-634-1903

National Council of Juvenile and Family Court Judges
P.O. Box 8970
Reno, Nevada 89507
702-784-4829

Family Violence State-of-the-Art Court Programs (1992,
    100 pages, $15/copy)

Treatment for Male Batterers

Strategy

While not an insurance policy against future abuse, mandated treatment programs for male batterers reduce the incidence of additional physical abuse of spouses.

Crime Problem Addressed

Domestic violence remains underreported in the United States. As mentioned above, annually an estimated 1.8 to 4 million women are assaulted by intimate partners. A 1994 Older Women's League study contends that 1.4 million women aged forty-five to sixty-five were physically abused by their partners. Consistently, statistics indicate that nearly all batterers who do not receive treatment abuse again. Treatment programs can reduce the likelihood of repeat abuse.

Key Components

The long-term counseling programs for batterers now mandated in some localities train batterers (90 percent of whom are men) to take full responsibility for their behavior, adopt new ways of communicating with their partner and children, learn to respect and appreciate the opinions of their family members, understand the effects of abuse on their partner and the children, and identify and change attitudes that lead to abusive behavior. The training occurs through several months of group counseling. While abused partners may also receive counseling, counseling of batterers is handled separately so that batterers cannot abuse or coerce their partner during counseling. In group counseling guided by psychologists, batterers challenge one another to change their attitudes and behaviors.

Key Partnerships

Community-based and court-ordered counseling programs for batterers rely on partnerships with police and court officials to locate men needing treatment referrals. Programs for male batterers join forces with victim assistance programs to track how male participants fare in their continuing relationships with wives and ex-wives.

Potential Obstacles

Many spouses, police personnel, and court personnel do not believe that counseling for batterers reduces the likelihood that battering will continue. That sentiment can make it difficult to obtain the resources needed to support the program. Also, most batterers strongly resist admitting to their abusive behavior, reducing the chances of progress through treatment.

Signs of Success

Founded in 1977 and located in three major metropolitan areas of Massachusetts, Emerge offers treatment to abusive males on sliding fee scales and works on the assumption that battering is a learned behavior that can be unlearned through counseling and education. The court-mandated program is divided into two stages. In the first stage, abusive men participate in eight group sessions, each lasting two hours, in which education and counseling help them plan how they will change their behavior. In the second stage, the men confront one another about their abusive behavior and learn how to develop positive relationships based on respect. The program is offered in Spanish as well as English. In the program's second stage, clients can choose a counseling group led by an African-American.

Local criminal justice officials rely on the program and believe it is effective. Increasingly, other jurisdictions are referring men to the program. Evaluations of the program indicate that 70 percent of male clients will repeat battering behavior, as opposed to nearly 100 percent of male batterers who receive no treatment.

Applying the Strategy

Males ordered by the court to participate in Anger Management Groups established through the Memphis Family Trouble Center meet once a week to learn communication skills and understand the difference between discipline and abuse. A year after their participation, only 12 of 120 men had been rearrested for domestic violence.

Contact Information

Emerge Program
18 Hurley Street
Cambridge, Massachusetts 02139
617-422-1550

Teach Teens To Prevent Dating Violence

Strategy

Educating teens about abusive relationships helps prevent domestic violence among adults.

Crime Problem Addressed

In dating situations, youth test their concepts of masculinity, femininity, respect, mutuality, and communication. Dating relationships reinforce unhealthy gender stereotypes unless they are based on clear communication, trust, and nonviolent ways of settling conflict. Acquaintance rape and other violence can result from an inability to build healthy adult relationships. In a 1992 *National Crime Victimization Survey*, over half of rape victims were younger than eighteen. Many victims of domestic violence, too, are young women. Experts believe that violence between dating teens is severely underreported. This strategy trains youth to prevent dating violence.

Key Components

Programs that help teens of both sexes prevent dating violence address relationship issues through school-based support groups for victims, intervention and counseling groups for offenders, training for school and health care personnel so that they recognize signs of dating violence, and a curriculum that teaches teens how to recognize signs of abusive behavior, get help, or help a friend in need. Many programs also create hotlines through which teens can report abuse or seek assistance. Schools can help to teach students the program's messages.

Key Partnerships

Usually operated through a partnership with a group that assists victims of domestic violence or an agency that serves youth, the school-based programs rely on trained youth who counsel peers, operate hotlines, and deliver curriculum lessons in the classroom. In addition, through performances the programs dramatize conflicts and gender stereotypes. Together with community-based agencies, the schools publicize services available to victims and batterers.

Potential Obstacles

Because of fear or embarrassment, many students are reluctant to seek help through counseling and hotline services. The curriculum and supporting materials inform them about available services and encourage them to approach teachers, peers, or community agencies for help. School administrators, reluctant to get involved in rela-

tionship issues, may resist using the curriculum and other services within the school. Program proponents should emphasize the curriculum's value in combating violence among students.

Signs of Success

The Dating Violence Intervention Project (DVIP) grew out of a partnership between a treatment program for batterers and a shelter for victims. Established in 1986, the Boston-area program aims to "prevent boys and girls from learning to accept violence in their earliest relationships." DVIP programs include "awareness weeks," assemblies and theater performances built around the theme of respect; three-session courses in which former victims and abusers train students to identify abusive behaviors, engage in respectful communication, and manage conflict; special class sessions; performances in which youth dramatize issues of violence and gender stereotypes; 24-hour hotline and counseling services; an eight-session course that explores the causes of dating violence and trains youth as prevention advocates; and training of school staff so that they can recognize signs of dating violence among students. Male students who threaten or abuse a female peer must participate in weekly counseling groups.

Student participants report that the program taught them characteristics of abusive relationships and ways to cope with being abused or help a friend. Twenty Massachusetts towns have now developed programs modeled after DVIP, which trained police officers and school officials from fifty towns. The program also trained fifty peer leaders in 1993. In 1994 the Governor's Commission on Domestic Violence endorsed a plan to bring DVIP-inspired initiatives to additional communities through intervention programs for batterers, training for school staff, and inclusion of dating violence prevention in conferences sponsored by the state's education department. The curriculum has also been used in Canada, New Zealand, and Australia.

Applying the Strategy

The Southern California Coalition for Battered Women offers *Skills for Violence-Free Relationships*, an education program for use with students aged thirteen to eighteen. Adapted for use by school personnel, shelter workers, and youth advocates, the curriculum incorporates lessons and lectures, role playing, and storytelling. A complimentary teacher's guide is available through the Minnesota Coalition for Battered Women.

The Williston, North Dakota, Network Against Teenage Violence developed the program *When Love Really Hurts: Dating Violence Curriculum.* Established in cooperation with the community's Family Crisis Shelter, the four-session text is designed for incorporation into social studies, health, history, or psychology classes. A list of resources that help victims supplements the text.

Contact Information

Director, Dating Violence Intervention Project
P.O. Box 530
Harvard Square Station
Cambridge, Massachusetts 02238
617-354-2676

Community Crisis Response Teams

Strategy

Violence claims two victims, the person or people victimized and the community, which experiences trauma, fear, and stress. Crisis response teams help residents, including witnesses of violence, cope with a violent incident and its aftermath.

Crime Problem Addressed

Each year in the United States, millions of residents fall victim to violent crime, which also causes fear and stress to neighbors, children, businesspeople, and other community members. This strategy attempts to provide immediate intervention and support by community groups and local government.

Key Components

The strategy depends on a multidisciplinary team of health professionals, counselors, police, and youth ready to respond immediately to violent crimes in the community. While on patrol or on referral from the police, the team visits neighbors, victims, and children in the community to help them cope with the trauma of violent crime and tell them where they can obtain counseling, medical assistance, or legal help. Some programs maintain contact with religious leaders, who may be called to the scene to help victims and their families. In communities with significant youth gang violence, the programs use community mediation techniques to diffuse gang rivalries and diminish the prospects of retaliation and additional violence.

Key Partnerships

The strategy's success relies on collaboration between complimentary service providers from local agencies and community groups. Individuals and groups must establish communication links to ensure that team members respond as needed to violent incidents.

Potential Obstacles

Participating agencies may find it difficult to provide enough staff to apply the strategy throughout the city.

Close cooperation between agencies and the police department helps in determining where services will most likely be needed, maximizes resources, and lessens response time.

Signs of Success

The Community Crisis Response Team of Cambridge Hospital includes health care workers, judges, teachers, parents, police, probation officers, social workers, and youth workers. Recognizing that violent crime victimizes all residents of a community, the program's creators designed it to coordinate agency response to neighborhood occurrences of extreme and traumatic violence. The program focuses on trauma debriefings and training staff to deal with the psychological trauma of victims, witnesses, and neighbors. The program's goal is to empower the community and foster its long-term resiliency through community crisis intervention. Using a National Organization for Victim Assistance handout on psychological trauma in children and adults, the team intervened at fifty-nine separate events and assisted more than seven hundred individuals in 1991.

Applying the Strategy

Washington, DC's Youth Trauma Team includes a group of psychologists, social workers, police officers, and recreation workers. Responding immediately to violent incidents, the team offers counseling and support to children and others in the neighborhood. The program receives support from Howard University's Violence Prevention Project, which offers an after-school program and a summer camp for children who have witnessed violence.

The pastor who directs Mobile, Alabama's Group Against Narcotics and Gangs intervenes at the scene of violent incidents on an on-call basis. Since 1990 his rapport with gang-involved youth has helped his team prevent violence on several occasions. The team mediates disputes among rival gang members and assists neighbors who feel threatened. The organization also offers "runaway or displaced" youth accommodations in a neighborhood "safe house."

Contact Information

Community Crisis Response Team
Victims of Violence Program
Cambridge Hospital
1493 Cambridge Street
Cambridge, Massachusetts 02139
617-498-1150

Director, Group Against Narcotics and Gangs
2496 B Government Boulevard
Mobile, Alabama 36606
334-471-8081

National Organization for Victim Assistance
1757 Park Road, NW
Washington, DC 20010
202-232-6682 or 800-TRY-NOVA

Teach Entrepreneur and Job Skills to Youth

Strategy

Programs that teach youth job skills and allow them to practice business techniques in an entrepreneurial setting bolster resiliency against delinquency and promote long-term prospects for employment.

Crime Problem Addressed

Criminal justice experts have long recognized lack of job skills, unstable employment history, and general unreadiness for employment as contributing factors in youth delinquency and violence. The primary goal of employment and entrepreneurial programs is to increase youth participants' income, but they also strengthen youth's positive social bonds to the community.

Key Components

Often based in a community organization or youth group and supported by a foundation or corporate sponsor, youth entrepreneur programs aim to boost the income of economically disadvantaged youth by focusing on responsibility, teamwork, job skills, and goal attainment. Youth in an entrepreneur program set personal and job-related goals. In some cases, the youth produce and market a product or service within their community, through cooperation with their peers. In other cases, the youth are paired with adult entrepreneurs who serve as mentors and positive examples of commitment to work and community life. Some programs "seed" individual youth with funds to start their own business ventures.

Key Partnerships

Youth participants receive support from agencies that teach job skills, advice on business techniques and financial management from local business leaders and mentors, "seed" funds from local foundations or corporations, and help from marketing and public relations professionals in planning how to publicize a product or service. Sponsoring agencies provide teamwork training and help finding a location for the business.

Potential Obstacles

Difficulty obtaining start-up funds is the most likely obstacle to a youth entrepreneur program. It is also hard to evaluate the effect of this kind of program on delinquency because youth who opt into the program have already demonstrated a desire to achieve. Other obstacles include locating and maintaining contacts with area business leaders and marketing experts who can advise the youth as needed and demonstrate support for the program.

Signs of Success

Baltimore-based Hoka-Hai Enterprises and Tico Enterprises use reclaimed lumber to construct small racks for bathroom soap. Youth involved in the community initiative receive part of the profits; the rest goes to a scholarship fund. The product is now distributed internationally through The Body Shop, a chain of stores selling cosmetics.

The Hunt Alternatives Fund of Denver, Colorado, provided grants for two youth entrepreneur programs. The Young Americans Education Foundation used its 1994 grant to bring their "Be Your Own Boss" entrepreneur training program to fifteen more low-income youth. The training emphasizes practical skills and motivates youth to think beyond the funds needed to start a business to the commitment needed to make a business succeed. Youth Biz entrepreneurs produce and market a line of silk-screened T-shirts and other products out of a storefront in northeast Denver. Since 1992 Youth Biz has taught responsibility, teamwork, and management skills and has helped young men and women earn income.

Applying the Strategy

The University of North Carolina at Durham, area businesspeople, and several county agencies collaborate in a partnership called Support Adolescents with Guidance and Employment (SAGE). SAGE offers an educational program in cultural values for African-American males aged thirteen to sixteen, a mentoring program, job training and placement, and an entrepreneurs program that pairs youth with adult African-American entrepreneurs. To date, the program has served 250 young men.

Contact Information

Young Americans Education Foundation
311 Steele Street
Denver, Colorado 80206
303-321-2954

Youth Biz
3050 Richard Allen Court
Denver, Colorado 80205
303-394-2919

Corporate Support for Antiviolence Projects

Strategy

Corporations contribute to or implement antiviolence campaigns using their products, services, and resources. The visibility of corporate community members helps publicize antiviolence efforts, reinforce the marketability of nonviolent products, and demonstrate support for communities troubled by violence.

Crime Problem Addressed

The level of violent crime in the United States remains unacceptably high. Corporate America's resources and high profile provide a prominent platform from which to advocate nonviolence. In this strategy, corporations join with state, community, or national partners to promote antiviolence events, campaigns, products, and services.

Key Components

Both on their own and in partnership with local groups, state agencies, or national organizations, corporations are increasingly promoting antiviolence messages and products. Joining others concerned about violent crime's effects on individuals and communities, corporations have sponsored local and national events, supported public education campaigns, changed their own marketing and sales practices, lent executives and services to violence prevention groups, donated services and facilities to antiviolence causes, and contributed funding for specific programs. Their contributions are orchestrated through corporate foundations, marketing divisions, or training departments.

Key Partnerships

Corporate partners seek out local, state, and national projects to support and assist. The resources they can invest in public awareness campaigns often lead to additional support for the project or event.

Potential Obstacles

Local and national antiviolence program coordinators must balance their interest in corporate sponsorship with the corporation's reputation and business practices unrelated to the program. As with any other funding source, overreliance on corporate support can leave a program vulnerable to decisions by corporate managers, who might decide to withdraw support for financial or other reasons.

Signs of Success

Since 1980 the Advertising Council has supported the National Citizens' Crime Prevention Campaign (NCCPC). The print, television, and radio public service advertisements that they help produce feature McGruff, the Crime Dog, a popular character who advocates prevention of crime and violence. A 1993 evaluation of the campaign revealed that one in five persons who had seen the advertisements on TV took action to prevent crime in their community. The media outlets that run the ads contributed $92 million in donated air time in 1994 alone. A 1994 Advertising Council campaign on domestic violence cosponsored by the Family Violence Prevention Fund generated more than twenty thousand calls to the toll-free number during the campaign's first four months.

Radio Shack®, marketer of consumer electronics and computer products through over six thousand stores nationwide, has entered into a partnership with the National Crime Prevention Council to provide six free training sessions on crime prevention to law enforcement and community groups at satellite locations throughout the country.

Applying the Strategy

Concerned about the effects of gun violence on youth, two of the nation's largest toy store chains decided in late 1994 to stop selling toy guns. Kay-Bee and Toys R Us, with one thousand and over six hundred stores, respectively, joined several other national retailers who stopped selling the toy weapons out of concern that using them reinforced in children violent behaviors that they witness in their neighborhoods and on TV.

USAA, a national insurance company based in San Antonio, Texas, encourages employees to volunteer for a company-sponsored mentoring program.

Allstate Insurance company served as the major corporate sponsor for the 1994 5K Race Against Violence: America's #1 Challenge. The proceeds from registration fees for the race, held in ten major cities, benefited local Boys & Girls Clubs and the NCCPC. In 1995 Allstate again sponsored the October event, contributing the proceeds to the NCCPC and to Big Brothers and Big Sisters organizations in participating cities.

Contact Information

Project Coordinator
Radio Shack
701 One Tandy Center
Fort Worth, Texas 76102
817-878-6707

Use State Laws and Ordinances To Combat Gangs

Strategy

State laws can help police enforce against youth gang crime, including graffiti, coercion of members, illegal trafficking in firearms, and drive-by shootings.

Crime Problem Addressed

Throughout the United States, thousands of youth gangs intimidate neighborhoods, traffick in illegal drugs and weapons, and commit violent crimes. This strategy aims to create laws and ordinances that, when implemented effectively, equip police and prosecutors with an effective tool against gang-related crime.

Key Components

Careful drafting of state laws on street gang activity requires knowledge of gangs' nature, extent, and relationship to crime. Laws drafted have classified buildings in which gang activity occurs as a nuisance that should be abated, increased penalties for drive-by shootings, made repeat vandalism a felony, prohibited the sale of graffiti implements (such as paint) to minors, and provided for special penalties for coercive behavior by gang members. The laws typically increase penalties for violations (e.g., upgrade violations to felonies) or impose mandatory minimum sentences for some offenses.

Key Partnerships

Effective implementation of state laws on these issues requires collaboration among legislators, state and local law enforcement officials, judges, prosecutors, probation officers, and school personnel. Partnerships among these professionals ensure effective application of laws that counter gang activity and remove chronic and violent offenders from the community.

Potential Obstacles

The cost of enforcing the laws can burden local police agencies. State law enforcement, local prosecutors, and the courts can help through coordinated enforcement strategies and selective application of the laws to community locations where gang activity is most prevalent.

Signs of Success

California's attorney general, legislature, and governor cooperated in designing a wide array of laws to combat gang violence in communities throughout the state. The partnership resulted in enactment of the California Street Terrorism Enforcement and Prevention Act, which focuses on criminal street gang organizations. The act provides for felony prosecution of active gang members, felony penalties against adults who coerce youth into joining a gang, and possible life terms in prison for murder convictions involving drive-by shootings. It also outlines penalties for graffiti vandalism and sale of illegal weapons. Other provisions call for publication of a gang prevention resource guide for community organizations and in-service teacher training in preventing gang violence and drug abuse.

The purpose of the National Youth Gang Center established by the OJJDP is to assist state and local jurisdictions in noting, analyzing, and sharing promising strategies for prevention and suppression of gang-related crime. The center also disseminates gang-related materials through the Juvenile Justice Clearinghouse.

Applying the Strategy

Cathedral City, California, applied the law to combat the city's gang problem. After GRASP used the law to identify gang members and enforce against their graffiti vandalism and violence, community incidents of graffiti dropped by more than two-thirds.

Contact Information

Crime and Violence Prevention Center
Office of the Attorney General
P.O. Box 944255
Sacramento, California 94244-2550
916-324-7863

Institute for Intergovernmental Research
(re: National Youth Gang Center)
P.O. Box 12729
Tallahassee, Florida 32317
904-385-0600

Juvenile Justice Clearinghouse 1-800-638-8736

Teach Children About Gun Safety

Strategy

Educating children about gun safety prevents accidental discharge of firearms by teaching children that only a trained adult should handle a gun.

Crime Problem Addressed

According to the National Center for Health Statistics, in 1990 in the United States 4,941 children younger than nineteen died from gunshot wounds, 538 of them having been shot accidentally. Most children accidentally killed with a gun die while playing with the gun in their own home or that of a friend. Every day, fifteen children younger than nineteen are killed with guns. This strategy seeks to educate children about guns' dangers so that they will stay away from guns they see in their homes, school, or neighborhood.

Key Components

Gun safety awareness and risk-prevention programs for children offer age-appropriate curriculum materials that can be incorporated into health education or social studies courses, strategies for involving youth in antiviolence activities, videos that outline situations students should avoid, and teacher training. School-based programs spread the program's message to students and parents. Most programs focus on educating children not involved with firearms, although some programs focus on turning gun-using children away from reliance on the weapon because of the dangers involved.

Key Partnerships

A 1991 Gallup poll revealed that over half of handgun owners keep their guns loaded at least part of the time. Another study showed that over half of gun owners don't keep their guns locked up. Children who live in homes in which guns are left loaded or not locked up are at increased risk of accidental death. School-based educational programs on gun safety should educate parents about the importance of keeping guns in the home secured and away from children. Parents can also help by reinforcing the message that students should stay away from guns, at home, at school, and in their neighborhood.

Potential Obstacles

Guns' availability in some communities and the increasing incidence of children carrying guns out of concern for their safety makes gun safety education more of a challenge. A program for younger children should leave them wary and informed, but not fearful.

Signs of Success

Responding to concerns about youth involvement in gun violence, in 1989 the Center to Prevent Handgun Violence launched the Straight Talk About Risks (STAR) pilot curriculum. The program was developed in cooperation with teachers, guidance counselors, parents, police, and a team of child development specialists.

The STAR curriculum teaches students how to peaceably resolve conflict, manage anger, avoid dangerous situations, and cope with negative peer pressure. The nation's first comprehensive program devoted to teaching children and teens about preventing gun violence, STAR offers curriculum materials, in both English and Spanish, for grades kindergarten through twelve; information on ways that children and their parents can help prevent crime and violence; bibliographies of reference materials and other resources for teachers, parents, and students; and videos geared to secondary school students. In each community that has adopted the program, the center has worked with the school district to train teachers. The center estimates that STAR can be implemented in thirty schools for $60,000, this includes training for 150 teachers, and obtaining materials for fifteen thousand students.

Schools throughout New Jersey; California; New York City; and Dade County, Florida, have implemented STAR. Schools in Dade County were among the first to pilot the curriculum. Their ongoing program includes a public education campaign, use of the curriculum, and safety training for parents. During Gun Safety Awareness Week, local TV stations support the program with public service announcements. A formal, in-depth evaluation of the program's long-term effect is under way.

Applying the Strategy

The volunteer-run Weapons Awareness Program established by the Department of Juvenile Justice in Spartanburg County, South Carolina, works with youth younger than sixteen who have been convicted of a gun offense, such as bringing a weapon to school. A weapons awareness seminar led by a police officer graphically shows the impact of gun violence on individuals. In the course on conflict management, which lasts eight to twelve weeks, counselors challenge youth to identify strategies for dealing with difficult situations peaceably. As of 1994, among forty-five program graduates, only one had been charged with another gun-related offense.

Contact Information

Education Division
Center to Prevent Handgun Violence
1225 I Street, NW, Suite 1100
Washington, DC 20005
202-289-7319

Director of Community Programs
Spartanburg County Judicial Center
180 Magnolia Street
Spartanburg, South Carolina 29301
803-585-5181

After-School Programs for Latchkey Children

Strategy

Safe and constructive after-school activities for latchkey children help prevent their involvement in dangerous or delinquent behavior and support their educational goals.

Crime Problem Addressed

Each day, the work schedules of America's parents leave many children unattended at home or unsupervised in the community. These children may be more vulnerable to the influence of delinquent peers or to academic difficulties if they need additional support to succeed. Failure in school and the influence of delinquent peers are both associated with delinquency among youth. This strategy allows youth to take advantage of an array of services designed to give them educational support and prevent delinquency and substance abuse.

Key Components

The programs that use the strategy are as varied as the communities in which the participating children live. However, latchkey programs commonly provide a secure location known to the neighborhood's children, educational support such as tutoring or special enhancement classes, recreation, and prevention education. The programs range from large-scale efforts run through major community-based organizations and recreational facilities to neighborhood-based tutoring centers in homes. Program staff plan assistance for the children, track their school performance and attendance, and communicate with parents to ensure the student's progress.

Key Partnerships

Program coordinators should seek parents' cooperation in helping children to learn and retain prevention information. Partnerships with schools increase knowledge of how program interventions improve grades, attendance, and behavior.

Potential Obstacles

Finding funds for the diverse activities that interest children and support their academic and physical development in a healthy atmosphere has challenged many local governments and community-based agencies that serve youth. Once programs are established, careful tracking of the effect on youth academics and delinquency provides information vital to long-term resource development.

Signs of Success

Local officials who wanted to make Tucson, Arizona, a "child-friendly city" established the KIDCO program, operated by the city's parks and recreation department. The city council added $500,000 to its 1992 budget so that the previously summer-only program could expand to include a literacy lab, activities that increase self-esteem, sports and other recreation, an arts camp, and educational information on healthy lifestyles. KIDCO provides thousands of breakfasts to participants in early morning programs, helps teens with job hunting, and hires college students to help out at the centers, which serve a growing number of latchkey children. The city's library system, its arts council, the local cable TV station, an interfaith council, and the University of Arizona all help with some aspect of the program. During summer 1993, Tucson experienced 52 percent fewer crimes than during summer 1992. Police attribute part of the decline to the enhanced services offered by KIDCO and other parks department projects.

Oakland's Kids House program pays parents and other Oakland residents $400 a month to offer a group of students supervision, snacks, and tutoring. The adults provide the service at their home. Support for the program comes from businesses and local foundations. Tutors are paid $7 an hour. In the first year of this small-scale program, the grades of 63 percent of the children improved.

Applying the Strategy

The Academic Career and Community Enhancement for Latchkey Children and Their Families (ACCEL) program, based at the Martin Luther King, Jr., Community Services Center of Freeport, Illinois, assists children living in or near public housing communities, nearly two-thirds of whom come from single-parent homes. The community's only free tutoring program, ACCEL provides a safe location, homework help, computer instruction, recreational activities through a partnership with the Boys & Girls

Club, a career club for older students, a science club staffed by local corporate volunteers, and in-home follow-up visits for discussions with parents. In 1994 the Center for Substance Abuse and Prevention presented the full-service program with an Exemplary Prevention Program Award for its contribution to preventing delinquency and substance abuse and to improving academic achievement.

Contact Information

Community Program Manager
Tucson Parks and Recreation Department
900 South Randolph Way
Tucson, Arizona 85716
602-791-4873

Hold Parents Accountable for Their Children's Behavior

Strategy

Parents held accountable for their children's delinquent behavior are more likely to reinforce appropriate behavior in the youth.

Crime Problem Addressed

Nearly 130,000 juveniles were arrested for major violent crimes in 1992. Teenagers are now more likely to be victims of violent crime than adults over age twenty-five. Over the past fifteen years, use of guns by youthful offenders has increased by nearly 20 percent. Juvenile offenders are responsible for one-third of all reported property crimes. This strategy addresses the youth behaviors that lead to status offenses and property crimes by holding parents legally and financially accountable for their children's actions.

Key Components

Localities across the nation have enacted ordinances in response to growing concern about the incidence of juvenile crime. In thirty-three states, local judges can require parents to pay restitution for crimes committed by their children. City councils have designed late-night curfew, truancy, graffiti, gang enforcement, and gun ordinances that impose penalties and possible arrest for parents whose children repeatedly violate the ordinances' behavior standards. In effect, the ordinances constitute a system of graduated sanctions against the parent and the youth.

Key Partnerships

City officials who design the ordinances and sanctions must work with police and other personnel responsible for

enforcing them to determine whether proposed sanctions will be effective deterrents for parents and youth.

Potential Obstacles

Parents and others may oppose passage of the ordinances on the grounds that parents should not be held responsible for their children's behavior when the children are not under their supervision. Also, the sanctions are not likely to be effective among parents who cannot pay the fines.

Signs of Success

Following the recommendation of a coalition of local government and grassroots crime prevention advocates, the city council in San Antonio, Texas, passed ordinances on juveniles and firearms, a daytime curfew to control truancy, a late-night curfew for juveniles, and graffiti removal. Each ordinance imposes fines on parents and juveniles. The late-night juvenile curfew helped reduce juvenile crime by 5 percent and juvenile victimization by 43 percent during curfew hours. In 1993, incidents of violent crime were 19 percent fewer than in 1991. Repeat violations of each ordinance have become less frequent as parents and youth have seen the penalties imposed.

Applying the Strategy

Silverton, Oregon, has become a model for communities interested in imposing ordinances that hold parents accountable for their children's behavior. In Silverton parents can be fined up to $1,000 if their child is found carrying a gun, smoking cigarettes, or using illegal drugs. Parents who agree to attend parenting classes can avoid the fines. Within the first two months after the law was passed in early 1995, seven parents were fined and many others registered for parenting classes.

Applying the strategy differently, a crime prevention group in Mobile, Alabama, proposed state legislation making it a felony to store a firearm improperly and unsafely in a location accessible to a child.

Contact Information

Crime Prevention Unit
San Antonio Police Department
214 West Nueva
San Antonio, Texas 78207
210-207-7615

Train Emergency Room Staff To Prevent Violence

Strategy

Violence prevention training for hospital staff and security policies regarding violent patients and visitors reduce the incidence of violence in hospital emergency rooms.

Crime Problem Addressed

A 1992 survey of 103 hospitals in Los Angeles and other urban areas of California cited in *Violence in Our Schools, Hospitals, and Public Places: A Prevention and Management Guide* revealed that nearly 60 percent of hospital staff had been injured by visitors or patients. A 1989 study of hospital crime in three hundred facilities across the country found a sharp increase in assaults on staff, half of which occur in emergency rooms. Two-thirds of emergency room nurses surveyed in 1991 reported that they had been assaulted on the job. This strategy combines training in violence prevention and awareness with security procedures, as part of a comprehensive effort to prevent violence.

Key Components

Training in violence prevention helps hospital staff to recognize potentially violent patients and visitors and handle violent people. Preventive security procedures include metal detectors at entrances, photo ID cards for staff, badges for visitors, patient processing policies that minimize waiting time for treatment, controlled access to hospital buildings, secure telephone communications by which staff can report incidents, locked doors to emergency rooms and treatment areas that are not in use, closed-circuit TV monitoring of waiting rooms and parking lots, and trained security guards.

Key Partnerships

Hospital administrators should develop partnerships with doctors, nurses, and staff to understand past events that raised security concerns and devise possible training strategies and security policies to prevent additional incidents, particularly attacks on staff. Administrators should also seek assistance from police or other crime prevention and security specialists who can assess security issues and recommend action.

Potential Obstacles

Staff training and physical changes in hospital facilities can be expensive. Partnerships with police can reduce training costs. Even expensive changes in hospital facilities can be cost-effective when they reduce staff fear, minimize the staff time lost because of injuries, and minimize maintenance costs resulting from violent incidents.

Signs of Success

Following a 1991 study of violence at hospitals throughout the state, the California Emergency Nurses Association successfully advocated a mandatory four-point action plan aimed at preventing violence and based on the best practices at different facilities. Among other recommendations, the legislature set guidelines for minimum safety features and assessments of needed changes in each facility, minimum educational requirements for staff who work in the emergency room, training standards for security staff and appropriate equipment, and special criminal penalties for violent acts against hospital personnel while they are on the job. Associations in other states now advocate similar policies, using the California law as a model.

Applying the Strategy

Six months after a metal detector was installed at a Detroit hospital, officials reported that they had detected 33 guns, 1,234 knives, and other weapons. A Los Angeles hospital revealed that, among trauma patients treated in one year, 25 percent of males and 31 percent of females had weapons on them when they were admitted. Detection of the weapons prevented possible attacks on hospital staff.

Contact Information

National Emergency Room Nurses Association
216 Higgins Road
Partridge, Illinois 60068
708-698-9400

International Association for Healthcare Security and
    Safety
P.O. Box 637
Lombard, Illinois 60148
708-953-0990

Incentives for Positive Behavior

Strategy

Incentives for positive social behavior in youth reduce the long-term likelihood of delinquency.

Crime Problem Addressed

Tens of thousands of youth are arrested in the United States each year. Many thousands more are identified as being at high risk for involvement in delinquent activity. Clear and consistent behavior standards help prevent such delinquency. This strategy aims to promote positive social behavior through specific incentives and rewards.

Key Components

Incentive programs offer youth access to special events, participation in recreational activities, and public recognition for their positive accomplishments, for example, in the form of awards. A variety of youth-serving and police agencies use the strategy to encourage healthy decision-making and positive leadership among youth.

Key Partnerships

Parents should encourage youth to participate and pursue the incentive as part of setting measurable personal goals. Programs should join with police and the schools to publicize the program and its incentive component. Corporations, foundations, and local businesses can provide valuable support for recognition events and donate prizes or services.

Potential Obstacles

The primary obstacle is difficulty finding the time and funds needed to organize an incentive or recognition program. Business or foundation partners and community organizations can help locate those resources or donate them. Some programs recognize deserving youth only with ceremonies, certificates, or scholarships because they do not want youth to expect prizes for all their achievements. The program seeks to foster self-esteem, not to provide youth with material things.

Signs of Success

Miami's Do The Right Thing (DTRT), a nonprofit organization that works with the city's police, promotes academic achievement by youth from low-income and minority communities. It enhances their self-esteem through recognition of their accomplishments at picnics, community-wide ceremonies, and prize-package giveaways. Each participant receives a T-shirt and certificate. Teachers, coaches, and parents nominate thousands of students. Ten finalists chosen by DTRT staff receive plaques, savings bonds, and prizes at an event covered by all the city's major media outlets. DTRT and high schools have teamed up to establish a scholarship program for students who demonstrate exceptional potential.

The city's police believe that the program has contributed to a decline, in recent years, in crime in the communities served. The police department's relations with the community's youth improved as neighbors began to associate the police with a positive program that engages and supports youth. In 1994 the program was included in the National League of Cities publication *Exemplary Programs in Criminal Justice*.

Applying the Strategy

The Stop, Think, Act, and Review (STAR) Program of the Tyler, Texas, police department encourages and rewards positive behavior in students throughout the elementary school system. After a school incorporates a fifteen-minute presentation on positive behavior into its curriculum, police "adopt" the school and visit periodically throughout the year, including during special school events. Each school holds a rally to recognize students with good behavior and give them certificates. The city also sponsors a community-wide recognition event at the end of the school year. Several participating schools have reported improved student attendance, lower suspension rates, and fewer disciplinary referrals since the program began.

Contact Information

Executive Director, Do The Right Thing
400 Northwest 2nd Avenue
Miami, Florida 33128
305-579-3344

STAR Program Coordinator
Tyler Police Department
711 West Ferguson Street
Tyler, Texas 75702
903-531-1048

Performance as Therapy and Education

Strategy

Programs that feature play therapy and performances communicate vital prevention messages and help children and youth deal with their feelings about anger, violence, and diversity.

Crime Problem Addressed

Every year in the United States tens of thousands of youth are arrested, thousands more are victimized by violent crime, and many others remain troubled about how to deal with peer pressure, anger, violence, and other issues they face. This strategy aims to present prevention messages in a performance or play-therapy format that entertains as it encourages youth to participate and helps them cope with their feelings.

Key Components

These programs are operated by a variety of groups, including community organizations active in prevention, youth centers, schools, and youth performance troupes sponsored by business or other community patrons. Although the performances vary in the topics they present, all encourage youth expression (through role plays and audience participation), provide substantive prevention information, and are followed by discussions that help the youth audience address problems and share ideas about how to solve them. The strategy's primary goal is to use performances to change attitudes and promote healthy behaviors and decisionmaking among youth. Another important goal is to increase youth participants' leadership skills. The most successful programs also involve parents or offer complimentary services such as hotlines and collaboration with counseling services.

Key Partnerships

Partnerships with schools, counseling services, teen centers, and parents strengthen the messages portrayed in the performance and discussed afterward. Schools, in particular, can provide performance space and audiences. Local businesses and corporate partners can contribute funds for performance space, supplies, and travel costs.

Potential Obstacles

Performance programs must emphasize prevention in an entertaining way. The material must suit the learning styles and capacities of the children or juveniles in the audience.

Signs of Success

Sydney, Australia's Family Planning Association and its police and education departments collaborated to design crime prevention workshops and a video project for youth. Students from several schools worked with police officers and youth workers on *Truth or Dare*, a video about dating violence and relationships. The students wrote, performed in, and produced the video with the support of a grant from the agencies. The video was then incorporated into an educational program for youth called *Making Sense of Sex*. Teens who had helped produce the video recruited over forty of their peers to serve as counselors on a teen hotline that fielded calls about violence and irresponsible sexual practices. The police credit the program with a decrease in violence against the gay community, a major problem in Sydney. A Rand Corporation report called *Community Action toward Youth Violence Prevention* noted that the program was able to "change the opinions and attitudes of youth toward minorities and gays and even reduced the amount of violence . . . in the year following the evaluation."

Applying the Strategy

Real Alternatives to Violence for Every Student is an educational program that uses skits, role plays, and performances to teach students how to manage conflict. The program is designed to work in conjunction with a school curriculum in conflict management for grades four through six. Kaiser Permanente, a major health insurer, provides support for the troupe of teen performers. The first performance in a school is followed two weeks later by sessions in which students develop skills in anger management and decisionmaking by using a life-size board game. Later, students in grades four through six work with mentors (usually ninth graders) on a long-term project intended to teach the younger students these skills. In this part of the program, called the Legacy Project, students create a play, musical event, or video to present to younger students. Parents get involved as mentors and support the program through home lessons. The troupe of performers and supporting staff from Kaiser Permanente work with schools throughout the process. The program has reached thousands of children.

Contact Information

Coordinator of Educational Theater Programs
Kaiser Permanente
2101 East Jefferson Street, Box 6122
Rockville, Maryland 20849-6122
301-816-6418

Teach Male University Students To Prevent Acquaintance Rape

Strategy

Education about rape prevention helps dispel gender stereotypes and promotes awareness of rape, battering, and sexual harassment.

Crime Problem Addressed

Sexual harassment, rape, and other sexual assault of women are among the most underreported crimes in the United States. According to national statistics, two-thirds of women victimized by rape or other sexual assault know their attacker. This strategy seeks to prevent acquaintance rape and other sexual assault by educating male university students about the effects of such violence on women and by using discussion to dispel gender stereotypes that hinder intimate relationships.

Key Components

Colleges and universities have become increasingly aware of the need to educate all students about acquaintance rape, other sexual assault, and sexual harassment. Psychology and sociology departments, sports teams, fraternal organizations, and other student groups can provide a forum for student discussion on these issues, challenging male students to examine their concepts of masculinity, power in relationships, consensual sex, relationships with women, and violence. Typically, interactive discussions include role plays, presentations by victims, and training of student volunteers so that they can bring prevention information to other students. Participants are challenged to think of ways to intervene effectively when peers harass or otherwise show aggression toward other students.

Key Partnerships

Sports teams, fraternal groups, service clubs, dormitory councils, and student government representatives should participate in, and help implement, education and awareness programs. School-based programs should work in partnership with community-based organizations that can offer counselors, speakers, and trainers. Events held by student organizations and sports teams provide opportunities to distribute educational materials to the student body. Student and community newspapers can direct students to education programs and support services.

Potential Obstacles

Attitudes about relationships, violence, rape, and appropriate behaviors for men and women cannot be changed quickly. Programs must make use of campus and community resources that can help reinforce prevention messages and ensure appropriate sanctions against students who violate university and community standards against violence and harassment.

Signs of Success

Tulane University's Men Against Rape project educates men about rape, helps them understand the meaning of consensual sex, and teaches male students how to help a victim of sexual assault. Since 1992 the New Orleans program has trained male volunteers to make presentations, guide discussions, publicize the program, and act as liaisons to athletic teams, other student groups, and the general student population. Part of the university's comprehensive program on crime prevention, Men Against Rape provides orientation seminars for incoming students, trains administrators and staff in rape awareness and prevention, and offers self-defense classes to interested students. The training sessions are popular among students, many of whom believe that "everyone should go through this program." The university also has off-duty city police officers patrol areas near the campus and operates an escort service and emergency phone system.

Applying the Strategy

Established by the Center for the Study of Sport in Society at Northeastern University, the Mentors in Violence Prevention (MVP) Project supports discussion groups and training sessions for male and female athletes at local universities.

Those who run the Boston-based program believe that student athletes enjoy a high status that increases their influence over peers. For this reason, it is especially important to educate student athletes about rape, battering, and sexual harassment. Using what it calls the *MVP Playbook*, the program guides students through role plays and discussions about on-campus parties, alcohol and its effect on dating relationships, harassment of gay and lesbian students, and violence in relationships. The program challenges male students to develop strategies for dealing with abusive behavior by a fellow student. In addition to working on campus with fraternities and student government, the program trains student athletes to make their own presentations to middle and high school classes.

Contact Information

Office of Crime Prevention and Victim Resources
6823 St. Charles Avenue
Department of Public Safety
Diboll Complex
New Orleans, Louisiana 70118
504-865-5381

Coordinator, Mentors in Violence Prevention Project
Center for the Study of Sport in Society
Northeastern University
360 Huntington Avenue, 161CP
Boston, Massachusetts 02115
617-373-4025

Use School Organization and Policy To Address Violence

Strategy

School activities and curricula, parent-school partnership efforts, and staffing all impact on violence in school settings. Schools that modify their organization to address these issues will experience less violence.

Crime Problem Addressed

Research reveals that most U.S. school districts have experienced increasing violence within the past five years. As many as one million students drop out of school each year. Amid these challenges, local governments face budget constraints that restrict the resources available for scholastic and athletic programs. Communities using this strategy recognize that a comprehensive review of administrative policy and school organization, as well as outreach to parents and other partners, helps them address violence on school campuses.

Key Components

As noted in *Guide for Implementing the Comprehensive Strategy for Serious, Violent, and Chronic Juvenile Offenders*, schools can combat juvenile crime through staffing, communications about school policies, and cooperative planning that involves parents, administrators, and teachers. Reviews of school organization and policy are particularly important in schools with low student achievement scores, high dropout rates, poor attendance, minimal parental involvement, considerable crime and violence, and high teacher turnover.

Key Partnerships

Whenever possible, any changes in school organization should be developed in partnership with parents, teachers, other staff, and students. Local agencies may assist the review process by identifying opportunities to bring needed services into the school or providing information on ways in which students and parents can find help in the community.

Potential Obstacles

School boards and administrators struggling with budget problems and burdened by administrative and supervisory duties may resist changes in school organization out of a fear that recommended changes will go unfunded or undone amid other pressing priorities. Parents, other agencies, and school staff can share ideas about ways in which volunteers, staff "loaned" from community groups and agencies, and low-cost policy changes and outreach programs can promote safety in the school.

Signs of Success

The OJJDP study describes school organization programs as promising, noting that these programs may strengthen the protective factors of bonding to school, healthy beliefs and clear standards for behavior, and skill to resist engaging in and becoming a victim of aggression. School organization interventions may address a number of risk factors, including transitions, laws and norms regarding delinquency and violence, academic failure, lack of commitment to school, association with delinquent and violent peers, and alienation and rebelliousness.

The study describes the key components of New Haven, Connecticut's school organization plan: integration of arts and athletic activities; parental involvement with teachers and other staff; a multidisciplinary mental health team to help manage student behavior; and a management team of teachers, administrators, parents, and staff who reviewed school policy and recommended additional interventions. After the program, an evaluation based on a small sample indicated that 92 percent of parents had visited their child's school and that students in middle schools had significantly higher grades, better achievement scores, and improved social skills.

Applying the Strategy

The Positive Action through Holistic Education Project in Charleston County, South Carolina, addressed school organization in four middle schools and four high schools in predominantly low-income neighborhoods. This successful program incorporated academic innovations, peer counseling programs, academic and behavior counseling, inservice training for teachers, and student participation in reviews of school policy. After the program, an assessment of students in participating schools revealed that they had significantly lower delinquency rates and many fewer school suspensions than peers in schools that did not participate in the program. Also, students who received counseling and tutoring fared better on standardized tests.

Contact Information

Child Study Center
Yale University
230 South Frontage Road
P.O. Box 207900
New Haven, Connecticut 06520-7900
203-785-5930

(re: Charleston County, S.C.)
Center for Social Organization of Schools
Johns Hopkins University
3505 North Charles Street
Baltimore, Maryland 21208

Gang Prevention Through Community Intervention With High-Risk Youth

Strategy

Coordinated intervention by the community and law enforcement personnel reduces the likelihood that high-risk youth with become involved in gangs. Involvement of police agencies, educators, job-training resources, parents, and community groups is essential to success.

Crime Problem Addressed

An estimated 4,881 violent youth gangs with nearly 250,000 members were responsible for 46,359 crimes in 1991. Communities in which gang activity is most prevalent generally have high concentrations of poverty and joblessness and poor coordination of prevention services among local government agencies and community organizations. This strategy addresses those conditions through a comprehensive approach that links the community and government in providing positive opportunities and demonstrating clear consequences for youth at risk for gang involvement.

Key Components

Programs that use this strategy combine service coordination, partnership between police and the community, suppression of gang activity through coordinated enforcement and prosecution, neighborhood mobilization, and job training for youth. The integrated strategies' chief goal is to reduce gang-related violent crime and youth involvement in gangs. Police, probation personnel, and prosecutors share information about gang activity, diffuse crises that arise from gang conflict, and refer at-risk youth to community-based services. Street outreach through community organizations and parents supplements partnerships among agencies to make well-integrated services available to the youth. Prevention efforts include job training and placement, recreation at safe locations, and mobilization of neighborhood residents and police in identifying community resources that serve youth.

Key Partnerships

For the strategy to succeed, the police and other enforcement agencies must work together to suppress gang activity by gathering information through community contacts. Also, police, local agencies, and community-based resources must work together to support youth and promote nonviolent activities in the neighborhood. The strategy must involve parents in prevention activities and support parents and other residents concerned about gang-related violence.

Potential Obstacles

Communities beset by gang-related violence may be less inclined to develop stable and effective partnerships with their city's police. Those partnerships must be built through sustained effort and clear policies regarding officers' responsibilities to residents. Residents may also be reluctant to become involved in violence prevention projects out of fear of the gang. Coordination among police, prosecutors, probation services, social agencies, churches, and other resources helps residents feel comfortable and supported in their involvement.

Signs of Success

Chicago's police department works closely with prosecutors, probation, job-training programs, community agencies, churches, parents, neighbors, and former gang members on the Gang Violence Reduction Program (GVRP). Focused on two gangs in the city's Little Village section, the project serves a community that experienced fifty-three gang-related crimes involving handgun use in the year before the program's inception. The program's primary goal is to reduce gang assaults and homicides on six police beats. It focuses on two hundred youth aged seventeen to twenty-five. The project team meets weekly to share information about gang activity, discuss interventions in gang conflicts, and plan enforcement strategies. Street workers concentrate on building relationships with current and former gang members, often as negotiators of truces among gangs or factions. The Neighbors Against Violence (NAV) group keeps police and prosecutors aware of residents' concerns about gang activity and violence. NAV has recruited block watch groups, church congregations, agencies that serve youth, and parents as members. Probation administrators focus on collaboration with youth-serving agencies and on jobs-development programs.

An evaluation by a University of Chicago researcher revealed that GVRP helped slow the increase in violent gang-related crime in Little Village. Gang homicides declined from fifteen in the year before the program began to seven in each of the two years since its inception. While violent activity of the gangs addressed by GVRP slowed, crime by other area gangs increased after the program began. The program is credited with substantially improved cooperation among police and probation staff who serve the community.

Applying the Strategy

Seattle is one of four cities that participate in a gang prevention program sponsored by the Administration for Children, Youth, and Families and supported by local business taxes. Youth aged twelve to eighteen are offered mentoring, recreation, training in social and life skills, and job placement assistance. Enforcement and suppression components include coordinated efforts by police and probation personnel to track violent offenders, visits to the homes of at-risk youth, job training, and child care for teen parents. Cooperation among the city agencies involved has improved. According to plans, the project will soon provide additional services for parents of gang-involved youth, as well as housing and other aftercare for youth released from a juvenile corrections facility.

Contact Information

School of Social Service Administration
University of Chicago
969 East 60th Street
Chicago, Illinois 60637
312-702-1134

Gun Interdictions

Strategy

Community-supported vigorous enforcement of existing gun laws can help reduce the incidence of gun-related violent crime.

Crime Problem Addressed

Between 1983 and 1992, juvenile arrests for weapons violations increased 117 percent. During the same time period, arrests of juveniles for murder rose by over 125 percent. In 1993, firearms were used in 7 of ten murders, with about half of the offenses committed by someone not related to or acquainted with the victim(s). This strategy aims to address all types of gun-related violent crimes in the targeted area.

Key Components

In this law-enforcement-led strategy, local police direct intensive patrols to specific geographic areas with high rates of gun-related incidents of violence. Selection of the patrol area is determined by analysis of gun-related crime data. The proactive patrols focus on traffic stops and other mechanisms to detect illegal or illegally concealed weapons and seize weapons. The patrols also try to gain the cooperation of the community to apprehend suspects in gun-related violent crimes. Activities of the patrols include search of suspicious persons and vehicles in the selected areas. In some communities where gun-related crimes have crossed jurisdictional borders, the strategy is implemented by a coalition of localities, in cooperation with county or state authorities.

Key Participants

Community support for the interdiction strategy is vital. The searches and seizures can raise controversy in communities where residents have not been consulted about the purpose and potential benefits of the strategy. Local law enforcement should seek community input in selection of the targeted area and establish mechanisms for residents to support the strategy through identification of "hot spot" areas where gun-related crimes have occurred.

Potential Obstacles

The strategy must be implemented by patrol officers adequately trained to be aware of civil liberties laws that provide guidelines for objective criteria which define appropriate searches. The budget of local law enforcement agencies must either allow for the overtime for officers to process increased arrests and citations or consider limitations on overtime funds in the design of gun law enforcement patrols. Outreach to resident groups and clear crime analysis data should help the department allay the concerns of the community and help clarify the potential benefits of the strategy to the neighborhood.

Signs of Success

An on-site study of one city's program by U.S. Department of Justice-sponsored evaluator at the University of Maryland concluded that use of intense patrols to seize guns prevented two gun-related crimes for every gun seized in the targeted area during the first six months the strategy was implemented in 1993.

Applying the Strategy

In 1993, the 80-block area known as Kansas City's Central Patrol District had a homicide rate 20 times the national average. Gun-related crime in the inner-city community declined by almost fifty percent after six months of directed, intensive patrols, traffic stops, and gun seizures. In the Central District, drive-by shootings dropped from 7 to 1, gun seizures increased by one-third, and officers made over 400 arrests for violation of local laws and 170 arrests on state and federal gun-related charges. Also, according to a study sponsored by the U.S. Department of Justice, "directed patrols [in Kansas City] were also shown to be, on average, about three times more cost-effective in getting guns off the street than routine police activity." Moreover, the decline in gun crimes in the targeted area did not result in increased gun-related crimes in any of the surrounding patrol areas. A city-wide version of this strategy was implemented in Indianapolis beginning in late 1994.

Contact Information

National Criminal Justice Reference Service
Box 6000
Rockville, Maryland 20850
800-851-3420

Ask for National Institute for Justice "Research In Brief" paper: *The Kansas City Gun Experiment* (NCJ #150855).

Bibliography

Books

Embry, Dennis D. *Reducing Youth Violent Crime by 50% with Proven Research-based Interventions through a Community-wide Partnership Approach.* Washington, DC: U.S. Centers for Disease Control and Prevention, 1994.

Jones, Michael A., and Barry Krisberg. *Images and Reality: Juvenile Crime, Youth Violence and Public Policy.* San Francisco, CA: National Council on Crime and Delinquency, 1994.

Krisberg, Barry. *Juvenile Justice: Improving the Quality of Care.* San Francisco, CA: National Council on Crime and Delinquency, 1992.

Periodicals

Allen, Pam. The Gould-Wysinger Awards: A Tradition of Excellence. *OJJDP Model Programs 1993,* February 1994.

Dating Violence Intervention Project Enters Fifth Year. *Transition House Newsletter* (Cambridge, Massachusetts), October 1991.

Domestic Violence and Abuse. *Sheriff,* November–December.

Gordon, Mary France. Domestic Violence Emerges as a Critical Issue for Public Safety Needs. *Nation's Cities Weekly,* October 1994, p. 16.

Glamser, Deeann. Communities Seek to Stem Youth Crime. *USA Today,* February 21, 1995, p. 01A.

Gun Dealers: Weeding Out the Trash. *U.S. News & World Report,* February 27, 1995.

Henderson, Andre. A Safer Way to Settle Differences. *Governing,* October 1994, pp. 42–43.

Levy, Doug. Campus Woes Flow from Binge Drinking. *USA Today,* December 7, 1994, p. 01D.

Mitchel, Leslie. Healthy Families America: Preventing Abuse by Supporting Parents. *Violence Update,* October 1994.

Moyers, Bill. There Is So Much We Can Do. *Parade,* January 8, 1995, pp. 4–6.

Partnerships to Prevent Youth Violence. *Bulletin: Community Partnerships* (DOJ and NCPC), August 1994.

Project Aims to Replicate Massachusetts Experiment. *Criminal Justice Newsletter,* June 15, 1994, pp. 2–3.

Reno Outlines Plans for Nationwide Instant Gun Checks. *Criminal Justice Newsletter,* June 15, 1994, pp. 5–6.

Santoli, Al. A Better Way to Protect Our Children. *Parade,* July 24, 1994, pp. 12–13.

Stopping Rape: Men Educate Men at Tulane University. *Catalyst* (NCPC), April 1993, pp. 1–2.

Youth in Corrections Reach Out to Victims. *Catalyst* (NCPC), November 1994, p. 6.

Public Documents

Ad Hoc Committee on the Reduction of Crime and Violence. *Final Report.* Greensboro, NC, 1992.

Bureau of Justice Assistance (DOJ). *Violent Crime and Drug Abuse in Rural Areas: Issues, Concerns, and Programs.* Washington, DC: U.S. Department of Justice, 1993.

———. *State and Local Conference on Responding to Change and Meeting Future Needs: Conference Summary.* Washington, DC: U.S. Department of Justice, 1994.

———. *State and Local Programs: Focus on What Works.* Washington, DC: U.S. Department of Justice, 1994.

———. *State and Local Programs: Preventing Drug Abuse and Violent Crime.* Washington, DC: U.S. Department of Justice, 1994.

———. *Highlights from 20 Years of Surveying Crime Victims: The National Crime Victimization Survey, 1973–92.* Washington, DC: U.S. Department of Justice, 1993.

City of Richmond Urban Violence Strategy. *Community Oriented Policing.* Richmond, VA, 1990.

———. *Violence Prevention Plan.* Richmond, VA, 1991.

City of Richmond Urban Violence Strategy II. *Focusing on the Child.* Richmond, VA, 1990.

Coping with Violence in the Schools: A Report of the 1993 Summer Conference of the Center for School Counseling Practitioners. Cambridge, MA: Harvard University Graduate School of Education, 1993.

Dating Violence Intervention Project. *Preventing Teen Dating Violence: A Three-Session Curriculum for Teaching Adolescents.* Cambridge, MA, 1993.

Family Violence Prevention Fund. *Marshalls against Domestic Violence: There's No Excuse.* San Francisco, CA, 1994.

Federation of Canadian Municipalities. *Youth Violence and Youth Gangs: Responding to Community Concerns.* Ottawa, Canada, 1994.

Justice Research and Statistics Association. *Criminal Justice Issues in the States: 1993 Directory,* Vol. 10. Washington, DC, 1993.

———. *Domestic and Family Violence: Highlighted Programs from the State Annual Reports.* Washington, DC, 1994.

National Institute of Corrections (DOJ). *The Intermediate Sanctions Handbook: Experiences and Tools for Policymakers.* Washington, DC: U.S. Department of Justice, 1993.

National Institute of Justice (DOJ). *Questions and Answers in Lethal and Non-Lethal Violence.* Washington, DC: U.S. Department of Justice, 1993.

———. *Boot Camps for Juvenile Offenders: Overview and Update.* Washington, DC: U.S. Department of Justice, 1994.

Office of Justice Programs (DOJ). *Comprehensive Strategy for Serious, Violent, and Chronic Juvenile Offenders: Program Summary.* Washington, DC: U.S. Department of Justice, 1994.

Office of Juvenile Justice and Delinquency Prevention (DOJ). *The Child Victim as a Witness.* Washington, DC: U.S. Department of Justice, 1994.

———. *What Works: Promising Interventions in Juvenile Justice.* Washington, DC: U.S. Department of Justice, 1994.

Office of the Attorney General. *Juvenile Justice Handbook for Cities: How the System Works and Resources for Texas Cities to Combat Juvenile Crime.* Austin, TX, 1994.

U.S. Attorney's Office. Serious Habitual Offender Comprehensive Action Program (SHOCAP). In *Resource Fair Program Summaries: Building Justice in Our Communities,* 11–12, 1994.

Youth Initiatives of the City of San Antonio. *City of San Antonio: A Program for Embracing Our Youth.* San Antonio, TX: City of San Antonio, 1994.

Youth Policy Institute. Safe School Grants Program. In *Youth Record,* Vol. 5, 1994.

Drugs

Drug use breeds crime. Individuals on drugs often commit violent acts or steal in order to support their habit. Dealers fight territorial wars, for drug markets, that often result in deaths.

Public apathy encourages youth to use drugs. To combat a newly expanding drug market, society must send a clear antidrug message.

The effort to reduce drug abuse must begin with prevention. Educating young children about drugs' perils can have lifelong benefits. Schools must warn students about drugs while providing a stable, safe environment in which to learn. Preventing drug abuse prevents drug trafficking.

Antidrug curricula reduce the chances that kids will start using drugs. Programs show drugs' dangers, demonstrate positive alternatives to narcotics, and emphasize the risks of alcohol abuse, which often leads to narcotics use. Educational programs also seek to build the self-esteem that enables youth to resist peer and other social pressures to try drugs. Drug Abuse Resistance Education (D.A.R.E.), a nationwide police-supported program that warns school children about the risks of substance abuse, educates youth by putting them in contact with police and social services.

A safe school environment is another important element of prevention; it allows students to focus on learning. Drug-free school zones with increased penalties for drug trafficking and use, gang activity, and weapons possession exist nationwide; their effectiveness depends largely on enforcement. Even if police resources are scarce, media public service announcements that state the penalties for crimes committed on school grounds can boost deterrence. Student drug offenses within one Tucson, Arizona, school zone dropped 43 percent after it was declared a drug-free zone.

Drug education outside of school must reinforce the values taught in the classroom. Studies show that parental involvement is critical to sending a clear antidrug message. Youth peer counseling programs can help stem substance abuse. Drug-free group activities decrease the incentive to use drugs as a means of socializing. Churches and other religious organizations also provide an excellent means of community outreach to discourage drug use. After churches in Cleveland, Ohio, held rallies against drug trafficking and vigils outside houses being used for drug transactions, dealers left the neighborhood.

Communities can also prevent youth from turning to drugs by offering positive alternatives to drug use and trafficking—such as youth centers, sports, job training, and public service activities. An Alternatives For Teens (AFT) program in Middleburg, Vermont, that provided activities for at-risk teens reduced the percentage of drug abuse among participants by over 75 percent.

Businesses can help reduce addiction and drug traffic, both among employees and throughout the community. Drug-testing programs can identify and deter use, increasing workplace safety and employee health. Businesses, particularly bars and restaurants, can decrease substance abuse in the community. Programs that train restaurant personnel to prevent underage or excessive drinking by patrons decrease the likelihood of drunk-driving crashes and discourage alcohol consumption by youth. Drug dealers can be prevented from using places of business for drug transactions. Restricting pay phones to outgoing calls denies drug dealers a free, unregistered phone line through which to establish operations. A program in Chicago that stopped pay-phone acceptance of incoming calls caused drug dealers to move on, increasing resident safety.

Substance abuse treatment programs are effective means of rehabilitating drug users. Community treatment and outreach strategies attempt to identify drug users and provide them with help at little or no cost. The presence of informal community treatment centers in areas with high rates of drug abuse allows residents to seek convenient, voluntary treatment. Medical and criminal justice professionals have determined that treatment programs in the criminal justice system are highly effective because the threat of imprisonment motivates drug addicts to stay in treatment until they are clean. Drug courts and pretrial intervention programs in which charges against a defendant are dismissed upon successful rehabilitation have excellent track records in several regions. These programs alleviate the case pressures of the criminal justice system while achieving positive behavior change rarely accomplished by incarceration alone. Success stories of treatment as a condition of probation or diversion abound. Among drug court defendants who participated in a Bro-

ward County, Florida, pretrial intervention program that places offenders in rigorous treatment programs, only one percent had returned to jail after one year.

Expanded law enforcement is critical to eradicating drug threats within communities. Traditional responses such as increased penalties for drug offenses and more police officers on the street reduce crime while increasing a community's sense of safety. It is also important to expand the means by which officers can detain drug dealers. Code enforcement of public safety laws and public misconduct charges can be used to counter drug activity. Cooperation with the community can help police locate drug offenders; 24-hour hotlines through which citizens can anonymously report drug-related activity encourage citizens to reclaim their communities and overcome the fears that accompany drug activity.

Neighborhoods can reduce drug-related activity by making environmental changes that reduce the ease with which illicit activity can take place. Physical changes, such as better street lighting and cleaner parks and public places improve surveillance, while restricting street access prevents drug dealers from turning an area into a center of illegal business.

This chapter contains strategies for countering the influence of drugs within a community. Examples of successful programs offer hope for overcoming the destruction caused by narcotics. Increased prevention, enforcement, and treatment can rebuild communities currently overwhelmed by the drug trade.

School-Based Curricula

Strategy

Schools provide the setting for curricula designed to prevent or reduce drug use among school-aged children.

Drug Problem Addressed

School-based programs reach those most vulnerable to the use of alcohol and other drugs—young people. Research indicates that young people who avoid using drugs, including alcohol, are much less likely to become frequent drug users later in life. Through school antidrug programs, the greatest number of youth receive antidrug education for an extended period.

Key Components

Antidrug curricula vary, but most include factual information about smoking, drinking alcohol, and using illegal drugs, including their serious health effects, and about positive alternatives to substance abuse. Exercises and role plays develop students' ability to refuse dangerous

substances, make decisions, solve problems, communicate, cooperate, and set goals; they also enhance family relationships, sensitivity to diversity, leadership skills, and self-esteem.

The curricula may include lectures, class discussions, guest speakers, written and oral exercises, performing arts, audiovisual materials, special assemblies, individual and group projects, and special youth-led events. Community antidrug programs can reinforce the curricula.

Some programs (e.g., D.A.R.E.) use an outside resource person such as a law enforcement officer or primary school teacher or facilitator; others (e.g., "Here's Looking at You, 200") use the classroom teacher in that role.

Key Partnerships

School-based antidrug programs bring together school teachers, staff, parents, law enforcement personnel, and other members of the community willing to come into the classroom and assist with antidrug instruction.

Potential Obstacles

Some schools have failed to develop or enforce clear anti-drug policies. Before a school adopts an antidrug curriculum, the administration should issue a strong statement on school policy that communicates zero tolerance of alcohol and other drug use, seizure of drugs and drug paraphernalia, penalties for drug activity, the school's working relationship with law enforcement agencies, and a commitment to protecting students' rights.

Schools should shop around, among tested and evaluated antidrug curricula, for one that is cost-effective and age-appropriate.

Signs of Success

School-based antidrug curricula have been intensely evaluated. Early evaluations indicated that knowledge of drugs was insufficient to affect behavior. Effective antidrug curricula taught life skills and helped young people make healthy choices. In 1990 *Science* published a study of junior high school programs focusing on social influences (such as peer pressure). The study found that such programs measurably reduce adolescent smoking and marijuana use, often the precursor to other drug use. Additional research by the Office of Substance Abuse and Prevention (OSAP) shows that school-based programs work well when incorporated into a broader framework of promoting health development in children and that efforts need to begin before and during elementary school.

Applying the Strategy

In Chicago's Logan Square neighborhood, many Hispanic youths learn to avoid the drug use through the Quest K-12 drug prevention program, supported by the local Lions' Club chapter.

In Waterloo, Iowa, the local crime prevention officer appears before elementary school children as McGruff the Crime Dog, teaching them to avoid drugs and protect their health.

In the police-sponsored D.A.R.E. program, uniformed officers come into the classroom for seventeen weeks of the school year to teach students the dangers of drug use, how to say no to drugs, and how to make good decisions about healthy lifestyles. D.A.R.E. trains these officers to help students resist the temptation to use drugs. D.A.R.E. is part of a comprehensive, four-pronged program to revitalize and clean up neighborhoods in Trenton, New Jersey. The program also includes a project to remove violent offenders, community-oriented policing, a Safe Haven program, and a social services program.

Contact Information

Chief, Trenton Police Department
225 North Clinton Avenue
Trenton, New Jersey 08609
609-989-4055

D.A.R.E. America
P.O. Box 2090
Los Angeles, California 90051
1-800-223-DARE (3273)

Drug Planning and Outreach
Office of Elementary and Secondary Education
U.S. Department of Education
400 Maryland Avenue, SW
Washington, DC 20202-6123
202-401-3030

Truancy Prevention

Strategy

Communities can provide high-risk youth, who are often truant from school and who may be using or dealing drugs, with early intervention services. Parents should also receive services.

Drug Problem Addressed

Some youth at high risk for drug use fail to benefit from school-based antidrug programs because they are frequently absent from or late for class. Studies show that young people who drop out of school are more likely to associate with other youth involved with crime and drugs, work at a job with limited potential for long-term stable income, and experience emotional difficulties as a result of alienation from peers still attending school.

Key Components

Students who are chronically absent from or late for school lack academic success. In turn, this lack of success diminishes their self-confidence. They may also lack positive peer relationships and feel strong antagonism toward school or schoolwork. These attitudes often lead a chronically truant student to become involved with alcohol or other drugs. A program that addresses truancy must be able to identify truant students, assess their specific needs, and intervene in a way that involves the students, their families, and school personnel. Anti-truancy programs work best when referrals are made to service providers in the community and parents offer encouragement. Students benefit from daily attendance monitoring, one-on-one counseling, and group sessions with drug-prevention specialists. Frequently, school staff act as role models and assist with behavior modification.

Key Partnerships

Anti-truancy programs involve efforts by parents, youth, social-service providers, and school personnel such as guidance counselors and teachers. Truant teens need to interact with peers in support groups that encourage alternatives to substance use.

Potential Obstacles

For the best results, anti-truancy programs must be long term. Parents may show interest and enthusiasm at first, but they may find monitoring their child burdensome and difficult and may need encouragement to continue to support the program.

Signs of Success

OSAP data on a three-year anti-truancy program in Pennsylvania show significantly improved attendance by formerly truant students. These data also reveal that 60 percent of the students referred to the anti-truancy program have a parent who abuses alcohol or other drugs. The program initiated an outreach effort to identify and assist families in need of alcohol, drug, or other services.

Applying the Strategy

The Community College of Beaver County in Monaca, Pennsylvania, has addressed the needs of truant students in its Absentee Prevention Program. It has developed a manual and a two-day training program for a team of specialists who have helped students who fail to attend school for a variety of reasons: poor parental attitude toward school, anxiety over poor performance, frequent illness, significant family events (divorce, a parent's loss of a job, death in the family), and drug or alcohol involvement. The program has been copied in other Pennsylvania school districts, New Jersey, and Michigan.

In Charleston, South Carolina, two truancy officers locate at-risk children who fail to attend school. During the summer months, the anti-truancy program focuses on building trust between the youth and the truancy officers who will work with them when school begins.

Contact Information

Director, Prevention Project
Beaver Valley Professional Center
1260 North Broadhead Road, Suite 302
Monaca, Pennsylvania 15061-2590
412-775-7904, ext. 213

Parental Involvement

Strategy

Programs and mechanisms that incorporate parental involvement in raising drug-free children can reduce drug use and strengthen community antidrug norms.

Drug Problem Addressed

When drug information and antidrug behaviors learned at school are not reinforced at home, young people are more likely to turn to substance abuse.

Key Components

The most important components of a parent-based strategy for drug prevention are factual education and support from other parents or community groups. Drug prevention efforts should include teaching parents the signs of drug use and informing them about drug paraphernalia. Parents should also be made aware of community resources if they are concerned that their children might be involved with alcohol or other drugs. An effective parent program strengthens communication between parents and children, supports parents who refuse to allow alcohol or other drugs at parties, provides information about sources of

alcohol and drugs, and reinforces other parents who are trying to keep their children drug free. In some communities, parents sign a pledge that they will not permit young people to bring alcohol or other drugs into their homes.

Key Partnerships

Parents can work with school personnel, other community residents who observe young people in after-school or evening activities, law enforcement, community service providers, and youth. In some communities, leaders of youth organizations and athletic coaches have worked effectively with parents interested in combating drug use among youth.

Potential Obstacles

Denial is a serious barrier to helping parents whose children are involved with alcohol and other drugs. Also, some parents may judge others too harshly, creating hostility within the parent support group. These barriers can be addressed through the expertise of trained family counselors or drug prevention specialists who are effective in communicating without expressing condemnation.

Signs of Success

In *Adolescents at Risk* (1990), J. D. Dryfoos reviews the success of adolescent drug prevention programs and concludes that the involvement of a caring adult in a parenting role is the "hallmark of effective prevention programs."

Project Info in Whittier, California, works closely with youth who show early signs of drug or alcohol abuse, and with their families. Founded as a research project, the program now provides direct services. A recent evaluation highlighted a 4 percent recidivism rate for youth participants.

Applying the Strategy

In Houston, the Self-Help for African People through Education program formed a Parent Awareness Network to unite the community in the fight against drugs and crime and to improve neighborhood conditions. With help from local schools, the parents met weekly at the schools and at a housing development and signed a pledge to work together to keep their children drug free.

The Scott Newman Center, with headquarters in California, has been part of a strong movement to increase parental awareness of drug problems and how they affect families. The center's program, Neighborhoods in Action, assists existing neighborhood groups by providing drug education and drug prevention materials, teaching basic parent-child communication skills, and helping to resolve problems that arise from drug use.

The Parents' Communication Network of Minnesota connects more than ten thousand families in the state with newsletters and other printed materials on alcohol and other drug use, parenting skills, party hosting and restrictions, and other issues that concern parents of elementary and teenage children. The network also keeps parents apprised of effective antidrug curricula, legislative efforts to prevent substance use, state and national resources in drug prevention, and health issues.

Contact Information

Program Coordinator
Parents' Communication Network of Minnesota
National Federation of Parents for Drug-Free Youth
P.O. Box 24392
Apple Valley, Minnesota 55124
612-432-2886

Neighborhoods in Action
Scott Newman Foundation
6255 Sunset Boulevard, Suite 1906
Los Angeles, California 90028
213-469-2029

Before- and After-School Programs

Strategy

School buildings are used before and after school hours to provide superior educational and recreational programs for youths.

Drug Problem Addressed

Latchkey children are particularly vulnerable to alcohol or other drug use because they are unsupervised by their parents or other responsible adults before and after school.

Key Components

Some schools permit children to arrive early, when parents must leave for work, and stay late in the afternoon to take advantage of tutoring, athletics, supervised programs, or playtime. Before- and after-school programs can be run by neighborhood volunteers, school staff, or organizations willing to conduct programs at schools. They can also be based at community centers or church buildings. It is important that the program not be viewed as a baby-sitting service or an extension of school time, but rather a time during which children's developmental needs are served. Successful programs provide opportunities for play, creativity, companionship, and relaxation.

Key Partnerships

School-based programs for latchkey youths can involve schools, churches or other religious organizations, neighborhood groups, volunteers, teens who are trained (and sometimes hired) to supervise young children, or parents who share in the responsibility of supervising youths. The municipal department of parks and recreation can also sponsor an after-school program.

Potential Obstacles

Child-care providers must comply with local and state regulations, including TB screenings and possible background checks. In addition, caring for children requires commitment and responsibility; supervisors must embody the substance-free message.

Signs of Success

Anecdotal evidence suggests that providing latchkey children with before- and after-school safe havens decreases their exposure to neighborhood drug or other criminal activity.

Applying the Strategy

A Hartford, Connecticut, school stays open before and after class hours because parents and others in the community identified the need for a safe, supervised place for children.

In Trenton, New Jersey, four schools have become Safe Havens from 3 p.m. to 9 p.m., providing positive recreational and other opportunities for youths who want to stay drug- and gang-free. The program, which also provides activities for adults, is funded through the city's Weed and Seed grant from the U.S. Department of Justice (DOJ).

Gaining Realization of Worth, a YMCA program in Phoenix, Arizona, is an activity-based after-school program that helps youth resist alcohol and other drugs by increasing their decision-making and survival skills, giving them healthy values, enhancing their self-esteem, and offering them positive group membership.

Contact Information

Project Director
YMCA of Phoenix and Valley of the Sun
350 North First Avenue
Phoenix, Arizona 85003
602-258-0077

Drug-Free School Zones

Strategy

Most communities have enacted laws that create legal "safe zones" around schools and other public areas frequented by young people. Violations of drug laws in those zones carry stiff penalties.

Drug Problem Addressed

This strategy addresses the problem of drug dealers and users who frequent schools and other public areas in order to sell drugs or lure young people to try drugs. In a 1989 Bureau of Justice Statistics (DOJ) survey, students reported that some drugs were readily available at schools.

Key Components

Most states have enacted laws to create drug-free school zones, although the degree of enforcement varies widely. These laws impose sharp penalties for drug sale or use, gang involvement, or carrying weapons if the offense occurs within a thousand feet of a school or within a park or other public area. In Illinois, legislation forbids students from bringing cellular phones onto school property except with the principal's permission. Some communities have extended the concept to parks and other public property. Signs marking drug-free zones warn potential offenders.

To protect young children, area residents may walk young children to and from school or enroll in a program that allows them to put signs in their windows indicating that their home is a "Safe House" for a child in need.

Key Partnerships

This strategy is most effective when schools work with parents, students, school personnel, police, and area residents.

Potential Obstacles

The most serious obstacle to this strategy is possible lack of enforcement, which can result from understaffing at local law enforcement agencies or lack of understanding of the law by area residents. In some areas a comprehensive publicity campaign which clarifies the law and underscores the severe penalties can overcome the obstacle.

Signs of Success

Some schools have reported a decreased drug presence around schools since the Federal Drug-Free School Zone Law went into effect in 1984. When Tucson, Arizona, instituted drug-free school zones, the number of students caught in possession of alcohol or drugs dropped by 43 percent.

Applying the Strategy

In a Houston, Texas, neighborhood, approximately two hundred volunteers take time each day to lead children safely to and from school. Their action protects the children and demonstrates their community's intolerance of drug use or other illegal activity near schools. Signs announcing drug-free school zones state that penalties for violations are severe.

In a Chicago neighborhood, a drug-infested block was declared a Narcotics Enforcement Area. Police reclaimed the area for residents by arresting drug dealers and making the block safe again.

Contact Information

Self-Help for African People through Education
SHAPE Community Center
3815 Live Oak
Houston, Texas 77004
713-521-0629

National School Safety Center
4165 Thousand Oaks Boulevard, Suite 290
Westlake Village, California 91362
805-373-9977

Incentives and Rewards for Healthy Choices

Strategy

Community-sponsored incentives and rewards reinforce attitudes and behaviors that support crime-free, drug-free, healthy lifestyles.

Drug Problem Addressed

Many young people feel peer pressure to use drugs. If they feel rewarded for healthy choices, they are more likely to stay drug free.

Key Components

Amid peer pressure, young people sometimes have difficulty remaining steadfast to a pledge of no alcohol or other drugs. By offering rewards in the form of store discounts, T-shirts, and special privileges, youth drug prevention organizations can support young people in their decision to avoid substance abuse. Many local businesses are willing to donate special items to young people or give them discount coupons. Performing arts groups can offer tickets to special concerts or plays. Restaurants can sponsor drug-free pizza parties, honoring youths who have stuck by their pledges to stay drug free. Free admittance to athletic events or to movies can reward youths and entice others to join the community's drug prevention effort.

The incentive or reward need not be a material thing but can take the form of local media coverage, a celebration banquet, a certificate of commendation, or the addition of an honoree's name to a plaque.

Key Partnerships

Local businesses often spearhead a partnership with community leaders in drug prevention to reward young people who stay clean. Community-based organizations can also offer special privileges or commendations to youth who are high achievers or good role models.

Potential Obstacles

This strategy's start-up is labor intensive. Although businesses are largely supportive, it may take numerous contacts and negotiations to secure their involvement. Also, it takes time to keep records updated and maintain business interest and commitment. Adequate staff time must be allocated in advance.

Signs of Success

The response from community residents and businesses has been extremely positive. Staff members at the Sheriff's Pass Program in Cape May, New Jersey, have received hundreds of requests from counties nationwide for information on initiating programs that use this strategy. The Sheriff's Pass Program has been successfully duplicated in Gloucester, New Jersey.

Applying the Strategy

In Cape May, New Jersey, more than a hundred local businesses have agreed to participate in the Sheriff's Pass Jail program. First, teens are educated about the legal consequences of drug use. Next they sign a drug-free pledge and obtain a photo ID that brings discounts at participating businesses on clothes, videos, haircuts, food, books, and other goods and services. Cards must be revalidated every two years; teens found to be involved with drugs lose their privileges.

Contact Information

Sheriff's Pass Jail Program
4 Moore Road, DN 301
Cape May Courthouse, New Jersey 08210-1097
609-463-6426

Easy Access to Prevention and Treatment Services

Strategy

When a community provides easy access to prevention and early intervention services, these services reach youth and adults who would otherwise go unassisted.

Drug Problem Addressed

Because of family, social, economic, or environmental factors, some children, and their parents, are particularly vulnerable to using alcohol and other drugs. Some troubled families fail to get help because services are too expensive, inaccessible, or unavailable during convenient hours.

Key Components

High-risk young people often need special intervention and drug-related services. Often, their parents also need assistance. Easy-access prevention and intervention services can be located at schools, churches, housing complexes, day-care centers, community centers, or storefronts. They can provide free family advocacy services, tutoring, family counseling, parenting classes, assistance for students who have been suspended or are in danger of being suspended from school for drug-related offenses, and information and referral to other community resources. Neighborhood-based assistance can also be extended to runaways, homeless youths, juvenile offenders, and youths who have been removed from home for their protection.

Key Partnerships

Community-based service providers must be part of a network that includes schools, parents, youth groups, and the local juvenile justice system. These providers must share information and coordinate services to identify and serve high-risk individuals.

Potential Obstacles

Often, at-risk individuals do not seek assistance until there is a crisis, and parents who are burdened with socioeconomic difficulties are often unsupportive if their children are in trouble. Many parents find it difficult to attend meetings or counseling sessions because of transportation problems, lack of child care, or restrictive job requirements. Others are apathetic or fearful regarding assistance programs.

Signs of Success

An OSAP evaluation of one easy-access intervention program for high-risk youths found that four of five major risk factors—frequency and amount of drug use—had been reduced in participating youth. OSAP also reported improved adolescent-adult communication.

Applying the Strategy

Pittsburgh's Addison Terrace Learning Center is located in a public housing project where many youths and their parents are involved in drug use. The center teaches parenting skills through a parent forum, has a child-care program and on-site playroom for the children of parents who seek treatment, and offers an on-site, income-producing print shop and job training for adolescents.

In Atlanta, the Bridge (Operation Higher Ground) program provides emergency shelter and counseling for runaway or homeless youths. The goal is to replace high-risk behavior, which can lead to or exacerbate drug use, with healthy behavior. In collaboration with Atlanta's public school system, the Bridge also operates an alternative school for youth who cannot attend regular classes while in a shelter. The program is part of National Families in Action.

The House Next Door, in Deland, Florida, offers family therapy to youths in trouble with drugs and to their families, with parent-training services in the homes of participating families. The program has documented a high rate of client retention and a decrease in drug use among youths.

Contact Information

Executive Director
National Families in Action
2296 Henderson Mill Road, Suite 300
Atlanta, Georgia 30345
404-934-6364

Youth-to-Youth Antidrug Strategy

Strategy

Communities use one of their greatest resources to combat drug use among youths—other youths.

Drug Problem Addressed

Young people are often reluctant to heed adults who warn them to avoid the use of alcohol and other drugs. Such youth frequently respond more to peer influence.

Key Components

Teens are resourceful and imaginative. When charged with developing programs and projects for reaching their peers with antidrug messages, young people nationwide have suggested and implemented a teen activity center, training for teens to help peers, puppet shows or other performances that dramatize an antidrug message, youth workshops, "fun days" that feature positive alternatives to drugs, peer counseling and mentoring, awareness campaigns, community patrols, school-based youth projects, antidrug murals, cross-age teaching, athletic contests with law enforcement sponsorship and participation, parent-teen talk sessions, and many other programs. One thing is critical in a youth-led, youth-focused program: let the program belong to the youth.

Key Partnerships

Youth should be the program's primary participants, although adults can be effective in supporting roles. Youths can seek the assistance and involvement of school personnel, community leaders, business professionals, law enforcement personnel, social service providers, religious leaders, and others.

Potential Obstacles

Some young people have more energy and enthusiasm than training. Supporting adults should ensure that young people acting as peer counselors or mentors, as project leaders, or in other positions of responsibility have sufficient training to do the job properly. Be careful, though: some adults have difficulty limiting themselves to supporting roles in youth programs. When adults take over, youths often lose interest in the program.

Signs of Success

In one neighborhood "good kids just stayed home," said one young girl whose mother was afraid to let her leave the house. When the young people in town developed a youth center with the help of some caring adults, there was a feeling of safety among the neighborhood residents. In collaboration with the local police department, the young people connected to this center produced a video to educate their peers about the dangers of using crack cocaine.

Applying the Strategy

In Evansville, Indiana, teens organized a Teen Council and sponsored a video on alternatives to drug use, identifying fun activities in the area that did not involve illegal substances.

In New York City, teens participated in Youth Unlimited (formerly Youth Force), training other teens in life skills and implementing a program (Take Back the Park) in which a group of teens identified as emotionally handicapped restored a children's garden in a park that had become littered with drug paraphernalia.

Members of the Natural Helpers Program in Hampton City, Virginia, train to help younger children avoid alcohol and other drugs. They have developed a New Students' program to help youths adjust to new school situations and a Peer Partner program to help ninth graders adjust to high school. Natural Helpers serve as drug-free role models and special friends.

Contact Information

Youth Unlimited
Citizens Committee for New York City
305 7th Avenue, 15th Floor
New York, New York 10001
212-989-0909

Alternatives to Drugs

Strategy

Saying no to drug use is only half the battle. Effective drug prevention requires a range of positive alternatives to which youths can say yes.

Drug Problem Addressed

Often, young people say that they started using alcohol or other drugs because there "just isn't anything else fun to do." An absence of positive activities increases the likelihood of substance abuse.

Key Components

Ideally, an antidrug program that focuses on positive alternatives to substance abuse will be designed and managed by youths. Adult support is frequently necessary, but the program should belong to the young people who will benefit from it.

Alternative programs have included youth centers where young people can "hang out" after school; job training; athletic contests; substance-free social events; performing arts events, such as theater, puppet shows, and concerts; community service projects; and tutoring. Each of these activities focuses on fun and accomplishment, while healthy living is the foundation. Adults can help with transportation, youth leadership training, and some details of organization.

Key Partnerships

All segments of the community—including parents and special-interest youth groups such as the Boy Scouts, Girl Scouts, or 4-H—can contribute to youth programs that focus on alternatives to substance abuse. Businesses can donate materials and refreshments; schools can assist with service projects; law enforcement can help organize athletic leagues and youth crime- and drug-watch activities.

Potential Obstacles

Alternative programs for youth can be impeded by difficulty in sustaining interest. Many young people have short attention spans and easily become bored. Program leaders must detect declining interest and re-energize the program through new activities. Difficulty in attracting adult volunteers qualified to work with young people will also hamper a program. Although young people drive these programs, success can rest with supportive adults. Without taking the lead, adults must help young people develop their own program.

Signs of Success

During the seven years of a youth alternatives program in Middleburg, Vermont, they raised the legal drinking age from eighteen to twenty-one and Students Against Drunk Driving (SADD) and Mothers Against Drunk Driving (MADD) formed local chapters. Among teen participants in an alternative adventure program for high-risk youth, the rate of involvement with alcohol or other drugs fell from 32 percent before the program to 7 percent afterward.

Applying the Strategy

A Waterloo, Iowa, couple started the African American Recreation Transformation System (AARTS) in a former bar that had gunshot holes in the wall and was next door to a bar known for employing young people in drug sales. A youth governing board enforced a strict code of conduct that permitted no alcohol or other drugs at the center and took part in AARTS's daily operation.

AFT has provided enjoyable substance-free events for teens in rural Middlebury, Vermont. The teens decide which events they want to organize, plan the events, and make the necessary arrangements. School guidance counselors, teachers, administrators, parents, and friends support the group.

Youths aged nine to seventeen who are at risk for alcohol or other drug abuse are encouraged to join Adventure Alternatives, operated by the Austin, Texas, Wilderness Counseling Service. The program provides professional counseling to youths and families, as well as adventure camping programs, lasting one to two weeks, that feature wilderness backpacking, campcraft, astronomy, nature study, map and compass reading, and outdoor cooking. An evaluation of the program revealed a significant decline in the use of alcohol and other drugs among participants who completed the program.

Contact Information

Iowa Citizens for Community Improvement
612 Mulberry Street
Waterloo, IA 50703
319-233-9920

Media Campaigns

Strategy

The mass media disseminate antidrug information and motivate the public to protect the community from drug-related activity.

Drug Problem Addressed

Communities may be in denial about their problems. Radio, television, and the print media reach a wide audience. Mass media campaigns are a cost-effective way to make the community aware of drug problems and solutions.

Key Components

Mass media antidrug campaigns can include public service advertising on TV or radio, print ads, flyers and other printed materials, as well as donations of space or materials by transit companies, utilities, and local businesses. Often, the ads and program messages are given a local framework to direct the attention of community residents to local problems. To be effective, the campaign must go beyond informing the public; it must also provide an avenue for action. Mass media advertising is often a part of national antidrug and anticrime efforts that may include antidrug events or activities for specially designated times of the year, such as the National Crime Prevention Council's (NCPC's) annual Crime Prevention Month in October or the National PTA's Drug Awareness Week held the first week of March.

Key Partnerships

Mass media antidrug campaigns involve most sectors of the community, including local radio and television stations, local newspapers and other print media, antidrug organizations, and business. Other community resources, such as journalism departments of local colleges or universities and journalism clubs at high schools, are also valuable partners in mass media campaigns.

Potential Obstacles

One potential obstacle to a mass media campaign is a lack of follow-up and sustaining effort after an initial burst of enthusiasm. In some communities, public interest in an antidrug campaign has gradually waned once media turned to other issues.

Signs of Success

A Bureau of Justice Assistance (BJA) study on the National Citizens' Crime Prevention Campaign (NCCPC) found that it resulted in a positive long-term change in citizens' behavior and attitudes towards crime and drug activity. The study found decreased fear of crime and more citizen action to prevent crime than had existed ten years earlier. Mass media campaigns have made a positive difference in crime and drug prevention.

Applying the Strategy

In Houston, Texas, local reporters and city officials were invited to take a bus tour through the city's most drug-ravaged ward. After footage of the event appeared on the evening news, residents reported that local services improved.

In communities in every state, the NCPC's McGruff the Crime Dog talks to young people about drug prevention and health. Most children recognize McGruff and say they trust him and would like to follow his advice.

Contact Information

National Crime Prevention Council
1700 K Street, NW, 2nd Floor
Washington, DC 20006-3817
202-466-6272 x121

Community Action

Strategy

A comprehensive public effort driven by neighborhood pride, a sense of community survival, and self-protection results in a successful antidrug campaign.

Drug Problem Addressed

Community mobilization strategies address local problems, such as drug dealers moving into or taking control of a community. Residents combat drug-related problems specific to a community, neighborhood, or block of homes or apartments by designing and implementing their own antidrug fight.

Key Components

Community mobilization usually follows heightened awareness of the nature and severity of local drug problems. This awareness often results from a highly publicized local incident or from information gathering that confirms neighborhood problems. Residents meet to determine appropriate action and initiate an antidrug plan.

Community mobilization strategies can include large- or small-scale rallies held at safe places such as shopping malls or community centers, community surveillance of crime and drug incidents, cleanup activities in parks and other public places, marches with banners and placards announcing residents' determination to keep their neighborhood drug free, or community picnics designed to encourage residents to get to know one another.

Key Partnerships

Community mobilization partners include residents, schools, local businesses, local officials, religious groups, neighborhood groups, law enforcement, and youth. Broad-range partnerships are key to successful community mobilization strategies.

Potential Obstacles

In the first stages of identifying local drug problems, fear of retaliation represents a major obstacle to community mobilization. Many community residents resist getting involved because they wish to protect their children, themselves, and their property. Often, anonymity assuages fear, as when police station hotlines do not require callers to give their names. As a community begins to feel stronger and more cohesive in fighting drug activity, fear usually subsides.

Signs of Success

Community mobilization has been at the core of much antidrug activity across the country. Some communities have reported increased community pride (Northwest Bronx Community and Clergy Association) and decreased fear, restored law and order (Union Miles Development Corporation, Cleveland), cessation of drug activity (South Austin suburb of Chicago and Union Miles in Cleveland), fear-free access to local parks (Waterloo, Iowa), and unification of a multi-ethnic community through a common purpose (Chicago).

Applying the Strategy

In the Northwest Bronx, a "We Are Drug Free" rally at a local shopping mall, attracted more than two thousand individuals. This rally signaled the beginning of the community's public stand against drug use and crime.

A coalition of ministers, the Union Miles Development Corporation, launched a major community drug prevention campaign in Cleveland, Ohio, by holding Good Friday prayer vigils outside several drug houses. The next morning, they held a neighborhood cleanup; in the evening, they marched to a tent meeting. On Easter Sunday the ministers held prayer services at the drug houses and inaugurated a week-long drug-reporting strategy. Area visitors, no longer afraid to walk down the streets, remarked that the community strategy restored law and order.

Young people in the Youth as Resources program have mobilized their peers across the state of Indiana to improve their neighborhoods. The programs include a wide range of students—among them, former school dropouts, Honor Society members, teen mothers, 4-H junior leaders, probationers, and class officers. Their projects, supported by the Lilly Endowment and guided by the NCPC, have ranged from a health fair with literature about the dangers of alcohol and other drugs to drug prevention education for young children.

Contact Information

Union Miles Development Corporation
12002 Miles Avenue
Cleveland, Ohio 44127
216-341-0757

"Hot Spot" Strategy

Strategy

Community residents help build evidence that certain areas are frequented by drug dealers by anonymously submitting critical information to law enforcement or other authorities.

Drug Problem Addressed

Drug dealers often operate out of specific neighborhood areas ("hot spots"), setting up business in abandoned buildings or storefronts. Sometimes they operate out of their cars by parking near certain intersections.

Key Components

Often, residents are afraid to call police about drug activity because they fear retaliation. Some communities have distributed "hot-spot" cards to residents, enabling them to anonymously report what they have observed. The cards request information about suspected drug dealers: their physical appearance, address, vehicle, and visible weapons, and the types of drugs they sell. These cards can be screened by a community organization or sent directly to the local police. The information assists police in monitoring areas reported to have heavy drug activity and in taking action to rid the community of the dealers. Police departments can also set up special phone lines to take information about hot spots, guaranteeing the caller anonymity.

Key Partnerships

Neighborhood residents become partners with law enforcement agencies by serving as police departments' eyes and ears. When a resident reports information, law enforcement agencies can act expeditiously, and with adequate evidence, to clean up a trouble spot.

Potential Obstacles

Some residents who cooperate with law enforcement fear retaliation from drug dealers. It is critical to assure resi-

dents that their identity will not be disclosed. Also, law enforcement must verify information before acting to close a crack house or other center of drug activity. Incorrect or incomplete information can lead to problems with false arrests.

Signs of Success

The Eastside Substance Abuse Awareness Program is a comprehensive, community-based substance awareness program in Wilmington, Delaware. Police reported that this program's hot-spot reporting and community policing efforts resulted in substantially increased citizen call-ins and drug-related arrests over a five-year period. The sixth year brought an encouraging drop in calls and arrests as drug activity declined in the neighborhood.

Applying the Strategy

Residents in Waterloo, Iowa, designed an antidrug strategy that includes distributing hot-spot cards to residents in areas identified as centers of drug activity. The cards, which help law enforcement personnel focus on drug dealers and crack houses operating in neighborhoods, resulted in increased arrests.

In the Eastside neighborhood of Wilmington, Delaware, residents worked with police to curb drug-related activity through an active hot-spot call-in program combined with community meetings, Neighborhood Watch, recreation programs, community policing, and referral to service providers.

Contact Information

Senior Planner
Criminal Justice Council
820 North French Street, 4th Floor
Wilmington, Delaware 19801
302-577-3430

Restrictions on Pay Phones

Strategy

Phone companies limit the use of public pay phones to outgoing calls in areas where drug dealers operate.

Drug Problem Addressed

Drug dealers often use public phones to arrange transactions. These dealers want to avoid using residential or business phones, or they are unable to qualify for regular phone service. By restricting pay-phone service so that dealers cannot receive incoming calls, phone companies interrupt drug dealers' business without inconveniencing honest residents.

Key Components

In many drug-ridden areas, residents are intimidated by groups loitering near public coin-operated phones used for drug transactions. Some dealers reportedly claim exclusive rights to these phones and threaten anyone who attempts to use them. Community residents can request that phone companies restrict pay-phone service to outgoing calls only, preventing dealers from using the phones to get callbacks from customers or from drug runners with beepers.

Key Partnerships

Community residents can work with the local phone company to change phone service to outgoing calls only. Businesses can join in a campaign to restrict pay phone use, which will reduce loitering and disruptive activity outside commercial buildings.

Potential Obstacles

Dealers could retaliate by damaging the phones, making them unusable.

Signs of Success

Reportedly, loitering around public phones decreases when a phone company restricts service.

Applying the Strategy

In Chicago's South Austin neighborhood, elderly residents were afraid to use the public phone outside a neighborhood church because drug dealers loitered there and intimidated the residents. The elderly, some of whom were unable to afford their own phones, were forced to go elsewhere to make calls, causing them considerable inconvenience and expense. The South Austin Coalition and Community Council asked Illinois Bell to intervene. Within a week, the phones near the church would accept only outgoing calls, the dealers moved on, and residents again felt safe in their neighborhood.

According to residents of Wilmington, Delaware's Eastside area, pay phones were attracting loiterers and suspicious activity. The phone company agreed to remove some of the phones and modify others so that they could no longer accept incoming calls, making them useless for drug transactions.

Contact Information

South Austin Coalition Community Council
5112 West Washington Boulevard
Chicago, Illinois 60644
312-287-4570

Community Partnerships

Strategy

Formal, ongoing partnerships among organizations have become the cornerstone of many drug prevention coalitions, providing a broad interdisciplinary base and avoiding wasteful duplication.

Drug Problem Addressed

Individual, narrowly focused drug prevention programs often duplicate efforts, are costly, and fail to have sustained results. Also, people most in need of assistance frequently fall through the cracks.

Key Components

In communities that build coalitions to prevent or reduce alcohol and other drug use, the lead official or agency identifies representatives from other groups, agencies, and organizations to serve on a governing committee. The task force determines the nature and extent of drug-related problems in the community and designs a work plan that includes a defined sphere of action, short- and long-term goals, and a detailed budget.

After an action plan is adopted, its implementation may require technical assistance, training, broad financing, and much time and effort. An evaluation program will provide guidance for program modification and gauge success.

Key Partnerships

Task force members should include law enforcement and criminal justice system representatives, leaders of community groups, social service providers, business leaders, elected officials, religious leaders, youth, media representatives, school representatives, private citizens, drug prevention experts, treatment providers, and other medical experts.

Potential Obstacles

A community drug prevention coalition can have trouble reaching a consensus on goals and objectives, sustaining interest, maintaining cooperation, coping with cultural diversity, setting realistic goals, tapping financial resources, and recognizing the community's limitations. Solutions to these problems come from patient dedication and commitment to a common goal: a drug-free community.

Signs of Success

In an evaluation of ten communities that formed coalitions and used a variety of strategies to combat local drug activity, each community reported positive results. Drug houses were closed and youth centers were opened, parents established peer networks, neighbors joined antidrug marches, and dealers were driven out of neighborhoods. Through collaboration, resources were combined in new ways to meet community needs. Agencies cooperated and combined talents to focus more effectively on local problems.

Applying the Strategy

In the maritime community of Gloucester, Massachusetts, the Gloucester Prevention Network is addressing the town's serious history of alcohol and other drug abuse through education, religious groups, parents, sports, youths, and the elderly. Each steering committee member addresses the problem in his or her own area. Participants in twelve neighborhood-based sports organizations for youth—which reach about seven thousand children—wear Network patches on their sports uniforms.

In Cuyahoga County, Ohio (which includes Cleveland and fifty-six other cities), violent crime increased and as many as 70 percent of arrestees tested positive for drugs. The area formed the Substance Abuse Initiative and focused on after-school programs and stronger neighborhood links with the Cleveland police, local clergy, social service agencies, neighborhood centers, business, block clubs, and other groups.

Contact Information

Substance Abuse Initiative
Project Director, Task Force on Violent Crime
300 Rockefeller Building
614 Superior Avenue, West
Cleveland, Ohio 44113-1306
216-781-2944

National Crime Prevention Council
Attn: Community Responses to Drug Abuse
1700 K Street, NW, 2nd Floor
Washington, DC 20006-3817
202-466-6272

Churches as Resources

Strategy

Churches and other religious institutions use their organizational strength and influence to rid communities of drug activity.

Drug Problem Addressed

Involving religious institutions in a community effort to reduce drug abuse can address drug problems in neighborhoods where religious influence is strong and religious groups can perform effective outreach. Religious groups can be particularly successful in communities with a large ethnic population not easily reached through other means.

Key Components

In many communities the church, temple, mosque, or other religious institution is the center of both spiritual and social activities. Such religious institutions can achieve community cohesion and implement programs to keep drugs from taking over neighborhoods. Religious groups can also spearhead campaigns against specific problems identified by the residents. Often, a common cause brings diverse religious communities together. Religious leaders can form coalitions or task forces to help plan and implement antidrug activities. Sometimes churches volunteer their space for weekday community meetings. Religious institutions in ethnically diverse communities can offer drug education classes and support groups for people new to the United States who are unable to speak English.

Key Partnerships

Religious leaders can work successfully with law enforcement, social service providers who can provide treatment or assistance for drug problems, leaders in the congregation or in religion-affiliated lay organizations, and community residents. In some communities, religious leaders belong to community-wide task forces that design and implement antidrug strategies.

Potential Obstacles

Religious leaders who participate in the strategy must feel involved in all stages of program planning and implementation. Volunteers recruited from church congregations must clearly understand the antidrug message. Program leaders must ensure that all volunteers conform to the well-defined drug prevention activities, both for their safety and the program's effectiveness. Community groups must recognize that pastors and other religious leaders have busy schedules and must attend to their regular church obligations. Also, many churches have limited cash resources for programs.

Signs of Success

The involvement of religious institutions in drug prevention has resulted in greater community cohesion, increased economic benefits for families at risk, and more expansive outreach to community members in need of drug prevention assistance. In Cleveland, outdoor prayer vigils reduced drug trafficking in several locations. In Los Angeles, a community church group succeeded in decreasing local alcohol-related problems by getting involved in alcohol licensing and zoning procedures.

Applying the Strategy

In Connecticut, Hartford Area Rallies Together has worked with police and churches to eradicate drug hot spots and create antidrug education programs. Church leaders in Hartford's Hispanic neighborhoods are currently focusing on increasing summer employment opportunities for youth and expanding drug treatment services.

The South Central Organizing Council of Los Angeles, a consortium of churches and labor unions, worked successfully with the city's planning and attorney's offices to modify city ordinances so that community groups could participate in licensing and zoning of alcohol outlets. The year after the change took effect (1983), twenty-one of twenty-five requests for liquor store permits were refused, and license revocation procedures were initiated against three existing outlets.

The Oakland Community Organizations, in California, is a federation of thirteen churches and community-based organizations that has used local ordinances and the police to eradicate drug activity. The federation has gathered an army of volunteers and for generated support within congregations.

Contact Information

Oakland Community Organizations
3914 East 14th Street
Oakland, California 93707
510-639-1444

Involve Local Businesses

Strategy

Local businesses, which have an important economic stake in a drug- and crime-free community, use their influence to promote drug-free norms and incentives and a generally healthy community.

Drug Problem Addressed

Drug activity in a neighborhood often drives business away, frequently destroying the area's economic underpinnings and opening the way to neighborhood decay.

Key Components

If a community is run-down or dying because of uncontrolled drug activity, businesses suffer economically and many are forced to relocate or close. Local businesses can get involved in community antidrug campaigns by contributing money for supplies, prizes, or awards; donating materials (e.g., flyers and T-shirts) and services (e.g., flyer duplication and distribution); setting up summer programs or projects for neighborhood youths; providing an office for weekend meetings; or lending visible support to a community mobilization campaign. Commercial establishments can also alert police to loiterers near their places of business. Neighborhood drug activity can cause businesses burglary or shoplifting losses. Strategies that clean up neighborhoods help businesses thrive. Business leaders and representatives are often effective members of community task forces or coalitions.

Key Partnerships

Community members, the local chamber of commerce, professional groups, and businesses can work together to maintain neighborhoods' economic health by being equal partners in an antidrug campaign.

Potential Obstacles

When businesses volunteer to participate in an antidrug effort, it is important that they receive public credit for their involvement. In some communities, local businesses have volunteered goods, services, and meeting space but have not felt appreciated when, for example, their premises were not cleaned up after being used for meetings.

Signs of Success

Communities report that local business sponsorship has contributed measurably to the implementation of several community programs. Through business donations, antidrug campaign organizers have been able to reward participants for their hard work. Such rewards are often key to sustained efforts to prevent or reduce drug abuse.

Applying the Strategy

Hartford's Area Rallies Together program succeeded in getting stiffer penalties for drug activity in drug-free zones, but it did not have enough money to erect signs announcing the penalties. The 3M company stepped in and donated the much-needed signs.

Businesses in Montgomery County, Maryland, joined with the county government to form a partnership—Business Against Drugs (BAD)—that encourages alcohol and other drug prevention efforts in county businesses. BAD is a forum through which businesses can exchange information that helps resolve drug problems in the workplace and community. Participating businesses have distributed materials on local antidrug programs.

The Summer Youth Employment and Training program, sponsored by the Private Industry Council of Atlanta, has found peer counseling, clerical, and maintenance jobs with the city's housing agency and parks division for hundreds of teenagers. When their summer jobs conclude, the youths recommend and recruit other young people for the following summer's employment and training programs.

Contact Information

National Institute on Drug Abuse
5600 Fishers Lane, Room 1005
Rockville, Maryland 20857
301-443-6480

National Clearinghouse for Drug and Alcohol Information
P.O. Box 2345
Rockville, Maryland 20847-2345
301-468-2600
1-800-729-6686

Enforce Local Codes and Ordinances

Strategy

Enforcement of local codes and municipal regulations that set standards for residential and commercial buildings' physical condition and maintenance can drive drug users and traffickers out of a neighborhood.

Drug Problem Addressed

Drug dealers move into neighborhoods and establish a foothold by operating out of abandoned or dilapidated housing or stores. The dealers' presence causes residents to retreat into their homes in fear. The drug activity can be accompanied by other crime.

Key Components

This innovative strategy uses the considerable powers of local regulatory agencies (housing, health, water and sewer, safety, fire, transportation/traffic) to enforce regulatory codes to rid a neighborhood of drug dealers and crack houses. Code violations include improper or inadequate building exits or fire escapes, broken sidewalks, and improper refuse disposal. When city agencies find code violations, property owners can evict the tenants (or illegal inhabitants) or clean up the property, bringing it within the code. Owners are encouraged to act promptly to avoid paying heavy fines.

Key Partnerships

The community can work closely with municipal regulatory and enforcement agencies by providing tips about code violations and unsafe or improper conditions at a specified address. The community can also inform law enforcement agencies of suspected drug activity at specific locations.

Potential Obstacles

As with many drug prevention strategies, some residents fear retaliation if they inform the police about drug activity. In this strategy, however, residents can report suspicious activity to regulatory agencies if they are afraid of talking directly to law enforcement.

Signs of Success

In communities employing this strategy, crack houses have been shut down and crime and drug activity have dramatically declined. Community residents have returned to public areas in their neighborhood without fear.

Applying the Strategy

Tampa, Florida's police department added more police officers and support personnel as part of its participation in Quick Uniform Attack on Drugs, a program that has reduced crime and drug activity. Program participants work with housing inspectors to close crack houses and with the departments of solid waste and parks to clean up streets and parks. They also use building condemnation to halt drug dealing.

Chicago's Operation Clean Sweep rids subsidized housing complexes of drugs through joint efforts of the city's departments of sewers, water, streets, utilities, and animal- and rodent-control units. Housing inspectors make unannounced visits to ensure that everything is working properly and in good repair. Teams inspect each unit and storage room and, when necessary, order repairs. Following the sweep, resident organizations and patrols maintain security. Residents over the age of seven are forbidden entry to the complex without a specially issued ID.

Oakland, California's Beat Health police unit worked closely with neighborhood coalitions, residents, and municipal agencies to shut down drug houses and restore lawfulness in neighborhoods invaded by drug dealers. By anonymously using hot-spot cards, hundreds of community residents reported suspicious activity. Law enforcement agencies monitored the targeted addresses and worked with regulatory agencies to shut down drug operations by enforcing standards and codes.

Contact Information

Oakland Police Department
Beat Health Unit
455 75th Street
Oakland, California 94607
415-287-6368

Hold Property Owners Accountable

Strategy

Communities use local ordinances, laws, and actions in small claims courts to hold property owners accountable for controlling and eliminating drug activity.

Drug Problem Addressed

Drug dealers and users move into neighborhoods and threaten residents' safety. Sometimes property owners' virtual abandonment of property offers ready havens for drug dealers and users.

Key Components

Community residents are successfully using local laws and ordinances against property owners whose buildings are occupied by drug dealers. By citing nuisance abatement laws, private citizens, local agencies, or city attorneys can file civil suits against property owners who permit specific nuisances or misconduct to occur on their property. Owners can be held accountable for noise pollution and gang activity. Penalties can include heavy fines, eviction, and property condemnation. In some communities the law states that any person who knowingly makes a building available for the purpose of unlawfully manufacturing or delivering a controlled substance is subject to a felony. Property owners can be taken to small claims court to recover damages inflicted on the neighborhood. Legislatures can pass ordinances regarding owners' level of maintenance and the activities occurring on their property. Since vacant and dilapidated housing provides a major opportunity for illegal drug use and sales, local ordinances can force property owners to maintain the premises, board up buildings if necessary, and be responsible for the conduct of those in the building.

Key Partnerships

Residents can join with attorneys, city agencies, and members of the criminal justice system to apply local laws to property owners. Neighborhood business owners and residents can work with law enforcement to call attention to properties being used for drug-related purposes.

Potential Obstacles

Although lawyers need not be involved in small claims court actions in some states, other legal transactions can be expensive. Some attorneys will work with communities for no fee, contributing their services for the neighborhood's benefit.

Signs of Success

Portland, Oregon, has closed more than four hundred drug houses by suing property owners under an ordinance that addresses crime occurring on their property. Oakland, California, residents helped secure confiscation of a crack house and a $10,000 penalty against the landlord through use of the state's nuisance abatement law.

Applying the Strategy

Based on the Portland model, Citizens for Community Improvement, in Des Moines, Iowa, informed police that drug dealing was taking place at a specified property. The chief of police warned the property owner that unless the activity ceased immediately, the property could be closed for a year and fines levied against the owner. After ten days, the city council can authorize the city attorney to begin civil court proceedings against the owner. If the owner does not evict the residents or take other necessary steps, a penalty is imposed.

In Miami Beach, Florida, the Nuisance Abatement Board hears complaints and evidence about drug-related nuisances and has the authority to sue to bring an injunction against persons causing the nuisance as well as against the property owner or agent. During an eighteen-month period, the police had received 120 calls for service at an apartment complex. Using the nuisance abatement ordinance, they made twenty arrests at the site, including nineteen for drug-related activities.

When the city of Baltimore recognizes a property as vacant and untended, it gives the owner notice to secure and maintain the property within thirty days. If the owner fails to do so, the city may convey the property to a recognized neighborhood association, which has the option of occupying the house and using it for positive community activity, auctioning it, or asking the city to manage the building.

Contact Information

Director
Des Moines Citizens for Community Improvement
2301 Forest Avenue
Des Moines, Iowa 50311
515-255-0800

Reinvest Assets Seized in Drug Raids

Strategy

Local law enforcement uses money or other assets seized in drug raids and arrests to help support local drug prevention programs.

Drug Problem Addressed

This strategy addresses the problem of scarce resources for implementing drug prevention programs.

Key Components

Federal, state, and local prosecutors are encouraging states to adopt a Model Asset Seizure and Forfeiture law that would uniformly permit drug prevention programs, among others, to benefit from money and property seized in drug-related arrests. Currently, many states lack mechanisms by which to transfer funds gained from drug and asset seizures to local jurisdictions.

Successful programs for asset seizure and forfeiture rely on legislation that defines the scope of seizures, adjudication procedures, and distribution of proceeds; court organization that facilitates drug-related civil and criminal proceedings and a cooperative and informed prosecutor and defense counsel with knowledge of civil forfeitures; properly trained law enforcement agencies that are able to identify assets that can be seized; the ability to conduct financial investigations; policies and procedures regarding adjudications and negotiated dispositions; property maintenance and inventory control; and systems that provide information to the program's administration and management.

Key Partnerships

Asset forfeiture laws frequently result from effective partnerships among law enforcement, prosecutors, courts, and community residents who bring these laws to the attention of local elected officials. An effective asset forfeiture program depends on information sharing among partners and cooperative negotiating with the criminal justice system.

Potential Obstacles

Several problems can interfere with asset forfeiture. In some cases, seized assets fail to be distributed at the local level due to a lack of communication and coordination. Also, the distribution process is not always equitable.

Signs of Success

The "Drug Use Is Life Abuse" program in Orange County, California, has been funded by money seized from local drug dealers. According to Sheriff Brad Gates, in three years the program took eighty million doses of drugs off the streets and $60 million away from drug dealers.

Applying the Strategy

Cleveland, Ohio's mayor has expressed a commitment to seeing that vacant houses seized in drug arrests be turned over to community organizations and rehabilitated for low- to moderate-income housing. The Union Miles Development Corporation in Cleveland is also supporting laws that would allow all neighborhoods with heavy drug activity to benefit from forfeited funds.

Washington State's Drug Education and Enforcement Account is funded through proceeds from forfeiture of real property (land, houses, etc.) that was used in drug transactions.

Washington, DC's mayor presented $568,000 seized from drug dealers to twenty-seven neighborhood organizations for drug and crime prevention. The money will be used to underwrite parenting classes, peer counseling, mentoring projects, an alcohol server training program for Hispanic hotel and restaurant workers, an antidrug theater project for youth, and a safe haven for young people who want a quiet place to study.

Contact Information

Executive Director
Union Miles Development Corporation
9119 Miles Avenue
Cleveland, Ohio 44105
216-341-0757

Senior Special Agent
U.S. Drug Enforcement Agency
400 6th Street, SW, Suite 2558
Washington, DC 20024
202-401-7492

LECC Coordinator
U.S. Attorney's Office
215 North 17th Street
P.O. Box 1228 DTS
Omaha, Nebraska 68101-1228
402-221-4774

Enforce Bans on Alcohol Sales to Minors

Strategy

Before communities introduce new antidrug measures, they can ensure that existing laws are enforced—especially laws that keep illegal substances out of children's reach—by banning the sale of alcohol to underage persons, the sale of drug paraphernalia, and the use of illegal ID cards.

Drug Problem Addressed

Resources for drug prevention programs are scarce and must be shared among many community efforts. Spending money to secure legislation or programs that already exist is not a wise use of limited funds.

Key Components

The sale of drug paraphernalia can be discouraged through such state laws as the model Drug Paraphernalia Act, which prohibits possession, manufacture, delivery, or advertising of drug paraphernalia.

Most states outlaw a variety of items designed for use with drugs: special pipes; farm and laboratory equipment used to cultivate or manufacture illegal drugs; and cigarette papers used with illegal drugs. States generally control the sale of drug paraphernalia in stores, while the federal government controls their sale through mail-order companies.

In Illinois, selling or delivering drug paraphernalia is a Class 4 felony carrying a minimum fine of $1,000 for each item. Any adult who sells or delivers drug paraphernalia to someone younger than eighteen is guilty of a Class 3 felony and faces a possible prison term of two to five years and a $10,000 fine. Communities and law enforcement officers can remind establishments that sell alcohol that there are penalties for sales to minors. Some communities have monitored bars and liquor, beer, and wine stores to ensure that they require proof of identification before a sale.

False ID cards present a problem for sellers of alcohol. In Montgomery County, Maryland, every establishment that sells alcohol must send at least one representative (bartender, manager, etc.) to a course that assists them in identifying underage drinkers and spotting fake IDs.

Key Partnerships

Retail and wholesale alcohol distributors, law enforcement agencies, and community residents working together can ensure that local drug and alcohol laws are upheld. Residents can bring pressure upon commercial establishments suspected of selling alcohol or drug paraphernalia illegally.

Potential Obstacles

Police and code enforcement agencies cannot patrol all licensed establishments to ensure compliance. Staff resources are typically limited, making public education and strict enforcement of sanctions against violators essential.

Signs of Success

Residents in a Chicago neighborhood mounted a campaign and removed drug paraphernalia from approximately three hundred area stores. These community efforts resulted in a statewide law to ban the sale of drug paraphernalia.

Applying the Strategy

College-level criminal justice students in Montgomery County, Maryland, serve as undercover agents to help enforce age restrictions on purchases of alcoholic beverages. In a carefully designed operation, the students seek to make purchases under police supervision. Merchants who sell illegally are prosecuted as appropriate.

The Nuisance Bar program of the Pennsylvania Liquor Control Board (PLCB) encourages citizens to report to local law enforcement agencies incidents of alcohol sales to minors or intoxicated persons, loud and noisy operations, or drug-related activities. A toll-free hotline is available for reporting purposes. If it is determined that the licensee

has abused the licensing privilege, the PLCB may refuse to renew the establishment's license. Since 1990, 359 bars have been refused a license renewal, 123 refusals are under appeal, and 631 licensees have been warned that if improper operations continue, their licenses may not be renewed the following year.

Contact Information

South Austin Coalition Community Council
5112 West Washington Boulevard
Chicago, Illinois 60644
312-287-4570

Pennsylvania Liquor Control Board
Bureau of Licensing
Central Office
112 Northwest Office Building
Harrisburg, Pennsylvania 17124-0001
717-783-8250

Drug Courts

Strategy

Drug courts that expedite drug-related cases through the criminal justice system can deter drug crimes.

Drug Problem Addressed

Because the criminal justice system moves slowly, offenders arrested for drug-related crimes often either are released or fail to receive adequate treatment. Frequently they return to the streets and the same drug-related activity.

Key Components

Drug courts selectively process felony drug cases to relieve crowded dockets, reduce case processing time, and establish mechanisms for dealing more constructively with drug defendants who may benefit from sentencing alternatives to incarceration. Drug courts are most successful when they have strong, consistent leadership and when the judge, assistant district attorney, and public defender serve long-term assignments that permit the development of expertise about antidrug enforcement. Defendants are often placed in rehabilitation programs with frequent monitoring and treatment requirements. After the program, they report back to the courts. By expediting the court process and reducing the demand for jail space, these courts can achieve substantial cost savings.

Key Partnerships

Drug courts succeed with the cooperation of law enforcement officers, prosecuting attorneys, court personnel, corrections officials, and rehabilitation and treatment providers. Community-based organizations can also be effective partners in the delivery of aftercare services to defendants released back into the community.

Potential Obstacles

According to the National Association of Drug Court Professionals, selecting a drug court judge requires careful attention. A judge who accepts the challenge must be willing to become a hands-on participant in the process and can make or break the court's efforts.

Signs of Success

According to *The CJER Journal*, a number of drug courts report that they have achieved remarkable success in reducing levels of drug abuse, incarceration, and criminal recidivism among drug-using offenders. In Broward County, Florida, the drug court is a pretrial intervention program for first-time felony drug offenders. Eligible offenders are expeditiously placed into designated court and treatment programs, which include urinalysis, counseling, fellowship meetings, acupuncture, education, vocational training, and aftercare. The BJA reports that only 1 percent of the Broward County drug court defendants returned to jail after one year, compared to 46 percent of first-time drug offenders placed on straight probation.

Applying the Strategy

Miami, Florida's drug court has also demonstrated this strategy's effectiveness. Between June 1989 and March 1993, approximately 4,500 defendants (representing nearly 20 percent of all arrestees in the county charged with drug offenses) entered Miami's Diversion and Treatment Program. Among defendants who successfully completed the program, only 11 percent were arrested again in the year following their participation.

The Drug Diversion Court in Jefferson County, Kentucky, includes meditation, optional acupuncture, group and individual treatment, remedial education, case planning, and court supervision through a three-phase program. Successful completion of the program results in dismissal of the underlying drug-related criminal charge.

In Philadelphia's Court of Common Pleas, an expedited drug court program reduced the average number of days from arraignment to disposition by 26 percent, increased the number of jail beds available by up to four hundred a day, achieved a 42 percent decrease in jury trials and an 18 percent increase in guilty pleas, and reduced the court's total criminal caseload by approximately 32 percent during the first year of operation.

Contact Information

Broward County Courthouse
201 SE 6th Street
Fort Lauderdale, Florida 33301
305-831-7095

National Association of Drug Court Professionals
901 North Pitt Street
Alexandria, Virginia 22314
703-706-0563

Empower Residents To Reclaim Public Housing

Strategy

Residents help law enforcement agencies reduce drug activity and maintain security by reporting illegal activity to authorities, forming neighborhood patrols, and screening visitors to their buildings. Such crime reduction efforts save money and improve the quality of life.

Drug Problem Addressed

Public housing and surrounding areas often have serious drug problems and accompanying crime and violence.

Key component

Special uniformed narcotics teams can purge public housing of drug activity, restore law and order, and educate citizens in tenant responsibility, crime and drug prevention, and basic security measures. Some public housing residents follow up the work of special law enforcement teams and take back their homes, parks, and play areas from drug dealers and users. They walk hallways and public spaces, report to police or housing authorities on building conditions and criminal activity, and discourage vandalism and drug dealing with their frequent, visible presence. Some patrol members receive rent abatements in exchange for hours worked. Police officers train residents in crime observation and prevention and provide patrols with flashlights, whistles, walkie-talkies, jackets, and caps.

Key Partnerships

Successful narcotics sweep programs in public housing depend on cooperation among housing residents, management, the local municipal housing authority, and law enforcement agencies.

Potential Obstacles

Drug activity is often accompanied by serious crime and violence, causing public housing residents to fear retaliation by drug dealers. Community empowerment evolves from a complex learning process. Residents should learn about the legal process, housing codes, and ways to use demographic data on crime to identify and solve problems.

Signs of Success

In Chicago, Operation Clean Sweep and resulting resident patrols controlled drug activity in at least sixty buildings. Authorities report that drug dealers have moved out of the buildings, there is less fear of crime, and residents have taken more responsibility for their own security in their buildings. In addition, vandalism and vacancy rates have declined. Narcotics enforcement in Denver public housing has reduced drug use, theft of personal property, and residents' fear of crime.

Applying the Strategy

Newport News Redevelopment and Housing Authority, in Newport News, Virginia, worked with residents in five of the area's ten public housing communities to organize a successful residential foot patrol. Residents received eight hours of in-class training on crime and safety and were provided with the necessary tools (hard hats, flashlights, etc.) to initiate a safety patrol in their neighborhoods. According to police reports, crime has decreased significantly, residents' sense of ease has increased, and there is more participation among all ages in outdoor leisure activities.

In 1992 the Bronx, New York, housing authority implemented a "Model Buildings" program in the Patterson Houses development. The program entailed a major anti-vandalism and -graffiti project designed with a gain-sharing component that put money saved back into the housing units. Tenant volunteers and housing officials worked diligently to restore two buildings, each with more than a hundred housing units, in the eight-building housing development. They covered walls with anti-graffiti shields that allow easy removal of graffiti, installed hall mirrors to deter criminals from lurking, and replaced broken windows, locks, and doors. In addition, around-the-clock tenant patrols were set up at hall stations to monitor building visitors and sign them in and out. After two months, the program saved the housing authority an estimated $5,000 in vandalism control. The buildings have been free of graffiti and other vandalism for three years and crime has noticeably decreased.

Contact Information

District Director
Patterson Houses
2430 Boston Road
Bronx, New York 10467
718-654-3626

U.S. Department of Housing and Urban Development
Crime Prevention and Security Division
451 7th Street, SW, Room 4118
Washington, DC 20410
202-708-1197

Screen Tenants

Strategy

Public housing managers can screen potential tenants and specify certain restrictions in leases to effectively control drug activity.

Drug Problem Addressed

Those who rent apartments in public housing may do so to set up headquarters for drug activity. Frequently, they have been evicted from other housing due to vandalism, public nuisance problems, failure to pay rent, or other problems.

Key Components

This strategy is multi-pronged and can be effective in many manager-tenant situations.

Often, managers have little information about potential renters. Access to a database such as the National Tenant Network (NTN), operative in some cities, can resolve this problem. Designed by a private company, NTN offers standard credit reports (to which housing managers have had legal access for many years) and information on past resident performance, including evictions and lease violations. The U.S. Department of Housing and Urban Development (HUD) has instituted its own computerized screening process for tenants in public, publicly subsidized, and market-rate housing.

In addition to having access to computerized screening, private housing managers can draw up leases that include specific bans on illegal drug activity. Under the terms of such leases, tenants who engage in drug trafficking can be evicted within thirty days.

The strategy encourages residents to work with local and federal authorities to enforce the Federal Asset Forfeiture Law, which allows the seizure of leases of tenants engaged in drug trafficking. Residents can help by providing authorities with evidence of drug activity to establish probable cause for warrants and other action.

Key Partnerships

An effective working relationship among housing residents, management, municipal housing authorities, law enforcement, and property owners can make this a successful antidrug strategy.

Potential Obstacles

If housing managers develop computerized tenant screening, program designers must ensure that the database does not include information that would be declared discriminatory or that would violate constitutional rights to privacy.

Signs of Success

In one area with computerized tenant screening, service subscribers report that the system has helped them screen out applicants who would have harmed the community, such as those involved in drug activity. The system has also been successfully used for fraud investigation in private house rentals.

Applying the Strategy

In San Francisco's Bay Area, thousands of public housing units have been rented to tenants first screened through a computerized system. Tom Matthews, executive director of the Alameda (California) Public Housing Authority estimates that the system eliminates about 10 percent of applicants on the basis of former eviction and resident performance reports. He comments, "It's hard to credit the screening system . . . with the reduction in drug-related activities we've seen in the past year and a half, but we do know we can spot and eliminate applicants who fit the profile of current drug use or dealing."

Contact Information

Executive Director
City of Alameda Housing Authority
701 Atlantic Avenue
Alameda, California 94501
510-522-8422

Vice President
National Tenant Network
P.O. Box 1145
Lafayette, California 94549
510-284-1204

Discourage "Happy Hours"

Strategy

Community residents can discourage commercial establishments that sell alcohol by the glass from promoting "happy hours" that glorify alcohol consumption.

Drug Problem Addressed

Young people receive mixed messages. They are told that alcohol is illegal for anyone younger than twenty-one, can cause serious injury or death when the drinker is operating a vehicle, and can cause serious health problems. At the same time, young people read or hear advertising that extols the pleasures of happy hours.

Key Components

The United States has banned TV advertising of some alcohol and tobacco products because of health risks associated with these products. The treasury department's Bureau of Alcohol, Tobacco, and Firearms has a congressional mandate to control alcohol advertising at the national level, but the law does not apply to local jurisdictions. Some states have adopted national codes for local and statewide advertising. In other states, communities should petition legislators and policymakers to regulate advertising of controlled substances more strictly.

Key Partnerships

Parents and young people can work with local establishments that serve alcohol to curb happy hour and other promotional advertising that glorifies alcohol consumption. Elected officials, the media, representatives of the hospitality industry, and legal organizations can join together to publicize the issue.

Potential Obstacles

In some cases, bar managers or owners will not comply with the community's wish that they tone down their advertising of happy hours. They will argue that their promotions bring in needed business. In such cases, economic pressure might be brought to bear on the bars, or local elected officials might be enlisted to assist with the issue.

Signs of Success

From Teton County, Wyoming, to Braintree, Massachusetts, jurisdictions around the country have banned promotion of alcoholic beverages through advertising featuring special prices. The U.S. Army has also forbidden happy hours at all clubs and bars on its bases. Parents need the support of bar and restaurant proprietors in convincing their children that underage drinking can lead to disaster. Community mobilization against happy hour advertising can take the form of boycotts and focused media attention.

Applying the Strategy

MADD reports that eighteen states have restrictions on establishments charging reduced prices for alcohol.

As a result of public hearings on the subject, Pennsylvania enacted regulations that placed restrictions on happy hours. The sale of alcohol at reduced prices is limited to two hours and must end before midnight. Also, establishments are prohibited from serving a person more than one drink at a time.

Contact Information

Director of Administration
Pennsylvania Liquor Control Board
Northwest Office Building
Harrisburg, Pennsylvania 17124-0001
717-783-8325

Mothers Against Drunk Driving
National Office
511 E. John Carpenter Freeway, Suite 700
Irving, Texas 75062-8187
214-744-MADD

Ban Drugs From Public Events

Strategy

Communities demonstrate intolerance of illegal substance use by establishing and enforcing policies forbidding alcohol or other drug use at sports or other public family-oriented events.

Drug Problem Addressed

Many adults believe that drinking alcohol is a necessary part of a "fun" day or event. Sports figures sometimes ceremoniously drink champagne to celebrate a victory. Ballparks are crowded with concession stands that sell beer. Young people quickly learn to associate fun with drinking, and some youths extend the concept to other drug use.

Key Components

Controlled alcohol consumption is legal for adults over twenty-one, but drinking isn't appropriate at all events, especially when young people are present. Communities can establish policies and distribute written rules that limit alcohol consumption at family-style events (e.g., county fairs, community parades or picnics, some sports events). Even if community or neighborhood tradition upholds the prohibition or restriction of alcohol consumption, it is necessary to clearly advertise drinking restrictions. If an event is held during the school year, ask the school to distribute flyers stating its policy on alcohol consumption. Groups can be encouraged to set up concession stands that sell alternative beverages such as hot chocolate or fresh lemonade.

Key Partnerships

Event organizers and sponsors, parents, and community leaders must cooperate to activate and enforce alcohol restriction at public events. Law enforcement agencies can play a supportive or monitoring role at family events. Local alcohol distributors can be asked to visibly support public policy statements about restricted alcohol consumption.

Potential Obstacles

It is critical to ensure that parents and other participants voluntarily comply with a no-alcohol policy. This strategy's value lies in the message it sends to young people. Non-compliance can negate the strategy's effectiveness and demonstrate to young people that rules and community attitudes don't matter.

Signs of Success

In San Diego, community mobilization against alcohol consumption at ball games resulted in new restrictions in Jack Murphy Stadium. In specially designated family sections, beer can no longer be served; the sale of alcohol anywhere in the stadium ceases at the end of the seventh inning in baseball games. Twelve of the twenty-six Major League baseball stadiums have either designated family sections or sections in which no alcohol is sold; twenty-four prohibit the sale of alcohol after a certain inning or time.

Applying the Strategy

In Messina, New York, parents and community leaders established a policy that no alcohol be served at sports arenas or gatherings such as picnics, parades, festivals, and family-oriented social events that include both parents and children.

Parents in Deerfield, Illinois, worked with parents from neighboring communities to patrol Lake Michigan's beach area, as a show of support for state and local policies against alcohol and other drug use on the beach and at beach parties.

A motor-sports racetrack near Denver has set aside one seating section in which adults may purchase and drink beer. Everywhere else in the stands the sale or consumption of alcohol is banned.

Contact Information

Major League Baseball
Public Relations
350 Park Avenue
New York, New York 10022
212-339-7800

Athletics for Drug Prevention

Strategy

Drug-free athletes and coaches serve as effective role models.

Drug Problem Addressed

A drug prevention program centered on sports and drug-free athletes will reach many young people uninfluenced by other programs. Athletes can effectively address the serious problem of illegal steroid use among young people.

Key Components

Sports activities stress fitness through healthy lifestyles. They offer the opportunity to teach young people about the dangers of alcohol and other drugs while promoting physical fitness and fun. They also allow youth to take pride in their individual accomplishments, increasing their self-esteem. Some sports programs have a leadership training component; they teach youth to become effective role models for their teammates and for younger students. Coaches serve as mentors and counselors to students who have personal or family problems. In some programs, athletes and their parents sign a pledge of no alcohol or drug use. Education about the dangers of steroid use should be part of any sports program.

Key Partnerships

Sports-based drug programs aren't limited to coaches and athletes. Parents and school staff must become involved. Sports programs also provide drug education opportunities for students who are team managers, coaching assistants, or members of pep squads or cheerleading teams. Forming booster clubs and encouraging schools to reinforce the antidrug message through tough policies and enforcement helps parents.

Potential Obstacles

The most serious obstacle to this program's success is that young people who fail to win or perform well sometimes feel inferior to their teammates. They need to learn how to lose as well as win. Athletics teach commitment, responsibility, and endurance.

Signs of Success

In 1983 the athletic department of Anderson High School, in Cincinnati, started a drug prevention program that the Federal Drug Enforcement Administration (DEA) adopted as a model in 1984. The program illustrates the influence that athletes have on their peers and coaches have on athletes. Based on the premise that drug prevention requires a team approach, Anderson High School's athletic department combined a comprehensive drug prevention program with their regular athletics and fitness regime. Using lesson plans, coaches educated the team about drugs and the ramifications of drug use. Athletes encouraged their teammates and peers not to use drugs. Team captains were held responsible for their teammates' choices about using or eschewing alcohol and other drugs. The program reduced the use of alcohol and other drugs 90 to 95 percent during the season and showed a similar reduction off-season.

The DEA's demand reduction section sponsors a program in which coaches attend workshops, seminars, and clinics in order to learn how to prevent drug use among young athletes. The athletes serve as school leaders and role models to other students who want to learn how to live drug-free.

Applying the Strategy

In Madison, Wisconsin, mentors from a local water-ski team give individual water-skiing instruction to forty at-risk girls and boys aged ten to eighteen. Through the sheriff's office, the lake patrol also instructs about water safety and the importance of not drinking alcohol while skiing or driving a ski boat. Madison Water Ski and the Boy Scouts of America provide information on drug-free water-ski activities across the country. The program can be adapted to other sports.

In the Police Athletic League, a national drug-free sports program for kids eight and over, San Diego students play ball with police officers who organize teams at neighborhood recreation centers or schools and incorporate drug prevention into the fun. The police officers act as teachers, mentors, friends, and role models.

Contact Information

Anderson High School
7560 Forest Road
Cincinnati, Ohio 45255-4378
513-232-2772

308 350 Tested Strategies to Prevent Crime

Drug Screening of Employees

Strategy

Businesses, schools, the criminal justice system, the federal government, major corporations, and other institutions use drug testing as a prevention tool.

Drug Problem Addressed

In some jobs, use of alcohol and other drugs poses serious—sometimes life-threatening—safety, security, and health risks.

Key Components

Drug screening through urine testing can be used either to deny applicants employment or to get help for employees who are using alcohol or other drugs. Testing can be used in the private sector, as a monitoring tool, to enhance on-the-job safety and productivity and to reduce drug-related impairment. Transportation workers, security guards, operators of heavy equipment, and school bus drivers are among employees frequently monitored through drug testing. A testing program can reduce the rate of absenteeism (which lessens productivity) and foster public trust. Many states have laws regulating the accuracy and confidentiality of workplace drug testing. Criminal justice employees are tested to maintain public confidence in the integrity and professionalism of law enforcement and to ensure public safety.

The federal government requires drug testing in such areas as defense contracting, nuclear energy, and public transportation, and many states have followed federal guidelines for their own employees. Some states also authorize private employers to test for drug use if they have a "reasonable suspicion" that an employee's performance has been affected by alcohol or other drugs. Effective drug testing may include screening of job applicants, random testing of all employees or those in sensitive positions, testing of any employee who wishes to participate in a drug-testing program, testing based on reasonable suspicion, special-condition testing (e.g., following an incident, accident, or unsafe practice), and follow-up testing performed after a person has tested positive or completed a rehabilitation program.

Key Partnerships

Successful drug-testing programs require partnership among employers (private or public), the local chamber of commerce (which can assist with antidrug workplace policy), law enforcement personnel, employees, and service providers who consult with employee assistance programs.

Potential Obstacles

Drug-testing administrators must pay heed to legal and procedural requirements regarding chain of custody for urine samples, employees' right to privacy, use of accredited laboratories, and the possibility of false positive tests.

Signs of Success

The armed forces, mass transportation companies, and the postal service all test employees to ensure public safety during the operation of vehicles and equipment. In Washington, DC, and nearby Maryland suburbs, Bell Atlantic maintains a strict policy on substance use that includes pre-employment drug screening and testing for cause or suspicion. A positive test can result in dismissal and, if illegal activity was involved, notification of law enforcement. According to the policy, drug testing is "designed to further ensure a productive and safe work environment for all employees." The company reports that the number of on-the-job accidents decreased following the 1987 implementation of an official substance abuse policy that permits drug testing.

Applying the Strategy

In Utah, drug testing is permitted for essentially all public and private job applicants and employees if the employer has a written policy, makes it available to the applicant or employee, confirms tests that are positive, and maintains proper documentation of samples.

The George Hyman Construction Company, in Bethesda, Maryland, bases its substance abuse policy on a commitment to fighting alcohol and drug abuse. Adherence to the policy is a condition of employment. The head of the human resources department says that the employee assistance program, including its substance abuse component, is "the most cost-effective and well-received benefit we have. . . . We are getting a remarkable response."

Contact Information

Bell Atlantic-Washington, DC
Director, Health Services
7833 Walker Drive, 2nd Floor
Greenbelt, Maryland 20770
301-397-5401

EAP Coordinator
Human Resources Department
George Hyman Construction Company
7500 Old Georgetown Road
Bethesda Metro Center
Bethesda, Maryland 20814
301-986-8100

Culturally Sensitive Drug Prevention Programs

Strategy

Communities can expand drug prevention programs to reach culturally diverse populations by training youth, families, schools, and service providers to be culturally knowledgeable and sensitive.

Drug Problem Addressed

Many communities lack appropriate cultural understanding, translated materials, and contact with ethnically diverse groups such as immigrants and refugees who have settled in the neighborhood. Frequently, traditional drug prevention strategies don't reach residents in multicultural communities.

Key Components

Drug prevention programs can obtain the trust of those new to the United States by working within their cultural traditions and serving the entire family, not just the youth. Often, parents new to America do not realize that their children have a problem with alcohol or other drugs, deny the problem, or wish to resolve it within their own family. Especially vulnerable to feelings of alienation, youth new to this country may resort to unhealthy ways of gaining social acceptance. Culturally sensitive drug prevention strategies must address the values of parents and succeeding generations.

To address problems among those new to this country, some police departments and service providers have hired community outreach personnel from the immigrant or refugee population as interpreters and links to the ethnic community. Anyone who works with immigrants or refugees needs a solid understanding of the group's values, social hierarchy, gender roles, cultural beliefs, and traditions.

Drug prevention programs can build on cultural traditions such as festivals; can be introduced into classes that teach English as a second language; can be part of a school ethnic-awareness program; and can reach adults through neighborhood associations, religious groups, health providers, local media, parent assistance training, and workplace programs. An ethnic community council can be formed to assess problems with alcohol and other drugs, design a plan to meet the needs of local ethnic groups, and develop ways of reaching community members through formal and informal service systems.

Key Partnerships

Culturally focused drug prevention efforts require the cooperation of law enforcement personnel, other service providers in the community, schools, both unassimilated and fully Americanized youth, and leaders of ethnic communities. Mutual assistance associations, which assist ethnic groups in the relocation process, can connect an ethnic community to drug prevention experts.

Potential Obstacles

Many obstacles interfere with successful ethnic drug prevention efforts: inadequate translation and interpreting services; an ethnic group's ignorance of U.S. law and the criminal justice process; a reluctance on the part of ethnic groups to seek help outside their community; and a distrust of law enforcement, often stemming from experiences in their native land.

Signs of Success

In many cities, police departments are hiring members of diverse ethnic groups to serve as liaisons between law enforcement and refugee or immigrant communities. In various cities, law enforcement officers report a higher incidence of reporting of drug-related crime, decreased victimization in ethnic communities, decreased use of drugs among youth, and a greater rapport between law enforcement and ethnic youth.

Applying the Strategy

San Francisco's Asian Youth Substance Abuse Project is a consortium of five community agencies serving Asian-American youth and immigrant and refugee youth from China, Japan, Korea, Vietnam, and the Philippines. The project's goal is to prevent alcohol and other drug problems among Asian youth by means of education, counseling, treatment, and referral services that meet each group's cultural needs.

Highland High School, in Salt Lake City, has instituted a Port of Entry program to help students who do not speak English learn about healthy living in the United States. The program refers students to the Asian Association of Utah, Hispanic Aid, and the Tolstoy Foundation (for Eastern European students).

Contact Information

Program Director
Asian Youth Substance Abuse Project
Asian American Recovery Services, Inc.
785 Market Street, 10th Floor
San Francisco, California 94103
415-541-9285

University Drug Policies

Strategy

Colleges and universities frequently struggle with problems of alcohol and drug use. They can mitigate these problems through policy enforcement, antidrug education, and social influence.

Drug Problem Addressed

A 1992 study of 140 college campuses conducted by the Center on Addiction and Substance Abuse at Columbia University found that substance abuse, particularly alcohol "binge drinking," has become as much a part of college life as studying. One in three college students now drink to get drunk. Ninety-five percent of violent crime on campus is alcohol related; 90 percent of all reported campus rapes occur when alcohol is being used by either the assailant or the victim; and 60 percent of college women who have acquired sexually transmitted diseases, including AIDS and genital herpes, were under the influence of alcohol during intercourse. College and university students are especially vulnerable to substance abuse because they are removed from parental supervision.

Key Components

University and college administrators must clearly and regularly publicize and enforce guidelines for the regulation of substance use on and off campus. Students and parents must know the policies and the consequences of policy violations; they can be spelled out in student handbooks, school brochures, and course schedules. Schools can ask students to create posters for dormitories and student gathering places. Most institutions brief incoming students about alcohol and other drugs during new-student orientation, student assemblies, or residence hall meetings. Schools can also reduce illegal alcohol use at local college hangouts by asking proprietors to enforce legal-age laws and check IDs. Fraternities, sororities, and other social groups must enforce clear policies on the use of alcoholic beverages at parties. Nonalcoholic beverages should be served at all official university events.

Key Partnerships

Colleges and universities can reduce the use of alcohol and other drugs among students if they team up with college staff, local law enforcement agencies, restaurants and bars near the campus, parents, residence-hall staff, fraternities and sororities, and high-profile student leaders and athletes.

Potential Obstacles

Schools have difficulty addressing excessive drinking on campus where nearly three-quarters of their students are legally underage. Teaching minors how to drink responsibly is technically illegal. Advocating moderation also puts schools in jeopardy of losing federal funding because laws prohibit them from having policies that inadvertently or directly condone the use of alcohol and other drugs. In addition, many school drug prevention programs suffer from relaxed enforcement, a school's tendency to protect students from consequences, students' ability to obtain false ID cards, and lack of compliance by the overall student body.

Signs of Success

A 1991 study of 94,253 students from Nebraska's twenty-six colleges and universities found that approximately 89 percent of the students consume alcohol; 47 percent reported becoming intoxicated at least once during the two weeks prior to the survey. As a result of these findings, the Nebraska Office of Highway Safety, received a federally funded grant initiative—Let's Intervene for Education (LIFE)—designed to help policymakers, prevention specialists, and health professionals address alcohol abuse on Nebraska's campuses. The program's primary goals were to prevent and reduce alcohol abuse and, as a result, prevent dangerous actions such as driving while intoxicated. Following a structured planning session, twenty-one college and university chief student-affairs officers formed a steering committee that meets quarterly to review ongoing activities and plan events free of alcohol. The program publishes a quarterly newsletter that it distributes to all participating prevention specialists and steering committee members. The program encourages support from all agencies concerned with alcohol abuse. It is also one of the few projects that directly involves all of a state's institutions of higher learning. The program has been adopted by Union Pacific Railroad (which has ninety thousand employees) and by school districts throughout Nebraska (as a means of educating teachers, administrators, and parents). It has also received a request from New York colleges and universities for LIFE training.

Applying the Strategy

Howard University, in Washington, DC, has had an antidrug policy since 1971 that addresses indiscriminate nonmedical use of prescribed drugs; possession or manufacture of drugs for exchange or transfer, and the selling of drugs. To complement its policy, the university sponsors lectures and seminars on drug-related topics and supports a referral program to area treatment centers for students with substance abuse problems.

Contact Information

Project Director
Drug Education and Prevention Program
University Counseling Service
Howard University
6th and Bryant Streets
Washington, DC 20059
202-806-6870

Nebraska Office of Highway Safety
P.O. Box 94612
301 Centennial Mall South
Lincoln, Nebraska 68509-4612
402-471-2515

Mentors as Role Models

Strategy

Some drug prevention programs pair high-risk young people with adult mentors who can influence their lifestyle choices.

Drug Problem Addressed

Due to the epidemic of broken families, single parents, teen parents, and runaway youth, many young people suffer from a lack of positive role models and guidance when they are considering the use of alcohol and other drugs.

Key Components

Mentoring programs foster close relationships between caring, supportive adults and young people identified as needing individual guidance and direction. The relationship, based on mutual respect and time spent together, can include special recreational, social, or academic activities that help the young person learn healthy lifestyle choices. The mentoring program doesn't have to focus specifically on drugs but can center on the drug-free example set by the adult.

A mentoring program should recognize children's special needs, ensure that the youth really want to be involved in the relationship (prior orientation can help determine genuine interest and commitment), and screen mentors to determine motivation and degree of commitment. The ideal mentoring relationship lasts a long time, allowing the youth to go through several developmental stages guided by the caring adult. Successful mentoring relationships often begin with a shared task, such as a community service project during which the youth and the adult can get to know each other. Successful mentoring programs have orientation sessions and regularly scheduled meetings among mentors to discuss problems and strategies.

Key Partnerships

Mentoring relationships are a partnership between a committed adult and a youth who needs adult guidance and companionship. Schools, religious organizations, and other community groups can be a part of a mentoring program, either by helping to identify adults who will make good mentors and youth who will benefit from mentoring or by sponsoring a mentoring program.

Potential Obstacles

This type of drug prevention effort requires the adult's commitment. Problems arise when a recruited adult fails to give the youth adequate time, show up for scheduled activities, or embody a drug-free lifestyle. Close screening of mentors is mandatory. Make sure both adult and youth understand that not all pairings work the first time.

Signs of Success

Research has long indicated that young people adopt the attitudes and activities of people they admire. In a mentoring program, the adult not only is a role model but becomes the young person's friend, advisor, and confidante. Participants in a Boston mentoring program note that crime in the area has declined since their program began.

Applying the Strategy

In Boston, faculty at the Wentworth Institute recognized the link between lack of economic opportunities for youth and drug involvement, as evidenced by the young people in a nearby housing project. They set up a mentoring program, focused on teaching computer skills, which quickly expanded to include breakfast for the young participants and an athletic period during the day. The faculty served as the mentors, teaching youth about computers' physical components, programming, the application of computers to crime prevention, the computerized analysis of sports statistics, and the creation of architectural designs. The Boston's metropolitan police have also donated time to the program.

In St. Louis, mentors work with seriously disadvantaged young people who are being released from juvenile corrections programs. Often these youth are sent home without the support they need to avoid returning to the drug- and crime-related activities they engaged in before their incarceration. Mentors provide aftercare to ease the youths' transition into their home environments.

Contact Information

Department Head, Math and Physics
Wentworth Institute of Technology
550 Huntington Avenue
Boston, Massachusetts 02115
617-442-9010

Arts-Related Prevention

Strategy

Drug prevention programs use arts activities as a positive alternative to drug use whereby nurturing a young person's creativity.

Drug Problem Addressed

This strategy offers an alternative path to young people who may not respond to other antidrug programs.

Key Components

Arts-related drug prevention programs offer a wide variety of fine arts projects that attract young people with visual, musical, or theatrical talent. The youth participate in designing a program or performance, constructing the stage props, creating promotional flyers, talking with the press to publicize the event, serving refreshments or arranging for concession stands, collecting tickets, and cleaning up after the event. The projects or events offer at-risk youth an alternative to drug use. They may also educate the public about alcohol and other drugs through their content.

Key Partnerships

Arts projects bring together young people, parents, schools, local adults involved in the performing arts, businesses that donate materials or services to the program, and the media.

Potential Obstacles

Obtaining and maintaining funding for art programs can be difficult. Programs need to clarify and emphasize the prevention content in the program when they seek funding. Identifying and recruiting adult supervisors and instructors can be challenging. Universities and community-based theatre programs can be a good source for this support.

Signs of Success

In 1993 the Learning Systems Group, in partnership with the U.S. Department of Education, initiated a national "Murals Reflecting Prevention" project to prevent youth involvement with alcohol, tobacco, and other drugs. To date, the program has involved over ten thousand students nationwide in expressing prevention themes. The student-designed murals have been displayed at exhibitions in several states and provide a novel approach to uniting youth and their communities around the issue of drug abuse.

Applying the Strategy

Action in the Arts has changed the lives of some young people in Greenville, South Carolina. In an area once overrun by "curb service drug dealing," about three hundred young people aged five to twenty-two now take roles in plays that depict the problems of substance abuse. The plays have been performed at housing projects, schools, city and county community centers, and town festivals. The youth are part of the theater company's advisory board, and local groups assist with costumes, sets, and production details.

In Evansville, Indiana, Teens As Resources Against Drugs (TARAD) sponsored an award given to Girl Scout Troop 902 for their presentation of puppet shows to younger students. The shows dramatized the dangers of alcohol and other drugs.

Another popular TARAD program is the Great American Medicine Show, a series of antidrug skits and songs performed by South Carolina youth at schools and community centers statewide. The show features Hans and Franz, adapted from television's "Saturday Night Live" characters, who offer to "pump you up" for drug abuse prevention.

Contact Information

Coordinator of Community and Resident Services
Greenville Housing Authority
P.O. Box 10047
Greenville, South Carolina 29603
803-467-3087

Drug Activity Hotlines

Strategy

Many communities and cities provide all-hours dedicated access to the police department, housing authority, crisis intervention service, or other emergency service so that callers can report drug activity. Community drug prevention efforts don't last only from nine to five, five days a week.

Drug Problem Addressed

Twenty-four-hour access to assistance assures residents that emergency drug situations will receive quick attention any time of the day or night.

Key Components

This strategy's key component is a special dedicated phone line operated by trained personnel at municipal agencies, hospitals, or community-based organizations. The police or sheriff's department can set up a "tip" line through which residents can anonymously report crime or drug activity information. Service providers can set up a hotline that will give emergency advice or referrals to teens in crisis. These lines are usually staffed by experts or by teens trained to talk with their peers and, when necessary, refer them to law enforcement professionals. Housing authorities have special lines to take information about drug activity in housing projects. Some national hotlines give information about specific drugs (e.g., 1-800-COCAINE), drug-related workplace problems (1-800-843-4971), alcohol problems (1-800-NCA-CALL), or emergency drug problems (1-800-662-HELP).

Key Partnerships

Effective partners in hotline or tip-line strategies include law enforcement units, referral services, youths, schools, hospitals and clinics, and local organizations that can provide emergency assistance.

Potential Obstacles

Volunteers who answer hotline calls must be carefully screened, trained, and monitored. Incorrect or inappropriate responses to an emergency call can result in injury or death. Callers with severe psychological problems must be handled by experts who can assist them quickly while convincing them to seek professional help.

In the case of a 24-hour tip line, authorities must verify information that is called in before action is taken.

Signs of Success

In a public assistance housing complex in Columbus, Ohio, the number of units identified as drug houses dropped from 251 to 5 after a phone line was established which provided leads for law enforcement. Callers were assured that they needn't give any names and that no one would be harmed. On average, the hotline received six hundred calls a week.

Applying the Strategy

Fifteen teens in Harlem, New York City, set up HOTLINE Cares, a bilingual (English and Spanish) crisis intervention and counseling program that provides immediate assistance to people involved with drug-related or other emergencies. Adults are in charge of the program's administrative details and train the teens to respond properly to calls.

We Turn In Pushers (1-800-78-CRIME) is a national hotline set up so that residents can help local police purge their neighborhoods of drug dealers. Callers, who can remain anonymous, are given a code that they can later use to find out what actions were taken as a result of their tip. If a tip leads to a conviction, the caller receives a cash reward of a thousand dollars.

Contact Information

Chief of Safety and Crime Prevention Coordinator
Metropolitan Housing Authority
960 E. 5th Ave
Columbus, Ohio 43201
614-421-4424

Safe Design of Public Areas

Strategy

Neighborhoods can reduce drug-related activity through environmental changes that make their communities less vulnerable and hospitable to drug dealers.

Drug Problem Addressed

Some communities are perfect hideaways for drug dealers and users. For example, the street lighting is poor or the traffic patterns permit quick getaways.

Key Components

Drug-related activity can be reduced if a neighborhood or community is physically designed to protect residents. Relevant physical improvements include better outdoor lighting, building of fences, and removal of abandoned vehicles.

Key Partnerships

Community residents can team up with municipal planners, architects, city agencies, law enforcement, traffic engineers, and utility companies to create a safer neighborhood environment.

Potential Obstacles

Often, municipal governments are willing to work with communities to improve a neighborhood's physical layout or design in order to reduce the presence of drug dealers and other criminals. The process frequently takes time because of the requirements of surveying, analysis, bidding for contracts, and delegating funds. In addition to technical issues, there are issues of eliminating residents' fears, establishing trust between law enforcement and residents, and working to design a model that increases the neighborhood's safety and appearance.

Signs of Success

In 1992 residents in the Five Oaks community of Dayton, Ohio, joined forces with local police and city planners to institute a "Neighborhood Stabilization" program. Thirty-five iron gates and twenty-six alley barricades were installed around the community in order to create defensible space. The gates and barricades effectively closed off open space previously occupied and used as a main thoroughfare by drug dealers and prostitutes. According to a report from Dayton's Office of Management and Budget, the initiative resulted in a 24 percent decrease in nonviolent crime and 50 percent decrease in violent crime.

Applying the Strategy

One year, 10 percent of Connecticut's homicides occurred in Bridgeport's east-side peninsula, an area locally known as "Beirut." In this area, local police authorities and city-planning officials have since implemented a street modification program called the Phoenix Project. In areas with heavy drug traffic, street barriers and traffic-control devices were installed to create one-way streets, make turn-offs onto side streets difficult, and make traffic flow easier to manage and monitor. The project included community mobilization and a sting operation that targeted dangerous gang leaders and drug dealers. The overall initiative resulted in an approximate 75 percent decline in crime and the area's lowest crime rate since 1972.

Contact Information

Chief, Bridgeport Police Department
300 Congress Street
Bridgeport, Connecticut 06604
203-576-7611

Dayton Police Department
Professional Standards Division
335 West Third Street
Dayton, Ohio 45402
513-449-1311

Drug-Free Social Events for Youth

Strategy

Schools and communities reduce alcohol-related injuries and fatalities when they set and enforce drug-free standards at celebrations such as proms, homecoming dances, or graduation festivities.

Drug Problem Addressed

Many youth are able to resist using alcohol or other drugs except at parties and other celebrations that offer easy access to illegal or restricted substances. These events frequently lead to tragedy.

Key Components

Drug-free football-related social events, homecoming events, school dances, and graduation celebrations prevent injuries and deaths from driving by teens under the influence of alcohol or other drugs. Drug-free events can provide refreshments or full meals, band music, contests, and door prizes. Students can select, and schools and parents can sponsor, special outings such as sports parties, picnics, or other activities. The events should be well advertised in the school. Students who drink alcohol or use illegal drugs should be reported to school authorities or law enforcement officials.

Key Partnerships

Student events free of alcohol and other drugs result from the combined efforts of schools, parent-teacher groups, organizations such as SADD and MADD, student leaders, local business sponsors, the media, law enforcement agencies, parents, and participating youth.

Potential Obstacles

Even if most students are willing to attend drug- and alcohol-free social events, small groups of students may refuse to participate. Sometimes parents will undermine the school's efforts by providing beer or other alcohol in their homes at private parties. This is discouraged if parents are asked to sign a pledge that they will supervise parties and prohibit the use of illegal substances.

Signs of Success

In 1990 Nationwide Insurance Company initiated the "Prom Promise" campaign in Richmond, Virginia; Columbus, Ohio; Knoxville, Tennessee; and the Piedmont region of North Carolina. The campaign was organized by local youth but implemented with nationwide assistance. One hundred and sixty schools enlisted in the program, and more than 80,000 students signed a pledge to remain drug- and alcohol-free on prom night. In 1993, 2,600 high schools in eighteen states participated, and over one million students signed the pledge. In 1994, more than three million students in 3,300 schools in twenty-two states and the District of Columbia participated in the campaign.

Applying the Strategy

The National Highway Traffic Safety Administration sponsors Project Graduation, a nationwide program, begun in 1980, that has reduced driving-related injuries and deaths following graduation parties.

In St. Mary's County, Maryland, Project Graduation followed the realization that 83 percent of the deaths of young people were related to the use of alcohol or other drugs. The program was partially funded through fines paid by people arrested for substance abuse crimes. Now, all students sign contracts in which they agree not to consume any illegal substance during graduation festivities. A student who breaks the contract can be arrested and prosecuted. The students work with the school administrator, a state trooper, and an adult project coordinator.

Parents of students at Klein Forest High School in Houston, Texas, sponsor Project After Prom, which offers all-night, drug-free events featuring movies, auctions, or other activities. They also offer and organize transportation for midnight movies, sponsored by a local theater, after fall football games.

Contact Information

Corporate Prom Promise Coordinator
Nationwide Insurance Company
One Nationwide Plaza
Columbus, Ohio 43215
614-249-7111 ext. 6022

Project Graduation
National Highway Traffic Safety Administration
U.S. Department of Transportation
400 7th St., SW, NTS-21
Washington, DC 20590
202-366-2724

Job Training and Employment Opportunities

Strategy

Communities can address drug dealing's economic appeal by offering young people beneficial career training and employment opportunities.

Drug Problem Addressed

Young people who enter the risky drug trade seek power, respect, or (most often) money. Some young people deal drugs to support their families. For many young people who have dropped out of school or who live in impoverished conditions, the future is unclear. They need money to survive, but they have not succeeded in getting a degree or developing marketable job skills. The possibility of large, fast financial gains often lures them into the illegal drug trade. Whether or not they themselves use drugs, they become a source of drugs for others; their profits depend on building a clientele.

Key Components

A successful employment-based program offers an alternative to drug dealing. Such a program must teach skills and provide employment opportunities. Training and employment programs must be structured to attract young people and offer incentives such as scholarships and future career development. Classes should be scheduled in convenient locations at convenient times, particularly if participants have other obligations such as school, family care, or jobs.

Key Partnerships

Job skills training brings together schools, businesses, students, employment agencies, and local organizations. Schools can identify students who need financial resources and are vulnerable to the lure of drug profits. Local businesses can assist with job training and donate computers or other equipment or materials. College students can serve as role models and mentors. Employment agencies can help graduates find jobs. Local organizations can help underwrite a jobs program.

Potential Obstacles

Instituting a job skills and employment program is costly and requires the financial and personnel support of community business and municipal agencies. Programs must be sufficiently strong and engaging to sustain participants' attention.

Signs of Success

Strictly Business, a youth entrepreneurship training project of Youth Unlimited, the Youth Leadership Center of the Citizens Committee for New York City, offers a positive alternative to troubled youth aged sixteen to twenty-one— such as those who have been gang members, drug dealers, or street hustlers. Teaching strong leadership, communication, management, and business skills, Strictly Business provides entrepreneurial training, technical assistance, and mentoring so that troubled youth can transform themselves and their communities. Participants work on earning a high school or general equivalency diploma. Participants who form a business partnership and complete business plans receive follow-up technical assistance and up to $2,500 in seed capital grants and loans through the Strictly Business Revolving Loan Program. This money helps them establish and operate legitimate businesses. Among the 182 youth who have participated in the program, 122 have completed their training requirements.

Applying the Strategy

One to One Partnership sponsors the PATHWAYS Initiative and provides up to $10,000 for economically disadvantaged children in grades four through ten who participate in their mentoring program. Participants earn equity in the $10,000 if they maintain a relationship with an adult mentor, perform community service, start a business, earn good grades, and participate in entrepreneurial, job, and life skills training. They can use the money to finance a college education, job training, a new business, or other positive venture. Currently, participants include 196 youth in eight cities (Atlanta, Boston, Detroit, Los Angeles, New York, Omaha, Philadelphia, and Richmond).

At Champ Cookies in Washington, DC, approximately fifty youth aged ten to seventeen earn an average of $50 a day baking and selling cookies. Using the slogan "It's dough money, not dope money," Champ offers inner-city youth a legal way to earn money. According to the organization, the students' $250 weekly take-home pay is comparable to that of most crack cocaine dealers. The youngsters learn all aspects of the business and attend weekly business workshops.

Contact Information

Program Coordinator
One to One Partnership
2801 M Street, NW
Washington, DC 20007
202-338-3844

Project Director
Citizens Committee of New York
Youth Unlimited/Strictly Business
305 7th Avenue, 15th Floor
New York, New York 10001

President
Champ Enterprises
1133 15th Street, NW, Suite 1200
Washington, DC 20005
202-293-1800

Train Those Who Serve Alcohol

Strategy

By informing those who serve alcohol in bars and restaurants about the dangers of alcohol consumption, communities can reduce alcohol-related injuries and deaths due to impaired driving.

Drug Problem Addressed

Research published in 1985 in *The Journal of Public Health Policy* indicates that more than 50 percent of intoxicated drivers involved in motor vehicle crashes have, shortly before, been in bars, in restaurants, or at sporting events licensed to sell alcoholic beverages. A 1989 study by the Marin Institute for the Prevention of Alcohol and Other Drug Problems found that 53 percent of people enrolled in driving-under-the-influence classes in Monterey County, California, had purchased their last drink prior to being arrested in a commercial drinking establishment. In some states, alcohol servers can he held liable for injuries or death from a customer's impaired driving.

Key Components

Alcohol server intervention programs focus on prohibiting the sale of alcohol to minors or intoxicated patrons and on promoting nonalcoholic beverages. An effective program trains servers to maintain certain standards of customer behavior (e.g. no excessively loud or unruly activities) and requires management to support servers who, when necessary, limit their customers' consumption. Commercial establishments can also be encouraged to provide alternative transportation for intoxicated customers. Some bars stop serving alcohol for a period of time before the bar closes; others close early, before a customer can consume too much. In some jurisdictions, plainclothes police officers serve as decoys to test alcohol service policies.

Key Partnerships

A broad range of partners can team up for an effective alcohol server strategy, including municipal agencies that regulate alcohol, law enforcement agencies, proprietors of commercial establishments, chambers of commerce or other business organizations, hospitality and tourist organizations, servers' unions, public health agencies, automobile associations, taxi companies, alcohol distributors, and community residents who live near bars and are concerned about impaired driving on their streets.

Potential Obstacles

Businesses often resist restrictions on serving alcohol because they fear loss of business. Restricting consumption in one bar can cause a customer to go to another to finish drinking. Also, because of high staff turnover in the hospitality industry, training should be ongoing.

Signs of Success

Evaluations indicate that server training reduces intoxication. In one assessment, fewer U.S. Navy patrons near a base were served to intoxication as a result of server training. In a rural university town, two actors posed as patrons in two bars to test the alcohol service policy and found that their requests for alcohol were denied when the server determined they had consumed excessively. In a third evaluation, the National Highway Traffic Safety Administration determined that a Techniques of Effective Alcohol Management program used at seven National Basketball Association arenas decreased the sale of alcohol and increased the sale of food and nonalcoholic beverages. Attendance also increased.

Applying the Strategy

In Thunder Bay, Ontario, Canada, four of eight taverns gave their servers training courses. Actors posing as patrons enacted scenarios that had been addressed in the courses, such as ordering double-strength drinks, drinking to intoxication, and arriving intoxicated. An assessment showed significant positive changes in knowledge and attitudes by servers who had taken the course. Trained servers were much more likely to intercede to prevent intoxication and to manage underage patrons properly.

Contact Information

Project Techniques for Effective Alcohol Management (TEAM)
National Highway Traffic Safety Administration
Office of Alcohol and State Programs
400 7th Street, SW
Washington, DC 20590
202-366-9588

Increase Police Presence

Strategy

Local law enforcement can provide increased police presence and problem-oriented service to areas where a high incidence of drug activity has been reported.

Drug Problem Addressed

Directed police patrols and other community policing techniques can address problems of drug activity and the residents' fear of crime and violence that often accompanies drug activity in a neighborhood.

Key Components

Community police patrol and an increased law enforcement connection to a neighborhood is based on two-way communication between citizens and police officers and follow-up action in response to local problems and concerns. Some communities request increased police patrolling at night or on weekends to deter crime and drug activity. Officers communicate regularly with residents, who help law enforcement identify and apprehend drug dealers and other criminals.

In some communities, increased police presence and community policing take the form of police-staffed satellite neighborhood stations that provide a wide variety of services, such as quick response to drug-related problems, antidrug education, referrals to community-based service providers, and youth programs. In Phoenix, Arizona, and Seattle, Washington, police who patrol on bicycles report that they make as many as five times more arrests than those who patrol in cars.

Key Partnerships

Directed patrol and community policing techniques are most effective when all community residents work with law enforcement. When there is a sustained and accessible police presence in the neighborhood, young people are more likely to develop positive relationships with police.

Potential Obstacles

In one neighborhood that implemented community policing and directed patrol techniques, police felt pressure to respond to the high volume of 911 calls, which decreased their time to otherwise address community concerns. Often, however, calls for service increase when a walking patrol strategy takes effect, due to increased confidence in law enforcement on the part of community residents.

Also, changes in policing techniques must have the full support of police management before they can succeed. Organizational and policy change within law enforcement agencies can be cumbersome.

Signs of Success

Within a three-month period of increased police patrols in a neighborhood in Chapel Hill, North Carolina, police made four drug-related arrests. After police set up operations out of office space provided by a housing project, they recorded an 84 percent decrease in criminal activity and a 64 percent reduction in calls for service.

Applying the Strategy

In the Eastside neighborhood of Wilmington, Delaware, walking police patrols resulted in such positive changes that when the police department proposed transferring the officers and assigning new ones to their locations, the community protested and the original officers stayed.

Increased late-night and weekend patrolling of neighborhoods has reduced drug-related activity and the fear of crime. Off-duty Chapel Hill police work under the auspices of a five-pronged drug elimination plan, working in partnership with residents who compiled a list of known drug dealers who operate on public property. Increased police presence and drug dealer arrests deter further neighborhood drug activity.

In nearby Greensboro, North Carolina, police have established four Police Neighborhood Resource Centers (PNRCs) in housing complexes seriously troubled by drugs and violent crime. The PNRCs are staffed at each site with two law enforcement officers and resident managers who oversee the operation. The officers attend residents' meetings and are involved with clubs that sponsor athletic activities and leadership training for youth.

The Ocala, Florida, Housing Authority provides office space to the police in each of the city's police districts. When the police moved in, residents began to step forward and work with them to rid the area of drug-related activity.

Contact Information

Captain, Ocala Police Department
P.O. Box 1270
Ocala, Florida 32678
904-629-8518

Educate Hotel and Motel Personnel

Strategy

Law enforcement can alert operators of hotels and motels to the signs of illegal use of rooms for drug manufacturing or other drug-related activity.

Drug Problem Addressed

Hotel and motel rooms are clandestinely used to manufacture and sell illegal drugs, such as methamphetamine. Not only is the manufacture of methamphetamine illegal, but the drug can cause serious harm through toxic contamination and fire or explosion.

Key Components

A drug manufacture awareness program for hotel and motel operators should alert them to signs of an intent to manufacture illegal drugs—such as registrants who request a specific room that is isolated and private, vans or trucks loaded with chemistry paraphernalia, evidence of large amounts of cash, refusal of maid service, activity at strange hours, efforts to conceal activity inside the rooms, strong chemical odors, and garbage containing broken flasks, beakers, tubing, or other chemical paraphernalia. Hotel and motel staff are advised to leave the premises if they suspect that someone is using a room as a methamphetamine lab. Motel and hotel operators should also be alerted to the signs of drug dealing—such as high traffic, numerous phone calls, visitors who park several blocks away and walk to the rooms, lookouts who loiter outside the room, and drug paraphernalia lying around the room. Hotel and motel operators who see such signs should call police immediately.

Key Partnerships

Hotel and motel operators and personnel should work closely with representatives of the hospitality industry, law enforcement, and residents in areas with heavy drug activity. Municipal departments that deal with emergencies, hazardous materials, and streets/traffic can also provide information to law enforcement if they are aware of suspicious activity.

Potential Obstacles

Drug dealers and those who illegally manufacture drugs may have radio scanners with which they monitor police bands. If the motel or hotel operator calls the police, the occupants may leave suddenly. If possible, the desk clerk should note the occupant's license plate number and other identifying information.

Signs of Success

Portland, Oregon, police officers and neighbors have worked with motel and hotel operators since 1987 to resolve drug-trafficking and prostitution problems in several neighborhoods. Officers are trained in problem-solving broker "partnership agreements" between business owners and residents. The agreements outline each group's responsibility to address crime-related concerns. Their success led the police bureau to include agreement guide-

lines in a problem-solving workbook for police and neighborhood service agencies.

Applying the Strategy

In Portland, Oregon, the mayor, police chief, public safety commissioner, and chief of fire, rescue, and emergency services distribute booklets explaining the dangers of clandestine drug labs and the appropriate action to take if a motel or hotel operator suspects that drug activity is occurring in a rented room. A state law restricts the use of rented rooms for drug activity and puts a burden on the hotel or motel operator to keep the room drug free. If the room is used for illicit drug manufacture, the hotel or motel owner must decontaminate it or be liable to legal action.

Contact Information

Portland Bureau of Police
1111 SW Second Avenue
Portland, Oregon 97204
503-823-0014

Make Drug Users Accountable

Strategy

Holding drug users accountable reduces drug use.

Drug Problem Addressed

This strategy addresses drug activity and related attitudes. Drug activity will remain high as long as drugs are in demand. Drug use will not decline as long as society sees it as harmful only to the individual user. Accountability programs target drug users who refuse to regard the consequences of their drug use as serious.

Key Components

Drug users must be held accountable for their actions. Many drug users deny that their drug use has anything to do with this country's "drug problem." In fact, their drug use finances drug-related murders, contributes to the deterioration of their cities and communities, and can lead to the injury or death of their own family members.

Police officers must make the arrest of drug users a top priority, and anyone arrested for a user offense must be punished. Several nights in jail will make a user reconsider his or her habits. Drug users should also undergo rehabilitation and drug tests, some of which are expensive.

Key Partnerships

Tough user accountability programs result from strict enforcement of antidrug policies in schools, public places, the

workplace, entertainment establishments, and other institutions, but the effort must have the support of family, the church and other religious groups, social groups, and youth groups. Judges, prosecutors, and legislators must ensure that users do not escape the consequences of their actions.

Potential Obstacles

Many criminal justice system officials treat drug-use cases as if they were inconsequential. When that attitude becomes apparent to a community's residents, antidrug programs lose their credibility.

Signs of Success

Some states (Alabama, Arizona, California, Georgia, Kansas, Kentucky, Louisiana, Maine, Nevada, Oklahoma) have statutes that call for the revocation of driving privileges for people convicted of drug offenses.

Applying the Strategy

"Do Drugs, Do Time" is the campaign warning for the user accountability program in Maricopa County, Arizona. The program, which has strong support from residents and the media, places drugs users in mandatory treatment programs or jail. The program has documented less recidivism and more money, from county jail fees, for antidrug programs.

A National Institute of Justice evaluation of the program revealed a 20 percent recidivism rate among participants. Even more promising, however, was the 8 percent recidivism rate among those who chose to enter the Treatment Alternatives to Street Crime and Drug Diversion program, a component of the "Do Drugs, Do Time" campaign.

Des Moines, Iowa's police department considers dealers only one part of the drug problem. In the past, when police officers arrived on the scene of a drug deal, they arrested only those possessing or selling drugs. Now, thanks to the city's user accountability program, the drug buyer or user must go through a court-approved rehabilitation program at his or her own expense. If the user is arrested a second time, the penalties are severe.

Maricopa County's program targets drug users and brings together law enforcement agencies, prosecution officials, and treatment facilities. Arrested users are charged with possession, which is a felony in Arizona, and are subject to loss of property, including their cars, through asset forfeiture. Arrestees who qualify may choose a pre-filing diversion program that requires treatment and drug testing.

Contact Information

Des Moines Police Department
25 East 1st Street
Des Moines, Iowa 50309
515-283-4800

Maricopa County Attorney's Office
Demand Reduction Program
301 West Jefferson, Suite 800
Phoenix, Arizona 85003
602-506-7799

To obtain a free copy of the evaluation report on the Maricopa County Demand Reduction Program, ask for NCJ 138225 when you call or write the following:

National Criminal Justice Reference Service
Box 6000
Rockville, Maryland 20850
1-800-851-3420

Prevent Gangs

Strategy

When a community and its law enforcement agencies focus their attention on purging the community of gang activity, some drug activity will also be removed.

Drug Problem Addressed

The presence of gangs in a community is often accompanied by drug warfare, drive-by shootings, turf battles, and the murder of innocent bystanders. Evidence suggests that members of youth gangs are particularly susceptible to recruitment into larger criminal organizations engaged in drug trafficking. For example, as reported by Irving Spergel in *Crime and Justice* (1990), Chinese-American youth gangs may be responsible for an increase in the heroin trade in New York City.

Key Components

Many law enforcement agencies are developing gang prevention strategies that target areas where gangs are involved in drug trafficking. Gangs and drugs are not always linked, but in cities in which gangs definitely participate in the local drug trade, police and sheriffs' departments sometimes use drug investigations to halt gang activity.

Drug prevention strategies rely heavily on parent and community education and on attracting youths to alternative activities. Teaching parents how to parent effectively, to be positive community members, and to recognize gangs and protect their children from them are key components of gang prevention efforts. Through events at schools, clubs, churches, or other meeting places, many programs help socially isolated families feel that they are valued members the community. Other programs focus on helping youth who feel a lack of direction, companionship, and belonging. In some communities, former gang members discourage other young people from joining gangs. The nature and extent of gang activity vary widely from area to area; strategies should address local problems.

Key Partnerships

Leaders in anti-gang, antidrug programs must educate and work with parents, school staff, adults who deal with youths, criminal justice personnel, and community residents.

Potential Obstacles

Due to the violence associated with many gangs, residents are frequently afraid to share information with law enforcement agencies. Gang behavior varies between cities, ethnic groups, and particular groups of young people. Stereotyping gang activity is not helpful in addressing the gang/drug problem.

Signs of Success

In Long Beach, California, once home to as many as nine thousand gang members, a program in which former gang members counsel gang members to get jobs or return to school reported a 92 percent rehabilitation rate. In Philadelphia, an African-American community and counseling center provided job placement and sponsored sporting events for gang members. The center, Philadelphia's House of Umoja, was credited with much of the decline in the city's gang activity.

Applying the Strategy

Jurisdictions Unified for Drug Gang Enforcement (JUDGE), in San Diego, is a multiagency task force that enforces probation conditions for drug- and gang-involved probationers. Its goal is to reduce violence and gang-related crimes by ensuring real consequences for violations.

JUDGE targets juvenile and adult street gang members on probation for narcotics offenses through undercover operations, drug testing, and coordination between probation officers and other law enforcement personnel.

In Stockton, California, the Unified School District's Anti-Drug/Gang program provides gang information packets, in a variety of languages, that explain why youths join gangs, how gangs operate, and how a person can recognize the presence of gangs. Parents of children suspected of gang involvement receive mailed information, followed up with individual conferences.

Contact Information

Community Youth Gang Services
144 S. Fetterly Avenue
Los Angeles, California 90022
213-266-4264

Educate the Elderly About Prescription Abuse

Strategy

Problems with substance use are not limited to youth. Many elderly people who take prescription and over-the-counter medications need education about the dangers of substance use.

Drug Problem Addressed

Often the elderly fail to receive or understand information about the medicines they take, whether they are prescribed or over the counter. Also, they may not appreciate the potentially fatal consequences of combining different drugs, including alcohol.

Key Components

Educating the elderly about drug use can be part of a community-wide antidrug strategy. Pharmacists, nursing-home or assisted-living personnel, all paramedical professionals, and families should also be taught about the risks of substance use among the elderly. Flyers can be made available at senior-citizen centers, churches or other religious institutions, nursing homes, hospitals, and other places where the elderly receive services. Public service announcements can increase awareness of some elderly people's difficulty taking medications correctly.

Key Partnerships

Elderly community residents often have limited contacts as they become more isolated due to physical and mental disabilities. A drug prevention strategy that targets the elderly should be designed by medical professionals and implemented as a collaborative effort with the older person's family, immediate friends, and helpers (such as day workers or nurses).

Potential Obstacles

The primary obstacle is difficulty communicating information about the dangers of a patient's taking excessive dosages, mixing medicines, or drinking alcohol while using certain medications. When necessary, a caregiver must take responsibility for proper administration of medication.

Signs of Success

Through the National Institute on Drug Abuse, the U.S. Department of Health and Human Services publishes *Using Your Medicines Wisely*, directed toward the elderly. Also, the American Association of Retired Persons has produced several publications that discuss potential problems with mixing of drugs.

Applying the Strategy

Pontiac, Michigan's Senior Citizen Substance Abuse Prevention project is a print and broadcast public service campaign to heighten awareness of the potential for taking medications incorrectly or unsafely. Aimed at the elderly, the program has recruited pharmacists and counselors to discuss responsible use of prescribed and over-the-counter drugs. Program efforts, which include dramatic skits that deliver the safety message, are coordinated with those of several regional substance abuse agencies.

In Kansas, Elder Ed is part of the state's drug prevention program, educating service providers and the elderly about the proper use of medications. Elder Ed teaches physicians and pharmacists to communicate effectively with their elderly clients—for example, by explaining how to maintain a medication schedule.

Contact Information

Coordinator of Services to the Aging
27725 Greenfield Avenue
Southfield, Michigan 48076
810-424-7019

Senior Program Specialist
Program Coordination and Development
Mental Health and Reminiscence
American Association of Retired Persons
601 E Street, NW
Washington, DC 20049
202-434-2277

Department of Public Health
101 Grove Street, Room 204
San Francisco, California 94102
415-554-2638

Prevention and Treatment Directed at Women

Strategy

An effective antidrug program that targets women addresses a wide range of potential physical and emotional consequences, for both women and their children, of substance abuse.

Drug Problem Addressed

Substance abuse by women threatens the women themselves and, if they are pregnant, their fetuses. Women who become aggressive or negligent when under the influence of alcohol or other drugs also harm family members.

Key Components

An antidrug program that focuses on women's problems must present clear, compelling information on physical and emotional health information and clearly define the law and the consequences of failing to obey it. Antidrug education for women should address the relationship between drug use and fetal alcohol syndrome, AIDS, reproductive problems, the birth of "crack babies," and emotional and physical problems. The program should also provide follow-up services for pregnant women in need of personal help, guidance in parenting, or child care services. A women's antidrug program should also underscore the effects of a mother's incarceration on her children. Outreach efforts are most effective when implemented in safe environments such as women's support groups and in accessible locations such as local health agencies or community centers.

Key Partnerships

A drug prevention campaign for women that addresses the dangers of alcohol and other drugs, especially during pregnancy, should involve medical and psychological service providers who specialize in women's health, family counselors, and parenting specialists. Other effective partners include neighborhood associations, schools, and religious groups that can assist with daily needs. In addition, the media, local businesses, alcohol retailers and distributors, and members of the hospitality industry can publicly address the problems of women who abuse substances.

Potential Obstacles

Women who feel isolated, powerless, and disenfranchised due to family or economic circumstances are particularly difficult to reach with drug prevention programs. Outreach efforts are most effective within safe environments, such as women's support groups. Often a woman's decision not to use alcohol or other drugs is linked to a major (possibly frightening) change in her circumstances, such as leaving her parents' home or her neighborhood or severing a relationship with a husband or other male companion.

Signs of Success

In Claremont, California, several neighborhood recovery centers, together with other local groups and the National Council on Alcoholism, mounted a campaign to reduce the number of alcohol-related birth defects. Their campaign persuaded most of the cities in San Diego County to adopt ordinances requiring the posting of alcohol-related educational signs in alcohol outlets and eating establishments.

Applying the Strategy

Each year, the San Diego County Department of Alcohol and Drug Services' Options for Recovery Program provides case management and residential treatment to over a thousand women recovering from alcohol and other drug addiction and also serve their 250 children. The Options project has several programs designed to meet the unique medical and other treatment needs of women and small children. The culturally sensitive programs include services targeted to African-American women, pregnant women, teens, and women needing residential treatment services. The program provides early intervention and ongoing therapy. Among the women who participated during one recent year, 91 percent gave birth to babies free of drugs.

The Center for Human Development, in Lafayette, California, offers a Pregnant Teens/Teen Parent program, including a teen mother support group, case management and advocacy for teen mothers, a support group for teen fathers, and a grandparent support group. In the program, young mothers earn income by running a store that offers inexpensive items for young mothers and their children.

A Tuba City, Arizona, program addresses the special needs of pregnant Navaho women and mothers of children with fetal alcohol syndrome. The program screens for the syndrome and refers women to services, including case management, health care, education counseling, and support services. The program was used as a model for other Indian Health Service projects focused on fetal alcohol syndrome.

In New York City, the Women's Action Alliance sponsors a Women's Alcohol and Drug Education Project aimed at helping underserved African-American, Hispanic, and low-income women, who are often battered, sexually abused, unemployed, and vulnerable to alcohol and other drug use. The project provides drug and alcohol education, a support system, intervention, and health and referral services. Participants are encouraged to join on-site chapters of Alcoholics Anonymous, Narcotics Anonymous, or Al-Anon groups as needed.

Contact Information

San Diego County
Department of Health Services Alcohol Program
P.O. Box 85222
San Diego, California 92138
619-692-8672

Leadership Training for High-Risk Youth

Strategy

Communities can train high-risk youth to become positive leaders, role models for their peers, and educators of other youths about the dangers of alcohol and other drugs.

Drug Problem Addressed

Training high-risk youth to help other high-risk youth maximizes the number of young people who are helped.

Key Components

Leadership training for high-risk teens has been a very successful component of community antidrug efforts. Teens who go through leadership training often develop a commitment to their community, personal responsibility, and a desire to help others. Teen leadership programs focus on preventing alcohol and other drug use, preventing teen pregnancy, developing community-building skills, and developing communication and other personal skills. Teens learn from other teens how to design and implement antidrug programs for their peers. These programs can include special drug-free events (such as beach trips, athletic events, and pizza parties), community service projects, neighborhood cleanups, and antidrug peer education.

Key Partnerships

Teens can be chosen for leadership training with the assistance of school personnel, parents, mentors, youth club leaders, law enforcement units, and service providers as well as other adults who have identified young people with influence over their peers. Leadership trainers can be drawn from a broad range of community residents, including business leaders, professionals, neighborhood leaders, and other youths.

Potential Obstacles

Adults may impede youth leadership training by attempting to dominate youth, failing to fulfill their commitments, or reacting negatively to any suggestions by teens. Youth training programs should recruit adults who have demonstrated a belief in teens' capabilities and an ability to let teens take the lead.

Signs of Success

In an evaluation of Portland, Maine's Peer Leader Program (PLP) for high-risk teens, the group got high marks for improving teens' leadership skills, interpersonal relationships, and ability to cooperate. The program successfully intervened in the lives of teens who were abusing alcohol and other drugs, were suicidal, or were experiencing family problems. It also improved school performance and increased community service among participants.

Applying the Strategy

PLP draws its participants from three large public housing projects, characterized by extreme poverty, cultural deprivation, and high rates of alcoholism and sexual and physical abuse. Sponsored by the Community Leadership Institute of Maine, PLP was initiated as a joint effort of the local housing authority, the Portland business community, local tenant associations, service providers, and the municipality of Portland. Teens lead the program's decision-making; they are involved in a training workshop, weekly meetings, planning of drug-free activities and events, and a media campaign that promotes community awareness of the program.

Contact Information

Assistant Director
Community Leadership Initiatives of Maine
P.O. Box 17801
Portland, Maine 04101
207-874-1140

Bibliography

Books

Cadwalader, Wickersham, and Taft. *A Civil War: A Community Legal Guide to Fighting Street Drug Markets.* Ann Arbor, MI: Edwards Brothers, 1993.

Conner, Roger, and Patrick Burns. *The Winnable War: A Community Guide to Eradicating Street Drug Markets.* Washington, DC: American Alliance for Rights and Responsibilities, 1991.

Jackson, Gail, ed. *Exemplary Programs in Criminal Justice: Innovations at the Local Level.* Washington, DC: National League of Cities, 1994.

Katcher, Brian S. *Prescription Drugs: An Indispensable Guide for People over 50.* New York, NY: Avon, 1993.

National League of Cities. *Front Line Reports: Local Strategies in the War against Drugs.* Washington, DC, 1989.

U.S. Department of Housing and Urban Development. *Together We Can . . . Meet the Challenge: Law Enforcement Strategies and Practices to Eliminate Drugs in Public Housing.* Washington, DC: Office of Public and Indian Housing, 1994

Weingart, Saul N., Francis X. Hartmann, and David Osborne. *Lessons Learned: Case Studies of the Initiation and Maintenance of the Community Response to Drugs.* Washington, DC: National Institute of Justice, 1992.

Periodicals

Cianfarano, Michael G. Berrien County's Drug Court. *Colleague* (Michigan Judicial Institute), October 1992.

Jackson Takes a Stand Community Partnership Project. *JTAS Speaks*, Fall 1993.

National Association of Child Advocates. *Youth Crime Prevention Programs Work* (fact sheet). Washington, DC, 1995.

Thomas, Pierre. Use of Drugs by Teenagers Is Increasing: Study Finds Sharp Rise in Marijuana Smoking, *Washington Post*, December 13, 1994, p. A1.

Youth Employment. *Home Front* (HUD), Washington, DC, Summer 1994.

Public Documents

American Bar Association. *Just Solutions: A Program Guide to Innovative Justice System Improvements.* Chicago, IL, 1994,

———. *Strategies for Courts to Cope with the Caseload Pressures of Drug Cases.* 1991.

American Society of Criminology. *Criminology*, vol. 30, 1992.

———. *Criminology*, vol. 32, 1994.

Area Agency on Aging. Senior Citizens Programs; Jackson County Alcohol and Other Drug Partnership; Health Promotion Program for Citizens of Jackson County; Cardiovascular Health Promotion. In *Health Promotion Initiatives.* Tallahassee, FL.

Bringing Everybody's Strengths Together (BEST). In *Resource Fair Program Summaries: Building Justice in Our Communities*, pp. 28–29. 1994.

Bureau of Justice Assistance (DOJ). *Crime Prevention in Overnight Lodging.* Washington, DC, 1991.

———. *Drugs and Crime Facts, 1993.* Washington, DC, 1993.

———. *Violent Crime and Drug Abuse in Rural Areas: Issues, Concerns, and Programs.* Washington, DC, 1993.

———. *State and Local Programs: Preventing Drug Abuse and Violent Crime.* Washington, DC, 1994.

Center for Substance Abuse Prevention. *Preventing Alcohol and Other Drug Problems in our Communities: Case Studies and Resources.* Rockville, MD, 1994.

Do Drugs, Do Time: An Evaluation of the Maricopa County Demand Reduction Program. *Research in Brief* (National Institute of Justice), October 1994.

Drug Case Management and Treatment Intervention Strategies in the State and Local Courts. Vol. 1. Washington, DC: American University, 1994.

Greater Tyler Drug-Free Business Initiative. In *Resource Fair Program Summaries: Building Justice in Our Communities*, pp. 39–40. 1994.

National Crime Prevention Council. *Given the Opportunity.* Washington, DC, 1992.

National Institute of Justice (DOJ). *What Price Justice?: A Handbook for the Analysis of Criminal Justice Costs.* Washington, DC, 1989.

————. *Report from the States on What Works at the State and Local Levels: A Compendium of Assessment and Evaluation Results.* Washington, DC, 1992.

Office of Technology Assessment. *Technologies for Understanding and Preventing: Substance Abuse and Addiction.* Washington, DC: U.S. Government Printing Office, 1994.

Ohio Valley Regional Development Commission; Youth Opportunities Unlimited. *Rewarding Adolescent Drug Abuse Resistance.* South Point, OH, 1993.

Pennsylvania Liquor Control Board. *"Nuisance Bar" Program.* 1993.

President's Commission on Model State Drug Laws. *The Importance of Immediate and Intensive Intervention in a Court-ordered Drug Rehabilitation Program.* Philadelphia, PA, 1993.

Rent Stabilization Association; New York City. *Drug-Free Neighborhoods: A Partnership of Owners, Tenants and Government Services.* New York, NY, 1990.

Responsible Hospitality Institute; Monterey-Santa Cruz Responsible Beverage Service Project. *Final Report: Place of Last Drink Prior to Arrest.* Scotts Valley, CA, 1993.

Syracuse-Onondaga Business Against Drugs (SO BAD). In *Resource Fair Program Summaries: Building Justice in Our Communities*, p. 33. 1994.

Ten Most Wanted Program. In *Resource Fair Program Summaries: Building Justice in Our Communities*, pp. 22–23. 1994.

TIP Drug Pushers out of Your Neighborhood. *Parents Today* (NCPC), vol. 2, no. 1.

Bias Crimes

Acts or threats of acts against people that grow out of the offender's hostility to the victim's ethnic or racial group, religious affiliation, gender, or sexual orientation are classified as bias or hate-motivated crimes.

In the early 1990s, FBI reports indicated that a hate crime occured every fourteen minutes in the United States. Owing to their potential to affect entire groups and communities of people—to give an impression that one group is excluded from the rest of society—bias crimes are uniquely destructive, with potentially devastating impacts for social cohesion. As the U.S. population continues to diversify, it is becoming increasingly urgent that we prevent hate from defining intergroup relations.

Strategies to diminish bias-motivated crimes should include at least three areas of response. Specific penalties that recognize the unique impact of hate crimes should be created to help deter potential offenders. Also, community and institutional programs to facilitate diversity education and multicultural interaction serve an essential function in preventing the social disharmony that spawns bias crimes. Further, counseling services for both victims and perpetrators of bias crimes minimize the damage inflicted by hate-motivated violence.

Law enforcement has initiated a variety of programs to deal with the problem of bias crimes. Programs exist in every state and on the federal level to ensure that hate criminals are punished severely. Despite the increased penalties for bias-motivated offenses, most of the law enforcement programs around the country have been unable to overcome the surge of hate crimes for a number of reasons: victims are afraid of reporting crimes to the police, fearing a biased criminal justice system and the potential stigmatization of being identified and labeled based on group membership; prosecution of hate criminals without confronting underlying causes and the facts of societal discrimination has the potential to intensify intergroup tensions; and support services to put victims in contact with the appropriate authorities are often inadequate.

The police and criminal justice system therefore should undertake programs to build community partnerships and to increase the public's faith in law as part of an effort to reduce hate crimes. Rapid responses to complaints about hate crimes signal intolerance of these crimes and help to prevent their recurrence. Specifically targeted police programs to reduce crimes motivated by hate have proven effective. A Boston program designated a team of officers to contend solely with hate crimes, allowing rapid responses to any threats. As a result, hate crimes were reduced by more than 50 percent.

Law enforcement sensitivity to language and cultural differences that may exist within a community helps lessen victims' fears about reporting crimes. Lincoln, Nebraska, and Garden Grove, California, recognizing the need for police outreach to immigrant communities, have programs that provide bilingual assistance to help bridge cultural gaps. The result has been a substantial increase in crime reports and improved community relations.

Similarly, it is critical to provide counseling for victims and victimized groups in order to facilitate recovery and empowerment that can help prevent further offenses from occurring. Services that assist victims of bias crimes in overcoming their trauma and programs that teach hate crime prevention to vulnerable groups signal community support for victims, thereby encouraging greater reporting of such offenses. Programs in Chicago; St. Paul, Minnesota; and Willows, California have all proven effective in establishing contact among victims, support services, and law enforcement.

The legal community must demonstrate its willingness to confront any discrimination within itself. Strategies to establish court observers, members of the community who observe criminal proceedings in order to determine whether the legal system conducts them fairly and without discrimination, have made courts more aware of biases that exist and measures that can be taken to eliminate them.

Perhaps even more important, bias crimes must be confronted at their roots, since they are often caused by a lack of education and underexposure to diverse sectors of society. School years are thus a crucial time at which discrimination can be confronted and hate crimes prevented. Indeed, education in any form acts as a barrier to bias crimes, since keeping youths from becoming alienated and disaffected goes a long way in stopping group interactions from being based upon fear and mistrust. Elementary school programs that increase student awareness and understanding of other cultures stem the ignorance that frequently underlies violence spawned by hate.

Green Circle, a nationally distributed program to promote diversity and understanding, works with local communities throughout the country to establish education programs that encourage children to confront their behaviors and challenge biases.

Media cooperation through public service announcements (PSAs) has the potential to increase cultural awareness and understanding among distinct groups, thereby advancing the goal of a community that embraces notions of diversity and rejects intolerance. Partnerships between local media and national organizations committed to increasing tolerance, such as the Anti-Defamation League, can create educational programming and advertisements that increase understanding among different groups and enhance harmonious community relations.

Those who have committed hate crimes can benefit from carefully designed education strategies. The combination of legal sanctions and counseling that involves the exposure of hate criminals to members of the group that they threatened or acted against can overcome the lack of knowledge about other people that often underlies these crimes. An Anti-Defamation League diversion and counseling program for juvenile bias crime offenders has seen no repeat of hate crime offenses among participants.

This chapter explores eleven innovative strategies that have been successfully implemented and are currently working to prevent the occurrence of bias crimes. Through a combination of enforcement, education, and sensitivity to issues of diversity, hate crimes can be controlled, both in their occurrence and in their impact on society.

Court Monitoring

Strategy

Recruiting community volunteers to monitor the performance of local courts or instituting a task force whose purpose is to analyze court performance promotes equitable decision-making in the criminal justice system.

Crime Problem Addressed

A tainted or biased court system adds to the greater societal problems and perpetuates bias crimes and behavior. The majority of cases that go through the criminal justice system are settled fairly; however, in certain cases people have been treated unjustly by the court based on their race, religion, gender, or sexual preference. Not only do court watch groups take action when they see wrongdoing, but their visibility alerts the courts that people are watching to ensure that decisions are made fairly. A self-monitoring court not only helps the court act justly, it sends

a message to the community that the courts serve the people.

Key Components

The fundamental element of court monitoring is to have *somebody* critically observe the courts. Community watch groups track both the behavior of the courts and the condition of the courthouses' facilities to ensure that there is no wrongdoing in the court procedures. Then, they report their findings back to the courts, the public, and the press. Often these watch groups are connected to community-based victim services or crime prevention organizations. The information that the court watchers gather is used to identify unfair court practices and to determine how to rectify these problems. A task force or commission is composed of community and legal professionals who clearly establish the issues pertinent to the court and the community they serve. The commission performs a variety of roles such as holding public hearings, using a research staff for projects, utilizing lawyers' surveys with regard to bias, and making recommendations for change.

Key Partnerships

The court watchers are not the nemeses of the courts but rather partners with the courts in that they work together to create an equitable and efficient system. The court watchers meet with court leaders to review performances and offer advice for improvement. Also important is the willingness of community members to volunteer to be court watchers. In order to solicit volunteers, activists publicize the need for equitable courts in the community. A commission or task force evolves out of interest from both court-related professionals and the public, and sometimes develops in the aftermath of specific incidents or cases. Additionally, there is a close partnership among the members of the commission.

Potential Obstacles

It can be difficult to find impartial court watchers who volunteer for reasons other than a personal agenda or particular closeness to a problem or group. Therefore, it is important to train volunteers and ensure that their purpose is to help maintain impartiality in the courts. Also, court watching is a time-consuming commitment, not only for the volunteers but also for the court leaders who take time to meet with them and respond to their concerns. Successful court watching requires the commitment of court officials if the court-watching program is to form partnerships and avoid adversarial relationships. Even after court monitors identify problems, the challenge of how to rectify the problems and how to implement changes remains.

Signs of Success

Court watchers are not concerned with the outcomes of the cases; instead, they turn their attention to the *perfor-*mance of the courts. Court watch programs usually result following a trend of injustices or a tip that a court is not acting impartially. Many people understand the value of court watchers. In fact, there are organizations of lawyers such as the Women's Bar Association of Maryland that support such programs. As for self-evaluation of courts, the National Center for State Courts published a manual which outlines how courts can create self-monitoring commissions. The manual presents all of the issues that need to be considered to effectively build and maintain a commission, such as partnerships, key issues, financing, and goals.

Applying the Strategy

After a report by the Joint Committee on Gender Bias in the Courts revealed that gender bias clearly existed in the Maryland court system, the Women's Bar Association of Maryland initiated a court watch program. The Fund for Modern Courts monitors courts in both rural and urban New York State. Cook County, Illinois, court watchers have developed a successful partnership with court leaders.

Contact Information

Court Watchers
The Women's Bar Association of Maryland
520 West Fayette Street
Baltimore, Maryland 21201
410-528-9681

Commissioner
National Center for State Courts
1700 North Moore Street, Suite 1710
Arlington, Virginia 22209
703-841-0200

Diversity and Tolerance Education in Schools

Strategy

Teaching tolerance in elementary schools reduces the incidence of hate crimes, racism, discrimination, and bigotry.

Crime Problem Addressed

Prejudice and intolerance in the United States are climbing as increasing numbers of minorities live in this country. According to a 1993 report issued by the FBI, data collected from 2,800 police departments in thirty-two states revealed 4,755 bias-related crimes. Because this figure does not include the majority of police departments, the actual figure is likely to be much higher. In many cases, such behavior results from lack of education and exposure to people who are different from oneself. Instituting school programs that teach students how to relate to others from different backgrounds and cultures helps students learn early in life how to appreciate diversity and relate peaceably to other people.

Key Components

Children are aware of racial and gender differences at a very young age, and by age twelve they have formed stereotypes. In fact, recent studies show that tolerance education is most effective between the ages of four and nine years. Therefore, it is important to teach tolerance to young children and continue reinforcing the message over time. Age-appropriateness is involved in the creation of the different curricula that educators have developed. For instance, part of the curriculum includes classroom exercises from newsletters and newspaper sections directed toward younger audiences. Additional methods include short theatrical productions and role-playing exercises.

Key Partnerships

Some school systems recognize the need to teach tolerance, soliciting outside resources to conduct educational programs. In other communities, local organizations realize the need for tolerance education and promote appropriate curricula. What students learn in the classroom needs to be reinforced in other aspects of their lives, which requires parental involvement. Schools also recruit community leaders from different groups, races, and ethnicities to teach that tolerance reaches into relationships at home, play, and school.

Potential Obstacles

Intolerance surrounds society; consequently, it may be difficult to monitor what is learned in the classroom in a noneducational setting. Additionally, communities as a whole must want to implement a tolerance education program in the schools. For instance, teachers need training and instruction on how to model ideas and present values.

Signs of Success

Educating students about other cultures, races, religions, and gender helps them understand people different from themselves. Understanding ultimately leads to greater tolerance. Instilling critical thinking skills, creating role-playing, and cooperative learning have proven effective teaching tools. Since 1957, the Green Circle Program based in Philadelphia has promoted awareness, understanding, and appreciation of diversity. Rather than prescribe values for children, Green Circle provides models for certain behaviors and lets the children evaluate their own behaviors. Green Circle serves groups and schools across the United States.

Applying the Strategy

In 1992, the American Bar Association's Young Lawyers Division (YLD) launched four Tolerance Education pilot projects in elementary schools, middle schools, high schools, and colleges throughout the country. The programs featured education about the law, open discussions, and mock trials. The South Carolina Bar YLD operates a tolerance education program for third and fourth graders in which attorneys go into the classroom and teach the students. According to one participating lawyer, both the students and the teachers loved the program, and the school invites the program back year after year. In fact, the YLD is currently working to implement the program in more South Carolina schools. At the conclusion of the program, it is evident that the students have a greater understanding of discrimination and prejudice. In fact, one of the third-grade students confronted his parents about their bias toward people unlike themselves. Other states are beginning to adopt the program as well.

Contact Information

American Bar Association, Young Lawyers Division
750 North Lake Shore Drive
Chicago, Illinois 60611
312-988-5000

Green Circle Program
1300 Spruce Street
Philadelphia, Pennsylvania 19107
215-893-8400

South Carolina Bar YLD
205 North Irby Street
P.O. Box 107
Florence, South Carolina 29503
803-662-6301

Multilingual Reporting and Education Services

Strategy

Reaching out to immigrants who do not speak English through bilingual crime prevention and reporting services (i.e., employing bilingual community service officers (CSOs)) helps law enforcement agencies improve community relations.

Crime Problem Addressed

As the number of immigrants in the United States increases, so does the number of immigrant residents who become targets of crimes or witnesses of crimes. Because many of the immigrants do not speak English, a great portion of these crimes go unreported. Additionally, some of the immigrants never report crimes because they feared the police in their homeland and may think they will have the same experience in this country. Employing bilingual police officers and posting bilingual notices helps bridge both language and cultural gaps. By reaching out to the immigrant communities, police gain access to and protect the immigrant community.

Key Components

Programs using this strategy often hire bilingual police officers and publicize crime prevention and crime reporting information in the language(s) of the local immigrant population. Furthermore, they strive to build a cultural understanding between the police and the immigrant community to create even better relationships and greater trust. One way the police reach out to the immigrant populations is to set up substations. Substations are police stations located in the immigrant community where the CSO works. These stations serve a dual purpose: first, they provide a community with a police presence that helps deter criminal activity; second, community members do not have to travel far to report crimes or problems.

Key Partnerships

Some states provide funding to the police department to either hire bilingual personnel or educate the department on preconceptions that immigrants may have about law enforcement and the law. Additionally, the police department works to create a relationship with the immigrant community so that its members feel they can turn to the police. Community-based organizations within those immigrant populations work with the police and the immigrant community to provide information, services, and activities. The CSO also works with the media to create crime prevention programming for the radio and crime prevention news releases for newspapers in the appropriate language. Because many police departments cannot afford to set up these substations, the project may depend upon support from local businesses.

Potential Obstacles

Gang members from immigrant populations may work against what the police and the other organizations are trying to establish for the community. Also, law enforcement agencies must make institutional commitments of money, time, and personnel.

Signs of Success

Increases in reported crimes to the police by immigrants and heavy use of crime reporting hotlines in the respective language are just two of the indications that this strategy works. Also, trust has grown between the immigrant community and the police. Furthermore, bilingual CSOs are receiving recognition and commendations for their work.

Applying the Strategy

The Garden Grove Police Department in California received a grant from the state to employ two bilingual CSOs to create liaisons with the growing Asian population. About 50 percent of the 143,000 persons in the city are Southeast Asians, mainly Vietnamese immigrants. The police department has substations in the heart of "Little Saigon," where most of the Vietnamese live. In addition to being present in the community and going into schools and businesses to speak to the Vietnamese population about crime prevention, the CSO also hosts a question-and-answer radio program in Vietnamese. Because of the overwhelming positive response, the radio station increased the length of the program from one to two hours. A recorded increase in crime reports followed (with the help of a hotline that does not require callers to leave their names), relations between the Asian community and the police improved, and the program has become a national model for bilingual hotlines.

Contact Information

Community Service Officer
Garden Grove Police Department
P.O. Box 3070
11301 Acacia Parkway
Garden Grove, California 92642
714-539-2284

Culturally Based Youth Leadership and Empowerment Programs

Strategy

Offering culturally based leadership training, counseling, and educational workshops empowers youth and helps them avoid delinquent behavior.

Crime Problem Addressed

School dropout, substance abuse, gangs, and lack of life skills are all problems that affect many youth. Providing alternate activities—educational and skill development and advisement sessions—offers youth the tools to become community leaders and to contribute to a better society.

Key Components

It is important to design a program to fit the needs of a particular community, for each community has to contend with its own situation. Each program, then, needs to plan with its community's needs and spirit in mind.

Key Partnerships

A multifunction program requires the partnerships of many different public and private organizations. Community leaders and government officials form a partnership, and they work with students and parents. It is also important to work with other neighborhood groups with similar missions, because the groups lend one another support and resources.

Potential Obstacles

When officials and police enter a community and want to help it, community members tend to be skeptical. In order to gain community cooperation, both the community and the officials must have confidence in one another.

Signs of Success

Many culturally based programs are successful. For example, Martin Luther King Community Services of Freeport, Illinois, delivers many programs and services for more than 800 high-risk youth. The majority of the youth are African-Americans living at or below the poverty line. The program integrates Black History Month and Martin Luther King Day and offers ongoing activities involving African-American ministers and community leaders. The goal is to reduce risks in as many facets of life as possible through educational enhancement programs, parent training and support, and partnerships among the family, school, and community. The program has been praised as accessible to people who want its services and successful

in providing after-school supervision and academic assistance. As a result of the work of Martin Luther King Community Services, the rate of young people succeeding in the school system (meaning they obtain a C grade or better) increased from 7 percent to 32 percent. The program also serves more than 280 teenaged and single parents. Of the group of 280, 60 percent received academic assistance to pursue higher education, and 60 of them found jobs.

Applying the Strategy

There are ASPIRA Clubs ("aspira" means "to aspire" in Spanish) located in Florida, New York, Pennsylvania, New Jersey, Illinois, and Puerto Rico which boast a 98.6 percent success rate of students who stayed in school. ASPIRA is a community-based organization that teaches youth leadership skills to promote positive change to the community. During the weekly club meetings, ASPIRA uses curriculum-based training prevention awareness program. The emphasis on cultural activities (e.g., celebration of various holidays) is one of the important components of the curriculum. Youth come to the program after being referred by the school or through peer recruitment. During the 1994-95 academic year, Miami ASPIRA reached out to more than 1,500 local youth. The program increased youth participation in the educational process and resulted in more youth graduating from high school and continuing on to college.

Contact Information

Raul Martinez
3650 North Miami Avenue
Miami, Florida 33137
305-576-1512

Martin Luther King Community Services of Illinois
Freeport Initiative
511 South Liberty
Freeport, Illinois 61032
815-233-9915

Ongoing Police-Cultural Organization Service Partnerships

Strategy

Providing a bridge between the community and law enforcement agencies creates partnerships for education and outreach through ethnic-oriented community organizations.

Crime Problem Addressed

Problems can erupt from a basic lack of cultural understanding. Immigrants to the United States are often un-

aware of some of its laws and customs because of language barriers. They may also have problems communicating with police officers. Also, long-time residents of a community often lack information about recent immigrant populations. When people cannot communicate well with one another, fear and frustration often result, which ultimately may cause rifts between cultural groups.

Key Components

Ethnic-oriented organizations provide both information to help particular ethnic groups better understand the United States, and educate the rest of the community about their culture and traditions.

Key Partnerships

A liaison from the ethnic group in the community works closely with the ethnic group, the community, and law enforcement agencies to create a dialogue that everyone understands. The liaison is responsible for such tasks as communication (e.g., presenting laws in English as a second language to children and adults), translating legal documents and human service information, providing mediation services, and coordinating events such as multicultural festivals for the entire community.

Potential Obstacles

The liaison has a delicate position, for he or she must gain the trust of an ethnic community while maintaining a close relationship with the law enforcement agencies and the greater community. People in the ethnic community may feel betrayed or hostile toward a liaison who also works with people outside of the community.

Signs of Success

Numerous communities have ethnic-oriented community organizations and liaisons to promote more harmonious relationships within the community as a whole. In many instances, police departments employ a community outreach person, or liaison, to assist with communications. In other cases, a community organization takes responsibility for such outreach programs. For example, St.

Rita's Asian Center in Bronx, New York, offers educational services, advocacy programs, translation services, crisis intervention, and victim assistance.

Applying the Strategy

In just a few years, Lincoln, Nebraska's Vietnamese population grew from a few hundred to more than 3,000 in a population of more than 100,000 people. Efforts by the police-employed liaisons and several police officers who have learned some Vietnamese have increased trust between the Vietnamese community and the law enforcement officers. In addition to liaisons, Lincoln has launched various community events aimed at cultural awareness. For instance, there was a school festival celebrating different cultures where students had the opportunity to experience food, dance, and costumes from other cultures. This type of exposure helps break down misconceptions and creates a community that better understands and appreciates all its members. Lincoln has recorded fewer racially motivated problems since implementing cultural awareness throughout the community.

Contact Information

Community Liaison
Lincoln Police Department
233 South 10th Street
Lincoln, Nebraska 68508
402-441-6350

St. Rita's Asian Center
2342 Andrews Avenue
Bronx, New York 10468
718-295-8175

Rapid Response to Reported Incidents

Strategy

Rapid and effective law enforcement response to hate violence demonstrates a tough attitude toward hate crime perpetrators while demonstrating sensitivity to the special needs of victims.

Crime Problem Addressed

Government and private sources have documented increasing reports of hate violence. These criminal acts, in which the victim is targeted because of race, religion, sexual orientation, or ethnicity, are designed to intimidate victims and other members of the victim's community and leave them feeling isolated, vulnerable, and fearful. These crimes have a special emotional and psychological impact on the victims and exacerbate racial, religious, or ethnic tensions in the community.

Key Components

Forty-six states and the federal government have established increased penalties for hate crimes. These laws reassure targets of hate violence and deter these crimes by imposing serious punishment on the perpetrators. The Hate Crime Statistics Act (HCSA), enacted in 1990, requires the FBI to collect hate crime data from state and local law enforcement officials. Tracking hate crime data encourages victims to report these crimes and can help police anticipate sensitive issues in the aftermath of an incident.

Key Partnerships

Municipalities establish an integrated hate crime response network, including liaisons to local prosecutors, human rights commissions, and community-based victim advocacy organizations. Community-based groups and victim support organizations work with law enforcement to urge residents to report hate crimes and assist at the investigation and prosecution stages, help reduce the victim's sense of isolation and vulnerability, and analyze hate crime data for both their own constituents and the media. Police departments adopt a written policy regarding procedures for effective response to hate violence and train officers in how to identify, report, and respond to such crimes as well as how to deal with victims.

Potential Obstacles

Many police departments have failed to report HCSA statistics, citing the burden of additional paperwork, fears about negative publicity, or budget constraints. Active police response to hate violence may result in increased reports and prosecutions over those of neighboring, less attentive departments. However, even in departments that have specific hate crime guidelines, ambiguity in some cases remains.

Signs of Success

Working with civil rights groups, the law enforcement community has played a leadership role in supporting hate crime, penalty enhancement, and data collection initiatives. Police authorities have long recognized that tracking crime can help departments create preventive strategies and allocate resources. Virtually every state has statutes about hate violence, and 47 percent of 109 police departments surveyed have instituted policies on bias-motivated crime. For instance, Montgomery County, Maryland, established the Office of Human Relations Commission to deal with bias crimes, providing an array of services and educational information to the community. The Anti-Defamation League has published a book highlighting a large number of other cities that have pursued similar policies. Implementing procedures and dealing effectively with such crimes sends a message to the community that this type of crime is a serious problem and will be treated as such.

Applying the Strategy

In 1978, the Boston Police Department was the first department in the country to establish a Community Disorders Unit. The department has nine detectives, three interpreters, two sergeants, one lieutenant, one police officer, and one secretary. In 1978, the department handled 609 bias crime cases, compared with only 276 cases in 1993. In fact, one year the department recorded as few as 158 bias crime cases. Whereas the department used to handle many repeat cases (i.e., the same family repeatedly being tormented), repeat cases are now very rare. These decreases in bias crimes resulted from the department sending a clear message.

Contact Information

Anti-Defamation League
823 United Nations Plaza
New York, New York 10017
212-490-2525

Boston Police Department
154 Berkeley Street
Boston, Massachusetts 02116

Media Campaigns About Community Standards for Tolerance

Strategy

Using media resources as an education vehicle builds awareness about diversity and decreases prejudice.

Crime Problem Addressed

Demographic studies show that the United States is becoming more diverse. By the year 2000, members of minority groups will form the majority of the population in more than fifty American cities. The change in population has increased bias-related crimes. Awareness programs create understanding, and this understanding builds a community of people who respect one another's differences.

Key Components

This strategy uses all forms of media, but primarily television and newspapers. The purpose is to educate viewers and readers and present information on other cultures, religions, and races; program content also promotes critical thinking about prejudices. The media cosponsor community events focusing on reducing prejudice and cover the events for the community. Examples of media programming are live specials and festivals, documentaries, and PSAs.

Key Partnership

The key partners are local media talents, educators, community members, and people in the private sector. The most important partnership is with a television station that agrees to provide both air time and technical and production support. Leaders of various racial, religious, and ethnic groups and local organizations should agree to act as consultants and proponents of the program. Furthermore, teachers receive training from the programming on how to teach and deal with diversity in the classroom. This project requires willingness to participate and active input from all of the partners.

Potential Obstacles

Soliciting the media requires an effective campaign by community leaders to convince the media and the public that bias crimes are a problem that affects the entire community.

Signs of Success

Spreading information via the media is an efficient and influential method to reach a large audience. In 1985, the Anti-Defamation League's Boston office successfully implemented "A World of Difference" (AWOD) program, which links media and educational resources to develop diversity awareness programming. Several of the programs that evolved from this project are now used in diversity awareness and anti-prejudice training sessions for more than 110,000 elementary and secondary school educators, for college students on more than 400 campuses, for more than 70,000 employees in a variety of workplaces, for law enforcement professionals, and for community organizations. AWOD has expanded internationally to Germany, South Africa, and Russia following invitations from those three countries.

Applying the Strategy

The Anti-Defamation League in Washington, DC, together with WUSA-TV, created a local AWOD campaign focusing on multicultural education training for teachers. Task forces of community leaders and local educators ensured that the materials addressed the concerns and needs of the greater Washington metropolitan area. In addition to live specials, documentaries, PSAs, and a special news series, there were several programs concentrating on the campaign. Because WUSA used the campaign as a guide for much of its programming, the anti-prejudice, pro-acceptance message permeated the fabric of the community.

Contact Information

Anti-Defamation League
1100 Connecticut Avenue, NW, Suite 1020
Washington, DC 20036
202-452-8320

Counseling for Offenders Involved in Hate Groups

Strategy

Enlisting young members of hate-crime groups into counseling programs helps dispel bias.

Crime Problem Addressed

As the United States becomes more and more diverse, there is a correlated increase in bias crimes, and groups of people commit criminal acts for reasons such as race, religion, and sexual orientation. Often, such biases derive from a lack of information and exposure to people who are "different." In "Hate Crime Laws: A Comprehensive Guide," the Anti-Defamation League says, "experience has shown that juvenile civil rights offenders are more likely than their adult counterparts to act out of ignorance rather than deeply ingrained attitudes."

Key Components

A counseling program presents an opportunity to educate hate-crime offenders (or even potential offenders) about those who are the object of their hate. Ultimately, the purpose of such counseling is to broaden hate-crime offenders' views of other cultures and, in doing so, change their values. Some effective "awareness" sessions include intensive counseling along with encounter sessions. During encounter sessions, hate-crime offenders come face to face with those they hate. For example, a teenager who spray-painted swastikas on a synagogue is given an opportunity to discuss religion with a rabbi.

Key Partnerships

To alter the viewpoints of perpetrators of hate crimes, the "hosts" of a counseling program establish a level of credibility through open dialogue. Other methods of reform include encounters with local judges who explain what may happen to offenders if they continue committing bias crimes and visits to county prisons where they are warned they may spend time. An important technique allows the offenders to meet the victims of hate crimes. Therefore, it is necessary to have victims volunteer who are willing to talk about their culture, race, or gender.

Potential Obstacles

Finding and engaging the more extreme members of hate-groups may be difficult, unless they are in court custody required by law officials to undergo education treatment and counseling. Also, it is a challenge to convince offenders that their values are wrong or unacceptable and to change long-held beliefs and promote new ways of thinking.

Signs of Success

Education is a powerful tool that opens up alternate avenues of thought and behavior. In many cases, members of hate groups are invited or chosen to participate in the programs, but others participate on a voluntary basis. In fact, one program's final report describes the following scenario: At the beginning of the three-day counseling program, a participant said that he did not need a "baby-sitter." By the third day, the same participant said that he wished he had been through such a program years earlier so that his life would have been much different. However, some participants attend out of mere curiosity about the program. According to reports by the Anti-Defamation League, the participants of "The Juvenile Diversion Program: Learning About Differences" have not been involved in further hate-crime activities since the program began.

Applying the Strategy

The Assistant U.S. Attorney initiated a three-day hate-crime prevention counseling program for teenage members of the Fourth Reich Skinheads of Orange County, California. The program consisted of three major components: intensive counseling, encounters with Holocaust survivors, and visits to a county jail and a federal courtroom. Although the program did not reach all of the skinheads, several changed their ways. In fact, the American Bar Association's *Just Solutions* publication reports, "Turtle, a 19-year-old wearing an Iron Cross on his jacket, renounced his membership in the Fourth Reich Skinheads, saying: 'I don't want to be a skinhead anymore. I don't want to be associated with people who kill for no reason.'"

Contact Information

Assistant U.S. Attorney
312 North Spring Street, Room 1424
Los Angeles, California 90012
213-894-2400

Anti-Defamation League
823 United Nations Plaza
New York, New York 10017
212-490-2525

Community-Based Dispute Mediation Services

Strategy

Providing mediation services prevents disputes from escalating into larger community problems and informs the community of the benefits of conflict management programs.

Crime Problem Addressed

As disputes in a community escalate toward and result in violence and remain unresolved, the problems continue to grow. But if people learn that these disputes can be discussed and usually resolved, they understand that alternate means of dealing with conflict exist.

Key Components

Community-based mediators who handle many types of disputes between community members have found bias disputes on the rise. Conciliation is a preventive measure because it intercepts problems before they escalate or multiply.

Key Partnerships

Community mediation services involve several partners. Mediation volunteers must be recruited and trained. In addition to individual parties seeking mediation services, referrals are made by small claims court, the police, the juvenile probation department, other city agencies, and schools. Sources for funding a mediation service can include private funds, state or local government, and direct service fees.

Potential Obstacles

Educating people about the benefits of mediation requires effective partnerships among local organizations, community members, and local government. Also, there is the possibility that after courts see the effectiveness of mediation, they may refer to lawyers for solutions rather than seek out community members.

Signs of Success

Requests and referrals for mediation services continue to grow in communities where these services are available.

Sources indicate that the great majority of "hearings" result in lasting written agreements.

Applying the Strategy

The Community Board Program in San Francisco, California, has grown from 20 volunteer mediators in 1977 to 300 volunteers and has mediated for upwards of 25,000 people. Additionally, the program has created conflict resolution training programs for schools, local government agencies, juvenile corrections facilities, and public housing committees. Volunteers represent the diverse population in San Francisco.

Contact Information

Community Board Program
Conflict Resolution Resources
1540 Market Street, Suite 490
San Francisco, California 94102
415-552-1250

Support for Victims

Strategy

Providing support services and educational programs helps victims of hate crimes.

Crime Problem Addressed

While it is important to punish and educate perpetrators of hate crimes and inform the public of the problem, it is equally important to provide services to the victims of hate crimes. Victims can benefit from services to help them cope with the many emotional, physical, and financial impacts of such crimes. Providing services for the victims helps them overcome the trauma and signals the community's intolerance for hate crimes.

Key Components

In addition to support groups for victims of hate crimes, groups who are targets for hate crimes often receive education on violence prevention, discrimination, and safety from community-based organizations and/or law enforcement agencies. This education prepares groups who may be victimized to avoid confrontation and suggests ways of handling it if it does occur. It also encourages people to report bias-related crimes.

Key Partnerships

Victim support outreach groups, religious institutions, or other community organizations offer services to members of groups targeted for hate crimes. Law enforcement agencies also play an integral role with the community members by responding to reports and preventing revictimization through education and visibility.

Potential Obstacles

First, support services must receive publicity so that people will report their victimization and seek help. Funding for such support services tends to be limited; therefore, it is important to have strong partnerships with different community-based organizations. Support services depend heavily on volunteers, so active participation and recruitment is important.

Signs of Success

Support groups for victims provide comfort, education, and open discussion for people in need. They are an effective means of uniting people who share the same problems, concerns, or interests. Additionally, victims are more apt to report their victimization if they know there is a recognized resource. In response to these facts, there are a growing number of services for minority groups and refugee communities. For example, the Willows Police Department provides the Southeast Asian refugees in the California community with translators, information on gang prevention, community crime prevention tactics, and other services. The St. Paul, Minnesota, Police Department provides services for St. Paul's Southeast Asian refugee population and focuses on gang prevention strategies.

Applying the Strategy

The Horizons Anti-Violence Project in Chicago offers services to victims of hate crimes. It particularly focuses on the gay community, but other groups can also solicit its services. From January 1988 to July 1994, Horizons has served 1,826 clients.

Contact Information

Horizons Anti-Violence Project
961 West Montana
Chicago, Illinois 60614
312-472-6469

Bibliography

Books

National Crime Prevention Council. *Building and Crossing Bridges: Refugees and Law Enforcement Working Together.* Washington, DC, July 1994.

American Bar Association. *Just Solutions: A Program Guide to Innovative Justice System Improvements.* Chicago, IL, 1994.

Kelly, Robert J. *Bias Crime: American Law Enforcement and Legal Responses.* Chicago, IL: University of Illinois at Chicago, 1993.

Periodicals

Delaware Valley Intergenerational Network. Intergenerational Programming for a Diverse Society. *Interchange,* Fall 1994, pp. 1–3.

Public Documents

Crime and Violence Prevention Center, California Attorney General's Office. *Violence Prevention: A Vision of Hope.* Sacramento, 1995.

Property Crime

Property crime—taking or damaging items that belong to others—traumatizes its victims while threatening further crime in the future. The property owner feels invaded and unjustly violated, much like the victim of a direct personal crime.

Serious disruptions of personal and financial life result from property crimes: A stolen car may prevent someone from going to work or providing child care; a vandal's destruction of a mailbox could stop the delivery of a Social Security check; the loss of personal property or irreplaceable mementos can consume a victim with fear and a sense of loss.

The failure to come to terms with property crimes creates a self-perpetuating problem, and it implies a symbolic lack of concern for the belongings of community members that encourages further theft and destruction. Authors George Kelling and James Q. Wilson coined the phrase "broken windows" to describe the accelerating cycle of crime that begins with disrespect for property and spirals toward violence. Increasing evidence of the correlation between property crimes and other crimes is emerging from gang patterns of threat communication and territorial markings with graffiti.

Recent statistics have shown some improvement in property crime rates, although the incidence of these crimes is still staggeringly high. Property crime is far and away the most frequently occurring crime, and while it did drop 2.3 percent between 1992 and 1993, there were still over 12 million property crimes reported to police in 1993. These offenses represented financial losses of more than $14.8 billion (*Uniform Crime Reports*, 1994). Clearly, there is a need for greater action to decrease the prevalence of property crimes.

Policies that seek to solve property crime through law enforcement measures are useful, but they are insufficient in isolation. Teenagers—major perpetrators of both vandalism and auto theft—tend not to respond to deterrent measures; recidivism rates for both types of crimes are high. Prevention can be achieved only when the community makes its intolerance of property crimes clear through educational programs, counseling, and citizen action to discourage such crimes.

Fortunately, community awareness and local action can alleviate property crime. For example, successful implementation of Neighborhood and Business Watch programs, combined with simple safety measures that residents can perform in conjunction with police, have been shown to reduce crime dramatically.

Technology has led to great improvements in crime and theft prevention, through both deterrence and an increased ability to retrieve stolen property. Many local awareness programs come at little to no cost while providing remarkably high returns—a bit of information is often the only motivation required for people to take action to stop property crimes.

Ongoing programs to clean up vandalism, in which police cooperate with the community, serve an educational function that deters property defacement; at the same time, the incentive to produce graffiti is diminished by its rapid removal, since the prestige of a visible message is lost.

Educational measures can often produce the greatest gains in property crime prevention. Contact among children, police, and firefighters provides an opportunity to have a positive role model deliver the message at an early stage that property crimes are wrong; these impressions have long-lasting effects in reducing crime. Indeed, fire prevention and safety programs in schools are still an excellent means of preventing arson.

Prevention programs that encourage citizens to take part in the eradication of property crimes can impart a sense of civic pride. Simple projects such as the beautification of an area provides residents with a greater appreciation for their neighborhood. Additionally, the cooperation of local police units and businesses such as insurance companies can make local initiatives to combat property crime highly effective in achieving neighborhood safety.

Several programs around the country have proven effective in reducing the incidence of property crimes. This section explores some of those strategies in six areas:

- Vandalism;

- Residential Burglary;

- Nonresidential Burglary;

- Larceny;

- Arson; and

- Auto Theft.

Citizens can organize and work with law enforcement to avoid becoming victims of property crime. Communities can empower themselves against such crimes. Action at all levels—national, state, local, and personal—provides the tools with which to erase the fear and destruction that property crimes create.

Graffiti Removal Policy/Tips

Strategy

Locations or objects prone to graffiti are identified and property owners are taught the most effective removal methods.

Crime Problem Addressed

Graffiti removal policies and tips seek to reduce or control vandalism. The tips can affect drug sales, robbery, and assault, to the extent that these are related to graffiti.

Key Components

A zero-tolerance policy for graffiti is established. Locations where most graffiti is found are identified and the responsibility for removing it is determined. Property owners should be advised of methods for removing graffiti and how to deal with the surfaces where it is found. Graffiti-removal services may be offered for individuals or organizations that are unable to remove graffiti.

Key Participants

Participants should include property owners victimized by graffiti: schools, government, businesses, recreation facilities, public transportation, utilities, public works, and shopping malls, among others. The police, a crime prevention organization, or other civic or business organization can identify and help remove graffiti.

Potential Obstacles

Getting property owners to expend the time and effort to remove graffiti may be difficult. Physical removal may not be easy. It may take three, four, or more attempts to remove it. In some instances, it will remain as a constant maintenance headache.

Signs of Success

The New York City Clean Car Program established a policy of cleaning any subway car with graffiti within two hours of its discovery. By 1989, all 6,400 subway cars were free from graffiti. (Sloan-Howitt and Kelling, Subway Graffiti in New York City, *Security Journal,* Vol. 1, No. 3, p. 131). A St. Petersburg, Florida, ordinance that requires businesses to remove graffiti has resulted in 85 percent of reported graffiti being removed within forty-eight hours (Graffiti, *Governing,* August 94, p. 40).

Applying the Strategy

The Community Crime Prevention/SAFE Program in Minneapolis developed a program to assist property owners plagued by graffiti. Brochures on how to remove graffiti were distributed. The police department provides free graffiti remover to residents and businesses.

Contact Information

Department of Neighborhood Services
Room 310-1/2 City Hall
350 South 5th Street
Minneapolis, Minnesota 55415-1388
612-673-5701

Discourage Graffiti Marketing

Strategy

Businesses are discouraged from marketing products that rely on or promote graffiti.

Crime Problem Addressed

Identifying graffiti marketing should discourage businesses from promoting or endorsing graffiti and vandalism.

Key Components

Marketers who use graffiti as backdrops for products or who promote graffiti-related designs should be contacted and made aware that their products appear to endorse graffiti and vandalism. They should be asked to stop selling such products.

Key Participants

Individuals and crime prevention groups must identify commercial products that promote graffiti.

Potential Obstacles

Many individuals and organizations claim that graffiti is an art form. Some organizations promote graffiti art as a form of positive expression for youth. Businesses may see graffiti as a useful tool to make products more marketable to today's youth.

Signs of Success

A community-based organization in San Diego wrote a letter of complaint to Warner Brothers concerning a T-shirt that appeared to promote and advocate graffiti. The T-shirt showed a Warner Brothers character standing in front of a wall covered with graffiti. Warner Brothers removed the shirt from the market when notified that although popular with youth, the activity depicted on the shirt was inappropriate.

Applying the Strategy

The National Graffiti Information Network contacted the Disney Company about the "Goofiti" Vest marketing by the company. The vest and advertising for it seemed to glorify graffiti. Based on the "alert" from the National Graffiti Information Network, Disney agreed that the vest sent the wrong message about graffiti and stopped selling it.

Contact Information

National Graffiti Information Network
P.O. Box 400
Hurricane, Utah 84737
801-635-0646

Graffiti-Resistant Materials

Strategy

Graffiti-resistant materials and paints are used in locations prone to graffiti and vandalism.

Crime Problem Addressed

Using materials that are resistant to graffiti deters graffiti by denying vandals the surfaces they need to commit their illegal acts.

Key Components

Responding to the growth in graffiti vandalism, many companies now offer paints and other coatings, bathroom fixtures, and other items that resist the application of graffiti by paint or marker. These products have a chemical makeup that makes it difficult for paint or ink to adhere to them. Many of these new products can be installed or applied at the time of construction. However, there are also many products that can be applied to existing surfaces to deter future graffiti.

Key Participants

Persons who have or expect to have a problem with graffiti should contact a hardware store, paint store, or other construction supplier for information about purchasing graffiti-resistant materials.

Potential Obstacles

These graffiti-resistant materials can add to costs of new construction and will require staff time to apply to existing surfaces. The products typically make it easier to remove graffiti, so removing existing graffiti will still require some cleaning.

Signs of Success

Several cities in California have passed ordinances that require graffiti-resistant coatings on surfaces up to a height of 10 feet. Philadelphia, Pennsylvania, has passed a local ordinance that requires that storefront security screens be constructed of open grill material rather than solid panels to deny the graffiti vandal a place to paint (From the Wall, *National Crime and Graffiti Prevention Network,* January 1994).

Applying the Strategy

In Los Angeles, California, graffiti is such a problem that the city has a staff person who tests graffiti-resistant and graffiti-removal products for quality. The Construction Specifications Institute produces a technical specifications listing of anti-graffiti coatings.

Contact Information

Los Angeles General Services
555 Ramirez Street, Room 150TA
Los Angeles, California 90012
213-485-5801

Offender Help With Paint-Outs

Strategy

Individuals arrested for painting graffiti are required to participate in a community service program to paint over graffiti.

Crime Problem Addressed

It is hoped that requiring graffiti offenders to paint over graffiti will discourage them from committing further graffiti.

Key Components

Use the community service option in the juvenile court to assign youthful offenders to paint out graffiti. Based on arrest for graffiti vandalism, referral by a police officer, juvenile probation officer, social service worker, or parent or guardian, youth can be placed in a program to paint out or paint over graffiti in their neighborhoods. Youth who enter the program and their parents should be provided an orientation and follow-up counseling about the seriousness of vandalism and graffiti. Paint and tools will have to be purchased or donated.

Key Participants

Police departments must work with the courts, offenders, and community service groups to conduct the paint-outs.

Potential Obstacles

Some youth may not take the option of participating in the program. The strategy requires strong enforcement of graffiti violations or no offenders will participate in the program.

Signs of Success

None of the nearly fifty juveniles who completed a juvenile offender paint-out program in Los Angeles was rearrested for a graffiti violation (Graffiti Paint Outs, *FBI Law Enforcement Bulletin,* June 1992).

Applying the Strategy

An offender paint-out program is a component of a comprehensive program in Los Angeles, California, to combat graffiti. Participants also receive counseling from police officers, professional counselors, and ex-convicts.

Contact Information

Office of Operations
Los Angeles Police Department
150 North Los Angeles Street, Room 717
Los Angeles, California 90012
213-485-4111

Adopt-A-Highway/Road

Strategy

Volunteers pick up litter from roads and highways.

Crime Problem Addressed

This program uses volunteers to control litter and vandalism by maintaining public roads and highways.

Key Components

Individuals, civic associations, employee groups, or Neighborhood Watch groups cooperate with local or state road officials to pick up litter from the highways. Participants select sections of road they would like to police and establish a schedule for picking up litter. Volunteers are provided safety vests and bags for depositing litter. Litter may be taken to a central drop off point or left on the roadside for pick-up by government highway personnel. Signs are used to denote areas of the road maintained by the volunteer groups.

Key Participants

Road officials and individuals and organizations with a concern about litter and vandalism participate in this program. The programs are usually coordinated with local or statewide litter control programs.

Potential Obstacles

The obstacle is the same for any volunteer activity with little reward—maintaining interest and participation. Participants also expose themselves to some danger by picking up trash along roads.

Signs of Success

In one state, Adopt-A-Highway volunteers cleaned about 1,400 miles of state roads in one year and provided the equivalent of $6 million of litter control services. The program involves more than 50,000 volunteers and since 1988 has collected enough trash to build a twenty-five-square-foot tower ten miles high.

Applying the Strategy

Most state highway departments support Adopt-A-Highway programs. Many local jurisdictions that maintain their own roads also support Adopt-A-Road programs.

Contact Information

North Carolina Department of Transportation
P.O. Box 25201
Raleigh, North Carolina 27611-5201
919-715-3188

Restrict Sales of Graffiti Tools

Strategy

By restricting the sale of items such as spray paint and markers, deny youth the tools to commit vandalism.

Crime Problem Addressed

Restricting sales denies youth the tools they need to commit graffiti.

Key Components

Merchants should be encouraged to restrict the sale of items that can be used by youth to commit vandalism. These items would include spray paint and marking pencils. Merchants can be asked not to sell these items to minors or to restrict their access. Several local jurisdictions have enacted laws that prohibit the sale of certain items used to create graffiti, such as spray paint or markers.

A policy on sale restrictions could be a requirement to participate in a Business Watch program.

Key Participants

Police agencies and community groups can encourage businesses to restrict sales or access of graffiti tools to youth. Local government officials representing road maintenance, public transportation, and other agencies that have the responsibility to clean up graffiti can work with local lawmakers to craft legislation to restrict sales.

Potential Obstacles

Restricting the access to graffiti tools places a burden on merchants and may reduce sales. Passing local ordinances may be difficult because the tools used by youth to draw graffiti do have legitimate purposes.

Signs of Success

Three states and more than two dozen major cities limit or ban the sale of spray paint to minors. (Graffiti, *Governing*, August 1994).

Applying the Strategy

California has had legislation for several years that prohibits the sale of spray paints to persons under eighteen years of age.

Contact Information

Los Angeles County Multi-Agency Graffiti Coalition (MAGIC)
120 South Spring Street
Los Angeles, California 90012
310-603-7462

Vandalism Prevention Curriculum

Strategy

School-based educational programs teach youth about the losses generated from vandalism.

Crime Problem Addressed

An educational curriculum can help define what vandalism is and demonstrate to youth its costs to society.

Key Components

A curriculum can be developed or obtained for use in schools to teach students what vandalism is and what it costs. It should include a teacher's manual and a student workbook. A curriculum using puppets may be useful with very young students. To augment classroom instruction, older students can be involved in a community service project to remove graffiti.

Key Participants

Educators can work with insurance companies, the police, and business groups to obtain or develop a school-based vandalism prevention curriculum.

Potential Obstacles

Educators are under a great deal of pressure to incorporate all types of programs into the educational process.

Signs of Success

Reported vandalism dropped 54 percent after the Project Pride vandalism curriculum was implemented in the Northside, Texas, Independent School District. A comprehensive prevention program in Holland achieved a 25 percent reduction in vandalism. The educational component turned out to be the most effective part of the program. Another evaluation four years later found that vandalism had been stabilized, with $2 million less damage. (*Report of the International Symposium on Vandalism,* Seattle, April 1989.)

Applying the Strategy

The Washington Metropolitan Area Transit Authority developed the Metro Awareness Program, a pre-kindergarten through twelfth grade anti-vandalism and safety curriculum. It was presented to 25,000 children in Washington, Maryland, and Virginia. The "Vandalism Game" developed as a 4-H project in Nebraska involved five lessons focused on the problem; attitudes, values, and environmental factors; characteristics of victims; characteristics of vandals; and alternative prevention methods. The lessons were for fifth- to eighth-grade students.

Contact Information

Metro Awareness Program
Washington Metropolitan Area Transit Authority
600 Fifth Street, NW
Washington, DC 20001
202-962-2276

Community Cleanups

Strategy

Community cleanups remove litter and graffiti and repair minor vandalism.

Crime Problem Addressed

Community cleanups can remove litter and graffiti and help repair minor vandalism. Doing so should help to keep locations prone to vandalism from evolving into locations where violence, drug dealing, and other crimes occur.

Key Components

A community cleanup committee should include representatives from local government, business, and neighborhood groups. An educational program can be developed, and police, public works, business, industry, and neighborhoods can report littering and dumping violations. Federal, state, or local funding sources can be identified to support cleanup activities. In New Jersey, businesses are taxed if they sell any of fifteen products designated by the state as likely to end up as litter.

Key Participants

Cleanups can be accomplished by individuals, families, blocks, neighborhoods, or communities. The greater the organization and support from government, business, and civic organizations, the broader the impact.

Potential Obstacles

Maintaining the continued participation of volunteers will present a challenge, especially since much of the work will involve cleaning up the same spots repeatedly.

Signs of Success

The Wipe Out Graffiti Program in Anaheim, California, is a volunteer organization that has removed over 3 million square feet of graffiti since 1989. The program involves more than twenty-five Adopt-A-Block groups and paint-outs twice a month. More than 90 percent of the materials used are donated by local businesses and civic groups (From the Wall, *National Crime and Graffiti Prevention News,* vol. 1, issue 2).

Applying the Strategy

From March to November 1993, the Rebound Plus Program to clean up neighborhoods in Yakima, California, picked up more than 440,000 pounds of garbage, 227 discarded appliances, and 521 old tires. The neighborhood cleanup program has been supported by more than 700 resident volunteers who have donated 3,200 hours of service.

Contact Information

Rebound Plus
103 South 7th Avenue
Yakima, Washington 98902
509-575-6246

Home Security Inspections

Strategy

Occupants of dwellings have their homes inspected by the police agency that assesses the security of the residence.

Crime Problem Addressed

Home security inspections are intended to reduce burglary or breaking and entering by making the home a more difficult target. The inspections may also diminish home robberies and larceny of property stored in the yard.

Key Components

The police department may offer inspections to the public at no cost. The service can be performed by a sworn officer, a civilian working for the policing agency, or a representative of the local Neighborhood Watch program. The inspector examines doors, door frames, door locks, windows, window locks, lighting, landscaping, fencing, and alarm systems for weaknesses in security. The inspector may provide the resident a written copy of the survey.

Key Participants

The police department is the key service provider. Neighborhood Watch groups can help by encouraging residents to have a home security survey completed. However, the key is the resident, who must request and agree to the survey. Insurance companies may provide incentives for home security inspections.

Potential Obstacles

Residents must request the survey, but the most difficult obstacle is follow-through. Many residents do not implement all or any of the recommendations. Participation in rental housing may be weak because residents may feel that the responsibility for security resides with the property owner.

Signs of Success

From 1977 to 1982, the Arlington County, Virginia, Police Department conducted 3,764 home security inspections. A study found that sixteen residences that implemented all security recommendations had been burglarized. Residences that implemented none or only part of the recommendations had sixty-three burglaries. The burglary rate for residences that had implemented all security recommendations was 1 per 190 residences. The residential burglary rate for the entire county was 1 per 49 residences (Arlington County Police Department, internal memo, January 29, 1982).

Applying the Strategy

The Tucson, Arizona, Police Department, like most police departments across the country, provides residential security surveys to the public at no cost.

Contact Information

Tucson Police Department
270 South Stone Avenue
Tucson, Arizona 85702-1917
520-791-4441

Residential Building Codes

Strategy

Security requirements are included in local or state residential building codes.

Crime Problem Addressed

Security requirements for residential building codes address home burglary.

Key Components

First, it is necessary to identify the authority for building codes in the locality. Many local and state building codes are based on standards developed by national or regional groups. The police can help to develop basic residential security requirements. They should address door and window locks, doors and windows, door frames, lighting, peepholes, and landscaping. Code officials can discuss the addition of security requirements to the building code. A formal proposal can then be developed and presented to building officials and local or state legislators.

Key Participants

Establishing security requirements will require the participation of the police, building officials, developers, builders, building associations, homeowners, and neighborhood associations.

Potential Obstacles

Most building codes do not address crime as a building issue. Safety issues addressed by most codes are safety from electrical hazards, falls, and other accidental injuries.

Many developers and builders oppose security requirements because of the additional construction costs.

Adding security to a statewide building code will be more difficult than dealing with a local code.

Signs of Success

Oakland, California, adopted the first commercial security ordinance in the nation. From 1964 until 1976, its commercial burglary rate increased only 20 percent, while the rate in the rest of the nation increased 200 percent. A building code was implemented in parts of Dade County, Florida, for new construction, and from 1975 to 1976 the burglary rate for homes fell 24 percent. Orange County, California, found that the chance of a forcible home entry was seven times greater if that home had not been constructed according to the county Building Security Ordinance Standards (*A Building Code for Minnesota*, Minnesota Crime Prevention Center, 1977).

Applying the Strategy

The Portland Police Department developed a set of security guidelines for the City of Portland that address doors, windows, and security hardware. They were adopted by the Crime Prevention Association of Oregon. The guidelines were also submitted to the Structural Code Advisory Board of the State of Oregon.

Contact Information

Portland Police Bureau
111 Southwest 2nd
Portland, Oregon 97204
503-731-3020

Insurance Premium Reductions

Strategy

Home and apartment insurance discounts are offered voluntarily or by legislative mandate to policyholders who implement basic residential security recommendations.

Crime Problem Addressed

The insurance discounts are intended to reduce burglary and to some extent larceny. They may also affect violent crimes that can result from a burglary if the home happens to be occupied.

Key Components

Certain insurance companies in the locality may offer premium reductions for the installation of basic home security devices. After determining what security improvements are required to qualify for the rate reductions, the police, Neighborhood Watch groups, and other civic associations can work to publicize the rate reductions.

Key Participants

Homeowners and apartment dwellers must cooperate with insurance companies to obtain the rate reductions. The police and Neighborhood Watch groups can help by making people aware of the rate reductions.

Potential Obstacles

The savings from rate reductions for home insurance policies are small, and some people may not bother with them. Theft is the smallest category of loss faced by companies in the home insurance market, so it is not a high priority.

Signs of Success

The Institute of Insurance in Great Britain reported that insurance costs dropped from £3.5 per £1,000 worth of contents to £2.5, the cheapest rate available, as the result of a Neighborhood Watch program that reduced crime by 75 percent. The highest insurance rates are in the highest crime areas, where rates are £10 per £1,000 worth of contents (*Crime Prevention News*, Home Office, Fall 1989).

Applying the Strategy

Texas mandates insurance rate reductions for home security improvements on the part of the homeowner. Some of the companies that offer rate reductions are State Farm, Allstate, Safeco, and GEICO.

Contact Information

Insurance Information Institute
110 William Street
New York, New York 10038
212-669-9200

Operation Identification

Strategy

Marking personal property with identifying marks discourages theft and increases the chances of identification if the property is stolen.

Crime Problem Addressed

Marking personal property for identification is intended to reduce burglary and larceny.

Key Components

Residents and businesses are requested to mark personal property with unique identifying numbers. Many localities use driver's license numbers that enable the police to locate the owner of the property more easily. Operation Identification is often a component of Neighborhood Watch along with home security inspections. Property marking can be used as an introductory program to get residents involved in other crime prevention programs. Some police departments make engravers available to help people mark their property. The police department may also supply window stickers allowing participants to "advertise" their participation in the program.

Key Participants

The police department, Neighborhood Watch group, or other civic organizations can work with residents to mark their personal property. The same approach can be used by businesses.

Potential Obstacles

The concept of the program is so simple that enlisting citizen participation may be difficult. If the availability of engraving tools is not communicated frequently, participation may be weak.

Signs of Success

Local surveys of burglary rates before and after households joined Operation Identification showed a 32.8 percent reduction in Seattle and a 24.9 percent reduction in St. Louis. Burglary rates at participating homes were reportedly 6.7 times lower than in nonparticipating homes in Denver and 18.7 times lower in Phoenix (Institute for Public Program Analysis, *Operation Identification Projects: Assessment of Effectiveness*, 1975).

Applying the Strategy

Operation Identification is a standard service offered by most police departments that provide crime prevention services, including the Cincinnati, Ohio, Police Department.

Contact Information

Cincinnati Police Department
310 Charles Drive
Cincinnati, Ohio 45214
513-352-3536

Neighborhood Watch

Strategy

Start a Neighborhood Watch to organize residents to watch out for each other and to report crimes or suspicious behavior to police.

Crime Problem Addressed

Neighborhood Watch can address all types of crime, but its primary focus is residential burglary and other crimes around the home, such as larceny and vandalism. Neighborhood Watch can also play a significant role in deterring criminals who would use a neighborhood for drug- or gang-related activities.

Key Components

The first step is to identify key leaders or persons most concerned about crime in the neighborhood and organize a meeting of these individuals to discuss safety. The police can be invited to a neighborhood meeting to discuss community safety, and volunteers can be solicited to serve as block watch leaders. The neighborhood may be divided by blocks and block leaders assigned to serve as points of contact. A communication network can be organized to pass along information about crime and security to residents. The police may provide training on recognizing and reporting suspicious activity and on home and neighborhood security. The watch may expand to foot or car patrols. Signs designate the area as a Neighborhood Watch community. The watch can provide a variety of safety and security information to residents.

Key Participants

Neighborhood residents can work with the police to establish watches. If a neighborhood organization already exists, it may be more efficient to make Neighborhood Watch a part of that organization.

Potential Obstacles

Many watch programs start in response to a serious crime incident or a rash of crimes. Once the number of crimes decreases, interest may subside. Maintaining participant interest is the greatest challenge.

Signs of Success

In Tucson, Arizona, a neighborhood suffering from crime formed a Neighborhood Watch group. About 400 people learned the basic techniques of how to watch out for crime and how to better secure homes. In just three weeks, seventeen arrests based on thirteen tips from citizens caused burglaries to drop by 30 percent (*Foundations for Action,* National Crime Prevention Council, 1990).

Applying the Strategy

Neighborhood Watch is used throughout the United States, Canada, and many other countries. More than 90 percent of U.S. police departments offer help in setting up Neighborhood Watch. The National Association of Town Watch, a non-profit organization, sponsors the National Night Out on the first Tuesday of August each year as a national day in support of anticrime efforts.

Contact Information

National Association of Town Watch
7 Wynnewood Road, Suite 215
P.O. Box 303
Wynnewood, Pennsylvania 19096
610-649-7055

Home Security Alarms

Strategy

Installing home security alarm systems helps to deter and detect burglars.

Crime Problem Addressed

Home security alarm systems are installed to prevent burglary. They may also deter physical attacks, which can take place if the home is occupied during the burglary.

Key Components

Residents should contact local alarm companies to find out the options and costs for residential alarm service. Continuing changes in technology make a great variety of alarm options available. Because there has been a problem with small, unprofessional alarm sales companies, homeowners should check with the local Better Business Bureau for suggestions about reliable alarm companies.

Key Participants

Homeowners contract with private security alarm companies to have home security alarms installed. Homeowners may also purchase alarm systems and install them.

Potential Obstacles

There are few obstacles to installing a home alarm system because they are available in a great variety of options and price ranges. Residents in apartments should check with the landlord about policies on installing alarms. Many localities now issue fines for alarms that exceed a given number of false or inaccurate reports.

Signs of Success

A study of three suburban localities in the Philadelphia area found that the burglary probability for nonalarmed homes was 2.7 times greater than that for alarmed homes.

This was especially true as the value of the residence increased. Nonalarmed homes in the upper value range were 3.1 times more likely to be burglarized than alarmed homes (Burglar Alarms and the Choice Behavior of Burglars, *Journal of Criminal Justice,* vol. 21, no. 5, 1993).

Applying the Strategy

The National Burglar and Fire Alarm Association works with alarm companies and associations throughout the United States to provide effective alarm service to residential and commercial customers.

Contact Information

National Burglar and Fire Alarm Association
7101 Wisconsin Avenue
Bethesda, Maryland 20814
301-907-3202

Street Access Restrictions

Strategy

Restricting access into neighborhoods makes travel into and through the neighborhood by nonresidents less convenient.

Crime Problem Addressed

Restricting access is primarily intended to reduce burglary and larceny, but it can also diminish rape, robbery, and assault. Reducing extra traffic flow may also reduce problems of litter and vandalism.

Key Components

Vehicular traffic in the neighborhood and surrounding areas should be assessed to determine whether neighborhood streets are used to a significant degree by nonresidents. The neighborhood may serve as a shortcut for drivers and walkers. Road officials must determine whether changes can be made to traffic flow to discourage nonresident traffic. Restricting traffic may require installing stop signs, restricting turns, or changing street directions. Closing off streets is an option, but it raises concerns about costs and free use of streets and roads, as well as concerns about emergency access.

Key Participants

Neighborhood residents must work with the police, other emergency service representatives, and transportation officials to restrict traffic access.

Potential Obstacles

Transportation officials will be concerned that changes may restrict traffic flow adversely. Fire and rescue personnel will want to ensure that changes do not affect their access to neighborhoods. There is also a potential for some people to see the access restrictions as an infringement on their right to use public roads. Changes will inconvenience neighborhood residents as well as outsiders.

Signs of Success

A Dayton, Ohio, neighborhood has implemented changes to traffic patterns. The targeted neighborhood experienced a 50 percent decrease in violent crime, a 26 percent decrease in total crime, and a 67 percent drop in traffic (Drawing Up Safer Cities, *Newsweek,* July 11, 1994, p. 57).

Applying the Strategy

Project Quiet Street in St. Louis discourages nonresident traffic in neighborhoods by modifying traffic patterns. Quiet Street is part of the Safestreet Program, which also involves Neighborhood Watch, home security, street lighting, and a community newsletter.

Contact Information

Operation Safe Street
City Hall, Room 417
1200 Market Street
St. Louis, Missouri 63103
314-622-3444

Increase Visibility and Surveillance

Strategy

Increasing the ability of neighbors, police, and others passing through the neighborhood to see the home deters crime.

Crime Problem Addressed

Increasing visibility of the home deters burglary, theft, and vandalism. It may also affect burglaries that escalate to robbery, rape, and murder.

Key Components

House and apartment dwellers need to understand the value of visibility around the home. Homes that have very visible doors and windows are less vulnerable to crime. People should be advised of problems created by overgrown or improperly placed shrubs and bushes, privacy fences, or clutter around the yard or house that may provide hiding places for criminals.

Residents can be encouraged to increase surveillance by keeping curtains open and orienting activities in the home so that they are near windows more often.

Key Participants

Homeowners or rental community managers must ensure that visibility around the dwelling is maintained.

Potential Obstacles

Many people choose privacy over safety. Maintaining visibility around the home is a simple maintenance chore that must be performed on a regular basis. Fence companies might be encouraged to market fences that strike a balance between privacy and security.

Signs of Success

A study of crime in public housing found that crime was lowest in buildings that had optimum opportunities for visibility and surveillance based on building orientation and street location. The crime rate for buildings that had minimal opportunities for visibility and surveillance was more than 100 percent higher (Oscar Newman, *Defensible Space*, 1972).

Applying the Strategy

The Tucson, Arizona, Police Department implemented a program called Safe By Design that advised homeowners about steps they could take to increase the visibility inside and outside their homes.

Contact Information

Tucson Police Department
270 South Stone Drive
Tucson, Arizona 85701-1917
520-791-4441

Cellular Telephone or Radio Patrols

Strategy

Users of cellular phones or two-way radios call in to report suspicious or dangerous activity.

Crime Problem Addressed

Communicating dangerous or suspicious situations by cellular phone or other two-way communication helps reduce all types of community crime. The phone also offers safety to the user because it provides instant communication.

Key Components

A cellular system must be set up to accept 911 calls. Owners of cellular phones can be provided basic information on recognizing and reporting suspicious or dangerous activities. This information can be sent out by the cellular phone company during regular mailings. Cellular phones can be purchased or donated to augment reporting by Neighborhood Watch groups. An orientation class or brochure on how to use cellular phones to report suspicious or dangerous situations is useful.

Key Participants

Local cellular telephone companies working with community groups and the police can establish these programs.

Potential Obstacles

The local cellular phone companies must have the capacity to establish a 911 telephone number. Not everyone can afford a cellular phone.

Signs of Success

Operation Interlock/Interwatch, established by the Association for a Better New York, provides two-way radios to businesses to give them direct access to police dispatchers. The program has expanded to all of Manhattan. A parking attendant credits the program with saving his life when he was able to call the police on his radio after being shot. Avis is experimenting with cellular phones in its rental cars in high-crime areas and major tourist destinations (*Reuter Business Report,* March 30, 1994).

Applying the Strategy

The Newport News, Virginia, Redevelopment and Housing Authority has used funds from a federal grant to establish a cellular phone-supported citizen patrol in two public housing communities. Ameritech Cellular Services donated cellular phones and free air time to a ten-city block watch group in Columbus, Ohio. Nine other midwestern cities will also be provided free phones and services.

Contact Information

Columbus Police Division
120 Marconi Boulevard
Columbus, Ohio 43215
614-645-4600

Voice Mail Information

Strategy

Citizens can call a telephone voice mail system to get tips about crime prevention and information about crime in the immediate neighborhood and the entire community.

Crime Problem Addressed

A voice mail information system can address all types of crime.

Key Components

The police department cooperates with a telecommunications organization to establish a system that enables citizens to call a telephone number to hear a variety of recorded messages on crime prevention topics. Callers should be provided a variety of topics they can access by using their telephone. Basic crime prevention tips are updated periodically; time-sensitive information about crime patterns, wanted persons, or important events is changed more frequently.

Key Participants

The police agency working with a local telecommunications company can put this strategy to work. The public must also be informed about how the system works.

Potential Obstacles

Some localities may not be able to afford to implement the system. Like all information systems, it must be maintained. The system must work properly and offer accurate and timely information.

Signs of Success

The Irdell County, North Carolina, Sheriff's Department has a telephone voice mail system named "Call McGruff." It lets children dial McGruff's own telephone number. The kids hear a short message or song about crime prevention and can leave their own message. A message left by one child said, "Thanks for coming to my school today and giving me the hug. I never get hugs at home." (NCPC, *Catalyst,* November 1992).

Applying the Strategy

Residents of Toledo, Ohio, can call the Telefact line twenty-four hours a day to get information about crime prevention, special crime alerts, block watch meetings, and even recorded messages from McGruff. Callers who select the Crime Information Hotline hear a recorded message on crime specific to a geographic area. The line received 9,300 calls in its first four months of operation.

Contact Information

Community Affairs Section
Toledo Police Department
2301 Nebraska Avenue
Toledo, Ohio 43607
419-531-4411

Outside Residential Lighting

Strategy

Adequate street and building lighting help make residents feel more secure.

Crime Problem Addressed

Providing adequate street lighting helps reduce the public's fear of crime in residential and commercial neighborhoods.

Key Components

Most local governments now offer some type of street lighting for residential neighborhoods. Residents can request that the locality upgrade or enhance the street lighting to improve safety. Residents can also upgrade lighting by contracting for additional lighting from the local power company or by installing additional lighting themselves. Maintenance is a key factor. Light fixtures must be cleaned periodically and bulbs must be changed. It is also important to use the appropriate type of lighting for the location and weather conditions.

Key Participants

Homeowners can work with local governments, power companies, and lighting suppliers to upgrade lighting in residential areas.

Potential Obstacles

Installing or upgrading lighting will be an expense. Many people in residential neighborhoods do not like efficient lighting of neighborhoods. Lighting fixtures that are not maintained will not be effective or efficient.

Signs of Success

Various studies of increased lighting have claimed crime reductions of 70 percent (Chattanooga), 60 percent (Gary, Indiana), and 85 percent (Indianapolis). An extensive study of improved street lighting implemented by many cities in the 1970s could not find statistical evidence that increased lighting reduced crime. It did find that increased lighting, especially uniformly placed lighting, reduced the fear of crime (*Street Lighting Projects,* Department of Justice, 1979).

Applying the Strategy

Most power companies offer consumer information on how to improve security lighting around the home. The National Association of Town Watch supports residential use of lighting to deter crime. During its annual Night Out Against Crime, it encourages participants to turn on exterior lights to make the neighborhood safer and to demonstrate support for Neighborhood Watch.

Contact Information

National Association of Town Watch
7 Wynnewood Road, Suite 215
P.O. Box 302
Wynnewood, Pennsylvania 19096
610-649-7055

Commercial Lighting

Strategy

Adequate street and building lighting deter nighttime criminial activities.

Crime Problem Addressed

Lack of adequate lighting allows criminals to commit burglary, theft, and vandalism against commercial buildings under the cover of darkness, thus reducing their chances of detection and capture.

Key Components

An effective security lighting system should discourage intruders and make detection highly probable should an entry be attempted. Business owners can contract with a lighting consulting firm, talk with the local police department, or evaluate the lighting themselves at night, looking for dark spots that burglars or vandals might use. Exterior lighting fixtures should be vandal resistant and designed for the purpose of providing security lighting. One of the most important points in security lighting is to provide uniform lighting. Interior lighting can also be used to provide visibility of high-risk areas.

Key Participants

Businesses, utility companies, and local governments must work together to provide adequate lighting for businesses and the streets and alleys surrounding them. Some localities have passed ordinances that mandate certain lighting levels.

Potential Obstacles

Initial investments for lighting can be high. Lighting fixtures must be properly installed and maintained or their effectiveness will be diminished.

Signs of Success

Various studies of increased lighting have claimed crime reductions of 70 percent (Chattanooga), 60 percent (Gary, Indiana), and 85 percent (Indianapolis). An extensive study of improved street lighting implemented by many cities in the 1970s could not find statistical evidence that increased lighting reduced crime. It did find that increased lighting, especially uniformly placed lighting, reduced the fear of crime (*Street Lighting Projects,* Department of Justice, 1979).

Applying the Strategy

All types of businesses use light to protect their property. Standards for providing interior and exterior artificial lighting for highways, sports, industrial complexes, security, and others have been established by the Illuminating Engineers Society. The standards are contained in the *Lighting Handbook,* which prescribes lighting levels for all types of environments.

Contact Information

Illuminating Engineering Society of North America
120 Wall Street, 17th Floor
New York, New York 10005
212-248-5000

Business Watch

Strategy

Businesses are organized into associations to become more aware of the threat of crime and ways to prevent it by helping each other, the neighborhood, and themselves.

Crime Problem Addressed

Business Watch aims to reduce robbery, burglary, vandalism, and larceny. Larceny includes shoplifting, credit card fraud, bad checks, and employee theft.

Key Components

Businesses organize into informal associations to help them develop a greater understanding of the crime problems they face and steps they can take to avoid victimization. The policing agency typically organizes the businesses, provides them crime prevention information, security surveys, and training, and sets up a system to communicate with the businesses on a regular basis. The businesses should be kept informed of crime trends and crimes that are being committed against area businesses.

Key Participants

The policing agency works with businesses and business associations to establish watch programs. If the businesses are in a residential area, the local Neighborhood Watch can also participate.

Potential Obstacles

Many businesses may not feel they have free time to devote to a project that does not show immediate profits.

Policing staff must ensure that Business Watch does not adversely affect business operations. The information passed on to businesses must also be timely and useful.

Signs of Success

A Business Watch program in Seattle, Washington, achieved a 48 percent reduction in commercial burglary from 1980 to 1990 (Seattle Washington Police Department). The Neighborhood Commercial Crime Prevention Program in Philadelphia has provided more than $800,000 in matching funds for security improvements for small businesses.

Applying the Strategy

The Philadelphia Neighborhood Commercial Crime Prevention Program performs security surveys for businesses, provides direct rebates for security improvements, conducts business crime prevention training, and serves as a liaison among the police, district attorney, and individual businesses in four state-designated enterprise zones.

Contact Information

Crime Prevention Services
1315 Walnut Street, Suite 600
Philadelphia, Pennsylvania 19107
215-790-2247

Display Business Address Numbers

Strategy

Businesses are required to prominently display address numbers on the front of the business and the rear if warranted.

Crime Problem Addressed

Prominently displaying address numbers allows the police to respond more effectively to businesses that are victims of any type of crime or disturbance.

Key Components

Businesses must be made aware of the importance of a prominently displayed address number in ensuring efficient service from the police department or any other emergency service agency. Local business associations can encourage businesses to display their address number as a commonsense marketing tool. If the police cannot locate the address, customers might have the same problem. A Business Crime Watch or association could provide numbers for businesses to apply.

Key Participants

Businesses, business associations, and emergency service personnel must work together to ensure that the address numbers of businesses are prominently displayed.

Potential Obstacles

The only real obstacle is indifference on the part of business owners.

Signs of Success

This strategy is self-explanatory, and many localities do require businesses to display address numbers. In localities without 911 emergency service, address numbers are very important for reporting emergencies at locations other than homes. The 911 enhanced emergency service can be adversely affected if emergency personnel cannot find an address number. Many localities have ordinances that require businesses or residents to display address numbers.

Applying the Strategy

Ann Arbor, Michigan, like many other localities, requires by city ordinance that all buildings have their address numbers prominently displayed.

Contact Information

Crime Prevention Unit Director
Ann Arbor Police Department
Ann Arbor, Michigan 48104
313-994-2979

Direct Deposit

Strategy

Payroll, Social Security, and other benefits are directly deposited into bank accounts by electronic fund transfer.

Crime Problem Addressed

Direct deposit is designed to discourage theft of checks from the mail. It also offers some protection from personal robbery, because recipients do not need to travel to a bank to cash a payroll or benefits check.

Key Components

The organization that issues the payroll or benefit check must make arrangements with the United States Treasury Department to participate in the program. The check issuer must then make clients aware of the program. Once an individual agrees to participate, compensation or benefits are deposited directly into checking, savings, or other accounts when these payments are issued.

Key Participants

Key participants are the United States Department of Treasury, employers or organizations that pay benefits, and recipients. The program is well established within the Treasury Department, and many employers and benefiting organizations participate.

Potential Obstacles

The primary obstacle is payroll or benefit recipients who do not wish to participate. Some persons are reluctant to participate because they want to ensure personally that a check is deposited or that cash is received. Most employers should have no problem participating in this program; however, some small businesses may find it somewhat burdensome.

Signs of Success

It is estimated that the direct deposit program has saved the federal government more than $60 million annually in operating costs while reducing the possibility of checks being stolen, forged, or lost. Direct deposit reduces the cost of a check from federal payroll or benefit payments from 30 cents to 4 cents (National Crime Prevention Council, *Foundations for Action,* 1990).

Applying the Strategy

Direct deposit is used by the federal government, state governments, and many local governments for payroll and

benefits. Many employers, large and small, also participate in the program.

Contact Information

Direct Deposit Program
Treasury Annex No. 1, Room 226
Madison Place & Pennsylvania Avenue, NW
Washington, DC 20226
202-874-7328

Pay-Before-You-Pump Gas Policy

Strategy

Business selling gas require customers to pay for the gas before they pump.

Crime Problem Addressed

Pay-before-you-pump reduces theft of gas by persons driving off without paying for it and internal theft by employees who take cash for gas they claim was stolen.

Key Components

The business selling gas must establish a pay-before-you-pump policy and communicate it to customers. This policy can be flexible, depending on location, time of day, and visibility of pumps. In some localities, the police department will not take reports of gasoline drive-offs if the business does not have a pay-before-you-pump policy.

Key Participants

The business selling gas, its employees, and its customers are the key participants. The police may refuse to take reports if some type of policy is not required.

Potential Obstacles

Many businesses contend that a pay-before-you-pump policy is an inconvenience to customers and has an adverse

impact on sales. Others are concerned that requiring customers to pay first implies that they may be dishonest.

Signs of Success

A study in Austin, Texas, estimated that a pay-before-you-pump policy would reduce gasoline drive-offs by 40 percent (Reducing Gasoline Drive-Offs: Designing a Less Convenient Environment, *Crime Prevention Studies,* vol. 2, 1994).

Applying the Strategy

Many convenience stores and gasoline retailers use pay-before-you-pump selectively, based on the crime rate where the business is located, the time of day, and visibility of particular pumps from the cash register. It is interesting to note that New Jersey and Oregon eliminate the opportunity for drive-offs, because state law prohibits customers from pumping their own gas.

Contact Information

National Association of Convenience Stores
1605 King Street
Alexandria, Virginia 22314
703-684-3600

Score/Cut Vehicle Inspection Stickers

Strategy

Vehicle inspection or locality license stickers are scored or cut after they are applied to the windshield.

Crime Problem Addressed

People steal inspection or license stickers to avoid paying vehicle inspection costs or local taxes. Scoring the stickers helps discourage their theft by destroying the sticker (or making it useless) if someone tries to remove it.

Key Components

The vehicle owner uses a razor knife to score or cut the sticker after it is applied to the vehicle windshield. The vehicle owner can also write down the type of car and license number before applying the sticker.

Key Participants

The vehicle owner is the primary participant. Vehicle owners can encourage inspection stations to take these steps when they inspect the vehicle. Some localities now distribute vehicle license stickers that will be destroyed or show void if removed.

Potential Obstacles

There are no real obstacles to this simple crime prevention strategy. However, for it to discourage theft, it must be used by as many people as possible, and everyone must know that the stickers "self-destruct" when removed.

Signs of Success

This is a simple, self-explanatory strategy that will make most theft attempts useless. For it to be effective, the locality must encourage the broadest use of this simple idea.

Applying the Strategy

When it replaces stolen inspection stickers for motorists, the Virginia Department of State Police scores the inspection stickers and writes the license number on the back of the sticker. Many localities now have their city license stickers manufactured to show void when they are removed from the vehicle windshield.

Contact Information

Virginia Department of State Police
Safety Division
7700 Midlothian Turnpike
Richmond, Virginia 23236
804-674-2000

Protect Credit Cards

Strategy

Information is made available to consumers to help prevent the theft and fraudulent use of credit cards.

Crime Problem Addressed

Protecting credit cards helps prevent their theft or fraudulent use.

Key Components

Major credit card companies supply information on how to prevent theft and fraudulent use of credit cards. This information could be handed out during a Neighborhood Watch meeting or included as advice given by the police or volunteers when a home security inspection is conducted. Credit card companies recommend that consumers shred all receipt carbons before disposing of them, shred information about preapproved credit cards before throwing it away, destroy old cards and cards no longer used, retain receipts from automated teller machines (ATMs) so thieves cannot get their account number, do not write ATM personal identification numbers (PINs) on the credit card, and do not share a PIN with another person.

Key Participants

Consumers must follow the advice provided by banks and credit card companies to protect credit cards.

Potential Obstacles

There are no obstacles. Credit card companies have taken many steps to protect credit cards. A great deal of the responsibility for protecting the card lies with the consumer.

Signs of Success

Facing Financial Fraud is a consumer education program developed by Citibank MasterCard and Visa to provide consumers and retailers with information on protecting themselves from different forms of financial fraud. Presented in conjunction with the U.S. Secret Service and Postal Inspection Service, this seminar has been presented to over 10,000 consumers (Tips to Prevent Credit Card Fraud, *Business Wire,* February 3, 1994).

Applying the Strategy

Citibank MasterCard and Visa have also introduced Photocard to allow consumers to have their picture and signature digitally imprinted on their cards. Citibank also provides a Lost Wallet Service. Citibank is the largest issuer of credit cards, with more than 30 million cards in circulation.

Contact Information

Facing Credit Card Fraud
Citibank Processing Center
P.O. Box 17029
Baltimore, Maryland 21203
800-967-6777

Use Security Sensor Tags

Strategy

Security sensor tags help to deter and detect the theft of high-value products from retail stores and other businesses.

Crime Problem Addressed

Applying security sensor tags to high-theft items that can be easily concealed, such as cassette tapes, film, batteries, and apparel, deters theft and helps detect shoplifting.

Key Components

A wide variety of electronic sensor security tags is available. The retailer contracts with a sensor tag company to purchase tags. The store applies tags to items that are frequently stolen. When a sale is made, the store clerk uses a special piece of equipment to deactivate or remove the tag. Sensor units set up in store doorways detect active tags on items that someone is trying to steal from the store. Some hospitals have also been applying sensor tags to the clothing of newborn babies or elderly patients to sound alarms if they are moved from or leave an assigned location. Reusable or disposable tags are available.

Key Participants

Retailers, hospitals, and others can purchase these systems from a several vendors. Staff must be trained in their use, and customers or clients should be made aware that they are being used.

Potential Obstacles

It normally takes a special tool to remove the tag, but some thieves have found ways to defeat the system. Staff must be trained not to become complacent about shoplifting and not to rely totally on the sensor system to detect shoplifters.

Retailers must be careful about liability arising from accusing a customer who walks through a tag sensor and sets off the alarm.

Signs of Success

The systems have proven so valuable that major companies such as Wal-Mart, K-Mart, and Home Depot are installing them on many of their retail items. Some of these companies are also pushing manufacturers to install sensor tags at the time of production to relieve stores of the task of applying sensor tags to retail items (Fearful of Theft, American Businesses Tag All, *Reuter Business Report,* March 22, 1994).

Applying the Strategy

Sensormatic is one of the leading sensor tag businesses and is responsible for about 85 percent of the U.S. department store market. It currently produces about 2.5 billion tags annually.

Contact Information

Sensormatic Electronics Corporation
500 Northwest 12th Avenue
Deerfield Beach, Florida 33442
305-427-9700

Fire Safety Education for Juveniles

Strategy

Arson by juveniles can be prevented through fire safety education.

Crime Problem Addressed

A total of 49 percent of arson arrests in 1992 were juveniles. Arson is one of the leading causes of death for children under five. More than 4,500 children die in fires each year in the United States. National statistics list youth under thirteen years of age as responsible for as many as 12 percent of fires started intentionally. By focusing on educating children about the dangers of fire, this strategy aims to prevent fires started by juveniles.

Key Components

Arson prevention curricula for youth use classroom exercises and discussion to review a number of topics, including the dangers of fire and flammable materials (matches) and the fact that they are not toys, what students should do in the event of a fire in their home, how to report a fire emergency, and the impact of fires on families and communities. Parents receive material on how to secure household items from children and other means of preventing firesetting by curious children in the home. Many schools with such curricula ask local firefighters to help present the material to students, particularly students in lower grades. Most programs also emphasize posting educational material in the school to reinforce the messages delivered through the curriculum.

Key Partnerships

Firefighters represent an important resource for schools with fire prevention education programs. They serve as role models for students, answering student questions about fires, arson, and their job. Parents help by reinforcing the lessons and keeping firestarting and flammable materials in the home out of reach of their children. The fire prevention education program should also work in cooperation with local mental health professionals in the event that students at risk of committing arson need counseling.

Potential Obstacles

Some communities may not be aware of fire prevention education programs or find it difficult to schedule curriculum modules among the many other core and elective subjects offered by schools. A partnership with local firefighting agencies helps provide volunteers to deliver the curriculum and support additional materials for the program.

Signs of Success

A National Committee on Property Insurance report, *Juvenile Firesetters Programs,* summed up the potential impact of the strategy by noting that "studies indicate that the long-term solution to juvenile firesetting lies in the education of pre-school through grade 12 students."

Applying the Strategy

The National Fire Protection Association (NFPA) has presented fire prevention curricula to 4 percent of the nation's students annually since 1979. Through its Learn Not to Burn program, NFPA has reached more than 1.3 million students annually with fire safety behavior and arson prevention education. Learn Not to Burn is credited with saving 451 people from life-threatening fire-related incidents.

Contact Information

Assistant Vice President for Public Affairs and Education
National Fire Protection Association
1 Batterymarch Park
Quincy, Massachusetts 02269-9101
617-984-7288

Disseminate Automobile Theft Prevention Devices

Strategy

Dissemination of automobile theft-prevention devices helps prevent car theft, securing the car owner's property and limiting losses for insurance companies.

Crime Problem Addressed

Millions of automobiles are stolen every year. This strategy seeks to deter auto thieves by making it more difficult and time-consuming to attempt to steal a vehicle. Increasing the time it takes to steal the vehicle reduces the ease of opportunity, leaving the thief more vulnerable to detection.

Key Components

States enact legislation to provide consumers discounts on comprehensive insurance for installation of car alarms and anti-theft devices such as "kill" switches on the ignition that prevent the car from starting. Alarms and other more sophisticated technologies can be expensive to install. Using "kill" switches or marking key component parts with vehicle identification numbers are more affordable, ranging from $25 to $75. Insurance companies inform clients about the potential savings from the installation of such devices and how they can help prevent theft. State agencies, non-profit organizations, and insurance companies promote or sponsor the installation of anti-theft devices.

Key Partnerships

Communication between state agencies (insurance regulation and attorney general) and insurance companies is necessary for the program to be effective. In particular, they should cooperate on campaigns to inform the public about anti-theft devices.

Potential Obstacles

Anti-theft systems are still somewhat expensive. *Consumer's Digest* estimates that the cost of what it terms "a decent alarm system" ranges from about $130 for one installed by the owner to well over $1,000 for a professionally installed system with a more elaborate array of protective and convenience features. While the purchase prices of such systems are high, the insurance savings that often accompany installation allow the device to pay for itself.

Signs of Success

Statistical data measuring the impact of anti-theft devices are scant. That said, most insurance and law enforcement officials agree that a wide range of anti-theft technologies have a deterrent effect on automobile theft. A National Insurance Crime Bureau "FACTPACT" concluded that, "while impossible to measure, the effectiveness of anti-theft devices is significant. Passive anti-theft devices such as engine kill switches—which disable a vehicle by shutting down the fuel system—are especially effective." To date, eleven states have implemented legislation requiring insurance discounts for cars with theft prevention devices.

Many insurance companies provide discounts for automobile theft prevention systems ranging from 5 percent (for driver-activated devices) to 35 percent (for automatically activated devices) of coverage costs. Lower insurance costs essentially pay owners for the systems. Reduced losses from stolen vehicles make lower premiums worthwhile for insurance companies. Massachusetts residents are eligible for a 35 percent discount on insurance if they install a Lo-Jack tracking and recovery system, which the company claims recovers the car in 95 percent of theft cases.

Applying the Strategy

Citizens for Auto Theft Responsibility (CAR), a non-profit agency based in Palm Beach, Florida, works to reduce auto theft through public awareness, education, and prevention. In cooperation with law enforcement, insurance companies, businesses, auto theft victims, the media, and crime prevention authorities, CAR evaluates theft prevention devices, develops public education materials, creates community-based theft prevention programs, and provides support to auto theft victims.

CAR and Shell Oil Corporation recently produced an "Answer Book" about auto theft prevention. Since 1990, CAR and local law enforcement agencies have sponsored ten "STOP AUTO THEFT!" rallies throughout Florida where they install prevention devices on theft-prone vehicles and disseminate educational material. The first rally received the Crime Prevention Program of the Year award from the Florida Crime Prevention Association. In 1993, the Florida Division of Motor Vehicles became a member of CAR, distributing thousands of auto theft prevention newsletters through driver's license offices. As a result of the focus on theft prevention awareness and devices, incidences of auto theft in West Palm Beach declined from 2,200 in 1987 to 1,400 in 1991.

Contact Information

Citizens for Auto Theft Responsibility
P.O. Box 3131
Palm Beach, Florida 33480
407-478-8990

Insurance Information Institute
National Insurance Crime Bureau
10330 Roberts Road
Palos Hills, Illinois 60465
708-430-2430

Anti-Theft Decals for Automobiles

Strategy

Anti-theft decals on cars, which direct law enforcement to stop vehicles during late-night hours, help officers recognize cars that may be stolen and enhance their ability to recover stolen vehicles.

Crime Problem Addressed

Millions of automobiles are stolen every year in the United States. This strategy aims to give law enforcement another tool to detect possible stolen vehicles.

Key Components

State law enforcement agencies provide decals for car owners to display on the vehicle. Vehicles with decals are registered with the program. Cars displaying the decal can be stopped by law enforcement agents for any reason between the hours of 1 a.m. and 5 a.m. During the stop, the officer verifies ownership by checking vehicle registration. If the car has been reported stolen or if the driver cannot produce identification to match registration documents, the officer can recover the stolen car, sometimes before the owner even realizes it is gone.

Key Partnerships

State attorney generals and law enforcement or crime prevention agencies develop and operate decal programs. The administering agency develops public education campaign and information materials on auto theft prevention targeted to car owners, working through local law enforcement agencies to publicize the program and encourage area drivers to promote use of the decals.

Potential Obstacles

Law enforcement agents may resist being required to identify decals and stop all cars with decals during the late-night hours. That is often the busiest time for law enforcement officers, when many emergency calls need rapid response. The time it takes to stop cars seems less burdensome, however, when contrasted with the time officers would have to spend investigating the theft of the same cars.

Signs of Success

The National Insurance Crime Bureau (NICB), a private insurance industry group, supports implementation of Combat Auto Theft Programs (CAT), the common term for auto decal theft prevention programs. NICB notes that such efforts "effectively heighten public awareness and establish a link among consumers, insurers and law enforcement."

Successful decal programs operate statewide in Rhode Island, New Jersey, and Florida and in select cities in California, Ohio, Minnesota, New York, Texas, Tennessee, and South Carolina. New York City reported more than 100,000 vehicles registered in its decal program by 1994. The annual theft rate of autos with decals is .7 percent. The rate for vehicles without decals is 7.1 percent. Many other localities are considering the program.

Applying the Strategy

As of early 1994, owners of more than 30,000 vehicles in Dallas, Texas, had obtained theft prevention decals. Of those vehicles, only .3 percent have been stolen. The comparable rate of theft for cars without decals is 1.64 percent. The Help Enforce Against Auto Theft (HEAT) program will soon cover the entire state. Legislators in several states reviewed the success of the Dallas and New York programs with an eye toward replicating these successful efforts.

Contact Information

T-CAP for a Better Dallas, Inc..
P.O. Box 147
Dallas, Texas 75221-0147
214-670-5593

Intervention To Prevent Recidivism Among Juvenile Arsonists

Strategy

Repeat offenses by juvenile offenders can be reduced through strategic therapeutic intervention.

Crime Problem Addressed

In recent years, as many as half of the arsonists arrested have been juveniles. An estimated one of eight fires in a recent year was set by an arsonist under thirteen years of age, often out of curiosity, out of revenge, or on a dare from a peer. Identification and therapeutic treatment to help identify the causes of firesetting significantly reduce the incidence of repeat offenses.

Key Components

Intervention programs for youthful arsonists work through the police, the juvenile court, and the fire department to identify offenders and direct them toward counseling or more intensive psychological assessments to determine the cause of the unlawful behavior and the most appropriate course of treatment. Not a substitute for punishment

for the offense, therapeutic interventions coordinated by mental health professionals in cooperation with fire department experts and schools focus on identifying triggers or causes for arson.

The programs seek to alter the delinquent behavior through behavior modification techniques, including rewards for positive behavior and clear consequences for delinquent or antisocial behavior. They emphasize the consequences of arson for individual victims and the community and build the offender's empathy for victims. The programs are operated by mental health agencies or counseling programs. Where arson is related to a serious mental health problem, the juvenile is referred to more intensive treatment outside the program.

Key Partnerships

Fire departments and mental health professionals represent vital resources for juvenile arsonist intervention programs. Their expertise in pointing out the impact of arson on communities and the deadly consequences for victims helps deter the youthful offender from repeating the offense. Schools can help by educating students about fire safety and arson prevention and referring students to counseling programs.

Potential Obstacles

The cost of counseling can prove a barrier for programs that do not rely heavily on volunteer resources. Partnerships among mental health, school, and fire safety agencies can coordinate resources to house and staff counseling and other related services for juvenile offenders.

Signs of Success

The National Committee on Property Insurance's *Juvenile Firesetters Programs: A Summary of Available Resources* notes the benefit of intervention programs, stating, "expressed in terms of non-recurring firesetting behavior, success rates of 90 to 100 percent drops in recidivism are indicated. These impressive results rank high among intervention programs dealing with juvenile anti-social or delinquent behavior." The Massachusetts-based National Fire Protection Association recommends intervention programs for prevention of repeat incidents by juvenile firesetters.

Applying the Strategy

Fall River, Massachusetts' Juvenile Firestarters Information Program is operated through the cooperation of the Fall River Firefighters Memorial Museum. It helps counsel juvenile arsonists and prevent additional incidents. The Maryland-based U.S. Fire Administration advises community and mental health groups about the establishment of arson intervention programs, including programs for juvenile offenders.

Contact Information

National Fire Service Support Systems, Inc.
20 North Main Street
Pittsford, New York 14534
716-264-0840

Fall River Juvenile Firesetters Information Program
418 Quequechan Street
Fall River, Massachusetts 02723
508-674-1810

Bibliography

Books

Plaster, Sherry, and Stan Carter. *Planning for Prevention: Sarasota, Florida's Approach to Crime Prevention Through Environmental Design*. Tallahassee, FL: Florida Department of Law Enforcement; Florida Criminal Justice Executive Institute; Programs and Research in Criminal Justice, 1993.

Periodicals

Wilson, James Q., and George L. Kelling. The Police and Neighborhood Safety: Broken Windows. *The Atlantic Monthly*, March 1982.

Public Documents

AIA/ACSA Council on Architectural Research: A Joint Council of The American Institute of Architects and Association of Collegiate Schools of Architecture. *Secure and Livable Communities: Crime Prevention Through Environmental Design*. Washington, DC, December 9–11, 1993.

Crime Concern. *A Practical Guide To Crime Prevention For Local Partnerships*. September 1993.

National Crime Prevention Council. Put a Stop to Auto Theft. *Topics in Crime Prevention*, November 1991.

U.S. Department of Housing and Urban Development. *Defensible Space: Deterring Crime and Building Community*. February 1995.

U.S. Department of Justice, Office of Justice Programs, Bureau of Justice Assistance. *The Systems Approach to Crime and Drug Prevention: A Path to Community Policing*. vol. I, issue 2, September 1993.

RESOURCE LIST

4-H
Extension Service
U.S. Department of Agriculture
14th & Independence, SW
Washington, DC 20250
202-720-5853

American Academy of Pediatrics
P.O. Box 927
Elk Grove Village, IL 60009-0927
708-228-5005

American Association of Retired Persons
601 E Street, NW
Washington, DC 20049
202-434-2222

American Bar Association
Standing Committee on Dispute Resolution
740 15th Street
Washington, DC 20005
202-662-1680

American Council for Drug Education
164 West 74th Street
New York, NY 10023
212-595-5810

American Council on Alcoholism
2522 St. Paul Street
Baltimore, MD 21218
410-889-0100 or 800-527-5344

American Society for Industrial Security
1655 North Fort Myer Drive
Suite 1200
Arlington, VA 22209
703-522-5800

Anti-Defamation League of B'nai B'rith
823 United Nations Plaza
New York, NY 10017
212-490-2525

Association of Junior Leagues International, Inc.
660 First Avenue, Second Floor
New York, NY 10016
212-683-1515

Big Brothers/Big Sisters of America
230 North 13th Street
Philadelphia, PA 19107
215-567-7000

Board of Young Adult Police Commissioners
Department of Police Services
One Union Avenue
New Haven, CT 06519
203-946-6276

Boys & Girls Clubs of America
National Headquarters
1230 West Peachtree Street
Atlanta, GA 30309
404-815-5700

Boy Scouts of America
P.O. Box 152079
Irving, TX 75015-2079
214-580-2000

Bureau of Justice Assistance
Office of Justice Programs
U.S. Department of Justice
BJA Clearinghouse
P.O. Box 6000
Rockville, MD 20850
800-688-4252

Bureau of Justice Statistics
Office of Justice Programs
U.S. Department of Justice, NCJRS
P.O. Box 6000
Rockville, MD 20850
Justice Statistics Clearinghouse
800-732-3277

Center for Community Change
1000 Wisconsin Avenue, NW
Washington, DC 20007
202-342-0519

Center for Democratic Renewal
P.O. Box 50469
Atlanta, GA 30302-9836
404-221-0025

Center for Substance Abuse Prevention
National Clearinghouse for Alcohol and Drug Information
P.O. Box 2345
Rockville, MD 20847-2345
800-729-6686

Center for the Study and Prevention of Violence
University of Colorado
Institute of Behavioral Science
Campus Box 442, Building #9
Boulder, CO 80309-0442
303-492-1032

Center to Prevent Handgun Violence
1225 Eye Street, NW, Suite 1100
Washington, DC 20005
202-289-7319

Children's Defense Fund
25 E Street, NW
Washington, DC 20001
202-628-8787

Child Welfare League of America
440 First Street, NW, Suite 310
Washington, DC 20001-2085
202-638-2952

Citizens Committee for New York City, Inc.
305 Seventh Avenue, 15th Floor
New York, NY 10001
212-989-0909

City Year
285 Columbus Avenue
Boston, MA 02116
617-927-2500

Community Board Program
1540 Market Street, Suite 490
San Francisco, CA 94102
415-552-1250

Community Relations Service
U.S. Department of Justice
5550 Friendship Boulevard, Suite 330
Chevy Chase, MD 20815
301-492-5969

Community Youth Gang Services
144 South Detterly Avenue
Los Angeles, CA 90022
213-266-4264

Corporation for National and Community Service
1201 New York Avenue, NW
Washington, DC 20525
202-606-5000

Crime Victims Research and Treatment Center
Department of Psychiatry and Behavioral Sciences
Medical University of South Carolina
171 Ashley Avenue
Charleston, SC 29425
803-792-2945

D.A.R.E. America
P.O. Box 2090
Los Angeles, CA 90051
800-223-DARE

Emerge
280 Green Street, Second Floor
Boston, MA 02139-3312
617-422-1550

Education Development Center
55 Chapel Street
Newton, MA 02158
617-969-7100

Family Violence and Sexual Assault Institute
1310 Clinic Drive
Tyler, TX 75701
903-595-6600

General Federation of Women's Clubs
1734 N Street, NW
Washington, DC 20036-2990
202-347-3168

Head Start Association
418 South Washington Street
Alexandria, VA 22314
703-739-0875

High/Scope Educational Research Foundation
600 North River Street
Ypsilanti, MI 48198
313-485-2000

The Home and School Institute, Inc.
1500 Mass. Avenue
Washington, DC 20036
202-466-3633

HUD Drug Information and Strategy Clearinghouse
P.O. Box 6424
Rockville, MD 20850
800-578-DISC

Institute on Black Chemical Abuse
2616 Nicollet Avenue South
Minneapolis, MN 55408
612-871-7878

International Association of Chiefs of Police
515 North Washington Street
Alexandria, VA 22314-2357
703-836-6767

International Society of Crime Prevention Practitioners
1696 Connor Drive
Pittsburgh, PA 15129-9035
412-655-1600

Just Say No International
2101 Webster Street, Suite 1300
Oakland, CA 94612
800-258-2766

Justice Research and Statistics Association
444 North Capitol Street, NW
Suite 445
Washington, DC 20001
202-624-8560

Kiwanis International
3636 Woodview Trace
Indianapolis, IN 46268-3196
317-875-8755

Mediascope
12711 Ventura Boulevard, Suite 250
Studio City, CA 91604
818-508-2080

National Aging Resource Center on Elder Abuse
College of Human Resources
University of Delaware
Newark, DE 19716
302-831-8546

National Alliance of Business
1201 New York Avenue, NW, Suite 700
Washington, DC 20005
202-289-2888

National Association for the Advancement of Colored People
4805 Mount Hope Drive
Baltimore, MD 21215-3297
410-358-8900

National Association for the Education of Young Children (NAEYC)
1509 16th Street, NW
Washington, DC 20036
800-424-2460

National Association of Elementary School Principals
1615 Duke Street
Alexandria, VA 22314-3483
703-684-3345

National Association of Neighborhoods
1651 Fuller Street, NW
Washington, DC 20009
202-332-7766

National Association of Police Athletic Leagues
618 North U.S. Highway 1
Suite 201
North Palm Beach, FL 33408
407-844-1823

National Association of Service and Conservation Corps
666 11th Street, NW, Suite 500
Washington, DC 20001
202-737-6272

National Association of State Boards of Education
1012 Cameron Street
Alexandria, VA 22314
703-684-4000

National Association of Town Watch
P.O. Box 303
7 Wynnewood Road, Suite 215
Wynnewood, PA 19096
610-649-7055

National Center for Community Policing
School of Criminal Justice
Michigan State University
East Lansing, MI 48824
517-355-2322

National Clearinghouse on Family and Youth
P.O. Box 13505
Silver Spring, MD 20911-3505
301-608-8098

National Black Youth Leadership Council
244 West 54th Street, Suite 800
New York, NY 10019
212-541-7600

National Burglar & Fire Alarm Association, Inc.
7101 Wisconsin Avenue, Suite 901
Bethesda, MD 20814-4805
301-907-3202

National Center for Missing and Exploited Children
2101 Wilson Boulevard, Suite 550
Arlington, VA 22201
800-842-5678

National Clearinghouse on Runaway and Homeless Youth
P.O. Box 13505
Silver Spring, MD 20911-3505
301-608-8098

National Clearinghouse on Child Abuse and Neglect Information
P.O. Box 1182
Washington, DC 20013-1182
800-FYI-3366

National Coalition of Hispanic Health and Human Services Organizations
1501 16th Street, NW
Washington, DC 20036
202-387-5000

National Committee to Prevent Child Abuse
332 South Michigan Avenue
Suite 1600
Chicago, IL 60604-4357
312-663-3520

National Conference of Christians and Jews
71 Fifth Avenue, Suite 1100
New York, NY 10003-3095
212-206-0006

National Congress of Parents and Teachers (National PTA)
330 North Wabash Street, Suite 2100
Chicago, IL 60611-3690
312-670-6782

National Council on Alcoholism and Drug Dependence
12 West 21st Street
New York, NY 10010
212-206-6770

National Council on Crime and Delinquency
685 Market Street, Suite 620
San Francisco, CA 94105
415-896-6223

National Crime Prevention Council
1700 K Street, NW, Second Floor
Washington, DC 20006-3817
202-466-6272

National Crime Prevention Institute
Brigman Hall
University of Louisville
Louisville, KY 40202
502-852-6987

National Criminal Justice Association
444 North Capitol Street, NW
Suite 618
Washington, DC 20001
202-347-4900

National District Attorneys' Association
99 Canal Center Plaza, Suite 510
Alexandria, VA 22314
703-549-4253

   American Prosecutors Research Institute
   703-549-9222

   National Center for Prosecution of Child Abuse
   703-739-0321

   National Drug Prosecution Center
   703-549-6790

National Exchange Clubs Foundation for the Prevention of Child Abuse
3050 Central Avenue
Toledo, OH 43606
419-535-3232

National Family Partnership
11159B South Towne Square
St. Louis, MO 63123
314-845-1933

National Fraud Information Center
815 15th Street, NW
Washington, DC 20005
800-876-7060

National Gay and Lesbian Task Force
2320 17th Street, NW
Washington, DC 20009
202-332-6483

National Governors' Association
Hall of the States
444 North Capitol Street, NW
Suite 267
Washington, DC 20001
202-624-5320

National Institute for Citizen Education in the Law
711 G Street, SE
Washington, DC 20003
202-546-6644

National Institute for Dispute Resolution
1726 M Street, NW, Suite 500
Washington, DC 20036
202-466-4764

National Insurance Crime Bureau
10330 South Roberts Road, Suite 3A
Palos Hills, IL 60465
708-430-2430

National League of Cities
1301 Pennsylvania Avenue, NW
Suite 550
Washington, DC 20004
202-626-3010

National McGruff House Network
66 East Cleveland Avenue
Salt Lake City, UT 84115
801-486-8768

National Network for Youth
1319 F Street, NW, Suite 401
Washington, DC 20004
202-783-7949

National Organization for Victim Assistance
1757 Park Road, NW
Washington, DC 20010
800-TRY-NOVA

National Organization of Black Law Enforcement Executives
4609 Pinecrest Office Park Drive
Second Floor, Suite F
Alexandria, VA 22312
703-658-1529

National Parents' Resource Institute for Drug Education
3610 Bekalb Technology Parkway
Suite 105
Atlanta, GA 30340
800-853-7867

National Safety Council
P.O. Box 558
1121 Spring Lake Drive
Itasca, Il 60143
800-621-7619

National School Safety Center
4165 Thousand Oaks Boulevard
Suite 290
Westlake Village, CA 91362
805-373-9977

National Sheriffs' Association
1450 Duke Street
Alexandria, VA 22314
800-424-7782

National Training and Information Center
810 North Milwaukee Avenue
Chicago, IL 60622-4103
312-243-3035

National Urban League, Inc.
Stop the Violence Clearinghouse
500 East 62nd Street
New York, NY 10021
212-310-9000

National Victim Center
2111 Wilson Boulevard
Suite 300
Arlington, VA 22201
703-276-2880

National Youth Leadership Council
1910 West County Road B
Roseville, MN 55113
612-631-3672

Office of Juvenile Justice and Delinquency Prevention
U.S. Department of Justice
Juvenile Justice Clearinghouse
P.O. Box 6000
Rockville, MD 20849-6000
800-638-8736

Police Executive Research Forum
1120 Connecticut Avenue, NW
Washington, DC 20036
202-466-7820

Police Foundation
1001 22nd Street, NW, Suite 200
Washington, DC 20037
202-833-1460

**Prejudice Institute and The
Center for the Applied Study of
Ethnoviolence**
Towson State University
Stephens Hall Annex
Towson, MD 21204
410-830-2000

**Preparing for the Drug-Free
Years Program**
Developmental Research and
Programs, Inc.
130 Nickerson, Suite 107
Seattle, WA 98109
206-286-1805

Scott Newman Center
6255 Sunset Boulevard, Suite 1906
Los Angeles, CA 90028
213-469-2029

Southern Poverty Law Center
Klanwatch Project
P.O. Box 548
Montgomery, AL 36101-0548
334-264-0286

U.S. Conference of Mayors
1620 I Street, NW
Washington, DC 20006
202-293-7330

U.S. Department of Education
Safe and Drug Free Schools Program
400 Maryland Avenue, SW
Room 1073
Washington, DC 20202
202-260-1856

**U.S. Department of Health and
Human Services**
Administration for Children, Youth, and
Families
330 C Street, SW, Room 2026
Washington, DC 20201
202-205-8347

U.S. Department of Justice
U.S. Drug Enforcement
Administration Demand Reduction
Section
600 Army Navy Drive
Arlington, VA 22202
202-307-7936

**Young Men's Christian
Association**
101 North Wacker Drive
Chicago, IL 60606
312-977-0031

**Young Women's Christian
Association**
726 Broadway
New York, NY 10003
212-614-2700

Youth Crime Watch of America
9300 South Dadeland Boulevard
Suite 100
Miami, FL 33156
305-670-2409

Youth Service America
1101 15th Street, NW, Suite 200
Washington, DC 20005
202-296-2992

Youth Volunteer Corps of America
6310 Lamar Avenue, Suite 125
Overland Park, KS 66202-4247
913-432-9822

INDEX

AAA. *See* American Automobile Association

AARP. *See* American Association of Retired Persons

AARTS. *See* African American Recreation Transformation System

Abandoned buildings, 175

Abduction prevention, 69–70

Abington, Pennsylvania, 129, 149, 150

About Face Program, 247

Absentee Prevention Program, 286

Academic Career and Community Enhancement for Latchkey Children and Their Families, 272

ACCEL. *See* Academic Career and Community Enhancement for Latchkey Children and Their Families

Access control, 161–162, 213–214, 349

Accion International, 233

Accountability programs, 319–320

Acquaintance rape prevention, 276

Action in the Arts, 312

Action messages, 5

ADAM. *See* Awareness and Development for Adolescent Males

Addison Terrace Learning Center, 290

Administration for Children, Youth, and Families, 278–279

Adolescent Violence Prevention Project, 249

Adolescents. *See* Youth

Adolescents at Risk, 101

Adopt-A-Block groups, 345

Adopt-A-Highway programs, 342–343

Adult bookstores, 173

Adult mentors. *See* Mentoring programs

Advance Parental Advisory, 3

Adventure Alternatives, 292

Advertising Council, 268

Advisory boards, 73–74

Advocacy for Women and Kids in Emergencies, 253

AEO. *See* Association for Enterprise Opportunity

African American Recreation Transformation System, 292

African-American youth
mentoring program for females, 103
rites of passage training for males, 103
Self-Esteem Through Performing Arts program, 58

Afrocentric approach, 107

After-school programs, 92, 271–272, 287–288

Alachua County (Florida) Sheriff's Department, 128

Alameda, California, 216, 228, 305

Alamo Rent-A-Car, 191

Alberta (Canada) Liquor Control Board, 138

Albuquerque, New Mexico, 42

Alcohol abuse prevention. *See also* Drug abuse prevention
discourage "happy hours," 305–306
parental involvement, 287
prevent sales to minors, 301–302
train servers, 316–317
treatment for women, 322–323
use in public parks, 185

Alcohol-addicted babies, 90

Alexandria, Virginia, 39

Alisco-Pico Recreation Center, 184

Allegheny County, Pennsylvania, 81

Allen School, 72

Allstate Insurance company, 269

Alpha collaboration, 92

Alpha Program, 57

Alternative school, 76–77

Alternatives program, 292

A.M. Best Company, 167

"America Against Crime," 9

American Academy of Pediatrics, 240

American Alliance for Rights and Responsibility, 214

American Association of Retired Persons, 39, 64, 124

American Automobile Association, 168

American Bar Association, 127, 144, 330

American College of Emergency Physicians, 186

American Truckers Association, 193

"America's #1 Challenge: U.S. Against Violence," 9

AmeriCorps, 63

Ameritech Cellular Services, 351

AMYS. *See* Aunt Martha's Youth Services

Anaheim, California, 345

Anger Management Groups, 264

Ann Arbor, Michigan, 125, 172, 182, 354

Annie Casey Foundation, 76

Anti-Crime Youth Council, 255

Anti-Defamation League, 334, 335

Anti-Drug/Gang program, 321

Antisocial behavior, 261

Apartment Watch, 45

Apprenticeships, 89–90

Architectural Design for Crime Prevention, 211

Arizona, 7, 80. *See also specific communities and programs*

Arizona Crime Prevention Association, 10

Arizona State University Prevention Resource Center, 86

Arkadelphia, Arkansas, 235

Arlington, Texas, 207

Arlington County, Virginia, 345

Arson, 121, 357–358, 360–361

Arson Early Warning and Prevention Program, 225–226

Arts-related drug prevention programs, 312

Asian Association of Utah, 309

Asian community, 28, 102, 331

Asian Law Enforcement Advisory Council, 143

Asian Youth Substance Abuse Project, 309

ASPIRA Clubs, 332

Asset seizure, 300–301

Associated Marine Institutes, 243

Association for a Better New York, 351

Association for Enterprise Opportunity, 233

ATF. *See* Bureau of Alcohol, Tobacco and Firearms

Athens, Ohio, 225
Athletics, 307
Atlanta, Georgia, 23, 90, 99–100, 180, 209, 290
ATMs. *See* Automated teller machines
Aunt Martha's Youth Services, 65
Austin, Texas, 19, 21, 59, 80, 175, 355
Automated teller machines, 124, 182
Automobile Association of Florida, 191
Automobile theft prevention
  decals, 359–360
  devices, 358–359
Avance program, 106
Avocado Theft Hotline, 139
AWAKE. *See* Advocacy for Women and Kids in Emergencies
Awards ceremonies, 48
Awareness and Development for Adolescent Males, 100
Awareness programs, 334–335
AWOD. *See* A World of Difference program

"Back the Blue" campaign, 24, 37
BAD. *See* Business Against Drugs
BALANCE. *See* Beautiful Ambitious Ladies Able to Negotiate Commitment to Self-Esteem and Excellence
Ballfields, 46
Baltimore, Maryland, 32, 88, 96, 106, 163, 235, 267, 300
Barriers, 218–219
Basic Center Project, 65
Batterers, 264. *See also* Domestic violence programs
Bay Area United Youth, 228
Baylor College of Medicine, 240
BB/BS. *See* Big Brothers and Big Sisters of America
Beacon School, 110
Beat Health police unit, 299
Beat officers, 132
Beautification projects, 14–15, 46, 228–229
Beautiful Ambitious Ladies Able to Negotiate Commitment to Self-Esteem and Excellence, 83
Before-school programs, 287–288
Begging, 189
Behavior problems, 90
Believe in Me program, 59
Bell Atlantic, 308
Bellevue Hospital, 187
Berkeley (South Carolina) Victims' Assistance Program, 39

Best Underwriting Guide for Commercial Standards, 167
Bethel African Methodist Episcopal Church, 32
Bethesda, Maryland, 308
Bias crimes
  counseling programs, 335–336
  court monitoring, 328–329
  culturally based leadership training, 331–332
  diversity and tolerance education, 329–330
  media campaigns, 334–335
  mediation services, 336–337
  multilingual services, 330–331
  overview, 327–328
  police-cultural organization service partnerships, 332–333
  rapid police response, 333–334
  victim support, 337
Bicycle patrols, 149–150, 180
Big Brothers and Big Sisters of America, 66, 102
Bigotry. *See* Bias crimes
Bilingual personnel, 330–331
Binghamton, New York, 70, 124
Birmingham, Alabama, 80, 262
Birth defects, 90
Block parties, 48
Block Watch, 117, 159
Blue Ridge Parkway, 183
Board of Young Adult Police Commissioners, 73–74, 123
Boise, Idaho, 171
Boot camps, 246–247
Boston, Massachusetts, 23, 93, 210, 249, 253, 311
Boston City Hospital, 260
Boston Police Department, 334
Boston Violence Prevention Project, 249
Boy Scouts, 136
Boys and Girls Clubs, 58, 72–73, 98, 120, 136
Bradenton, Florida, 61
Bradford, England, 192
Brandeis University, 54
Bridge program, 290
Bridgeport, Connecticut, 159, 162, 314
"Bridging the Gap," 6
Brighton Neighborhood Improvement Program, 34
Bristol, England, 192
British Home Office, 158
Broadcast television. *See* Media resources
Bromley-Heath Resident Management Corporation, 210

Bronx, New York, 304, 333
Brooklyn, New York, 34, 226
Broward County, Florida, 302
Buddy system, 23
Buffalo Grove, Illinois, 169
Building codes, 29–30, 346
Bullying, 251–252
Bureau of Alcohol, Tobacco and Firearms, 85, 131, 254
Bureau of Justice Assistance, 8, 22, 35, 37, 146, 149
Bureau of Narcotics Investigation, 150
Burglary prevention, 16
Burns International, 179
Buses, 188, 190
Business address numbers, 172, 354
Business Against Drugs, 298
Business Crime Council of South Texas, 17
Business districts. *See also* Businesses
  cash control, 167–168
  crime prevention education, 164
  fax information networks, 165–166
  hotel/motel security standards, 168
  insurance loss control, 166–167
  safety and security assessments, 164–165
  workplace safety inspections, 166
Business ethics, 229–230
Business incubator program, 224–225
Business Task Force, 35
Business Watch, 16, 165, 235–236, 353
Businesses. *See also* Business districts
  anticrime groups, 16–17
  drug abuse prevention, 297–298
  graffiti removal, 160–161
  law enforcement cooperation, 137–138
  lighting, 352–353
  mentoring programs, 89–90
  pay-before-you-pump gas policy, 355
  security guidelines for high-risk businesses, 155
  security systems, 17–18
Butz Learning Progressive Center, 77
Buy-back programs, 25

Cabbies on Patrol program, 121
Cable television. *See* Media resources
California, 139, 343. *See also specific communities and programs*
  Department of Alcohol and Drug Services, 322
  Department of Food and Agriculture, 139
California Drug Abatement Act, 177

California Emergency Nurses Association, 273
California Governor's Office, 86
California Legislative Research Office, 45
California Office of the Auditor General, 53
California State University, 242
California Street Terrorism Enforcement and Prevention Act, 269
California Wellness Foundation, 69, 255
California Youth Authority, 246
Cambridge, Massachusetts, 105, 266
Campus Opportunity Outreach League, 66
Cape May, New Jersey, 289
CAR. *See* Citizens for Auto Theft Responsibility
Cardboard police officers, 169
Career advancement guidance, 54
Career Beginnings, 89
Career mentorship programs, 89–90
Caring Area Residents meetings, 135
CASA. *See* Court-Appointed Special Advocates program
Cash control, 167–168
CAT. *See* Combat Auto Theft Programs
Cathedral City, California, 95, 242, 269
Caught in the Crossfire, 43, 94
CCNYC. *See* Citizens Committee for New York City
CCP. *See* Comprehensive Competencies Program
CCTV. *See* Closed circuit television
Cedar Rapids, Iowa, 103
Celebrating Neighborhoods that Work, 48
Cellular One, 40
Cellular telephone patrols, 40, 350–351
Center for Human Development, 323
Center for Intergenerational Learning, 64
Center for Media and Public Affairs, 3
Center for Substance Abuse and Prevention, 272
Center for Successful Child Development, 97
Center for the Study of Sport in Society, 276
Center for Urban Expression, 145
Center for Youth Development and Policy Research, 53–54
Center to Prevent Handgun Violence, 240, 270
Centers for Disease Control and Prevention, 103

Central Florida Hotel and Motel Association, 168
Central Patrol District, 279
Centros Sor Isolina Ferre in Ponce Playa, 38
The Challenge of Community Policing, 149
Challenger Boys and Girls Club, 73
Champ Cookies, 316
Chapel Hill, North Carolina, 318
Character Education Program, 71
Charleston County, South Carolina, 277
Charlotte, North Carolina, 96, 172
Chattanooga, Tennessee, 57
Cherokee County, South Carolina, 102
Chicago, Illinois, 65, 97, 100, 103, 104, 105, 225, 235, 239–240, 278, 295, 337
Chicago Housing Authority, 43, 209, 212
Chicago Public School District, 194
Chicano Family Center, 120
Chief's Award of Merit, 132
Child abuse
    court-appointed special advocates, 88–89
    in-home counseling services, 97
    intervention to prevent foster care placement, 107
    teaching crime prevention to children, 69–70
    teen pregnancy prevention programs, 99
    victim assistance, 252–253
Child and Adolescent Mental Health Demonstration Project, 87
Child Care Management Services, 19
Child in Need of Assistance Mediation Project, 89
Child Molestation programs, 124
Child Witness to Violence Project, 260
Children. *See also* Child abuse; Youth
    community-based health services, 92–93
    counseling for violence witnesses, 260
    crime prevention techniques, 69–70
    ensure affordable child care, 18–19
    gun safety education, 270–271
    latchkey, 271–272, 287–288
    physically and mentally challenged, 70, 124
    victim assistance, 252–253
Children Cope with Divorce, 67
Children's Defense Fund, 99
Children's Fund, 76
Children's Hospital, 186, 253

"Choices" program, 255
Churches
    drug abuse prevention, 296–297
    mentoring programs, 31–32
    rites of passage training, 103
Cincinnati, Ohio, 60, 142, 307, 347
CIS. *See* Cities in Schools
Citibank MasterCard and Visa, 356
Cities in Schools, 102, 109
Citizen Observer Patrols, 39
Citizen patrol groups, 33–34, 121
Citizen Police Academy, 141
Citizens and Their Courts: Building a Public Constituency, 4
Citizens Committee for New York City, 33, 142–143, 158, 316
Citizens for Auto Theft Responsibility, 359
Citizens for Community Improvement, 299
Citizens Reclaiming Our Neighborhoods from Crime, 24, 37
CITY. *See* Community Intensive Treatment for Youth
City agencies, 133
City Children 2007, 76
City Livability Award, 148
City-wide crime problems
    access restrictions, 161–162
    code enforcement teams, 156–157
    CPTED for parking structures, 162–163
    CPTED ordinances, 155–156
    crime prevention councils, 158–159
    crime prevention programs for women, 157–158
    graffiti removal, 160–161
    high-risk business security guidelines, 155
    insurance premium reductions for security improvements, 163
    live-in police officers, 160
    safer neighborhood design, 159
    utility employee watch, 157
Civil Bicycle Patrol, 150
Civil Translators Pilot Program, 144
Civitas Initiative, 239–240
Claremont, California, 322
Clean-Land initiative, 46
Clean Sweep operation, 212
Cleanup projects, 217–218
Cleveland, Ohio, 9, 26, 31, 46, 95, 137, 146, 161, 293, 300
Cleveland, Tennessee, 251
Climate of Hope, 37
Climb Theatre group, 20

Closed circuit television
    in public housing, 210–211
    in schools, 195–196
Coalition for a Non-Violent City, 254
Coca-Cola Valued Youth Program, 69
Code enforcement teams, 140, 156–157
Code of conduct, 196
Codes and ordinances, 29–30,
    298–299
College of William and Mary, 91
College students
    acquaintance rape prevention, 276
    crime prevention education, 256–257
    as role models for youth, 66
    safety programs, 128
    school drug policies, 310–311
    as volunteers in youth programs,
        20–21
Columbus, Ohio, 128, 242, 351
Combat Auto Theft Programs, 360
Comer School, 57
Commission on Families and Children,
    253
Commission on the Future of Virginia
    Judicial System, 126
Committee for Children, 239
Common Enterprise, 241
Common Ground, 145
Commonwealth Fund, 89
Communication skills, 19–20, 69
Communications Network, 141
Community Action Guide, 44
Community Affairs Division, 241
Community-based programs
    domestic violence victim support,
        103–104
    health services for children, 92–93
    parent education and support, 106
Community-based supervision, 80–81
Community Board Program, 240, 337
Community Coalition to Prevent Black
    Homicide, 249
Community coalitions, 35–37, 117–118
Community College of Beaver County,
    286
Community concerns, 74–75
Community courts, 126
Community Crime Patrol, 128
Community crime prevention
    programs, 40. *See also* Public
    education; *specific communities*
Community Crime Prevention/SAFE
    Program, 161, 340
Community Crisis Response Teams,
    43, 266
Community Development Block Grants,
    232

Community Development Corporations,
    232
Community Disorders Unit, 334
Community events
    celebrate neighborhood
        accomplishments, 47–48
    law enforcement-sponsored, 135
    promote crime prevention, 23–24
Community groups, 32–33. *See also
    specific communities*
Community Information Exchange, 8
Community Intensive Supervision
    Program, 81
Community Intensive Treatment for
    Youth, 80
Community Leadership Institute of
    Maine, 323–324
Community media. *See* Media
    resources
Community meetings, 137
Community mobilization
    access to safe urban open space, 46
    beautification projects, 14–15
    business anticrime groups, 16–17
    celebrate neighborhood
        accomplishments, 47–48
    citizen patrols, 33–34
    codes and ordinances, 29–30
    college students as volunteers, 20–21
    combate crime, violence, and drug
        abuse, 37
    community groups, 32–33
    crime prevention services for the
        elderly, 22–23
    crime tip rewards, 41–42
    directories of services, 47
    drug abuse prevention, 21–22,
        293–294
    ensure affordable child care, 18–19
    faith institution-supported mentoring,
        31–32
    home and business security systems,
        17–18
    job banks, 28–29
    law enforcement partnership, 116–117
    law enforcement support, 36–37
    local government crime prevention
        coalitions, 35–36
    local media coverage, 30–31
    neighborhood associations, 32–33
    neighborhood-based service centers,
        15–16
    Neighborhood Watch, 45
    overview, 13–14
    problem solving education for youth,
        19–20
    promote prevention, 23–24

    provide positive alternatives to gang
        activity, 24–25
    reduce the number of handguns,
        25–26
    reinforce community standards
        against violence, 43–44
    reinforce prevention themes through
        performances, 40–41
    senior citizens as volunteers, 39
    support programs for mentally ill
        offenders, 26–27
    support needs of recent immigrants,
        27–28
    use technology to promote safety and
        crime prevention, 40
    victim assistance services, 42–43
    violence prevention education for
        youth, 19–20
    youth development programs, 38
Community ombudsman, 130
Community-oriented policing, 142,
    146–148
Community Policing Media and
    Outreach program, 141
Community Policing Officers, 146–147
Community Policing vehicles, 149
Community Reinvestment Act, 232
Community resource centers, 109–110
Community Responses to Drug Abuse,
    22, 37
Community service, 108–109
Community Service Officers, 129, 145,
    330–331
Community service projects, 55
Community Street Coordinator, 134
Community Support Program, 27
Comprehensive Competencies
    Program, 57
*Comprehensive Crisis Management
    Planning*, 206
*Comprehensive Strategy for Serious,
    Violent, and Chronic Juvenile
    Offenders*, 84, 87, 88
Conference of Chief Justices, 4
Conference of State Court
    Administrators, 4
Conflict mediation, 257–258
Connecticut, 67, 106. *See also specific
    communities and programs*
    Department of Children and Youth
        Services, 106
Conroe, Texas, 250
Construction Specifications Institute,
    342
Consumer Research and Service
    Development Project, 126

Controlling Crime in the School, 200, 205
Convenience Store Security Act, 155
Convenience stores, 167–168, 174
Cook County, Illinois, 67
COOL. *See* Campus Opportunity Outreach League
COP. *See* Citizen Observer Patrols
Cops on the Block program, 160
Cornwall, New York, 205
CORP. *See* Crime Prevention Program
Corporate project support, 268–269
Corporation for National and Community Service, 18, 102
Corporation for Public Broadcasting, 255
Corpus Christi, Texas, 7, 60, 67, 130, 253
Correctional facilities, 243–244
Corrections programs, 79
Council for Spanish Speaking, 28
Council of Neighborhood Associations, 36
Council on Families in America, 67
Counseling programs
    for bias crimes offenders, 335–336
    for children who witness violence, 260
    for divorcing parents, 67–68
    for domestic violence victims, 103–104
    for runaway and homeless youth, 65
County Juvenile Court Victim Restitution Program, 99
Court-Appointed Special Advocates program, 88–89
Court-based programs, 263
Court monitoring, 328–329
Court of Common Pleas, 303
Court School programs, 89
Court systems. *See also* Law enforcement
    community input on improving, 126
    drug courts, 302–303
    educational programs, 127
    gun courts, 262
    small claims courts, 30, 177
    for youth, 81–82
Courts Community Advisory Board, 126
CPOs. *See* Community Policing Officers
CPTED. *See* Crime Prevention Through Environmental Design
Crack cocaine, 117
CRDA. *See* Community Responses to Drug Abuse
Credit cards, 356–357

"Crime, Drugs and Subsidized Housing," 211
Crime Bill of 1994, 233, 234
Crime data analysis, 118–119
Crime Information Hotline, 351
Crime Prevention Action Plan, 20, 35
Crime Prevention Association of Oregon, 346
Crime Prevention Bulletin, 9
Crime prevention councils, 158–159
Crime prevention expo, 9
Crime Prevention Information Center, 7–8
Crime prevention programs
    for businesses, 164
    for college students, 256–257
    for department staff, 132
    for the elderly, 22–23
    for female youth, 60–61
    multilingual materials, 144
    for public housing residents, 216–217
    for school personnel, 208
    use technology, 40
    for young children, 69–70
    for youth, 110–111
Crime Prevention Section, 17
Crime Prevention Through Environmental Design
    ordinances, 155–156
    for parking structures, 162–163
    for subways, 188–189
    training of law enforcement officers, 125
Crime reporting hotline, 201–202
Crime Stoppers International, 42
Crime tip rewards, 41–42
Crime Watch, 117
Crime Watch Coalition, 159
Criminal justice system. *See also* Court systems; Law enforcement
    community meetings, 137
    youth interaction with, 123
Crisis hotlines, 111–112
Crisis planning, 206–207
Crisis response teams, 266–267
Crop theft, 139
Cruising control techniques, 170–171
CSCD. *See* Center for Successful Child Development
CSP. *See* Community Support Program
Cultural Diversity Project, 10
Culturally based leadership training, 331–332
Culturally diverse populations, 145, 309, 329–330
Curfews, 62–63, 95–96
Cuyahoga County, Ohio, 296

Dade County, Florida, 64, 134, 270, 346
Dads on Patrol, 205
Dallas, Texas, 8, 41, 156, 165, 206–207, 360
Danville, Virginia, 165
D.A.R.E. *See* Drug Abuse Resistance Education
Data-gathering techniques, 119
Dating violence prevention, 265–266
Day treatment, 79–80
Daytime curfews, 95–96
Dayton, Ohio, 71–72, 159, 162, 314, 349
DC Hospital Center, 247–248
DEA. *See* Federal Drug Enforcement Administration
Decatur, Georgia, 256
Deerfield, Illinois, 306
"Defensible Space: Deterring Crime and Building Community," 213
Deland, Florida, 290
Delinquency. *See* Juvenile delinquency
Denver, Colorado, 267
DePauw University, 66
Des Moines, Iowa, 30, 299, 320
Detroit, Michigan, 17, 20, 181, 186, 236
Development Research Programs, 58
Developmental problems, 90
Direct Deposit program, 354–355
Directories of services, 47
Discrimination. *See* Bias crimes
Disney Company, 341
Diversion programs, 251, 303
Diversity education, 329–330
Division of Mental Health, Developmental Disabilities, and Substance Abuse Services, 87
Divorcing parents, 67–68
Do Drugs, Do Time campaign, 5, 319–320
Do The Right Thing campaign, 274
DOJ. *See* U.S. Department of Justice
Domestic violence programs, 103–104, 105, 263, 265
Dorchester, Massachusetts, 129, 145
Dorchester Youth Collaborative, 120
Dorset, England, 187
Downtowns. *See* Business districts
Dress codes, 197
Dropout prevention programs, 56–57, 60–61, 69
DRP. *See* Development Research Programs

Drug abuse prevention. *See also*
  Alcohol abuse prevention
  arts-related prevention, 312
  athletics for prevention, 307
  ban drugs from public events, 306
  before- and after-school programs,
    287–288
  churches as resources, 296–297
  codes and ordinances, 298–299
  community mobilization, 293–294
  community partnerships, 21–22, 37,
    295–296
  culturally sensitive prevention, 309
  drug courts, 302–303
  drug-free school zones, 288
  drug-free social events for youth,
    314–315
  educate hotel and motel operators,
    318–319
  education programs, 59
  employee screening, 308
  gang activity prevention, 320–321
  hold drug users accountable, 319–320
  hot spot strategy, 294
  hotlines, 313
  incentives and rewards, 289
  increase police presence, 317–318
  involve local businesses, 297–298
  job training, 315–316
  leadership training, 323–324
  media campaigns, 292–293
  mentors as role models, 311–312
  overview, 283–284
  parental involvement, 100, 286–287
  pay phone restrictions, 214, 295
  peer influence, 290–291
  police cooperation with residents,
    150–151
  for pregnant women, 90–91
  prescription abuse by the elderly,
    321–322
  prevention and treatment services
    access, 289–290
  property owners' responsibility,
    299–300
  provide alternatives, 291–292
  public areas design, 159, 313–314
  public housing areas, 303–304
  school-based curricula, 284–285
  street-level drug purchases, 212
  tenant screening, 304–305
  truancy prevention, 285–286
  university drug policies, 310–311
  using assets seized in drug raids,
    300–301
  for women, 322–323

Drug Abuse Resistance Education,
    132, 285
Drug-addicted babies, 90
Drug and Gang Elimination Program,
    217
Drug courts, 302–303
Drug Education and Enforcement
    Account, 301
Drug Enforcement Agency, 5
Drug-Free Public Housing Task
    Force, 220
Drug-free zones, 72, 136, 198–199
Drug Paraphernalia Act, 301
DTRT. *See* Do The Right Thing
    campaign
Duke University, 87

Early Adolescent Helper Program, 109
Early pregnancy prevention programs,
    60–61
Earn-It restitution program, 98, 245
Eastside Substance Abuse Awareness
    Program, 294
Economic development
  Arson Early Warning and Prevention
    Program, 225–226
  business ethics promotion, 229–230
  Business Watch programs, 235–236
  community beautification, 228–229
  ensure affordable housing, 230–231
  housing development planning, 227
  incubate businesses, 224–225
  micro-credits to small-scale
    businesses, 232–233
  overview, 223–224
  targeted lending, 234–235
  using HUD resources, 231–232
Economic Development Initiative, 232
Edmonton, Alberta (Canada), 138
Educators for Social Responsibility, 258
Effective Strategies for School Security,
    204
Elder Ed, 321
Elderly. *See* Senior citizens
Electronic mail, 40
Electronic town meetings, 7
Elementary school children. *See* Youth
Elgin, Illinois, 160
Elmira, New York, 97
Emerge, 263, 264
Emergency rooms, 186–187, 273
Emotional problems, 86–87
Employee safety training, 168–169
Employment training, 54, 315–316
Empowerment programs, 211–212
Empowerment Zones, 232

English as a Second Language classes,
    129, 131
"Enough is Enough" campaign, 37
Enterprise Communities, 227, 232
Enterprise Zone, 227
Entertainment districts
  abandoned buildings demolition, 175
  operating hour curtailment, 173–174
  photograph illegal behavior, 176
  small claims courts, 177
  traffic control, 174
  trash patrol, 175–176
  uniforms for workers in public,
    177–178
  vehicle seizure, 178
  zoning laws, 173
Entrepreneur programs, 267
Escort services, 192
ESL. *See* English as a Second
    Language classes
Ethnic groups
  business crime prevention and, 170
  partnership with law enforcement,
    122, 143–145
  service partnerships, 332–333
Evansville, Indiana, 56, 291, 312
Even Start program, 106
Exact change policy, 188
*Exemplary Programs in Criminal
    Justice: Innovations at the Local
    Level*, 82
EZ. *See* Enterprise Zone

Facing Financial Fraud, 356
Fact Sheet, 82
Fairfax County, Virginia, 102, 144,
    164, 259
Fairfax Peer Survivors Group, 259
Faith institution-supported mentoring,
    31–32
Fall River, Massachusetts, 361
Family and Youth Services Bureau,
    65, 83
Family Assessment Services Team, 134
Family Augmenting Approach to
    Prevention, 85
Family Crisis Shelter, 266
Family management skills, 106
Family Planning Association, 275
Family Planning Perspectives, 100
Family Preservation Services, 107
Family-school partnerships, 91–92
Family Start, 106
Family therapy programs, 86–87, 261
Family Trouble Center, 133
Family Violence Prevention Fund, 268

Family Violence State-of-the-Art Court Programs, 263
Fargo, North Dakota, 10
Farm Bureau, 139
Farm Watch, 236
"Fathering encouragement," 68
Fax Alert program, 165
Fax information network, 165–166
FCCI. *See* Fulton-Carroll Center for Industry
FDC. *See* Flatbush Development Corporation
Fear of crime, 23, 171, 178
Federal Bureau of Investigation, 5, 90, 121
Federal Court Interpreters Act, 144
Federal Drug Enforcement Administration, 307
Federal Drug-Free School Zone Law, 288
Federation of Inner-City Community Organizations, 36
Female youth
  crime prevention programs, 60–61
  gang prevention programs, 82–84
  leadership development programs, 56
  pregnancy prevention programs, 61, 99–100
Fences, 218–219
Fetal alcohol syndrome, 323
FINCA. *See* Foundation for International Community Assistance
Fire codes, 30
Fire safety education, 357–358
Fires. *See* Arson
Flatbush Development Corporation, 226
Fleetwatch Program, 17, 157, 236
Florence V. Burden Foundation, 32
Florida, 191. *See also specific communities and programs*
Florida Division of Motor Vehicles, 359
Florida Environmental Institute, 243
Florida Independent Gasoline Retailers Association, 174
Focus on Children, 67
Foley (Minnesota) Public Schools, 195
For Which We Stand: A Statement of Purpose, Principles and Ethics, 230
Ford Foundation, 226
Fort Bragg, North Carolina, 87
Fort Lauderdale, Florida, 100
Fort Myers, Florida, 60
Fort Stockton, Texas, 77
Fort Wayne, Indiana, 108
Fort Worth, Texas, 29, 34, 78, 121, 131
Forum on the Prevention of Adolescent Female Gang Involvement, 83

Forums. *See* Town hall forums
Foster care, 107
Foundation for International Community Assistance, 233
Fourth Reich Skinheads, 336
Fredericksburg, Virginia, 176
Freeport, Illinois, 272, 332
Fresh Start Program, 105
Fresno, California, 241
Friendly Persuasion, 61
Friends of the Family, 106
Ft. Lauderdale, Florida, 185
Fulton-Carroll Center for Industry, 225
Fulton County, Georgia, 254
Fund for Modern Courts, 329
FYSB. *See* Family and Youth Services Bureau

Gainesville, Florida, 128, 257
Gaining Realization of Worth, 288
Galveston, Texas, 185
Gang Intelligence Files, 95
Gang prevention programs
  community intervention, 278–279
  drug activity prevention, 320–321
  for female youth, 82–84
  information networks, 241–242
  law enforcement intervention for youth at risk, 130–131
  multiagency interdiction teams, 242
  provide positive alternatives, 24–25
  school curricula, 85–86
  school dress code policies, 197
  use state laws, 269–270
Gang-Related Activity Anti-Suppression Program, 95, 269
Gang Resistance Education and Training program, 85–86, 131
Gang Resource Intervention Program, 78
Gang Violence Reduction Program, 278
Garden Grove Police Department, 331
Garland, Texas, 73
GED. *See* General Equivalency Diploma
Gender bias, 329
General Equivalency Diploma, 77
George Hyman Construction Company, 308
George Mason University, 257
Georgia Power Company, 169
Girl Scouts, 61, 136
Girls. *See* Female youth
Girls, Inc., 61
Glenarden, Maryland, 184
Gloucester Prevention Network, 296
Good Grief Program, 260

Governing magazine, 80, 81
Government agencies, 125. *See also specific agencies*
Graffiti
  community cleanups, 344–345
  discourage marketing, 341
  enforcement, 94–95
  offender paint-outs, 342
  removal by businesses, 160–161
  removal policy, 340
  resistant materials, 341–342
  restrict sales, 343
Graham, North Carolina, 245
Grameen Bank, 233
Grandfriends, 64
GRASP. *See* Gang-Related Activity Anti-Suppression Program
Grassroots community coalitions, 36, 117–118
GREAT. *See* Gang Resistance Education and Training program
Greater San Antonio Crime Prevention Commission, 35
Greater San Antonio (Texas) Crime Prevention Commission, 20
Green Circle Program, 330
Green Cities Initiative, 46
Greensboro, North Carolina, 318
Greenville, North Carolina, 122
Greenville, South Carolina, 70, 190, 312
Greenwich, Connecticut, 220
GRIT. *See* Gang Resource Intervention Program
Group Against Narcotics and Gangs, 266
Gun court, 262
Gun exchanges, 9
Gun-free School Zones Act, 201
Gun-free zones, 72, 200–201
Gun licensing regulations, 253–254, 279–280
Gun safety education, 270–271
GVRP. *See* Gang Violence Reduction Program

Habitual offenders, 244–245
Hampton, Virginia, 33, 291
Handguns, 25–26
Handicapped people, 124
"Happy hours," 305–306
Harlem, New York, 4, 313
Hartford, Connecticut, 22, 178, 249
Hartford Area Rallies Together, 297, 298
Harts, West Virginia, 92
Hate Crime Statistics Act, 333

Hate crimes. *See* Bias crimes
Hawaiian Department of the Attorney
General, 6
Hayward, California, 125, 140
HCSA. *See* Hate Crime Statistics Act
Head and Spinal Cord Injury Prevention
Program, 248
Head Start Program, 66, 93
Health awareness education, 59
Health care professionals, 239–240
Health codes, 30, 140
Health education programs, 99
Health services, 15, 92–93
Healthy Communities, Healthy Youth, 71
Healthy Neighborhoods Initiative, 33
Healthy Start, 91
Heartwood Ethics Curriculum
program, 71
HEAT. *See* Help Enforce Against Auto
Theft
Help Enforce Against Auto Theft, 360
Hennepin County, Minnesota, 26
Henry Ford Hospital, 186
Hertz, 191
*High Risk: Children Without a
Conscience*, 97
Higher Education Amendments of
1992, 256
Highway truck drivers, 192–193
Highways, 342–343
HIPPY. *See* Home Instruction Program
for Preschool Youngsters
Hispanic Aid, 309
Hispanic community, 28, 83
Hmong community, 170
Hoffman Estates Peer Jury program, 82
Hoka-Hai Enterprises, 267
Home Instruction Program for
Preschool Youngsters, 97
Home Loan Guarantee Program, 232
Home Security and Burglary Victims
Program, 18
Home security inspections, 345
Home security systems, 17–18,
348–349
Home Visitation Program, 97–98
Homeless youth. *See* Runaway and
homeless youth
Homeowner associations, 18
HomeQuest, 53
Honolulu, Hawaii, 28, 122
Horizons Anti-Violence Project, 337
Hospital-based programs, 247–248
Hospital security, 185–187
Hospital staff, 239–240, 273
Hospital Watch, 187
Hot spots, 294

Hotels
drug manufacture awareness
program, 318–319
security standards for, 168
HOTLINE Cares, 313
Hotlines. *See also specific hotlines*
crisis support, 111–112
drug abuse prevention, 313
for reporting crime, 201–202
House Next Door, 290
House of Umoja, 84–85, 321
Housewise/Streetwise, 70
Housing development planning, 227
Housing violations, 140
Houston, Texas, 70, 101, 120, 129, 169,
205, 315
Houston Teen Court, 82
"How to Evict Drug Dealers from
Public Housing," 209
Howard University, 94, 266, 310
HUD. *See* U.S. Department of Housing
and Urban Development
Hunt Alternatives Fund, 267

Ida B. Wells Public Housing
Development, 43
Idaho Youth Ranch, 107
Identification cards, 202–203
IFS. *See* Intensive Family Services
system
Illinois
Department of Children and Family
Services, 244
Illinois Criminal Justice Authority, 244
Illuminating Engineers Society,
172, 353
*Images and Reality: Juvenile Crime,
Youth Violence and Public
Policy*, 80
Immigrants and refugees
partnership with law enforcement,
122, 143–145
support needs of, 27–28
Travelers and Immigrants Aid, 59
Immigration Pro Bono Development
Project, 144
"Impact of Crime on Victims," 246
In-home counseling services, 97–98
In-school probation, 249–250
Incentive programs, 274
Indian Health Service, 323
Indiana, 293. *See also specific
communities and programs*
Department of Labor, 166
Indianapolis, Indiana, 41, 108

Indochinese Mutual Assistance
Association, 256
Infant mortality, 90
Information brochures, 140
Information fairs, 9–10
Initiative for Assisting Disadvantaged
Children Award, 77
Initiative groups, 211–212
Injury Prevention and Control Unit, 249
Innovative Neighborhood-Oriented
Policing Program, 146, 149, 151
INOP. *See* Innovative Neighborhood-
Oriented Policing Program
Institute for Social Analysis, 226
Institute for Social Research, 75
Insurance Information Institute, 163
Insurance loss control, 166–167
Insurance premium reductions, 163,
346–347
Intensive Family Services system, 107
Intensive intervention, 78–79, 107
Interagency Council for Immigrant
Services, 122
Intercultural Development Research
Association, 69
Intercultural Mutual Assistance
Association, 135
Intergenerational programs, 63–64
International Association of Chiefs of
Police, 39
Interpreters, 144
Intervention, 78–79, 107
Irdell County, North Carolina, 351
ISA. *See* Institute for Social Analysis

Jackson, Mississippi, 217
Jacksonville, Florida, 131
Jane Boyd Harambee House, 103
Jefferson County, Kentucky, 303
JIPS. *See* Juvenile Intensive Probation
Supervision
Job banks, 28–29
Job skills training, 54, 59, 267–268,
315–316
Joint Parks Department and Police
Guild Program, 142
*Journal of Emotional and Behavioral
Problems*, 88
JUDGE. *See* Jurisdictions Unified for
Drug Gang Enforcement
Judge Baker Children's Center, 93
Judicial system. *See* Criminal justice
system
Junior Achievement programs, 89–90
Junior Cadet program, 90
Junior Police Academy, 131

Jurisdictions Unified for Drug Gang Enforcement, 321
Just for Girls, 61
Just Solutions, 127
Justice Achievement Award, 126
Juvenile and family courts, 88
Juvenile Conference Committee, 98
Juvenile delinquency. *See also* Gang prevention programs
    community programs, 38
    prevention programs for female youth, 60–61
    risk factors, 84
    therapy programs, 261
"The Juvenile Diversion Program: Learning About Differences," 336
Juvenile Firestarters Information Program, 361
Juvenile Intensive Probation Supervision, 81
Juvenile Justice: Improving the Quality of Care, 79
Juvenile Justice Clearinghouse, 269
Juvenile Upgrading Motivating Program, 251
Juvenile Work Restitution Program, 245
Juveniles. *See* Youth

Kaiser Permanente, 275
Kansas City, Kansas, 279
Kay-Bee, 268
Keene, New Hampshire, 98, 245
Kentucky Highlands Investment Corporation, 227
Kentucky Teen Leadership Conference, 74
KIDCO program, 271
Kids Health Fairs, 91
Kids House program, 92, 271–272
King County, Washington, 104, 105
Kiosks, 213
Knoxville, Tennessee, 162, 216, 220

La Familia agency, 28, 92
Lafayette, California, 323
Lafayette County, Mississippi, 195
Lakewood, Colorado, 141
Landlords, 177
Lansing, Michigan, 21, 135, 147–148
Lansing Neighborhood Network Center, 15–16
Las Vegas, Nevada, 57
Latchkey children, 271–272, 287–288
Late Night Retail Workers Crime Protection, 166

Latin Women in Action, 104
Law enforcement. *See also* Court systems
    analyze crime data from community, 118–119
    antigang programs for youth, 130–131
    bicycle patrols, 149–150
    citizen patrol, 121
    city agencies partnership, 133
    code enforcement, 139–140
    community meetings, 137
    community mobilization, 116–117
    community ombudsman, 130
    community policing planning, 146–147
    community support for, 36–37
    control drug trafficking, 150–151
    cooperation with businesses, 137–138
    cooperation with grassroots organizations, 117–118
    crime prevention training for department staff, 132
    educate residents about operations, 140–141
    identify community needs, 147–148
    increase police presence, 317–318
    involvement in schools, 128–129
    mobile service vehicles, 148–149
    multiagency support, 134, 141–142
    operations education, 140–141
    outreach to diverse communities, 143–144
    overview of link to community, 115–116
    partnership with public housing residents, 121–122
    programs for diverse groups of youth, 145
    quality-of-life improvements, 142–143
    rapid response to reported incidents, 333–334
    rural community partnerships, 138–139
    Safe Havens, 136
    service partnerships, 332–333
    sponsor community events, 135
    storefront police stations, 129
    support of vulnerable members of the community, 124
    training in prevention for other local agencies, 125
    translators and interpreters, 144
    youth interaction, 120, 123
Law Enforcement Gang Information Network, 241

Law-related education, 110–111
Law-Related Education Program for Adjudicated Youth, 111
Leadership Institute, 33
Leadership training, 55–56, 323–324, 331–332
Learn Not to Burn program, 358
Learning academies, 77
Learning Progressive Center, 77
Learning Retreats, 64
Learning Systems Group, 312
Legacy Project, 275
Legal services, 4
Lehigh County, Pennsylvania, 250
Let's Intervene for Education, 310
License stickers, 355–356
LIFE. *See* Let's Intervene for Education
Life skills training, 102–103
LIFT. *See* Neighborhood Leveraged Investments for Tomorrow program
Lighting
    commercial, 352–353
    public housing areas, 220–221
    residential, 352
    retail districts, 171–172
Lighting Handbook, 172, 353
Lights out policy, 203–204
Lilly Endowment, 56
LIMO. *See* Local Intercampus Mobile Operation program
Lincoln, Nebraska, 144, 333
Linking Lifetimes, 64
Literacy, 106
Litter, 342–343
Little Rock, Arkansas, 219
Live-in police officers, 160
Local government agencies, 35–36, 38, 75–76
Local Intercampus Mobile Operation program, 192
Local media, 30–31
Long Beach, California, 14, 143, 321
Los Angeles, California, 25, 46, 73, 123, 184, 191, 255, 342
Louisville, Kentucky, 122
Lowell, Massachusetts, 143
LPC. *See* Learning Progressive Center

Macon, Georgia, 56, 69
MAD DADS. *See* Men Against Destruction: Defending Against Drugs and Social Disorder
MADD. *See* Mothers Against Drunk Driving

Madison, Wisconsin, 307
Mail order shopping, 193
Making Sense of Sex, 275
Male batterers, 264
Mall watch, 181
Malls
　automated teller machine safety, 182
　bicycle patrol, 180
　mall watch, 181
　police substations, 181–182
　security staff, 179
　valet parking, 179–180
Manchester, New Hampshire, 221
Marathon County, Wisconsin, 17
Maricopa County, Arizona, 319–320
Marquette Bank, 124
Marquette University, 192
Martin Luther King Community
　Services, 332
Maryland, 106, 107, 137. *See also*
　specific communities and programs
Massachusetts, 79–80. *See also specific*
　communities and programs
Massachusetts Committee on Criminal
　Justice, 145
Mat-Su Alternative School, 77
Maternal and Child Health Bureau,
　90–91
Matteson, Illinois, 204–205
Mayors United on Safety, Crime, and
　Law Enforcement, 35
MBL. *See* Midnight basketball league
McGruff the Crime Dog, 5, 70, 268,
　285, 293, 351
Meade County, South Dakota, 111
Media resources
　community outreach, 8–9
　crime prevention programs, 5–6
　develop crime prevention coalitions,
　　2–3, 30–31
　drug abuse prevention, 292–293
　promote nonviolent images of youth,
　　254–255
　tolerance campaigns, 334–335
Mediation services, 336–337
Memphis, Tennessee, 31, 36, 133, 247
Memphis Family Trouble Center, 264
Men Against Destruction: Defending
　Against Drugs and Social
　Disorder, 34, 118
Men Against Rape project, 276
Mental Health Association, 253
Mental health screening, 93
Mentally ill offenders, 26–27
Mentoring programs
　for at-risk youth, 101–102
　career mentors, 89–90

drug abuse prevention, 311–312
faith institution-supported, 31–32
for female youth, 61
peer-to-peer, 69
Mentors in Violence Prevention
　project, 276
Mercer, Pennsylvania, 87
Messina, New York, 306
Methuen, Massachusetts, 176
Metro Awareness Program, 344
Miami, Florida, 16, 200, 274, 300
Michigan, 127. *See also specific*
　communities and programs
Michigan State Diversion Project, 251
Micro-credits, 232–233
Middleburg, Vermont, 292
Midnight basketball league, 184
Midtown Community Court, 126
Military personnel, 87
Military-style training, 246–247
Milwaukee, Wisconsin, 27, 28, 261
Mini-stations, 220
Ministorage theft, 10
Minneapolis, Minnesota, 64, 161, 340
Minneapolis Way to Grow, 76
Minneapolis Youth Organization, 76
Minnesota, 20, 44, 101. *See also specific*
　communities and programs
Minnesota Coalition Against Domestic
　Violence, 105
Minnesota Coalition for Battered
　Women, 265
Mississippi State University, 208
Missouri, 79–80. *See also specific*
　communities and programs
Mobile, Alabama, 209, 216, 266
Mobile police units, 7–8
Mobile service vehicles, 148–149
Model Assets Seizure and Forfeiture
　law, 300
Model Buildings program, 304
Moderately priced dwelling units,
　230–231
Monaca, Pennsylvania, 286
Monitoring programs, 250–251
Monroe County, Kentucky, 205
Monroe Foundation, 124
Montgomery, Alabama, 196, 207
Montgomery County, Maryland,
　230–231, 253, 298, 302, 334
Monticello, Arizona, 97
Moreno Valley (California) Youth
　Court, 82
Motels
　drug manufacture awareness
　　program, 318–319
　security standards for, 168

Mothers Against Drunk Driving,
　118, 292
Motorola, Inc., 230
Movies. *See* Media resources
Movimento Ascendencia program,
　83–84
Moving Up, 54
MPDUs. *See* Moderately priced
　dwelling units
Mujeres Latinas en Acción, 104
Multiagency support teams, 134,
　141–142
Multicultural programs, 145
Multilingual services, 144, 330–331
Multnomah County (Oregon)
　Community and Court Services
　Agency, 78
"Murals Reflecting Prevention," 312
MUSCLE. *See* Mayors United on
　Safety, Crime, and Law
　Enforcement
Music recording industry. *See* Media
　resources
Mutual Assistance Associations, 144
MVP. *See* Mentors in Violence
　Prevention project
MVP Playbook, 276

Narcotics Enforcement Area, 288
National Arbor Day Foundation, 46
National Association for Court
　Management, 126
National Association of Convenience
　Stores, 169
National Association of Juvenile and
　Family Court Judges, 53
National Association of
　Neighborhoods, 33
National Association of Town Watch,
　45, 348, 352
National Burglar and Fire Alarm
　Association, 349
National Business Incubation
　Association, 225
National Campaign to Reduce Youth
　Violence, 255
National Center for Community
　Policing, 15
National Center for Juvenile Justice, 98
National Center for Service Learning in
　Adolescence, 109
National Center for State Courts, 329
National Citizens' Crime Prevention
　Campaign, 5, 268
National Community Services Trust
　Act, 108

National Conference on Student Community Services, 66

National Council of Juvenile and Family Court Judges, 81, 263

National Council on Alcoholism, 322

National Council on Crime and Delinquency, 79, 80

National Court-Appointed Special Advocate Association, 88

National Crime Prevention Council, 9, 37, 55–56, 70, 111

National Dropout Prevention Center, 56, 95

National Education Association, 205

National Education Goals 2000, 92

National Fire Protection Association, 358

National Foundation for the Improvement of Education, 56

National Graffiti Information Network, 341

National Highway Traffic Safety Administration, 315, 317

National Institute of Citizen Education and the Law, 111

National Institute of Justice, 85, 98, 246–247

National Insurance Crime Bureau, 360

National Leadership Summit, 66

National League of Cities, 82, 103–104

National Night Out, 45, 348

National Organization for Victim Assistance, 43

National Organization of Student Assistance Programs and Professionals, 77

National Park Service, 178

National Parks and Recreation Association, 60

National Rifle Association, 262

National School Boards Association, 195, 196

National School Safety Center, 165, 196, 201, 202, 252

National Sheriff's Association, 39

National Tenant Network, 216, 304

National Youth Employment Coalition, 53–54

National Youth Gang Center, 269

Nationwide Insurance Company, 315

Natural Helpers Program, 291

NAV. *See* Neighbors Against Violence

NBIA. *See* National Business Incubation Association

NCCD. *See* National Council on Crime and Delinquency

NCCPC. *See* National Citizens' Crime Prevention Campaign

NCPC. *See* National Crime Prevention Council

NCPN. *See* Non-Custodial Parents of Nebraska

NDS. *See* Neighborhood Defender Service

Nebraska Office of Highway Safety, 310

Neglected children. *See* Child abuse

Neighbor Woods, 46

Neighborhood Anticrime Center, 33

Neighborhood associations, 32–33

Neighborhood-based information centers, 7

Neighborhood-based service centers, 15–16

Neighborhood Block Watch Fund, 45

Neighborhood Business Banking Program, 233

Neighborhood Cleanup Program, 14

Neighborhood Commercial Crime Prevention Program, 353

Neighborhood Defender Service, 4

Neighborhood Development Company, 33

Neighborhood Enhancement Operation Network, 16

Neighborhood Environmental Assessment Team, 134

Neighborhood festivals, 48, 135

Neighborhood Grant Partnership Program, 36

Neighborhood House of North Richmond, California, 69

Neighborhood improvement, 14, 36, 143

Neighborhood Initiative, 46

Neighborhood Leadership Institute, 158–159

Neighborhood Learning Centers, 76

Neighborhood Leveraged Investments for Tomorrow program, 232

Neighborhood Network Center, 15, 135, 147–148

Neighborhood Partnership Department, 36

Neighborhood Partnership Program, 14–15

Neighborhood Resource Centers, 8

Neighborhood Resource Team, 134

Neighborhood Service Team, 73

Neighborhood Stabilization program, 159, 314

Neighborhood Task Force, 35

Neighborhood Watch, 7, 18, 23, 45, 117, 124, 132, 147, 158, 347, 348

Neighborhood Watch Advisory Board, 45

Neighborhoods in Action, 101, 287

Neighbors Against Violence, 278

NEON. *See* Neighborhood Enhancement Operation Network

Network Against Teenage Violence, 266

Nevada, 107. *See also specific communities and programs*

New Community Corporation, 227

New Haven, Connecticut, 73, 94, 123, 132, 157, 216, 218, 228, 255, 260, 277

New Jersey Supreme Court Task Force, 144

New Mexico Center for Dispute Resolution, 258

New Orleans, Louisiana, 63, 91

New Students' program, 291

New York, New York, 8, 33, 54, 89, 109, 110, 142–143, 158, 163, 187, 215, 291

New York City Clean Car Program, 340

New York City Housing Authority, 209, 211

New York City Taxi and Limousine Commission, 191

New York Transit Authority, 189

Newark, New Jersey, 227

Newport News, Virginia, 24, 37, 159, 175, 351

Newport News Coalition, 117

Newport News Redevelopment and Housing Authority, 304

Newsletters, 140–141

Newspapers. *See* Media resources

NFIE. *See* National Foundation for the Improvement of Education

Niagara County Hotline and Drug Abuse Program, 112

NICB. *See* National Insurance Crime Bureau

Night Out Against Crime, 352

NIJ. *See* National Institute of Justice

Noble Neighbors group, 184

Noise and nuisance abatement codes, 30

Non-Custodial Parents of Nebraska, 68

Non-emergency police services, 130

Nonviolent entertainment, 3

Nonviolent offenders, 79–80, 81, 249–250

Norfolk, Virginia, 26, 134, 175

North Carolina Mental Health Service Program for Youth, 87

North Flatbush, New York, 225–226

North Shield, England, 190
Northeastern University, 276
Northside, Texas, 344
Northwest Bronx, New York, 22
Northwest Bronx Community Clergy
    Coalition, 38
Northwest Victims Services, 259
NOVA. *See* National Organization for
    Victim Assistance
NRA. *See* National Rifle Association
NSBA. *See* National School Boards
    Association
NSSC. *See* National School Safety
    Center
NTN. *See* National Tenant Network
Nuisance abatement, 30, 300
Nuisance Bar program, 302
NVS. *See* Northwest Victims Services
NWBCCC. *See* Northwest Bronx
    Community Clergy Coalition

Oakland, California, 22, 25, 43, 92, 94,
    156, 212, 256, 271–272, 299, 346
Oakland Community Organization,
    140, 297
Oakland Crack Task Force, 117
Ocala, Florida, 318
Occupational Safety and Health
    Act, 166
Office of Human Relations
    Commission, 334
Office of Juvenile Justice and
    Delinquency Prevention, 24–25,
    82, 84, 87, 88, 98, 244, 269
Office of Substance Abuse and
    Prevention, 285
OFY. *See* Opportunities for Youth
    Program
Ohio State University, 128
OJJDP. *See* Office of Juvenile Justice and
    Delinquency Prevention
Oklahoma City, Oklahoma, 63, 96, 203
Older Resident Program, 23
Omaha, Nebraska, 34, 90, 103, 118
Ombudsmen, 130
Omnibus Budget Reconciliation
    Act, 227
On-line databases, 7–8
One to One Partnerships, 102, 316
Oneida County, New York, 205
Open space, 46
Operation Clean Sweep, 299, 303
Operation Commitment, 36
Operation Crime Watch, 144
Operation Drive Out Crime, 31
Operation Higher Ground, 290
Operation I.D., 241

Operation Identification, 16, 347
Operation Interlock/Interwatch, 351
Operation NEON, 16
Operation Safe Street, 18
Opportunities Fair, 23
Opportunities for Youth Program, 19
Options for Recovery Program, 322
Orange County, California, 336, 346
Orange County, Florida, 150
Ordinances, 29–30, 155
OSAP. *See* Office of Substance Abuse
    and Prevention
OTO. *See* One to One Partnerships
Out-of-home placement, 107
Outdoor challenge education, 52–53
Outreach Center, 32
Outreach programs, 140
Oxford, Mississippi, 194, 204
Oxnard, California, 6, 40, 244

PACE. *See* Police Assisted Community
    Enforcement program
PAL. *See* Police Activities League
Palm Beach, Florida, 359
PAN. *See* Parent Awareness Network
Panhandling, 189
Parent Awareness Network, 101, 287
Parent education and support, 106
Parent Teacher Associations, 57, 118
Parents
    family-school partnerships, 91–92
    held accountable for children's
        behavior, 272–273
    involvement in drug abuse
        prevention, 100–101, 286–287
Parents Anonymous, 112
Parents as Educational Partners
    Program, 92
Parents as Teachers program, 97
Parents' Communication Network,
    101, 287
Park Watch, 183
Parking structures, 162–163
Parks. *See also* Public areas
    extended park operating hours,
        183–184
    Park Watch program, 183
    restrict alcohol use, 185
    safety of, 46
    take back the parks campaign, 184
Partners Against Violence Network, 7
Pasadena, California, 71, 254
PAT. *See* Parents as Teachers program
Paths to Prevention program, 21
PATHWAYS Initiative, 316
PAVNET. *See* Partners Against Violence
    Network

Pay-before-you-pump gas policy, 355
Pay phone restrictions, 214, 295
Peace Posse, 69
Peer group pressure, 40–41
Peer juries, 81
Peer Leader Program, 323–324
Peer Partner program, 291
Peer Power, 100
Peer-to-peer instruction, 68–69
Pennsylvania Commission on Crime and
    Delinquency, 250
Pennsylvania Liquor Control Board, 302
Pennsylvania State Police, 193
Performance programs, 275
Performing arts programs, 40–41,
    58–59
Philadelphia, Pennsylvania, 24, 64, 84,
    104, 184, 189, 259, 303, 353
Phoenix, Arizona, 5, 18, 48, 63, 81,
    86, 131, 184, 207, 221, 288
Phoenix Project, 159, 314
Photocard, 356
Photograph illegal behavior, 176
Pinellas County (Florida) Community
    Partnership Program, 37
Pittsburgh, Pennsylvania, 71, 290
Pittsburgh Public Housing Authority, 90
Placement services, 54
Play therapy, 275
Playgrounds, 46
PLCB. *See* Pennsylvania Liquor Control
    Board
PLP. *See* Peer Leader Program
PNRCs. *See* Police Neighborhood
    Resource Centers
Points of Light Foundation, 102
Police. *See* Law enforcement
Police Activities League, 120
Police Assisted Community
    Enforcement program, 134
Police Athletic League, 120, 307
Police Beat Health program, 156
Police-Community Partnership
    Program, 133, 136
Police in residence program, 221
Police Neighborhood Resource
    Centers, 318
Police Officer Placement Solution
    program, 221
Police Resource Officers, 132
Police substations, 129, 181–182
Ponce, Puerto Rico, 38
Pontiac, Michigan, 321
Poole General Hospital, 187
Port of Entry program, 309
Portage County (Ohio) Municipal
    Court, 127
Portland, Maine, 323–324

Portland, Oregon, 28, 40, 98, 120, 141, 143, 170, 176, 178, 319, 346
Positive Action through Holistic Education Project, 277
Postpone Sexual Involvement, 99–100
Pregnancy prevention programs, 61, 99–100
Pregnant Teens/Teen Parent program, 323
Prejudice. *See* Bias crimes
Prenatal care, 90–91
President's Community Development Banking and Financial Institutions Bill, 232
Preventing Adolescent Pregnancy program, 61
The Prevention of Youth Violence: A Framework for Community Action, 103
Prince Georges County, Maryland, 173, 199–200, 204
Prince William County, Virginia, 182
Private Industry Council of Atlanta, 298
Problem solving education, 19–20
Progress program, 106
Project After Prom, 315
Project First-Class Male, 100
Project Graduation, 315
Project Image, 103
Project Info, 101, 287
Project Link, 91
Project Payback, 98
Project Pride vandalism curriculum, 344
Project Quiet Street, 349
Project Yes! Yes to Education and Skills, 86
Prom Promise campaign, 315
Property crimes. *See also* Graffiti
Adopt-A-Highway programs, 342–343
anti-theft decals for automobiles, 359–360
business address numbers, 354
Business Watch, 353
cellular telephone patrols, 350–351
commercial lighting, 352–353
community cleanups, 344–345
credit card protection, 356–357
direct deposit, 354–355
fire safety education, 357–358
home security alarms, 348–349
home security inspections, 345
increased visibility and surveillance, 350
insurance premium reductions, 346–347

juvenile arsonist intervention, 360–361
Neighborhood Watch, 348
Operation Identification, 347
overview, 339–340
pay-before-you-pump gas policy, 355
residential building codes, 346
residential lighting, 352
security sensor tags, 357
street access restrictions, 349
theft prevention devices for automobiles, 358–359
two-way radio patrols, 350–351
vandalism prevention curriculum, 344
vehicle inspection stickers, 355–356
voice mail information, 351
Prostitution, 118
Providence, Rhode Island, 262
Proyecto Pastoral, 255
PSA. *See* Public service advertising
Psychology Today, 67
PTAs. *See* Parent Teacher Associations
PTP. *See* Paths to Prevention program
Public areas
business districts, 164–168
city-wide crime problems, 155–163
entertainment districts, 173–178
hospitals, 185–187
malls, 179–182
overview of crime problems, 153–154
parks, 183–185
public housing, 209–210
public transportation, 188–193
retail businesses, 168–172
safe design of, 313–314
schools, 194–208
Public buses, 188, 190
Public education
advocacy for nonviolent entertainment, 3
community special events and information fairs, 9–10
Crime Prevention Information Center, 7–8
crime prevention programs on local cable television, 5–6
expand access to public officials, 6–7
involve media representatives in coalition work, 2–3
local public service advertising, 5
outreach through community media, 8–9
purpose of, 1
speaker's bureaus, 10–11
steering committee, 2
targeted legal services and education, 4

Public health programs, 248–249
Public Health Service, 90–91
Public housing
access control, 213–214
cleanup projects, 217–218
closed circuit television, 210–211
crime prevention and awareness training, 216–217
drug abuse prevention, 303–304
enforcement of trespass law, 210
enhanced outdoor lighting, 220–221
eviction, 209
fencing, 218–219
partnership with law enforcement, 121–122
pay phone restrictions, 214, 295
police-in-residence program, 221
resident initiative groups, 211–212
security headquarters location, 219–220
tenant screening, 215–216
undercover street-level drug purchases, 212
voluntary resident patrols, 214–215
youth leadership development, 56
Public Housing Authority, 22
Public Housing Crime Interdiction Through Community Policing Program, 209, 216
Public information, 140
Public Information Task Force, 35
Public officials, 6–7
Public/Private Ventures, 54
Public service advertising, 5
Public transportation
cameras on buses, 190
CPTED for subways, 188–189
escort services, 192
exact change policy, 188
highway watch, 191–192
prohibit panhandling in subways, 189
rental vehicle identification, 190–191
taxi security screens, 191
use technology to shop or work, 193
Pueblo (Colorado) Family and Youth Services Bureau, 83

QOP. *See* Quantum Opportunities Program
Quality-of-life improvements, 142–143
Quantum Opportunities Program, 54
Quest K–12 drug prevention program, 285
Quick Uniform Attack on Drugs, 298–299
Quincy, Massachusetts, 98, 104, 263

Racism. *See* Bias crimes
Radio. *See* Media resources
Radio Shack, 268
Rand Corporation, 53
Rape prevention education, 265–266, 276
Real Alternatives Program, 69
Real Alternatives to Violence for Every Student, 275
Rebound Plus Program, 345
Recidivism rates, 53
Recognition of Program Merit, 53
Recreation centers, 59–60
Recreational events. *See* Community events
Redevelopment, 47–48
Redevelopment and Housing Authority, 351
"Reducing School Violence: Hot Topics and Usable Research," 202
Refugee Substance Abuse Prevention Project, 59
Refugees. *See* Immigrants and refugees
Regulating Land Use: The Law of Zoning, 173
Rehabilitation Institute of Chicago, 248
Rehabilitation services, 243–244
Reintegration, 80–81
Religious organizations, 103, 296–297
Remote Office, 193
Rental vehicles, 190–191
Research and Training Associates, 97
Resident Officer Program, 221
Resident patrols, 214–215
Residential treatment, 79–80
Residents in Force for Freedom, 212
Resolving Conflict Creatively Program, 258
Resource centers, 7–8, 109–110
Resource list, 363–366
Resource mothers, 91
Restitution to victims, 98–99, 245–246
Retail businesses. *See also* Businesses
    business address numbers displayed, 172
    cardboard police officers, 169
    control cruising, 170–171
    culturally sensitive business crime prevention, 170
    employee safety training, 168–169
    enhanced lighting, 171–172
Retired Senior Volunteer Project, 18, 64
Retirees. *See* Senior citizens
Revere, Massachusetts, 144
Revitalization projects, 47–48
Richmond, Maine, 139

Richmond, Virginia, 176, 180
Richmond Youth Against Violence, 239
RIFF. *See* Residents in Force for Freedom
Ringling School of Art and Design, 156
Rites of passage training, 102–103
Road Watch, 193
Roads, 342–343
Robbery prevention, 16
Robert Taylor Homes, 97
Robert Wood Johnson Foundation, 87
Rochester, Minnesota, 135
Rocky Mountain Business Watch, 165
Role models
    college students, 66
    drug abuse prevention, 311–312
Rotary International, 229
Rouse Company, 179, 180
RSVP. *See* Retired Senior Volunteer Project
Runaway and homeless youth, 64–65
Rural communities, 138–139

Sacramento, California, 28, 92
SADD. *See* Students Against Drunk Driving
Safe By Design, 350
Safe City Initiative, 33
"Safe Corridors," 22
Safe Haven programs, 72–73, 136, 288
Safe Houses, 288
Safe Neighborhood Parks Act, 46
SAFE STREETS, 217
SAFE teams, 156
Safer Cities, 158
Safestreet Program, 349
Safety and security assessments, 164–165
Safety codes, 30
SAGE. *See* Support Adolescents with Guidance and Employment
Saginaw, Michigan, 215
Salem, Oregon, 157
Salt Lake City, Utah, 125, 130, 309
San Antonio, Texas, 2, 56, 60, 62, 90, 96, 106, 150, 241, 272
San Bernardino, California, 131
San Clemente, California, 183
San Diego, California, 41, 53, 201, 204, 214, 256, 322
San Francisco, California, 46, 69, 76, 177, 240, 309, 337
San Jose, California, 42, 63, 96, 128
San Juan Capistrano, California, 197
San Leandro, California, 75
Sangamon County, Illinois, 45

Santa Ana, California, 119, 128, 138
Santa Fe Mountain Center, 53
Sarasota, Florida, 156
Sasha Bruce Youthwork, 65
Savannah, Georgia, 57, 148, 160
Savannah High School Health Center, 93
Savannah Silent Witness program, 42
Save Our Sons And Daughters, 20
Schaumburg, Illinois, 181
"School Crisis Prevention and Response," 202
School dropout, 56–57
School Police Services, 201
School resource officers, 128, 207
School Safety Check Book, 196
School-to-Work programs, 53–55
School Violence: A Survival Guide for School Staff, 205
"School Violence: Preparing In-Service Teachers," 208
Schools
    closed circuit television surveillance, 195–196
    code of conduct, 196
    as community resource centers, 109–110
    control access to school buildings, 194
    crime reporting hotline, 201–202
    crisis planning, 206–207
    diversity and tolerance education, 329–330
    dress code, 197
    drug abuse prevention curricula, 284–285
    drug-free zones, 198–199, 288
    gun-free zones, 200–201
    ID cards, 202–203
    law enforcement involvement, 128–129
    prevent bullying, 251–252
    reduced nighttime lighting of buildings, 203–204
    school resource officers, 207
    staff training, 208
    student crime watch, 199–200
    telephones in classrooms, 205
    vandalism prevention curriculum, 344
    violence prevention, 238–239, 277
    volunteer school security patrols, 204–205
Scott Newman Center, 101, 287
SDO. *See* Station Duty Officer
Search Institute, 71
Seattle, Washington, 28, 45, 47, 88, 142, 151, 198, 202, 239, 353

Seattle Team for Youth, 83

Seattle Violence Prevention Project, 112

Second Chances, 67

Second Step, 239

Security Applications in Industry and Institutions, 195

Security Awareness for Employees, 169

Security Awareness Program, 169

Security headquarters, 219–220

Security screens, 191

Security sensor tags, 357

Security staff, 179

Security systems, 17–18

Self-esteem, 68

Self-Esteem Through Performing Arts: A Prevention Strategy for African-American Youth, 58

Self-Help for African People through Education, 101, 287

Self-protection, 16, 69–70

Senior citizens
 crime prevention services, 22–23
 home security, 18
 law enforcement support, 124
 prescription abuse, 321–322
 as role models for youth, 63–64
 "Safe Corridors," 22
 as volunteers, 39

Senior Citizens Substance Abuse Prevention project, 321

Senior Response Unit, 23

Sensormatic, 357

Serious Habitual Offender Comprehensive Action Program, 244–245

Service centers, 15–16

Service Station Dealers of Florida, 174

Service support teams, 141–142

Services directories, 47

Services to Assist Youth Team program, 57

SET. *See* Special Emphasis (Police) Teams

Set Straight on Bullies, 252

Seven-Eleven stores, 167–168

Sex education programs, 99

Sexual abuse, 69–70. *See also* Child abuse; Rape prevention education

Sexual Assault Services Coordinator, 257

SHAPE. *See* Self-Help for African People through Education

Shell Oil Corporation, 359

Sheriff's Pass Program, 289

Shining Star program, 57, 59

SHOCAP. *See* Serious Habitual Offender Comprehensive Action Program

Showcase Neighborhood Program, 148

Silver Spring Neighborhood Center, 261

Silverton, Oregon, 272

Single-parent households, 63

Sisters in Spirit, 103

Skills for Violence-Free Relationships, 265

Small Business Administration, 232

Small claims courts, 30, 177

SMART Moves, 72–73

Smith County, Texas, 39

Social activities. *See* Community events

Social development, 84

Social intervention, 25

Social services agencies, 15, 88

SOSAD. *See* Save Our Sons And Daughters

South Austin Coalition and Community Council, 295

South Berkeley, California, 177

South Central Organizing Council of Los Angeles, 297

South Seattle (Washington) Crime Prevention Council, 151

South Shore Bank, 235

Southeast Regional Center for Drug-Free Schools and Communities, 57, 59

Southeastern Michigan Spinal Cord Injury Center, 247

Southeastern Regional Vision for Education, 202

Southern Bell Corporation, 90

Southland Corporation, 155, 168

Southwest Key Day Treatment Program, 80

Spartanburg County, South Carolina, 271

Speaker's bureaus, 10–11

Special Emphasis (Police) Teams, 212

Special populations, 124

Specialized Treatment Services, 87

Specified Crime Property Ordinance, 30

Springfield, Illinois, 157

St. Louis, Missouri, 18, 23, 97, 349

St. Mary's County, Maryland, 315

St. Paul, Minnesota, 33, 178

St. Petersburg, Florida, 14–15, 36, 48, 57, 92, 135, 340

St. Rita's Asian Center, 333

Stampede Technologies, 193

STAR. *See* Stop, Think, Act, and Review Program; Straight Talk About Risks Project

STARS. *See* Success Through Academic and Recreational Support

State Justice Institute, 4

Station Duty Officer, 130

Status offenses, 95

STAY. *See* Services to Assist Youth Team program

Staying Safe at School, 197

Stockton, California, 321

Stop, Think, Act, and Review Program, 274

Stop Firearm Injury program, 240

Storefront police stations, 7, 129

Straight Talk About Risks Project, 250, 270

Stranger Danger Program, 70, 124

Strategy on Elementary School Theater for Violence Prevention, 41

Street access restrictions. *See* Access control

Street Gangs: Current Knowledge and Strategies, 85

Strengthening Programs For Youth, 54

Strictly Business, 316

Strong Families, Strong Schools: Building Community Partnerships for Learning, 92, 109

Student Assistance Program Teams, 250

Student code of conduct, 196

Student crime watch, 199–200

Student Security Advisory Council, 200

Students Against Drunk Driving, 292

Students Taking a Right Stand program, 69

The Study Circle Handbook: A Manual for Study Circle Discussion Leaders, Organizers, and Participants, 241

Study Circles Resource Center, 241

Substance abuse. *See* Alcohol abuse prevention; Drug abuse prevention

Substance Abuse Initiative, 296

Substations. *See* Police substations

Subways
 CPTED for, 188–189
 graffiti removal policy, 340
 prohibit panhandling, 189

Success Through Academic and Recreational Support, 60

Suicide prevention, 70

Summer of Safety, 18

Summer Youth Employment and Training program, 298

Sunrise, Florida, 182

Super 8 Motel, 168

Supervised Parent Visitation Center, 67–68

Supplemental parents, 85
Support Adolescents with Guidance and Employment, 268
Support programs
for domestic violence victims, 103–104
for juvenile offenders, 250–251
multiagency teams, 134
for parents, 106
for young parents, 97
for youth, 141–142
Suppression activities, 25
Surrogate families, 84–85
Surveys, 74–75, 126, 146
Sydney, Australia, 275

TABS. *See* Truant and Burglary Suppression program
Tackling Drug Problems in Public Housing, 209
Tacoma, Washington, 39, 197, 202, 212, 213, 217, 218, 221
"Take a Bite Out of Crime" message, 5
Tampa, Florida, 218, 243, 298–299
TARAD. *See* Teens As Resources Against Drugs
Targeted lending, 234–235
Tarrant County (Texas) Advocate Program, 78
Taxi security screens, 191
TCAP. *See* Tarrant County (Texas) Advocate Program; Teenage Community Alternative Program
TCC. *See* Teens, Crime, and the Community program
Teacher's Education Idea Guide, 44
Technical Resource Center and Leadership Training Institute, 33
Techniques of Effective Alcohol Management program, 317
Technology, 40
Teen Awareness Group, 93
Teen Clinic, 93
Teen Connection Teen Theater, A Practical Guide, 41
Teen Connections, 61
Teen Council, 291
Teen courts, 81–82
Teen pregnancy prevention, 99–100
"Teen Summit," 255
Teen survival booklets, 249
Teenage Community Alternative Program, 82
Teenagers. *See* Youth
Teens, Crime, and the Community program, 111

Teens As Resources Against Drugs, 312
Teens on Target program, 25, 256
Tele-Court, 127
Telecommuting, 193
Telefact line, 351
Teleshopping, 193
Television. *See* Media resources
Tempe, Arizona, 132, 141, 151
Temple University, 64
Tenant screening, 215–216, 304–305
Texas, 80, 163, 347. *See also specific communities and programs*
Texas Attorney General, 59
Texas Cities Action Plan, 7, 8
Theater programs, 41
Therapy programs, 86–87
Think First program, 248
Thomas Jefferson Research Center, 71
THRIVE. *See* Truancy Habits Reduced, Increasing Valuable Education program
TIA. *See* Travelers and Immigrants Aid
Tico Enterprises, 267
Tipton (Indiana) Community School Corporation, 197
Together for a Safe Campus, 128, 257
Toledo, Ohio, 351
Tolerance education, 329–330
Tolstoy Foundation, 309
Topeka, Kansas, 195
Topsfield Foundation, 241
Toronto, Canada, 158, 162
TOV. *See* Turn Off the Violence campaign
Town hall forums, 137, 146
Toys R Us, 268
TPL. *See* Trust for Public Land
Traffic control, 174
Training schools, 80
Training Teams, 10
Transition Resource Teachers, 57
Transitional Living Program for Homeless Youth, 65
Translators, 144
Trash patrol, 175–176
Trauma Team, 266
Travelers and Immigrants Aid, 59
Treatment Alternatives to Street Crime and Drug Diversion program, 320
Treatment services, 289–290
Tree planting, 46
Trenton, New Jersey, 136, 285
Trespass law enforcement, 210
Tri-Agency Resource Gang Enforcement Team, 242
TRIAD, 39

TRT. *See* Transition Resource Teachers
Truancy Habits Reduced, Increasing Valuable Education program, 96
Truancy prevention, 95–96, 285–286
Truant and Burglary Suppression program, 96
Trucking companies, 192–193
Trust for Public Land, 46, 228
Truth or Dare, 275
Tuba City, Arizona, 323
Tucson, Arizona, 45, 53, 119, 271, 345, 348, 350
Tulane University, 276
Turn Off the Violence campaign, 3, 44
Turnpikes, 193
Tuscaloosa, Alabama, 99
Tutoring program, 59, 69
Two-way radio patrols, 157, 350–351
Tyler, Texas, 274

Ujima project, 256
UMCA programs, 288
Unemployment, 28
Uniforms, 177–178
Union City, New Jersey, 133, 136
Union Miles Development Corporation, 293, 300
Union Pacific Railroad, 310
United Way, 47, 70
University of Florida, 128, 257
University of Illinois, 66
University of Maryland, 88
University of Michigan, 75
University of Mississippi, 208
University of Nebraska, 74
University of North Carolina, 267–268
University of Southern Mississippi, 208
University of Texas School of Social Work, 21
University of Virginia, 208
University of Washington, 66
University students. *See* College students
Upward Movement program, 84
Urban Empowerment Zone, 235
Urban Forestry Program, 14
Urban Initiatives, 64
Urban League, 100
Urban Los Angeles program, 46
Urban open space, 46
U.S. Army, 87
U.S. Attorney's Office, 5, 137
U.S. Conference of Mayors, 148
U.S. Department of Education, 57, 92, 109, 142

U.S. Department of Health and Human Services, 65, 90–91
U.S. Department of Housing and Urban Development, 56, 160, 209, 231–232
U.S. Department of Justice, 5, 8, 22, 24, 29, 37, 53, 85, 98, 244
U.S. Department of Labor, 54
U.S. Fire Administration, 361
U.S. Park Service, 183
USAA Casualty Insurance Company, 89–90, 269
User accountability programs, 319–320
Using Your Medicines Wisely, 321
Utah, 67, 79–80, 308. *See also specific communities and programs*
Utah Council for Crime Prevention, 2
Utility employee watch, 157

Valet parking, 179–180
Values-based curricula, 71–72
Vancouver, Canada, 162
Vandalism, 94
Vehicle inspection stickers, 355–356
Vehicle seizure, 178
Vera Institute of Justice, 4
Victim assistance
  bias crimes, 337
  for children, 252–253, 260
  community-based services, 42–43
  domestic violence programs, 263
  law enforcement support, 124
  restitution, 98–99, 245–246
  for senior citizens, 22–23
  support programs, 93–94
Victim Witness Assistance Program, 259
Victimization prevention programs, 70, 143–144
Videotape illegal behavior, 176
Vietnamese community, 129, 331, 333
Violence-free zones, 72
Violence in Our Schools, Hospitals, and Public Places, 201
Violence in the Schools: How America's Schoolboards Are Safeguarding Your Children, 195
Violence prevention. *See also* Gang prevention programs; Victim assistance
  acquaintance rape prevention, 276
  after-school programs, 271–272
  boot camps, 246–247
  community-based programs, 19–20
  community mediation, 240–241

comprehensive curricula, 238–239
conflict mediation for school-age children, 257–258
corporate project support, 268–269
corrections combined with treatment, 243–244
crisis response teams, 266–267
dating violence prevention, 265–266
educate college students, 256–257
family therapy, 261
gun court, 262
gun interdictions, 279–280
gun licensing regulations and ordinances, 253–254
gun safety education for children, 270–271
habitual offenders, 244–245
health care professionals training, 239–240
in-school probation, 249–250
incentive programs, 274
involving youth, 255–256
job skills for youth, 267–268
monitoring and support programs, 250–251
overview, 237–238
parents held accountable for children's behavior, 272–273
partnership between law enforcement and city agencies, 133
performance programs, 275
prevent bullying in schools, 251–252
promote nonviolent images of youth, 254–255
public health programs, 248–249
reinforce through performances for youth, 40–41
restitution by juvenile offenders, 245–246
teach juveniles consequences of violence, 247–248
train emergency room staff, 273
treatment for male batterers, 264
use school organization, 277
Violence Prevention Project, 266
Violent Crime Coordination Group, 137
Violent Crime Task Force, 35
Violent Juvenile Offender Program, 243
Virginia, 173. *See also specific communities and programs*
Virginia Crime Prevention Association, 165
Virginia Department of State Police, 176, 356
Virginia Judicial Council, 126
Virginia National Guard, 175

Virginia Youth Violence Project, 208
VisionQuest, 53
VJO. *See* Violent Juvenile Offender Program
Voice mail systems, 351
Volunteer Sponsor Program, 102
Volunteers
  college students, 20–21, 66
  mentoring programs, 31–32
  resident patrols, 214–215
  as school security patrols, 204–205
  senior citizens, 39

Walbridge Caring Communities Program, 107
Walking buddies, 72
Walking/running races, 9
Walls of the City, 95
Warminster Township (Pennsylvania) Police Department, 124
Warner Brothers, 341
Washington, 166, 301. *See also specific communities and programs*
  Department of Labor and Industry, 166
Washington, DC, 9, 65, 94, 121, 174, 186, 188, 189, 233, 266, 301, 310, 316, 335
Washington Community Violence Prevention Program, 247–248
Washington Metropolitan Area Transit Authority, 344
Wasilla, Alaska, 77
Waterloo, Iowa, 118, 292, 294
Wausau, Wisconsin, 236
We Help Ourselves, 70
We Turn In Pushers hotline, 313
Weapons and Violence Reduction Program, 78
Weapons Awareness Program, 271
Weed and Seed grants, 24, 29, 288
Wentworth Institute, 311
Westminster, California, 170, 242
White collar crime, 229
Whittier, California, 101, 287
WIC. *See* Women, Infants, and Children's Program
Wichita, Kansas, 47
Wilderness Counseling Service, 292
Williston, North Dakota, 266
Willows, California, 145
Wilmington, Delaware, 294, 295
Window watch program, 210
The Winnable War: A Community Guide to Eradicating Street Drug Markets, 198, 214

Wipe Out Graffiti Program, 345
Wisconsin Correctional Service, 27
Witness support. *See* Victim assistance
Women. *See also* Female youth
  crime prevention programs for,
    157–158
  drug abuse prevention, 322–323
Women, Infants, and Children's
    Program, 93
Women Against Abuse program, 104
Women in Municipal Government, 104
Women's Action Alliance, 323
Women's Alcohol and Drug Education
    Project, 323
Women's Bar Association of Maryland,
    329
Woodgate Fathers organization,
    204–205
Workplace safety inspections, 166
A World of Difference program, 335
WUSA-TV, 335

Yakima, California, 345
YAPC. *See* Board of Young Adult Police
    Commissioners
YAR. *See* Youth as Resources
YCB. *See* Youth Coordinating Board
YCWA. *See* Youth Crime Watch of
    America, Inc.
YFA. *See* Youth Futures Authority
YIP. *See* Youth Initiatives Program
YLD. *See* Young Lawyers Division
Yonkers, New York, 241
Young Americans Education Foundation,
    267
Young Lawyers Division, 330
Young v. American Mini Theaters, 173
Youth. *See also* Children; Drug abuse
    prevention; Gang prevention
    programs; Violence prevention
  adult mentors, 89–90, 101–102
  alternative school sites, 76–77
  college students as volunteer
    resources, 20–21, 66
  community-based health services,
    92–93
  community-based support for
    domestic violence victims,
    103–104
  control cruising, 170–171
  counseling for divorcing parents,
    67–68

Court-Appointed Special Advocates,
    88–89
crime prevention programs for female
    youth, 60–61
crime prevention techniques for
    young children, 69–70
crisis hotlines, 111–112
curfews, 62–63, 95–96
dating education, 105
day and residential treatment for
    offenders, 79–80
dropout prevention, 56–57
family-school partnerships, 91–92
fire safety education, 357–358
graffiti enforcement, 94–95
in-home counseling for young
    parents, 97–98
individual and family therapy
    programs, 86–87
intensive community-based
    supervision, 80–81
intensive intervention, 78–79, 107
interaction with law enforcement and
    the judicial system, 123
intergenerational programs, 63–64
intervention for arsonists, 360–361
law enforcement programs for
    diverse groups, 145
law-related education, 110–111
leadership development, 55–56
multiagency youth service support
    teams, 141–142
outdoor challenge education, 52–53
overview of programs for, 51–52
parent education and support, 106
parental involvement programs,
    100–101
peer-to-peer instruction, 68–69
performing arts programs, 58–59
police-sponsorship of positive
    activities for, 120
pregnancy prevention, 99–100
prenatal care for pregnant women,
    90–91
problem solving education, 19–20
programs for runaway and homeless
    youth, 64–65
recreation centers, 59–60
reinforce prevention themes through
    performances, 40–41
restitution to victims, 98–99
rites of passage training, 102–103
safe haven facilities, 72–73, 136

school-to-work programs, 53–55
schools as community resource
    centers, 109–110
surrogate families, 84–85
surveys of concerns, 74–75
teen courts, 81–82
truancy reduction through daytime
    curfews, 95–96
values-based curricula, 71–72
victim and witness support, 93–94
youth advisory boards, 73–74
youth-designed and youth-led
    community service, 108–109
youth policy and programs, 75–76
Youth, Family, and Neighborhood
    Vitality, 19
Youth Action Corps., 63
Youth advisory boards, 73–74
Youth Advisory Commission, 75
Youth Advocate Programs, 78
Youth Alive, 25, 43, 94, 256
Youth and Education Task Force, 35
Youth and Elderly Against Crime
    project, 64
Youth as Resources, 55–56, 108,
    256, 293
Youth Biz, 267
Youth Commission, 82
Youth Coordinating Board, 76
Youth Corrections Centers, 53
Youth Crime Watch of America,
    Inc., 199
Youth Futures Authority, 76, 93
Youth Initiatives Program, 76
Youth Intervention Program, 131, 142
Youth Involvement Network, 47
Youth Leadership Center, 316
Youth Opportunity Centers, 19
Youth Support Teams, 142
Youth Trauma Team, 94
Youth Unlimited, 291, 316
Youth Violence Project, 208
Youth Yellow Pages, 47
YWCA, 61
YWCA New Entrepreneurs, 90

Zero-tolerance policy, 199, 201, 340
Zero-tolerance zone, 73
Zoning laws, 173